EDUCATING STUDENTS

WITH

MILD DISABILITIES

Edited by

Edward L. Meyen

University of Kansas

Glenn A. Vergason

Georgia State University

Richard J. Whelan

University of Kansas

LOVE PUBLISHING COMPANY®
Denver, Colorado 80222

Library of Congress Catalog Card Number 92-74809

Copyright © 1993 Love Publishing Company
Printed in the U.S.A.
ISBN 0-89108-230-1

Contents

Preface

THIS BOOK has two simple, yet major, areas of emphasis. First, it explores perspectives on educating students with mild disabilities. Perspective in this sense means to see clearly the developments that are forming the foundation for special education and related services to students with mild disabilities. The second area focuses on practices built upon the perspectives guiding special education at this time in its history. Accordingly, the two major sections are titled New Perspectives and New Practices.

When we use the term "mild disabilities," we are including the traditional categories of learning disabilities, mental retardation, and emotional disturbance. These three classifications and the general category of "mild" encompass more than 70% of the students ages 6–21 served under the Individuals with Disabilities Education Act, passed by Congress and signed by the President in 1990.

The chapters under each of the major sections are recent articles that have appeared in *Focus on Exceptional Children*. They were selected based upon their fit with the two main topical areas and, more important, upon the useful information they convey to professionals in special education. Each article is preceded by a brief editorial abstract pointing out some key features and areas for thought.

Under the New Perspectives section the articles range in content from the controversy surrounding the regular education initiative—a clear policy issue of utmost importance to the profession—to consideration of the effects of cultural and linguistic variables on the academic achievement of students from underrepresented groups in our society. Other topics include motivation, collaboration between regular and special educators, configurations of secondary programs for students with mild disabilities, and transition from formal schooling to the world of work. Still other articles discuss the importance of students with mild disabilities learning to self-regulate their academic and social behaviors. Finally, instructional models for teaching learning strategies provide another approach to serving students with mild disabilities. For example, rather than special education teachers' attempting to teach all of the academic content across subject fields, they concentrate on teaching students strategies for learning and using content information in problem solving and critical thinking in the daily challenges of school.

Under the New Practices section, the articles provide information and guidelines for teacher/learning interactions in instructional settings. For example, curriculum-based measurement as a problem-solving assessment procedure is a practice whose time has come. Proficiency in this knowledge and skill domain will enable teachers to contribute to the new educational reform expectation that all children can learn and that learning will be evaluated by predetermined outcomes instead of standardized multiple-choice tests. The curriculum-based measurement approach allows special educators to make informed decisions based upon how students actually perform within a curriculum as contrasted to a test that may or may not address the student's knowledge and skill.

Other articles within this section deal with the curriculum areas of whole language, reading, and mathematics. The article on the Foxfire Pedagogy brings together practices that have been successful in educating students at risk and those with mild disabilities and offers a comprehensive approach to helping these students become engaged with the curriculum and develop a commitment to lifelong learning.

We have tried to select the articles with a simple goal in mind: to bring to practitioners and teacher educators the best and most current knowledge regarding perspectives and special education practices for students with mild disabilities. In this era, when more and more special educators are rethinking the role of special education within the entire regular education context, they are naturally turning to a review of past and current practices and are looking for ways in which the entire education profession can work together to enable students with mild disabilities to gain the utmost knowledge and skills from their instructional experiences. This requires us to find ways to collaborate more with our colleagues in general education. It also requires us to view the continuum of educational services as beginning with the presumption that all children with disabilities are entitled to be educated in a general education environment to the extent possible and still receive a free appropriate public education. This is a departure from some past practices, in which the label applied to the child—legislation and regulations to the contrary—almost universally predicted placement along a continuum. The thought, though rarely expressed, was that if the student is mentally retarded, that is why we have special classes. This contrasts with truly individualized decision making based upon the student's current levels of educational performance that is now required for placement in the least restrictive instructional setting.

These are exciting times. If the ferment in education today is channeled into constructive policies and actions, students with disabilities will surely benefit.

Some articles in *Educating Students with Mild Disabilities* reflect the recent changes in the titles of the federal laws; others do not. However, the substance and intent of federal policies and laws has not been altered, and the included articles remain up-to-date and highly relevant.

Part I:
New Perspectives

The field of special education for students with mild disabilities is quite different now from what it was even a few years ago. These changes are the result of greater diversity in social/cultural conditions, more diversity in exceptionalities, stronger advocacy by parents, and continued emphasis on the least restrictive environment, especially as it is interpreted in including students with disabilities in regular education. These changes have forced special educators to examine what they are doing, how they are rendering their services, the effectiveness of programs. This first section examines a variety of new perspectives, all of which have had, or may have in the future, a significant effect on students with disabilities.

In the first article, Vergason and Anderegg point out that special education has been through some difficult times, with advocates of the regular education initiative suggesting that all students with disabilities be served in the mainstream and not by pullout programs. Others have argued that the resource room and the service delivery system effectively serve children. Though the discussion continues in the literature, Vergason and Anderegg indicate that both sides need to realize that special education has a repertoire of effective instructional approaches that can be employed in resource rooms and in regular classes. They review the approaches that have been shown to be effective.

The second article, by Whitaker and Prieto, examines the greater diversity in schools and especially the effects of bilingualism on students' achievement. This diversity exists whether the students are in the mainstream or some other place in the service delivery system. The authors recognize the limitations but also point out some positive effects of differences in linguistic backgrounds.

Special education and regular education also must address motivation among students with mild disabilities because motivation and expectancy are so closely tied to our success. The third article, by Mehring and Colson, focuses on motivational theories and the results of research on motivation that allow programmatic and curricular changes to enhance student performance and the school's holding power.

Closely related to sociocultural expectancy and motivational variables with students who have disabilities has been the current movement toward students' regulating their own learning. The article by Graham, Ellis, and Reid presents much of the research and programmatic information on this topic. The approaches include instructing students to manage their own behavior and use their own metacognition and metamemory to assist them with behavior and learning.

Likewise, in his article on employment as an outcome, Edgar provides some sobering statistics on dropouts versus the holding power of schools for students with exceptionalities. Large numbers of students with disabilities drop out, and Edgar suggests that the present curriculum actually may be working against them in the employment arena. Students in programs that are most tailored to their abilities and future needs are more likely to remain in school. On the other hand, a curriculum for those with mild disabilities that is the same as or part of regular education may result in lower expectancy and a greater likelihood of their dropping out of school and not becoming effective citizens.

In this section, we also examine several models that can help us more effectively address students with disabilities. Perceiving the increasing emphasis on special education as a support system in regular education, Simpson and Myles offer a practical model for collaboration with regular education. It is a guide toward greater mainstreaming, especially if resource teachers are to become collaborative teachers.

On the other hand, Zigmond presents an approach for students with learning disabilities in secondary education that many will see as producing more restrictive environments. If, however, the reader follows Zigmond's careful review of the research, Edgar's data on dropouts among those with mild disabilities, and the need for a different secondary curriculum, the intensive programs she recommends will not seem so foreign.

The above-described articles, together with the model for teaching learning strategies presented by Ellis, Deshler, Lenz, Schumaker, and Clark, provide a background of approaches for addressing special needs. This is one of the most widely adopted models in the United States. The authors emphasize strategies such as organization, metacognition and metamemory, note taking, paraphrasing, and study skills. Research has demonstrated the effectiveness of the learning strategies approach from elementary through high school.

The Whites describe how two school systems have incorporated special education and regular education teachers in a team-teaching relationship. They outline the process for effectively starting and conducting such a program in enough detail to allow others to avoid the usual pitfalls. They also address some of the unique differences implementing the program in a middle school environment.

Last, Truesdell and Abramson provide a different perspective on academic behavior and grades for mainstreamed students. It is easy for parents and advocates to push for mainstreaming on a programmatic basis, and these authors provide some sobering information for systems, parents, and advocates. Although mainstreamed students often are placed in lower tracks with "regular" students, this study and others found that mainstreamed students passed most of their school courses and often without much assistance from special educational personnel. Those who favor mainstreaming and those who argue for less can both find direction in this article for adjustments in programs.

The first section of this book certainly offers a variety of new perspectives. The second section builds on these articles and offers some practical approaches for educating students with mild disabilities.

The authors review the proposals of the regular education initiative or, as it is now called, inclusive education. It calls for integrating all students with disabilities into regular education and for special education to become a part of regular education and a support system working cooperatively with regular educators. While acknowledging the criticisms voiced during the last 15 years against the resource room approach for students with mild disabilities, Vergason and Anderegg maintain that effective practices are available regardless of the geography of placement. The authors recommend peer tutoring, direct instruction, cognitive training, curriculum-based instruction, cooperative learning, instructional alignment, and learning strategies as effective approaches, supported by research.

Beyond the Regular Education Initiative/Inclusion and the Resource Room Controversy

Glenn A. Vergason and M.L. Anderegg

Having written a number of articles during the last two years refuting the claims of proponents of the regular education initiative (REI) (Anderegg & Vergason, 1988, 1989a, 1989c, 1990; Vergason & Anderegg, 1989a, 1989b, 1990a, 1990b) and having talked with educators from across the United States and Canada, we have come to these conclusions:

1. Most special educators are in favor of improving relations with regular education.
2. Most special educators also favor working cooperatively with regular education.
3. Most special educators likewise want to improve the delivery system through implementation of the least restrictive alternative (Turnbull, 1990).

Rather than continuing the debate about REI, which will accomplish little, much can be accomplished by shifting our emphasis, in this article, to practices that have stood the test of time, research, and application.

Slavin (1989) has indicated that educators, in general, have been only too willing to implement new educational techniques without waiting for hard educational research to demonstrate their replicated effectiveness. Slavin reviewed several examples of educational practices that have been widely implemented, only to learn later that the practices were not effective.

In special education, examples such as the work of Ault, Wolery, Doyle, and Gast (1989) indicate that, in the area of moderate and severe disabilities, many strategies that are being implemented have actually not been studied in depth. These researchers looked at 31 investigations. Of the 78 possible comparisons on 13 identified strategies, Ault et al. found that only 19 of the possible comparisons had been studied and 8 of the 19 had been addressed in only one study.

In contrast, we have found that many strategies and techniques have been thoroughly examined and found to be effective in a wide range of applications with mildly disabled students. These strategies have yet to be implemented widely by frontline special educators—and should be.

After having read the literature thoroughly, including studies that proponents of inclusion have claimed to demonstrate the ineffectiveness of resource rooms (Haynes & Jenkins, 1986; Rich & Ross, 1989), we found, upon careful examination of the data, that these studies actually reflect favorably on resource rooms (Vergason & Anderegg, 1990b, 1991). This technology and other practices, we believe suggest that special education is not beyond salvage and in fact has much to contribute. Much of our opinion is based on practices that have been so effective in replication that we are recommending them as methods for improving the outcomes of students in regular education and special education. Implementation of these practices will not depend on the type of service delivery system and can make special and regular education more effective.

PROGRAMS RECOMMENDED FOR USE

After developing a list of a number of teaching practices that we planned to recommend to special educators, we discovered a similar list by Meyen (1990). He did not have time or space to explain his list, but the similarity of his list to ours was striking. He likewise was recommending his list as practices that should be employed on a large scale.

The programs and techniques we recommend to special educators include: peer tutoring, direct instruction, cooperative learning, self-instructional training, curriculum-based measurement (CBM), instructional alignment, and learning strategies. This is not an all-inclusive list, but if only these practices were put to widespread use, we would be delighted.

Special educators work with children who usually do not profit from seatwork as much as other students may (Zigmond, 1990). These children lack the ability to maintain vigilance during independent work. The advantages Bloom (1984a, 1984b) showed with tutorial instruction are lost with the special education child while the teacher is tutoring others in the class. Thus, mainstreamed students may not be engaged during much of the instructional time. Perhaps the deficits in the engaged time of mainstreamed students explains, in part, the high dropout rate of students with mild disabilities (Butler-Nalin & Padillo, 1989) and the large number of regular education courses in which students with mild disabilities are making failing grades (Wagner, 1989). We believe one way to begin to address these problems is through peer tutoring and the other techniques we recommend to decrease the amount of unengaged time and improve achievement of learners with disabilities.

Peer Tutoring

Special education literature contains numerous studies on the effectiveness of peer tutoring (see Jenkins & Jenkins, 1985; Lloyd, Crowley, Kohler, & Strain, 1988). Locating negative findings from the literature on peer tutoring is difficult because this practice helps those who tutor as much as those who are being tutored. Peer tutoring, however, does require preliminary training and continued retraining to be the most effective (Cohen, Kulik, & Kulik, 1982; Maheady, Sacca, & Harper, 1988).

Some students with behavior disorders have actually expressed more positive behaviors after tutoring nondisabled students in lower grades. And cross-age instruction enhances peer tutoring because the student in the lower grade is not maintained in an inferior role of always receiving help. The lack of equal status and its effects are discussed in an article by Cole, Vandercook, and Rynders (1988). Special educators should not place students, especially those with disabilities, in a role that may be damaging to self-esteem. Therefore, knowledge of the effects of status may aid teachers in taking counteracting steps. Cross-category tutoring also offers the potential to improve the self-esteem of learners with disabilities and assist other students in the program as well.

Cross-age tutoring has been shown to be highly effective with students who have learning disabilities and those who have mental retardation. Relevant studies have shown greater success for one-to-one peer tutoring than for teacher-led, small-group instruction (Jenkins, Mayhall, Peschka, & Jenkins, 1974). Both tutoring and peer tutoring are highly effective instructional approaches, and we will see, under instructional alignment, just how powerful these can be. An additional advantage of peer tutoring is the high cost-effectiveness of such programs (Levin, Glass, & Meister, 1984). To us, trying to implement a program for students with mild disabilities without peer tutoring is like trying to row a boat without oars!

Direct Instruction

Another highly effective instructional practice, direct instruction, was first introduced to the literature by Rosenshine (1976) in relation to effective instruction. Its suggested use here is more related to the work of Engelmann and his colleagues (Becker, Engelmann, Carnine, & Rhine, 1981; Engelmann & Carnine, 1982). Direct instruction implies attention to the curriculum as much as to the techniques of teaching. The latter, however, has been the more emphasized element of the approach. Direct instruction and its advocates have come mainly from Ohio State University (Stephens, 1977; Stephens, Hartman, & Lucas (1983) and the University of Oregon (Gersten & Carnine, 1986).

The components of direct instruction include explicit step-by-step teaching strategy, student mastery of each step, strategy correction for student errors, gradual fading from teacher direction, adequate systematic practice, cumulative review, and a teaching format that anticipates potential errors (Gersten & Carnine, 1986). The benefits of this approach are well documented.

Becker and Carnine (1981) showed that students involved in direct instruction make more overall academic gains; and slow/immature learners are helped as well by direct instruction (Doyle, 1983). Improvements were also demonstrated in targeted comprehension skills (Singer & Dolan, 1982), and direct instruction was far more effective than traditional approaches in teaching math word problems (Darch, Carnine, & Gersten, 1984). Direct instruction further was found to be highly effective in teaching the use of savings accounts to students with mild retardation (Bourbeau, 1984) and street crossing to students with moderate to severe mental retardation (Horner, Jones, & Williams, 1985).

To appreciate this system fully, teachers are urged to read an article by Gersten, Woodward, and Darch (1986). They present the usual reading exercise from a Houghton-Mifflin textbook, emphasizing how the coverage of oceanographer, tides, and currents are not appropriately presented for individuals with learning and behavioral deficiencies. They then carry through, showing how these and other types of lessons are taught by direct instruction. They present the critical features as:

1. Teach an implicit step-by-step strategy.
2. Develop [the strategy] at each step.
3. Develop strategy (or process) corrections for student errors.
4. Gradually fade from teacher directed activities toward independent work.
5. Use adequate, systematic practices with a range of examples.
6. Use cumulative review. (p. 19)

Some researchers favor direct instruction because the methods are closer to those of regular education (Reynolds, Wang, & Walberg, 1987). That contention, however, appears to be grounded in a misconception of what occurs in the regular classroom. Regular education instruction is centered more on the masses and fails to address the systematic nature of direct instruction, the latter's emphases being on success in learning and adjustment of the curriculum and learning tasks. Some studies report that regular teachers say they are employing direct instruction as the most frequent method of instruction (Ysseldyke, Thurlow, Wotruba, & Nania, 1990). In the same study, which obtained results from 197 full-time regular education teachers who had students with disabilities in their classes, 58% of the elementary school teachers and 51% of the high school teachers "reported no differences in their classroom instructional arrangements due to the presence of students with handicaps" (p. 5). The difference between an adjustment of curriculum and learning tasks and the lack of accommodation Ysseldyke et al. reported may demonstrate definitional differences Reynolds et al. overlooked.

In our way of thinking, these teachers certainly were not using direct instruction as special educators define it and showed little cognizance of the necessity to modify curriculum and instruction. The proper employment of direct instruction with all its precision would seem to bring superior results in resource and regular classrooms.

Cooperative Learning

Cooperative learning offers another encouraging technique for resource teachers, consultant teachers, and regular class teachers with learning handicapped students. A couple of recent studies (Putnam, Rynders, Johnson, & Johnson, 1989; Tateyama-Sniezek, 1990) offer a word of caution, but we believe the general technique has great merit.

Basically, a teacher who uses cooperative learning will employ group assignments to accomplish instructional goals. Although it is beyond the scope of this article to explain fully this technique, a teacher decides which cooperative approach to employ, how goals will be assigned, if at all, how much direction to give the group, and whether to structure it so everyone in the group will have some necessary part of the solution.

It is true that a wide diversity in student abilities may actually work against completion of the task, but cooperative learning does offer an opportunity for students of differing ability levels to contribute to accomplishing a task and to learn to work with people of a variety of abilities and disabilities (Johnson & Johnson, 1986; Johnson, Johnson, Warring, & Maruzama, 1986). To accomplish this, the teacher must structure the task for the groups and develop, in each grouping, a role for every individual.

For example, the multiple levels of Bloom's task taxonomy (1984a) can be incorporated toward completing the final product, with each learner contributing tasks at his or her personal optimal level. Thus, some students would be involved in activities in the knowledge and application tasks while others could be dealing with the higher order processes of synthesis and evaluation.

It does little good to mainstream a student only to have the group exclude the individual beyond observation of the activity. Students with disabilities always have had ample opportunity to observe without participation. A mainstream placement, on the other hand, is intended to include participation. Some professionals (Orelove & Sobsey, 1987) believe that partial participation is acceptable but such limited involvement does little for learners with disabilities. Thus, we should seek maximum use of techniques with a high potential for participation.

Self-Instructional Training

Self-instructional training has variations such as cognitive behavior modification (Swanson & Kozleski, 1985) and self-control curriculum (Edwards & O'Toole, 1985), but the emphasis of such training is still on teaching cognitive control of a specific behavior related to learning, such as attention (Lewis & Blampied, 1985) or memory (Deshler, Schumaker, & Lenz, 1984; Pressley, Scruggs, & Mastropieri, 1989). This may involve the disabled student's own knowledge of thinking or memory strategies or even self-monitoring of academic processes (Sheinker, Sheinker, & Stevens, 1984).

When one of our doctoral students at Georgia State University proposed self-instructional training using labels printed on the pages of books, with statements such as "eyes on work," "pay attention," and similar phrases, his committee was not impressed. The results of the study, however, provided strong support for the effectiveness of this approach (Davis, 1984; Davis & Hajicek, 1985; Davis, Uhlir, & Kelly, 1986). Self-instruction and other cognitive training offer much to the teacher in terms of improvement in learning as well as social behaviors. Similar kinds of cognitive training through therapeutic writing is being used for controlling depression, for example (L'Abate, Boyce, Frazier, & Russ, 1992).

Curriculum-Based Measurement (CBM)

Curriculum-based measurement (CBM) amounts to taking daily samples of student performance and using these as measures of the effectiveness of instruction. One form of implementation simply involves recording the number of errors made in one minute of reading with the number of errors plotted daily or weekly. Zigmond (1990) has shown that this technique can demonstrate to a teacher if the instruction is appropriate. If the instructional curve goes up, the teacher continues the present instruction. A downward curve, on the other hand, suggests abandoning that instructional technique and selecting a new approach based on the deficits revealed in the downward curve.

Because proponents of the REI, inclusion, and some reform movements advocate a noncategorical approach and request waivers from traditional assessment measures (Reynolds, Wang, & Walberg, 1987), it becomes increasingly important that teachers have ways of demonstrating achievement before and after instruction. With CBM, students are not likely to get lost or to stagnate either in regular education or in special education. This technique's effectiveness and diversity over content areas have been well documented (Deno & Fuchs, 1987; Fuchs & Fuchs, 1986; Marston, 1988). CBM offers a means for improving the quality of both regular and special education and will decrease referrals to special education.

Instructional Alignment

The concept of instructional alignment comes out of the writing of Cohen (1987) and is based on the work of Bloom (1984a, 1984b) and Carroll (1963). Bloom's work centers on instructional effectiveness and is intended to quantify the effectiveness of instruction. Much of his work involves looking for group methods that are as effective as one-to-one tutoring, and he has developed techniques for accomplishing what is termed *mastery learning*. In this context, mastery learning involves systematic instruction combined with feedback and correction to improve learning. Mastery learning differs little from task analysis and reinforcement as used in special education.

Bloom has used the regular classroom as the instructional setting. Through mastery learning he has demonstrated that a class of 30 students with mastery learning can achieve 1 mean standard deviation above traditional regular class instruction or Sigma 1. Bloom (1984b) also has demonstrated that tutorial instruction (teacher-student ratios of 1:1, 1:2, and 1:3) with feedback can produce mean performance levels of 2 standard deviations or 2 Sigma above traditional methods. Researchers, including Bloom sought ways to go beyond 2 Sigma, but without success until the work of Cohen (1987).

Cohen employed the construct of instructional alignment. He applied Bloom's technology but also inserted a preliminary step of determining and teaching prerequisite skills. Special educators may be familiar with this technique as part of task analysis. Another term that could be employed would be *readiness skills* or precursors of the instruction. Using this approach, Cohen has gone beyond Sigma 2.

The implications of these results for special education are clear. One-to-one or small-group instruction with corrective feedback is highly effective if properly done. Further, incorporating the precursor or readiness skills for the tasks to be taught can raise our success rate even higher. The low pupil-teacher ratio can be effective, but it also can be one of the greatest detriments to effective instruction in special education.

Resource teachers typically teach one or two students in a tutorial fashion while other students work individually and often are off-task. In such a case, unless the teacher uses grouping, student achievement is impeded. If the teacher emphasizes individual seatwork with his or her monitoring and offering assistance, some students will receive only 5 minutes of instruction per hour. Zigmond (1990) has shown that simple grouping can raise engaged time from 9% to 42% of the time.

Special educators and regular educators can scarcely afford to have students idle or *not* receiving intensive instruction. Thus, grouping plus Bloom's mastery learning and the techniques of instructional alignment seem highly desirable.

Learning Strategies

Learning strategies have been demonstrated to be effective methods for teaching coping skills to students who have learning disabilities and mental retardation, especially high school students (Sheinker, Sheinker, & Stevens, 1984; Deshler & Schumaker, 1984; Larson & Gerber, 1987; Scruggs & Mastropieri, 1986, 1988). As more students have been mainstreamed, it has become necessary for teachers to apply techniques that teach students self-monitoring behaviors such as notetaking, memory strategies, paraphrasing, and extraction of main ideas. These monitoring skills differ somewhat from the cognitive management skills discussed earlier but differ little from what has been labeled as coping skills for survival in regular classrooms. Thus, cognitive skills, as well as social skills, can be taught under the guise of learning strategies.

To these strategies Zigmond (1990) has added teacher-pleasing behaviors, which include getting to school, being on time, having books and other appropriate materials on hand, and recording homework assignments. These teacher-pleasing behaviors might better be referred to as prerequisites to successful high school programming.

In two recent nationwide studies the lack of school success appeared in the same cluster of prominent at-risk factors as absenteeism (Butler-Nalin & Padillo, 1989; Frymier, 1989; Lombardi, 1990). The techniques we have discussed here, though not difficult to teach or to learn, when matched to the student's specific needs and cognitive level, can reduce the student's at-risk status and make the difference in maintaining these students in school.

SUMMARY

Suggestions have been offered for techniques that can assist special educators and regular educators in maintaining students with disabilities in mainstream settings, assuring that these students receive an education appropriate to their functioning successfully and independently in academic situations. Many of these techniques can be applied equally well in regular education, and special educators should not lose sight of this fact. By the same token, it would be erroneous to believe, as some educators seem to, that every special education technique would contribute equally in all settings.

This article recommends the use of peer tutoring, direct instruction, cooperative learning, self-instructional training, curriculum-based measurement, instructional alignment including Bloom's mastery learning, and learning strategies. Although their originators may consider each of these approaches as separate, they have common denominators: an emphasis on engagement of the learner, the presence of task analysis or precursors to learning, the application of theory to instruction, systematic application of precision to the process, and the belief that all student learning can be fostered by application of these methods. Each has demonstrated the capability to transcend settings.

Before we toll the bell for special education, we should implement the most substantial technology our research affords us. This idea is not original with us. Such use of our technology was visualized and recommended by Deno in 1970 while PL 94–142, the Education for All Handicapped Children Act, was still only a dream. We wholeheartedly recommend implementing what we know works while we continue to seek better solutions.

REFERENCES

Anderegg, M.L., & Vergason, G.A. (1988). An analysis of one of the cornerstones of the regular education initiative. *Focus on Exceptional Children, 20* 1–7.

Anderegg, M.L., & Vergason, G.A. (March, 1989a). No more teachers: Bah, humbug: An answer to Stainback and Stainback. *TASH Newsletter, 15*(11), 7, 10.

Anderegg, M.L., & Vergason, G.A. (1989b, March). The regular education initiative: What CEC members ought to know. *Confederation,* 2–3.

Anderegg, M.L., & Vergason, G.A. (1989c). The rest of the story: An answer to "The regular education initiative, A force for change in general and special education." *Education & Training of the Mentally Retarded, 24,* 100–101.

Anderegg, M.L., & Vergason, G.A. (1990). *Four data based objections to the regular education initiative.* Submitted for publication.

Ault, M.J., Wolery, M., Doyle, P.M., & Gast, D.L. (1989). Review of comparative studies in the instruction of students with moderate and severe handicaps. *Exceptional Children, 55*(4), 346–356.

Becker, W., & Carnine, D. (1981). Direct instruction: A behavior theory model for comprehensive educational intervention with the disadvantaged. In J. Bijou & R. Ruiz (Eds.), *Behavior modification.* Hillsdale, NJ: Erlbaum.

Bloom, B.S. (1984a). The search for methods of group instruction as effective as one-to-one tutoring. *Educational Leadership, 41,* 4–17.

Bloom, B.S. (1984b, June/July). The 2 Sigma problem: The search for methods of group instruction as effective as one-to-one tutoring. *Educational Researcher, 13,* 4–15.

Bourbeau, P. (1984). *An experimental analysis of the generalization of teaching skills from the classroom to trained and untrained bank settings in the community.* Unpublished doctoral dissertation, University of Oregon, Eugene.

Butler-Nalin, P., & Padillo, C. (1989, March). Dropouts: The relationship of student characteristics, behaviors, and performance for special education students. Paper presented at Council for Exceptional Children International Convention, San Francisco.

Carroll, J.B. (1963). A model of school learning. *Teachers College Record, 64,* 723–733.

Cohen, P.A., Kulik, J.A., & Kulik, C.C. (1982). Educational outcomes of tutoring. *American Educational Research Journal, 19,* 237–248.

Cohen, S.A. (1987). Instructional alignment: Searching for a magic bullet. *Educational Researcher, 16*(6), 16–20.

Cole, D.A., Vandercook, T., & Rynders, J. (1988). Comparison of two peer interaction programs: Children with and without severe disabilities. *American Educational Research Journal, 25*(3), 415–439.

Darch, C., Carnine, D., & Gersten, R. (1984). Explicit instruction in mathematical problem solving. *Journal of Educational Research, 4,* 155–165.

Davis, R.W. (1984). Cognitive behavior modification and performance of exceptional learners in mathematics. *Tennessee Educational Leadership, 11*(2), 76–80.

Davis, R.W., & Hajicek, J.O. (1985, August). Effects of self-instructional training and strategy training on a mathematics task with severely behaviorally disordered students. *Behavioral Disorders, 10*(3), 275-282.

Davis, R.W., Uhlir, R., & Kelly, L.J. (1986, Summer). Strategies and self-instruction for behaviorally disordered students: A direct instruction approach. *Directive Teacher, 8*(1), 18–19.

Deno, E. (1970, November). Special education as developmental capital. *Exceptional Children, 36*, 229–237.

Deno, S.L., & Fuchs, L.S. (1987). Developing curriculum-based measurement systems for data-based special education problem solving. *Focus on Exceptional Children, 19*(8), 1–16.

Deshler, D.D., & Schumaker, J.B. (1984). An instructional model for teaching students how to learn. In J.L. Graden, J.E. Zins, & M.J. Curtis (Eds.), *Alternative educational delivery systems: Enhancing instructional options for all students* (pp. 391–411). Washington, DC: NASSP.

Deshler, D.D., Schumaker, J.B., & Lenz, B.K. (1984). Academic and cognitive interventions for LD adolescents (Part 1). *Journal of Learning Disabilities, 17*, 108–117.

Doyle, W. (1983). Academic work. *Review of Educational Research, 53*(2), 159–199.

Edwards, L.L., & O'Toole, B. (1985). Application of the self-control curriculum with behavior disordered students. *Focus on Exceptional Children, 17*(8), 1–8.

Engelmann, S., & Carnine, D. (1982). *Theory of instruction.* New York: Irvington.

Frymier, J. (1989). *A study of students at risk: Collaborating to do research.* Bloomington, IN: Phi Delta Kappan Educational Foundation.

Fuchs, L.S., & Fuchs, D. (1986). Effects of systematic evaluation: A metaanalysis. *Exceptional Children, 53*, 199–208.

Gersten, R., & Carnine, D. (1986). Direct instruction in reading comprehension. *Educational Leadership, 43*(7), 70–78.

Gersten, R., Woodward, J., & Darch, C. (1986). Direct instruction: A research-based approach to curriculum design and teaching. *Exceptional Children, 53*, 17–31.

Haynes, M.C., & Jenkins, J.R. (1986). Reading instruction in special education resource rooms. *American Educational Research Journal, 23*(2), 161–190.

Horner, R., Jones, D., & Williams, J. (1985). Teaching generalized street crossing to individuals with moderate and severe mental retardation. *Journal of Association for Persons with Severe Handicaps, 10*(2), 71–78.

Jenkins, J., & Jenkins, L. (1985). Peer tutoring in elementary and secondary programs. *Focus on Exceptional Children, 17*(6), 1–12.

Jenkins, J.R., Mayhall, W.F., Peschka, C., & Jenkins, L.M. (1974). Comparing small group and tutorial instruction in resource room. *Exceptional Children, 40*, 245–250.

Johnson, D.W., & Johnson, R.T. (1986). Mainstreaming and cooperative learning strategies. *Exceptional Children, 52*, 553–561.

Johnson, D.W., Johnson, R.T., Warring, D., & Maruzama, G. (1986). Different cooperative learning procedures and cross-handicap relationships. *Exceptional Children, 53*(3), 247-252.

L'Abate, L.C., Boyce, J., Frazier, L., & Russ, P.A. (1992). Programmed writing: Research in progress. *Comprehensive Mental Health Care, 2*, 45–62.

Larson, K.A., & Gerber, M.M. (1987). Effects of social metacognitive training for enhancing overt behavior in learning disabled and low achieving delinquent. *Exceptional Children, 54*(3), 201–212.

Levin, H., Glass, G., & Meister, G.S. (1984). *Cost-effectiveness of four educational interventions.* Stanford, CA: Institute for Research on Education Finance & Governance.

Lewis, R.O., & Blampied, N.M. (1985). Self-management in a special class. *Techniques: A Journal for Remedial Education & Counseling, 1*, 346–354.

Lloyd, J., Crowley, E.P., Kohler, F.W., & Strain, P.S. (1988). Redefining the applied research agenda? Cooperative learnings, prereferral, teacher consultant, and peer-mediated interventions. *Journal of Learning Disabilities, 21*, 43–52.

Lombardi, T.P. (1990, April). *The relationship between special education and students at risk: Report from the Phi Delta Kappan National Study.* Paper presented at Council for Exceptional Children International Convention, Toronto.

Maheady, L., Sacca, M.K., & Harper, G.F. (1988). Classwide peer tutoring with mildly handicapped high school students. *Exceptional Children, 55*(1), 52–59.

Marston, D. (1988). The effectiveness of special education: A time series analysis of reading performance in regular and special education settings. *Journal of Special Education, 21*(4), 13–26.

Meyen, E. (1990). Quality instruction for students with disabilities. *Teaching Exceptional Children, 22*(2), 12–13.

Orelove, F.P., & Sobsey, D. (1987). *Educating children with multiple disabilities.* Baltimore: Paul Brookes.

Pressley, M., Scruggs, T.E., & Mastropieri, M.A. (1989). Memory strategy research in learning disabilities: Present and future directions. *LD Research, 4*(2), 68–77.

Putnam, J.W., Rynders, J. E., Johnson, R.T., & Johnson, D.W. (1989). Collaborative skill instruction for promoting positive interactions between mentally handicapped and nonhandicapped children. *Exceptional Children, 55*(6), 550–557.

Reynolds, M.C., Wang, M.C., & Walberg, H.C. (1987). The necessary restructuring for special and regular education. *Exceptional Children, 53*(5), 391–398.

Rich, H.L., & Ross, S.M. (1989). Students' time on learning tasks in special education. *Exceptional Children, 55*(6), 508–515.

Rosenshine, B. (1976). Classroom instruction. In N. Gage (Ed.), *The psychology of teaching methods: The seventy-fifth yearbook of the National Society for the Study of Education.* Chicago: University of Chicago Press.

Scruggs, T.E., & Mastropieri, M.A. (1986). Improving the test-taking skills of behaviorally disordered and learning disabled children. *Exceptional Children, 53*(1), 63–68.

Scruggs, T.E., & Mastropieri, M.A. (1988). Teaching test-taking skills to behavior disordered students. *Behavior Disorders, 13,* 240–244.

Sheinker, A., Sheinker, J.M., & Stevens, L.J. (1984). Cognitive strategies for teaching the mildly handicapped. *Focus on Exceptional Children, 17*(1), 1–15.

Singer, H., & Dolan, D. (1982). Active comprehension: Problem solving scheme with question generalization for comprehension of complex short stories. *Reading Research Quarterly, 2,* 166–186.

Slavin, R.E. (1989). The PET and the pendulum: Faddism in education and how to stop it. *Phi Delta Kappan, 71,* 752–758.

Stephens, T. (1977). *Teaching skills to children with learning and behavior disorders.* Columbus, OH: Charles Merrill.

Stephens, T., Hartman, A., & Lucas, U.H. (1983). *Teaching children basic skills: A curriculum handbook.* (2nd ed.). Columbus, OH: Charles Merrill.

Swanson, H.L., & Kozleski, E.B. (1985). Self-talk and handicapped children's academic needs: Applications of cognitive behavior modification. *Techniques: A Journal for Remedial Education & Counseling, 1,* 367–379.

Tateyama-Sniezek, K.M. (1990). Cooperative learning: Does it improve the academic achievement of students with handicaps? *Exceptional Children, 56*(5), 426–437.

Turnbull, H.R., III. (1990). *Free appropriate public education: The law and children with disabilities.* Denver: Love.

Vergason, G.A., & Anderegg, M.L. (1989a, February). *Data-based objections to the regular education initiative.* Paper presented at Supervision Leadership Meeting for Oakland School District, Pontiac, MI.

Vergason, G.A., & Anderegg, M.L. (1989b). Save the baby: A reply to Wang, Reynolds, and Walberg. *Phi Delta Kappan, 71*(1), 61–63.

Vergason, G.A., & Anderegg, M.L. (1991a). Preserving the least restrictive alternative in special education. In W. Stainback & S. Stainback (Eds.), *Issues in special education.* New York: Allyn & Bacon (in preparation).

Vergason, G.A., & Anderegg, M.L. (1990b). The regular education initiative and special education reform in California. *The Journal: California CEC, 39*(3), 8–9.

Vergason, G.A., & Anderegg, M.L. (1991b). Rich & Ross: A mixed message. *Exceptional Children, 57,* 475–476.

Wagner, M. (1989). *The school programs and school performance of secondary school students classified as learning disabled: Findings from the National Longitudinal Study of Special Education.* Menlo Park, CA: SRI.

Ysseldyke, J., Thurlow, M., Wotruba, J., & Nania, P. (1990). Instructional arrangements: Perceptions from general education. *Teaching Exceptional Children, 22*(4), 4–8.

Zigmond, N. (1990). Rethinking secondary school programs for students with learning disabilities. *Focus on Exceptional Children, 23*(1), 1–16.

Glenn Vergason is a professor of special education and the coordinator of the Special Education Administration Program at Georgia State University, Atlanta. M. L. Anderegg is an assistant professor of curriculum and instruction at Kennesaw State College, Georgia.

○ 2 ○

This article examines the positive and negative effects of bilingual instruction with special attention to the added effects of bilingualism on children with disabilities. Although early research studies suggested only negative effects, more recent research points to positive effects on cognition and achievement. They voice caution, however, about research in this area because of methodological errors that have to be corrected in future research. Also, much more research is needed on effects of bilingualism on individuals with disabilities.

The Effects of Cultural
and Linguistic Variables
on the Academic Achievement
of Minority Children

Joseph H. Whitaker and Alfonso G. Prieto

Research on bilingual/bicultural education and on bilingual/bicultural issues is broad and represents a variety of theoretical perspectives, which can be categorized into four general domains:

1. The effects of bilingualism and second-language acquisition.
2. The effects of bilingualism on social development and social interaction.
3. The effects of bilingualism on academic performance, cognition, and cognitive development (Rueda, 1983a, 1983b, 1985).
4. Theoretical considerations (Piagetian, linguistic, metacognitive, metalinguistic, and information processing) involved in language and cognition (Whitaker, 1983).

In relation to the last two areas of research, current theory proposes that certain features of the bilingual/bicultural environment may result in positive effects on the cognitive and academic performance of the bilingual/bicultural child. Additionally, a threshold level of language proficiency may be necessary for the positive cognitive effects of bilingualism to occur.

When factors other than specific disability or anomalous cognitive development (such as race, culture, or gender) are added to the research picture, however, many questions arise that are at present unanswered. For example: Should bilingual education be considered an available alternative for handicapped language minority children? Do certain groups of handicapped children have such a difficult time acquiring one language that bilingual programs should not be considered? If indeed certain cognitive advantages can be gained from proficiency in two languages, perhaps students in this group should have available the option of this potential remedial tool in conjunction with other interventions (Rueda, 1983a).

Obviously, before any decision can be made about the possibility of using bilingual/bicultural education as an educational intervention with language minority handicapped children, the above questions must be addressed. But, more important, how bilingualism affects cognitive performance must be determined. The following review of the literature examines the research on bilingualism, language, cultural, and racial factors and how they relate to cognition, with special attention to the cases in which bilingualism and anomalous cognitive development are involved.

RESEARCH ON BILINGUALISM AND COGNITION

A large number of studies have attempted to relate bilingualism specifically to cognitive development and academic achievement. In the following review these studies have been classified according to whether they support either positive or detrimental consequences of bilingualism. Then we will attempt to account for the discrepancies found in these diverse investigations.

Negative or Mixed Effects of Bilingualism on Cognition

An early study by Darcy (1946) reported significant differences between the mean IQ scores achieved by monolingual and bilingual subjects on the Stanford-Binet Intelligence Scale. These differences were consistent when subjects were divided according to age and gender and also when the age groups and genders were combined. Conversely, when differences in the mean IQs were determined for both language groups on the Atkins Object-Fitting Test (Atkins, 1931), significant differences in favor of the bilingual group were found. The differences were consistently in favor of the bilinguals when the groups were divided according to age and gender and also when the age groups and genders were combined.

The above results were substantiated by the differences found between the mean mental ages achieved by the two language groups on the Stanford-Binet and on the Atkins test. In every age and gender division the mental ages of the monolinguals surpassed those of the bilinguals on the Stanford-Binet scale, whereas on the Atkins test the performance of the bilinguals was consistently superior to that of the monolinguals.

The monolingual and the bilingual subjects of this study were matched closely as to number, gender, socioeconomic status (SES), and age within 6-month intervals. Further, the performance of the bilingual subjects was significantly inferior to that of the monolingual subjects on the Stanford-Binet scale but significantly superior to the performance of the monolingual subjects on the Atkins test. Therefore, it may be concluded that the bilingual subjects tested using the Stanford-Binet in Darcy's (1946) investigation may have experienced language differences because performance on the Stanford-Binet would require subjects to have a substantial command of English.

Studies that claim to demonstrate the negative effects of bilingualism appear to suffer from a failure to adequately define bilingualism either operationally or theoretically, or to adequately control for language proficiency. Consequently, researchers such as Yela (1975) concluded that bilingualism reduced subjects' performance on semantic tasks. Brown, Fournier, and Moyer (1977) found that Mexican-American children scored significantly lower on tests that focused on science concepts and Piagetian concrete reasoning than did their Anglo-American counterparts. The population used in the Brown et al. (1977) study consisted of rural Colorado Mexican-American and Anglo-American fifth-graders. Identification of Mexican-American subjects was based on their having a Spanish surname or Spanish being spoken at home.

In an examination of the creative functioning of bilingual and monolingual third-through fifth-grade students using a regular and translated version of the Torrance Test of Creative Thinking (Torrance, Wu, Gowan, & Aliotti. 1970), monolingual subjects scored significantly better on the measures of fluency and flexibility at every level. The bilingual group performed significantly better than the monolingual group on the measure of elaboration, although statistical significance was reached at only one grade level for the measure of originality.

A longitudinal study by Barik and Swain (1976) compared students receiving instruction in a French immersion program with students in the regular English programs. Three groups of students were evaluated annually using the Otis-Lennon Mental Ability Test. The immersion pupils outperformed the English-program students, although initial differences between the groups are difficult to attribute to language learning or type of program.

A comparison of the performance of Spanish-English bilinguals with English-speaking monolinguals on the PPVT and Raven's Coloured Progressive Matrices was done in a study by Myers and Goldstein (1979). Subjects were selected from intact classrooms at three levels (kindergarten, third, and sixth grades), in which all students were of low SES. Although there were no significant differences on the Raven's test between the two groups, the monolingual children performed significantly better than the bilingual students on the PPVT.

Using a Piagetian measure of conservation, De Avila and Pulos (1979) found no significant differences in performance between monolingual Spanish-speaking, monolingual English-speaking, and bilingual first-grade students. It was hypothesized that failure to find differences might have been due to the possibility that bilingual advantages may occur at an earlier or later stage of development or to the fact that balanced bilinguals were rare in the sample.

Gorrell, Bregman, McAllister, and Lipscomb (1982) compared two groups of bilingual students (Vietnamese-English and Spanish-English) to a group of monolinguals on the block design subtest of the WISC–R and on three spatial role-taking tests of increasing complexity. The bilingual subjects were found to perform better than the monolinguals on the block design subtest but not on the measures of spatial role taking.

Positive Effects of Bilingualism on Cognition

Peal and Lambert (1962) designed a study to examine the effects of bilingualism on the intellectual functioning of children and to investigate the relationship between bilingualism, school achievement, and students' attitudes toward the second-language community. Bilinguals performed better than monolinguals on verbal and nonverbal intelligence tests—a clear reversal of previously reported findings (e.g., Darcy, 1946).

The French-English bilingual children who were subjects in the Peal and Lambert study, as a result of wider experiences in two cultures and languages, appeared to have advantages that the monolinguals did not. Experience with two language systems resulted in mental flexibility, superior concept formation, and more diversified set of mental abilities. On the other hand, monolingual children appeared to have a more unitary structure of intelligence, which they had to use for all types of intellectual tasks. The bilingual children also were further ahead in school than the monolinguals, and they achieved significantly better than their classmates in the study of English. Their superior achievement in school appeared to be dependent on verbal facility.

In the previously mentioned study by Torrance et al. (1970), monolingual and bilingual Chinese and Malayan children in the third, fourth, and fifth grades of Singapore schools were administered Figural Form A of the Torrance Test of Creative Thinking (Torrance, 1966). Test booklets were translated into the subjects' native languages, and all instructions were given in the school's language of instruction, which was Chinese, Malayan, or English. Fluency, flexibility, and elaboration were scored using the standard guides for scoring all versions of this form of the test. A guide for scoring originality was based upon data from the Singapore culture, according to the same general principles as were used in developing the original scoring guide for the United States version of the test.

Overall, the monolinguals performed better than the bilinguals on fluency and flexibility, but the direction of the trend was reversed for originality and elaboration. The overall difference for elaboration was significant, but there was no significant difference for originality. If corrections are made for number of responses, the trend toward superiority of the bilinguals over the monolinguals on originality and elaboration becomes even stronger.

Ianco-Worrall (1972) designed several experiments to test Leopold's (1961) observations on the earlier separation of word sound from word meaning by bilingual compared to matched monolingual children. Attention to meaning or to sound of words was tested with the Semantic and Phonetic Preference Test, a two-choice test in which similarity between words could be interpreted on the basis of shared meaning or shared acoustic properties.

The notion that bilingualism leads to earlier realization of the arbitrary nature of name-object relationship was tested with the questioning technique developed by Vygotsky (1962). The technique calls for an explanation of names, whether names can be interchanged, and, when names are interchanged in play, whether the attributes of the objects change along with their names. The results supported Leopold's observations. Of the young 4- to 6-year old bilinguals, 54% consistently chose to interpret similarity between words in terms of the semantic dimension.

The conclusion drawn is that bilinguals who are brought up in a two-language environment reach a relatively high level of semantic development 2 to 3 years earlier than their monolingual peers. A high percentage of the bilingual children perceived relationships between words in terms of their symbolic properties rather than their acoustic properties.

Application of Piagetian constructs to the study of bilingualism also can be found in the literature. The advantage of Piagetian tasks is that they can be administered so that the content of the task, but not necessarily the language in which the instructions are given, can be standardized, and also the experimenter can take care to assure that subjects understand the task at hand. This is certainly important when assessing the cognitive performance of groups for whom valid and reliable assessment has been a problem.

For example, Feldman and Shen (1971) designed a study to demonstrate that 5-year-old bilinguals have advantages that would be expected from their having two languages: in object constancy, in naming, and in the use of names in sentences. Additionally, it was suggested that object constancy should be in advance of naming (as Piaget suggested) and that naming should be in advance of using names in sentences. Specifically, monolingual and bilingual 5-year-old children were compared in their ability at tasks involving object constancy, naming, and use of names in sentences. These three tasks, which constitute a natural sequence of language skills, were all found to be easier for bilinguals than for monolinguals. This was most clear on nonverbal measures. Further analysis indicated that switching names in sentences was superior in bilinguals, but the knowledge of names and facility for acquiring new names was equivalent in the two groups.

A study by Liedtke and Nelson (1968) considered the experience of becoming bilingual at an early age and tested the effect on mental development. Certain aspects of concept development of bilingual and monolingual children then were compared. A test of concepts of linear measurements was constructed to serve as the primary instrument. The test (Concepts of Linear Measurement Test) consisted of six subtests, which dealt with the following aspects of linear measurement: (a) reconstructing relations of distance, (b) conservation of length, (c) conservation of length with change of position, (d) conservation of length with distortion of shape, (e) measurement of length, and (f) subdividing a straight line.

The resulting mean for the bilingual sample on the Concepts of Linear Measurement Test was significantly higher than the mean for the monolingual sample, which is in agreement with Peal and Lambert's (1962) finding that bilingualism has favorable effects on intellectual functioning. The mean for the bilingual sample on the conservation part of the test also was significantly higher than the mean for the monolingual sample. If the implication of the higher score is that the concept is more advanced and more highly developed, bilingual children manifest a better understanding of the concept as compared to monolingual children of the same age.

The mean for the bilingual sample on the measurement part of the test was significantly higher than the mean for the monolingual sample. This suggested that the measurement concept also had developed to a more advanced stage in the bilingual subjects.

Overall, the results seem to indicate that the linguistic and cultural experience of the bilinguals was an advantage. Additionally, the results indicate that being bilingual or becoming bilingual accelerates the normal process of some components of mental development.

Limitations of the Research

After a review of the above studies, results may be difficult to interpret because of the methodological errors in group assignment, controlling for language proficiency, and defining bilingualism. This includes failure to control for linguistic variables and proficiency—specifically, a lack of the use of measures or controls for language proficiency. Alter considering the previously reviewed articles, the need for tighter linguistic control over the definition of bilingual and monolingual groups becomes readily apparent.

Results of the Feldman and Shen (1971) study, for example, are questionable because of the criteria for assignment to subject groups. Assignment to the bilingual group was made on the basis of the children's "understanding of several simple Spanish questions and ability to speak Spanish at home." Further, no information was provided concerning the nature of these questions or how the ability to speak Spanish at home was defined or ascertained.

Similarly, in the Liedtke and Nelson (1968) study, the criterion for assignment to the bilingual group was based on teacher observation. The group was defined as "children who had used two languages before entering school and who were exposed to both languages at home." No data were provided as to the actual level of proficiency for either the bilingual or monolingual groups. This study, like the Feldman and Shen (1971) one, was weakened by the lack of appropriate linguistic controls.

Research Controlling for Languages Proficiency and Bilingualism

If bilingualism does accelerate cognitive functioning, the cognitive advantages of bilinguals should manifest themselves in studies that carefully control for language proficiency and that carefully operationalize and define bilingualism. These variables were carefully controlled in the Duncan and De Avila (1979) study on bilingualism and cognition, as reported in Table 1. The primary purpose of the study was to assess the English/Spanish relative linguistic proficiency of four groups of Hispanic-background children in grades 1 and 3 and, on the basis of that assessment, to describe the relationship between degree of bilingualism and cognitive functioning, as measured by performance on a test of neo-Piagetian intellectual development and two tests of field dependence/independence.

An important finding of the Duncan and De Avila study was that the proficient bilingual children significantly outscored all other monolingual and limited-proficiency bilingual children on tasks of cognitive perspectivism and scored higher on tasks of cognitive perceptual components of field-dependent cognitive style. These findings clearly support the hypotheses regarding the advanced cognitive functioning of proficient bilinguals (Peal & Lambert, 1962; Ianco-Worrall, 1972; Duncan & De Avila, 1979; Cummins, 1978).

Cummins (1978) investigated the effects of bilingualism on the development of children's awareness of certain properties of language and on their ability to analyze linguistic input. Bilingual children at two grade levels (grade 3 and grade 6) demonstrate significantly greater awareness of the arbitrary nature of word-referent relationships and also were better able to evaluate nonempirical contradictory statements.

An important feature of the above examples is that they involve knowledge of linguistic processes. An even more important feature, however, is that the level of abstraction is free of content, and, as a result, metalinguistic or metacognitive awareness may not be necessarily related to any particular language or sociocultural circumstance and possibly can apply to other situations or experiences. One could expect, then, that the effects of bilingualism on cognitive or metacognitive processes might be manifest on other types of tasks. As a matter of fact, one of the primary features defining metacognitive and metalinguistic awareness is the individual's understanding of the arbitrary use of language.

More recent research has been conducted using subjects who have mild mental retardation. Rueda (1983b) examined the cognitive performance of children who are mentally retarded with moderate levels of language proficiency in Spanish and English in comparison to a matched group of monolingual English children. In spite of the study's limitations (small sample sizes, only moderate proficiency on the part of the bilingual subjects, and failure to measure the language skills of the monolingual sample), it was found that the bilingual group did not suffer any harmful effects as a result of exposure to two languages. In fact, there were differences in favor of the bilingual group on some items of the metalinguistic tasks.

Whitaker, Rueda, and Prieto (1985) compared the performance of three groups of 7- and 8-year-old mildly retarded children. Four dependent measures were used (three Piagetian tasks assessing conversation skills, reconstructive memory, recognitory memory, and one information processing task) to test the hypothesis that bilingualism would positively affect cognitive performance. Results indicated that the high-proficiency bilinguals' performance was significantly superior on three of the four dependent measures.

Summary of Research on Bilingualism and Cognition

A summary of studies investigating the effects of bilingualism on various cognitive measures is presented in Table 1. As the previous discussion indicates, there is suggestion of both negative and positive effects of bilingualism on the educational, intellectual, and academic performance of language-minority students.

Several of the studies suffer from methodological and theoretical errors, including: (a) sample bias, (b) deficiency in sample selection with regard to the control of language pro-

TABLE 1   Positive and Negative Effects of Bilingualism on Cognitive Performance

Author(s)	Date	Subjects	Measures	Results
Darcy	1946	2 yrs, 6 mos	Stanford-Binet Intelligence Test	Bilinguals scored lower (Stanford).
		4 yrs, 5 mos	Atkins Object-Fitting Test	Bilinguals favored (Atkins).
Peal & Lambert	1962	10-yr-olds	Lavoie-Laurendeau Group Test Raven Progressive Matrices Thurstone Primary Mental Abilities	Bilinguals performed better than mono-linguals on verbal and nonverbal intelligence tests.
Liedtke & Nelson	1968	Grade 1 N = 50	Piagetian Concept Formation	Bilinguals performed higher.
Torrance et al.	1970	3rd, 4th, 5th Graders	Torrance Test of Creative Thinking	Monolingual—higher on fluency, flexibility. Bilingual—higher on elaboration; not sig-nificant for originality.
Feldman & Shen	1971	5-yr-olds	Object Constancy (Piagetian), Naming, Sentences	Bilinguals performed better on all three tasks.
Ianco-Worrall	1972	4- 6-yr-olds	Questioning Technique	Bilinguals reach a stage of semantic development 2-3 years earlier than monolinguals.
Barik & Swain	1976	Ss* in French Immersion Program vs. Regular English Program	Otis Lennon Mental Ability Test	Immersion pupils out-performed English program pupils.
Brown et al.	1977	5th Graders N = 150	Science Concepts Test	Bilinguals scored lower.
			Piagetian Concrete Reasoning	Bilinguals scored lower
Cummins	1978	Grade 3 N = 80	Language Objectivity	Bilinguals show greater awareness of arbitrary nature of language.

*Ss = Spanish-speaking

TABLE 1 (continued)

Author(s)	Date	Subjects	Measures	Results
Duncan & De Avila	1979	N = 202 Mex-Am N = 54 (Urban) Mex-Am N = 79 P.R.-Am N = 45 Cuban-Am N = 43 1st-3rd grades	Cartoon Conservation Scale (CCS) LAS Child Embedded Figures Test Draw-A-Person	Proficient bilinguals significantly out- performed all other groups.
Myers & Goldstein	1979	Monolingual SPA Monolingual ENG Matrices Bilingual	PPVT Raven Coloured Progressive	No difference on Raven's. Monolinguals out- performed bilinguals on PPVT.
De Avila & Pulos	1979	1st Graders Monolingual SPA Monolingual ENG Bilingual	Piagetian Measure of Conversation	No significant difer- rences between the three groups.
Gorrell et al.	1982	Vietnamese- ENG Spanish- English Monolinguals	WISC-R Block Design Three spatial role-tasks	Bilinguals performed better on block design but not on spatial role- taking tasks.
Rueda	1983	Bilingual ENG-SPA Monolingual ENG EMH	Measures of Metalinguistic Awareness	Bilinguals performed equally, if not better, on various tasks.
Whitaker et al.	1985	Bilingual ENG-SPA EMH	Piagetian— Conservation, Reconstructive Memory, Recognitory Memory	Proficient bilinguals performed better than monolinguals on three of four measures
		Monolingual ENG EMH	Information Processing	

ficiency, (c) test bias, and (d) procedural errors (Were subjects tested in their native language?). These errors may limit interpretation of the research.

From Table 1, it is apparent that differences in favor of bilinguals have been found in the studies that utilized Piagetian measures and metalinguistics measures. Theoretically, this has been explained by certain methodological factors such as control for language proficiency, and by certain features of the bilingual environment and experience. It includes the observation that Piagetian-based tasks may be better indicators of cognitive differences because they are not heavily language-dependent.

EDUCATIONAL CONSIDERATIONS

At this point we can attempt to tie the previously cited findings concerning bilingualism and cognition to the unique educational needs of the language minority/bilingual exceptional child and point out some areas of continuing educational concern. The studies that reported negative educational, intellectual, and cognitive consequences for certain groups of bilinguals are indicators of practices that have caused minority children to be overrepresented in special education. Further, biased assessment instruments and practices and inadequate educational programs have done little to serve the needs of the students in question. Children from cultural and linguistic groups different from those of children in the majority culture, and particularly those from low SES environments, historically have been educationally underserved.

In making an effort to remedy these problems, attention to certain areas is crucial. These include, but are not limited to: (a) appropriately identifying and assessing the bilingual exceptional child, (b) alleviating the impact of biased assessment instruments and practices, (c) developing relevant and appropriate instructional programs and materials, (d) minimizing the impact of certain negative special education labels, (e) developing adequate bilingual and English as a Second Language (ESL) programs, and (f) modifying certain expectations and attitudes of teachers and administrators. Each of these areas of concern will be examined briefly.

Appropriately Identifying and Assessing the Bilingual Exceptional Child

The consequences of using inappropriate identification and assessment instruments, procedures, and techniques indeed can be quite serious for the bilingual exceptional child. One consequence of inappropriate procedures and instruments is overrepresentation in special education, which often leads to overall poor school progress for the bilingual exceptional child (Oakland, 1979; Mercer, 1971). Poor progress results from placement in programs that are unsystematic, inadequate, inappropriate, undeveloped, or simply nonexistent (Rodriguez, 1982; Baca, 1980).

Adequate identification and assessment of the bilingual exceptional child must include factors such as language, culture, and socioeconomic status (Ambert, 1982). But few assessment instruments have been developed or modified that can assess, in a fair manner, different cultural and linguistic groups (Baca & Bransford, 1982; Bernal, 1979;

Ambert, 1982). Even if adequate instruments were available, a more serious problem exists: insufficient numbers of professionals have been adequately trained in administration and interpretation of such instruments (Hilliard, 1980; Ortiz, 1985). The situation is improving somewhat, though. For example, recent research has been conducted in identification of language disorders in Spanish-speakers (Ambert, 1986); techniques for minimizing inappropriate referrals of language minority students to special education (Ortiz & Maldonado-Colón, 1986); methods of assessment and data interpretation of linguistically and culturally different students referred for disabilities or disorders (Maldonado-Colón, 1986) and assessment of reading problems (Viera, 1986).

Alleviating Bias in Assessment Practices

As mentioned, one severe consequence of using biased instruments and assessment procedures results in overrepresentation of minority groups in special education (Mercer, 1974). Generally, such biased instruments and procedures fail to detect a distinct learning impairment but, rather, detect an inability to function adequately in English, which may result in special education placement because of cultural or dialectical differences (Ambert, 1982). An even more serious consequence, however, is that the placement is usually in a more restrictive special education program. This results in an associated problem of negative label impact (stigma, discrimination, embarrassment) and lowered teacher expectations (Jones, 1976). The pattern appears to be continuing.

Developing Relevant and Appropriate Educational Programs

Appropriate educational programs for the bilingual exceptional child, and in particular the preschool exceptional and limited English-proficient (LEP) gifted and talented, are virtually nonexistent. But if any attempt were made to develop relevant and appropriate programs, certain considerations would have to be taken into account. For example, poor academic performance on the part of many bilingual exceptional children can be traced to curriculum that is historically and culturally irrelevant (Banks, 1981) and to IEPs that fail to address certain learner traits because of the nature of the IEP process (Ambert & Dew, 1982). To partially alleviate this problem, Ambert and Dew (1982) suggest that:

> IEPs for exceptional bilingual students specify: (a) instructional strategies which take into account linguistic facility, academic skill levels, modality and cognitive style preference; (b) the language(s) of instruction; (c) curricula, and materials designed specifically for linguistically and culturally diverse populations; and (d) motivators and reinforcers which are compatible with the learner's cultural and experiential background.

The language of instruction for bilingual exceptional children should be consistent with what is known about relationships between the native and the second language. For example, using the native language to promote certain conceptual skills may be more effective as a basis for the acquisition of English oral and literacy skills (Cummins, 1984).

Effective teaching skills, which involve utilization of both the native language (Spanish) and English can assist the teacher in mediating instruction and thus assist bilingual exceptional children's understanding of information and task expectations so they can obtain more accurate feedback regarding their performance (Omark & Erickson, 1983; Baca & Cervantes, 1984).

To minimize incompatibilities between bilingual exceptional children and standard school curricula, it is generally agreed that certain perspectives of the child's culture and heritage should be taken into account, although there is disagreement on exactly how they should be dealt with. As an example, some cultural and heritage enrichment programs appear to be compensatory in nature and reflect certain deficiencies in the home; as a result, care must be taken to adequately incorporate culture and heritage in the educational curriculum without adding any undue negative connotations (Banks, 1979).

Minimizing Negative and Inappropriate Special Education Labels

The impact of negative labels has concerned educators for some time (Dunn, 1968; Hobbs, 1975; McMillan, Jones & Aloia, 1974). Additionally, the educational relevancy (aside from funding) of certain special education labels is increasingly being questioned (Howell & Morehead, 1987).

Probably the most serious consequences of negative labels center on teacher expectations and student attitudes. As an example, Prieto and Zucker (1981) demonstrated that even special education teachers considered special education placement more appropriate for Mexican-American children than for their Anglo counterparts. Interestingly, some expectations seemed to take precedence over identical educational and psychological evaluation information in hypothetical case studies. Attempts to alleviate these problems should center on developing generic-type programs that emphasize academic skills and place less reliance on labels.

Developing Adequate Bilingual and ESL Programs

This concern focuses on the specific type of program established by the local education agency. It usually involves choosing between the transitional program and a maintenance program. But, as Rodriguez, Prieto, and Rueda (1984) have stated:

> There are a variety of ways to describe the different types of programs that may be used. One way to address the problem is by "non-response," that is, to ignore that non-English speakers exist in the school. Another way can be termed "extinction," that is, to forbid the use of the non-English language.

In the area of ESL, a major theoretical difference involves the distinction between language learning and language acquisition, with acquisition being the generally preferred model. As Krashen (1982) explains, language acquisition takes place best when students are provided input that is comprehensible, interesting and relevant, not grammatically sequenced, and in sufficient quantity. Methods to accomplish this include Total Physical Response (Asher, 1972), "suggestopedia" (Bushman & Madsen, 1976), and the Natural Approach (Krashen & Terrell, 1982). For the bilingual exceptional child, these methods may offer language codes that are simplified and encourage more active involvement in the learning process.

MODIFYING TEACHER-ADMINISTRATOR EXPECTATIONS AND ATTITUDES

Teacher and administrator attitudes not only set the tone of the classroom but, more important, also shape and determine the nature of classroom interaction between student and teacher, and between students. Although the literature on precise effects of teacher expectations on the performance of minority and exceptional children is vague and controversial, evidence does suggest that teachers hold some negative attitudes toward minority-group children (Jones, 1976). Certain student characteristics upon which teachers seem to base their negative expectations have been identified. These include low academic achievement, low SES, and, curiously, the use of nonstandard language, be it English or Spanish (Brophy & Good, 1974).

The expectation that bilingual exceptional children will benefit from the regular mainstreamed classroom, particularly if this placement is with an inexperienced or insensitive teacher, could in the end be harmful to the student. Consequently, parents, teachers, and the student should be prepared well in advance of any such placements, with emphasis placed on the students' similarities rather than their differences.

Finally, Cummins (1986) has suggested that education reform is necessary if linguistic and culture-minority children are to succeed in school. According to him, this reform must include changes in (a) how teachers interact with students, (b) how the schools respond to minority communities, and (c) the general attitude of the dominant culture toward minority cultures within the society. Teachers must increase both oral and written communication with minority students and allow them to develop some responsibility for what they learn. Second, the schools have to develop better relationships with minority communities and encourage them to become involved in the decision-making processes that affect the educational experiences of their children. Third, the attitude of the dominant culture must begin to reflect equality toward minority culture rather than continue to view them as inferior. When these changes occur, minority children's educational experiences will be altered and the possibility of their academic success will increase.

REFERENCES

Ambert, A.N. (1982). The identification of LEP children with special needs. *Bilingual Journal, 6*(1), 17–22.

Ambert, A.N. (1986). Identifying language disorders in Spanish-speakers. *Journal of Reading, Writing & Learning Disabilities International, 2*(1), 21–41.

Ambert, A.N., & Dew, N. (1982). *Special education for exceptional bilingual students: A handbook for educators.* Milwaukee: Midwest National Origin Desegregation Assistance Center.

Asher, J.J. (1972). Children's first language as a model for second language learning. *Modern Language Journal, 53,* 3–17.

Atkins, R.E. (1931). *The measurement of the intelligence of young children by an object-fitting test.* Minneapolis: University of Minnesota Press.

Baca, L. (1980). *Policy options for insuring the delivery of an appropriate education to bilingual/bicultural handicapped children.* Reston, VA: Council for Exceptional Children.

Baca, L., & Bransford, J. (1981). Meeting the needs of bilingual handicapped children. *Momentum* (pp. 26–29, 49–51), Boulder, CO: University of Colorado.

Baca, L., & Cervantes, H. (Eds.). (1984). *The bilingual special education interface.* St. Louis: Times Mirror/Mosby College Publishing.

Banks, J.A. (1981). *Multi ethnic education: Theory and practice.* Boston: Allyn & Bacon.

Barik, H.C., & Swain, M. (1976). A longitudinal study of bilingual and cognitive development. *International Journal of Psychology, 11*(4), 251–263.

Bernal, E.M. (1979). *The education of culturally different gifted.* Chicago: National Society for the Study of Education.

Brophy, J.E., & Good, T.L. (1974). *Teacher-student relationships: Causes and consequences.* New York: Holt, Rinehart & Winston.

Brown, R.L., Fournier, J.F., & Moyer, R.H. (1977). A cross-cultural study of Piagetian concrete reasoning and science concepts among rural fifth-grade Mexican and Anglo-American students. *Journal of Research in Science Teaching, 14*, 329–334.

Bushman, R., & Madsen, H. (1976). A description and evaluation of suggestopedia—a new teaching methodology. In J. Fanselow & R. Crymes (Eds.), *On TESOL '76* (pp. 29–38). Washington: TESOL.

Cummins, J. (1978). Bilingualism and the development of metalinguistic awareness. *Journal of Cross-Cultural Psychology, 9*(2), 131–149).

Cummins, J. (1984). *Bilingualism and special education: Issues in assessment and pedagogy.* Clevedon, Avon, England: Multilingual Matters, Ltd.

Cummins, J. (1984). Empowering minority students: A framework for intervention. *Harvard Educational Review, 56*(1), 18–36.

Darcy, N.T. (1946). The effects of bilingualism upon the measurement of the intelligence of children of preschool age. *Journal of Educational Psychology, 37*(1), 21–43.

De Avila, E.A., & Pulos, S.M. (1979). Bilingualism and cognitive development. In M.K. Poulsen & G.I. Lubin (Eds.), *Piagetian theory: The helping professions.* Los Angeles: University of Southern California Press.

Duncan, S.E., & De Avila, E.A. (1979). Bilingualism and cognition: Some recent findings. *NABE: The Journal for the National Association for Bilingual Education, 4*(1), 15–50.

Dunn, L.M. (1968). Special education for mildly handicapped—Is much of it justifiable? *Exceptional Children, 46*(8), 584–588.

Feldman, C., & Shen, M. (1971). Some language-related cognitive advantages of bilingual five-year olds. *Journal of Genetic Psychology, 118*, 235–244.

Gorrell, J.J., Bregman, N.J., McAllister, H.A., & Lipscomb, T.J. (1982). A comparison of spatial role-taking in monolingual and bilingual children. *Journal of Genetic Psychology, 140*, 3–10.

Hilliard, A.G. (1980). Cultural diversity and special education. *Exceptional Children, 46*(8), 584–588.

Hobbs, N. (1975). *Issues in the classification of exceptional children.* San Francisco: Jossey-Bass.

Howell, K.M., & Morehead, M.K. (1987). *Curriculum-based evaluation in special and remedial education.* Columbus, OH: Merrill.

Ianco-Worrall, A.D. (1972). Bilingualism and cognitive development. *Child Development, 43*, 1390–1400.

Jones, R.L. (1976). Evaluating mainstream programs for minority children. In R.L. Jones (Ed.), *Mainstreaming and the minority child.* Reston, VA: Council for Exceptional Children.

Krashen, S. (1982). *Principles and practice in second language acquisition.* Elmsford, NY: Pergamon Press.

Krashen, S., & Terrell, T. (1982). *The natural approach: Language acquisition in the classroom.* Elmsford, NY: Pergamon Press.

Leopold, W.F. (1961). Patterning in children's language learning. In S. Saporta (Ed.), *Psycholinguistics.* New York: Holt, Rinehart & Winston.

Liedtke, W.W., & Nelson, L.D. (1968). Concept formation and bilingualism. *Alberta Journal of Education Research, 14*(4), 225–232.

Maldonado-Colón, E. (1986). Assessment: Interpreting data of linguistically and culturally different students referred for disabilities or disorders. *Journal of Reading, Writing, & Learning Disabilities International, 2*(1), 73–83.

McMillan, D.L., Jones, R.L., & Aloia, G. (1974). The mentally retarded label: A theoretical analysis and the review of research. *American Journal of Mental Deficiency, 79*, 241–261.

Mercer, J.R. (1971). Sociocultural factors in labeling mental retardates. *Peabody Journal of Education, 48*, 188–203.

Myers, B., & Goldstein, D. (1979). Cognitive development in bilingual and monolingual lower-class children. *Psychology in the Schools, 16*, 137–142.

Oakland, T. (1979). Research on the Adaptive Behavior Inventory for children and the estimated learning potential. *School Psychology Digest, 8*(1), 63–70.

Omark, P., & Erickson, J. (Eds.). (1983). *The bilingual exceptional child.* San Diego: College-Hill Press.

Ortiz, A.A. (1985). Language and curriculum development for exceptional bilingual children. In P. Chinn (Ed.), *Education of culturally and linguistically different exceptional children.* Reston, VA: Eric Clearinghouse on Handicapped & Gifted Children.

Ortiz, A.A., & Maldonado-Colón, E. (1986). Recognizing learning disabilities in bilingual children: How to lessen inappropriate referrals of language minority students to special education. *Journal of Reading, Writing, and Learning Disabilities International, 2*(1), 43–56.

Peal, E., & Lambert, W.E. (1962). The relation of bilingualism to intelligence. *Psychological Monographs, 76*(27), 1–23.

Prieto, A.G., & Zucker, S.H. (1981). Teacher perception of race as a factor in the placement of behaviorally disordered children. *Behavior Disorders, 7*(1), 34–38.

Rodriguez, R.F. (1982). *The Mexican-American child in special education.* Las Cruces, NM: Clearinghouse on Rural Education & Small Schools.

Rodriguez, R.F., Prieto, A.G., & Rueda, R.S. (1984). Issues in bilingual multicultural special education. *NABE: Journal for the National Association for Bilingual Education, 8*(3), 55–65.

Rueda, R. (1983a). *Research in language and cognition with handicapped and non-handicapped bilingual children.* Paper presented at Symposium on the Handicapped Hispanic Child: Research and Implications for Educational Practice, Texas A & M University, College Station.

Rueda, R. (1983b). Metalinguistic awareness in monolingual and bilingual mildly retarded children. *NABE: The Journal for the National Association for Bilingual Education, 8*(1), 55–67.

Rueda, R. (1985). Cognitive development and learning in mildly handicapped bilingual children. In Chinn, P. (Ed.), *Education of culturally and linguistically exceptional children.* Reston, VA: Council for Exceptional Children.

Torrance, E.P. (1966). *Torrance tests of creative thinking: Directions manual and scoring guide: Figural Test Booklet A.* Princeton, NJ: Personnel Press.

Torrance, E.P., Wu, J., Gowan, J.C., & Aliotti, N.C. (1970). Creative functioning of monolingual and bilingual children in Singapore. *Journal of Educational Psychology, 61*(1), 72–75.

Viera, D.R. (1986). Remediating reading problems in a Hispanic learning disabled child from a psycholinguistic perspective: A case study. *Journal of Reading, Writing and Learning Disabilities International,* (2)1, 85–97.

Vygotsky, L.S. (1972). *Thought and language.* Cambridge, MA: M.I.T. Press.

Whitaker, H.J. (In press). Theoretical considerations in bilingualism and cognition. *NABE: The Journal for the National Association for Bilingual Education.*

Whitaker, J.H., Rueda, R.S., & Prieto, A.G. (1985). Cognitive performance as a function of bilingualism in students with mental retardation. *Mental Retardation, 26*(6), 302–307.

Yela, M. (1975). Compresión verbal y bilingüismo. *Revista de Psicología General y Aplicado, 30*(6), 1039–1046.

Joseph Whitaker is an assistant professor in special education at Inter American University of Puerto Rico. Alfonso Prieto is a professor in special education at Arizona State University.

○ 3 ○

Without motivation, students, especially students with disabilities, will not achieve and become productive citizens. The authors review the various theories of motivation and their implications for special education. In addition, they look at the effects of anxiety, structure, self-concept, teacher expectancy, and other factors on motivation. Differences in motivation or expectancy for success are noted in students with disabilities. The authors give suggestions for instituting programs to remediate or induce higher levels of motivation, especially in students with disabilities.

Motivation and Mildly Handicapped Learners

Teresa A. Mehring and Steven E. Colson

Motivation affects learning, and learning affects motivation (Sprinthall & Sprinthall, 1987). Regular educators and special educators daily are faced with questions regarding motivation in the students for whom they are responsible. What factors influence students' motivational levels? Can a teacher motivate students? What techniques are effective in motivating students?

The school can contribute to development of emotional and motivational problems in very specific ways (Hallahan & Kauffman, 1988; Paget, Nagle, & Martin, 1984; Pullis & Cadwell, 1985). Teachers may be insensitive to individual student needs; they may hold expectations for achievement or conduct that are too high or too low; and they may communicate to the student who does not meet expectations that he or she is inadequate or undesirable. In addition, instruction may be offered in skills for which the student has no real or imagined use. All of these factors may influence the level of motivation that a regular or special education student brings to the learning environment.

Despite the critical link between motivation and learning, little research has been conducted to investigate this correlation in mildly handicapped students. Investigating the effects of motivation on school success and learning in students with mild learning and behavior deficiencies (mental retardation, learning disabilities, and behavior disorders) could provide important information to special and regular educators.

Several researchers have found that motivation to learn differs in students with mental retardation (MacMillan, 1982; Polloway & Epstein, 1985; Polloway & Smith, 1983; Robinson & Robinson, 1976; Zigler, 1962). After experiencing failure, mentally retarded students tend to display reduced motivation and lack efficient learning even on simple tasks. Reschly (1987) calls this tendency the "failure set phenomenon" (p. 43). Individuals with mental retardation also tend to attribute success or failure to external variables (luck, difficulty of the task) rather than to internal factors (personal ability or amount of effort expended on the task).

Research with students who have learning disabilities (LD) has reported motivation and attribution deficits similar to those found in investigations with students who have mental retardation. Adelman and Taylor (1983, 1984) reported that LD students display an external locus of control for reinforcement and tend to attribute success to external factors. Deshler, Schumaker, and Lenz (1984) emphasized the existence of motivation factors that must be considered in developing interventions with LD students.

Most students with behavior disorders (BD) are also underachievers at school, as measured by standardized tests. Students who are affected by a behavior disorder usually do not achieve at the level expected for their mental age, and they relatively seldom achieve academically advanced performance. Some children are already dysfunctional when they come to school. Others develop disorders during the school years—perhaps in part because of damaging experiences in the classroom itself (Hallahan & Kauffman, 1988).

Most human motives are learned or acquired. Motives also affect perception. Many theorists have attempted to explain where motivation comes from and how it can be changed. An understanding of current motivation theories is critical to special education teachers, school psychologists, and regular classroom teachers who work with mildly handicapped learners. Theory assists us in understanding why some students display certain behaviors—behaviors that we often call "lack of motivation."

MOTIVATION THEORIES

Not until the early 20th century did anyone experimentally validate the link between learning and motivation. In the 1980s virtually all psychologists and an increasing number of regular and special educators have become concerned with the impact of motivation variables on human behavior. Implicit in the literature on underachievement and overachievement is the assumption that motivation and emotional variables play a crucial, if not *the* crucial, role in academic success.

Instinct Theory

Before observations of other cultures by anthropologists Margaret Mead and Ruth Benedict, many early Western psychologists thought that what they observed in their own culture was true the world over. Because it was assumed that motives such as competition, power, status, approval, and achievement were present among all people everywhere, the term *instinct* was used. Early in this century McDougall (1908) authored the first book on the subject, titled *Social Psychology*. In it, he stated that all social life was the result of inherited instincts. According to McDougall, people were destined to play out preprogrammed instincts that were built into their biological natures. Students achieved academically because of an achievement instinct. Students not so blessed were doomed to a school life of academic frustration, and nothing could be done to change it.

By the mid 1920s psychologists had dismissed instinct theory as unscientific and ludicrous. We now know that social motives differ widely throughout the world and that social motives are learned or acquired, not inherited.

Needs/Drives Theory

According to needs/drives theory, motivation has two identifiable components: needs and drives. Needs are based on some deficit within the person. The deficit may be physiological or psychological. Physiological needs are obvious—water, food, sex, sleep, warmth, and so on. Psychological needs are more subtle and less easily identified—approval, affection, power, prestige, and so on.

Drives are based on needs, but they have the added feature of an obvious change in behavior; they imply motion of some sort. When we experience a drive, we are motivated to pursue actions that will lead to a reduction in the drive. A good example might be hunger. If an individual goes without food for a while, the result is discomfort or internal tension. This drive motivates the individual to obtain food. Eating reduces the drive and restores physical and psychological balance.

All humans are born with a small set of unlearned biological drives. Twelve biological motives that Madsen (1973) and others have described are:

hunger	excretion
thirst	oxygen
sex	rest/sleep
nurturance (parenting)	activity (stimulation/arousal)
body temperature	security
pain avoidance	aggression

These biological motives gradually develop into a larger, more diverse set of drives acquired through learning. Murray (1938) referred to learned drives as being *psychogenic*. According to Murray, most individuals have drives for achievement, recognition, affiliation, dominance, acquisition (of possessions), exhibition, and play.

Maslow (1970) postulated that all humans are motivated to satisfy or reduce a common set of needs that are qualitatively different and that could be arranged hierarchically on a scale from low to high priority These are given in Figure 1. When needs at the physiological level are satisfied, an individual becomes concerned with higher-level needs. Satisfaction of a level of needs activates needs at the next level.

	self-actualization (realization of potential)
Being Needs	aesthetic (order and beauty)
	cognitive (knowledge and understanding)

- -

	esteem (achievement; gaining of recognition, respect, status)
Deficiency Needs	belonging and love (affiliation and acceptance)
	safety and security (long-term survival and stability)
	survival/physiological (hunger, thirst, etc.)

Source: From *Motivation and Personality* (2nd ed.) by A. H. Maslow, 1970, New York: Harper & Row.

FIGURE 1   Maslow's Hierarchy of Needs

Maslow's theory may be identified by teachers who note that hungry students are less likely to pay attention in school than those who have had enough to eat. Even if they obtain a good meal, children who have experienced hunger are likely to experience the hunger drive as a continuing force and often begin planning how to obtain their next meal as soon as they finish eating. Students who are physically uncomfortable for any reason are less likely to be attentive because they are preoccupied with attempts at reducing their discomfort.

Safety and security are two other needs identified by Maslow. Infants and children need to satisfy safety and security needs almost daily. During their early years children are relatively helpless and most in need of stable and orderly environments. When a child's or an adolescent's world is disrupted suddenly by loss of a parent through divorce, serious illness, or death, psychological security needs often dominate. Children are easily frightened by strange environments or environments in which they feel threatened.

Once children feel safe, they turn toward affiliation needs to achieve fulfillment. Friendships, love relationships, and group acceptance emerge as dominant concerns. According to Maslow, if an individual has difficulty satisfying love and belonging needs, maladjustment—and sometimes psychopathology—may result. Students who have difficulty getting along with their classmates or teachers often have trouble reaching their academic potential. School is the first real testing ground for establishing their place among children. If they fail in social relationships, school can become a hostile environment associated only with fear and anxiety. Maslow suggested that teachers should perceive school not only as a place where students learn facts and skills but also as a place where they can develop important interpersonal relationships.

The fourth need Maslow identified is self-esteem. Esteem needs involve recognition as a human being. These needs include self-respect as well as respect from others. From self-respect comes confidence, independence, and freedom. Respect from others generates a sense of appreciation and prestige. If these needs are not satisfied, children become preoccupied with their perceived inadequacies and with possible rejection by others. Teachers should provide opportunities for students to learn to respect themselves. One of the most important roles a teacher plays is that of model. Teachers who relate to students honestly and respectfully tend to generate this attitude in their students.

When the needs described so far are more or less satisfied, individuals turn to higher-level needs for intellectual achievement, aesthetic appreciation, and, finally, self-actualization. According to Maslow, self-actualized people are fulfilled people. They perceive reality easily and are comfortable with it. They accept themselves and others. They feel free to think and act spontaneously. They approach problems with no personal biases. They value time they can spend by themselves as well as time they spend with others. Their thinking is not rigidly tied to cultural values, and they feel brotherhood among all human beings. They enjoy a small number of rich relationships with people of both sexes. They enjoy work involved in reaching goals. They are relatively free of prejudice and jealousy. They have a sense of humor and the ability to be creative.

Maslow called the four lower-levels needs—survival, safety, belonging, and esteem—deficiency needs. When these needs are not met, motivation increases to find ways of satisfying them. When they are satisfied, the motivation for fulfilling them decreases. Maslow labeled the three higher level needs—intellectual achievement, aesthetic appreciation, and self-actualization—being needs. When they are met, a person's motivation does not cease; instead, it increases to seek further fulfillment. Unlike deficiency needs, being needs can never be completely fulfilled.

Maslow's theory can provide important information for understanding motivation. Even so, it has been criticized because people do not always appear to behave as the theory would predict. Most of us move back and forth among different types of needs and may be motivated by different needs at the same time. Regardless of criticism, Maslow's hierarchy does provide a way of looking at the full person, whose physical, emotional, and intellectual needs are interrelated.

Cognitive Theory

One of the central assumptions in cognitive theory is that individuals are motivated by variables other than external events or physical conditions such as hunger. When we succeed or fail at a task, we naturally think about who or what was behind our success or failure. We look to assign responsibility, and to understand the causes of our performance. We make attributions about who or what was responsible for how we performed. Attributions also are the source of our feeling good, bad, or indifferent after we succeed or fail.

Attributions can be classified along three dimensions: the source (locus) of control, stability, and controllability (Weiner, 1986). The source of control can be either internal or external. Saying that you did well on a test because you're good in math is an example of attributing success to an internal characteristic—ability. If you believe you did well because the teacher was lenient, you are attributing your success to an external factor—the teacher.

Stability, or the lack of it, is another characteristic of attribution. Suppose you fail an exam. An unstable attribution might refer to effort (I didn't study as much as I should have). A stable attribution might refer to perceived discrimination on the part of the teacher (she's always tough on girls).

Attributions also vary along a dimension called "controllability." If you believe that the difficulty of the task was responsible for your failure (I didn't do well because the questions were too hard), you're describing a cause beyond your control. If you failed the test because you lost your notes and couldn't study, you're attributing your failure to a factor that you can control.

The internal/external dimension seems to be closely related to feelings of confidence, self-esteem, pride, guilt, or shame. If success or failure is attributed to internal factors (i.e., skill, effort), success will lead to pride and increased motivation, whereas failure will lead to shame. If the causes are seen as external, gratitude could follow success and anger could follow failure. This dimension is closely related to Rotter's (1954) idea of *locus of control.* Sometimes individuals believe they are responsible for their own fate and like to work in situations where skills and effort can lead to success. Other people tend to have an external locus of control and generally believe that people and forces outside of themselves control their lives. These individuals prefer to work in situations where luck determines the outcome.

The stability dimension seems to be closely related to expectations about the future. If, for example, students attribute their success (or failure) to stable factors such as ability or difficulty of the test, they are likely to expect to succeed (or fail) on similar tasks in the future. But if they attribute the outcome to unstable factors such as mood or luck, they are likely to expect changes in the future when confronted with similar tasks.

The control dimension is related to both confidence and future expectations. A student who attributes a high grade on an American History exam to controllable factors takes pride in the grade and expects to achieve a similar grade on future tests. But if the student thinks the grade had very little or nothing to do with controllable factors (Boy, did I luck out!), he or she is likely only to feel grateful and hope that the good luck will continue.

According to cognitive theory, how we classify attributions can affect our performance on future tasks. If you believe a failure is controllable (say, the result of low effort), you may be spurred by that failure to do better next time. If you believe, however, that you cannot control who or what caused the failure, you may not even try to improve your performance. Failure itself is not always harmful; what does the damage is attributing failure to causes over which you have no control.

A major component of cognitive theory that is related to locus of control is *learned helplessness*, described as the perception that one has no control over events. Learned helplessness develops when students or teachers believe that what happens has little or nothing to do with how much effort they expend (Abramson, Seligman, & Teasdale, 1978). Many students from minority groups, poverty backgrounds, and special education settings develop extremely negative self-concepts when they perceive that no matter what they do or can do, their teachers expect them to do better or differently. Persistent students who are also higher achievers tend to attribute success to what they're doing. Low achievers and less persistent students more frequently attribute success to external causes. These are the students who tend to exhibit learned helplessness (Dweck, 1975).

Young children usually start school with high self-concepts. No one has taught them that they can't succeed. At first, when they have difficulty, they attribute it to bad luck or to the task at hand. Gradually, as they learn (or are told) through repeated exposure that they are incompetent, they learn to attribute failure to themselves (Buys & Winefield,

1982). Internal attributions can cause students who feel helpless to have intense feelings of shame and self-doubt (Covington & Omelich, 1981). At this point, whether students believe that they have failed because of external causes or lack of ability (internal causes), they're equally likely to believe in their helplessness and stop trying. Attribution patterns are fairly stable over time and situations, but training programs *can* break self-defeating attributions in students (Bar-Tal, Raviv, and Bar-Tal, 1982).

Covington and Beery (1976) described two types of students: success-oriented and failure-avoiding. Success-oriented students tend to believe that they can handle most academic challenges. They do not view ability as an important issue in learning. These students view success and failure as related to quality of efforts. Bar-Tal (1982) found that success-oriented students attribute success to ability and effort and failure to lack of proper effort. Success improves further confidence; failure signals a need to try harder. Success-oriented individuals are not threatened by failure when it does occur because it doesn't reflect on their ability. Failure can be used to motivate already successful students.

Failure-avoiding students tend to have a different set of attributes. They attribute failure to lack of ability and attribute success to external factors such as luck or easiness of the task (Weiner & Kukla, 1970). These students blame themselves for failure but take little credit for success. They feel they have little control over their academic destiny. They try to minimize pain by trying to avoid failure. Severely failure-oriented students develop learned helplessness. The individual sees no relationship between effort and attainment of goals.

Attribution theory literature suggests that low-achieving students are not all unmotivated. Many are very motivated—but to avoid failure rather than to succeed. Teachers should spend more time learning about student beliefs about causes for success and failure. Kifer (1975) found that changes in locus of control and self-concept both occur gradually and with repeated experience with success or failure. One important goal is to establish classroom conditions in which students learn that proper effort can lead to success.

Other Factors Influencing Motivation to Learn

In addition to the theoretical perspectives described, several additional factors have been associated with the link between motivation and academic performance. These include (a) anxiety, (b) self-concept, (c) teacher expectations, (d) the learning process, (e) goal structure, and (f) incentives for learning.

Anxiety

Several behaviors of highly anxious students in learning situations account for their low performance levels. Hill and Wigfield (1984) found that highly anxious students respond similarly to those with learned helplessness; they tend to avoid failure because they fear negative evaluations. They avoid evaluative situations and choose easy tasks in which success is more certain. They also engage in failure-avoiding strategies. Anxious students do not attend to tasks in sufficient detail; they are preoccupied with negative self-references or worry. As the teacher is presenting material, anxious students are likely to be thinking about inadequacies that may make attempts to learn the material more difficult.

Anxious students have difficulty when instructional methods require them to rely on short-term memory or when they are asked to perform quickly. They have difficulty learning material that is not well organized. Anxious students tend to perform better when the teacher structures information. Anxiety also may cause the student to have social and academic problems. Highly anxious students have lower self-concepts, blame themselves for failure, and daydream excessively.

Self-Concept

Self-concept—one's ideas or perceptions about oneself—is one of the most important single factors affecting behavior (Combs & Avila, 1985). Educators have become increasingly aware of the impact that an individual's self-concept and self-esteem have on classroom behavior and achievement. Students' problems in school may be solely attributable to the lack of a positive self-concept (Combs & Avila, 1985).

The relationship between self-concept and achievement has been discussed extensively in the psychology literature. Students' self-concept can be an important aspect in understanding how they deal with academic tasks. Many students are caught in a vicious cycle; they believe they cannot perform well in a certain activity and they avoid it. Because they avoid it, they fail to get practice in the activity and do not perform well when they are asked to respond in class. The negative experience caused by the inability to respond correctly only reinforces their initial belief about their inability. This cycle becomes a self-fulfilling prophecy. A negative self-image can be self-perpetuating. Over time it can have a negative impact on academic achievement.

Teacher Expectations

Although debate and research continues, Rosenthal and Jacobson's (1968) investigation of teacher expectations does point out a serious concern. In the classroom a teacher's incorrect beliefs about a students' abilities or behaviors can bring about the behaviors the teacher expects. Several researchers have found that teacher expectations can influence student performance (Cornbleth, Davis, & Button, 1974; Good, 1970; Pippert, 1969). Two kinds of expectation effects can occur: self-fulfilling prophecy and sustaining expectation effect.

Self-fulfilling prophecy occurs when teacher beliefs about students are incorrect, but student behavior comes to match the initially inaccurate expectation. The sustaining expectation effect occurs when teachers *are* fairly accurate in their assessment of student abilities and respond to students based on those judgments. The problem arises when students show some improvement but the teacher does not alter his or her expectations to take account of the improvement. The chance to raise expectations, provide more appropriate teaching and thus encourage higher student achievement is lost.

Good and Brophy (1984) found that once teachers have formed expectations about a student, they treat that student in accordance with those expectations. Students who are expected to achieve tend to be asked more and harder questions, are given more chances and longer time to respond, and are interrupted less often than students who are expected to do poorly (Allington, 1980; Cornbleth, Davis, & Button, 1974; Good & Brophy, 1984; Rosenthal, 1983).

Students for whom teachers have high expectations are given clues and prompts—communicating their beliefs that the student can answer the question (Rosenthal, 1983). Teachers tend to be more encouraging in general toward students for whom they have high expectations. They smile at these students more often and show greater warmth through nonverbal responses such as leaning toward the student and nodding their heads as students speak (Woolfolk and Brooks, 1982, 1985). In contrast, with students for whom expectations are low, teachers ask easier questions, allow less time for answering, and are much less likely to give prompts.

Good and Brophy (1984) noted that teachers demand better performance from high-achieving students, are less likely to accept a poor answer, and praise them more for good answers. Teachers are more likely, on the other hand, to accept or even reinforce inadequate answers from low-achieving students or criticize students for wrong answers. Low-achieving students receive less praise than high-achieving students for similar correct answers. On tests when the answer is almost right, the teacher is more likely to give the benefit of the doubt (and better grade) to high-achieving students (Finn, 1972).

This inconsistent feedback is confusing for low-ability students. Imagine how difficult it is to learn if your wrong answers are sometimes praised, sometimes ignored, and sometimes criticized, and your correct answer receives little recognition (Good, 1983).

A student's achievement motivation, aspiration level, and self-concept may all be affected by teacher expectations. Many students use the teacher's behavior as a mirror in which to see themselves. If the reflection says they are incapable, self-esteem is likely to suffer. Brophy (1982) found that, in general, the self-esteem of students who are young, dependent, conforming, or who really like the teacher is the most likely to be affected by teacher views.

The Learning Process

Keller (1983) suggested that four major dimensions of the learning process affect motivation:

1. Interest—learner curiosity.
2. Relevance—learner perception that instruction is related to personal needs or goals.
3. Expectancy—learner-perceived likelihood of success and extent to which the student views success as being under personal control.
4. Satisfaction—a learner's intrinsic motivation and reaction to extrinsic rewards.

Clearly, for learning to occur, one must pay attention to a stimulus. According to Keller, interest is more likely to be maintained if curiosity is stimulated and if students have an opportunity to explore and manipulate various objects physically or intellectually. Personal motivation also will increase when individuals perceive that an instructional task will satisfy a basic need, motive, or value. An individual's expectation for success or failure also can affect performance.

Teachers can increase expectations for success by providing successful experiences on meaningful, *not* trivial or easy, tasks. They also can use instructional strategies that offer students personal control over success. Feedback that helps students relate success to personal ability and effort also may increase student motivation.

In general, students benefit from feedback and information that has pleasurable rather than aversive consequences. They enjoy having the opportunity to make decisions and to be rewarded occasionally for tasks for which they are at least partially responsible.

Goal Structure

Johnson and Johnson (1978, 1987) have found that motivation can be influenced greatly by the ways in which we relate to the other people who are also involved in accomplishing a particular goal. Johnson and Johnson have labeled this interpersonal factor the *goal structure* of the task. The three basic structures are: cooperative, competitive, and individualistic.

Cooperative	Students work together to accomplish shared goals.
Competitive	Students work against each other to achieve goals that only a few students can attain.
Individualistic	One student's achievement of the goal is unrelated to other students' achievement of the goal.

Several studies have shown that when the task involves complex learning and problem-solving skills, cooperation leads to higher achievement than does competition, especially for low-ability students (Davis, Laughlin, & Komorita, 1976; Edwards & DeVries, 1974; Slavin, 1977). Johnson and Johnson (1987) found that cooperative settings are more likely to produce higher levels of motivation to learn, because interaction patterns encourage and support efforts to achieve. Their research has shown improved learning in cross-ethnic and cross-handicapped groupings. Many experts have pointed out detrimental effects of competition in the classroom. Holt (1982) found that students who fear failure in competitive situations spend most of the day figuring out strategies to protect themselves in the classroom. Competition appears to motivate students to avoid failure rather than to focus on learning.

All three goal structures are effective under certain conditions and are relevant to specific goals and objectives of a lesson. Knowing when to use cooperative, competitive, and individualistic learning is an important instructional decision that teachers must make.

Incentives for Learning

Not every lesson successfully completed will enhance a sense of competence. Some activities necessarily involve drill and repetition. A student may feel competent enough to not have any intrinsic interest in working on the task to improve his or her competence. In this case, the teacher may decide to provide extrinsic reinforcement for successful completion of work.

Some students—those with less ability, a low need for achievement, inadequate preparation, a history of failing a particular subject, or a poor academic self-concept—may need extra incentives at the outset in order to tackle what, for them, is a difficult task. In these situations the teacher may plan the lesson to include systematic reinforcement.

Caution should be observed, however, because external rewards used inappropriately can undermine students' natural interest in a subject (Cohen, 1985; Deci, 1975).

REMEDIAL STRATEGIES TO INCREASE MOTIVATION

Apparent lack of motivation in a student may result from a variety of underlying reasons such as those postulated in the theories and factors just described. Unfortunately, there is no panacea or cure-all for motivation deficits. Various intervention approaches have been described in the education and psychology literature. Several of these suggested techniques and strategies will be described. Initially, however, teachers may want to consider interacting closely with the student to attempt to get a better feel for the conditions that may be at the heart of the motivation deficit. *The Teacher-Student Motivation Planning Form* (Figure 2) may provide an appropriate format for teacher-student interaction.

Teacher-Student Motivation Planning Form

The *Teacher-Student Motivation Planning Form* provides a format for recording and monitoring decisions about motivation planning, as well as information about the student's present level of performance. This is given in Figure 2. Some parts of the form are to be completed prior to a teacher-student conference; others are to be completed after intervention, when results and possible revised plans are being made. Teachers are urged to fill in each part of the form so that it will provide as complete a profile as possible.

The Teacher-Student Motivation Planning Form consists of the following sections: General Information, Current Student Behavior, Desired Student Behavior, Teacher's Attributions, Student's Attributions, Previous Plan and Results, Current Plan, Results, and Revised Plan.

General Information
This part of the form provides space for the student's name, school, date of birth, age, grade in school or specific class period, teacher's name, and the current date.

Current Student Behavior
The teacher's goal for this student behavior is to be stated; for example, "To pass this course, Bill must turn in each homework assignment."

Teacher's Attributions
Performance is the only visible indicator of achievement motivation. When a student succeeds or fails at a task, we naturally think about who or what was behind the success or failure. Here the teacher would describe his or her own attributions about the current student behavior. Teachers may attribute student success to the student's home conditions, effort, interest, and their own teaching skill. The teacher must honestly look at his or her perception of the student behavior. Often, teachers will see a variety of interrelated factors—some of which the teacher can control (length of assignment, reinforcers, grading

Student: _____   School: _____

Date of Birth: _____   Age: _____   Grade/Class: _____

Teacher: _____   Date: _____

Current Student Behavior:

Desired Student Behavior:

Teacher's Attributions:

Student's Attributions:

Previous Plan (if any) and Results:

Current Plan:

    Realistic Short-Term Goal:

    Modifications Necessary for Success:

    Assessment:

    Next Conference Date:

Results:

Revised Plan (if necessary):

FIGURE 2   **Teacher-Student Motivation Planning Form**

procedures) and those he or she cannot (student's physical health, parental cooperation, and lack of time for homework because of employment or family demands).

Student's Attributions

During a conference situation, in which a sense of rapport and true nonthreatening concern have been expressed, the student is asked for attributions concerning the behavior. Students probably will attribute their performance to some combination of effort, ability, mood, task difficulty, and luck. Teachers are cautioned to record the student's answers without judgmental responses or facial expressions.

Previous Plan and Results

Unfortunately, many students have a long history of social and academic behaviors that interfere with success. In this section teachers should list any previous classroom intervention to modify this behavior. They will want to probe the student and professional colleagues about previous attempts to modify this type of behavior. For example, an explanation of past token economies and contingency management techniques could be described, along with their results. If previous attempts have failed, the teacher will want to carefully consider whether other similar measures would be successful.

The teacher also may gain important insights on how to modify previously unsuccessful techniques. The student should be asked about the success or failure of previous interventions. Often the student's perception of these attempts adds anecdotal information that will guide the planning process.

Current Plan

After completing the previous sections, the teacher and student collaboratively decide on a course of action. A realistic short-term goal must be agreed upon. In most cases teachers cannot expect a complete reversal of current student behavior overnight. Likewise, students cannot expect to continue an undesirable classroom behavior without at least some modification. Once again, an atmosphere of mutual respect and commitment to change will facilitate the creation of a realistic goal.

Usually some modifications will have to be considered if a realistic short-term goal is to be reached. As an example, the teacher might give serious consideration to the types of homework being assigned. Because homework is designed as an independent activity, a student may need more time in teacher-directed and dependent activities before this type of homework can be completed.

The assessment phase of the current plan should state how both teacher and student will record the progress or lack of progress; for example, "Both Bill and Mrs. Jones will record each math assignment at the beginning of class." Having the student record his or her own performance helps put ownership of the realistic short-term goal with the student.

The last decision to be made in this section is to schedule a future conference to discuss the results. Because this planning form is geared to realistic short-term goals, a subsequent conference probably should be scheduled within days or weeks of the plan's implementation.

Results

This section should include a descriptive analysis of the plan's effectiveness, along with supporting data. If the results show that the short-term goal has not been met, the teacher should go on to the next section, Revised Plan.

Revised Plan

The process is repeated. A new conference would be held, during which both the student and the teacher formulate a new strategy with particular emphasis on not repeating the parts of the previous plan that contributed to its failure.

Guidelines for Classroom Motivation

Once teachers have a clearer idea of variables influencing current student motivation and performance in the classroom, more appropriate goals and intervention strategies can be targeted. Although many educators and cognitive psychologists now believe that children are responsible for their own learning (Reid & Hresko, 1981), classroom teachers still control the vast majority of instructional variables. Various strategies and techniques that have been presented in the education and psychology literature on student motivation are discussed next. These guidelines have proven effective for some students in some situations.

Competitive, Noncompetitive, and Cooperative Learning Structures

Some students thrive in situations in which competition is essential for success. A spelling bee or a multiplication fact card game with only one "real winner" are two examples of competitive classroom structures. When all participants are evenly matched, a competitive game or contest can be exciting and rewarding for all, especially if winners are likely to change from one match to the next.

Noncompetitive structures emphasize individual learning and individual effort. In a sense, students do compete, but only with their own past performance. This kind of structure allows for more winners and permits a greater number of students to feel competent.

In a cooperative learning structure, students usually work in small groups for group rewards. All members of a group, both high and low achievers, learn to work together for rewards that each member will share. When properly introduced and supervised, this type of classroom arrangement can be successful. Optimally, cooperative learning allows each student to display his or her strength while becoming more aware of the needs of others.

Choosing a competitive, noncompetitive, or cooperative learning structure is an individual teacher decision. Different activities within any given day may successfully incorporate one or more structures. Certainly the world outside the classroom demands a shift from structure to structure. Why should the child's world within the classroom be any different?

Unidimensional and Multidimensional Classrooms

Rosenholtz and Simpson (1984) have stated that most teachers expect all students to be working on similar tasks at any given time. Even in classrooms for children with special needs, teachers typically expect this same type of conformity, albeit with more individual flexibility than regular classrooms. This type of classroom is commonly referred to as "unidimensional."

Unidimensional classrooms can be stressful for students who are performing significantly above or below the normal range of achievement. Often, teachers unknowingly contribute to this stress by placing an individual student in an activity that he or she is developmentally unprepared to master. Hudson, Colson, and Braxdale (1984) have proposed a hierarchy of levels of teacher presentation to match each child's current level of functioning. For example, one student may *recall* the capital of Kansas as Topeka, while another may need several choices because he or she is functioning at the lower *recognition* level.

In multidimensional classrooms, individual students often work on different tasks. The key to success in these types of classrooms rests on the accuracy of assessment information gathered on individual students. Norm-referenced tests, which provide scores that are mistakenly matched to grade-level curricula, further complicate teachers' attempts to structure successful multidimensional classrooms. Current curriculum-based assessment tools, such as the *Hudson Education Skills Inventory* (Hudson, Colson, Welch, Banikowski, & Mehring, 1989), give teachers more accurate information to plan appropriate instruction for a wide range of student performance within the same classroom.

Intrinsic and Extrinsic Reinforcers

During various activities some students appear to be unaffected by environmental variables. Motivation without apparent reward is called *intrinsic*. Some theorists believe that intrinsically motivated students have developed self-reinforcement processes that can be traced back to some earlier, external reinforcer. For example, a student may have initially turned in assignments in the best handwriting because the teacher rewarded this effort with a sticker or praise. Now this same student may turn in the same quality penmanship for internal feelings of satisfaction of a job well done.

Children with special needs may require a varied menu of both intrinsic and extrinsic rewards. Too often, educators insist that classroom rewards be either all intrinsic or all extrinsic. Motivating all behavior with extrinsic rewards can set up unrealistic expectations for the child outside the classroom. Likewise, asking students to rely solely on intrinsic motivators hardly approximates life for most adults. How many workers would continue to be effective for purely intrinsic rewards, forsaking paychecks and praise from co-workers and supervisors?

Systematic reinforcement, in the form of teacher praise, free time, or the chance to play educationally relevant games, may make school life more pleasant and may assist students to become more involved in learning. Token economies also have been found to be effective in improving the academic and social behaviors of many exceptional students (McLaughlin, 1975; O'Leary & Drabman, 1971). Cohen (1973) and others have found contingency management contracting to be a particularly effective method of external motivation at the secondary level.

Motivational Techniques in Teaching

Gage and Berliner (1988) have listed 15 techniques that are supported by research as increasing motivation in the classroom.

1. Begin the lesson by giving students a reason to be motivated.
2. Tell students exactly what you want accomplished.
3. Have students set short-term goals.
4. Give verbal and written praise.
5. Use tests and grades judiciously.
6. Capitalize on the arousal value of suspense, discovery, curiosity, and exploration.
7. Occasionally do the unexpected.
8. Whet the appetite.
9. Use familiar material for examples.
10. Use unique and unexpected contexts when applying concepts and principles.
11. Make students use what they have previously learned.
12. Use simulations and games.
13. Minimize the attractiveness of competition.
14. Minimize any unpleasant consequences of student involvement—i.e., use positive reinforcement.
15. Understand the social climate of the school. (pp. 378-389)

Dembo (1988) suggested several additional classroom applications for enhancing student motivation:

1. Focus and maintain student attention through arousing student curiosity. This can be accomplished by introducing something that is novel, different, or unusual.
2. Consider varying levels of ability in students, and encourage them to put forth maximum effort consistent with their ability. Differentiated assignments, materials, and evaluation standards will assist students to set more realistic aspirations. Assisting students to experience success will lead to increased achievement motivation.
3. When students do not experience success, give feedback in the form of concrete steps that will lead to improvement.
4. Actively involve students in the learning process. Provide them with opportunities to "select activities, assignments, due dates, and those with whom they work, as well as their own methods and pace of learning" (p. 210).
5. Reduce anxiety by providing sufficient time to complete assignments, tests, and other work.

Structured learning situations rather than independent study, discussion groups, or other types of student-directed learning activities also may be beneficial. Diagrams, outlines, and other organizational strategies also can aid in reducing anxiety. Teaching students relaxation techniques may be an additional option. Dembo's most important suggestion is that teachers should not wait for students to become motivated; the teacher should *act*!

Brophy and Kher (1985) suggested that in order to develop positive motivation, negative attitudes must be eliminated. Specific strategies for overcoming negative attitudes include the following:

1. Be a patient, encouraging teacher who supports learning efforts.
2. Provide an appropriate match between student ability and task difficulty.
3. Provide tasks that are sufficiently varied and interesting.
4. Be a teacher who generally presents tasks as learning opportunities with which he or she will assist students rather than as ordeals to be endured to get good grades or to please the teacher. (p. 445)

Increasing Achievement Motivation/Improving Student Attributions

Students with high achievement needs but equally high failure fears are likely to select relatively easy, clearly manageable tasks. Students with high achievement motivation, and little fear of failure are likely to select tasks that more fully test their limits. Teachers can help students engage in goal-relevant tasks by reducing fear of failure, helping to develop positive achievement motivation, and manipulating task incentives. Differential assignments also may have major effects on student performance. It is critical to help students perceive the relationship between their efforts and success. One way to facilitate this perception is to teach students how to explain success or failure on the basis of actual causal factors (I failed the test because I went to the ballgame last night instead of studying) rather than on the basis of habit (I failed because I'm stupid). Assisting students in learning how to set realistic goals also improves motivation and positive attributions toward learning.

Peer Tutoring

Buddy systems or peer tutoring can be used to effectively motivate student behavior. This technique has the added advantage of allowing peer tutors to be responsible for assisting other students and increasing their own subject matter knowledge. Training peer tutors through teacher modeling or role playing appropriate tutoring behaviors increases the effectiveness of the peer tutoring model.

Motivation Strategies

Good and Brophy (1986) described forty specific strategies which could be implemented in classrooms to improve motivation. Since this listing is far too numerous and detailed to summarize in this article, the reader is encouraged to go directly to the source listed in the reference section. Strategies are grouped into five major categories including: task design and selection strategies, strategies that involve imposing external reward systems, effective instruction strategies, success oriented strategies, and metacognitive strategies.

Van Reusen, Box, Schumaker, and Deshler (1987) designed an *Educational Planning Strategy*. The initial goal of this strategy was to train students to be more actively involved in the development of their individualized educational programs. The skills acquired as the result of instruction in this strategy, in addition, would assist most students to be more knowledgeable about their own learning and social strengths and weaknesses and equip them with specific skills to interact more confidently in a variety of settings. The strategy has proven to be effective in assisting students to take a more active role in decision making.

SUMMARY

Current research indicates a strong correlation between motivation and effective learning in regular and special needs students. Research also tells us that motivation levels *can* be changed over time. Before embarking on an intervention plan, however, teachers may find value in reviewing basic theories of motivation in an attempt to detect variables that may be affecting student motivation. The *Teacher-Student Motivation Planning Form* provides a format and process that teachers might use to facilitate this investigation. Once factors influencing student motivation are identified, alternative strategies may be implemented to influence students' active involvement in the learning process. There is no single motivation-enhancing intervention approach. Different techniques or strategies are effective with each student. Methods also may have to be varied over time or as effectiveness decreases. Reemphasis of Dembo's (1988) comment is an appropriate summary statement: Teachers should not wait for students to become motivated: They should *act*!

REFERENCES

Abramson, L., Seligman, M., & Teasdale, J. (1978). Learned helplessness in humans: Critique and reformulation. *Journal of Abnormal Psychology, 87*, 49–74.

Adelman, H. S., & Taylor, L. (1983). *Learning disabilities in perspective.* Glenview, IL: Scott, Foresman.

Adelman, H. S., & Taylor, L. (1984). Enhancing motivation for overcoming learning problems. *Annual Review of Learning Disabilities, 2,* 102–109.

Allington, R. (1980). Teacher interruption behaviors during primary-grade oral reading. *Journal of Educational Psychology, 71,* 371–377.

Bar-Tal, D. (1982). The effects of teachers' behavior on pupils' attributions: A review. In C. Antaki & C. Brieson (Eds.), *Attribution and psychological change: A guide to the use of attribution theory in the clinic and the classroom.* London: Academic Press.

Bar-Tal, D., Raviv, A., & Bar-Tal, Y. (1982). Consistency of pupil's attributions regarding success and failure. *Journal of Educational Psychology, 74,* 104–110.

Brophy, J. E. (1982, March). *Research on the self-fulfilling prophecy and teacher expectations.* Paper presented at annual meeting of American Educational Research Association, New York.

Brophy, J., & Kher, N. (1988). Teacher socialization as a mechanism for developing student motivation to learn. In R. Feldman (Ed.), *Social psychology applied to education.* Cambridge: Cambridge University Press.

Buys, N., & Winefield, A. (1982). Learned helplessness in high school students following experience of non-contingent rewards. *Journal of Research in Personality, 16,* 118–127.

Cohen, H. L. (1973). Behavior modification and socially deviant youth. In C. E. Thorenson (Ed.), *Behavior modification in education: Seventy-second yearbook of the National Society for the Study of Education* (Part 1). Chicago: University of Chicago Press.

Cohen, M. (1985). Extrinsic and intrinsic motivation. In M. Alderman & M. Cohen (Eds.), *Motivation theory and practice for preservice teachers* (pp. 6–15). Washington, DC: Eric Clearinghouse on Teacher Education.

Combs, A. W., & Avila, D. L. (1985). *Helping relationships: Basic concepts for the helping professions* (3rd ed.). Boston: Allyn & Bacon.

Cornbleth, C., Davis, O. L., & Button, C. (1974). Expectations for pupil achievement and teacher-pupil interaction. *Social Education, 38,* 54–58.

Covington, M., & Beery, R. (1976). *Self-worth and schooling.* New York: Holt, Rinehart & Winston.

Covington, M., & Omelich, C. (1981). As failures mount: Affective and cognitive consequences of ability demotion in the classroom. *Journal of Educational Psychology, 71,* 796–808.

Davis, J., Laughlin, P., & Komorita, S. (1976). The social psychology of small groups: Cooperative and mixed-motive interaction. In M. Rosenzweig & L. Porter (Eds.), *Annual Review of Psychology, 27,* 501–542.

Deci, E. (1975). *Intrinsic motivation.* New York: Plenum.

Dembo, M. H. (1988). *Applying educational psychology in the classroom* (3rd ed.). New York: Longman.

Deshler, D., Schumaker, J., & Lenz, K., (1984). Academic and cognitive interventions for LD adolescents. *Annual Review of Learning Disabilities, 2,* 57–66.

Dweck, C. (1975). The role of expectations and attributions in the alleviation of learned helplessness. *Journal of Personality & Social Psychology, 31,* 674–685.

Edwards, K. J., & DeVries, D. L. (1974). *The effects of teams-games-tournament and two instructional variations on classroom student attitudes, and student achievement* (Rep. No. 172). Baltimore: Center for Social Organization of Schools, Johns Hopkins University.

Finn, J. (1972). Expectations and the educational environment. *Review of Educational Research, 42,* 387–410.

Gage, N. L., & Berliner, D. C. (1988). *Educational psychology* (4th ed.). Boston: Houghton Mifflin.

Good, T. (1970). Which pupils do teachers call on? *Elementary School Journal, 70,* 190–198.

Good, T. (1983). *Recent classroom research: Implications for teacher education.* An invited address delivered at annual meeting of American Association of Colleges for Teacher Education, Chicago.

Good, T., & Brophy, J. (1984). *Looking in classrooms.* New York: Harper & Row.

Good, T. L., & Brophy, J. E. (1986). *Educational psychology* (3rd ed.). New York: Longman.

Hallahan, D. P., & Kauffman, J. (1988). *Exceptional children: Introduction to special education* (4th ed.). Englewood Cliffs, NJ: Prentice-Hall.

Hill, K. T., & Wigfield, A. (1984). Test anxiety: A major educational problem and what can be done about it. *Elementary School Journal, 85,* 105–126.

Holt, J. (1982). *How children fail.* New York: Delta.

Hudson, F., Colson, S., & Braxdale, C. (1984). Instructional planning for dysfunctional learners: Levels of presentation. *Focus on Exceptional Children, 17*(3), 1–12.

Hudson, F., Colson, S., Welch, D., Banikowski, A., & Mehring, T. (1989). *Hudson educational skills inventory.* Austin, TX: PRO-ED.

Johnson, D., & Johnson, R. (1978). Many teachers wonder . . . will the special needs child ever really belong? *Instructor, 87,* 152–154.

Johnson, D., & Johnson, R. (1987). *Learning together and alone: Cooperative, competitive, and individualistic learning* (2nd ed.). Englewood Cliffs, NJ: Prentice-Hall.

Keller, J. (1983). Motivation design of instruction. In C. Reigeluth (Ed.), Instructional-design theories and models: An overview of their current status. Hillsdale, NJ: Erlbaum.

Kifer, E. (1975). Relationships between academic achievement and personality characteristics: A quasi-longitudinal study. *American Educational Research Journal, 12,* 191–210.

MacMillan, D. (1982). *Mental retardation in school and society* (2nd ed.). Boston, MA: Little, Brown.

Madsen, K. B. (1973). Theories of motivation. In B. B. Wolman (Ed.), *Handbook of general psychology.* Englewood Cliffs, NJ: Prentice-Hall.

Maslow, A. H. (1970). *Motivation and personality* (2nd ed.). New York: Harper and Row.

McDougall, W. (1908). *An introduction to social psychology.* London: Methuen.

McLaughlin, T. F. (1975). The applicability of token reinforcement systems in public school systems. *Psychology in the Schools, 12,* 84–89, 369–370.

Murray, H. A. (1938). *Explorations in personality.* New York: Oxford University Press.

O'Leary, K. D., & Drabman, R. S. (1971). Token reinforcement programs in the classroom: A review. *Psychological Bulletin, 75,* 379–398.

Paget, K. D., Nagle, R. J., & Martin, R. P. (1984). Interrelationships between temperament characteristics and teacher-student interactions. *Journal of Abnormal Child Psychology, 12,* 547–560.

Pippert, R. A. (1969). *A study of creativity and faith* (Monograph No. 4). Manitoba Department of Youth and Education.

Polloway, E. A., & Epstein, M. H. (1985). Current research issues in mild mental retardation: A survey of the field. *Education & Training of the Mentally Retarded, 20,* 171–174.

Polloway, E. A., & Smith, J. D. (1983). Changes in mild mental retardation: Population, programs, and perspectives. *Exceptional Children, 50,* 149–159.

Pullis, M., & Cadwell, J. (1985). Temperament as a factor in the assessment of children educationally at risk. *Journal of Special Education, 19,* 91–102.

Reid, D. K., & Hresko, W. P. (1981). *A cognitive approach to learning disabilities.* Austin, TX: PRO-ED.

Reschly, D. (1987). Learning characteristics of mildly handicapped students: Implications for classification, placement, and programming. In M. C. Wang, M. C. Reynolds, & H. J. Walberg (Eds.), *Handbook of special education: Research and practice—Learner characteristics and adaptive education* (Vol. 1). New York: Pergamon Press.

Robinson, N., & Robinson, H. (1976). *The mentally retarded child* (2nd ed.). New York: McGraw-Hill.

Rosenholtz, S. J., & Simpson, C. (1984). The formation of ability conceptions: Developmental trend or social construction? *Review of Educational Research, 54,* 31–63.

Rosenthal, R. (1983). The Pygmalion effect lives. *Psychology Today,* pp. 56–63.

Rosenthal, R., & Jacobson, L. (1968). *Pygmalion in the classroom: Teacher expectation and pupils' intellectual development.* New York: Holt, Rinehart & Winston.

Rotter, J. (1954). *Social learning and clinical psychology.* Englewood Cliffs, NJ: Prentice-Hall.

Slavin, R. (1977). Classroom reward structure: An analytic and practical view. *Review of Educational Research, 47,* (4), 633–640 (Rep. No. 172). Baltimore: Center for Social Organization of Schools, Johns Hopkins University.

Sprinthall, N. A., & Sprinthall, R. C. (1987). *Educational psychology: A developmental approach* (4th ed.). New York: Random House.

Van Reusen, T., Box, C., Schumaker, J., & Deshler, D. (1987). *The education planning strategy.* Lawrence, KS: EXCELLENTerprises.

Weiner, B. (1986). *An attributional theory of motivation and emotion.* New York: Springer-Verlag.

Weiner, B., & Kukla, A. (1970). An attributional analysis of achievement motivation. *Journal of Personality & Social Psychology, 15,* 1–20.

Woolfolk, A. E., & Brooks, D. (1982). Nonverbal communication in teaching. In E. Gordon (Ed.), *Review of research in education* (Vol. 10). Washington, DC: American Educational Research Association.

Woolfolk, A. E., & Brooks, D. (1985). The influence of teachers' nonverbal behaviors on students' perceptions and performance. *Elementary School Journal, 85,* 514–528.

Zigler, E. (1962). Rigidity in the feeble-minded. In E. P. Trapp & P. Himelstein (Eds.), *Readings on the exceptional child* (pp. 141–162). New York: Appleton-Century Crofts.

Teresa Mehring is an assistant dean at the Teachers College, Emporia State University, Kansas. Steven Colson is an adjunct professor of special education and an educational diagnostician at the Children's Rehabilitation Unit, University of Kansas Medical Center, Kansas City.

$\circ$ 4 $\circ$

The authors describe a model by which special educators can support general education through collaboration in regular classrooms. Central to the model is the development of flexible departmentalization, program ownership, identification and development of supportive attitudes, student assessment to determine effectiveness, and classroom modifications to support mainstreaming. Simpson and Myles discuss each of these program concerns and offer suggestions based on the authors' success in developing programs of this nature.

General Education Collaboration: A Model for Successful Mainstreaming

Richard L. Simpson and Brenda Smith Myles

The Education for All Handicapped Children's Act (EHA) was designed to improve the quality of education received by children and youth with exceptionalities, including provisions for an appropriate education in the least restrictive environment. Thus, EHA requirements stipulate that students be removed from general education programs only when the nature or severity of their exceptionality is such that education in regular classrooms, even with the use of supplementary aids or services, cannot be conducted satisfactorily (Office of the Federal Register, 1987). For many children and youth with mild disabilities, this requirement has been translated to mean education in resource room and other pull-out programs (U.S. Department of Education, 1987).

Critics argue that service provision outside the regular classroom has led to discontinuity in instruction (Wang, Reynolds, & Walberg, 1986), reduction of curricular options for students with exceptionalities (Stainback & Stainback, 1984), and education with a limited scope. As a result, children and youth with disabilities are prevented from gaining skills that would facilitate their full-time reentry into regular classrooms (Dunn, 1968). Alleged byproducts of pull-out and other segregated programs include lower self-concept and self-esteem for students with disabilities than for nonhandicapped peers

(Rogers & Saklofske, 1985); less than adequate social skills (Madden & Slavin, 1983); and lack of preparation for adulthood, manifested by a high rate of unemployment among people with exceptionalities (Will, 1984).

The present educational system also has proven inadequate for students without labeled exceptionalities (Reynolds, Wang, & Walberg, 1987). Specifically, at least 20% of nonlabeled children and youth experience difficulty in regular classrooms. "These children are commonly described as slow learners, students who exhibit social, conduct, and behavior difficulties; possess low self-esteem; or have problems in understanding or using language (Will, 1986, p. 413).

Prompted by these issues, educators, policy makers, researchers, and theorists have called for a variety of educational reforms, all designed to serve more effectively and efficiently mildly handicapped and at-risk students in general education programs. Although specific methodologies vary, reform procedures consistently identify general and special education collaboration and shared decision making as essential ingredients for success. Yet, in spite of general acceptance of a need for greater cooperation and involvement between regular and special education, few models for achieving such collaboration have been presented. In particular, conceptual and procedural models that offer a broad perspective (i.e., focus on educational practices, environmental factors, and personnel considerations) are needed. In response, we offer the General Education Collaboration Model, designed to support general educators through collaboration with special educators.

GENERAL EDUCATION COLLABORATION MODEL

The General Education Collaboration Model, illustrated in Figure 1, is designed to support general educators working with exceptional children by means of collaboration with special educators or having special educators in the classroom. Based on shared input, shared responsibility, and shared decision making (AASA/NAESP/NAASP School-Based Management Task Force, 1988; Bauwens, Hourcade, & Friend, 1989; Crisci & Tutela, 1990), the model facilitates integration of students with mild to moderate learning and behavior difficulties into general classrooms; at the same time, it provides assistance that allows students to be successful. The model emphasizes both instructional variables and learner behaviors, based on the rationale that instructional variables and learner behaviors cannot be separated from instructional settings (Salend, 1990).

The following four major assumptions underlie the General Education Collaboration Model:

- The general educator assumes primary responsibility for teaching; the special educator's role is to provide support and resources to enhance student success.
- Social and academic interactions in the general education classroom are beneficial for all students, including those with disabilities.
- Students, parents, and school personnel prefer education in the general education classroom to pull-out and other segregated programs.

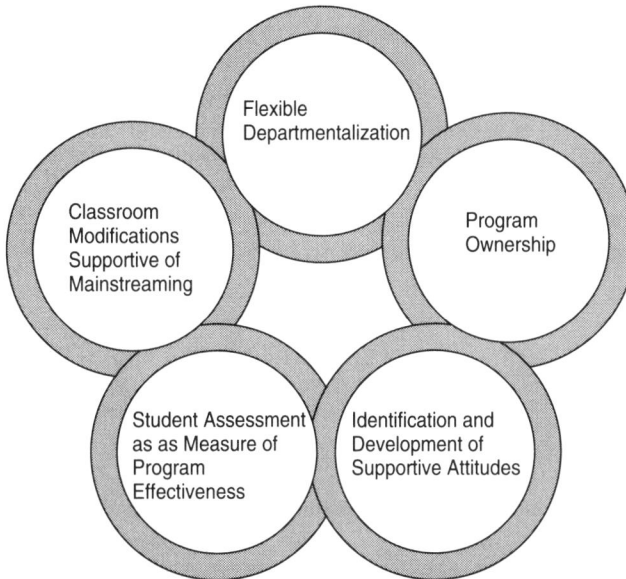

FIGURE 1   *Essential Elements of General Education Collaboration Model*

- Contingent upon appropriate support and resources, most general education teachers and administrators are willing and capable to serve students with mild to moderate disabilities in general classrooms.

COMPONENTS OF THE MODEL

The General Education Collaboration Model is based on five essential elements:

1. Flexible departmentalization (Jones, Gottlieb, Guskin, & Yoshida, 1978; Lawrence & Lorsch, 1967; Margolis & McGettigan, 1988).
2. Program ownership (Roubinek, 1978).
3. Identification and development of supportive attitudes (Heller & Schilit, 1987; Hersh & Walker, 1983).
4. Student assessment as a measure of program effectiveness (Jones et al., 1978; Rogers & Saklofske, 1985).
5. Classroom modifications that support mainstreaming (Myles & Simpson, 1989, 1990; Simpson & Myles, 1989).

Although each model component is presented as a discrete item, in actuality components are interwoven; each component significantly affects the others and cannot operate effectively in isolation. In fact, for school reform and mainstreaming to be effective, all components of the model must be in place.

Flexible Departmentalization

Departmentalization recognizes that individuals within a school organization each have unique job functions. In fact, their roles often are designed such that educators are able to function independently. To provide an optimal education for *all* students, however, departmentalization must allow for coordination, communication, and control.

Coordination here refers to the orchestration of defined roles for service delivery personnel. In recognition of this need, Judy Schrag (1990), Director of the U.S. Office of Special Education Programs, observed that:

> Special education program enhancements include better coordination across special programs and general education, increased roles of the building principals, continued exploration of the circumstances under which students with special needs can be educated in the regular classrooms and exploration of refinements in our assessment and classification procedures. (p. 7)

Coordination of special and general education programs requires that individuals be aware of their own responsibilities, as well as the responsibilities of others. Thus, much of the teacher discontent concerning mainstreaming programs stems from a lack of orchestration (e.g., role duplication or conflict) of school personnel responsibilities (McCoy & Prehm, 1987).

As it relates to departmentalization, *communication* serves as the basis for developing a collaborative relationship. Hence the need to involve all school organization members, including administrators, parents, teachers, support personnel and students. Communication ensures that involved persons are working toward the same purpose and that each individual provides program implementation feedback. Improved communication is the *sine qua non* of effective general-special education collaboration.

The need for shared decision making and participatory management has been recognized for some time. In his book, *Eupsychian Management: A Journal*, Maslow (1962) presented a management theory based on humanistic psychology and the premise that optimal involvement of all participants in decision making results in (a) the well-being of all involved, and (b) an efficient organization that meets the needs of the individual. As in society in general, schools are not operating under Maslow's ideal; moreover, they likely never will. Yet, the advantages of involving a variety of participants (e.g., teachers, administrators, parents, students, members of the community) in decision making and in creating a supportive environment are increasingly being recognized (Clune & White, 1988; Mertens & Yarger, 1988; Sickler, 1988; Walberg & Lane, 1989; White, 1989).

In the context of departmentalization, adoption and implementation of an effective *control system* is another critical issue. The control system should address the following questions: How long will the alternative service delivery model (e.g., mainstreaming, support services) be in place before efficacy issues are addressed? Who holds responsibility for those issues? Are there assurances for shared decision making? What criteria will be used in the decision-making process (Jones et al., 1978)?

Program Ownership

Historically, issues related to mainstreaming have been the domain of special education (McIntosh, 1979). Thus, special educators have assumed responsibility for determining if and when special needs students can be served appropriately in general education settings, which general education programs and instructors will best meet mainstreamed students' needs, and how mainstreaming may best be accomplished. This system, in combination with other ill-considered mainstreaming activities, has retarded general educators' participation in and embracement of mainstreaming practices. Knoff (1985), for instance, reported that many general educators feel imposed on by mainstreaming, consider themselves unprepared to teach students with disabilities, and are put upon by mainstreaming practices.

Significant improvements in the mainstreaming system can be expected only with the support of and close working relationship between general and special educators (Roubinek, 1978). In this regard, the General Education Collaboration Model stresses shared responsibility by general and special educators for students with disabilities. Accordingly, general educators must accept responsibility for mainstreamed students placed in regular education programs. In return, general educators can expect full participation in the decision-making processes associated with mainstreaming along with appropriate support (e.g., training, consultation). The importance of shared ownership and ownership clarification cannot be underestimated (Heller & Schilit, 1987; Hersh & Walker, 1983).

Identification and Development of Supportive Attitudes

The advantages of placing students with disabilities in general education classes have been well established. Thus, pursuing what the National Association of Retarded Citizens (1973) referred to as "an existence as close to normal as possible" (p. 72) for persons with disabilities, parents and professionals have increasingly endorsed both the least restrictive environment concept and mainstreaming. At one time mainstreaming was considered radical. Today, however, it is estimated that most students with disabilities receive part of their education in regular class settings (U.S. Department of Education, 1987). Moreover, many educators have accepted the philosophy of mainstreaming students with mild handicaps in regular classes, a recognition that bodes well for a continuation of this trend. Yet, in spite of this backing, limited attention has been given to preparing general classroom settings to accommodate students with disabilities.

In particular, selecting teachers, school staff, and students who are aware and supportive of students with disabilities is a basic requirement for successful mainstreaming (Hersh & Walker, 1983). As Martin (1974) cautioned, unless educators develop strategies for creating an accepting environment for students with disabilities, "we will be painfully naive, and I fear we will subject many children to a painful and frustrating educational experience in the name of progress" (p. 150). Reister and Bessette (1986) also contended that integration programs can be successful only to the extent that they create an educational environment in which children and youth with disabilities thrive, develop, and experience acceptance. Such a supportive environment requires strategies that assure not only that appropriate instructional materials and procedures are used, but that social, emotional, and attitudinal concerns receive proper attention.

The overall atmosphere within a school determines the extent to which the General Education Collaboration Model or any alternative mainstreaming strategy will be accepted and employed (Gersten & Woodward, 1990). Hence, attitudes of administrators, teachers, parents, and students must be assessed to determine to what extent these essential people are prepared and willing to accommodate students with disabilities in regular class settings.

With regard to *administrator* attitudes, O'Rourke (1980) found a significant relationship between teaching personnel and building principals' attitudes toward students with exceptionalities. Hence, principals' positive attitudes, as well as administrative support for working with all students (including those with exceptionalities), must exist if mainstreamed students are to receive optimal educational benefits (Heller & Schilit, 1987; McIntosh, 1979). Indeed, we recommend that administrative personnel should be selected, partly, on the basis of their integration attitude and their willingness to accommodate both disabled and normally developing students. Administrator attitudes toward students with disabilities can be modified (Donaldson, 1980); however, it is more efficient to select for educational leadership positions individuals who demonstrate positive attitudes toward mainstreaming and students with special needs, and who are, thus, able to establish a positive school atmosphere.

Positive *teacher* attitudes are also essential determinants of mainstreaming success. Research on teacher attitudes toward mainstreaming has shown that general education teachers generally perceive themselves to be ill equipped to deal with students with disabilities (Miller, 1990). Yet, they agree that mainstreaming is a positive educational practice, contingent on appropriate teacher support and training (Knoff, 1985; Moore & Fine, 1978; Reynolds, Martin-Reynolds, & Mark, 1982; Stephens & Benjamin, 1981; Williams & Algozzine, 1979). Myles and Simpson (1989) reported that 86% of general educators surveyed were willing to accept an exceptional child in their classrooms on a full-time basis, given appropriate support and training. Without support and training less than 33% of the respondents were willing to accept mainstreamed students in their general classrooms.

Mainstreaming success also hinges on the leadership and involvement of *parents*, both those with exceptional and with normally developing children (Heller & Schilit, 1987). Indeed, the activities and lobbying of parent groups led to the largest special education system reform in history (i.e. Public Law 94-142).

Many parents of children with disabilities report that they are willing to place their children in general classrooms, contingent on appropriate support and individualization (Myles & Simpson, 1990; Simpson & Myles, 1989). Of the parents of children with learning disabilities surveyed by Abramson, Wilson, Yoshida, and Hagerty (1983), 72% responded that educating handicapped and nonhandicapped children together would improve the handicapped children's academic achievement. In a related study 79% of parents surveyed by Abelson and Weiss (1984) agreed that handicapped and nonhandicapped children could learn in the same classroom, but 40% of the participating parents stated that handicapped children's educational gains would come at the expense of the quality of other students' education. As noted, most parents whose children have had mainstreaming experiences appear to support those programs, contingent on appropriate services and attitudes.

Recognizing the importance of *student* attitudes, Simpson (1987) observed that a noteworthy factor in the success or failure of mainstreaming is whether normally developing students accept, understand, and interact with peers with exceptionalities. Clearly, mainstreaming programs must include methods and procedures that facilitate normally achieving students' awareness and acceptance of exceptional students in the mainstream (Sasso, Simpson, & Novak, 1985). In the absence of this component, students with exceptionalities will fail to become fully integrated in mainstreamed settings.

As we suggested, *individuals with whom children and youth with disabilities will interact in general education settings* must be maximally supportive. Relative to the General Education Collaboration Model, therefore, teachers, administrators, and other adult staff members (e.g., custodians, cafeteria workers) must receive information about individuals with disabilities along with facts on the rationale and advantages of integration and mainstreaming. As a part of this process, adults need opportunities to discuss their mainstreaming roles and their attitudes and feelings regarding mainstreaming. Thus, a supportive general educational environment for students with disabilities is best developed by combining information with discussion opportunities.

Procedures for positively modifying the *attitudes and behavior of normally developing children and youth* toward their disabled peers is also a basic element of the General Education Collaboration Model. Nonhandicapped students require information and experiences designed to (a) familiarize them with the characteristics and needs of children and youth with disabilities, (b) foster more accepting attitudes toward individuals with disabilities, and (c) promote better interactions between handicapped and nonhandicapped students. Positive attitudes toward students with disabilities do not occur automatically; hence, this frequently overlooked mainstreaming element must be planned.

Use of *curricula and procedures* designed to facilitate better understanding and sensitivity toward students with disabilities has proven significant in integration programs (Fiedler & Simpson, 1987). Accordingly, the time and resource investment required to work with classmates of children and youth with disabilities appears to be cost-efficient and utilitarian.

Not all students are candidates for mainstreaming. Thus, selection of students most acceptable for integration must be based on both objective and subjective criteria. Objective criteria may include aptitude and achievement eligibility levels. Subjective criteria may include student motivation, social responsibility, and behavior. Although student mainstreaming criteria will vary from setting to setting, exceptional students must be assigned to general education classes to possess the basic skills necessary to allow them to be successful and accepted.

Student Assessment as a Measure Of Program Effectiveness

Assessment is a key component of any program serving students with exceptionalities and acts as an ongoing part of the instructional strategy (Carroll, 1974). In fact, evaluation is a key component of PL 94–142. To facilitate successful mainstreaming, assessment must be comprehensive, encompassing student achievement, self-concept, and social integration.

Decisions pertaining to *student achievement* include types of assessment measures (or specific instruments) as well as the frequency with which they are used. Because norm-referenced standardized tests may be unacceptable for students with exceptionalities, many educators prefer curriculum-based assessment methods. As noted by Marston, Fuchs, and Deno (1986), curriculum-based assessment measures allow for (a) reliability, (b) curricula compatibility, (c) validity with respect to criterion achievement measures, (d) ease and repetition of administration, and (e) sensitivity to student growth. Thus, curriculum-based assessment methods allow for consistent validation of instructional effectiveness and student growth.

Self-concept is a construct that correlates with school achievement and social adjustment. Thus this variable must be monitored and, if necessary, addressed through social skills instruction and other intervention programs. Results of investigations of the self-concept of students with mild exceptionalities have been conflicting; some report that the self-concept of students with mild handicaps does not differ from that of nonhandicapped peers (Coleman, 1984; Stone, 1984; Yauman, 1983); others note a marked discrepancy between the self-concepts of handicapped and nonhandicapped students (Ribner, 1978). At least in part, researchers attribute these equivocal research results to service delivery model differences. That is, resource room students who use normally achieving peers as a reference group appear to have lower self-concepts than resource room students who compare themselves with exceptional peers. But students with learning disabilities who use exceptional peers as a reference group appear to have self-concepts commensurate with those of nonhandicapped students (Coleman, 1984; Yauman, 1983). Preliminary studies of self-concept of students served in an alternative service delivery model revealed no differences between the self-concept of normally achieving and exceptional students (Hudson & Myles, 1989; Wang & Birch, 1984). To be conclusive, however, these results must be submitted to further investigation.

Social integration refers to the relationships between students. With respect to mainstreaming, social integration involves relationships between students with exceptionalities and normally achieving peers in terms of physical proximity, interactive behavior, assimilation, and acceptance (Kaufman, Gottlieb, Agard, & Kukic, 1975). Positive and accepting relationships between children with disabilities and their normally achieving peers are crucial to successful mainstreaming to the extent that exceptional students' rejection by or isolation from nonhandicapped peers could doom for failure an otherwise successful mainstreaming program (Reister & Bessette, 1986).

As suggested earlier, general education students must be made aware of the needs and characteristics of their exceptional classmates. Traditionally, little has been done to prepare general education students to interact with exceptional peers. Thus, significant change can and must occur via specific curricula and teaching strategies that facilitate normally developing students' interactions with persons with exceptionalities (Newman & Simpson, 1983).

Recognizing the importance of mainstreamed student success, we contend that ongoing assessment in a variety of areas is crucial to the success of the General Education Collaboration Model. Such assessment should be multifaceted, taking into account the "whole" child in terms of both self-concept and social integration.

Classroom Modifications Supportive of Mainstreaming

Researchers have demonstrated interest in classroom modifications that influence the educational process. In addition, the National Education Association (NEA) has taken a leadership role in this area. Harris (1974), NEA president, challenged schools to initiate reform to foster educational improvement, recommending, for example, that schools reduce class size and obtain the services of more specialists. A myriad of other modifications designed to enhance mainstreaming has also been suggested (Hersh & Walker, 1983).

Class Size

In his call to improve schools, Harris (1974) indicated that the educational system could improve if the average class size were reduced to 10 students. Harris's recommendation was supported by the results of an NEA survey (Teacher Opinion Poll, 1975a). When asked to state the importance of class size to (a) academic achievement, (b) social and personal development of pupils, and (c) teacher job satisfaction, 80% of teachers surveyed responded that small class size is extremely important. In a related study, 78% of general educators surveyed stated that class size is an important issue in mainstreaming. This group of teachers indicated that a maximum class size of 15 to 19 students is required to accept and accommodate one mainstreamed exceptional student (Myles & Simpson, 1989).

Although challenged (Robinson, 1990), a body of empirical data supports reduced class size. According to McKenna and Olson (1975), for example, a class size of 25 or fewer students would lead to: (a) wider variety of instructional methods, (b) better classroom management and fewer discipline problems, (c) improved teacher attitudes, and (d) improved student attitudes. Smith and Glass (1980) reported similar findings when class size was reduced to fewer than 15 to 20 students.

Thus, small class size seems to contribute to the academic achievement of mainstreamed students as well as to positive teacher and student attitudes. Therefore, the General Education Collaboration Model suggests that classes be small enough to allow teachers to meet the individual needs of students and to provide successful mainstreaming experiences.

Consultation

According to Idol and West (1987), school consultation in special education has flourished. At least 26 states currently have policies that mandate consultation (West & Brown, 1987). In addition, consultation appears to have general educator support. Approximately half of educators surveyed by Myles and Kasselman (1990) reported that they used collaborative consultation, although a formalized consultation program was not in place in their schools. Further, 95% stated that they would use collaborative consultation for exceptional and at-risk students if it were available in their schools. When asked to select modifications needed to mainstream an exceptional student, 65% of the 100 teachers polled by Myles and Simpson (1989) selected consultation.

In a data-based analysis of consultation, Miller and Sabatino (1978) compared student academic performance in a resource room with performance in a consultation model. Results showed that student academic performance gains were equivalent for both models. According to Miller and Sabatino:

> One could argue that the consultation model was surprisingly effective, since academic gains were on par with the direct service approach. That is, regular teachers seemingly became as effective in delivering instruction to special children within their classes as resource teachers were in intensive, 'out of mainstream' classes." (p. 89)

Concurring with the position taken by Miller and Sabatino, we contend that consultation between general and special educators is necessary to the success of the General Education Collaboration Model. This vehicle provides general education with information and support regarding the characteristics and needs of students with exceptionalities.

Inservice Programs

Inservice has been viewed as contributing to program change. Although the efficacy of traditional inservice programs has been challenged (Fullan, 1985), it appears that effective inservice may assist teachers in mainstreaming students with exceptionalities. In 1975 nationwide NEA survey, teachers were asked which classroom modifications would result in improved education (Teacher Opinion Poll, 1975b, p. 14). Opinions were diverse, totaling more than 16 different suggestions, including additional inservice programming.

According to a number of studies, teacher inservices may be desirable in implementing mainstreaming programs. For example, Myles and Simpson (1989, 1990) and Simpson and Myles (1991) found that parents of exceptional children, support service staff, and general educators favor inservice programs as a vehicle to enhance mainstreaming of students with mild handicaps. Approximately half of those surveyed selected this mainstreaming option.

The General Education Collaboration Model supports continued inservice programs as a means of enhancing the knowledge base of general educators through both group and individual training. Group inservice is well suited for providing a general body of information regarding student characteristics and needs, and individual training can give general educators specific information and feedback opportunities.

Paraprofessionals

Paraprofessionals play an important role in special education, as evidenced by the large number of people employed in this role. As of 1980, more than 80,000 paraprofessionals worked in special education public schools (Pickett, 1980). Research suggests that special educators are aware of the contributions that aides make in the classroom. Paraprofessionals are far less widespread in general education programs, though, suggesting that they are perceived to play a minor role in supporting mainstreamed students.

Regardless of the current use of paraprofessionals in general education programs, the General Education Collaboration Model is based on the premise that paraprofessionals are needed, to varying degrees, to support the mainstreamed students. Karagianis and Nesbit (1983) agreed with this assessment, noting that teachers' aides are "a necessary adjunct to the regular classroom where the teacher has a defined responsibility for handicapped children" (p. 19). General educators appear to concur; 65% of those surveyed by Myles and Simpson (1989) saw paraprofessionals as necessary facilitators of mainstreaming.

Paraprofessionals should be available to general education teachers who serve children and youth with disabilities. Specifically, paraprofessionals may assist teachers with a variety of tasks, including (a) reinforcing previously instructed concepts, (b) documenting student progress, and (c) assisting with daily planning. Paraprofessionals also can perform time-consuming tasks such as toilet training and modifying written materials (Kargianis & Nesbit, 1983; McKenzie & Houk, 1986).

Planning Time

Additional planning time was another frequently selected modification among general educators in the 1975 NEA poll (Teacher Opinion Poll, 1975b). Respondents selecting this modification suggested that increased planning time would improve teacher efficacy. With regard to mainstreaming, planning time takes on even greater importance. According to approximately half of general educators and ancillary staff surveyed, additional planning would be required if one student with an exceptionality were to be placed full-time in a mainstreamed setting. The majority of respondents indicated that they would prefer one hour of daily planning time (Myles & Simpson, 1989; Simpson & Myles, 1991). Parents did not view this mainstreaming option to be as important as school personnel did (only one-quarter indicated that one hour of daily planning was a necessary mainstreaming modification) (Myles & Simpson, 1990).

Teachers need adequate planning to be able to individualize academic tasks and plan optional or additional activities that can enhance the performance of students with exceptionalities. This time also is needed to allow general education personnel to consult with other education personnel or work with a paraprofessional. Hence, the General Education Collaboration Model incorporates adequate planning time as essential for general education teachers assigned to work with exceptional students. Additionally, the school day should be organized such that general and special educators share common blocks of time for planning.

Support Services

Availability of support service personnel has been seen to facilitate mainstreaming. Thus, the majority of general educators surveyed by Hudson, Graham, and Warner (1979) reported that although support service personnel were not generally available, they were needed to provide mainstreaming assistance.

Results similar to those of Hudson et al. (1979) were reached by Larrivee and Cook (1979), Moore and Fine (1978), and Knoff (1984). Those authors found that the availability of support services impacted teacher attitudes positively. Specifically, teacher attitudes toward mainstreaming seemed more positive when support services were available. In fact, in one study general educators indicated that, without assistance from resource personnel, they would not generally support full-time mainstreaming for students with learning disabilities or mental retardation (Knoff, 1984).

Further, both parents and support service personnel agree that support services play an important role in mainstreaming. Over half of the parents surveyed (Myles & Simpson, 1990) and three-fourths of ancillary staff surveyed (Simpson & Myles, 1991) responded that support staff availability was necessary to mainstreaming. Based on these findings, teachers are generally accepting of mainstreaming and having special students in their classes if they can rely on personnel for necessary support (Larrivee & Cook, 1979). Thus, based on sound professional practice, the General Education Collaboration Model maintains that these resources are essential for successful maintenance of students with disabilities in regular classrooms.

CONCLUSIONS

The myriad needs of children, youth, and their families and the ever-changing needs of society demand new ways of providing an appropriate education to children and youth with behavior and learning problems. Schrag (1990) reminded us that "the students we serve in special education today are not the students that we served five years ago. There is an increase in the number of students with learning and behavior problems because of poverty, child abuse, ethnic and language diversity, teen pregnancy, and drug dependence" (p. 2). Hence, legislators, educators, and the general public are increasingly demanding change, observing that education will either need to evolve or dissolve.

Students with special needs will continue to pose a special challenge to schools. Thus, educational change must include a methodology for more effectively serving these children and youth. The increasing reliance on general educators to assume responsibility for high-risk and disabled students demands an efficacious support system. A multifaceted system that takes into consideration shared input, responsibility, and decision making between general and special educators is needed to ensure an appropriate education for all. The General Education Collaboration Model, with its emphasis on meeting student, parent, teacher, and administrator needs, is a valuable contribution to this undertaking.

REFERENCES

AASA/NAESP/NAASP School-Based Management Task Force. (1988). *School-based management: A strategy for better learning.* Arlington, VA: American Association of School Administrators.

Abelson, A. G., & Weiss, R. (1984). Mainstreaming the handicapped: The views of parents of nonhandicapped pupils. *Spectrum, 2,* 27–29.

Abramson, M., Wilson, V., Yoshida, R. K., & Hagerty, G. (1983). Parents' perceptions of their learning disabled child's educational performance. *Learning Disability Quarterly, 6,* 184–194.

Bauwens, J., Hourcade, J., & Friend, M. (1989). Cooperative teaching: A model for general and special education integration. *Remedial & Special Education, 10*(2), 17–22.

Carroll, A. W. (1974). The classroom as an ecosystem. *Focus on Exceptional Children, 6*, 1–12.

Clune, W. H., & White, P. A. (1988). *School-based management: Institutional variation, implementation, and issues for further research.* New Brunswick, NJ: Rutgers University Center for Policy Research in Education.

Coleman, J. M. (1984). Handicapped labels and instructional segregation: Influences on children's self-concepts versus the perceptions of others. *Learning Disability Quarterly, 6*, 3–11.

Crisci, P. E., & Tutela, A. D. (1990). Preparation of educational administrators for urban settings. *Urban Education, 11*(4), 414–430.

Donaldson, J. (1980). Changing attitudes toward handicapped persons: A review and analysis of research. *Exceptional Children, 43*, 504–516.

Dunn, L. (1968). Special education for the mildly retarded—Is much of it justifiable? *Exceptional Children, 35*, 5–22.

Fiedler, C., & Simpson, R. L. (1987). Modifying the attitudes of nonhandicapped high school students toward handicapped peers. *Exceptional Children, 53*(4), 342–351.

Fullan, M. (1985). Change processes and strategies at the local level. *Elementary School Journal, 85*(5), 391–421.

Gersten, R., & Woodward, J. (1990). Rethinking the regular education initiative: Focus on the classroom teacher. *Remedial & Special Education, 11*(3) 7–16.

Harris, J. A. (1974). Drastic proposals for educational improvement. *Today's Education, 63*(4), 5.

Heller, H., & Schilit, J. (1987). The regular education initiative: A concerned response. *Focus on Exceptional Children, 20*, 1–6.

Hersh, R., & Walker, H. M. (1983). Great expectations: Making school effective for all students. *Policy Review Studies, 2*, 147–188.

Hudson, F., Graham, S., & Warner, M. (1979). Mainstreaming: An examination of the attitudes and needs of regular classroom teachers. *Learning Disability Quarterly, 3*(2), 558–562.

Hudson, F. G., & Myles, B. S. (1989). *An evaluation of the adaptive behavior, problem behavior and self-concept of students with mild-to-moderate learning disabilities in an alternative service delivery model: Class within a class.* Unpublished manuscript, University of Kansas, Lawrence.

Idol, L., & West, J. F. (1987). Consultation in special education (Part 2): Training and practice. *Journal of Learning Disabilities, 20*(8), 474–494.

Jones, R. L., Gottlieb, J., Guskin, S., & Yoshida, R. K. (1978). Evaluating mainstreaming programs: Models, caveats, considerations, and guidelines. *Exceptional Children, 44*, 588–601.

Karagianis, L., & Nesbit, W. (1983). Support services: The neglected ingredient in the integration recipe. *Special Education in Canada, 53*(3), 18–19.

Kaufman, M. J., Gottlieb, J., Agard, J. A., & Kukic, M. B. (1975). Mainstreaming: Toward an explication of the construct. *Focus on Exceptional Children, 7*, 1–12.

Knoff, H. M. (1984). Mainstreaming attitudes and special placement knowledge in labeling versus nonlabeling states. *Remedial & Special Education, 5*(6), 7–14.

Knoff, H. M. (1985). Attitudes toward mainstreaming: A status report and comparison of regular and special educators in New York and Massachusetts. *Psychology in the Schools, 22*, 410–418.

Larrivee, B., & Cook, L. (1979). Mainstreaming: A study on the variables affecting teacher attitude. *Journal of Special Education, 13*(3), 315–324.

Lawrence, P. R., & Lorsch, J. W. (1967). *Organization and environment.* Boston: Harvard Business Press.

Madden, N. A., & Slavin, R. E. (1983). Mainstreaming students with mild handicaps: Academic and social outcomes. *Review of Educational Research, 53*, 519–569.

Margolis, H., & McGettigan, J. (1988). Managing resistance to instructional modifications in mainstreamed environments. *Remedial & Special Education, 9*, 15–21.

Marston, D., Fuchs, L., & Deno, S. (1986). A comparison of standardized achievement tests and direct measurement techniques in measuring pupil progress. *Diagnostique, 11*, 77–90.

Martin, E. (1974). Some thoughts on mainstreaming. *Exceptional Children, 41*, 150–153.

Maslow, A. S. (1962). *Eupsychian management: A journal.* Homewood, IL: Richard D. Irwin Publishers.

McCoy, K. M., & Prehm, H. J. (1987). *Teaching mainstreamed students: Methods and techniques.* Denver: Love Publishing.

McIntosh, D. K. (1979). Mainstreaming: Too often a myth, too rarely a reality. *Academic Therapy, 15*, 53–59.

McKenna, B. H., & Olson, M. N. (1975). Class size revisited. *Today's Education, 64*, 29.

McKenzie, R. G., & Houk, C. S. (1986). Use of paraprofessionals in the resource room. *Exceptional Children, 53*(1), 41–45.

Mertens, S., & Yarger, S. J. (1988). Teaching as a profession: Leadership, empowerment, and involvement. *Journal of Teacher Education, 39*(1), 32–37.

Miller, L. (1990). The regular education initiative and school reform: Lessons from the mainstream. *Remedial & Special Education, 11*(3), 17–22.

Miller, T. L., & Sabatino, D. A. (1978). An evaluation of the teacher consultant model as an approach to mainstreaming. *Exceptional Children, 44*(1), 86–91.

Moore, J., & Fine, M. J. (1978). Regular and special class teachers' perceptions of normal and exceptional children and their attitudes toward mainstreaming. *Psychology in the Schools, 15*, 253–259.

Myles, B. S., & Kasselman, C. J. (1990). *Collaborative consultation: The regular educator's view.* Manuscript submitted for publication.

Myles, B. S., & Simpson, R. L. (1989). Regular educators' modification preferences for mainstreaming mildly handicapped children. *Journal of Special Education, 22*(4), 479–492.

Myles, B. S., & Simpson, R. L. (1990). Mainstreaming modification preferences of parents of elementary-age children with learning disabilities. *Journal of Learning Disabilities, 23*(4), 234–239.

National Association for Retarded Citizens. (1973). *The right to choose.* Arlington, TX: Author.

Newman, R. K., & Simpson, R. L. (1983). Modifying the least restrictive environment to facilitate the integration of severely emotionally disturbed children and youth. *Behavioral Disorders, 8*(2), 103–112.

Office of the Federal Register, National Archives and Records Administration. (1987). *Code of federal regulations: Education.* Washington, DC: U. S. Government Printing Office.

O'Rourke, A. P. (1980). A comparison of principal and teacher attitudes toward handicapped students and the relationship between those attitudes and school morale of handicapped students. *Dissertation Abstracts International, 40*(7-A), 3954.

Reister, A. E., & Bessette, K. M. (1986). Preparing the peer group for mainstreaming exceptional children. *Pointer, 31*, 12–20.

Reynolds, B. J., Martin-Reynolds, J., & Mark, F. D. (1982). Elementary teachers' attitudes toward mainstreaming educable retarded students. *Education & Training of the Mentally Retarded, 17*, 171–176.

Reynolds, M. C., Wang, M. C., & Walberg, H. J. (1987). The necessary restructuring of special and regular education. *Exceptional Children, 53*, 391–398.

Ribner, S. (1978). The effects of special class placement on the self-concept of exceptional children. *Journal of Learning Disabilities, 11*, 60–64.

Robinson, G. E. (1990). Synthesis of research on the effects of class size. *Educational Leadership, 47*(7), 80–90.

Rogers, H., & Saklofske, D. H. (1985). Self-concepts, locus of control and performance expectations of learning disabled children. *Journal of Learning Disabilities, 18*, 273–278.

Roubinek, D. (1978). Will mainstreaming fit? *Educational Leadership, 35*, 410–411.

Salend, S. J. (1990). *Effective mainstreaming.* New York: Macmillan.

Sasso, G. M., Simpson, R. L., & Novak, C. G. (1985). Procedures for facilitating integration of autistic children in public school settings. *Analysis & Intervention in Developmental Disabilities, 5*, 233–246.

Schrag, J. (1990). Charting the course for the 1990's. In L. M. Bullock & R. L. Simpson (Eds.), *Monograph on critical issues in special education: Implications for personnel preparation* (pp. 2–8). Denton: University of North Texas.

Sickler, J. L. (1988). Teachers in charge: Empowering the professionals. *Phi Delta Kappan, 375*, 354–356.

Simpson, R. L. (1987). Social interactions of behaviorally disordered children: Where are we and where do we need to go? *Behavioral Disorders, 12*, 292–298.

Simpson, R. L., & Myles, B. S. (1989). Parents' mainstreaming modification preferences for children with educable mental handicaps, behavior disorders and learning disabilities. *Psychology in the Schools, 26*, 292–301.

Simpson, R. L., & Myles, B. S. (1991). Ancillary staff members' mainstreaming recommendations for students with exceptionalities. *Psychology in the Schools, 28*(1), 26–32.

Smith, M. L., & Glass, G. V (1980). Meta-analysis of research on class size and its relationship to attitudes and instruction. *American Educational Research Journal, 17*(4), 419–433.

Stainback, W., & Stainback, S. (1984). A rationale for the merger of regular and special education. *Exceptional Children, 51*(2), 102–111.

Stephens, T. M., & Benjamin, L. B. (1981). Measures of general classroom teachers' attitudes toward handicapped children. *Exceptional Children, 46*, 292–297.

Stone, B. (1984). Ecological view of self-concept. *Remedial & Special Education, 5*, 43–44.

Teacher opinion poll: Class size. (1975a). *Today's Education, 64*, 109.

Teacher opinion poll: Professional satisfaction. (1975b). *Today's Education, 64*, 14.

U. S. Department of Education. (1987). *Ninth annual report to Congress on the implementation of the Education of the Handicapped Act.* Washington, DC: Author.

Walberg, H. J., & Lane, J. J. (1989). *Organizing for learning: Toward the 21st century.* Reston, VA: National Association of Secondary School Principals.

Wang, M. C., & Birch, J. W. (1984). Comparison of a full-time mainstreaming program and a resource room approach. *Exceptional Children, 51*, 33–40.

Wang, M. C., Reynolds, M. C., & Walberg, H. J. (1986). Rethinking special education. *Educational Leadership, 44*, 26–31.

West, J. F., & Brown, P. A. (1987). State departments of education policies on consultation in special education: The state of the states. *Remedial & Special Education, 8*(3), 45–51.

White, P. A. (1989, September). An overview of school-based management: What does the research say? *NASSP Bulletin*, 1–8.

Will, M. (1984). Let us pause and reflect—But not for long. *Exceptional Children, 51*, 11–16.

Will, M. (1986). Educating children with learning problems: A shared responsibility. *Exceptional Children, 52*, 411–416.

Williams, R. J., & Algozzine, B. (1979). Teachers' attitudes toward mainstreaming. *Elementary School Journal, 80*, 63–67.

Yauman, B. E. (1983). Special educational placement and the self-concepts of elementary school age children. *Learning Disability Quarterly, 3*, 30–35.

Richard Simpson and Brenda Smith Myles are with the Department of Special Education, University of Kansas, Lawrence.

○ 5 ○

Criticism of resource rooms and greater pressure from advocates have resulted in a need for modifications in service delivery. Some have advocated collaboration or special educators working with regular class teachers. This article describes successful programs in which students with disabilities and regular class students make up a joint class, with a special educator and the regular class teacher both conducting the instruction. The article points out the necessary administrative and inservices necessary to accomplish successful programs.

A Collaborative Model for Students with Mild Disabilities in Middle Schools

Alan E. White and Lynda L. White

The Individuals with Disabilities Education Act of 1990 (PL 101-476) and implementing regulations are responsible for shifting students with disabilities from one educational setting to another. Earlier efforts had been aimed at serving students with disabilities in special programs as a part of the public schools but not necessarily with general education students. This was followed by a movement to establish all programs for special students on the general education campus. Educators also identified and classified more students with mild disabilities and moved them from regular classes into special education resource classrooms. Approximately 15 years elapsed before Americans came to understand that what is really needed for many students with disabilities is to place them back into a more normalized regular classroom setting and educate them with their nondisabled peers.

This movement is not that unusual. The simple recognition of a need to help students with disabilities in school has always been an underlying theme of special education, and no one could argue with that idea. It seems, however, that we have been quite guilty of trying to educate those with disabilities by moving them away from the regular curriculum via a separate special education track. In doing so, we have succeeded in isolating the students physically and socially and have severely limited their opportunity for exposure to the established regular education curriculum. This is especially true for students with mild learning disabilities, behavior/emotional disorders, and intellectual disabilities.

BACKGROUND

Over many years, the pull-out delivery of service was the mainstay of school programs for the majority of students with disabilities. Large numbers of programs for the gifted, remedial, and non-English speaking students also employed this model. This delivery system has come under scrutiny as a result of policy, litigation, and research in special education. Wang and Baker (1986) and Wang and Zollers (1990), for example, demonstrated the educational benefit of participation in regular classes. The investigations of Stainback and Stainback (1989, 1990) also provide clear indicators for inclusive educational approaches.

The efficacy of interaction with nondisabled peers in a regular class setting is now fortified by a more practical need for comparable instruction in curriculum content for students with disabilities. Likewise, attention to learning styles, behavioral strategies, augmentive communication, and motivational techniques are examples of special education instruction that can take place in the regular education classroom.

Designing and implementing an instructional model for integrating students with disabilities into the regular classroom setting is a process of defining and redefining the requirements of the least restrictive environment under the Individuals with Disabilities Education Act (IDEA). Models that broadly fall into this concept are those of collaborative teaching, team teaching, inclusion, pull-in, and similar terminology used to describe integrated instructional procedures. The emphasis on joint efforts by general and special education is found more often at the secondary level but is becoming increasingly accepted as appropriate for middle and elementary age groups as well.

Many state and local school systems have developed required curriculum content for middle school students, designed to meet the unique learning needs of students in grades six through eight. The delivery of services for special education students in these grades, however, has not been modified at the same pace as the changing national emphasis on the middle school learner. In many instances, the traditional pull-out program of elementary school special education continues into the middle school program. Nevertheless, the middle school team approach by grade level and the instructional design for each specific grade level form a ready foundation for implementing the collaborative or team-teaching efforts of regular and special education students.

The purpose of this article is not to try to convince educators of the need of instructing students with disabilities in regular classes. A significant body of information already exists in research, law, and policy, plus common sense, that not only supports but actually demands that we offer similar educational opportunity to disabled and nondisabled students alike. Rather, we present a systematic approach for implementing a middle school collaborative model for the delivery of service to students with mild disabilities.

AN OVERVIEW

Various terms have been used to describe a combined instructional model for general and special education. In this article, collaboration refers to a single classroom combining disabled and nondisabled students, with instruction by one special education teacher and one general education teacher. The model for collaborative special and regular educational instruction is applicable to the high school and elementary levels, but the discussion here is directed specifically to the middle school level.

Students entering the sixth through eighth grades are well suited for the collaborative teaching model. The separation of students by grade and, more important, the emphasis on instructional teaming at the middle school level provide a ready avenue for collaborative teaching.

COMPONENTS OF THE MODEL

Major components of the model are denoted in Figure 1.

Program Design

Some school systems may not begin the collaborative teaching effort without a systemwide adoption of instructional philosophy for all special education programs. Decisions should be made with regard to the issues of inclusion and the regular education initiative positions, such as those expressed by Will (1986), Lilly (1986), or of Hallahan, Keller, McKinney, Lloyd, and Bryan (1988). Villa and Thousand (1990) provide strategies to promote a system philosophy for including special education students in the regular education mainstream. It is recommended that systems first demonstrate success of the program by establishing one or more pilot projects.

However the system chooses to approach initial implementation, the program philosophy and program design must be the result of joint regular and special education decision making. Special education staff cannot hope to implement a collaborative teaching

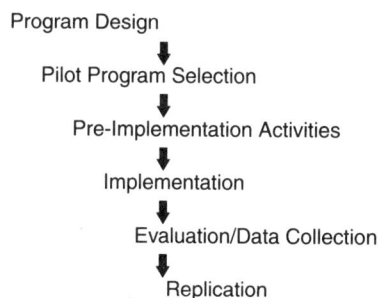

Program Design
↓
Pilot Program Selection
↓
Pre-Implementation Activities
↓
Implementation
↓
Evaluation/Data Collection
↓
Replication

FIGURE 1   *Major Components of the Collaborative Teaching Model*

model together with regular education instruction without advance planning, discussion, and agreement with system-level curriculum personnel.

Pilot Program Selection

Prior to implementing a model for delivery of services to students with mild disabilities, school districts may choose to identify a pilot site. School districts with small student enrollments might target one class or one grade in a school. Larger districts with several middle schools may select more than one school for participation during the initial implementation year. We do suggest that the number of pilot sites be limited because of the significant impact of staff training and data collection. Working through problems on a small scale during the first year allows orderly expansion later on.

Site Pre-Selection Activities

Prior to selecting the site, information should be gathered and reviewed to determine potential success of the model in a specific school. Types of information to be considered may include:

1. Local school administrative support
   —Does the school principal support the concept of collaborative teaching?
   —Will the model receive the necessary attention during development of the school's master schedule?
   —Can the regular and special education teachers have common planning time?
   —Will the model have support of parents and the community?
   —Will the principal support the school's selection as a pilot site?

2. Local school teacher support
   —Do special and regular education teachers support the philosophy of collaboration?
   —Are both groups willing to plan, provide instruction, and evaluate student performance collectively?
   —Is there potential for a positive "match" of regular and special education teachers?
   —Are both groups open to change as it relates to the instructional process?
   —Are there teachers with similar classroom behavior management strategies?
   —Are there teachers who have demonstrated the ability to share teaching responsibilities and to work together effectively? .
   —Can teachers collectively plan for positive parent involvement?
   —Will teachers be returning to the school the following year?
   —Does the school have more than one special education teacher?
   —Are there teachers who are willing to participate in data collection activities?

3. Special education student information
   —What data are available on special education students by area of disability and by grade level?

A data grid such as that presented in Figure 2 may assist school staff in gathering information regarding the number of students and periods per day of service as required in the students' IEPs. The maximum number of students served during each instructional period may be restricted by state or local regulations. The format of the grid, however, may be useful in identifying a group of students with common disabilities and grade levels. An appropriate number of students with the same grade placement and similar IEP goals and objectives could constitute a potential group for collaborative teaching.

Data collected might reflect, for example, that eight learning disabled students in the seventh grade have IEP goals and objectives focusing on the broad areas of reading comprehension and written expression skills. If the IEPs of these same students recommend two periods per day in special education, the eight special education students could be scheduled into a regular class for the determined curricula area. In addition, if collaborative opportunities exist, IEPs can be modified according to due process to allow more participation of special education students in a general education classroom.

Pilot Site Selection

Once data on potential sites have been collected, a review by special and regular education administration is recommended. Sites are rated as to potential effectiveness for a pilot program, followed by a final determination of sites. The local schools are officially contacted and their willingness to participate is confirmed.

Pre-Implementation Activities

Teacher Selection

After pilot sites have been selected, the participating teachers should be identified. According to Stalvey, Dye, and Goldblatt (1985), the most critical factor for pilot success is the selection and match of teachers involved. White, Spurgeon, Jackson, and Green-Folks (1991) suggest that selection criteria be based on:

—common interest and willingness to participate in collaborative teaching.

—established relationships between regular and special educators in the school.

—similar behavior management strategies.

—ability to share responsibilities of planning, presenting instruction, and evaluating students.

—demonstration of a plan for positive parent involvement.

	No. of Students/No. of Periods		
	6th Grade	7th Grade	8th Grade
Learning Disabilities			
Emotional/Behavior Disorders			
Mild Intellectual Disabilities			

FIGURE 2   ***Site Selection Data Grid***

Actual selection of a teacher team may occur formally or informally. A formal method suggested in Figure 3 by White et al. (1991) may utilize a teacher survey to assess attitudes toward collaborative teaching. Several other inventories are available for assessment, such as the *Learning Styles Inventory* (Silver & Hanson, 1980). The informal method, more feasible in most instances, consists of a meeting of interested teachers to discuss possibilities, interest in the model, and their ability to work together as a team. Even though formal instruments and inventories are useful, the most crucial issue is the willingness and commitment of teachers to work together in teams. Determination of teachers' characteristics, whether by formal or by informal means, is necessary to insure success. The pilot site should begin with one selected team for initial implementation.

Student Selection and Scheduling

Information on number of students, categories of disability, periods of service, and IEP goals and objectives should be available from data gathered during the site selection stage. The co-teaching team reviews the data and identifies the largest group of students in the same grade and with similar IEP goals and objectives. Table 1 presents data on a middle school that serves 60 resource students with mild disabilities through special education.

In this scenario, review of the data may reveal that of the sixth-grade LD students, eight have IEP goals in the language arts area and two students have goals for math. Then a sixth-grade language arts group could be considered for co-teaching. Selection of the students might be limited to the grade level taught by teachers participating in the pilot.

Teacher _____	Date _____		
A collaborative teacher will:	Agree	Disagree	No Opinion
1. Provide increased effective interaction among regular and special education teachers.			
2. Work to improve student self-esteem.			
3. Increase teacher/student awareness of individual differences.			
4. Provide lower teacher/pupil ratios.			
5. Provide for intensive interdisciplinary common planning.			
6. Allow for students to problem-solve and improve self-management skills.			
7. Allow for more flexibility in scheduling.			
8. Provide for generalization and transfer of learning strategies.			
9. Provide for cooperative learning experiences.			
10. Provide exposure to an increased awareness of regular education curriculum.			

Source: From Cobb County School District, Cobb County, Georgia.

FIGURE 3   Collaborative Teaching Survey

TABLE 1   *Example Middle School Data*

Area of disability	6th	7th	8th
Learning Disabled	10	12	12
Emotional/Behavioral	5	7	7
Mild Intellectual	3	2	2

If an eighth-grade language arts teacher is a willing participant, the co-teaching team would review and select appropriate eighth-grade students.

When selecting students, other considerations are:

1. Prior success in a regular education setting.
2. Student success in other cooperative learning situations.
3. Consideration of class content and student IEP objectives.
4. The degree of student behavior management required.

Students who do not meet these criteria may not be selected and thus continue to receive services through the traditional resource model. When all considerations have been applied to individual students, the team can determine the final group for inclusion in the collaborative teaching class. The school schedule then should include this group of students in the class. In many instances the pilot group is scheduled first to avoid difficult and often unpopular schedule changes later.

Parent Notification

Parents of students participating in the pilot should be included in the planning process. This may be done through an announced group meeting of parents with students who are considered for the model. Also, IEP meetings can be used—or may be required if the amount of time in special education or goals and objectives are to be modified. If the amount of time or goals and objectives remain the same, a less formal meeting or discussion may be held with the parents.

The special education administrators should review local due process procedures to assure that all requirements of the system are maintained. Regardless of the procedure, parents should be informed of the background, philosophy, and procedures to be used in the collaborative model. The increased participation with nondisabled students should be approached in a positive manner. Hanline and Halvorsen (1989) indicate that parental involvement during this transitional process is important to success.

Staff Training

Teachers participating in the collaborative model also must be assisted in adjusting to the change, because implementing the model is an ongoing process that is not limited to a single event. Staff training for co-teachers must occur prior to implementation of the model. Even though training activities often focus on routine tasks such as timelines, data collection, and the like, a significant amount of time in the initial training session should center on changing certain mindsets or paradigms (". . . because that's the way it's always been done") and stressing the importance of sharing and working together.

If more than one school is involved, all participating teachers and administrators can be trained at the same time, although teacher teams should participate in activities together. Bonding activities and simulations proved successful in districts such as the Cobb County School District, Georgia, where collaborative models are in place. Communication is the key to successful collaborative teaching and activities that build rapport and strengthen communication are critical, during initial implementation as well as throughout the entire pilot phase. Initial training should provide teachers with a repertoire of communication strategies that will help them get started as a team and serve as a resource if communication issues develop later.

Implementation

The Instructional Process

The goal of instruction is student performance and achievement.

In a two-year study by the National Association of State Boards of Education, Roach (1991) reported:

> States are exploring "outcome-based" education. They are shifting the focus away from processes and "input" measures such as the number of textbooks in a school and types of courses offered. Instead, there is an interest in performance, achievement, and "outcome" measures such as student knowledge and skills, student participation in social experiences, student participation in community and school life, and student satisfaction.
>
> The "model" chosen for instruction should address all these areas. In the collaborative teaching model, the regular and special education teachers share responsibility of the instructional process by jointly planning, presenting and evaluating the instruction.

Planning Phase

Planning for instruction is vital to instructional effectiveness. Common planning time should be scheduled for both teachers in the collaborative model. Administrative support is required to allow for this planning time in the schedule. During the planning phase, the general education teacher responsible for content pinpoints the concepts and material to be taught. The special education teacher suggests various modes and forms of presenting the information (Stalvey et al., 1985). Special educators bring to the team specialized skills in the areas of diagnosis and assessment, individualized instruction, and classroom management. The general educator's knowledge of course content for middle school curricular areas provides the foundation for instruction. Planning emphasizes not only what is to be taught in content but also how it is to be taught employing various methodologies.

Included in the planning phase is joint decision making by both teachers regarding the method for evaluating instructional lessons. Among various evaluative considerations are completion of assignments, earning daily points, turning in homework, class projects, and participation in cooperative learning activities. For example, both teachers may agree on the use of an assignment notebook to address the improvement of organizational skills. The planning encompasses the needs of all disabled and nondisabled students.

Planning time also provides the opportunity to review daily, weekly, or other results of student performance. The development, scoring, and weighting of tests and other assessment measures should be agreed upon jointly as part of the district's required grading procedures. Consideration and completion of final grades is a shared effort for all students in the class.

Instructional Phase
Lesson presentation is a responsibility of both teachers. This process has to be shared to prevent one teacher from becoming subordinate to the other. Students should not be given the impression that one assumes the role of "teacher" and one of "helper." Shifting of leadership in lesson presentation prevents negative role patterns from developing.

Lesson presentation can be shared using techniques such as the following.

1. The general education teacher presents new information to the class. The special education teacher writes notes on the chalkboard for students to copy. At the conclusion of the presentation, the special education teacher reviews the main points of the lesson from the chalkboard and leads class discussion.

2. The special education teacher organizes students into cooperative learning groups and presents an activity or assignment for each group to complete. Both teachers move about the room and answer questions, providing assistance to the groups as they work. When work is complete, groups share their work with the class as both teachers provide feedback.

3. Both teachers, prior to a test, have planned and developed questions for a competition as a study session, using a *Jeopardy* format. The special education teacher serves as the moderator, covers the rules, and conducts the game. The general education teacher serves as time-and-score keeper and conducts a summary review at the end of the game.

4. Both teachers assist students in developing organizational skills through the use of individual student notebooks. Both teachers direct disabled and nondisabled students through a process that may include: maintaining weekly logs by outlining daily required topics or issues and properly placing them in an appropriate section. Teachers share in a weekly notebook check of all students to maintain current and useful study guides.

Classroom management is the responsibility of both teachers. Each teacher shares the responsibility for modeling behavior, intervening in situations of inappropriate behavior, and planning strategies to assure a team approach in maintaining an orderly classroom. Again, advance planning and agreement on behavioral approaches is necessary to create a positive learning environment.

Presentation of facts to be learned does not assure mastery by all students. Presentation of concepts accompanied by study sheets, highlighted textbooks, color coding, clear directions, tips on how to identify main ideas, and multimodality approaches make the content meaningful. Although each of these methods may be found in a classroom, it is essential to select methodology that matches *what* students are to learn with *how* they learn. The excitement of learning will be maintained in this model as teachers identify their own individual talents, talents of the teaching team, and talents of individual students in the class.

Instructionally, collaborative teaching involves planning, presenting, and evaluating by both teachers. The interaction of curriculum content and specialized methodology presented in Figure 4 is the significant characteristic that makes this model unique. The strengths of both regular and special education are shared during a common classroom period to produce what can be a more effective instructional opportunity through collaborative teaching.

Evaluation and Data Collection

School districts implementing the collaborative teaching model should evaluate its effectiveness in a number of areas. The main focus should be on student outcomes, but additional feedback from teachers, administrators, and parents should be considered as well. Progress in academic areas should be assessed by reviewing mastery of IEP goals and objectives and final reported grades. Homework, class participation, organization skills, and other areas also should be included in the review of progress for all students in the program. Additional data should be assessed for student attitudes toward participation in the pilot.

Individualized Education Program

For students with disabilities, objectives mastered should be reviewed at the end of the pilot or during the routine annual IEP review. A data collection form should be kept for each student, reflecting the IEP objectives. These data can be summarized at the conclusion of the pilot. Prior to beginning the pilot program, the IEP committee should establish an expected percentage of mastery of goals by students with disabilities.

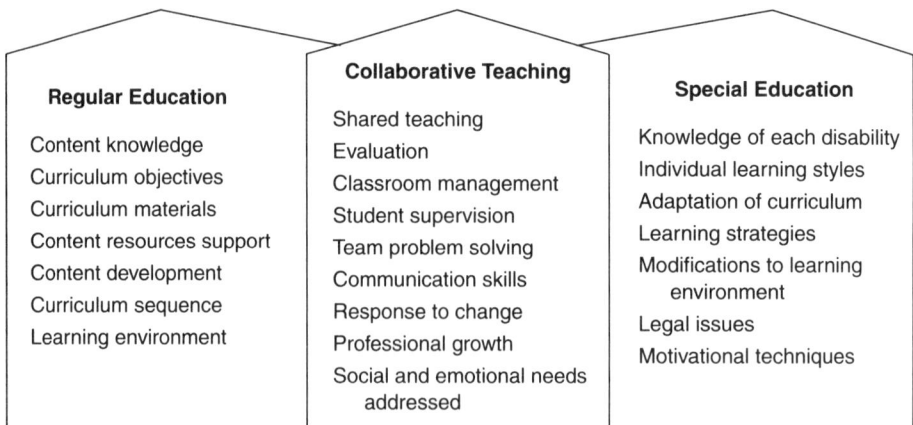

Regular Education	Collaborative Teaching	Special Education
Content knowledge	Shared teaching	Knowledge of each disability
Curriculum objectives	Evaluation	Individual learning styles
Curriculum materials	Classroom management	Adaptation of curriculum
Content resources support	Student supervision	Learning strategies
Content development	Team problem solving	Modifications to learning environment
Curriculum sequence	Communication skills	Legal issues
Learning environment	Response to change	Motivational techniques
	Professional growth	
	Social and emotional needs addressed	

FIGURE 4   Content and Methodology Interaction

Report Cards

Data from report cards should be reviewed for each student in the pilot and should not be limited to a single grade in the pilot class. Each of the academic, social, organizational skills, and other areas should be included for review and comparison. The kind and type of data available on report cards may differ between school systems, and identification and selection of data to be reviewed should be decided prior to implementation.

Student Attitudes

Pre- and post-assessment of student attitudes should be included as a data collection component. An initial student survey should be administered during the first two weeks and again during the final two weeks of the pilot term. Survey topics might include student attitudes toward having two teachers in one classroom, interest in the subject area, preference toward being in a regular, resource, or collaborative classroom, opinion of school, desire to participate in class, and willingness to work with other students. Topics should be assessed for both the disabled and nondisabled students in the class. A summary of the survey should be reviewed for the entire class and by each subgroup.

Teacher Attitudes

Attitudes of the teachers involved should be recorded throughout the pilot period. The pilot coordinator or other appropriate staff member should record responses to questions during the informal discussion and feedback sessions. Classroom observations and discussions should be maintained for review. The assessment of teacher attitudes might include opinions of perceived success or failure in providing curriculum content, increased learning for all students involved, student discipline, team efforts, and grading procedures, for example.

Administrator Attitudes

The school principal and other building administrators should be interviewed to assess the leadership perception of the collaborative model pilot. Central office administrators in both regular and special education also should observe the class and be interviewed. Administrative staff members should give their opinion of the program's strengths and weaknesses, along with specific suggestions and comments. The pilot coordinator should summarize all the information gained from the administrative assessment.

Parent Survey

One of the most important data collection aspects is the perception of parents regarding the success of the pilot program. Their feedback is necessary to indicate if their child's IEP needs are being met through collaborative teaching and whether they have observed changes in their child's behavior. In some cases, parents are able to compare the child's attitude toward school, the pilot class, and instruction between team teaching and the traditional resource or pull-out model. The parent questionnaire provided in Figure 5 may be used to summarize parental opinion as part of the data collection effort.

The pilot program coordinator and other involved administrators should analyze all of the data collected to determine the effectiveness of the collaborative teaching class. Re-

Parent Name _____   School _____

Student Name _____   Date _____

Please circle your response:

1. My child's participation in the collaborative teaching project:
   a. had a positive effect on my child.
   b. was not a positive experience for my child.
   c. did not seem to be very different from previous years.

2. Do you think the collaborative teaching project helped your child to be more successful in other subjects?
   a. Yes, it helped in other subjects.
   b. No, it did not help.
   c. I am not sure if it made a difference.

3. How do you think your child responded to the collaborative teaching project?
   a. preferred having the special education teacher come into the regular classroom.
   b. preferred leaving the regular classroom to go into the special education resource
      room.
   c. does not seem to have a preference.

4. Academically, I believe my child has:
   a. made more progress this year.
   b. made less progress this year.
   c. made about the same progress as in previous years.

5. Behaviorally, I believe my child has:
   a. made more progress this year.
   b. made less progress this year.
   c. made about the same progress as in previous years.

6. Please complete the following statements:
   a. My child would rather be in a collaborative teaching class because

   _____
   _____
   _____

   b. My child would rather be in a special resource class because

   _____
   _____
   _____

   c. I also would like to comment or suggest that

   _____
   _____
   _____

FIGURE 5   ***Parent Questionnaire***

view of the data should be a group process designed to arrive at specific implications and decision making for continuation and modification of the collaborative approach.

Pilot Replication

Decisions regarding the success of a pilot class may result in consideration to expand or replicate the pilot at additional sites. The data collection process and decision making regarding the data should lead to the replication decision. Systems typically add one or two programs at a time, depending on the overall size of the district. Expansion of the program should be made through the step-by-step procedure used in the pilot.

SUMMARY

The collaborative teaching model was designed as an alternative to the traditional resource, or pull-out, model for serving students with mild disabilities. Development of a middle school model should include consideration of opinions and concerns of teachers, administrators, parents, and students. The message seems clear that we can maintain instructional integrity for students with and without disabilities through a model that teaches both groups at the same time, in the same room. A collaborative teaching model also should be considered for other age groups of disabled students and, because the model's instructional planning and strategies may be appropriate, it can be applied to at-risk populations as well.

Collaborative teaching should be viewed as an arrangement between specialists in content and methodology that delivers the strengths of both special and general education within a single instructional setting. Stalvey et al. (1985) described a ripple effect as an incidental advantage of co-teaching. One teacher's strategy is observed by another, who uses it in a different setting, where it is observed by another teacher, and so on. A similar effect has been noted in students, who experience success from observing a learning strategy from another student, who uses it later, and so on. This exchange happens again and again because teachers and students take advantage of learning events that work in producing success.

Finally, we recognize that the collaborative model should not be considered as the best and only way to provide instruction. Some students will continue to be best served through a pull-out model to meet their individual learning needs. We are suggesting, however, that using the collaborative model at the middle school level significantly expands learning opportunities for many different types of students when they are educated together.

REFERENCES

Hallahan, D. P., Keller, C. E., McKinney, J. D., Lloyd, J. W., & Bryan, T. (1988). Examining the research base of the regular education initiative: Efficacy studies and the adaptive learning environments model. *Journal of Learning Disabilities, 21*, 29-34.

Hanline, M. R., & Halvorsen, A. (1989). Parent perceptions of the integration transition process: Overcoming artificial barriers. *Exceptional Children, 55*, 487–492.

Lilly, M. S. (1986). The relationship between general and special education: A new face on an old issue. *Counterpoint, 6*, 10.

Roach, V. (1991). Special education: New questions in an era of reform. *Issues in Brief* (National Association of State Boards of Education) *11*, 1–7.

Silver, H. F., & Hanson, J. R. (1980). *The TLC learning style inventory*. Moorestown, NY: Hanson Silver & Associates.

Stainback, S., & Stainback, W. (Eds.). (1990). *Support networks for inclusive schooling—Interdependent integrated education*. Baltimore: Paul H. Brookes.

Stainback, S., Stainback, W., & Forest, M. (Eds.). (1989). *Educating all students in the mainstream of regular education*. Baltimore: Paul H. Brookes.

Stalvey, K., Dye, B., & Goldblatt, J. (1985). *Team teaching: A resource guide*. Cobb County, GA: Cobb County School District.

Villa, R., & Thousand, J. (1990). Administrative supports to promote inclusive schooling. In S. Stainback & W. Stainback (Eds.), *Support networks for inclusive schooling—Interdependent integrated education* (pp. 201–218). Baltimore: Paul H. Brookes.

Wang, M. C. & Baker, E. T. (1986). Mainstreaming programs: Design features and effects. *Journal of Special Education, 19*, 503–521.

Wang, M. C. & Zollers, N. (1990). Adaptive instruction: An alternative service delivery approach. *Remedial & Special Education, 11*, 7–21.

White, L., Spurgeon, J., Jackson, P., & Green-Folks, N. (Eds.). (1991). Cobb County School System Special Education Department procedures manual—collaborative teaching model—middle school pilot, 1991–92. Cobb County, GA: Cobb County School District.

Will, M. C. (1986). Educating children with learning problems: A shared responsibility. *Exceptional Children, 52*, 411–415.

Alan White is the director of Special Services for the Marietta City School District, Marietta, Georgia. Lynda White is a supervisor, Special Education Department, for the Cobb County School District, Marietta, Georgia.

○ 6 ○

Zigmond examines the research on the effectiveness of programs for students with learning disabilities. She concludes that we have much reason to question the effectiveness of our present programs. As opposed to many other special educators, Zigmond does not believe special programs should be abandoned. In fact, she thinks the lack of structure and intensive instruction in mainstream classrooms is part of the problem. She recommends programs with even more restrictive environments and supports her contentions with an effective research base.

Rethinking Secondary School Programs for Students with Learning Disabilities

Naomi Zigmond

Nearly 15 years have passed since enactment of the Education for All Handicapped Children Act (PL 94-142) and the federal government's assurance of a free and appropriate public education for students with handicaps. During that time the numbers of students served in special education programs has grown to nearly 4.5 million, an increase of 21% over 1976 –77 counts.

Nowhere has the change in size and scope of special education services been more astounding than in the field of learning disabilities (LD). In the 15 years just passed, the number of students identified and served in programs for students with learning disabilities has increased by more than 145%. Every state in the nation has seen an increase in service rates in learning disabilities, with the service rates for students of secondary school age accounting for the greatest change. According to the *Eleventh Annual Report to Congress* (U.S. Department of Education, 1989) 1,025,010 students 12 to 17 years old have been diagnosed as LD and are receiving special education services.

Before passage of PL 94-142, only a small body of literature specifically addressed the characteristics and needs of adolescents with learning disabilities. It is not that learning disabilities were not thought to exist in adolescents and young adults. Indeed, early descriptions of students with dyslexia and related learning disabilities often included case studies of students in the age range of 12 to 21 years (see Critchley, 1964, pp. ix–xi; Johnson & Myklebust, 1967, pp. 229–232). But secondary school-aged students with learning disabilities were not considered a distinct population with distinct characteristics and programming needs.

The tide certainly has turned in the past decade and a half. Since 1975, there has been an enormous expansion of concern for, programming with, research on, and literature about students with learning disabilities in high school, and in the process of moving from school to work or further education. After reviewing past service delivery models and efficacy data, two models of services are proposed here. These models incorporate four components that I believe have potential for meeting the goals of a meaningful high school education and a smooth transition to life beyond school, each with important implications for staffing and teacher preparation as well as for general school policy and administration.

EARLY SERVICE DELIVERY MODELS: THE CSDC EXPERIMENTS

In the mid-1970s, special education programs for students with learning disabilities at the elementary level were commonplace, but few school districts provided programs for students with learning disabilities in secondary schools. After PL 94–142 was passed in 1975, schools were legally mandated to provide appropriate services for students with learning disabilities until graduation from high school or until age 21 (or age 25 in some states) and school districts undertook widespread efforts to develop secondary-level special education programs.

Of course, school authorities were not only responding to the mandate; parents and educators had a growing realization that, despite the emphasis on, and the optimism associated with, early intervention efforts, the learning difficulties of students with learning disabilities were not being ameliorated in the elementary grades. Many of these youngsters were leaving elementary school special education programs poorly equipped in the academic skills necessary for success in high school. Furthermore, many students were being identified as learning disabled in the intermediate and middle school grades and were entering high school having had no opportunity for early intervention.

Most of the new approaches to secondary school services for students with learning disabilities grew out of the network of Child Service Demonstration Centers (CSDCs) funded by the Bureau of Education for the Handicapped (BEH) between 1975 and 1977. These included:

1. The Parallel Alternate Curriculum for Secondary Classrooms, developed in Arizona.
2. Strategies to Increase Learning Efficiency Among LD Adolescents, developed in Kansas.
3. The Model Resource Room Project, developed in Michigan.
4. The Oklahoma Child Service Demonstration Center.

5. The Synergistic Education Model: A Comprehensive Plan for Learning Disabled, developed in Texas.
6. The Pittsburgh Child Service Demonstration Center (see Riegel & Mathey, 1980).

These CSDC models had in common a commitment to the concept of mainstreaming, consideration of the students' learning and behavioral characteristics, a focus on students with mild to moderate learning disabilities, attention to characteristics of the high school settings in which the students operated, design of specific, replicable methodologies of instruction, incorporation of motivational strategies, and attention to the importance of generalization and maintenance of skills.

But the CSDC models also differed on a number of important dimensions. For example, in the Kansas model, the primary focus for change was the student; in the Arizona model, it was the school environment; in the remaining models, both the students and the environment were targets for change efforts. A fundamental philosophy of the Kansas model was that students with learning disabilities must and can learn to become autonomously successful in academic and social environments, even if those environments often seem hostile and resistant. In contrast, developers of the Arizona model believed that students' academic and behavioral deficiencies could not be ameliorated and that students with learning disabilities would be successful in high school only if mainstream content demands (i.e., the environment and curriculum) could be modified to accommodate the disabilities and deficiencies of the students. The Oklahoma, Michigan, Texas, and Pittsburgh models incorporated strategies to promote change both in student behaviors and in mainstream curricular and instructional processes.

Another dimension upon which the CSDC models varied was the setting in which primary interventions were designed to take place. For example, in the Kansas model, primary interventions were designed for the resource room setting. In the Arizona model, mainstream content subject classes were the target sites for intervention. In the Oklahoma, Michigan, Texas, and Pittsburgh models, interventions were designed for both resource room and mainstream class settings.

Some of the CSDC models emphasized direct services to students, whether by the special education resource room teacher (Kansas) or by the mainstream teacher (Arizona). Others featured a combination of direct and *indirect* services to students through consultation to mainstream teachers (Oklahoma, Michigan, Texas, and Pittsburgh).

The CSDC models also varied significantly with regard to instructional emphasis. The Kansas model emphasized instruction in a wide range of learning strategies (i.e., techniques, principles and rules that would enable the student to learn independently and to solve problems) in lieu of basic skills instruction. The Oklahoma model combined remediation of academic skill deficiencies with training in compensatory strategies. The Texas model combined reading remediation to promote comprehension and vocabulary development with a social-behavioral program to build stronger self-concepts, develop communication skills, foster self-responsibility, and teach problem-solving strategies. The Pittsburgh model provided for basic skills remediation in reading or mathematics along with instruction in nonacademic skills (self-management, social, organizational, and study skills) that the developers believed were necessary for survival both within and outside the school setting.

Federal funding for the CSDC network ended within 2 years, although pressures on school districts to provide secondary school programs intensified. Forced to move quickly, school districts developed a plethora of hastily conceived adaptations of the CSDC models without the funding for technical support that might have ensured adequate implementation. By 1979 the most common service delivery model for secondary school-aged students with learning disabilities was simply an adaptation of the elementary school resource room—primary placement in mainstream classes with part-time instruction provided by special education personnel (Deshler, Lowrey, & Alley, 1979).

Most of these resource room programs continued the elementary school emphasis on remediation of basic skills (reading, writing and mathematics); the goal was competence in basic literacy and numeracy. But many resource room teachers also provided instruction to students with LD designed to help them achieve better grades in mainstream content subject classes, assisted students in completing regular class assignments, offered drill exercises to prepare students for an upcoming test in a mainstream class, arranged with mainstream content subject teachers to allow for administration of chapter tests or final exams by the resource teacher in the resource room (thus permitting more time for oral presentation of test items), and arranged for students to tape mainstream class lectures in lieu of taking notes. For many LD teachers and their students these additional "tutorial" activities gradually consumed all of the resource room time, and little time was left for remedial instruction, or for the other curricular elements introduced in the CSDCs, such as social or survival skills or learning strategies.

EVIDENCE OF PROGRAM EFFECTIVENESS

Dropout Rate

Special education programs are supposed to be nurturing, sustaining, and personalized, somewhere in the school system where students with handicaps can find special education teachers who care, who explain the importance of sustaining an interest in high school, who make learning relevant and accessible, and who help students to succeed. These are the very elements that have also been associated with successful dropout prevention programs (see Wehlage, Rutter, Smith, Lesko, & Fernandez, 1989)—attention to individual student needs, small student-teacher ratios, more opportunities for personal counseling, and utilization of individualized and diversified instructional strategies. So, if high school programs for students with learning disabilities are implemented appropriately, we should expect students with LD to be staying in school.

My colleagues and I spent 6 years working with special education and mainstream administrators, supervisors, and teachers in a large urban school district, to refine implementation of the Pittsburgh CSDC model of secondary school services for students with learning disabilities. By 1981 the model program had been in place long enough so that 52 students who had entered high school in 1977–78 as ninth graders and had been placed in the LD program should have been in 12th grade. We set out to document the progress of these 52 adolescents (see Levin, Zigmond, & Birch, 1985). We expected to find the students in 11th or 12th grade, some fully mainstreamed, some still being served in special education resource rooms, all showing improved basic skills and getting ready for the world of work. Instead, as far as we could determine, 47% of the students with LD had dropped out of school, a rate far in excess of the 36% dropout rate for nonhandicapped students reported by the host school district for the same time period.

The Levin et al. (1985) sample was very small, but the findings deeply troubled us. We had worked hard with the school district to develop a secondary school LD program that was sensible and meaningful. We had taught teachers how to help students make it in their mainstream classes. We had trained one special education teacher to function in a consulting teacher role to help students with learning disabilities and their mainstream teachers alike. We had data to indicate that a large percentage of the students with learning disabilities who came to school were earning passing grades (Zigmond, Levin, & Laurie, 1985). Disappointed to discover that students for whom we had designed this "special" education were abandoning it, we embarked on a second study to verify our original dropout findings.

Zigmond and Thornton (1985) located and interviewed students with LD from the same urban school district who should have been in the graduating class of 1982, and a control sample of non-learning-disabled students from the same high schools. Students were part of the LD or non-LD groups based on their status as ninth graders in the 1978–79 school year. Of the 60 LD participants in the study, 28 had completed high school and 32 had left school before graduation, a 53% dropout rate among high school students with LD. In sharp contrast, the dropout rate for non-LD participants was 27%.

A third follow-up study of the 1983 graduating class confirmed the finding again: 39% of students with LD who entered ninth grade in the 1979–80 school year dropped out before graduating from high school, as compared with 22% of nonhandicapped peers (Thornton & Zigmond, 1988). The picture that was emerging was that students with learning disabilities in this urban area seemed to be leaving high school at nearly twice the rate of nonhandicapped classmates. And follow-up studies in a neighboring blue-collar community (Morrow, Thornton, & Zigmond, 1988) and in rural Virginia (deBettencourt, Zigmond, & Thornton, 1989) showed that the phenomenon was not limited to the urban school.

Nor were we the only researchers to be reporting alarmingly high dropout rates among students served in special education programs in secondary schools. In Vermont, Hasazi and her colleagues reported that 34% of public school youth with mild disabilities were not completing a high school education (Hasazi, Gordon, & Roe, 1985). The reported dropout rate of youth with LD in several school districts in Florida was pegged at 31% (Fardig, Algozzine, Schwartz, Hensel, & Westling, 1985). In a large Alabama county school district, Cobb and Crump (1984) reported a dropout rate of 42% among students with learning disabilities. In a middle class suburban school district in the Midwest, White, Schumaker, Warner, Alley, and Deshler (1980) found that 26% of the youth with learning disabilities had dropped out.

In its *Tenth Annual Report to Congress* (U.S. Department of Education, 1988), the Office of Special Education Programs (OSEP) reported that in the 1985–86 school year,

26,644 students with learning disabilities, aged 16 through 21, dropped out of high school before completing their education, an average of 148 students each school day. This figure, which OSEP believed to be an underestimate, represented about 26% of all students with learning disabilities who left school that year and was nearly double the dropout rate reported by the National Center for Educational Statistics for the general school-aged population (see Rumberger, 1987). Data reported for the subsequent year (U.S. Department of Education, 1989), and data from the National Longitudinal Transition Study being carried out at SRI International under contract from OSEP confirm the finding (see U.S. Department of Education, 1989, p. 70).

My colleagues and I consider the dropout rate to be indirect evidence of the efficacy of secondary school programs for students with learning disabilities, and we find these dropout data compelling and disturbing. Surely if school programs were meeting students' needs, high school students with learning disabilities would not be leaving school! The dropout rates alone force a rethinking of special education services at the secondary school level.

But does it matter that students with learning disabilities are dropping out? Are those who leave school early just as well off in terms of employment and post-school adjustment as their counterparts who stay? Do the dropouts get a "jump on the job market?" Do they get some practical experience out there on the streets that is even better for them than what they get in school? A series of studies on the employment and post-school adjustment of graduates and dropouts over the past few years has provided the data to answer these questions: There is a significant differential in employment patterns and post-school adjustment of youth with LD who are dropouts or graduates.

In 1985, we reported that among urban youth, 75% of graduates with LD were employed at the time of follow-up, 18 to 28 months after graduation (see Zigmond & Thornton, 1985). This contrasted sharply with the employment figures for high school dropouts; only 47% of dropouts with LD were employed. High school leavers who returned to complete their GED were not much better off than those who did not; only 37.5% of youth with LD who had GEDs were holding jobs at the time of the follow-up interviews.

In some communities, of course, the job market is extremely good and *everyone* (graduates and dropouts, disabled and nondisabled) can find a job; such was the case in a rural Virginia study (see deBettencourt et al., 1989). In other communities the job market is extremely poor and *no one* can find a job, not graduates or dropouts, disabled or nondisabled; such was the case in the blue-collar community studied by Morrow et al. (1988). But in most of our work, and in the work of others across the nation, in terms of the transition from school to work, it pays for students with learning disabilities to stay in high school and graduate. Nevertheless, special education programs for these students seem to have minimal holding power, and many students with learning disabilities drop out of school to face uncertain, grim futures on the streets.

Achievement

Many researchers have reported academic achievement levels in reading and mathematics among adolescents with learning disabilities that are consistently low, 3 to 5 years behind actual grade placement at entrance to ninth grade (see Cobb & Crump, 1984; Levin, et al., 1985; Norman & Zigmond, 1980; Schalock et al., 1986; Thornton & Zigmond, 1987a; Warner, Alley, Schumaker, Deshler, & Clark, 1980; Zigmond & Thornton, 1985). Unfortunately, students with learning disabilities do not seem to recoup these basic skill deficiencies during their years of attending secondary school resource room programs (Zigmond & Thornton, 1985; Gregory, Shanahan, & Walberg, 1986) and, in fact, the gap between achievement scores and grade expectancy level actually seems to widen as students with learning disabilities progress through high school (Norman & Zigmond, 1980; Warner et al., 1980).

The follow-up studies we completed speak to this point as well. We have had the opportunity to assess basic skill levels among dropouts, who in general completed only 1 or 2 years of a high school LD program, and graduates, who had at least 4 years. Their achievement levels are essentially the same. Data taken from Zigmond and Thornton (1985), Thornton and Zigmond (1987b) and deBettencourt et al. (1989) illustrate a persistent finding: Special education programs at the high school level fail in their attempts to improve the basic skills of adolescents with LD. Many students with learning disabilities enter ninth grade barely literate and leave high school after 1, 2, 3, or 4 years, with literacy skills virtually unchanged.

COMPONENTS OF AN EFFECTIVE HIGH SCHOOL PROGRAM FOR STUDENTS WITH LD

Over the past decade, several researchers have attempted to delineate factors associated with low achievement and premature school leaving. The results have implicated environmental and family background factors including low socioeconomic level, large family size, established patterns of dropping out in parents and siblings, and nonintact families (Bachman, 1972; Tseng, 1972; Kowalski & Cangemi, 1974; Lloyd, 1976; Hewitt & Johnson, 1979; Hill, 1979; Mare, 1980), individual student characteristics including race, gender, IQ, and achievement level (Cervantes, 1965; Combs & Cooley, 1968; Kowalski & Cangemi, 1974; Lloyd, 1976; Kaplan & Luck, 1977; Hammontree, 1978; Stoughton & Grady, 1978; Hill, 1979; Howell & Frese, 1982; Rumberger, 1983), and grade retentions and high absence rates (Schreiber, 1962; Curley, 1971; Dean, 1973; Kowalski & Cangemi, 1974; Kaplan & Luck, 1977; Mahood, 1981).

Implicit in much of this research is the assumption that a better understanding of the characteristics of low achievers and dropouts and of their families and communities will lead to the development of school policies and programs that will reduce the number of adolescents who fail to graduate. The intent is noble, but the results have been negligible because the focus on social, family, and personal characteristics does not carry any obvious implications for reshaping school policies and practices.

We share the view of Wehlage and Rutter (1986) that to increase the effectiveness and the holding power of schools, *alterable* school conditions must be identified. So, in our research and writing over the past decade, instead of focusing on environmental and family background factors or immutable student characteristics, we have concentrated on school program variables—the curriculum and student schedules—and on student *be-haviors* in and around school—behaviors that students can control and that schools can teach. These also have been shown to contribute to low achievement and dropping out, and they can be reshaped and redirected.

Four components appear to be essential to more effective secondary school programming for students with learning disabilities: intensive instruction in reading and mathematics; explicit instruction in "survival" skills; successful completion of courses required for high school graduation; and explicit planning for life after high school.

Intensive Instruction in Basic Skills

Our own research has shown that many high school graduates of secondary school LD programs score at poorer than eighth-grade proficiency on a basic skills assessment in reading. Operationally, as the writing sample in Figure 1 illustrates, this means they are barely literate and unable to make functional use of written communications. They also

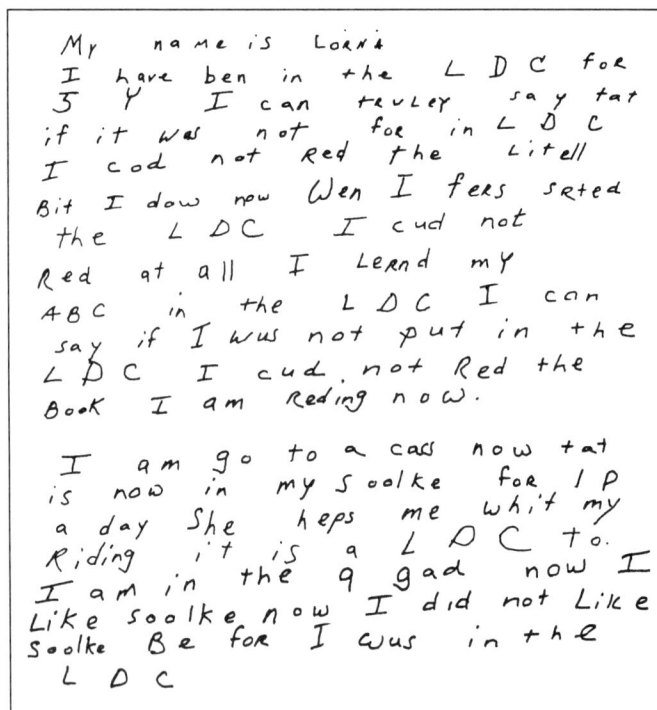

Note: She uses *LDC* to mean *learning disabilities class*;
        Y in the third line means *years*;
        1p in the second paragraph means *1 period*.

FIGURE 1   *Composition Written by a Ninth-Grade Girl with Learning Disabilities*

are incapable of meeting the increasingly high demands for literacy that are present in today's reform-minded mainstream high school. As our recent data have shown (see Donahoe & Zigmond, 1990), many students with learning disabilities are now earning failing grades in mainstream courses such as social studies, which place heavy demands on reading and writing, and even in less academically oriented courses such as health.

Some would say that the problem lies within the student; by adolescence, ability to learn basic skills plateaus and further progress in reading proficiency cannot be expected (see Alley & Deshler, 1979). Nevertheless, our observational studies of instruction in LD resource rooms at the secondary school level would assign the culprit elsewhere.

Figures 2, 3 and 4 summarize data gathered from four 42-minute observations in each of eight LD resource rooms in high schools in a large urban school district. Using a time-sample protocol (described fully in Zigmond, 1988), observers coded three dimensions of the

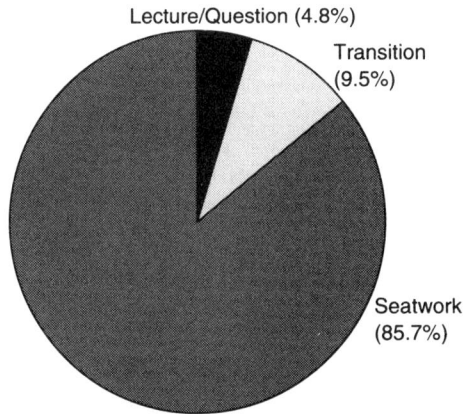

Lecture/Question (4.8%)

Transition (9.5%)

Seatwork (85.7%)

FIGURE 2 *Activity Structures in Eight LD Resource Rooms*

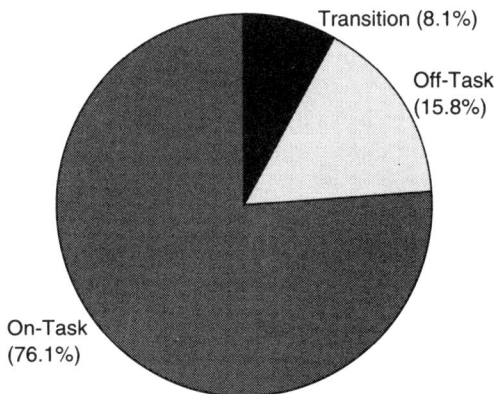

Transition (8.1%)

Off-Task (15.8%)

On-Task (76.1%)

FIGURE 3 *Student Behaviors in Eight LD Resource Rooms*

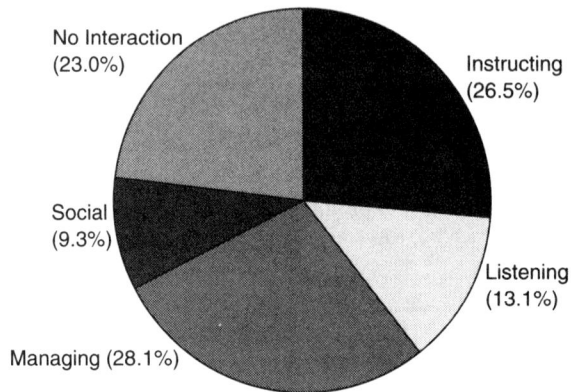

FIGURE 4   Instructional Interactions in Eight LD Resource Rooms

classroom experience: the activity structure of the class, the behaviors of the students with LD being observed, and the nature of the instructional interactions between teacher and students. Activity structure meant how the teacher arranged the class and the assignments. Observers coded activity structures as lecture or large-group question/answer format, small-group lessons, independent seatwork, or transition (when no activity was assigned to students). Figure 2 shows that students spent more than 85% of their resource room time assigned to independent seatwork and no time assigned to small group instruction.

Student behaviors were coded into one of three categories: on-task, off-task, or transition (no task to be done). Figure 3 shows that students in these LD resource rooms were on-task more than three fourths of the time.

Instructional interactions characterized how the teachers spent their time during each 42-minute period. Teachers could be instructing, listening (to student questions or student answers), managing the flow of academic activities (giving directions for an assignment, telling students to find materials or worksheets or a particular page in a book), socializing with students, or not engaged in any sort of interaction at all with students. Figure 4 shows that LD resource room teachers spent, on the average, slightly less than 40% of each class period in instructional interactions (instructing and listening), most of these one-to-one interactions with students as they completed worksheets at their desks. Teachers spent about 28% of class periods telling students what to do but not teaching them how to do it, and another 23% of class time not interacting with students at all. These data suggest that high school students with learning disabilities may not be making progress in basic skills because they are receiving so little teaching!

Literacy

We have all heard and read about the crisis of adult illiteracy in the United States. Depending upon the definition of literacy used, the figures on adult illiteracy range from 23 to 78 million Americans (Kozol, 1985), or a minimum of one in five adults who are totally or functionally illiterate. And numbers alone do not adequately portray the complexity of the problem. A disproportionate number of the individuals included in the figures are unemployed, poor, and disadvantaged minorities (Nickerson, 1985).

Students with learning disabilities who leave high school unable to read join this swelling mass of adult illiterates. High school programs for students with learning disabilities *must* provide intensive, relentless instruction in basic literacy skills to prepare students with LD for independence, employment flexibility, and job security.

Reading Instruction

Instruction in reading at the secondary school level has to be interesting and imaginative. Goals of the reading instruction are to make students independent, fluent readers, confident enough in decoding skills to be willing to attack unfamiliar text in a popular magazine, a novel, a technical manual, or a mainstream textbook. Reading instruction should be individualized but should not be delivered as predominantly one-to-one instruction. Assignments should be based on an analysis of the entering skills of each student, but instruction should be directed to the group, because this arrangement affords *all* students assigned to the special education teacher during a particular class period more opportunities for teacher-directed instruction and less time on independent seatwork.

Under no circumstances should high school students with learning disabilities simply be placed in a basal reading text series and taught a developmental reading program. Instead, reading lessons should be organized around a three-part curriculum: decoding; vocabulary, comprehension, and fluency; and writing. Time is short, and careful attention must be paid not only to teaching the most critically needed literacy skills but also to building students' self-confidence as readers.

Phonics Review and Decoding

Each year, students probably will need an intensive phonics review emphasizing word parts and word families, not individual sound-symbol associations (see Bradley & Bryant, 1985; Fayne & Bryant, 1981; Williams, 1980; Graham & Johnson, 1989). Decoding strategies such as those emphasized in the Glass analysis techniques also should be reviewed (Glass, 1978). Rapid drill and practice of words in isolation might be suitable for the early part of the school year, but soon after that, decoding strategies should be practiced in continuous narrative and expository text.

Vocabulary Development

Although skills are important, the major part of each reading period should be devoted to text-based activities for developing vocabulary, comprehension, and fluency. Text materials should include short stories or novels from a variety of genres (mysteries, real-life adventures, science fiction), selected for high interest and motivation. Most students with learning disabilities have never had the experience of not being able to put down a book, of wanting to read to the end to find out how it all turns out. Few students with LD think of themselves as readers competent enough to read for entertainment or distraction. Class time, as well as homework, could be devoted to reading a whole book, although the teacher could read parts of the book aloud, to move the action along. Requiring repeated readings (see O'Shea, Sindelar, & O'Shea, 1987) might help students get through particularly difficult or dense sections of the book and also are useful for developing fluency and enhancing comprehension.

During text reading, opportunities should be afforded to review decoding strategies for words in context and to develop vocabulary through semantic mapping and group discussion (see Calfee, 1976; McKeown & Beck, 1988). Teachers also should teach students strategies for understanding the structure of narrative text and engage students in plot and character analyses using graphic organizers such as those depicted in Figures 5 and 6. But mostly, with narrative texts, students should be encouraged to read for the pleasure of reading.

Work on narrative text should be alternated (in 4- to 6-week cycles, perhaps) with work on expository text. Now, popular magazines, newspapers, or science, social studies, or health textbooks can be used as vehicles for developing strategies to cope with expo-

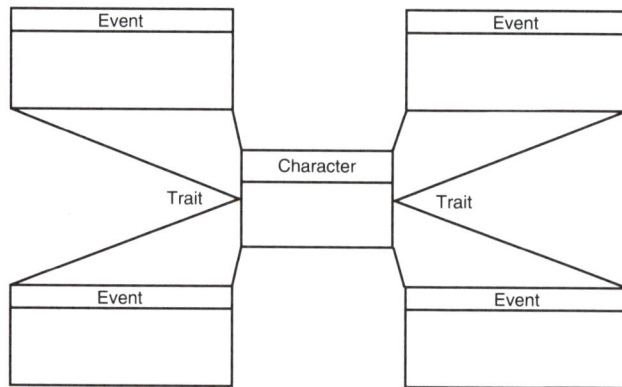

FIGURE 5   *Graphic Organizer for Character Analysis*

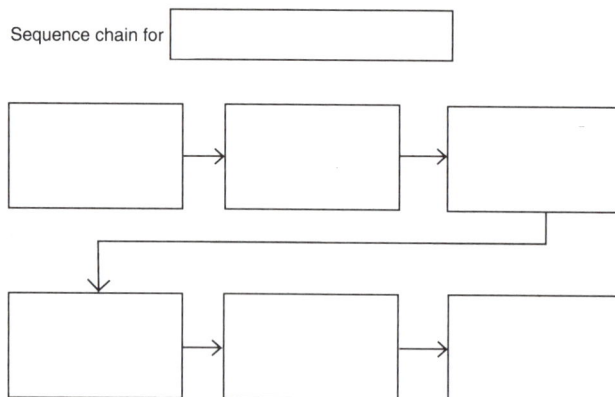

FIGURE 6   *Graphic Organizer for Plot Analysis*

sition. Strategies involving summarization, mental imagery, self-questioning, question answering, and so forth, reviewed by Graham and Johnson (1989), should be taught and practiced. Of particular use might be the reciprocal teaching strategy introduced by Palinscar and Brown (1984), which involves summarization, questioning, clarifying, and predicting, or the self-monitoring strategies reviewed by Wong (1986). Opportunities for vocabulary development should not be overlooked in expository text reading, again using semantic mapping and graphic organizers to help students see relationships among word meanings and concepts.

Writing

Finally, some part of each week of reading instruction must be devoted to writing. Writing activities should be an extension of the reading comprehension lessons and should build on the semantic maps and graphic organizers used in discussions of text. Strategies for improving the quality and technical adequacy of student writing, discussed extensively by Deshler (Alley & Deshler, 1979) and Graham and Harris (1989a, 1989b), should be incorporated into the writing part of the reading curriculum as well.

Measuring Learning

At regular intervals, perhaps as frequently as twice per week, curriculum-based measures (CBM) should be taken with students who are reading well below the eighth-grade level, to determine whether they are profiting from instruction. Students may be asked to complete 1-minute oral readings from grade-appropriate text material (see Deno & Mirkin, 1977) or to complete maze tasks delivered via computer (see Fuchs, Hamlett, Fuchs, Stecker, & Ferguson, 1988). Performance data then should be graphed and analyzed for trend. These CBM data provide a global indicator of reading fluency, a measure that is sensitive to improvements in reading performance over time.

If CBM data show a student making steady improvements (see Figure 7), the teacher can feel confident that the reading program is working. If a student's CBM data indicate a level or downward trend (see Figure 8), the teacher is informed that a change in the instructional program is warranted, that "business as usual" is no longer appropriate for this student. The change may involve tutoring the student in a strategy the rest of the class has mastered, changing the intensity and frequency of teacher feedback to the student during reading instruction, changing the nature of the assignments during independent seatwork, changing the incentives for student performance (see Howell & Morehead, 1987). Whatever the change, continual monitoring of CBM data will inform the teacher of the success of the new approach or of the need to continue to adjust instruction.

Math Skills

Intensive instruction in basic skills is not, of course, limited to reading and writing domains. Math skills of high school students with LD also demand considerable attention. Many students have not acquired fluency in basic math facts by the time they enter ninth grade. More important, they don't understand or feel comfortable using mathematics in everyday life—in shopping, measuring, estimating prices, solving problems.

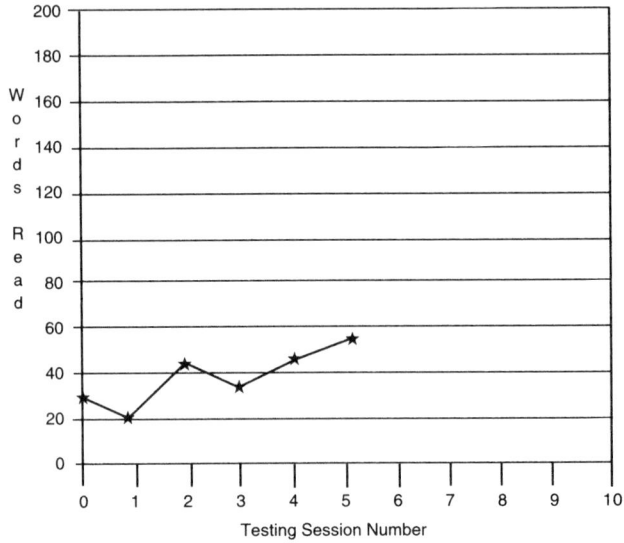

FIGURE 7   J.B.'s CBM Scores

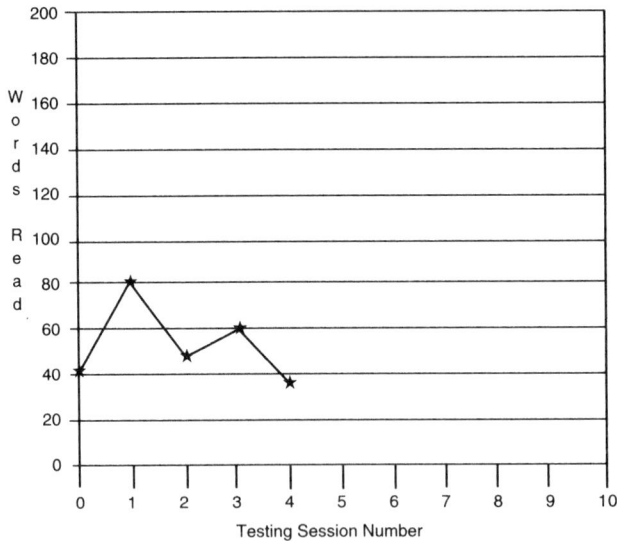

FIGURE 8   C.A.'s CBM Scores

A functional math curriculum should teach students basic algorithms up through simple algebra but emphasize problem solving and practical applications of math concepts. Lloyd and Keller (1989) provide excellent suggestions for effective math instruction for students with LD, which could be used at the secondary school level. Problem-solving strategies being explored by Cawley and his colleagues (see Cawley, Fitzmaurice, Shaw, Kahn, & Bates, 1978, 1979a, 1979b; Cawley, Fitzmaurice-Hayes, & Shaw, 1988) also are particularly relevant in teaching mathematics to students with LD in secondary school.

Explicit Instruction in Survival Skills

Several years ago we introduced readers of *Focus on Exceptional Children* to a curriculum for teaching coping skills to adolescents with learning disabilities (Silverman, Zigmond, & Sansone, 1981). We have not changed our minds about the importance of these survival skills to the successful functioning of high school students with learning disabilities, nor about the need to teach these skills explicitly. A survival skills curriculum would have three strands: behavior control, teacher-pleasing behaviors, and study skills/test-taking strategies. Descriptions of the objectives of each of these strands and sample activities were provided in Silverman et al. (1981). Some extensions of these ideas are provided next.

Behavior Control Activities

Behavior control activities are designed to help students who are always getting into trouble, who consistently do the wrong things, and who often are suspended or punished. These students do not seem to understand the role they play in creating the conflicts in which they are continually involved. In behavior control activities, the goal is to help students alter their locus of control from external ("I'm not at fault; someone else made these things happen to me") to internal ("I behaved in a certain way so these things happened; if I behave differently, different things might happen"). Students learn to take responsibility for their actions. They learn alternative ways of responding to situations that arise in the everyday course of school. They learn that they can change their school lives because they can change their own behaviors.

As is the case in all three strands of the school survival skills curriculum, teaching behavior control relies heavily upon simulations and role playing to help students learn to recognize what they and others do in school situations, the impact of one's behavior on other people, alternative ways of responding to specific situations, and the consequences of behaving one way or another. Early experiences in teaching behavior control in secondary schools have taught us that students with learning disabilities cannot use simulations or role playing effectively without explicit instruction in how to observe and document. So we spend time, initially, teaching students to use a graphic to organize their observations and record their feelings and impressions. An example of one such graphic is presented in Figure 9.

Once students are good observers, efforts can be concentrated on the content rather than on the process of the simulation or role play. Now we introduce a problem-solving strategy to help students become analytic about their experiences in school and their personal responsibility for events and consequences. The graphic displayed in Figure 10 becomes the basis for a group discussion on alternative ways of responding to situations such as the following:

Role Players

1. _____(_____)　2. _____(_____)　3. _____(_____)
　　　　　Role　　　　　Initials　　　　　　Role　　　　　Initials　　　　　　Role　　　　　Initials

Situation _____

Directions: Place an "X" on each line below to describe the role players' behaviors. Focus on the role or behaviors rather than on the individual playing it.

Verbal Behaviors
What I Heard

Role Player

(Loudness)

Comfortably Heard　　1 _____　Not Comfortably Heard
　　　　　　　　　2 _____
　　　　　　　　　3 _____

(Rate of Speech)

Easy to Follow　　1 _____　Difficult to Follow
　　　　　　　2 _____
　　　　　　　3 _____

(Tone of Voice)

Pleasant　　1 _____　Unpleasant
　　　　　2 _____
　　　　　3 _____

Nonverbal Behaviors
What I Saw

Role Player

(Eye Contact)

Engaged in Eye Contact　　1 _____　Avoided Eye Contact
　　　　　　　　　　2 _____
　　　　　　　　　　3 _____

(Body Proximity)

Comfortable Distance　　1 _____　Uncomfortable Distance
　　　　　　　　　2 _____
　　　　　　　　　3 _____

(Body Positions/Movement)

Open and Accepting　　1 _____　Closed and Rejecting
　　　　　　　　2 _____
　　　　　　　　3 _____

Feelings
How I Reacted

Role Player

Calm/ Comfortable　　1 _____　Uneasy/ Uncomfortable
　　　　　　　　2 _____
　　　　　　　　3 _____

FIGURE 9　　***Graphic to Teach Students to Observe and Analyze Role-Playing***

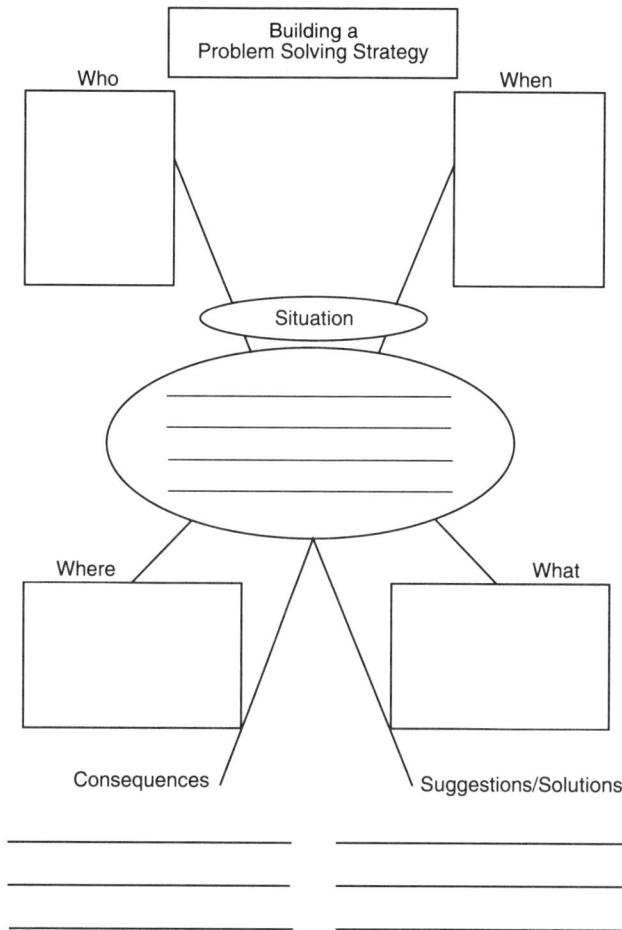

FIGURE 10   Graphic for Development of Problem-Solving Skills

As you are walking down the hall with a few of your friends, you see someone you know way down at the other end of the building. You call to him. Right at that moment, a teacher steps out of her classroom. She is very upset that you have disturbed her class while they are taking an important test.

You are standing in line at the cafeteria. As you are waiting, two students attempt to cut in front of you. You have been waiting patiently for some time, and you think this is unfair.

Students analyze the situation, discuss alternative ways of behaving, act out the various ways, and analyze the probable consequences of each scenario. Some role playing is videotaped so that the action can be replayed, observed, and stopped for extended discussion. Then, after practicing alternative behaviors within the safe environment of the resource room, students are encouraged to try new behaviors in their interactions around the school. They also are encouraged to keep track of the extent to which using behavior control strategies changes the rate at which they are assigned suspensions, detentions, demerits and so forth.

Teacher-Pleasing Behaviors

Teacher-pleasing behaviors focus on the behaviors students use to cope with rules and demands within their classes. This part of the curriculum helps students acquire behavior patterns that usually lead teachers to consider students more positively. Most students learn, in an incidental fashion, that certain behaviors ingratiate students with the teacher. These students learn to make eye contact, look interested in the lesson, volunteer responses in class, look busy. Many students with learning disabilities do not learn these behavior patterns, and their failure to display teacher-pleasing behaviors puts off the teacher.

The student with LD often needs to be taught, explicitly, how to act like a "good" student. Since writing the *Focus on Exceptional Children* article in 1981, my colleagues and I have developed scripts for 20 lessons on teacher-pleasing behaviors (see Zigmond, Kerr, Schaeffer, Farra, & Brown, 1986). During one of the earliest lessons, students complete a School Survival Skills Scale, a self-assessment of school-appropriate behaviors. Then each student compares the self-generated profile with one derived from a Scale completed by one of his or her mainstream teachers. The exercise helps students become aware of their own behaviors and of differences in how they view themselves in regular classes and how mainstream teachers view them in these same classes. The remaining lessons cover four basic aspects of behavior, as follows:

Attendance
- Coming to school
- Coming to class
- Coming on time
- Coming prepared

Assignment Completion
- Keeping track of assignments
- Turning in classwork/homework

Attentiveness
- Being more "on-task"
- Responding to teacher requests
- Asking questions/making comments

Compliance behavior
- Reducing disruptive behavior
- Talking more "appropriately"

Instructional formats and activities vary considerably from lesson to lesson to maintain student interest and active participation. For example, we use a pencil-and-paper task for an activity on remembering (see Figure 11). This remembering activity comes just before a simulation task on how to use an assignment book (Figure 12). In contrast, we use a Q-sort-like task to get students to think about appropriate classroom behavior. The statements in Figure 13 are each printed on a 4x6 card, and each student receives an entire deck of 16 cards. Students silently read the statements on the cards and sort the cards into two piles representing "cool" and "not cool" classroom behaviors. Then the students engage in a group discussion of the cards in each pile.

An important aid in teaching students to use new teacher-pleasing behaviors involves self-monitoring strategies. Students contract to perform first one, then more and more of the target behaviors. Students daily record whether they performed these behaviors, on self-monitoring forms checked by the special education teacher at regular intervals. The number of skills that students self-monitor increases gradually until students are recording their performance on as many as seven or eight skills. Figure 14 is a sample of a self-monitoring form used in the School Survival Skills Curriculum (Zigmond et al., 1986), on which students are recording behaviors of coming to class; arriving on time; bringing notebook, paper, and text; staying on task; following directions; asking questions; answering questions; and entering assignments in an assignment book for one mainstream class for one week of school. Figure 14 shows this self-monitoring form.

Study Skills and Test-Taking Strategies

Study skills and test-taking strategies help students with LD organize their time, approach a textbook, take notes from a lecture or a text, organize information, study for tests, and take tests. The goals of the study skills component of the school survival skills curriculum is to teach students strategies for gathering and retaining information that they will use in completing assignments and fulfilling the requirements of content subject courses. Students are taught systematic methods for approaching classroom tasks and for

Name _____

Date _____

Directions: Put a check in the appropriate box.

Have you ever forgotten:

	Often	Some-times	Almost never
1. to bring in a field trip permission slip?			
2. to study for a test?			
3. to bring in your homework?			
4. to find a newspaper or magazine article?			
5. to attend chorus or football practice?			
6. to hand in a book report?			
7. to bring in something you did for extra credit?			
8. to bring your just-washed gym clothes from home?			
9. to bring lunch or lunch money?			
10. to bring in an excuse for being absent?			

FIGURE 11   *School Survival Skills Curriculum: Task on Remembering*

compensating for deficiencies in basic skills. The activities of this component draw heavily on the work of Deshler and his colleagues (see Alley & Deshler, 1979) as well as on time-honored study skills such as SQ3R (see Alexander, 1985; Schumaker, Deshler, Alley, Warner, & Denton, 1982).

Successful Completion of Courses Required for Graduation

When students with learning disabilities are assigned to resource room programs, they take most of the courses they need in order to graduate from high school in the main-

---

"WHAT IF . . . ?" WORKSHEET

What if you are monitoring yourself and keeping track of assignments in your English class, and . . .

1. Today is Monday of Week 1
   . . . you have an essay to write, which is due in English class on Tuesday. What do you write in your Assignment Book?

2. Today is Tuesday of Week 1
   . . . you have a test on Friday in math class. What do you write in your Assignment Book?

3. Today is Wednesday of Week 1
   . . . you are supposed to read pages 192–241 in your English Literature book for Thursday. What do you write in your Assignment Book?

4. Today is Thursday of Week 1
   . . . your English teacher says, "Do the assignment on page 42. I will collect it at the end of class today." What do you write in your Assignment Book?

5. Today is Friday of Week1
   . . . your social studies teacher tells you that term projects are due the next Friday. What do you write in your Assignment Book?

TURN TO NEXT PAGE
WE ARE STARTING A NEW WEEK NOW.

6. Today is Monday of Week 2
   . . . you have to write another essay for English class on Wednesday. What do you write in your Assignment Book?

7. Today is Tuesday of Week 2
   . . . your English assignment (an essay), which was due on Wednesday, has been postponed until Thursday. What do you write in your Assignment Book?

8. Today is Wednesday of Week 2
   . . . your science teacher tells you that Friday you have to make up the unit test that you missed when you were absent last week. What do you write in your Assignment Book?

9. Today is Thursday of Week 2
   . . . you didn't have an English assignment on Wednesday because there was an assembly and you did not have English class. What did you write in your Assignment Book?

FIGURE 12   *Practice Task to Learn to Use an Assignment Book*

Card Number

1. Even if I'm daydreaming, I keep my eyes open and look at the teacher.
2. When the teacher asks a question, I raise my hand even if I'm not sure of the answer. If she calls on me, I'll ask her, politely, to repeat the question.
3. It is O.K. for me to correct the teacher during the lecture if he or she makes a mistake.
4. It is O.K. to sharpen my pencil while the teacher is talking.
5. During a class discussion I take the opportunity to comb my hair.
6. During English class I am doing my homework for math class.
7. When I need help with my work, I raise my hand and wait for the teacher to come.
8. I don't bring my text to class so that I don't have to do the work assigned.
9. Sometimes I use the dictionary during class time.
10. It is O.K. to talk to my friends during class if I whisper.
11. I don't understand the assignment sheet, so I ask for help.
12. If someone gets in trouble during class, I stop what I am doing to see what's going on.
13. I copy from the chalkboard only the words that make sense to me.
14. If I think I can't do an assignment, I just put it down.
15. I never participate in class discussions.
16. Classtime is a good chance for me to read a magazine or the paper.

FIGURE 13   "Cool" and "Not Cool" Classroom Behaviors

Date Given _____

Name_____   Due Date_____

Directions: Put a check (✔) if you did each step.
Put an "X" if you did not.

Period	Class	Room	Monday Date	Tuesday Date	Wednesday Date	Thursday Date	Friday Date
			Went to class ____ Got there on time ____	Went to class ____ Got there on time ____	Went to class ____ Got there on time ____	Went to class ____ Got there on time ____	Went to class ____ Got there on time ____
REMEMBER TO USE YOUR ASSIGNMENT BOOK!			Brought to class pen/pencil____ paper/ notebook ____ text ____	Brought to class pen/pencil____ paper/ notebook ____ text ____	Brought to class pen/pencil____ paper/ notebook ____ text ____	Brought to class pen/pencil____ paper/ notebook ____ text ____	Brought to class pen/pencil____ paper/ notebook ____ text ____
			Be on task/ working/ following directions ____	Be on task/ working/ following directions ____	Be on task/ working/ following directions ____	Be on task/ working/ following directions ____	Be on task/ working/ following directions ____
			Asked questions ____	Asked questions ____	Asked questions ____	Asked questions ____	Asked questions ____
			Answered questions ____	Answered questions ____	Answered questions ____	Answered questions ____	Answered questions ____

FIGURE 14   Self-Monitoring Form H from the School Survival Skills Curriculum

stream. Our research shows that students with LD in these courses cut class frequently and are often late to the classes they do attend (Zigmond, Kerr, Brown, & Harris, 1984). They arrive without a writing implement, notepaper or textbook at least 30% of the time (Zigmond et al., 1984). Their mainstream teachers characterize them as being poor at organizing themselves and their time, taking notes, identifying main ideas in lectures or texts, following directions, and completing and turning in assignments (Barrett, 1986; Zigmond, Kerr, & Schaeffer, 1988).

Despite these deficiencies, some students with learning disabilities do not fare too badly. Zigmond et al. (1985) found that only 20% of secondary school students with LD in a large urban school district failed more mainstream courses than they passed. Overall passing grades were obtained in approximately 75% of courses, and more than 30% of the students passed everything they took. But Donahoe and Zigmond (1990) found that 5 years later in this same school district, although approximately 75% of ninth graders with LD passed mainstream health courses, only 60% passed science and less than 50% earned passing grades in social studies.

Students with learning disabilities who are successful in high school participate actively and efficiently in the educational process. They can describe the skills that are important for making it in high school, and their behavior is consistent with their rhetoric (Brown, Kerr, Zigmond, & Harris, 1984). In contrast, the unsuccessful high school students seem to function in a more passive, less efficient manner, and their behavior is not consistent with their apparent knowledge of school rules and expectations (Kerr, Zigmond, Schaeffer, & Brown, 1986; Zigmond et al., 1988; Zigmond et al., 1984). Consistently, across studies and research teams, students with learning disabilities who fail mainstream courses can be differentiated from those who pass on the basis of class attendance behaviors (failing students have significantly higher absence rates) and proficiency in learning strategies and organizational skills (Alley & Deshler, 1979; Barrett, 1986; Donahoe & Zigmond, 1990; Warner et al., 1980; Zigmond et al., 1988).

In designing a secondary school program for students with LD, something must be done about these failure rates because the consequences of failing courses needed for graduation are serious. Our data (Thornton & Zigmond, 1986) show that students who fail to accumulate sufficient numbers of required credits to pass ninth grade inevitably drop out of high school before graduation. Passing ninth grade does not guarantee successfully completing high school, but failing ninth grade is devastating to students with learning disabilities.

Three approaches can be taken to this problem:

1. School survival skills and strategies training may make the student more capable of coping with the demands of the mainstream.
2. A consulting teacher may be able to influence mainstream teachers to alter the demands of the mainstream environment to accommodate students' learning difficulties (Miller, Leinhardt, & Zigmond, 1988).
3. Students could be placed in less demanding courses to meet graduation requirements (Hartwell, Wiseman, & Van Reusen, 1979).

Explicit Planning for Life After High School

More and more educators have begun to recognize the need to provide adolescents who are learning disabled with opportunities to prepare them for a successful transition to life after high school. Several studies, our own included, indicate that a small proportion of students with learning disabilities (12%–30%) continue on to 2- and 4-year colleges after graduating from high school (see White et al., 1980; Cobb & Crump, 1984; Association for Children and Adults with Learning Disabilities, 1982; Zigmond & Thornton, 1988; Hoffman et al., 1987). These students need help in selecting appropriate higher education institutions, in arranging for adapted versions of college entrance examinations, and in completing the applications for admission.

The non-college-bound students need help in planning what they will do with their lives, what occupations might be satisfying, and what training might be needed both in high school and after it. As part of transition planning, many students with learning disabilities are being counseled into a vocational education high school track, but placement in vocational education does not guarantee a successful transition. In fact, Zigmond and Thornton (1985) found no basis for assuming that mainstream vocational education programs better prepared students with LD for the world of work than the more traditional academic curriculum. In their first follow-up sample, the post-high school employment picture was no better for the 10 students with learning disabilities who were vocational education graduates than for the 16 students with LD who were graduates of a regular high school curriculum.

Thornton (1987) further explored the relationship between completing an intensive mainstream skill-centered vocational training program in high school and post-school employment patterns. She interviewed a sample of young adults with learning disabilities who had graduated from high school nearly 2 years prior to follow-up. Thornton hypothesized that the skills acquired in vocational training experiences would give vocational education graduates with LD an advantage in the post-school employment market over graduates with LD who had not taken vocational education courses. Again, the hypothesis was not confirmed. The two groups showed no differences on several measures of post-school adjustment, including employment rates (approximately 61% in both groups) and percentage of time employed since graduating from high school (approximately 50% for both groups). Furthermore, only 35% of the vocational education graduates were in post-school employment or training that even remotely related to their high school vocational education curriculum.

A second measure of the benefits of vocational education for students with LD relates to the assumption among vocational educators that enrollment in vocational training classes in high school tends to hold in school students who otherwise might drop out (Weber & Silvani-Lacey, 1983). Thornton and Zigmond (1987b) examined the holding power of mainstream vocational education for adolescents with LD by analyzing the risk status of those enrolled in vocational programs in a large urban school district. We assigned a dropout risk status to all students on the basis of their ninth-grade attendance and course completion. We found that the holding power of vocational education for students with LD at greatest risk for dropping out was minimal, at best, because the majority of high-risk students with LD left school before entering their third year of high school (i.e., before they could access their first skill-centered mainstream vocational training courses).

Students with LD who persisted in school long enough to enroll in the vocational education track were actually low-risk in terms of school dropout (based on ninth-grade attendance and course completion data) and were expected to finish high school regardless of their course choices. Furthermore, the few high-risk students with LD who persisted in school long enough to access vocational training courses still left school before graduation.

Many students with LD want to learn practical skills during their years in high school. Figure 15 is an indication of one student's desire to do this. Nevertheless, school personnel charged with developing appropriate transition planning opportunities for students with LD must recognize that enrollment in vocational education programs in the junior and senior years may not be the only answer.

TWO MODELS OF SERVICE DELIVERY

A comprehensive high school program for students with learning disabilities must contain the four components just discussed: intensive instruction in basic skills, explicit instruction in survival skills, successful completion of courses required for graduation from high school, and explicit planning for post high school life. The challenge for schools is to construct an efficient and affordable service delivery model with the appropriate combination of special and mainstream educational experiences to address these components,

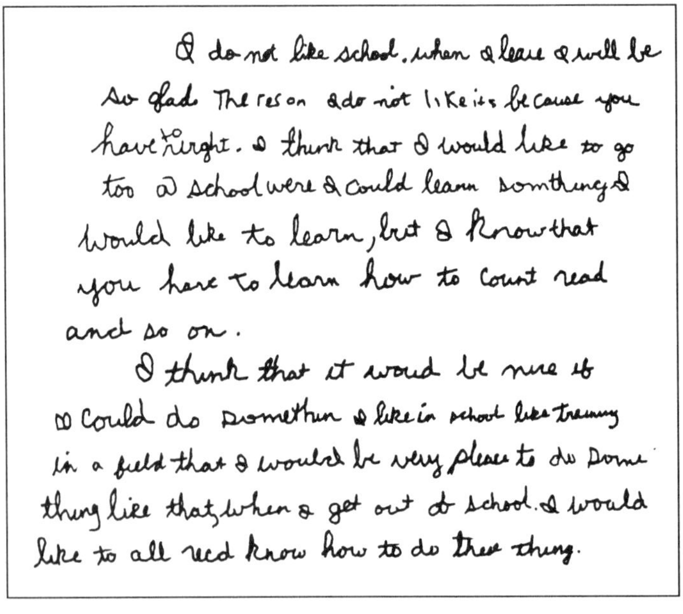
I do not like school. when I leave I will be
So glad. The reson I do not like it is because you
have to right. I think that I would like to go
too a school were I could learn somthing I
would like to learn, but I know that
you have to learn how to count read
and so on.
I think that it woud be nice if
I could do somethin I like in school like training
in a field that I would be very please to do Some
thing like that when I get out of school. I would
like to all red know how to do thes thing.

FIGURE 15 ***Composition Written by a Ninth-Grade Boy with Learning Disabilities***

and at the same time to develop an appealing and motivating educational program that holds students in school.

The best model will accomplish little if students abandon it early in their high school careers. I propose two ways in which the four components can be organized into a comprehensive high school program for students with learning disabilities. The models differ in the extent to which they rely on direct services from special education personnel and in their emphasis on preparation for work as contrasted with postsecondary education or training.

Model One: Less but Very Special Special Education

The first model for special education services at the secondary school level could be subtitled "Back to the Future" because it looks much like the model of services first proposed in our 1975 CSDC (see Zigmond, 1978). In this model, special education personnel are responsible for educating students with LD for three periods per day in ninth grade and two periods per day in the remaining years of high school. The mainstream high school program is offered to the students for the remainder of the school day. Model One utilizes the special education resource room as the service delivery setting and has five features:

1. *Students with LD are assigned to mainstream classes for math, content subjects required for graduation, and elective courses.* Students with LD are scheduled to take basic math courses with nonhandicapped students who likewise are not proficient in math. Basic, applied math courses offered in the mainstream are used to meet the math requirements for graduation. Students also are scheduled into mainstream science, social studies, and health classes so as to profit from learning these subjects from a content specialist.

2. *One special education teacher is assigned as a support or consulting teacher to work with mainstream teachers in whose classes students with LD are placed.* Many students with LD do not have the skills to manage the setting demands of the mainstream. In contrast to the individualized instruction in secondary school resource rooms, the majority of student time in mainstream academic classes is spent in teacher-directed, large-group instruction (Zigmond et al., 1984) with the instructional configuration most likely to be individualistic and competitive (Johnson & Johnson, 1978). Regular class teachers spend a great deal of time lecturing and at a speed that often makes note taking difficult (Moran, 1980).

    Mainstream content subject teachers offer few opportunities for student involvement in discussion and rarely present advanced organizers to help students listen more effectively or check on student comprehension of the content delivered by asking students to paraphrase what they have heard. Mainstream teachers typically evaluate competence through written products and infrequently provide direct oral feedback and reinforcement (Moran, 1980). Few regular class teachers spend time teaching test-taking skills (Cuthbertson, 1978). Teachers assume that students are capable of gaining knowledge of the material to be tested from reading textbooks or from absorbing information presented in lectures and class discussions. Few teachers offer students in a mainstream class the opportunity to re-take a test on which they have performed poorly.

A special education teacher in the role of support or consulting teacher will work with mainstream faculty to change their attitudes, expectations, and teaching and testing styles. The support or consulting teacher role has been shown repeatedly to facilitate successful integration of students with LD into mainstream academic courses (see Graden, Casey, & Bonstrom, 1985; Polsgrove & McNeil, 1989; West & Idol, 1987; Laurie, Buchwach, Silverman, & Zigmond, 1978), although to be effective, the role of consulting or support teacher in a high school must be considered a full-time indirect service special education job, not an activity tacked onto the job of a direct service resource room teacher.

3. *Additional special education teachers are responsible for yearly English/reading courses, one survival skills class, and a supervised study hall, which students with LD are scheduled to take each year of high school.* The curriculum of the English/reading courses over the four years of high school would follow the pattern outlined earlier in this article. It would include attention to decoding, vocabulary, comprehension and fluency, and writing. It would emphasize text-based instruction, make heavy use of graphic organizers in developing vocabulary and concepts, teach strategies for coping with narrative and expository text, and use curriculum-based measurement in reading to monitor student progress and signal needed changes in the instructional program.

The survival skills course would be offered to all ninth-grade students with learning disabilities, and to any student assigned to the LD program after ninth grade or transferring into the high school after ninth grade. Attention would be paid to teaching behavior control, teacher-pleasing behaviors, and study skills.

Each year, students would be scheduled for a study hall supervised by an LD teacher. This study hall would provide an opportunity for the students to receive guidance on homework assignments, to be coached to use reading comprehension strategies, learning strategies, and study skills that they have been taught in the English/reading and survival skills courses, and to receive tutoring, if necessary.

4. *From the start of ninth grade, students with LD interact regularly with a counselor for transition planning.* A counselor who is knowledgeable about the needs of students with handicaps is assigned to counsel students with LD on transition planning beginning early in ninth grade. Outcomes of these discussions are reflected in the selection of elective courses over the 4-year period so that students develop a growing sense of direction and purpose. The counselor helps students who are college-bound in the application process as early as the end of the sophomore year, when it may be appropriate to begin taking college entrance examinations.

5. *Courses required for graduation are spaced evenly throughout the four years to re-duce academic pressures, particularly in ninth grade.* Students never take a full load of courses, because each year includes a study hall. In addition, one required course traditionally scheduled for ninth grade is slipped to eleventh grade to in-

crease the likelihood that students will pass required courses in ninth grade and beyond and persist in school.

Figure 16 provides a 4-year schedule of courses for students in Model One. The
schedule is designed to meet graduation requirements in the Commonwealth of Pennsylvania and assumes that, for their elective courses, students will be guided to take the two
courses in arts or humanities that round out the requirements. The schedule also assumes
that students carry seven classes at a time and are scheduled for each of them 5 days per
week. The program of study outline in Figure 16 contains all four of the essential components of an effective LD program: intensive instruction in basic literacy skills (delivered by a special education teacher) and functional math skills (delivered in the mainstream); explicit instruction in survival skills (available as a course to be taken in ninth
grade); opportunities for success in courses required for graduation (through the availability of a full-time consulting teacher, a shift in the scheduling of required courses, and
a reduced schedule that incorporates a study hall supervised by a special education
teacher); and explicit planning for post-school life (through counseling and judicious
scheduling of six elective courses).

Model One is, however, appropriate only for certain students with learning disabilities. Students who are college-bound should be exposed to subject matter taught by main-

Year 1	Year 2	Year 3	Year 4
English/ Reading*	English/ Reading*	English/ Reading*	English/ Reading*
Math	Math	Math	
Social Studies		Social Studies	Social Studies
	Science	Science	Science
Survival Skills*			
Study Hall*	Study Hall*	Study Hall*	Study Hall*
PE/Health	PE	PE/Health	PE
Elective**	Elective**	Elective**	Elective**
	Elective**		Elective**

  * Course taught by special education teacher.

 ** Electives selected with advice from counselor to meet distribution require-
    ments for graduation, college entrance requirements for students consider-
    ing post-secondary education, and/or student's vocational interests.

Note: This schedule meets Pennsylvania requirements for graduation.

FIGURE 16   ***Four-Year Course Schedule for Students with Learning Disabilities
in Model One***

stream content subject specialists, and they have to test themselves in a context larger than special education. Model One provides these college-bound students with that opportunity. In addition, students who are uncertain about their plans beyond high school and who do not want to limit their postsecondary education or training options would be well served in Model One, if they have sufficiently developed language and social skills to cope with mainstream content demands.

One advantage of Model One is that most special education teachers currently in the field feel comfortable teaching English/reading, although most of these teachers will need considerable inservice training to help them change the direction and emphasis of the curriculum. They also will need training in how to teach survival skills. Furthermore, in implementing this model, special education teachers will have to be enjoined against drifting into tutoring in content subjects during English/reading and survival skills instruction.

In implementing Model One, administrators will face at least two challenges. One will be to develop a school climate that promotes accommodation to students with learning differences in the mainstream. Principals play a key role in setting the tone of a school building, and their support will be critical to accomplishing changes in mainstream attitudes and instructional styles needed if students with learning disabilities are to be accommodated successfully. The second challenge facing administrators will be to support the role of a full-time consulting teacher, troubleshooting with teachers and students across the school. Teachers who do not have direct service responsibilities are uncommon in secondary schools, yet this role will be critical to successfully implementing Model One.

Model One, the *resource room model*, is consistent with the mandate of PL 94-142 for education of students with handicaps in the least restrictive environment. It combines opportunities for special instruction with opportunities to accumulate mainstream academic credits to meet high school graduation and college entrance requirements. But the Model One service delivery alternative is not for everyone.

Model Two: More Special Education

Restructuring, the rising tide of the school reform movement, is part of the response of the education community to criticisms originating in the *A Nation At Risk* report (National Commission on Excellence in Education, 1983). The basic agenda of the restructuring movement has been to increase the academic pressure on the schools, to increase achievement in core skills, to increase student competence in higher-order thinking skills, to produce a high school graduate who is better prepared to enter the workforce so that America can compete successfully with Europe and the Pacific Rim countries. Restructuring at the high school level has meant tougher, more uniform standards; increased graduation requirements in mathematics, science, foreign languages, and technology; harsher grading; less leniency.

The restructuring of mainstream education has come at a time of intense pressure to restructure special education, as well. Many researchers, practitioners, and policymakers in the special education community have been calling for a restructuring of services for "hard-to-teach" students and have proposed that regular education classrooms can be made to work effectively for *all* students. That pressure to return students with disabilities to mainstream instruction is known as the *regular education initiative* (Will, 1986). Advocates of the regular education initiative (REI) assume that schools are prepared to accept a wider range of abilities and to deliver a diversity of educational options within the regular classroom.

The reality is quite different, especially at the high school level, because the restructuring effort in special education is simply not compatible with the restructuring effort in regular education. The mainstream reform effort sets rigid standards for acceptable school behavior; special education reform asks mainstream teachers to expand their tolerance of individual behavioral differences. The mainstream reform effort increases the rigor of the curriculum; the special education reform asks teachers to be more flexible, more thoughtful, more selective in curriculum coverage. The mainstream reform effort introduces uniform testing programs and grading guidelines; the special education reform asks teachers to adapt testing procedures and grading standards to accommodate students with special needs.

Recognizing the impact of mainstream reform efforts on high school teachers and high school programs, Model Two calls for *increasing* the level of responsibility of special education personnel for educating students with learning disabilities in secondary schools. Five features define the Model Two high school program:

1. *All basic skills are taught by a special educator and instruction in basic skills is linked to transition planning.* Special education personnel would be responsible for teaching all English/reading and math courses required for graduation. These courses would not be simple modifications of the mainstream high school curriculum. Instead, the curriculum of these courses would address the functional skill needs of the students in the classes and be coordinated with the vocational education courses being taken by the students concurrently. Explicit discussions on the relevance of reading and math skills to vocational pursuits would be a regular part of the courses, as would discussions of job possibilities after completion of high school.

2. *Required "content" subjects are co-taught by special educators.* Students with learning disabilities would be scheduled to take science, social studies, or health in mainstream classes co-taught by a mainstream specialist and a special education teacher. The curriculum would parallel the curriculum taught in other basic content courses in the mainstream but might utilize text material written at a more readable level. Also, the course might cover some material less deeply and some material more deeply than the more traditional mainstream counterpart.

3. *Vocational education is provided in the mainstream and coordinated with transition planning provided within special education.* Beginning in the freshman year of high school, students would be scheduled into regular vocational education courses. The first 2 years of vocational courses would involve extensive exploration of job possibilities, including some on-the-job internships to "try on" vari-

ous jobs, and would be scheduled for two periods per day. By the junior year, exposure to vocational/technical training would continue to occupy two periods per day, but vocational training would become more intense and involve sustained training in one occupation for 2 years. At the same time, vocational education teachers would work closely with special education personnel on skills students need to master the vocational content. These skills would be reinforced in the basic skills courses being taken by students concurrently. Also, special education and vocational education personnel would work with the students' counselors to be certain that coordinated transition planning is taking place.

4. *All ninth-grade students with learning disabilities will take a required course on survival skills taught by a special educator.* A survival skills course would provide incoming ninth graders with an orientation to the rules and demands of high school and teach the students behavior control, teacher-pleasing behaviors, and study skills expected of a high school student.

5. *Students' schedules would reflect a light academic load in ninth grade to ensure successful completion of the first year of high school.* During ninth grade, students would be scheduled to complete two vocational education courses and the elective requirements in art or humanities would be delayed until eleventh and twelfth grades. This would reduce the academic press of that first year in high school and increase the likelihood that students will have a successful year.

Figure 17 provides a summary of a 4-year high school program for students with LD that meets basic requirements for graduation in the Commonwealth of Pennsylvania. Again, the schedule in Model Two assumes that students carry seven classes at a time.

Model Two would be especially suitable for students who enter high school with minimal competence in basic skills and who have no aspirations to attend college. It has several advantages:

1. Students with learning disabilities are sheltered from the demands of mainstream classes and are less likely to earn failing grades; if they earn passing grades in required courses, students are more likely to persist in school until graduation.

2. Required academic courses are distributed fairly evenly throughout the 4 years, and two additional courses in arts or humanities required for graduation are not scheduled until the junior and senior years so that the ninth-grade curriculum is not quite so formidable.

3. Students have at least two periods per day of more practical coursework with explicit future-oriented planning; if vocational education really does have holding power, vocational courses beginning as early as ninth grade should "hook" students who are at greatest risk for dropping out.

4. Students are likely to be interacting throughout the day with a smaller network of teachers and fellow students, creating a more personalized "school within a school" climate that also could function to hold students in school.

Year 1	Year 2	Year 3	Year 4
English/ Reading*	English/ Reading*	English/ Reading*	English/ Reading*
Math*	Math*	Math*	
Social Studies*	Social Studies*		Social Studies*
	Science*	Science*	Science*
Survival Skills*			
PE/Health*	PE	PE/Health*	PE
Voc Ed	Voc Ed	Voc Ed	Voc Ed
Voc Ed	Voc Ed	Voc Ed	Voc Ed
		Elective**	Elective**

*   Course taught by special education teacher.
**   Courses co-taught by mainstream and special educators.
*** These courses would have to meet graduation requirements of two credits in Art and/or Humanities.
Note: This schedule meets Pennsylvania requirements for graduation.

FIGURE 17   Four-Year Course Schedule for Students with Learning Disabilities in Model Two

5. Students in Model Two will have been carefully prepared for the transition into the world of work or postsecondary job training and would have some immediately usable skills for entering the job market.

Although Model Two offers some distinct advantages for students with LD, it will be difficult to implement well because of staffing problems, as well as state and local school policy constraints. There are two staffing issues to consider. First, given the enhanced role of special education personnel in the model, a high school adopting Model Two may have to increase the numbers of its special education staff.

Second, special education teacher preparation programs simply do not prepare special education teachers as high school content subject specialists, so teachers will not be prepared for instructional duties in science, social studies, and health. We have observed secondary school content subject classes being taught by special educators; the teachers are so ill-at-ease with the subject matter that they cannot provide interesting elaborations or explanations of the content, and they cannot answer students' questions accurately. Furthermore, special education teachers have probably not had training in models of co-teaching and collaboration. Students with learning disabilities who are in this model will be seriously shortchanged unless teacher preparation programs address these deficiencies or school districts provide content updates for special education personnel given these new assignments.

Issues at the policy level also plague Model Two. First, graduation requirements set at the state level often consist of more than course titles. Curricula are defined for courses that will count toward meeting graduation requirements. Courses taught by special education personnel to students with LD may, by design, deviate from the prescribed curriculum, to make them more relevant and more suitable to the students' skill and cognitive levels. A waiver may be required for these adapted courses to be counted toward high school graduation.

Second, a single high school may not have sufficient numbers of students with LD to warrant offering co-teaching in the entire special education high school curriculum (four English courses, three math courses, three social studies courses, three science courses, and one health course) in a single year. Instead, co-teaching in social studies, science, and health courses may have to be offered on a rotating basis so that, over the course of four years, all courses will have been available to students with LD. This rotational system may make staffing easier, but students with LD who transfer in or out of a given high school during the 4 years may have difficulty getting all the courses they need.

CONCLUSIONS

The secondary school is a complex environment that many students find difficult to negotiate. For students with LD it presents formidable challenges. A poorly designed high school program can undermine students' self-concept and drive students from school before they are fully prepared. A well designed high school program provides opportunities to learn what has not yet been mastered, to develop social and interpersonal skills, to prepare for the world beyond public schooling.

An appropriate and effective secondary school program can fortify young people who have learning disabilities with the self-confidence and skills needed to function effectively in postsecondary education or employment, or in personal and social relationships. Our task is to organize schooling to provide opportunities for these things to happen regardless of the cost or how much change it requires of us. It is a challenging task, but it is a challenge we simply must meet.

I wish to acknowledge the support and cooperation of Dr. William Penn, Director of the Division for Exceptional Children, Pittsburgh Public Schools, without whom the work described in this article could not have been done. I also acknowledge grant support from OSEP through the divisions of Personnel Preparation and Innovation and Development (directed and field-initiated research), whose funds made much of this work possible.

REFERENCES

Alexander, D. F. (1985). The effect of study skill training on learning disabled students retelling of expository material. *Journal of Applied Behavior Analysis, 18,* 263–267.

Alley, G., & Deshler, D. (1979). *Teaching the learning disabled adolescent: Strategies and methods.* Denver: Love Publishing.

Association for Children and Adults with Learning Disabilities. (1982, September/October). *ACLD vocational committee survey of learning disabled adults: Preliminary report. ACLD News Briefs,* pp. 10–13.

Bachman, J. G. (1972). Anti-dropout campaign and other misanthropies. *Society, 9.*

Barrett, D. (1986). *An analysis of policy variables relating to secondary learning disabled students who are mainstreamed into academic content areas.* Unpublished doctoral dissertation, University of Pittsburgh.

Bradley, L., & Bryant, P. (1985). *Rhyme and reason in reading and spelling.* Ann Arbor: University of Michigan Press.

Brown, G. M., Kerr, M. M., Zigmond, N., & Harris, A. L. (1984). What's important for student success in high school? "Successful" and "unsuccessful" students discuss school survival skills. *High School Journal, 68*(1), 10–17.

Calfee, R. (1976). Sources of dependency in cognitive processes. In D. Klahr (Ed.), *Cognition and Instruction.* New York: Erlbaum.

Cawley, J. F., Fitzmaurice-Hayes, A. M., & Shaw, R. A. (1988). *Mathematics for the mildly handicapped: A guide to curriculum and instruction.* Boston: Allyn and Bacon.

Cawley, J. F., Fitzmaurice, A. M., Shaw, R. A., Kahn, H., & Bates, H. III, (1978). Mathematics and learning disabled youth: The upper grade levels. *Learning Disability Quarterly, 1,* 37–52.

Cawley, J. F., Fitzmaurice, A. M., Shaw, R. A., Kahn, H., & Bates, H. III, (1979a). LD youth and mathematics: A review of characteristics. *Learning Disability Journal, 2,* 29–44.

Cawley, J. F., Fitzmaurice, A. M., Shaw, R. A., Kahn, H., & Bates, H. III, (1979b). Math word problems: Suggestions for LD students. *Learning Disability Quarterly, 2,* 25–41.

Cervantes, L. F. (1965). *The dropout.* Ann Arbor: University of Michigan Press.

Cobb, R., & Crump, W. (1984). *Post-school status of young adults identified as learning disabled while enrolled in learning disabilities programs (Final report U.S.D.E. Grant No. G008302185).* Tuscaloosa: University of Alabama.

Combs, J., & Cooley, W. (1968). Dropouts in high school and after school. *American Educational Research Journal, 5,* 343–363.

Critchley, M. (1964). *Developmental dyslexia.* Springfield, IL: Charles C. Thomas.

Curley, T. J. (1971, March). *The social system: Contributor or inhibitor to the school dropout* (ED 049-344). Washington, DC: U.S. Dept. of Health, Education, and Welfare.

Cuthbertson, E. (1978). *An analysis of secondary testing and grading procedures.* Unpublished master's thesis, University of Kansas, Lawrence.

Dean, J. S. (1973, October). A plan to save dropouts: School-within-a-school. *Clearing House, 48,* 98–99.

deBettencourt, L., Zigmond, N., & Thornton, H. S. (1989). Follow-up of post-secondary age rural learning disabled graduates and dropouts. *Exceptional Children, 56*(1), 40–49.

Deno, S. L., & Mirkin, P. K. (1977). *Data-based program modification: A manual.* Reston, VA: Council for Exceptional Children.

Deshler, D. D., Lowrey, N., & Alley, G. R. (1979). Preparing alternatives for LD adolescents: A nationwide survey. *Academic Therapy, 14,* 389–397.

Donahoe, K., & Zigmond, N. (1990). High school grades of urban LD students and low achieving peers. *Exceptionality, 1,* 17–27.

Fardig, D., Algozzine, R., Schwartz, S., Hensel, J., & Westling, D. (1985). Post-secondary vocational adjustment of rural, mildly handicapped students. *Exceptional Children, 52*(2), 115–121.

Fayne, H. R., & Bryant, N. D. (1981). Relative effects of various word synthesis strategies on the phonics achievement of learning disabled youngsters. *Journal of Learning Disabilities, 73,* 616–623.

Fuchs, L. S., Hamlett, C. L., Fuchs, D., Stecker, P. M., & Ferguson, C. (1988). Conducting curriculum-based measurement with computerized data collection: Effects of efficiency and teacher satisfaction. *Journal of Special Education Technology, 9*(2), 73–86.

Glass, G. G. (1978). *Glass-analysis for decoding only.* Garden City, NY: Easier to Learn, Inc.

Graden, J. L., Casey, A., & Bonstrom, O. (1985). Implementing a prereferral intervention system: Part 2. The data. *Exceptional Children, 51,* 487–496.

Graham, S., & Harris, K. R. (1989a). Cognitive training: Implications for written language. In J. Hughes & R. Hall (Eds.), *Cognitive behavioral psychology in the schools: A comprehensive handbook* (pp. 247–279). New York: Guilford.

Graham, S., & Harris, K. R. (1989b). Improving learning disabled students' skills at composing essays: Self-instructional strategy training. *Exceptional Children, 56*(3), 201–214.

Graham, S., & Johnson, L. A. (1989). Teaching reading to learning disabled students: A review of research-supported procedures. *Focus on Exceptional Children, 21*(6), 1–12.

Gregory, J. F., Shanahan, T., & Walberg, H. (1986). A profile of learning disabled twelfth-graders in regular classes. *Learning Disability Quarterly, 9*(1), 33–42.

Hammontree, T. (1978). Profile of a dropout. *Florida Vocational Journal, 3,* 26–28.

Hartwell, L. K., Wiseman, D. E., & Van Reusen, A. (1979). Modifying course content for mildly handicapped students at the secondary level. *Teaching Exceptional Children, 12,* 28–32.

Hasazi, S., Gordon, L., & Roe, C. (1985). Factors associated with the employment status of handicapped youth exiting high school from 1979 to 1983. *Exceptional Children, 51*(6), 455–469.

Hewitt, J. D., & Johnson, W. S. (1979). Dropping out in Middletown. *High School Journal, 62,* 252–256.

Hill, C. R. (1979). Capacities, opportunities, and educational investments: The case of the high school dropout. *Review of Economics & Statistics, 61,* 9–20.

Hoffman, F. J., Sheldon, K. L., Minskoff, E. H., Sautter, S. W., Steidle, E. F., Baker, D. P., Bailey, M. B., & Echols, L. D. (1987). Needs of learning disabled adults. *Journal of Learning Disabilities, 20*(1), 43–52.

Howell, F., & Frese, W. (1982). Early transition into adult roles: Some antecedents and outcomes. *American Educational Research Journal, 19*(1), 51–73.

Howell, K., & Morehead, M. K. (1987). *Curriculum based evaluation in special and remedial education.* Columbus, OH: Merrill Publishing Co.

Johnson, D. J., & Myklebust, H. R. (1967). *Learning disabilities.* New York: Grune & Stratton.

Johnson, D. W., & Johnson, R. T. (1978). Cooperative, competitive, and individualistic learning. *Journal of Research & Development in Education, 12*(1), 3–15.

Kaplan, J., & Luck, E. (1977). The dropout phenomenon as a social problem. *Education Forum, 42,* 41–56.

Kerr, M. M., Zigmond, N., Schaeffer, A., & Brown, G. (1986). An observational follow-up of successful and unsuccessful high school students. *High School Journal, 70*(1), 20–24.

Kowalski, C., & Cangemi, J. (1974). High school dropouts—A lost resource. *College Student Journal, 8,* 71–74.

Kozol, J. (1985). *Illiterate America.* New York: Plume Publishers.

Laurie, T., Buchwach, L., Silverman, R., & Zigmond, N. (1978). Teaching secondary learning disabled students in the mainstream, *Learning Disability Quarterly, 1*(4), 67-72.

Levin, E. K., Zigmond, N., & Birch, J. W. (1985). A follow-up study of 52 learning disabled adolescents. *Journal of Learning Disabilities, 18,* 2–7.

Lloyd, D. N. (1976). Concurrent prediction of dropout and grade of withdrawal. *Educational & Psychological Measurement, 36,* 983–990.

Lloyd, J. W., & Keller, C. E. (1989). Effective mathematics instruction: Development, instruction, and programs. *Focus on Exceptional Children, 21*(7), 1–10.

Mahood, W. (1981, January). Born losers: School dropouts and pushouts. *National Association of Secondary School Principals Bulletin, 65,* 54–57.

Mare, R. D. (1980). Social background and school continuation decisions. *Journal of American Statistical Association, 75,* 195–305.

McKeown, M., & Beck, I. (1988). Learning vocabulary: Different ways for different goals. *Remedial & Special Education, 9,* 42–52.

Miller, S. E., Leinhardt, G., & Zigmond, N. (1988). Influencing engagement through accommodation: An ethnographic study of at-risk students. *American Educational Research Journal, 25*(4), 465–488.

Moran, M. R. (1980). *An investigation of the demands of oral language skills of learning disabled students in secondary classrooms* (Research Report #1). Lawrence: University of Kansas, Institute for Research in Learning Disabilities.

Morrow, D., Thornton, H., & Zigmond, N. (1988). *Graduation and post-secondary adjustment: Follow-up of urban-bound learning disabled students.* Final Report. Pittsburgh: University of Pittsburgh.

National Commission on Excellence in Education. (1983). *A nation at risk: The imperative for educational reform.* Washington, DC: U.S. Dept. of Education.

Nickerson, R. S. (1985). *Adult literacy and technology* (Report No. 351). Champaign, IL: University of Illinois, Center for the Study of Reading. (ERIC Document Reproduction Service No. ED 266 420).

Norman, C.A., & Zigmond, N. (1980). Characteristics of children labeled and served as learning disabled in school systems affiliated with child service demonstration centers. *Journal of Learning Disabilities, 13,* 542–547.

O'Shea, L. J., Sindelar, P. T., & O'Shea, D. J. (1987). The effects of repeated readings and attentional cues on the reading fluency and comprehension of learning disabled readers. *Learning Disabilities Research, 2,* 103–109.

Palinscar, A. S., & Brown, A. L. (1984). Reciprocal teaching of comprehension-fostering and comprehension-monitoring activities. *Cognition & Instruction, 1,* 117–175.

Polsgrove, L., & McNeil, M. (1989). The consultation process: Research and practice. *Remedial & Special Education, 10*(1), 6–13.

Riegel, R. H., & Mathey, J. P. (1980). *Mainstreaming at the secondary level: Seven models that work* (Bulletin #1427). Wayne County, MI: Intermediate School District.

Rumberger, R. W. (1983). Dropping out of high school: The influence of race, sex, and family background. *American Educational Research Journal, 20*(2), 199–220.

Rumberger, R. W. (1987). High school dropouts: A review of issues and evidence. *Review of Educational Research, 57,* 101–121.

Schalock, R. L., Wolzen, B., Ross, J., Elliott, B., Werbel, C., & Peterson, J. (1986). Post-secondary community placement of handicapped students: A five year follow-up. *Learning Disability Quarterly, 9*(4), 295–303.

Schreiber, D. (1962). School dropouts. *National Educational Association Journal, 51,* 50–59.

Schumaker, J. B., Deshler, D. D., Alley, G. R., Warner, M. M., & Denton, P. H. (1982). Multipass: A learning strategy for improving reading comprehension. *Learning Disability Quarterly, 5,* 295–304.

Silverman, R., Zigmond, N., & Sansone, J. (1981). Teaching coping skills: A school survival skills curriculum for adolescents with learning disabilities. *Focus on Exceptional Children, 13*(6), 1–20.

Stoughton, C. R., & Grady, B. R. (1978). How many students will drop out and why? *North Central Association Quarterly, 53,* 312–315.

Thornton, H. (1987). *A follow-up study of learning disabled young adults who participated in mainstream vocational education programs.* Unpublished doctoral dissertation, University of Pittsburgh.

Thornton, H., & Zigmond, N. (1986). Follow-up of post-secondary age LD graduates and dropouts. *LD Research, 1*(1), 50–55.

Thornton, H. S., & Zigmond, N. (1987a, April). *Predictors of dropout and unemployment among LD high school youth: The holding power of secondary vocational education for LD students.* Paper presented at annual meeting of American Educational Research Association, Washington, DC.

Thornton, H. S., & Zigmond, N. (1987b, April). *Post-secondary follow-up of learning disabled and non-handicapped completers of mainstream vocational education programs.* Paper presented at annual meeting of American Educational Research Association, Washington, DC.

Thornton, H. S., & Zigmond, N. (1988). Secondary vocational training for LD students and its relationship to school completion status and post school outcomes. *Illinois School Journal, 67*(2), 37–54.

Tseng, M. S. (1972). Comparisons of selected personality and vocational variables of high school students and dropouts. *Journal of Educational Research, 65*(10), 462–466.

U. S. Department of Education. (1988). *To assure the free appropriate public education of all handicapped children: Tenth annual report to Congress on the implementation of the Education of the Handicapped Act.* Washington, DC: Government Printing Office.

U. S. Department of Education. (1989). *To assure the free appropriate public education of all handicapped children: Eleventh annual report to Congress on the implementation of the Education of the Handicapped Act.* Washington, DC: Government Printing Office.

Warner, M. M., Alley, G. R., Schumaker, J. B., Deshler, D. D., & Clark, F. L. (1980). *An epidemiological study of learning disabled adolescents in secondary schools: Achievement and ability, socioeconomic status, and school experiences* (Research Report #13). Lawrence: University of Kansas, Institute for Research in Learning Disabilities.

Weber, J., & Silvani-Lacey (1983). *Building basic skills: The dropout.* Columbus: Ohio State University, National Center for Research in Vocational Education.

Wehlage, G. G., & Rutter, R. A. (1986). Dropping out: How much does school contribute to the problem? *Teachers College Record, 87,* 374–392.

Wehlage, G. G., Rutter, R. A., Smith, G. A., Lesko, N., & Fernandez, R. R. (1989). *Reducing the risk: Schools as communities of support.* New York: Falmer Press.

West, J. F., & Idol, L. (1987). School consultation (Part 1): An inter-disciplinary perspective on theory, models, and research. *Journal of Learning Disabilities, 20,* 388–408.

White, W., Schumaker, J., Warner, M., Alley, G., & Deshler, D. (1980). *The current status of young adults identified as learning disabled during their school career* (Research Report #21). Lawrence: University of Kansas, Institute for Research in Learning Disabilities.

Will, M. (1986). *Educating students with learning problems: A shared responsibility.* Washington, DC: Office of Special Education and Rehabilitative Services, U. S. Department of Education.

Williams, J. P. (1980). Teaching decoding with an emphasis on phoneme analysis and phoneme blending. *Journal of Educational Psychology, 73,* 697–704.

Wong, B. Y. L. (1986). Metacognition and special education: A review of a view. *Journal of Special Education, 20*(1), 9–29.

Zigmond, N. (1978). A prototype of comprehensive services for secondary students with learning disabilities. *Learning Disability Quarterly, 1*(1), 39–49.

Zigmond, N. (1988, April). *Evaluating staff development initiatives using direct observations of teacher and student behavior.* Paper presented at annual meeting of American Educational Research Association, New Orleans.

Zigmond, N., Kerr, M. M., Brown, G. M., & Harris, A. L. (1984). *School survival skills in secondary school age special education students.* Presented at annual meeting of the American Educational Research Association, New Orleans.

Zigmond, N., Kerr, M. M., & Schaeffer, A. L. (1988). Behavior patterns of learning disabled adolescents in high school academic classes. *Remedial & Special Education, 9*(2), 6–11.

Zigmond, N., Kerr, M. M., Schaeffer, A. L., Farra, H. E., & Brown, G. M. (1986). *The school survival skills curriculum.* Pittsburgh: University of Pittsburgh.

Zigmond, N., Levin, E., & Laurie, T. E. (1985). Managing the mainstream: An analysis for teacher attitudes and student performance in mainstream high school programs. *Journal of Learning Disabilities, 18*(9), 535–541.

Zigmond, N., & Thornton, H. S. (1985). Follow-up of post-secondary age LD graduates and dropouts. *Learning Disabilities Research, 1*(1), 50–55.

Zigmond, N., & Thornton, H. (1988)). Learning disabilities in adolescents and adults. In K. Kavale (Ed.), *Learning disabilities: State of the art and practice.* San Diego: College Hill Press.

Naomi Zigmond is affiliated with the Department of Instruction and Learning at the University of Pittsburgh.

$\circ$ 7 $\circ$

Edgar reviews extensive employment data, which indicate that after high school only about 60% of individuals with disabilities become employed. He says that special education believes it can "fix" these children while they are in the mainstream, but the evidence suggests it has not been successful in doing so. He argues for changes in education that more directly address the problem by providing better vocational training, altering the outcomes/goals of secondary education, developing mentor programs, or completely changing secondary education.

Employment As an Outcome for Mildly Handicapped Students: Current Status and Future Directions

Eugene Edgar

Special education serves a group of students who have a wide range of disabilities, from students with the most profound and disabling conditions to those with speech impairments only. By entrance into high school, however, some 70%–80% of all special education students are accounted for in the three categories of learning disabled, mildly mentally retarded, and emotionally disturbed (U.S. Department of Education, 1988). This article focuses on the employment outcomes of this group of students, referred to broadly as mildly disabled.

DEFINING THE POPULATION

Although much has been written about the characteristics of mildly disabled students, considerable debate remains about the etiology and exact nature of these conditions and, indeed, even about the ability of current technology to quantify the disabilities of students labeled learning disabled, mildly mentally retarded, and emotionally disturbed (Dunn, 1968; Gould, 1981; Hallahan & Kauffman, 1978; Heller, Holtzman, & Messick, 1982; Hobbs, 1975; Newkirk, Bloch, & Shrybman, 1978; Ysseldyke, Algozzine, & Richey, 1982). In a previous report, I referred to this group of students as the "nonquantifiably disabled" (Edgar & Hayden, 1985). These students come to special education not by their choice but, rather, by a specific process.

This process starts with identification resulting from their low or deviant performance. Professionals, usually teachers, nominate students as potential candidates for special services because of their performance in the classroom. Formal testing for eligibility determination takes place, and students who "qualify" are admitted into special education. This "Academy Award approach" has received much abuse from the field. Yet the practice persists.

The method of entrance into special education by this population is important to consider for a number of reasons. First, this group of students is heterogeneous on many dimensions. Even within a diagnostic category, great disparity exists between individual student abilities and needs. Therefore, extreme care must be given to any analysis that attempts to lump these students together. Second, reliance on the nomination approach results in overrepresentation of students from the underclass. Minorities and poor people are far more likely to be referred for special education than are middle-class white students. Males, also, are overrepresented in this population. Although this may be an artifact of special education procedures, the more likely cause is the unwillingness of regular education to accommodate this population (Heller, Holtzman, & Messick, 1982).

Given the demographic projections for the next 20 years (Hodgkinson, 1985; Wetzel, 1987), we can expect a major increase in the type of students who fall into these special education categories. Perhaps our entire system of schooling will change to accommodate this influx of culturally diverse students and thus negate the need for special education (Gartner & Lipsky, 1987; Singer & Butler, 1987). Then again, perhaps the special education system will be called upon to respond to the needs of these students. Regardless of the likelihood of changes in the overall education system, special education faces a major challenge in the near future: how best to prepare these mildly handicapped students for productive lives as adults.

PURPOSE OF SPECIAL EDUCATION

Special education has been concerned primarily with one basic issue: how best to teach children with disabilities. Our intent has been to devise procedures that would result in an increased behavioral repertoire for our students. This has led us to think about "how to teach" (the technology of instruction), "what to teach" (the content of our curriculum), and most recently "where to teach" (the debate on integration, mainstreaming). Certainly the first two questions (how and what) have dominated our thoughts and energies and are basically the parameters of education. The "where" issue can be viewed either as a method issue (how best) or as a policy issue broader than education (recognition of human rights). Regardless of which question is addressed, however, there is an implication that "correct" answers to these questions will result in better outcomes for our students. But just exactly what are these outcomes supposed to be?

Certainly enhanced behavioral repertoires are part of the desired outcomes of special education. We desire that our graduates be competent in reading, knowledgeable about our political process, committed to our social structure, job-ready for employment, able to care for their personal needs, and capable of contributing to society. We want our students to be competent. But is that all we desire? I contend that most of us truly believe we are increasing the probability that our students will have a "good quality of life." Although we focus on skill building (and knowledge and attitudes), we sincerely believe these skills will make a difference in the lives of our students.

For mildly handicapped students, the relationship between special education and regular education, especially at the secondary level, is, at best, unclear. Should special education students be mainstreamed into the regular curriculum (with added support), or should an alternative curriculum be developed? Part of the answer to this debate can be found if we can agree upon an outcome for mildly handicapped students. The Office of Special Education and Rehabilitative Services (OSERS) took a major step in this direction publishing the "Bridges Model" (Will, 1984). This model has been generally accepted by the field of special education. We have come to view special education as "an outcome-oriented process encompassing a broad array of services and experiences that lead to employment" (Will, 1984, p. 1).

What is still unresolved is whether this goal can be accomplished in the mainstream for mildly handicapped students or whether alternative programs are needed. The least restrictive environment (LRE) mandate of PL 94-142 challenges special education to find methods of keeping students in the regular curriculum. Basic human rights philosophy, especially in light of the overrepresented underclass in mildly handicapped programs, also suggests a more inclusive approach.

Additionally, there is considerable support for the notion that all students—those planning to continue their formal education beyond high school, as well as those who plan to enter the work force immediately—need the same set of experiences. Chester Finn, the current Assistant Secretary for Research and Improvement in the U.S. Department of Education, advocates this view. Finn has identified three missions for schools: to prepare students with skills for (a) the social system in which we live, (b) personally fulfilling lives, and (c) the next phase of their lives, whether it be higher education or employment (Finn, 1986).

A similar view, but with a rationale based on adolescent development, is provided by Wehlage (1983). In comparing specific skill training outcomes (job training) to training in more general coping skills (e.g., self-management, conflict resolution, problem solving), Wehlage advocates for the latter. With this approach, schools can be viewed as a metaphor for life (Susan Hasazi, personal communication June, 1988).

So how can schools perform these functions? First, we must take a look at how successful the schools have been to date, and then speculate on what could be done in the future.

CURRENT DATA BASE ON OUTCOMES IN SPECIAL EDUCATION

The 1980s have produced a mass of follow-up and follow-along studies of graduates of special education (Catterall & Stern, 1986; Clemmons & Dodrill, 1983; Edgar, Levine, Levine, & Dubey, 1988; Fardig, Algozzine, Schwartz, Hensel, & Westling, 1985; Gil & Edgar, 1988; Hasazi, Gordon, & Roe, 1985; Hasazi et al., 1985; Horn, O'Donnell, & Vitulano, 1983; Levin, Zigmond, & Birch, 1985; Linden & Forness, 1986; Mithaug, Horiuchi, & Fanning, 1985; Ross, Begab, Dondis, Giampiccolo, & Meyers, 1985; Wehman et al., 1982; White, Schumaker, Warner, Alley, & Deshler, 1980; Zigmond & Thornton, 1985; Sitlington, 1987). Undoubtedly I have missed additional studies. The point is: Data on outcomes are not lacking. I will attempt to summarize the highlights of findings regarding these students.

Available data suggest that about 50% of all high school students do not go on to higher education (Hamilton, 1986). On the other hand, there is a growing trend toward the idea of lifelong learning, and the probability that in the future a majority of the American adult population will be engaged in formal education of some sort (Hodgkinson, 1985). Regardless, many individuals move directly from high school into the work force. The majority of mildly handicapped students attempt to make this transition. How do they do?

Unfortunately, many of the follow-up studies do not break out their results by type of disability. Overall, about 60% of mildly disabled students find employment within a year of exiting the school system. When type of disability is controlled, however, employment rates vary from 70% for learning disabled students (Zigmond & Thornton, 1985) to 47% for mildly retarded students (Hasazi, Gordon, Roe, Hull, Finck, & Salembier, 1985). Students labeled as emotionally disabled obtain employment at a rate of 60% (Neel, Meadows, Levine, & Edgar, 1988). Nonhandicapped students tend to be employed at a rate of 70% (Edgar et al., 1988) to 75% (Hasazi et al., 1988).

Overall, males from special education obtain employment at a higher rate than do females (Hasazi et al., 1985; Hasazi et al., 1988; Edgar, 1987; Edgar et al., 1988). Interestingly, this discrepancy is not noted with the nonhandicapped population (Hasazi et al., 1988; Edgar et al., 1988).

Graduates tend to have higher employment rates than do those who exit the schools prior to graduation (Hasazi, Gordon, & Roe, 1985; Salembier, 1985; Zigmond & Thornton, 1985; Edgar, 1987). Although the employment rates vary by study and by disability, a rule of thumb is that dropouts are employed at about half the rate of graduates.

The types of jobs obtained by special education graduates, as well as their nonhandicapped peers, are entry-level jobs, with low salaries, few if any benefits, and minimal opportunity for advancement. Universally, the studies have found that the family/friend network is the primary method used to obtain employment.

In summary, we can conclude that mildly handicapped students as a group have more difficulty finding employment than do their nonhandicapped peers. Students labeled mildly mentally retarded do less well than any other subgroup. Females from special education do less well than their male counterparts, which does not seem to be the case with the nonhandicapped population. All jobs tend to be low-paying, with few benefits.

There is little evidence to support the idea that differential schooling results in different outcomes. But the ability of the family (or friends) to assist individuals in obtaining work is apparent. The bottom line is that graduates do much better than dropouts in finding jobs.

EDUCATIONAL PARADIGM

What does education try to do for mildly handicapped students? In my view, the overall belief is that we (in education) can "fix" these students. Our attempts to alter instructional procedures while we keep students in mainstream settings imply that we have the technology to overcome their disabilities. Is that possible?

Although education comprises a wide range of theories, the "fix-up" paradigm is rather simple. A human is a combination of genetic make-up and environmental influences. Manipulation of the genetic structure and regeneration of nerve cells remain beyond our current technology. Environment, however, is another matter. Education is based on the premise that behavioral repertoires, attitudes, feelings, and mental states *can* be manipulated through arrangement of the external environment. Careful thought is given to organizing and sequencing experiences in such a manner that human characteristics are altered in a desired direction. The gifts of Fröebel, the controlled learning environment of Guggenbühl, the sequencing of tasks by Itard, the errorless learning of Montessori, the discovery of adolescence by G. Stanley Hall, Dewey's idea of active learning, Piagetian developmental sequences, the operant learning of Skinner—all are milestones in the development of a pedagogy.

There is absolutely no doubt that current state-of-the-art educational technology will (and does) produce massive positive changes in human beings. With few exceptions, a well designed and implemented program of special education, given enough time, will produce competent behavioral repertoires in almost all human beings. With careful planning, collaborative use of resources, American ingenuity, tenacity, commitment, and time, our goals of an improved quality of life for our students can be achieved. Or so goes current thought.

Over the past few years, I have come to question this line of thinking. I have been an educator all my professional life and, until recently, had simply "accepted" these ideas. I also accepted the notion that, overall, most people in this country are doing better (in terms of quality of life) than they were, say, 10 years ago. These two ideas blend together to form a type of *incrementalism*—we are on the right track; we just have to keep slogging along, adding a little here and there, and eventually we will succeed. I no longer believe this.

I am not convinced that our current educational system is producing the outcomes we think it should. With the exception of students with visual disabilities only, hearing impairment only, and physical disability only, there is little evidence that special education students can be prepared to compete with their nonhandicapped peers. Special education has been effective only with students whose prosthetic environments allow them to input or output information. With few exceptions, however, students with impaired mental abilities (i.e., retardation, learning disabilities) continue to compete at a disadvantage with their nondisabled peers. The fix-up paradigm is not working very well for these students in terms of post-school success. Specifically, in terms of students finding employment, I would argue that the social status of the family has much more influence than does type of schooling.

SOCIAL JUSTICE

A number of data sets can be used to review the current political status in the United States. The pastoral letter on Catholic social teaching and the U.S. economy is one excellent source (Economic Justice for All, 1986). According to this document, an estimated 33 million Americans live below the poverty level, with an additional 20–30 million very needy people. Between 1968 and 1978, merely 25% of our population lived under the poverty level at one time or other. Since 1973, the proportion of people living below the poverty level has increased by one third. The top 10% of our population controls 86% of our wealth. Although this group remains stable, members of the middle class are falling into the underclass. We are becoming a country of relatively few who have much and many who have little.

The employment situation in this country continues to deteriorate. Eight million persons are actively looking for work (7% of the work force), with an additional 5% working in part-time jobs who want full-time work or who have given up looking for work. Since 1979, 2 million heavy industry jobs have been lost, which were replaced by 500,000 jobs for nurse's aides, 500,000 janitorial openings, 400,000 fast-food positions, and 100,000 office clerk slips. Half of these new jobs pay poverty-level wages (Robertson, 1988). Most of the new jobs pay no benefits and offer no career ladder opportunities.

Health-care delivery in the United States is a national disgrace. We rank 19th in the world in infant mortality and, for our African-American population, the infant mortality rate places us 28th in the world (Children's Defense Fund, 1988). Our medical technology is first class; our health delivery system is third rate.

The homeless in our country are increasing at an alarming rate. In *Rachel and Her Children* (1988), Jonathan Kozol paints a picture of despair for thousands of homeless people. But the homeless are not confined to New York City and Chicago. Families with young children live in cars, under bridges, and on sidewalk heat vents in Minneapolis, Seattle, and Nashville. Some home-based programs for preschool handicapped children provide services to children living in cars. Head Start programs are being developed in shelters for homeless families.

These trends of increasing poverty and increase in size of the underclass have been present for the last two decades. Ever since World War II, there has been a steady increase, or a leveling, of the percentages of poor people. Things are not getting better.

If these data are accurate, I contend that our current educational theory offers little hope for solving the problem of unemployment among students with mild disabilities. No matter how hard we work our students, competent though they may well be, they will not be competitive with the top 70% of our *adequately* employed population. The data suggest that what will make the difference are family connections. Students with "connected" families will get jobs. Students without such connections will be unable to escape poverty. The cycle will be unbreakable through standard educational intervention.

ALTERNATIVE SOLUTIONS

To my way of thinking, we have a serious problem in terms of employment outcomes for special education students. As an aside, I should note that I firmly believe there is much more to the quality of life than employment. Friends, experiencing joy, feelings of self-esteem, adventure and excitement, freedom of choice, reasonable living situations—the range of events, feelings, and experience we all value—make up quality. I believe that we, as educators, always must keep these values clearly before us. In our society, employment, and the money earned from employment, plays a critical rule in everyone's quality of life—hence the focus on employment. But we must remain aware that employment and jobs do not guarantee quality of life (Halpern, 1985; Halpern, Nave, Close, & Nelson, 1986).

What are some possible solutions for special education to consider? I will suggest a few, in an increasing order of radical change.

Beef Up Vocational Training

Vocational education programs for students with special needs have been in place for a number of years. More recently, considerable effort has been directed toward adapting regular vocational education programs to meet the needs of students from special education (Meers, 1980). Some programs have expanded on-the-job training to include actual paid work while the students are still in school. These efforts all share a common philosophy: Certain general work skills (e.g., dependability, following directions, accepting feedback, appropriate social interaction, honesty) can be taught. In addition, people can acquire specific job or technical skills that will increase their employability.

Attempts to implement programs such as these have ranged from K–12 career education (Brolin, 1983) to relatively short-range intensive intervention. To date, results have been less than spectacular. Proponents often claim that poor results are a result of improper program implementation. And the current trend toward higher academic standards has decreased funding and interest in vocational programs in many areas.

Although I believe that programs like these should be continued and expanded, I doubt if they will have a major long-term impact on the overall issue. The students most in need of such programs often are excluded because of behavioral or general attitude problems. Unless placement and follow-along support programs are available, many of the students with appropriate skills will not locate or maintain employment after graduation. If my earlier analysis of the current social-economic situation is correct, there are simply not enough jobs available that pay "livable" wages for youth entering the job market. Still, I would like to see an increase in educational funds to vocational education, especially in terms of postsecondary options for mildly disabled students.

Alter Instructional Goals

Many recommendations have been made to alter the desired outcome of secondary education (Wehlage, 1983; Finn, 1986). Most of these focus on strengthening students' problem-solving skills and coping ability as alternatives to academic outcomes. I always have been intrigued with these recommendations but never have clearly understood how programs such as these could be implemented.

A recent publication has provided an outline of such an instructional model (Mithaug, Martin, Agran, & Rusch, 1988). This problem-solving model is based on the idea that students fail to achieve success after school because they are not taught to set their own goals or to make decisions for themselves. Rather, according to Mithaug et al., our current instructional procedures teach students to be dependent on teachers for making all learning decisions. Thus, current instructional procedures, while focusing on basic academic or vocational skills, actually create dependent learners. This results in students not being skilled in pursuing lifelong learning opportunities. Further, these students are poorly prepared to compete for jobs that require on-the-job learning for advancement.

Mithaug and his colleagues recommend that students should be taught the following skills: goal setting, planning, independent learning, self-evaluation, and adjustment. Their curriculum, *How to Teach Success Strategies to Students with Special Needs* (Mithaug, Martin, & Husch, 1988) focuses on the instructional strategies to teach these skills, which include assessing decision making and teaching independent performance, self-evaluation, goal setting, and making adjustments. These curriculum recommendations are logical and address many of the problems with our current instructional practices. Whether the procedures are successful, however, remains to be seen. Virtually no data exist on the long-term outcomes of such instruction. As with enhanced vocational programs, the Mithaug et al. strategies appear to be worthy of considerable further study.

Develop Mentor Programs

One of the consistent findings of follow-up studies of high school graduates is the importance of the family/friend network in obtaining jobs and, indeed, coping with the problems of everyday life. The influence of this network may be more powerful than the type of instruction a student receives, or even his or her disability.

Adjustment to adult life is difficult for almost all people. For those with disabilities, this adjustment is even more of a problem. In the specific area of employment, Hamilton (1986) points out that American industry is not willing to give youth responsible positions. Only more mature individuals (age 22 and above) seem to have the opportunity to acquire meaningful employment. Hamilton calls this the "floundering period" in the lives of youth. For those who attend college or join the military, the floundering period is not as obvious as for those who attempt to enter the job market upon exiting from high school.

This transition period, from high school to the adult world, is the time that is most difficult for special education students. Because few attend postsecondary education, most flounder in the job market or attempts at employment. Often the students try one job and another, perhaps community college or some form of specialized vocational training, and then another job.

Andrea Zetlin and her colleagues (Zetlin & Hosseini, 1987; Zetlin & Murtaugh, 1987) have conducted a number of ethnographic studies of mildly handicapped students during this transition time frame. Those authors have clearly documented the floundering period and the importance of mentors. Mentors are adults to whom youth turn for advice, counsel, and perhaps financial assistance, but always friendship. For some youth, parents, older brothers or sister, or family friends fill this role (the family/friend network). For others, however, no one fills this role. These young adults flounder without help.

For students who do not have a well developed family/friend network, a mentor system would provide a meaningful support service. How to develop and implement such a system has yet to be proposed—much less tested. Certainly, depending on volunteers or existing social services (public or private) will not be sufficient. I believe that fruitful research could be pursued in this area.

Develop an Alternative System

As logically seductive as the above three proposals may seem, I do not believe any of them will be adequate to deal with the multiple problems facing youth with disabilities. These youth—the majority from poor families with few powerful social networks—attend a schooling system in which they fail every day. Their performance in academics is clear to them, to their teachers, and to their peers. There is no way that their self-esteem cannot be seriously damaged. Their social interactions are impaired. Those who are placed in self-contained special education classrooms suffer from the stigma of isolation and segregation. Those who are mainstreamed suffer daily abuse from their peers. The schools make few accommodations, either for learning style or for functional content.

Day after day these students are requested to do tasks they cannot do, tasks that hold little significance for their lives, tasks that bring them failure and ridicule. And we speculate about why so many complain (are "non-compliant"), or act out, or choose not to come to this setting (drop out), or drug out, or tune out. And this applies not only to mildly handicapped special education students but to a large proportion, perhaps 30%, of nonhandicapped students as well. Some of these students (both handicapped and non-handicapped) come from families that "make them" go to school. So they tolerate the "abuse" from the schools. Upon graduation, those with family connections make it. Those without family connections flounder. Students who come from families that do not make them attend school drop out. The results are the same: They flounder unless their families have connections. Why attend school?

The time is ripe for a major change in secondary education. Special education should take the lead, but this is THE opportunity for the regular education initiative at the secondary level. We (in special education) should invite those in regular education who are attempting to deal with high-risk youth to join together and form a coalition for developing a meaningful alternative secondary option for youth who are not headed directly for college. This alternative must be socially valued (not the "dumbbell" school), provide opportunities for youth to engage in activities valued by the adult society, focus on problem solving and coping skills, provide opportunities to learn, practice, and demonstrate valued vocational skills, and include ongoing mentor support systems.

Pie in the sky? Perhaps. Yet other countries have options that include major components of this proposal. Hamilton (1986) reports on apprenticeship opportunities in West Germany. Saha (1985) provides a detailed report on the Australian system in which up to 60% of youth *choose* an alternative to high school. For students who choose to leave school to pursue an alternative schooling (e.g., vocational, apprenticeship) that leads to employment, this choice must be considered appropriate and rational.

Could we not develop rational, appropriate alternatives such as these in the United States for mildly handicapped and other students? Might not such a system prevent drop-outs, tune-outs, and drug-outs? Could we not offer students a viable method to enter our society and be productive members of the adult community that does not include attending our current high schools? Could we not offer a meaningful alternative to students from the underclass, be they disabled or not, to partake in our society? I think it is time to try.

Those of use who work in special education and other human services often deal with the parts of our society in which the system is not functioning well. We interact with people who face discrimination because of disability or other factors. We encounter those living in poverty. We interact with young adults and their families who have no hope; who have lost faith in improving their lot; who are adrift, frustrated, in despair, lonely; no longer looking, with joy, to the morrow. We deal with the underbelly of our society.

Many of our colleagues in other areas of work do not have personal experience with this population. Their jobs and social circles insulate them from the part of the world we see. They read reports that our society is basically well and healthy, that those who are hungry simply do not know where to go for free food, that those who are unemployed are lazy, or alcoholic, or coddled by our welfare system. They read that the answer to the drug problem is learning how to say no, that the homeless are a few mentally ill people or transients who choose that lifestyle, that infant mortality is caused by factors other than the lack of health care, that our society is on the right track and the poor have the opportunity to "fix themselves" and partake of the fruits of our country.

We have a moral and ethical duty to inform our fellow citizens that our system has major problems, that many of our citizens live in deep despair with no way out, and that we must develop bold initiatives to make things right. We should be compelled to inform others that our society, founded on a belief system that values individual dignity and personal compassion, must respond to its own ills—not to bad-mouth our way of life but, rather, to show the world, and ourselves, that our way of life is really good.

At a minimum, we must ensure that all our citizens, disabled and nondisabled, male and female, employed and not employed, young and old, have daily food, a place to live, access to basic health care, and reasonable hope that their lives, and the lives of their children, will get better. This should be an entitlement we provide for all our citizens.

REFERENCES

Brolin, D. (1983). *Life centered career education: A competency based approach* (rev.). Reston, VA: Council for Exceptional Children.

Catterall, J., & Stein, D. (1986). The effects of alternative school programs on high school completion and labor market outcomes. *Educational Evaluation & Policy Analysis, 8*(1), 77–86.

Children's Defense Fund. (1988). *Health of America's children: Maternal and child health data.* Washington, DC: Author.

Clemmons, D.C., & Dodrell, C.B. (1983). Vocational outcomes of high school students with epilepsy. *Journal of Applied Rehabilitation Counseling, 14,* 49–53.

Dunn, L.M. (1968). Special education for the mildly retarded: Is much of it justifiable? *Exceptional Children, 35,* 5–22.

Economic Justice for All. (1986). *A pastoral letter on Catholic social teaching and the U.S. economy.* Washington, DC: National Conference of Catholic Bishops.

Edgar, E. (1987). Secondary special education: Is much of it justifiable? *Exceptional Children, 53,* 555–561.

Edgar, E., & Hayden, A.H. (1985). Who are the children special education should serve and how many children are there? *Journal of Special Education, 18,* 523–539.

Edgar, E., Levine, P., Levine, R., & Dubey, M. (1988). *Washington state follow-along studies 1983–1987: Final report.* Seattle, WA: University of Washington, Experimental Education Unit, Child Development Mental Retardation Center.

Fardig, D.B., Algozzine, R.F., Schwartz, S.E., Hensel, J.W., & Westling, D.L. (1985). Post secondary vocational adjustment of rural mildly handicapped students. *Exceptional Children, 52,* 115–121.

Finn, C.E. (1986). A fresh option for the non-college-bound. *Phi Delta Kappan, 68*(4), 234–238.

Gartner, A., & Lipsky, D.K. (1987). Beyond special education? Toward a quality system for all students. *Harvard Educational Review, 57,* 367–396.

Gould, S.J. (1981). *The mismeasure of man.* New York: W.W. Norton.

Hallahan, D.P., & Kauffman, J.M. (1978). Labels, categories, behaviors: ED, LD, and EMR reconsidered. *Journal of Special Education, 11,* 139–147.

Halpern, A.S. (1985). Transition: A look at the foundations. *Exceptional Children, 51*(6), 479–486.

Halpern, A.S., Nave, G., Close, D.W., & Nelson, D. (1986). An empirical analysis of the dimensions of community adjustment for adults with mental retardation in semi-independent living programs. *Australia & New Zealand Journal of Developmental Disabilities, 12,* 147–157.

Hamilton, S.F. ((1986). Excellence and the transition from school to work. *Phi Delta Kappan, 68*(4), 239–242.

Hasazi, S., Gordon, L., & Roe, C. (1985). Factors associated with the employment status of handicapped youth exiting high school from 1979 to 1983. *Exceptional Children, 51,* 455–469.

Hasazi, S., Gordon, L., Roe, C., Hull, M., Finck, K., & Salembier, G. (1985, December). A statewide follow-up on post high school employment and residential status of students labeled "mentally retarded." *Education & Training of the Mentally Retarded,* 222–234.

Hasazi, S.B., Johnson, R.E., Gordon, C.R., & Hall, M. (1988, April). *A statewide follow-up survey of high school exiters: A comparison of former students with and without handicaps.* Paper presented at AERA meeting, New Orleans.

Heller, K.A., Holtzman, W.H., & Messick, S. (Eds.). (1982). *Placing children in special education: A strategy for equality.* Washington, DC: National Academy Press.

Hobbs, N. (1975). *The futures of children: Categories, labels, and their consequences. Report on the Project on Classification of Exceptional Children.* San Francisco: Jossey-Bass.

Hodgkinson, H.L. (1985). *All one system: Demographics of education—kindergarten through graduate school.* Washington, DC: Institute for Educational Leadership.

Horn, W., O'Donnell, J., & Vitulano, A. (1983). Long-term follow-up studies of learning-disabled persons. *Journal of Learning Disabilities, 16,* 542–555.

Kozol, J. (1988). *Rachel and her children.* New York: Crown Publishers.

Levin, E., Zigmond, N., & Birch, J. (1985). A follow-up study of 52 learning disabled students. *Journal of Learning Disabilities, 13,* 542–547.

Linden, B.E., & Forness, S.R. (1986, September). Post-school adjustment of mentally retarded persons with psychiatric disorders: A ten-year follow-up. *Education & Training of the Mentally Retarded.*

Meers, G.D. (1980). *Handbook of special vocational needs education.* Rockville, MD: Aspen Systems Corp.

Mithaug, D.E., Horiuchi, C.N., & Fanning, P.N. (1985). A report on the Colorado statewide follow-up survey of special education students. *Exceptional Children, 51*(5), 397–404.

Mithaug, D.E., Martin, J.E., Agran, M., & Rusch, F.R. (1988). *Why special education graduates fail: How to teach them to succeed.* Colorado Springs, CO: Ascent Publications.

Mithaug, D.E., Martin, J.E., & Husch, J.V. (1988). *How to teach success strategies to students with special needs.* Colorado Springs, CO: Ascent Publications.

Neel, R.S., Meadows, N., Levine, T., & Edgar, E.B. (1988). What happens after special education: A statewide follow-up study. *Behavioral Disorders, 13,* 209–216.

Newkirk, D., Bloch, D., & Shrybman, J. (1978). *An analysis of categorical definitions, diagnostic methods, diagnostic criteria and personnel utilization in the classification of handicapped children.* Reston, VA: Council for Exceptional Children.

Robertson, J.O. (1988, February 20). A new depression is moving closer. *Seattle Times,* A-11.

Ross, R.T., Begab, M.J., Dondis, E.H., Giampiccolo, J.S., Jr., & Meyers, C.E. (1985). *Lives of the mentally retarded: A forty-year follow-up study.* Stanford, CA: Stanford University Press.

Saha, L.J. (1985). The legitimacy of early school leaving: Occupational orientations, vocational training plans, and educational attainment among urban Australian youth. *Sociology of Education, 58,* 228–240.

Singer, J.D., & Butler, J.A. (1987). The Education for All Handicapped Children Act: Schools as agents of social reform. *Harvard Educational Review, 57,* 125–152.

Sitlington, P.L. (1987). *Iowa statewide follow-up data.* Des Moines, IA: Department of Education.

Wehlage, G.G. (1983). The marginal high school student: Defining the problem and searching for policy. *Children & Youth Services Review, 5,* 321–342.

Wehman, P., Hill, M., Goodall, P., Cleveland, P., Brooke, V., & Pentecost, J.H. (1982). Job placement and follow-up of moderately and severely handicapped individuals after three years. *Journal of the Association for the Severely Handicapped, 7,* 5–16.

Wetzel, J.R. (1987). *American youth: A statistical snapshot: Youth and America's future.* Washington, DC: William T. Grant Foundation, Commission on Work, Family and Citizenship.

White, W.J., Schumaker, J.B., Warner, M.M., Alley, G.R., & Deshler, D.D. (1980). *The current status of young adults identified as learning disabled during their school career* (Research report #21). Lawrence: University of Kansas, Institute for Research in Learning Disabilities.

Will, M. (1984). Bridges from school to working life. *Programs for the handicapped.* Washington, DC: Office of Special Education & Rehabilitative Services, Office of Information & Resources for the Handicapped.

Ysseldyke, J.E., Algozzine, B., & Richey, L. (1982). Judgment under uncertainty: How many children are handicapped? *Exceptional Children, 48,* 531–534.

Zetlin, A.G., & Hosseini, A. (1987). *Moving toward adult status: Six case studies of mildly learning handicapped young adults who left school.* Unpublished paper, School of Education, University of Southern California, Los Angeles.

Zetlin, A.G., & Murtaugh, M. (1987). *Friendship patterns of mildly learning handicapped and nonhandicapped high school students.* Los Angeles: University of Southern California, School of Education.

Zigmond, N., & Thornton, H. (1985). Follow-up of postsecondary-age learning disabled graduates and dropouts. *Learning Disabilities Research, 1*(1), 50–55.

U.S. Department of Education (1988). *Tenth annual report to Congress on the implementation of the Education of the Handicapped Act.* Washington, DC: U.S. Government Printing Office.

Partial support for developing this article was provided by a grant (#G008530049) from the Office of Special Education and Rehabilitative Services (OSERS), U.S. Department of Education. Points of view stated here do not necessarily represent official positions of OSERS. Connie Pious provided assistance in preparing this manuscript.

Eugene Edgar is a professor of education at the University of Washington, Seattle.

○8○

Teachers often have thought they are responsible for providing motivation, instruction, and reinforcement to students. In recent years, however, there has been a growing realization that the most effective learning and behavior control occur through self-regulation. Graham, Harris, and Reid describe the four basic components of self-regulation: self-instruction, goal setting, self-monitoring, and self-reinforcement. They define each component and discuss how teachers can help students develop these skills.

Developing Self-Regulated Learners

Steve Graham, Karen R. Harris, and Robert Reid

An important characteristic of human beings is our ability to understand and regulate our own behavior. Theologians, philosophers, and psychologists have long viewed self-control as a distinguishing characteristic of the human species, and for a variety of religious, political, philosophical, and practical reasons, the call to personally cultivate self-understanding and self-control has been sounded repeatedly throughout the ages (Zimmerman & Schunk, 1989). The philosopher Aristotle, for instance, praised the virtues of self-awareness. Likewise, the notable American statesman and inventor Benjamin Franklin was a staunch proponent of self-regulation. He used an assortment of self-regulation procedures in his own struggles for self-improvement. At one point during his life, he defined 13 virtues (e.g., temperance, order) that he wished to develop, established the goal of increasing each virtue in turn during the space of a week, monitored instances of success and failure, and recorded the daily results. If, at the end of the week, no offenses were recorded against the virtue, he extended his goal to include the next virtue listed (cf. Zimmerman & Schunk, 1989).

Students with special needs can use the same types of self-regulation procedures to improve their academic performance and interactions in social situations (cf. Gresham, 1985; Hallahan & Sapona, 1983; Harris, 1982; Harris & Graham, 1992). They can apply self-regulation procedures such as goal setting, self-monitoring (which includes self-assessment and self-recording of performance), self-instructions, and contingent self-reinforcement to academic tasks.

THE RATIONALE FOR SELF-REGULATION

People use self-regulatory procedures such as goal setting, self-monitoring, and self-evaluation to help them accomplish specific tasks. Just as self-regulation procedures such as goal setting can be used to organize a person's overall approach to a task, they also can play a contributing, but less persuasive, role in how a person accomplishes a task. Self-regulatory mechanisms often are combined (as basic building blocks), for instance, with other cognitive routines to form a program for accomplishing a specific task (Brown & Campione, 1981). Scardamalia and Bereiter (1985) suggested that in addition to contributing to the immediate accomplishment of a task, self-regulatory mechanisms can further contribute to development of the cognitive system. The use of self-assessment, for example, generates information that may change how a person approaches a task.

These uses of self-regulation can be illustrated further by examining several real-life examples. First, a runner we know uses goal setting to organize and direct her running program. She sets weekly distance goals, monitors her progress daily, and reinforces herself with praise or more concrete rewards when she meets her goals. Second, many children we have observed use self-regulation procedures in combination with task-specific cognitive strategies to help them accomplish academic assignments. To get ready for a spelling test, for instance, one of our former students first did a self-test to determine which words he needed to study. He then studied these words using a specific word study strategy. During the course of study, he periodically reassessed his progress to determine when he knew the words well enough to earn a passing grade.

Similarly, in our own program of research (see Graham, Harris, MacArthur, & Schwartz, 1991; Harris & Graham, in press), we have taught students with learning disabilities (LD) how self-regulation procedures can help them better use the academic strategies they are acquiring. When teaching a strategy for writing, for instance, we encourage children to develop an inner dialogue (self-instructions) to guide how they apply the strategy. Moreover, we encourage students to set goals for using the strategy and monitoring its application. Combining these self-regulatory procedures with other strategy instruction components contributes to students' learning and use of academic strategies (cf. Sawyer, Graham, & Harris, 1991) and can result in changes in how students approach and view an academic task (Graham & Harris, in press).

The self-regulatory mechanisms that children use can be fostered and improved through instruction (Harris, 1982; O'Leary & Dubey, 1979; Scardamalia & Bereiter, 1985). This is especially important for students receiving special services. The problems that many students with special needs experience are related in part to problems in the self-regulation of organized strategic behaviors (cf. Harris, 1982; Licht, 1983).

The basic rationale for helping students with special needs learn to better use processes for self-regulating their behavior is to promote the development of self-regulated learners—students who independently plan and self-regulate goal-directed behaviors. Improving students' self-regulation abilities is important in academic settings for at least three reasons (Harris & Graham, in press).

1. Learning to self-regulate their behaviors allows students to become more independent. In addition to the many positive benefits this creates for students, it also reduces demands on teacher time.

2. Learning to use self-regulation procedures often increases students' level of task engagement; thus, in addition to facilitating learning, it may decrease disruptive or off-task behaviors.

3. Perhaps most important, self-regulation techniques enable students to monitor and regulate their own academic performance.

In short, these procedures empower students.

Four basic components of self-regulation are *self-instructions, goal setting, self-monitoring,* and *self-reinforcement.* Although each component is described separately here, they are closely related and can be used either independently or in combination. As mentioned, we use these same procedures as part of an instructional approach to help students with special needs develop academic strategies. We refer to this approach to strategy instruction as "self-regulated strategy development" and direct the reader who would like more information to Graham and Harris (1987); Graham, Harris, and Sawyer (1987); and Harris and Graham (1992, in press).

SELF-INSTRUCTIONS

Self-instructions involve speaking to ourselves to direct or regulate our behavior. This self-directing dialogue may be overt (spoken aloud) or covert (inside the mind). When writing, for example, authors constantly talk to themselves (either overtly or covertly). Some of this personal dialogue involves rehearsing or fine-tuning what they intend to say. Other parts of this dialogue are aimed at orienting, organizing, and structuring writers' composing behaviors. This self-speech (or private speech) is not intended for communication with others; it is directed to the self and is used to drive what the writer does.

Development of self-speech during early childhood is thought to be critical in the development of self-regulated behavior. According to Vygotsky (1934/1962), even toddlers' early egocentric speech may be a nascent form of self-regulation. Meichenbaum and Goodman (1979) noted that young children's egocentric speech can act as a self-command, as a reinforcer, or as an aid to mark the rhythm of an action. As children grow and develop, they gradually become able to use self-speech to consciously understand situations, to focus on problems, and to surmount difficulties (Harris, 1990; Zivin, 1979).

Overt self-speech typically increases until about age 7 (Fuson, 1979; Vygotsky, 1934, 1962). It then decreases until, by ages 8 to 10, it becomes primarily covert as the child's cognitive capabilities increase and he or she is aware that speaking aloud in the presence of others is not socially acceptable. This process may be delayed in some children, including those with learning problems (cf. Zivin, 1979). This covert self-speech is viewed as the immediate precursor to "pure thought."

Students can use self-speech or self-instructions in a variety of ways to strengthen their performance in academic situations. Self-instructions can help them understand the nature and demands of an academic assignment or problem; produce effective, relevant, and efficient strategies for accomplishing tasks; and monitor the use and effectiveness of these strategies. As other applications self-instructions in the classroom can be used to:

— direct attention to salient events, stimuli, or aspects of a problem.
— interpret or control automatic or impulsive responses.
— create and select among alternative actions.
— focus students' thinking.
— aid memory for steps and procedures.
— direct the execution of a sequence of actions or steps.
— cope with anxiety, frustration, or other emotional reactions.
— spell out criteria for success.

In addition, self-instructions can improve task orientation (resulting in a more positive approach to academic tasks), increase and maintain on-task behaviors (through increasing the amount of engaged time), and provide means for dealing with situations involving success or failure (Harris, 1982, 1990; Harris & Graham, 1992).

To illustrate how self-instructions (and a few other self-regulation techniques you will encounter later) might work, imagine an experienced teacher beginning to plan a lesson. Because she is experienced, she has little need for self-speech as she gets ready to plan. As she begins the planning process, she engages in self-speech as well as other cognitive processes: imagining, anticipating, and self-monitoring. Her internal dialogue might go like this: "What's the point of this lesson? Okay, I want them to understand how to solve this kind of word problem." As she works, her internal dialogue consists of abbreviated messages to herself such as, "They might not be able to do . . . ," "Maybe this would be better," "Last year this worked pretty well." These routine steps usually are taken care of with little or no self-speech.

When encountering a problem, however, the amount of self-speech increases, resulting in statements such as, "How am I going to teach them this concept?" As she begins to work on the problem, she finds herself muttering out loud, 'No, no, no, that just won't work." Evaluating students' anticipated responses, she decides, "This is too difficult, I need a much clearer example to illustrate this point." As she continues planning, she might make the following self-reinforcement and self-evaluation statements to herself: "That's it!"; "This is going to be a great lesson." As time passes, she reaches the point at which she becomes fatigued and is tempted to stop. Coping messages help her stay on-task and meet the goal she set to finish the lesson plan: "I can do this if I just keep at it. Then I can relax and it won't bother me later and I can enjoy the rest of the evening."

Forms and Levels of Self-Instruction

Teachers can help students learn to use at least six different forms of self-instructions (each of which can be used at two different levels) (Harris & Graham, 1992; Meichenbaum, 1977). Table 1 provides examples of each form and level. The self-instructions

TABLE 1   The Basic Forms of Self-Instructions, with Examples

Forms of Self-Instruction	Examples
1. Problem Definition (Sizing up the nature and demands of the task)	What is it I have to do here? What am I up to? What is my first step?
2. Focusing Attention and Planning (attending to the task at hand and generating a plan)	I have to concentrate, be careful . . . think of the steps. To do this right, I have to make a plan. First I need to . . . , then . . .
3. Strategy (engaging and implementing strategies)	First I will write—brainstorm as many ideas as I can. The first step in writing an essay is . . . My goals for this essay are . . . ; I will self-record on . . .
4. Self-evaluating and Error Correcting (evaluating performance, catching and correcting errors)	Oops, I missed one; that's okay—I can revise. Am I following my plan?
5. Coping and Self-Control (subsuming difficulties or failures and dealing with forms of arousal)	Don't worry—worry doesn't help. It's okay to feel a little anxious; a little anxiety can help. I'm not going to get mad; mad makes me do bad. I need to go slow and take my time.
6. Self-Reinforcement (providing reward)	I'm getting better at this. Wait 'til my teacher reads this! Hooray—I'm done!

Source: Adapted from *Helping Young Writers Master the Craft: Strategy Instruction and Self-Regulation in the Writing Process* by K.R. Harris and S. Graham, 1992, Cambridge, MA: Brookline Books. Reprinted by permission.

illustrated can help students comprehend the nature of the task or problem they are trying to solve, produce strategies for tackling the problem, use the strategies generated to mediate behavior directly and effectively, evaluate and modify strategies and performance as needed, increase independence, and improve generalization and maintenance of strategic performance. Depending upon the task or problem, students might use any or all of the forms and levels of the self-instructions illustrated.

Forms of Self-Instruction

1. *Problem definition* statements. These require students to ascertain the nature of the task and what is required to accomplish it. One way to do this is self-questioning (cf. Wong & Jones, 1982). Students ask themselves questions about the task and, in answering, provide possible solutions. A student might ask, "What do I need to do here? I need to write a report about the book I read; I need to remember to include the plot, character, and setting."

2. *Focusing attention and planning.* As the name implies, these statements help students focus on the task at hand and create a plan of action (e.g., choosing a strategy or determining appropriate steps to solve a problem). Here, a student's personal di-

alogue might include, "Before I start writing, I'll find the plot, character, and setting and make notes about each."

3. *Strategy* statements. Strategy statements help students engage and implement task-relevant or self-regulation strategies. An example might be, "I'll use my writing strategy: TAP and count. TAP means I need to consider my topic, audience, and purpose. Count means I have to think about the parts of what I'm going to write."

4. *Self-evaluation and error correction* statements. This type of statement helps students evaluate their progress and detect and correct errors. An example could be, "Let's see, did I include plot, character, and setting? Oops, I forgot setting. That's okay; I can revise."

5. *Coping and self-control* statements help students surmount difficulties or failures. These also can be used to deal with stress, anxiety, anger, frustration, or other feelings that interfere with performance. An older student confronted with a difficult task might say, "Okay, this isn't rocket science; I can do this," helping the student deal with fear of failure. Another example of coping and self-control statements is, "It's okay if I make a mistake; I can correct it later."

6. *Self-reinforcement.* These statements are used to reward progress, cope with problems, or increase persistence. Self-reinforcement statements include, "Good job" and "I'm making progress." Other examples of self-reinforcement statements are:

> **Awesome!**
> **That was my best job!**
> **Wonderful!**
> **Outstanding!**
> **Splendid!**
> **Fantastic job!**
> **Excellent!**
> **Keep up the good work!**
> **Wow!**
> **Terrific!**
> **Great!**
> **Nice job!**
> **Well done!**
> **Good job!**
> **Terrific!**
> **Super!**
> **I'm a genius!**

When working with students, teachers need not worry about or label what category a self-statement fits into. Instead, they should focus on helping students decide what types of self-statements will aid them, and assist if necessary in their formulation. Self-statements should be in the students' own words. Student-created self-statements are preferable to those developed by the teacher. When our students have devised self-statements, they generally have used categories such as "things to help me get going" (problem definition and focusing and planning self-instructions might be used here) and "what I say when I'm finished" (self-reinforcement and self-evaluation and error correction could come into play here).

Usually, starting with a single type of self-instruction that fits a child's specific need is best. Using too many types of self-instructions all at once or too quickly may cause students to become confused or overwhelmed. After students have grown accustomed to a particular form of self-instruction, new ones can be added. We have found that students with severe learning problems can quickly master self-instructions, and are soon ready to expand their repertoire (Harris & Graham, 1992).

Levels of Self-Instruction

Self-instructions can occur at two levels: (a) task-approach and (b) task-specific. *Task-approach statements* are appropriate for a wide variety of problems and situations. Task-approach statements often serve metacognitive functions, as they increase students' awareness and control of their own cognitive functioning. These global statements may be particularly useful in helping students generalize self-regulated behavior to other settings or tasks. The statement, "What do I need to do here?" is a problem definition statement at the task-approach level. Conversely, the self-statement, "I need to write down the steps in my spelling strategy" is a problem definition statement at the task-specific level. *Task-specific* statements are more helpful in improving performance on a given task but they typically have little potential for generalizability.

At present, it is not known if any of the six forms of self-instructions (at either level) is more effective than the others. We do not believe this is a critical issue for classroom practice, however. Students should simply be encouraged to develop self-instructions that meet their needs, regardless of the form or level. Teachers should concentrate on helping students generate both task-approach and task-specific self-instructions.

Teaching Students to Use Self-Instructions

A puzzle was rigged (it could not be successfully completed) to study the private speech of children with and without learning problems (Harris, 1986a). As expected, the normally achieving children used a number of strategies to try to complete the puzzle, and they produced a sizable amount of relevant, helpful self-speech. The children with learning problems, on the other hand, typically did not approach the task strategically and used irrelevant self-statements, many of which were negative. Examples of children using irrelevant self-statements included one girl who talked at length about what she would do at her Brownies meeting (which wouldn't take place for another 4 days), and a boy who sang a song about taking a trip to Idaho. Negative statements included "I hate puzzles" and "I'm no good at puzzles." Most of the students with LD stopped trying to work the puzzle before ever reaching the rigged piece.

Toward the end of the study, an adorable young man with a crewcut and horn-rimmed glasses, wearing a coat and bow tie, came to work on the puzzle. After explaining the task, the student was asked to complete the puzzle and then went to the other end of the room. Things appeared to be going as they had with the other students with LD. The student seemed to become frustrated quickly. Just when he seemed about to quit, however, he pushed himself back from the table, folded his hands in his lap, took a deep breath, and chanted, "I'm not going to get mad; mad makes me do bad." The "Little Professor" used the same self-instruction many times while working on the puzzle. He was able to fit more pieces and persisted longer than any of the other children with learning problems.

Curious as to how the little boy had come to use self-speech in this way, his teacher was contacted. The teacher, who was not familiar with the term *self-speech* or research in this area, simply believed that what we say to ourselves affects what we do. During weekly class meetings students helped one another identify problem areas and develop self-statements to deal with their problems. The Little Professor had identified getting mad as a problem that had prevented him from doing his best. Together, the class had worked out the procedure of his pushing back his chair, taking a deep breath, folding his hands, and using the self-statement. The teacher initially had helped by explaining the rationale for self-instructions, helping the students develop their own self-instructions, modeling their use, and cuing students when the self-statement was appropriate. The Little Professor obviously had mastered use of this self-statement—including being able to generalize its use across settings.

Teaching students to use self-instructions usually is done in much the same way as it was by the Little Professor's teacher. First the teacher and student(s) discuss the importance of what we say to ourselves and how the things we say can hurt or help us. Many of our students report primarily the spontaneous use of negative self-speech, of which they readily offer examples. Next the teacher assists students in developing meaningful self-instructions in their own words. Seeing someone else (preferably a peer) successfully use self-instructions (modeling) is a critical component in the learning process. One effective technique is for teacher and student to model and share, both formally and informally, how self-instructions can be used in given situations or for specific tasks. After self-statements have been determined, students are prompted and assisted in the use of the statements as necessary. This assistance is gradually faded as the students become more able to use the self-instructions appropriately and independently.

The teacher and students should regularly and collaboratively evaluate the efficiency and effectiveness of the self-instructions learned. If a student has stopped using self-instructions, the teacher should ascertain why. In some instances students may need only a reminder to remember to use their self-statements or may need to make a slight change in their self-statements. In other cases a more extended booster session may be necessary. Self-instructions may have to be remodeled, and procedures for prompting their use might have to be reinstated.

Students can use self-instructions alone or can combine these with other self-regulation techniques such as goal setting, self-monitoring, and self-reinforcement. Students with more severe learning problems may profit from gradually learning multiple self-regulation procedures. Students who are already using effective self-regulation strategies may not require help in this area, or they may profit from developing one or two new self-regulation strategies.

Practical Tips

Self-instructions generally are most effective when they are matched to the student's verbal type and language level. As mentioned, students' self-instructions should be in their own words. Although a teacher may initially model a self-instruction or a set of self-instructions, students should individually choose the wording of their own self-instructions. Also, if a student decides on a statement created by another student, the teacher should make sure the statement is meaningful and appropriate for the second student. Self-instructions that students do not truly understand and feel comfortable with will do little good. Finally, students typically abbreviate or modify their self-instructions over time. This is desirable as long as the self-instructions continue to work, but sometimes changes in self-instructions lessen their effectiveness or subvert their purpose. Teachers should be alert to this possibility.

When teaching self-instructions, the teacher has to be enthusiastic and modeling has to be done with appropriate phrasing and inflection. *Self-instructions cannot be taught in a mechanical, rote-learning fashion.* The student must be an active participant and collaborator in the design, implementation, and evaluation of self-instructions. The student should not be viewed as merely a passive recipient. Moreover, the model (whether the teacher or a peer) must have a positive, favorable relationship with the student. Self-instructions can be modeled on an impromptu basis and in informal situations such as games, discussions, and other everyday occurrences. Even though live models are preferable, other alternatives, such as cartoon characters and drawings, have been successful aids. Written lists of statements, tape-recorded statements, and videotaped models also have been used effectively.

Another useful technique is to ask the target student to be a model for other students. This gives the target student an extra incentive to learn to use self-instructions. Videotaping students saying their self-instructions also can be motivational. One teacher we know rewards students for mastering self-instructions by videotaping them as they apply what they have learned. These videotapes are used later to show other students how self-statements can be employed and facilitate performance.

Students have to realize that there is a connection between self-instructions and actions. Students need to know that merely saying the right things without doing the action or task will not likely be effective. If students have a great deal of difficulty achieving correspondence between saying and doing, their self-instructions may be too difficult or inappropriate. Teachers should be sensitive to the possibility that some students may need help in developing the connection between self-instructions and the behavior or cognition they are meant to affect.

Older students, who are more aware that talking to oneself is viewed as embarrassing or inappropriate, sometimes resist overt verbalizations. Students should not be forced to use overt verbalizations (or any kind of self-regulation procedures for that matter). Nevertheless, some techniques can be employed to circumvent this. One successful tactic with older students is to present self-instructions as "thinking out loud" rather than "talking to yourself out loud" and stressing that the overt use of self-instructions will be temporary. Group discussions in which individuals, including adults, share how they use self-speech both overtly and covertly can also help. Another tactic is to explain to students that hearing them use the self-instructions is necessary initially to be sure they are doing this appropriately. Students need to be told that their eventual goal is to use the self-instructions covertly and that they can progress to this stage quite quickly. If a student continues to be reluctant about overt self-instructions, allow that student to practice away from other students who might overhear, or let the student speak into a microphone (students usually see this as different from talking out loud to themselves).

Self-instructions appropriate to students' needs and characteristics (including language and cognitive capacity) and the task at hand rarely interfere with performance. Overt verbalizations, however, can interfere with behaviors that are timed, occur quickly, require reflexive reactions, or involve complex processing (Harris & Graham, in press a; Zivin, 1979). For example, we have found that complex self-instructions are cumbersome for many young children who are learning to print (Graham, 1983). Self-instructions should be evaluated carefully by the student and the teacher alike to ensure that they are both appropriate and do not interfere with performance.

GOAL SETTING

Goal setting provides a useful heuristic for attacking many educational difficulties. For instance, a student writing a term paper for a history class might decide to write a paper on Abraham Lincoln that will be 10 pages long, focus on the Civil War, and receive at least a "B" grade. The student might further operationalize some of these criteria by developing a practical plan that specifies a sequence of actions for attaining goals: "I'll get two books on Lincoln, read them to locate important events and information, make a tentative decision about what to include in the paper, and keep track of how many pages I write." While carrying out the assignment, the student might also periodically assess if the plan and goals are working out. If they are not, the student might decide to redefine the initial plans or a specific goal: "I can't cover all of this in 10 pages, so I'll make the paper a couple of pages longer."

In real life, the process of goal setting is not always this neat, nor are the goals always so clear-cut. Nevertheless, heuristics such as goal setting give learners a means for making a complex problem such as writing a term paper more manageable and less threatening (Graham, MacArthur, Schwartz, & Voth, in press). In examining goal setting, we first consider how the act of setting goals can facilitate performance.

Dimensions of Goal Setting

Across a diverse range of tasks from increasing productivity to losing weight, goal setting has been shown to be an extremely powerful tool (Johnson & Graham, 1990; Locke, Shaw, Saari, & Latham, 1981). One reason goal setting is so effective is that goals work to enhance motivation. The anticipated satisfaction and desire of attaining a goal provides an incentive to mobilize and sustain effort until the goal is reached or exceeded. Goal setting is also effective because goals focus attention on what has to be accomplished and foster the development of a plan of action for obtaining the desired results.

Goals further serve an informational function by allowing a person to compare present performance against the standard embodied in the goal (Bandura & Schunk, 1977; Schunk, 1985). Noting progress in obtaining a desired goal can boost one's personal sense of efficacy, which in turn can increase motivation for accomplishing the goal. For school-age children, goal setting can lead to increased task engagement, faster learning, and a heightened sense of personal accomplishment (Schunk, 1985, 1989).

Goal Properties

Goals exert their effects through their properties (Schunk, 1989). Three properties that are especially critical are specificity, difficulty, and proximity.

Specificity

Goals should supply a clear and specific standard for performance. For instance, a goal such as "Write a paper citing 20 references" will elicit better performance than a vague goal such as "Do some referencing" or no goal at all (Latham & Yukl, 1975). Specific goals give students a clear indication of what is required. This makes it easier for them to plan and assess their progress.

Difficulty

Goal difficulty refers to how challenging a goal is for a specific person. Challenging goals lead to better performance than easy goals; goals that can be achieved with little or no effort provide little incentive to mobilize effort or resources (Johnson & Graham, 1990). As Masters, Furman, and Barden (1977) accurately noted, "Any standard provides an incentive for improvement only until it is reached" (p. 218). A caveat, however, is in order. More difficult goals can lead to better performance only with both a commitment to obtaining the goal and the ability to achieve the goal.

Proximity

Goals also may differ in proximity. *Proximal goals* are near at hand and can be completed quickly (e.g., "Do ten algebra problems before the end of class today"). In contrast, *distal goals* can be completed only in the future (e.g., "Make a detailed observation of the mating patterns of the common sparrow"). Proximal goals produce higher levels of performance than do distal goals (Bandura & Simon, 1977). Distal goals are often too far removed in time to stimulate a person to mobilize resources in the here and now. We have all put off distal tasks (such as that term paper) until the last minute.

In summary, goals that are specific and challenging are superior to goals that are vague and easy. Furthermore, goals that can be accomplished more immediately (proximal goals) are superior to goals that can be accomplished only in the long term (distal goals).

Other Factors

Successful goal setting also depends on a number of other factors. Two of these are feedback and participation in setting goals.

Feedback

Of particular importance is knowledge about how good a job one is doing in achieving the desired goals. Successful goal setting is dependent on feedback or knowledge of results (Locke et al., 1981). Feedback influences performance by cuing individuals to increase effort when progress is lagging, to reset easy goals to more challenging ones, and to establish new goals when they have accomplished old ones. Timely and frequent feedback is especially helpful because it encourages evaluation and control of behaviors proactively. For children, feedback can be obtained from teachers or peers, or through self-assessments. Obviously, students will be more successful in evaluating their progress when goals are explicit and easily measured.

Participative Goal Setting

Who creates or sets the goals also can influence the power of goal setting. Goals can be assigned by the teacher, determined by the student, or participative. Participative goals involve both the teacher and student in developing or selecting goals. Having a student choose one or more from a set of goals conjointly developed by the teacher and the student is one example of participative goal setting. Participative goals should be emphasized initially, as many students (especially young children and students with learning problems) have difficulty setting reasonable and realistic goals for themselves (Graham & Harris, 1989). Thus, if possible, teachers should resist the temptation to provide students with desirable goals. Instead, teachers should involve students in the goal-setting process, as this leads to higher levels of commitment to achieve goals and a sense of ownership (Locke et al., 1981). Regardless of the approach, the teacher's ultimate objective is to have students establish their own goals independently.

In participative goal setting, teachers need to be sensitive to the match between goal selection and the individual student's ability to accomplish (or approach for accomplishing) selected goals. If selected goals repeatedly exceed a student's capabilities, the effectiveness of goal setting will be seriously undermined, possibly leading the student to devalue the goal-setting process. Mismatch between capabilities and goal difficulty can be mediated by helping students develop or access effective strategies for accomplishing the desired objective.

Obviously, acceptance of a goal and commitment to attain it are critical to the success of the goal-setting process. One way in which teachers can foster goal acceptance and commitment is by being supportive. Teachers should attend closely to students' opinions and feelings about goals, encourage questions, and query students on the actions they might perform to meet goals. Goals are also more likely to be accepted if they are perceived as being valuable. Unfortunately, for many students with special needs, academic goals often do not meet this criterion. One way to make academic goals more valuable to these students is to link accomplishment to an external reinforcer such as 15 minutes of free time. (Before using external rewards, however, we recommend that you consider the self-reinforcement procedures discussed later in this article.) Nothing works like success. Students who have a history of successfully meeting their goals are more likely to have the confidence to set and achieve even more demanding goals.

SELF-MONITORING

Self-monitoring occurs when a student determines whether a target behavior has or has not occurred and then records the result in some way (Nelson, 1977; O'Leary & Dubey, 1979). Thus, by definition, self-monitoring contains two components: (a) self-assessment and (b) self-recording. Determining whether a behavior has or has not occurred is *self-assessment.* Students may self-assess many aspects of a specific behavior (e.g., occurrence, duration, intensity, frequency). Although self-assessment can be done alone, it works best for most students in combination with self-recording (Harris & Graham, 1992). Because of this synergy, we will discuss self-monitoring as involving both self-assessment and self-recording. In practice, once students become adept at self-monitoring, they may choose to use self-assessment alone; however, self-recording necessarily involves appraisal and thus will always be used in combination with self-assessment.

Self-Assessment

Self-assessment requires students to be "observers" of their own behaviors or cognitions. What can be self-monitored is not limited just to overt behaviors. For example, students might ask themselves whether they were paying attention during seatwork activity or they might count how many times they mentally rehearsed specific facts and generalizations for an upcoming test.

Because self-assessment prompts students to compare their performance to a criterion for acceptable performance, it is often a good idea (at least initially) to help students spell out the standards that constitute acceptable performance ("I am on-task when I am _____ ; or "I have completed a spelling practice when I correctly write my word without looking at my list"). Even more important, the task or procedure chosen for self-assessment should be meaningful to the student and realistic in terms of his or her abilities.

Because the basic goal for any self-regulation procedure is independent performance, students need to learn how to direct and manage their own self-assessments. Therefore, all self-assessment procedures must be appropriate to the student's functional or developmental level, or the teacher should provide support and assistance until the student can conduct the self-assessments independently. When providing support, the teacher should remember not to co-opt the self-assessment process; the "self" is the central component in self-monitoring.

An example of teacher support gathered from our own field experience involves students who self-assessed the number of times they correctly practiced a spelling word during a study period. As students used this procedure, the number of times they correctly practiced spelling words increased. One student, however, started having some difficulty in applying the procedure, as she had trouble counting past 50 and was completing many more practices than this. Rather than counting for her, which would possibly subvert the process, the teacher gave her paper with consecutively numbered slots for each practice response. When using the paper, the student was directed to mark out any incorrect response as it occurred and not to proceed to the next slot until she had substituted a correct response. When the student was finished studying, she simply determined what number she had stopped at and recorded this number on her graph.

Finally, even though students can self-assess many facets of performance, it is usually best to begin with one aspect that is well within the student's capabilities. Additional elements can be addressed following improvement in the initial area. Goal setting can play a role in this process. If goals have been set previousy, either the goals themselves or the procedures used to attain the goals can be self-assessed, with the criteria for acceptable performance stated in the goal. For example, a student might set a goal of reading 20 pages of an assigned book each day until finishing the book. The student could then self-assess the number of pages read each day until the terminal goal was met.

Self-Recording

Self-recording involves writing down the results of the assessment. Individual tally sheets, charts, or graphs are frequently used for self-recording. Because these media present a visual record of students' performance over time and allow them to see their progress graphically, students often find them to be highly motivating (Reid & Harris, 1989). Interestingly, the use of graphs often results in spontaneous, unprompted goal setting. Self-recording graphs also may stimulate students to exceed previous performance levels. Sample self-recording graphs are shown in Figures 1 and 2.

Teaching Self-Monitoring to Students

Teaching students to self-monitor is straightforward. It often can be accomplished in only 15–30 minutes. After this initial instruction, students typically can use self-monitoring independently. The steps in teaching students to self-monitor are grounded empirically in research in both self-monitoring and cognition (e.g., Hallahan & Sapona, 1983; Harris, 1986b; Mahoney & Thoresen, 1974; Reid & Harris, 1989). The steps presented should serve as a guide and are intended to be flexible. They should be modified as necessary to meet the needs of the teacher and the learner.

Step 1. The first step involves determining and explicitly defining the target behavior the student will self-monitor. The target behavior ("behavior" is used broadly here; targets

Describing Words

Name _____

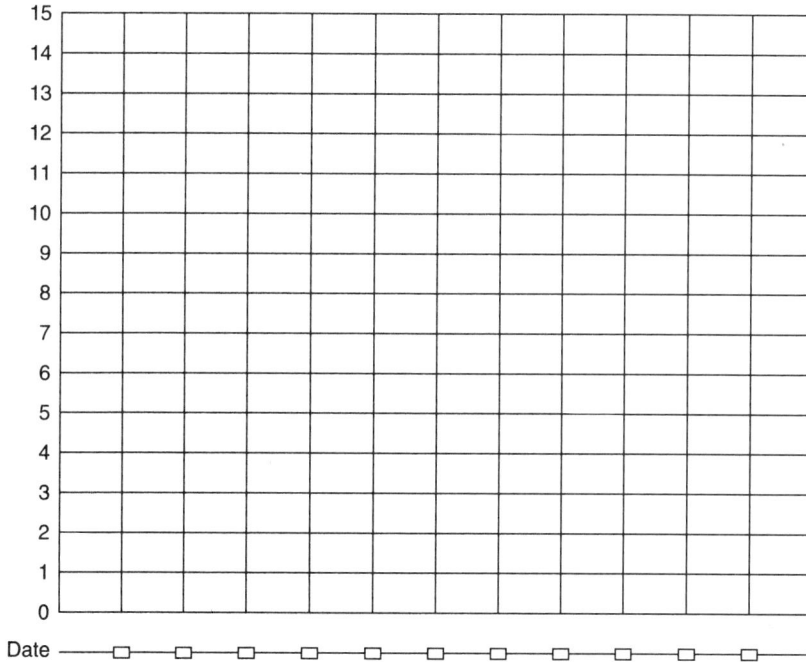

Fill in the number of describing words you used in your story.

Source: Adapted from *Helping Young Writers Master the Craft: Strategy Instruction and Self-Regulation in the Writing Process* by K.R. Harris and S. Graham, 1992, Cambridge, MA: Brookline Books. Reprinted by permission.

FIGURE 1   *Example of a Simple Recording Graph*

could be feelings, thoughts, academic products, processes for achieving a goal, etc.) or event should be defined clearly and precisely and must be easily understood by the student. For example, "doing good in math" might be a student's goal, but this would be nearly impossible for the student to self-monitor. More realistically, the student might monitor how many arithmetic problems were completed correctly during seatwork activities or on homework assignments and self-record the results using a graph such as the one shown in Figure 2. The student must be able to independently evaluate and self-record the behavior or event chosen for self-monitoring. The efficacy of self-monitoring may be reduced greatly if the student cannot independently self-assess the target behavior.

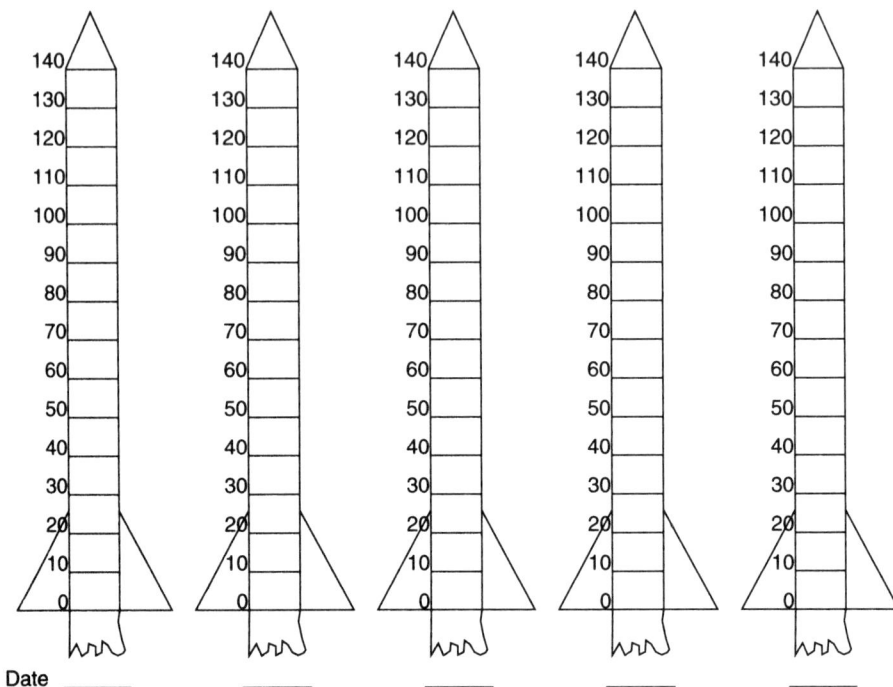

Date _____   _____   _____   _____   _____

Fill in the number of problems you did correctly on the graph.

Source: Adapted from *Helping Young Writers Master the Craft: Strategy Instruction and Self-Regulation in the Writing Process* by K.R. Harris and S. Graham, 1992, Cambridge, MA: Brookline Books. Reprinted by permission.

FIGURE 2   *Example of a Recording System Using Rockets*

It is preferable for the teacher and the student to collaboratively determine target behaviors, define criteria, and establish monitoring and recording procedures. Although collaboration is generally preferable, in some instances the instructor may need to determine and define target behaviors and procedures prior to meeting with the student. The following steps should be followed and the general principles presented apply, however, regardless of whether behaviors are determined collaboratively or by the teacher.

Step 2. Before initiating any self-assessment or self-recording, the teacher should collect information on the student's current level of performance on the target behavior of interest. This need not be a laborious, time-consuming process. For the previous math problem example, information collection might simply involve obtaining past examples of work. In contrast, targets such as being on-task can be more difficult to assess. What is most important is to gain an accurate picture of the student's current performance, not to collect reams of data. One purpose of this information is to allow teachers to assess the effectiveness of the intervention. It also can support goal setting and demonstrate progress after independent self-monitoring has begun. One note of caution: If knowledge of present performance is going to be a negative experience for the student, it is preferable not to share this data.

Step 3. During this step the student learns about self-monitoring. The teacher or the student may put forward a target for self-monitoring (if the target for self-monitoring is not determined until this point, the operational defining of the target discussed in Step 1 should be done here as well). The teacher and the student would then briefly note why the target is important, and the teacher would introduce and discuss the rationale for self-monitoring, discuss the benefits the student will derive, and enlist the student's active cooperation and commitment. The need for the student's willing involvement is not a trivial issue; self-monitoring interventions are unlikely to succeed if students are merely told to self-monitor. With self-monitoring (and other self-regulation procedures), the student is the "active ingredient" and actually runs the intervention after the initial training. Consequently, the student must be an enthusiastic partner rather than a rote follower.

Although teachers should be enthusiastic about self-monitoring and present it in a favorable light, they should avoid sweeping promises or statements of unrealistic benefits. Self-monitoring alone may not be sufficient for some students to improve their performance. For instance, weighing yourself each morning probably will not be enough to lose weight if you have no plans for cutting down what you eat or increasing exercise.

Step 4. After explaining the purpose of self-monitoring and gaining the student's cooperation, the teacher instructs the student in how to use the self-monitoring procedure (Steps 3 and 4 may occur together). In this step the teacher and student discuss (a) what will be self-assessed (e.g., the number of long-division problems correctly completed), (b) the criterion for success (e.g., follow all the division steps and get the correct answer), (c) how to self-record the target behavior (e.g., count up all the problems that met the criterion and graph the number), and (d) when self-monitoring will be done (e.g., during the practice session in the morning).

We use the following procedure with many students to help them learn to self-monitor: The teacher (or another student who has facility with self-monitoring) models the process, verbalizing what is being done at each step. Next the teacher asks the student to verbalize the steps and provides support when necessary. After the student can successfully verbalize the steps, he or she models and verbalizes them independently. Finally, the teacher and the student decide on a time to evaluate the effectiveness of self-monitoring and assess the student's reaction to the self-monitoring procedure. Some students are able to learn to self-monitor with a simple explanation and demonstration; adequate instruction, however, is a must, as the student must clearly understand the self-monitoring procedure to be able to carry it out independently.

When independent self-monitoring begins, the teacher should determine if the student is correctly performing the self-monitoring procedure. The self-monitoring procedure has to be carried out correctly and on a regular basis. If the procedure evokes confusion or problems, a short booster session to review or reteach the procedure should be conducted. Some students may benefit from (at least in the beginning stages) aids such as cards with the self-monitoring steps printed on them as a reminder. Teachers often need not be too concerned if self-recorded data are not extremely accurate; accuracy does not seem to be critical for self-monitoring interventions to be effective (Hallahan & Sapona, 1983; O'Leary & Dubey, 1979). If self-monitoring seems to be done correctly but does not result in improved performance, it may be necessary to teach the student to self-record more accurately, provide feedback or reinforcement (preferably social reinforcement) for accurate self-monitoring, or change the target behavior that is self-monitored.

If self-monitoring is agreeable to the student and is effective, self-monitoring should continue until the student and the teacher agree that it is no longer necessary. In practice, students enjoy using self-monitoring procedures, and self-monitoring can be used over long periods (Hallahan & Sapona, 1983; Harris, 1986b; Reid & Harris, 1989).

Practical Considerations

Self-monitoring is not a learning strategy. It should not be done exclusively to develop a skill or to teach new skills. Teaching students to self-monitor the number of division problems completed correctly, for instance, will have little effect if the student does not possess an effective long-division strategy (Reid & Harris, 1989). For self-monitoring to have meaningful effects, students must have the ability or knowledge to perform the process or to create the product that will be self-monitored. Self-monitoring also can be combined effectively with other instructional techniques such as strategy instruction (see Harris & Graham, 1985, for an example).

Teachers should not combine self-monitoring with rewards that are contingent on students' self-recorded data. Rewards based on students' self-records often lead to cheating or inaccurate self-recording. The student's focus then shifts from self-regulating to obtaining the reward. Students' self-recording is typically accurate, and self-monitoring is effective without extrinsic rewards or reinforcers (e.g., Hallahan & Sapona, 1983; Reid & Harris, 1989).

Although the student actually runs the intervention, the teacher has to show interest, to regularly evaluate the student's self-records, and to give positive social reinforcement for effort and achievement. With a supportive teacher, self-monitoring is pleasant and students are willing to self-monitor over long periods. In our experience, students often choose to continue self-monitoring even when given the option to stop.

Finally, deciding when or if self-monitoring should be terminated or a new target should be set should be done collaboratively. If a decision is made to terminate self-monitoring, the teacher and the student may want to phase out self-monitoring gradually rather than abruptly. A "weaning process" is often desirable; it can lead to maintenance of performance gains. This could be done by gradually cutting back on the days when the student self-monitors or by eliminating a step or more in the self-monitoring process (e.g., eliminating the self-recording step and using only self-assessment).

SELF-REINFORCEMENT

Self-reinforcement occurs when a student chooses a reinforcer and self-administers it when a criterion for performance has been met or exceeded. Self-reinforcement can be used alone and may be as effective as teacher-administered reinforcement (cf. O'Leary & Dubey, 1979; Rosenbaum & Drabman, 1979). In principle, self-reinforcement requires students to have full control over available reinforcers and freely impose contingencies for the self-administration of these reinforcers in the relative absence of any external influences (i.e., without the teacher's supervision). In the classroom, this level of control may not be possible, at least initially. As with all self-regulation processes, the effective transition from collaborative evaluation and reinforcement from others to self-evaluation and reinforcement is often gradual.

This process is analogous to the natural development of other self-regulation processes (Zimmerman & Schunk, 1989). At first, parents and other adults provide the child with standards for reinforcement. The child learns through interactions with adults that meeting or exceeding standards usually produces a positive response and that failing to meet standards may evoke little response or a negative response. Gradually children come to respond to their own behavior in self-rewarding (or self-punishing) ways. Whereas self-punishment is inadvisable, helping students to learn to self-reinforce, or to improve self-reinforcement procedures already in place, should play an integral role in helping them become self-regulated learners.

In practice, self-reinforcement usually is not done by itself. Rather, it is employed in conjunction with the other self-regulation procedures already discussed in this article. For example, we have found that many students respond nicely to simple, self-reinforcing statements (as discussed in the previous section on self-instruction) when they are used in combination with goal setting or self-monitoring. Using positive self-statements as a form of self-reinforcement tends to be easy for students to do and follows naturally from both goal setting and self-monitoring. It is hard to imagine students reaching meaningful goals and not rewarding themselves with positive self-statements.

Teaching Self-Reinforcement to Students

Self-reinforcement involves four basic components (Harris & Graham, 1992):

1. Determining the standards for earning a reward.
2. Selecting the reinforcer to be earned.
3. Evaluating performance.
4. Self-administering the reinforcer.

Students can be taught to self-reinforce both as they work and once a task or product has been completed. For example, as they work, students can self-reinforce the completion of subgoals for accomplishing the task, the generation of a new idea for completing the task, and so forth.

In helping students learn to apply self-reinforcement principles, the teacher and the student both need to play an active role. To illustrate, in initiating the change from other-reinforcement to self-reinforcement, the teacher and the student can set performance levels that will earn an agreed-upon amount of reinforcement. For example, if increasing the rate of homework completion is a desirable goal, the teacher and the student can jointly set standards for reinforcement. If the student wants more time on the computer (student-determined reinforcer), the teacher and student could look at the student's rate of homework completion and decide that each homework assignment successfully completed will earn the student 3 minutes of computer time.

During the initial phase of implementation, the teacher might (depending upon the child's age and competence) be responsible for ascertaining that the homework has been completed successfully; however, the teacher and the student would gradually shift responsibility to the student. When this occurs, the teacher becomes an observer, offering suggestions and advice when the need arises.

Practical Considerations

With self-reinforcement, one of the first issues that must be addressed is to determine the level or standard of performance that must be obtained for reinforcement to be forthcoming. As noted in the section on goal setting, many students need guidance during this step to set reasonable and appropriate standards. Students may, for example, adopt a lenient standard of performance. In helping students learn to self-reinforce, stringent standards usually result in higher performance levels than do lenient standards. Nonetheless, the level at which standards are set should be tempered by knowledge of students' abilities and current functional levels. "Stringent" is a relative term. What is lenient for one student may be unrealistic for another.

Students who set overly lenient standards for themselves may need prompting on more appropriate standards or may need the teacher's assistance in setting realistic standards. One approach is to allow fairly lenient standards initially but to increase the standards progressively. This method is particularly helpful with students who lack confidence or who have a great deal of anxiety regarding the target task. Conversely, some students set unrealistically high standards. This is not good, because self-reinforcement is unlikely to occur. These students also need assistance in setting reasonable expectations for themselves.

Similar problems arise when students evaluate their progress toward the goals or standards they plan to self-reinforce. Some students judge their own performance more harshly than their teacher does; others are easier on themselves than the teacher is. To obtain accurate self-evaluations, some students need to work closely with the teacher at first. Accurate self-evaluations are particularly difficult for students when less objective processes and products are to be evaluated, such as how well they cleaned up after an art project or how well they understood a reading assignment. For this reason, self-reinforcement instruction should begin with more concrete aspects of performance such as: (a) Were all the parts of an essay present? or (b) How many comprehension questions did I answer correctly?

The actual procedure a student uses to self-reinforce should be clear and specific. In our experience, if these procedures are determined conjointly by the teacher and the student, they work best. Making a concrete record of the procedure to be employed is a good idea. This avoids misunderstandings and also gives the student a written set of steps to follow if he or she needs a reminder.

While self-reinforcement is occurring, the teacher should administer social reinforcement, especially social reinforcement for engaging in self-reinforcement. This need not be elaborate; praise, a hug, smile, or pat on the back will do the job nicely. Social reinforcement should continue throughout the intervention. Social reinforcement from peers, parents, and teachers continues to be important. Over time, students should be encouraged to shift from tangible reinforcers (if these are being used) to self-praise and positive self-statements. These forms of reinforcement may eventually replace tangible reinforcers to a great extent; even competent adult performers (such as the authors of this article) however, sometimes welcome tangible self-reinforcement.

Finally, students' motivational characteristics often play an important role in the success or failure of self-reinforcement. Students who are motivated by feelings of self-satisfaction and who view success or failure as a function of their effort (or lack of effort) may respond positively to self-reinforcement and find that it results in better performance. In contrast, students who see success or failure as the result of external agencies and as being fundamentally beyond their control may have more difficulty with self-reinforcement. This does not contraindicate the use of self-reinforcement with these students. On the contrary, it may help instill motivation based on self-satisfaction and help them recognize the importance of their own efforts. These students, however, may require a more gradual transition from teacher reinforcement to self-reinforcement, more time and assistance to attain competence in using self-reinforcement, and help in developing effort attributions (cf. Licht, 1983).

CONCLUSIONS

Even though the development of self-regulation processes is an important part of learning and maturing, we would not advocate self-regulation instruction with every student in every setting. Some children already possess effective self-regulation strategies. In fact, some children are so good at regulating their behavior that they regulate not only their own behavior but that of their peers and sometimes their teachers as well (Meichenbaum & Beimiller, in press). We would like to encourage the reader, however, to apply the types of procedures and strategies discussed here as a complement or possible alternative to more traditional procedures. Exclusive reliance on methods that are solely directed and administered by others with students who have difficulty regulating their own behavior may well be teaching a hidden curriculum—namely, that only others can control the student's behavior. One of the primary values of teaching students procedures for regulating their own behavior is that is provides them with basic and powerful tools for self-empowerment.

REFERENCES

Bandura, A., & Schunk, D. (1981). Cultivating competence, self-efficacy, and intrinsic interest through proximal self-motivation. *Journal of Personality and Social Psychology, 41,* 586–598.
Bandura, A., & Simon, K. (1977). The role of proximal intentions in self-regulation of refractory behavior. *Cognitive Therapy & Research, 1,* 177–193.

Brown, A., & Campione, J. (1981). Inducing flexible thinking: A problem of access. In M. Freidman, J. Das, N. O'Connor (Eds.), *Intelligence and learning* (pp. 515–529). New York: Plenum.

Fuson, K. (1979). The development of self-regulating aspects of speech: A review. In G. Zivin (Ed.), *The development of self-regulation through private speech* (pp. 135–218). New York: Wiley.

Graham, S. (1983). The effects of self-instructional procedures on LD students' handwriting performance. *Learning Disability Quarterly, 6,* 231–234.

Graham, S., & Harris, K. R. (1987). Improving composition skills of inefficient learners with self-instructional strategy training. *Topics in Language Disorders, 7,* 66–77.

Graham, S., & Harris, K. R. (1989). Cognitive training: Implications for written language. In J. Hughes & R. Hall (Eds.), *Cognitive behavioral psychology in the schools: A comprehensive handbook* (pp. 247–279). New York: Guilford.

Graham, S., & Harris, K. R. (in press). Self-instructional strategy development: Programmatic research in writing. In B. Wong (Ed.), *Intervention research with students with learning disabilities: An international perspective.* New York: Springer Verlag.

Graham, S., Harris, K. R., MacArthur, C., & Schwartz, S. (1991). Writing and writing instruction with students with learning disabilities: A review of a program of research. *Learning Disability Quarterly, 14,* 89–114.

Graham, S., Harris, K. R., & Sawyer, R. (1987). Composition instruction with learning disabled students: Self-instructional strategy training. *Focus on Exceptional Children, 20,* 1–11.

Graham, S., MacArthur, C., Schwartz, S., & Voth, T. (in press). Improving LD students' compositions using a strategy involving product and process goal-setting. *Exceptional Children.*

Gresham, F. (1985). Utility of cognitive-behavioral procedures for social skills training with children: A critical review. *Journal of Abnormal Child Psychology, 13,* 411–424.

Hallahan, D. P., & Sapona, R. (1983). Self-monitoring of attention with learning disabled children: Past research and current issues. *Journal of Learning Disabilities, 16,* 616–620.

Harris, K. R. (1982). Cognitive-behavior modification: Application with exceptional students. *Focus on Exceptional Children, 15,* 1–16.

Harris, K. R. (1986a). The effects of cognitive-behavior modification on private speech and task performance during problem solving among learning disabled and normally achieving children. *Journal of Abnormal Child Psychology, 14,* 63–76.

Harris, K. R. (1986b). Self-monitoring of attentional behavior vs. self-monitoring of productivity: Effects on on-task behavior and academic response rate among learning disabled children. *Journal of Applied Behavior Analysis, 19,* 417–423.

Harris, K. R. (1990). Developing self-regulated learners: The role of private speech and self-instructions. *Educational Psychologist, 25,* 35–50.

Harris, K. R., & Graham, S. (1985). Improving learning disabled students' composition skills: Self-control strategy training. *Learning Disability Quarterly, 8,* 27–36.

Harris, K. R., & Graham, S. (1992). *Helping young writers master the craft: Strategy instruction and self-regulation in the writing process.* Boston: Brookline Books.

Harris, K. R. & Graham, S. (in press). Self-regulated strategy development: A part of the writing process. In M. Pressley, K. R. Harris, & J. Guthrie (Eds.), *Promoting academic competence and literacy: Cognitive research and instructional innovation.* New York: Academic Press.

Johnson, L., & Graham, S. (1990). Goal setting and its application with exceptional learners. *Preventing School Failure, 34,* 4–8.

Latham, G., & Yukl, G. (1975). A review of research on the application of goal setting in organizations. *Academy of Management Journal, 18,* 824–845.

Licht, B. (1983). Cognitive-motivational factors that contribute to the achievement of learning-disabled children. *Journal of Learning Disabilities, 16,* 483–490.

Locke, E., Shaw, K., Saari, L., & Latham, G. (1981). Goal setting and task performance: 1969–1980. *Psychological Bulletin, 90,* 125–152.

Mahoney, M., & Thoresen, C. (Eds.) (1974). *Self-control: Power to the person.* Belmont, CA: Wadsworth.

Masters, J., Furman, W., & Barden, R. (1977). Effects of achievement standards, tangible rewards, and self-dispensed achievement evaluations on children's task mastery. *Child Development, 48,* 217–224.

Meichenbaum, D. (1977). *Cognitive behavior modification: An integrative approach.* New York: Plenum Press.

Meichenbaum, D., & Biemiller, A. (in press). In search of student expertise in the classroom: A metacognitive analysis. In M. Pressley, K. R. Harris, & J. Guthrie (Eds.), *Promoting academic competence and literacy: Cognitive research and instructional innovation.* New York: Academic Press.

Meichenbaum, D., & Goodman, S. (1979). Clinical use of private speech and critical questions about its study in natural settings. In G. Zivin (Ed.), *The development of self-regulation through private speech* (pp. 325–360). New York: Wiley.

Nelson, R. O. (1977). Methodological issues in assessment via self-monitoring. In J. D. Cone & R. P. Hawkins (Eds.), *Behavioral Assessment: New directions in clinical psychology.* New York: Brunner/Mazel.

O'Leary, S., & Dubey, D. (1979). Applications of self-control procedures by children: A review. *Journal of Applied Behavior Analysis, 12,* 449–465.

Reid, R., & Harris, K. R. (1989). Self-monitoring of performance. *LD Forum, 15,* 39–42.

Rosenbaum, M., & Drabman, R. (1979). Self-control training in the classroom: A review and critique. *Journal of Applied Behavior Analysis, 18,* 467–485.

Sawyer, R., Graham, S., & Harris, K. R. (1991). Theoretically based effects of strategy instruction on learning disabled students' acquisition, maintenance, and generalization of composition skills and self-efficacy. Manuscript submitted for publications.

Scardamalia, M., & Bereiter, C. (1985). Fostering the development of self-regulation in children's knowledge processing. In S. Chipman, J. Segal, & R. Glaser (Eds.), *Thinking and learning skills: Current research and open questions* (Vol. 2, pp. 563–577). Hillsdale, NJ: Lawrence Erlbaum.

Schunk, D. (1985). Participation in goal setting: Effects on self-efficacy and skills of learning-disabled children. *Journal of Special Education, 19,* 307–317.

Schunk, D. (1989). Self-efficacy and cognitive achievement: Implications for students with learning disabilities. *Journal of Learning Disabilities, 22,* 14–22.

Vygotsky, L. (1962). *Thought and language.* Cambridge, MA: MIT Press (Original work published 1934).

Wong, B. Y. L., & Jones, W. (1982). Increasing metacomprehension in learning-disabled and normally-achieving students through self-questioning training. *Learning Disability Quarterly, 5,* 228–240.

Zimmerman, B., & Schunk, D. (1989). *Self-regulated learning and academic achievement: Theory, research, and practice.* New York: Springer Verlag.

Zivin, G. (Ed.). (1979). *The development of self-regulation through private speech.* New York: Wiley.

Steve Graham is a professor and Karen R. Harris is an associate professor at the University of Maryland, College Park. Robert Reid is an assistant professor at the University of Nebraska, Lincoln. Authorship for this article was determined alphabetically.

○ 9 ○

Educators have endorsed the strategies approach that came out of the University of Kansas Institute on Learning Disabilities. These learning strategies emphasize the individual's personal approach to learning: how the person thinks, memorizes or learns, studies, and organizes or conducts other personal learning tasks. Research has shown these learning strategies to be effective at the elementary through high school levels. The authors review basic instructional principles and the components of an instructional model that may facilitate generalization of the strategy training.

An Instructional Model for Teaching Learning Strategies

Edwin S. Ellis, Donald D. Deshler, B. Keith Lenz, Jean B. Schumaker, and Frances L. Clark

Over the past decade, remedial and special educators have become increasingly aware of the need to identify and use instructional techniques and curricula that promote their students' independence and success in the academic and social realms. Many educators have begun teaching their students strategies as a primary means for achieving this goal. *A strategy is an individual's approach to a task;* it includes how the person thinks and acts when planning, executing, and evaluating performance on a task and its outcomes (Deshler & Lenz, 1989). Many types of strategies are required for an individual to effectively and efficiently complete the array of academic tasks encountered in school. The use of specific learning strategies helps an individual approach the learning tasks.

For example, one might use the learning strategy Multipass (Schumaker, Deshler, Alley, & Denton, 1982) to learn the important information in a textbook chapter. Likewise, a student might use Error Monitoring Strategy (Schumaker, Nolan, & Deshler, 1985) to find and correct errors in a written product.

Learning strategies such as these have been designed to enable students to effectively and efficiently meet the academic demands they encounter in their school environments

151

(Deshler & Schumaker, 1988; Putnam, 1988). Many studies have demonstrated that learning disabled and other low-achieving students are able to master various learning strategies and to independently apply them to meet the demands of elementary, secondary, and postsecondary settings (e.g., Deshler & Schumaker, 1986; Harris & Graham, 1985; Palincsar & Brown, 1984; Pressley, Goodchild, Fleet, Zajchowski, & Evans, 1989; Wong & Jones, 1982).

Although several approaches to teaching learning strategies have been described and many appear promising, exactly what constitutes a set of "best practices" for facilitating acquisition and generalization of strategies by students at various age and performance levels has remained unclear. To address this issue, researchers at the University of Kansas Institute for Research in Learning Disabilities (KU-IRLD) have spent the past 15 years focusing on the specification of a set of best practices for teaching strategies to adolescents who are not succeeding in school settings. This research has been conducted primarily with adolescents with learning disabilities and other mildly handicapped populations, and the major goal associated with the research has been to teach strategies that these students can successfully apply to classroom assignments in secondary mainstream settings.

Instead of focusing on teaching simple strategies that can be applied to laboratory tasks, KU-IRLD research has focused on teaching "strategy systems" for approaching the complex learning tasks encountered in mainstream settings. Each strategy system is a collection of simple strategies integrated into one instructional routine that a student can use to effectively meet a curriculum demand (Deshler & Lenz, 1989). One example of a strategy system is the FIRST-Letter Mnemonic Strategy (Nagel, Schumaker, & Deshler, 1986), which includes strategies for creating lists of information and memorizing those lists in preparation for a test. Naturally, the notion of what constitutes effective learning strategy instruction has evolved as more and more of these strategies have been created, as additional research has been conducted, and as more than 25,000 teachers have taught these learning strategies to students and provided feedback about the process.

Two important domains that can have an effect on the ultimate success or failure of strategy training are: (a) a student's knowledge of critical skills and information related to strategy use including the student's motivation to learn and use the strategy, and (b) general instructional principles that have been found to be important in teaching learning strategies to students. A *working* model of the instructional methodology that has emerged and that reflects a series of instructional stages will be presented here. The term "working model" is appropriate because of the continuing evolution of ideas regarding the instructional process related to learning strategies. An earlier version of this model first appeared in Deshler, Alley, Warner, & Schumaker (1981). Although the instructional procedures described in this earlier work have been found to be effective for many students, much has been learned about the technology involved in teaching learning strategies that can potentially increase the likelihood of strategy acquisition and generalization. The model presented in this article represents the evolution of the original model to this point in time and will be used as a framework upon which future KU-IRLD research regarding methodology for teaching learning strategies will be based.

CRITICAL FACTORS AFFECTING STRATEGIC PERFORMANCE

For training in the use of learning strategies to have a significant impact on student success, the instruction must be intensive and extensive (Pressley, Goodchild, Fleet, Zajchowski, & Evans, 1987; Slavin, 1989). Of the many factors that may affect the ultimate success or failure of strategy training, two important domains are: (a) students' knowledge of critical skills and information that are potentially related to a strategy's use, and (b) students' motivation to learn and use the strategy. Figure 1 provides a summary of what a number of professionals (e.g., Pressley, Snyder, & Cariglia-Bull, 1987; Swanson, 1989; Wong, 1985) view as the essential components of these two domains.

With regard to these two domains, this figure summarizes the critical types of knowledge and skills associated with learning and using a new strategy. In addition, it highlights some of the teaching behaviors that characterize the instructional practices emphasized by less effective strategy teachers and more effective strategy teachers.

The Knowledge Domain

Successful learning and performance are contingent on the type and level of knowledge a student possesses across four areas. These areas include: (a) *process knowledge*, related to the essential cognitive and metacognitive strategies required for problem solving, (b) *semantic knowledge*, related to what the student already knows and can automatically access for use in problem solving, (c) *procedural knowledge*, related to how skills and strategies are organized to promote successful task completion, and (d) *conditional knowledge*, related to judging when and how strategies should be applied.

Process Knowledge
To effectively employ a learning strategy, students must possess essential process knowledge. Process knowledge includes knowing how to perform specific cognitive strategies (e.g., summarizing, question generating, predicting, monitoring to confirm) that might be required when performing a specific step of the learning strategy. For example, in the reading comprehension strategy called the Paraphrasing Strategy (Schumaker, Deshler, & Denton, 1984), illustrated in Figure 2, the second step of the strategy, "Ask yourself, 'What were the main idea and details in this paragraph?'", cues the student to use a self-questioning cognitive strategy after a paragraph has been read to identify the main ideas and details.

Process knowledge also involves knowing how to use the metacognitive self-regulation processes associated with effective application of these cognitive strategies when performing a specific step of a learning strategy. For example, metacognition comes into play while applying self-questioning (a cognitive strategy) within the second step of the Paraphrasing Strategy. Students may check the first sentence of the paragraph, generate a hypothesis about what they believe is the main idea, and then skim the rest of the paragraph to confirm their hypothesis. As new information from the paragraph is gained, however, students, realizing that what they thought was the main idea is not, modify the hypothesis to conform with what they have learned. This process, monitoring the accu-

KNOWLEDGE DOMAIN

MOTIVATIONAL DOMAIN

	Process Knowledge	Semantic Knowledge	Procedural Knowledge	Conditional Knowledge	Belief Systems	Self-motivation Techniques
Critical features of knowledge and skills associated with learning and using a new strategy	Knowledge of various cognitive strategies used when performing a strategy step Metacognitive knowledge • awareness of thinking style • use of self-regulation processes	Mastery of basic prerequisite skills for a strategy Acquired content-knowledge base	Knowledge of strategy steps Knowing why each step is important Knowing how to use self-instruction to cue use of steps	Knowledge of match or mismatch between problem's critical features & the strategy Recognition of environmental cues to use the strategy Recognition of need to adapt the strategy to meet various conditions	Beliefs about: • self • value of task • commitments to other strategies	Use of self-statements • coping • affirmation Use of goal-setting Use of self-reinforcement
Observations of less effective strategy teachers	Teachers not usually taught to think in information-processing terms Teachers often unaware of own mental processes	Many students do not possess prerequisite skills; tendency to ignore prerequisites or teach them and the strategy at the same time Some teachers have not identified stratgey prerequisites	Often focus only on procedure, not thinking processes involved in the procedure Often focus on rote memorization of procedure	Due to perceived time constraints, instruction of conditional knowledge is often sacrificed	Tendency to either ignore or be intimidated by students' beliefs	Tendency to reinforce extrinsic orientation by . . . • setting goals for students • use of exaggerated praise • use of extrinsic reinforcers
Observations of more effective strategy teachers	Teachers overtly model covert self-regulation thoughts	Prerequisites are identified and mastered by students prior to strategy instruction Content-knowledge base is expanded by linking new information to existing knowledge structures	Instruction focuses on facilitating students' elaboration of strategy procedure (what doing and why) • overall procedure • each step of the procedure	Extensive guided and independent practice is provided to facilitate and expand conditional knowledge	Teach students to: • use affirmation statements • use self-coping statements • set goals & monitor progress • use self-reinforcement techniques	

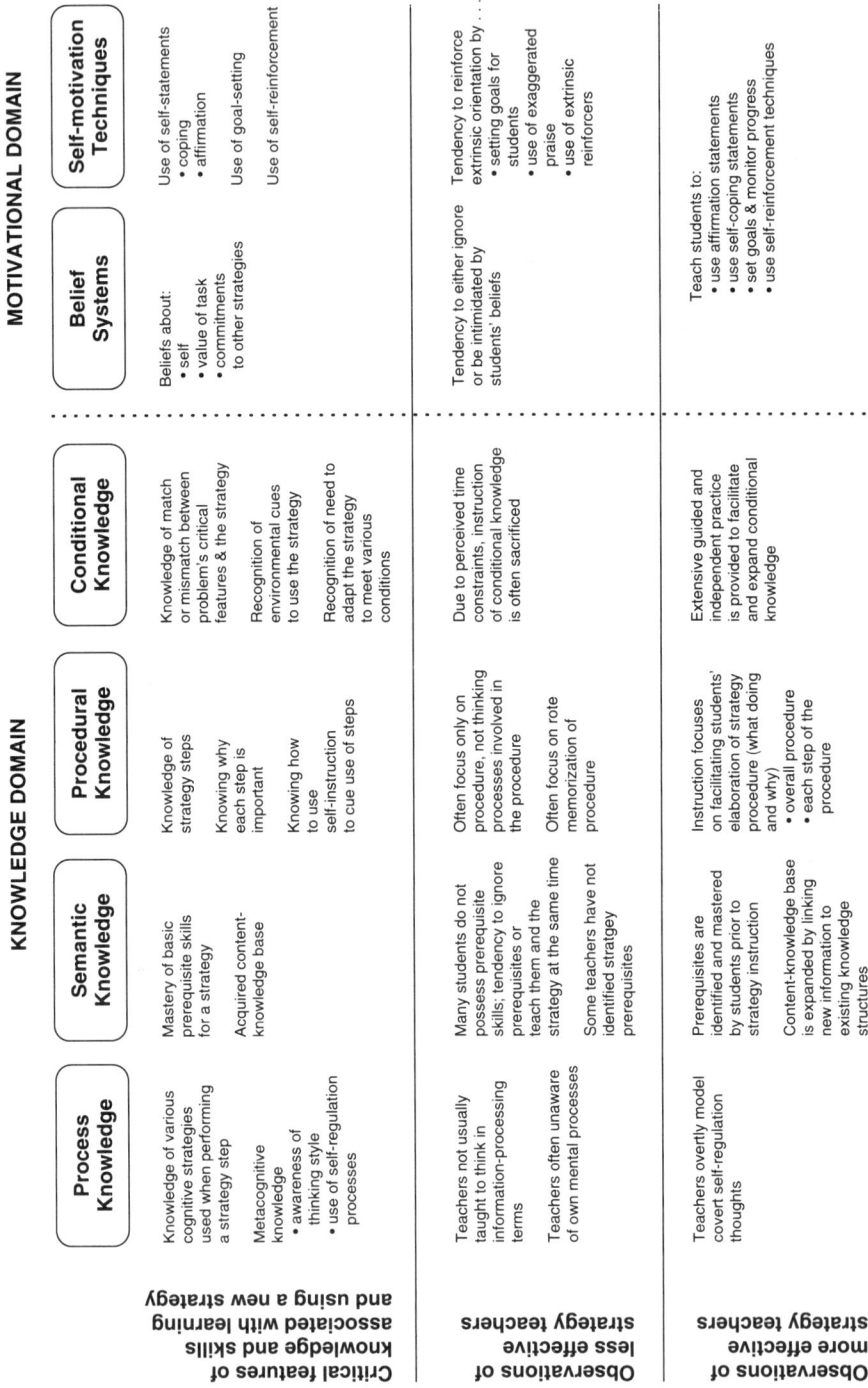

FIGURE 1   Critical Factors Affecting Strategic Performance

Read a paragraph

As you are reading the paragraph, look for a topic sentence or clue words that reveal the main idea and details.

Ask yourself, "What were the main idea and details in this paragraph?"

Ask yourself, "What was this paragraph about?" and "What should I remember about it?"

Put the main idea and details into your own words

Say, "This paragraph is about _____."

FIGURE 2   *The Paraphrasing Strategy*

racy of the hypothesis and modifying it as necessary, illustrates metacognition in action. Thus, a student who possesses this type of knowledge has a repertoire of cognitive and metacognitive processes and knows how and when to appropriately apply them.

Unfortunately, many teachers are not taught to think about how their students process information, and they often are unaware of their own mental processes (Pressley et al., 1987). Thus, when attempting to teach a new strategy, less effective teachers often fail to adequately model the critical cognitive and metacognitive processes involved when performing a specific step of a learning strategy. Instead, they tend to model self-instruction at the most rudimentary level.

For example, the teacher might say, "Let's see, the next step of the RAP Strategy is 'A'—Ask myself, 'What were the main idea and details in this paragraph?'" and then jump to naming a main idea ("Let's see, one main idea is that you should travel light when backpacking."). Here, the teacher modeled self-cuing of the next step of the strategy but failed to model any of the cognitive and metacognitive processes involved in determining the main idea.

An effective-strategy teacher would perform aloud all of the processes involved in asking oneself questions, reviewing the topic sentence, forming a hypothesis, checking the remainder of the paragraph to confirm or reject the hypothesis, and recycling the processes when necessary, as well as stating the outcome of the processes (naming the main idea). To be effective strategy teachers, then, covert thinking processes should be overtly modeled and mental "leaps" should be avoided.

Semantic Knowledge

In addition to knowing how to perform cognitive and metacognitive strategies, a student must possess semantic knowledge, to initially master a new learning strategy and to subsequently employ the strategy to meet the demands of mainstream environments. One aspect of semantic knowledge concerns students' mastery of prerequisite skills necessary to perform the strategy (e.g., prior to teaching students an error monitoring strategy to use in correcting mechanical errors in their writing, the teacher must ensure that they have knowledge of key capitalization and punctuation rules). One of the critical features of an effective learning strategy is that it enables students to strategically apply known skills or procedures. As a result, students must have the necessary skills in their repertoires before they can learn how to strategically apply them.

Unfortunately, when teaching a new strategy, less effective teachers often attempt to teach these prerequisite skills and the strategy simultaneously. Other less effective strategy teachers fail to even identify the required prerequisite skills, and thus they entirely ignore teaching them during the instructional process. Attempting to teach a strategy at the same time as teaching the prerequisite skills or ignoring these skills altogether often results in frustrated students and discouraged teachers. For strategy instruction to be efficient, students must have mastered these skills before strategy instruction begins.

A second aspect of semantic knowledge concerns the degree of acquired knowledge (content-area information) students should possess before attempting to apply a new learning strategy. For example, application of the Paraphrasing Strategy for enhancing reading comprehension is extremely difficult when the material the student is reading addresses a topic about which the student has little semantic knowledge; a strategy for writing well organized paragraphs is of little use when attempting to write on a topic about which the student knows very little; a strategy for identifying words when reading is of little use when the word to be identified is not in the student's listening vocabulary.

The implications associated with these problems are threefold. *First*, teachers must ensure that instruction is continuously provided, building the student's background knowledge in the content areas in which strategies will be employed so the student can benefit from the application of strategies. Furthermore, instruction in the content areas must facilitate students' connection of new information they are taught with the information they already possess. Apparently many teachers presume that students will automatically make these associations, but many students do not (Lenz, Alley, & Schumaker, 1987).

Second, students should be expected to learn content and meet the demands of content learning situations in order to practice and perfect strategy applications. Removing students from learning situations or reducing content learning demands inhibits the potential for both strategy and content acquisition (Ellis & Lenz, 1990).

Third, support-class teachers and content-area teachers must define their roles and responsibilities concerning responsibility for content and strategy acquisition. The appropriate personnel should discuss and assume the responsibilities associated with employing specific procedures for promoting strategy acquisition and generalization, as described in this article, as well as the responsibilities associated with strategically enhancing content delivery (Deshler & Schumaker, 1988; Ellis & Lenz, 1990; Lenz & Bulgren, 1990; Lenz, Bulgren, & Hudson, 1988; Schumaker, Deshler, & McKnight, 1989)

By addressing these areas, students will likely retain more information and subsequently will be able to independently learn more content when using learning strategies. If these areas are not addressed, students will retain less of the information, which in turn will limit the efficacy of the strategy. Students will know less and, thus, will be less able to apply the strategies they know.

Procedural Knowledge

Having process knowledge and semantic knowledge is not sufficient to enable a student to successfully perform a strategy. Students also must possess procedural knowledge, which concerns what students know about the specific procedures, or routines, to be used when performing a strategy. Procedural knowledge is related to how familiar students are with the specific steps of a given strategy, how they are sequenced, and why each step is essential to completing the learning task. Procedural knowledge also includes the skills involved when employing self-instruction to use the strategy steps when encountering a barrier to task completion. During instances such as these, students' procedural knowledge allows them to regulate their use of the strategy steps in solving the problem before them.

Less effective strategy teachers tend to limit the information they communicate about a strategy by only rudimentarily addressing procedural knowledge at the expense of facilitating comprehension of the procedures and communicating information about the thinking processes required. Often, the focus is on rote memorization of the strategy steps rather than on promoting the student's understanding of what each step entails and why the steps are important to the overall problem-solving process.

To facilitate acquisition of procedural knowledge, more effective teachers prompt students to verbally elaborate on the strategic process, both on a global level (e.g., they ask students to describe what the overall procedure is designed to do and why) and on an atomistic level (e.g., they ask students to specify the overt and covert behaviors that each step in the procedure is designed to cue students to use and why these are important to the overall problem-solving procedure). Students should be able to describe, in their own words, what they are generally doing when they perform the strategy and what they hope to accomplish as a result of using it. In addition, they should be able to describe each step of the strategy, what it is designed to do, and why it is important to the problem-solving routine.

Conditional Knowledge

Many students demonstrate high levels of competency when applying a new learning strategy while interacting with training materials, but they rarely, if ever, use it to meet the learning demands outside of the remedial setting. In short, they may have gained process, semantic, and procedural knowledge, but they have not gained enough conditional knowledge to make the strategy a functional problem-solving tool in the "real world." Conditional knowledge is the information students use to recognize a match or mismatch between the critical features of a given problem and the capability of a specific strategy to solve the problem. For example, they may not recognize that the critical features of a task related to writing a current-event report for a social studies class (e.g., explaining one's reaction to a news item) match a strategy for point-of-view writing (Ellis, Courtney, & Church, in press). Thus, learning a new strategy involves learning the conditions under which the strategy should be used. Students must learn to recognize the naturally occurring cues in the environment that signal opportunities to use the new strategy.

Students also must be able to adapt a learned strategy to match different but similar demands. For example, when the teacher directs students to write a book report using their own words to describe the book, they should be able to adapt the Paraphrasing Strategy (a reading comprehension strategy) to translate information into their own words for the book report. Unfortunately, although many teachers value strategy instruction enough to devote some instructional time to it, they often sacrifice instruction related to promoting conditional knowledge so that they can proceed to instruction in other strategies, skills, or content-area information. Sadly, the net result is often a total waste of time because students never learn how to generalize the strategies they have learned, and thus rarely use the strategies in the situations for which they had been taught and do not adapt them for use in other situations.

To expand conditional knowledge so that generalization is more likely to occur, a number of instructional initiatives on the part of the teacher appear desirable:

- Conducting guided and independent practice accompanied by individual feedback on a wide variety of stimulus materials with varying levels of difficulty.
- Providing opportunities for students to discuss and elaborate on use of and adaptation of the strategy.
- Facilitating goal setting related to generalization.
- Establishing the expectation of generalization.
- Structuring specific and varied transfer activities.

In summary, when teaching learning strategies to students, four types of knowledge must be addressed if they are to be expected to effectively learn and apply the new strategies to meet the demands of mainstream settings. *Process knowledge* enables students to perform the necessary cognitive and metacognitive strategies included in a learning strategy. *Semantic knowledge* enables students to perform other necessary skills involved in the strategy and provides them with a knowledge base upon which strategy use can build. *Procedural knowledge* enables students to put together the cognitive and metacognitive strategies and other nonstrategic skills into a fluid sequence. *Conditional knowledge* enables students to adapt the learning strategy where necessary and to apply it in appropriate situations outside of the remedial setting.

The Motivational Domain

The second domain of critical factors affecting strategic performance concerns students' motivation to learn and use a strategy. Student motivation can play as critical a role in the learning process as varying levels and types of knowledge. Typically, students targeted for learning strategy instruction are the same students who have been described as unmotivated and inactive participants in the educational setting (Deshler, Schumaker, & Lenz, 1984). Unfortunately, many educators identify fixed personality traits, such as temperament, as the cause of motivational problems and thereby preclude intervention in the motivational domain. A more profitable approach to the motivational problem considers students' belief systems and their use of self-motivation techniques as important targets of the instructional program.

Belief Systems

What students believe about themselves, the problems or tasks they encounter, the underlying principles to which they attribute the occurrence of certain actions or outcomes, and the effectiveness of the problems-solving strategies designed to address these problems can have a significant impact on their receptivity to learn and subsequently employ new strategies. For example, some students who have experienced a history of failure and who view themselves as incapable are skeptical of interventions designed to enable them to become capable. Many of these students have a tendency to rely on others for direction, goal setting, and reinforcement.

Students' beliefs about the relative merits of performing academic tasks naturally impact the extent to which they are willing to exert energies to undertake the tasks. For example, if they do not value the content they are learning in science class (i.e., do not believe the knowledge will be helpful to them), they will be less likely to complete science assignments and less likely to apply strategies to those assignments.

Likewise, students' beliefs in their old learning habits will have an impact on their willingness to learn new ways of approaching academic tasks. Many students seem to be thoroughly committed to using less efficient or effective strategies when learning or performing and are thus less willing to learn or use new strategies.

Some teachers seem to be intimidated by what they perceive to be students' beliefs. They perceive the student as resistant to learning, in general, and to strategy instruction, in specific, and consequently teach new learning strategies in a rudimentary or nondemanding fashion so that their rapport with students is not jeopardized. This instruction is less than effective because students do not receive the corrective feedback necessary to master the new strategy, and they often do not receive sufficient opportunities to practice using the strategy.

Effective strategy teachers use a variety of techniques to help their students alter their belief systems with regard to academic performance and use of strategies. *First*, they engineer instructional arrangements to promote and reinforce independence on the part of students. The more that students find that they are able to independently make choices and proceed through the learning process, the more likely they will adopt beliefs that are congruent with the notion that they can be effective learners.

Second, they communicate high expectations for their students through their words and actions. Students are more likely to believe that they can achieve challenging goals if others in their environment believe that they can achieve them as well.

Third, they help students identify and analyze beliefs that underlie their behavior as ineffective learners. The Control Model, developed by Bennett (1987), provides a framework for teachers to use in helping students identify the underlying beliefs they have adopted to meet certain needs (the need to feel important, or to have self esteem, the need for variety, the need to love and be loved, the need for survival, and so on), which ultimately govern much of their behavior. Through discussion of this model, teachers can, if necessary, help students understand how their beliefs might be functioning to undermine their success.

Fourth, they help students discard unproductive beliefs through a variety of means:

- They carefully orchestrate the types of assignments given to individual students. Thus, each assignment is carefully planned so that the student is afforded an opportunity to connect success with use of the strategy. Through a series of successes, students can begin to discard the belief that they cannot be successful and to adopt the belief that they can be successful when they use the strategy.
- The teachers tune into their students' verbal and physical behaviors so that they can identify students whose belief systems are incompatible with successful strategy usage.
- Once students are identified, effective teachers spend considerable time prompting the students' verbal expression of negative beliefs, discussing the impact of these beliefs on performance, modeling positive self-talk, prompting positive self-talk, and providing feedback about self-talk.
- The teachers permeate their strategy instruction with rationales and statements that connect use of the strategy with benefits the students can achieve for themselves.
- When success has been realized, these teachers spend time with the students comparing current performances with previous performances and celebrating the progress students have made. A major aspect of this comparison process involves helping students discover and articulate how their beliefs about themselves, their environment, and the strategies they have recently acquired have changed over time.

In short, through an emphasis on student beliefs, teachers help students see their surroundings and themselves within those surroundings in a significantly different way. Seeing things (or oneself) in a "different way" has been referred to as a "paradigm shift." Kuhn (1970) referred to the power of paradigm shifts in science that have enabled researchers to break with tradition and their old ways of thinking and to enable them to make new discoveries and breakthroughs as a result of their new or altered paradigm. Similarly, Covey (1989) has argued that the effectiveness and productivity of individuals can be greatly enhanced if they shift their paradigm concerning their beliefs about their potential for learning and their abilities to successfully cope with setting demands, given their mastery of an array of learning and social strategies.

Self-Motivation Techniques

To independently employ learning strategies to meet the demands of mainstream classes, students must be sufficiently motivated over a sustained period of time. Within a learning strategies context, McCombs (1984) has addressed the notion of sustained motivation through a concept called "continuing intrinsic motivation to learn." This concept has been defined as "a dynamic, internally mediated set of metacognitive, cognitive and effective processes that can influence a student's tendency to approach, engage in, expand effort in, and persist in learning tasks in a continuing, self-directed basis" (p. 200). This definition implies that students must know themselves as learners and realize that they are responsible for their own learning. McCombs further argues that the overriding purpose of self-motivation training is to promote in students a perception of self-efficacy and personal control. These perceptions underlie students' ability to take positive self-control and change negative attitudes and orientations toward learning.

Capable learners seem to employ a number of motivation strategies, including self-coping and affirmation statements, establishing their own goals, and reinforcing themselves. Ultimately, students mastering the use of a new strategy also must master the use of self-motivation strategies. Regrettably, many teachers take on the responsibility for motivating students rather than teaching students to motivate themselves. For example, some teachers employ only extrinsic motivational systems to motivate students. Such systems focus on the teacher establishing goals for students, awarding the students tokens or points for completed work, exchanging these tokens for extrinsic reinforcers, and delivering exaggerated praise in conjunction with appropriate performance. Although use of extrinsic reinforcement often produces immediate short-term benefits, some authors have suggested that its use in isolation from other motivational tools creates dependency in students and tends to reinforce external locus-of-control beliefs rather than to facilitate independence (e.g., Ellis, 1986; Ellis, Lenz, & Sabornie, 1987b; Litch & Kistner, 1986; Wittrock, 1986).

Although effective strategy teachers might make use of some form of extrinsic motivational systems (e.g., points, grades, parties, trips) to encourage learning, they also teach their students self-motivational techniques in conjunction with teaching them learning strategies. For example, they teach their students how to set annual goals for learning and how to present these goals at their IEP conferences in such a way that the goals are included in their formal educational plans (VanReusen, Bos, Schumaker, & Deshler, 1987; VanReusen, Deshler, & Schumaker, 1989). They teach their students to set personal goals, to make positive affirmation and self-coping statements to motivate themselves as they work through a task, to evaluate their own performances, to use self-reinforcement and self-correction procedures, and to monitor progress toward their goals (Seabaugh & Schumaker, 1981).

Thus, the instructional process is driven by student goals, not teacher goals. In addition, during the process of instruction on a given strategy and across strategies, teachers fade their mediation of the instructional process and expect the student to take more and more responsibility for learning. This transfer of responsibility prepares students to face the demands of mainstream educational environments, where self-motivation is required.

To summarize, motivational factors play a critical role in promoting strategic learning and performance. If students are to learn to use strategies effectively and efficiently, teachers should be aware of these factors and actively address them throughout the instructional process.

BASIC INSTRUCTIONAL PRINCIPLES

Pressley, Borowski, & Sullivan (1985) have argued that good strategies are "composed of the sufficient and necessary processes for accomplishing their intended goal, consuming as few intellectual processes as necessary to do so" (p. 140). Similarly, good strategy instruction incorporates procedures that are based on sound instructional principles and are sufficiently powerful to enable students to acquire a new strategy as quickly and as efficiently as possible. The following principles have been found to facilitate this type of strategy instruction.

1. *Teach prerequisite skills before strategy instruction begins.*

Because most learning strategies are designed to enable students to use skills in a problem-solving context, skills that are required for successful strategy use should be mastered *before* instruction in the actual strategy begins. To facilitate prerequisite skill instruction, students' skills must be assessed to determine whether they have mastered the skills necessary for successful application of a specific learning strategy. Some skills may require only a brief review, whereas others may require more intensive instruction. As a general rule, students should have mastered prerequisite skills well enough to fluently apply them. For example, instruction in the Paraphrasing Strategy (in which students are expected to read and paraphrase the content of a paragraph) may have to be preceded by instruction in a related prerequisite skill area such as paraphrasing smaller information chunks (e.g., one sentence). Similarly, if students are to be taught the Sentence Writing Strategy (Schumaker & Sheldon, 1985), instruction in the strategy is enhanced if students first learn how to identify subjects, verbs, and prepositions.

Teaching the necessary prerequisite skills prior to strategy instruction has two main benefits. The first is that teachers will be working only with students who are prepared to benefit from instruction in the given strategy; hence, the necessary steps already have been taken to prevent students from failing. In addition, instruction in the strategy will be more efficient because using instructional time to cover prerequisite skills in the middle of strategy instruction will not be necessary. This will allow students to travel a relatively straight and uninterrupted path between the initial introduction and description of the strategy and the actual application of the strategy to classroom assignments. A straight path can enhance the motivation of students to learn additional strategies.

2. *Teach regularly and intensively.*

For students with learning disabilities to successfully master complex learning strategies to a point of fluency, these strategies have to be taught on a consistent basis. Ideally, this means *daily* exposure to strategies instruction with ample practice opportunities programmed into an instructional period. Thus, activities that prevent or interrupt daily instruction (e.g., assemblies, standardized tests, trips to the counselor's office) must be kept to a minimum. In addition, regular attendance must be required and encouraged.

A key to ensuring intensive instruction is for both teachers and students to set daily, weekly, and semester goals related to strategy acquisition and generalization. Students should set semester goals that specify the strategies they want to learn. Daily and weekly goals they set should delineate the skills they want to acquire in the process of mastering the new learning strategy. During goal setting, students should consider two factors as they work on setting a goal: (a) a "quantity factor," specifying how much work will be accomplished during a given period of time (e.g., "Today I will complete five word problems in math using the problem-solving strategy I am learning"), and (b) a "quality factor," specifying what kinds of behaviors or attitudes a student will try to incorporate during completion of the task (e.g., "As I attack each problem, I will tell myself the steps of the strategy and remind myself that I can be successful in math when I use the strategy").

Students should set target dates for completing given instructional components, refer to these goals regularly, and adjust performance accordingly to meet them. In the absence of ambitious goals for strategy acquisition and generalization, students often tend to prolong the time spent mastering a given strategy. Given the many deficits most low-achieving students and students with learning disabilities exhibit, the limited instructional time available must be used optimally, and every effort must be made to prevent students from getting "bogged down" in learning a given strategy.

Teachers likewise should set goals regarding how much to accomplish with each student in a specified time. Without clearly defined goals, it is easy to fall a little behind schedule each week, resulting in significant slippage by the end of the semester. Well defined and ambitious goals tend to increase the intensity of instruction as well as students' overall progress. By openly sharing their goals with their students, teachers can effectively model for students how to set goals and express the personal value they have found in doing so on a regular basis.

3. *Emphasize personal effort.*

Students need to understand that successful problem solving, in the simplest terms, is related to choosing a strategy that can effectively address the demand of the setting and then trying as hard as possible to use the strategy properly. Teachers should remind students regularly that academic success results when students put forth significant personal effort in applying an appropriate learning strategy to a problem they are facing. In short, they should teach their students that the key elements in the formula for successful problem solving in an academic setting are:

Appropriately chosen learning strategy + personal effort = successful problem solving

Frequent reference to this formula in discussing progress and providing feedback to students can enhance students' understanding that they have to exert personal effort to ensure success. Using this formula over a sustained time can increase students' understanding of the learning process.

4. *Require mastery.*

Research has shown that students are more likely to generalize a given learning strategy (the major instructional goal) when they can proficiently perform the strategy at the specified mastery levels (Schmidt, Deshler, Schumaker, & Alley 1989). Specifically, two dimensions constitute mastery performance: (a) *correct performance* of a given strategy and (b) *fluent use* of the strategy. Typically, the early phases of strategy instruction focus on students acquiring and performing the correct strategy routines. After they have learned the routines in the correct order, the instructional emphasis must shift to increasing the speed and fluidity with which students use the strategy. The strategy must be integrated in their repertoires at the automatic level (Pressley, Johnson, & Symons, 1987). Older students often are required to acquire, store, or express large amounts of information quickly. If a learning strategy is to serve these students well, they must feel that they are more efficient at tackling a task or assignment with the strategy than without it.

Nevertheless, establishing a mastery criterion appropriate for all students is difficult. Although a tenth-grade student who is reading at the fourth-grade level must first demonstrate mastery of a strategy on fourth-grade materials, the instructional goal is for him or her to perform at a mastery level on tenth-grade materials. Unfortunately, the instructional time that must be expended to achieve the goal of mastery on tenth-grade materials may not justify the tradeoffs that must be made with regard to other instructional activities.

Extending the time period over which mastery is achieved might be necessary for some students. For example, if a student is having difficulty mastering the verbal expression of the different routines of a strategy, proceeding to a subsequent instructional stage and allowing the student to use a cue card when practicing with the strategy rather than relying on the student's memory might be necessary. This process may not only enable mastery of the strategy more quickly and reduce student frustration, but it also may afford the student multiple opportunities for exposure to the steps of the strategy in other contexts and circumstances, thus helping to compensate for what was not mastered at an earlier instructional stage.

5. *Integrate instruction*

The instructional methodology discussed in the next section is presented as a set of instructional stages that, on the surface, seem to be linear in nature. Although the stages are arranged in a logical order, beginning with a pretest of the student's skills and ending with specific generalization activities, strategy instruction seems most effective when several of the instructional methods are integrated throughout the entire series. For example, the generalization activities seem to be most effective if generalization is forecasted and emphasized in all the instructional stages. That is, even as early as the Pretest Stage of the instructional methodology, students' attention can be focused on generalization by emphasizing how they will be able to use the strategy in a broad array of settings and situations once they have mastered it (Ellis, Lenz, & Sabornie, 1987a, 1987b).

Similarly, teachers can continually identify situations in which an additional demonstration of the strategy or a substep of a strategy would be advantageous for students. For example, when giving feedback to the student on his or her performance of the strategy, modeling might be helpful to show the student what to do on the next practice attempt. Teachers also might effectively give students multiple opportunities to verbalize the steps of the strategy and the reasons for each step or substep of the strategy by regularly asking them to name and explain certain aspects of the strategy they are learning. This can even be done at times typically considered to be "noninstructional." For example, when students are being dismissed from class, the teacher can require them to "earn their way out of the room" by repeating a certain step of a strategy, by specifying why a certain step is useful, or by suggesting a situation in which the strategy can be used. Consistently expecting students to perform in this fashion can do much to help them achieve mastery. In short, strategy teachers have to be sensitive to any student who may need repeated exposure to an instructional technique (e.g., another model) or to any whose learning can be enhanced by recycling through a given stage once again.

6. *Emphasize covert processing.*

Throughout the instructional process, teachers should deliberately discuss and demonstrate the covert processes involved in performing the strategy. Applying a learning strategy to meet a specific academic task demand often involves using covert processes (cognitive strategies such as visual imagery, prioritizing, hypothesis generating, relating new information to prior knowledge, or paraphrasing; and metacognitive strategies such as problem analysis, decision making, goal setting, task analysis, and self-monitoring). Thus, instruction in the use of a learning strategy should address the covert processes involved in applying the learning strategy. For example, when teaching a learning strategy that contains a step designed to cue the student to paraphrase the main idea of a paragraph, an effective teacher will *explain* and *demonstrate* the cognitive processes one might use to find and state the main idea. The teacher also will coach students to perform these cognitive processes effectively and efficiently.

Roehler and Duffy (1984) have called instruction that emphasizes covert processing "direct explanation" (p. 265). In short, they argue that effective teachers focus not only on the mechanical aspects of learning and performing but also on directly teaching students to understand and use the covert processes involved in the task. A less effective teacher, on the other hand, might simply instruct (with *no* explanation or demonstration) the student to perform the covert behavior and then provide feedback with regard to whether the desired outcome was attained (e.g., whether students generated the correct main idea).

7. *Emphasize generalization in the broadest sense.*

Over time, the focus of instruction should shift from teaching students to use a task-specific learning strategy to meet the demands associated with a specific problem domain to a focus on how strategies can be used to address similar problems in other domains. Although a task-specific learning strategy is typically designed to target a problem that might be encountered in a specific academic domain (e.g., studying for a test), instruction in that strategy must impact the student beyond the scope of the original problem domain. Students should learn to be flexible and to adapt the processes involved in the task-specific strategy to meet a variety of needs in other problem domains.

For instance, if students are being taught to organize and prioritize in the context of studying for tests, they also might be taught how to apply these skills in other problem-solving contexts. Original instruction might focus on how ideas can be depicted in a manner that clearly communicates relationships, as well as on the processes used to prioritize what should be memorized first, second, third, and so on. Later, after students have mastered application of the skills within the context of studying for a test, these same skills might be addressed within the context of a paragraph-writing task or a note-taking task. Naturally, the more experience students have in learning the skills associated with categorizing and prioritizing in specific contexts, the more readily they will be able to apply them in previously unencountered contexts.

A WORKING INSTRUCTIONAL MODEL
FOR TEACHING LEARNING STRATEGIES

The working model presented here has been operationalized by specifying a sequence of eight instructional stages (See Table 1). The specific instructional stages have been identified to denote different emphases in the instructional process. The procedures described for each stage relate to this emphasis and have been organized into specific phases of instruction. In addition, the procedures associated with each stage of instruction are employed over various time periods and are unique to each stage of instruction. The time frame can range from as short as one instructional period to as long as several weeks for a given instructional stage.

TABLE 1   ***A Working Model for Teaching Learning Strategies***

Stages of Strategy Acquisition and Generalization

Stage 1: Pretest and Make Commitments
> Phase 1: Orientation and pretest
> Phase 2: Awareness and commitment

Stage 2: Describe
> Phase 1: Orientation and overview
> Phase 2: Presentation of strategy and remembering system

Stage 3: Model
> Phase 1: Orientation
> Phase 2: Presentation
> Phase 3: Student enlistment

Stage 4: Verbal Practice
> Phase 1: Verbal elaboration
> Phase 2: Verbal rehearsal

Stage 5: Controlled Practice and Feedback
> Phase 1: Orientation and overview
> Phase 2: Guided practice
> Phase 3: Independent practice

Stage 6: Advanced Practice and Feedback
> Phase 1: Orientation and overview
> Phase 2: Guided practice
> Phase 3: Independent practice

Stage 7: Posttest and Make Commitments
> Phase 1: Confirmation and celebration
> Phase 2: Forecast and commit to generalization

Stage 8: Generalization
> Phase 1: Orientation
> Phase 2: Activation
> Phase 3: Adaptation
> Phase 4: Maintenance

Two important instructional elements have been incorporated into each instructional stage to promote learning and motivation: (a) the use of organizers, and (b) principles of goal attainment. Because these elements are standard across implementation of each instructional stage, they will be reviewed at this point and only the aspects unique to a specific instructional stage will be addressed as each instructional stage is described.

First, each instructional stage uses advance, lesson, and post organizers to promote learning. Each lesson begins with an advance organizer. The purpose of this organizer is to help the teacher: (a) gain the students' attention, (b) review relevant learning, (c) make the connection between previous learning and the current instructional goals, (d) focus students' attention on the relationship between the activities of the day's lesson with the overall goal of mastering the new strategy, (e) personalize the lesson for students so they understand the benefits they will receive through the learning process, and (f) communicate specific learning and performance expectations. As each instructional stage is implemented, the teachers should use lesson organizers to further cue organization, state expectations, prompt the integration of new information with previously learned information, and make relationships clear. Finally, a post organizer is provided that prompts students to review learning and evaluate whether expectations for learning and performance have been met.

Second, each instructional stage incorporates the process of setting and evaluating goals related to strategy learning. To accomplish this, students set their own performance goals for the lesson and, at the end of the lesson, evaluate their performance. Progress is noted on a chart, and the student decides what must be accomplished in the next instructional period.

An overview of the key instructional behaviors associated with each stage of strategy acquisition and generalization, following the outline of Table 1, is presented next. The instructional stages are described in terms of the major focus of instruction, expected outcomes, and critical components and processes associated with each stage.

Stage 1: Pretest and Make Commitments

Consistent with the underlying principle that instruction should be driven by student goals, the major purpose of Stage 1 is to have students *want to* make a commitment to learn the strategy. The intent of this stage, therefore, is to motivate students to learn a new strategy by making them aware of: (a) a specific setting demand encountered in many of their classes, (b) how they are performing with regard to this demand, and (c) the existence of alternative approaches or strategies for meeting this demand. Students also are informed about the results obtained by other students with similar learning habits and entry-level skills who previously learned the new strategy. In short, through a discussion with the teacher, students are led to the following conclusions: (a) They are not meeting a specific setting demand in school, and, as a result, they are at-risk for failure; (b) their failure is not innate but, rather, is a function of not knowing the best strategy for the task at hand; (c) an alternative approach (strategy) can be used to produce success once it is learned and applied through consistent effort on their part; and (d) other students with similar difficulties in school have experienced success after using the new strategy.

Another purpose of this first instructional stage is to establish a baseline related to how each student is currently performing in meeting the targeted setting demand. By carefully observing students as they perform tasks related to the setting demand and by discussing with students how they approach specific tasks and how they feel when they are trying to respond to different task demands, teachers can determine students' current learning habits and anticipate the relative degree of instructional intensity required to teach the new strategy.

This stage has two phases of instruction: (a) an initial orientation combined with a pretest, and (b) a phase in which students become aware of their deficits and make a commitment to learn. When these two phases have been completed, a signed goal statement indicating a commitment to learn and apply the strategy and a record of the student's baseline performance should have been produced.

Phase 1: Orientation and Pretest

The purpose of the orientation and pretest phase is to introduce students to the importance of jointly (the teacher and the student) determining *how* students are approaching a specific curriculum demand (e.g., storing information from a lecture). Students need to understand, at this point, that the purpose of the probes or "tests" in this stage is not the same as tests given in the regular classroom. Here, the purpose is to try to figure out what strategies the student uses effectively and what current strategies/learning habits should be modified or changed altogether. Thus, the students need to know that how they score on the pretest will have no bearing on their grade in the course.

Students also need to understand that the deficits to be identified through the pretesting process are specific to the task or setting demand, and they do not indicate generalized deficiencies or inadequacies in the student. Often, students with a long history of academic failure have difficulty separating their worth as individuals from difficulties they may have in completing a specific task. During this phase, the teacher should:

1. Give students rationales for this phase of the instructional process.
2. Provide an overview of the entire Pretest Stage and point out how it is tied into the rest of the instructional process.
3. Discuss how decisions will be made regarding instruction on strategies in the area being assessed. Specifically, inform students that they will have a major voice, through the goal-setting process, in determining whether to work on a given strategy.
4. Assess how students perform relative to a specific setting demand. Include observations of students' strategic *processes* and *products*. The processes to be observed include the general approach students might use to accomplish the task and the specific behaviors they display while approaching the task (e.g., what a student does when attempting to take notes). The result of these processes is a product (e.g., a record of how much of the critical information the student was able to include in notes, how well this information was organized, and the like).

5. Use materials and tasks from the regular classroom, the setting where students must ultimately demonstrate mastery with the strategy, as the vehicles for the assessment process.
6. Score the student's products, compare each student's scores to the set mastery criteria, and determine whether the strategy is appropriate for each student who took the pretest.

Phase 2: Awareness and Commitment

One purpose of this phase is to make students aware of what was learned about them as learners as they were observed performing tasks and through analyzing the products they produced. In essence, this information represents their current habit(s) in coping with setting demands. A second purpose is to give students a general idea of the strategy they can choose to learn as an alternative to their current approach to the task. Finally, students will make commitments related to learning the new strategy, and the teacher will make a commitment to students to teach the strategy in a manner that will promote the student's mastery and generalization of the strategy. As a part of this phase, the teacher should:

1. Review pretest results. Care should be taken to discuss the student's performance according to *categories* of strengths and weaknesses. If the strengths and weaknesses are characterized in relation to categories, students will more easily understand their performance and the areas in which they need improvement. As a result, they will be able to focus their goal setting and effort on these areas.
2. Briefly describe the alternative strategy for meeting the specific demand, including the potential benefits of using the strategy to increase success at school, home, and work.
3. Describe what is required (in terms of time, energy, and commitment) to learn the new strategy.
4. Describe the kinds of results other students have achieved after learning the strategy.
5. Ask the student if he or she is willing to make a commitment to learn the new strategy in light of the information that has been presented.
6. Explain the commitment the teacher is willing to make to effectively teach the strategy.

Stage 2: Describe

The purpose of this instructional stage is to describe the new strategy in such a manner that students can: (a) become aware of the overt *and* covert processes involved in performing the new strategy; (b) become aware of how the steps of the strategy are used to approach academic tasks, and solve problems and how self-instruction is used to regulate use of the steps; (c) clearly see how this new strategy is different from their current habit of problem solving; and (d) become motivated to learn and apply the new strategy. In short, the teacher clearly "paints a picture" of what the new strategy is all about and how its use will alter learning and performing.

The Describe Stage of strategy acquisition and generalization has two phases of instruction. First, students receive an orientation and overview of the strategy and its application to specific setting demands. Second, they are made aware of the specific strategy steps and of their application to specific academic tasks.

Phase 1: Orientation and Overview

The purpose of the first phase of the Describe Stage is to orient students to different reasons for adopting the new strategy as an alternative method of problem solving. Students also are made aware of where and when the strategy is used appropriately and when not to use it. In addition, the importance of students' actively listening and comparing the new strategy with how they typically approach tasks is stressed. During this phase, the teacher should:

1. Ensure that students understand the rationales for learning the strategy and how the strategy can affect success across a wide number of settings.
2. Describe the general characteristics of situations in which the strategy can be used. Discuss examples of those situations and emphasize its relevance in school, home, work, and leisure settings.
3. Prompt the students to compare their old learning habits with the strategy as the discussion proceeds so they can discuss the differences at the end of the lesson.

Phase 2: Presentation of Strategy and Remembering System

During this instructional phase students are exposed to the overall intent of the strategy as well as to the nature and purpose of each of the instructional steps. Instruction should emphasize both the overt and covert processes involved in effectively using the strategy. As a part of this phase of instruction the teacher should:

1. Describe the strategic processes involved in using the overall strategy. For example, students should be told that a given strategy is effective because it helps them *transform* (e.g., cluster, organize, paraphrase) material into a form that is easier to understand and remember.
2. Describe, explain, and guide students to understand the overt and covert processes involved in each of the steps. This explanation should underscore for students the importance of the role of self-instruction when performing a strategy. That is, students should realize that they should understand the steps well enough to be able to talk their way through implementation of the strategy to both guide and monitor its successful application. Thus, the focus initially is *not* on learning to perform the steps of the strategy but, rather, on how one must use self-instruction to regulate use of the strategy steps.
3. Explain to students how to remember the strategy by discussing the remembering system used with the strategy.
4. Ensure that students understand the relationship between the remembering system and what is involved in applying the learning strategy, with particular emphasis on the process of self-instruction.

5. Through an open discussion, encourage students to compare and contrast the new strategic approach to their old approaches. This instruction should focus on how self-instructional use of the strategy steps differs from what they typically do when attempting to meet the setting demand.
6. Guide students to set individual goals for learning the strategy.

Stage 3: Model

Research suggests that learning disabled and other low-achieving students may not use self-talk effectively to guide their performances (Warner, Schumaker, Alley, & Deshler, 1989). Thus, teachers should teach students these cognitive behaviors as well as the overt physical acts they need to perform as they complete a given task. The Model Stage of instruction is fundamental for teaching and demonstrating these cognitive behaviors. A frequently made mistake in the instructional process is to confuse the Describe Stage of instruction with the Model Stage. That is, teachers traditionally have not been trained to demonstrate their thought processes by "thinking aloud." Once this instructional process is mastered, teachers can greatly enhance students' understanding of the strategy as well as the speed with which it is learned. In short, this step is considered to be the "heart of strategy instruction" (Schumaker, 1989). The Model Stage has three major phases.

Phase 1: Orientation

During this phase the teacher *reviews previous learning* by covering the nature and purpose of the strategy steps and where and when the strategy can be applied. In addition, the teacher *personalizes the strategy* so that students understand how its use will benefit them. The teacher also *defines the lesson content*, providing an explanation of what a model is and how it can help students as learners, and a brief description of the activities in the lesson. Finally, the teacher *states expectations* regarding student involvement during the lesson (such as instructions for students to watch the demonstration, pay particular attention to what the teacher says and does, and imitate what has been demonstrated).

Phase 2: Presentation

This phase of the Model Stage consists of a teacher demonstration of the strategy. The demonstration includes all the elements of how to think and act while performing the strategy. It should be fluid and organized; thus, preparation and prior practice on the teacher's part are critical. Specifically, the demonstration emphasizes the cognitive acts required to perform the strategy through a thinking-aloud process. Care should be taken to provide a balanced demonstration that shows enough of the cognitive processes involved to enable the student to understand application of the strategy without bogging down the demonstration in a manner that will make the strategy seem difficult and cumbersome. As a part of this phase, the teacher should:

1. Emphasize three types of cognitive processes while thinking aloud. *First*, the teacher demonstrates *self-instruction* by modeling how to cue oneself to use the next step of the strategy (e.g., "Let's see, the next step is 'Insert a letter'."). *Second*,

the teacher models how to do *problem solving* (e.g., "Hmmmm . . . I have a problem. There are nine items in this list, and I should only have seven. I know! I'll put four items together because they're all related to plants, and the other five can be grouped together because they're all related to animals."). *Third*, the teacher demonstrates the *monitoring* required while performing a strategy (e.g., "Let's see, where am I? I just finished checking for punctuation errors; next I need to check for spelling errors.").

2. Demonstrate how to *perform the task*. Merely describing a performance (telling what to do) does not provide a true model of the thinking processes and physical acts that students can imitate. Therefore, the entire strategy must be demonstrated, and performance with regard to the whole task must be shown.
3. Avoid making mental leaps between specific steps or actions. Students will have difficulty making correct decisions throughout a strategy if they do not see the major thinking processes involved in performing the strategy.

Phase 3: Student Enlistment

During this phase students are *prompted* to gradually perform more and more of the required thought processes and physical acts themselves. They become the demonstrators. Initially, students can be prompted to name the next step. Once mastered, they should be prompted to say what they would say as they: (a) check their progress, (b) evaluate their performance, (c) make adjustments, and (d) problem solve. By involving students, the teacher can check their understanding of the strategy steps and the processes involved in performing them.

Frequently, students will not be able to explain the covert processes involved in a strategy during the formal Model Stage of instruction. Students often find "thinking out-loud" about the strategic processes to be difficult until they begin to understand how the strategy is applied. This level of understanding gradually emerges as instruction proceeds. Forcing students to "think out-loud" before they are ready can sometimes bog down instruction and make the strategy seem difficult to use. Therefore, students should be enlisted in a way that prompts maximum involvement at a level that is appropriate and at which success is guaranteed. Students can be enlisted in the modeling process more fully as part of the practice and feedback stages of instruction. As a part of this phase of instruction, the teacher should:

1. Require students to use the actual words they would say to themselves in using the strategy.
2. Provide feedback including correction and expansion of student responses during the exercise.
3. Prompt as much self-talk as possible.
4. Engineer as much success as possible by assigning tasks that students are likely to complete successfully and by prompting involvement that is easy at first and that gradually becomes more complex.
5. Draw students' attention to good performance models, and emphasize the importance of imitating the processes they have seen and heard.

Stage 4: Verbal Practice

The focus of this instructional stage is on ensuring comprehension of the process involved in applying the new strategy. To effectively use self-instructional processes while performing a strategy, students need to be able to use their own language structures to communicate with themselves about the strategic process. Thus, the instructional emphasis during this stage is on facilitating student mediation or elaboration of the key information presented to them so that it is restructured in terms of students' prior knowledge. Two major phases are part of this instructional stage: verbal elaboration and verbal rehearsal.

Phase 1: Verbal Elaboration

The purpose of this phase is to facilitate explanation of key information associated with the strategy in the students' own words. Initially, the focus of instruction is on facilitating students' ability to elaborate on what the overall strategic process is designed to accomplish and generally what the process involves. The obvious prerequisite to students' being able to elaborate on the processes of a strategy is for them to clearly understand the intent of the overall strategy. Once students are able to describe the "big picture" in their own words, the focus of instruction shifts to facilitating student elaboration of the specific strategy steps. Here, while looking at the list of the strategy steps, students describe what each step is designed to do and *why* it is an important component of the overall strategic process. Once students can accurately describe the strategy steps, they should be asked to elaborate on the role of self-instruction with regard to performing the strategy.

Phase 2: Verbal Rehearsal

Before students can be asked to use a given strategy, they must learn to name the strategy steps at an automatic level. Thus, students are expected to commit the strategy steps to memory via rote rehearsal. Steps are memorized to fluent 100% mastery levels so that steps can readily serve as self-instructional cues for what to do as the strategy is performed. A procedure called "rapid-fire practice" is used to promote memorization of the strategy steps. In this method, the teacher points to each student in succession and requires contribution of the next step of the strategy. This exercise begins slowly, and students are called on in a predictable order. As they become more familiar with the steps of the strategy, the speed of the practice is increased and students are called on randomly. Students' verbal mastery of the steps is checked individually until they reach the mastery criterion.

Stage 5: Controlled Practice and Feedback

This stage of instruction has several instructional goals. One is to give students ample opportunity to practice using the new strategy with materials or in situations largely devoid of many of the demands found in regular-class settings. A second goal is to build students' confidence and fluency in using the strategy. Third, controlled practice is a major tool in helping students gradually take over (from teachers) the responsibility of mediating effective use of the strategy in their life.

Practice using the strategy is controlled along three major dimensions: (a) the type of instructional materials used, (b) the context within which the strategy is practiced, and (c) the amount of teacher/peer mediation employed. Each of these dimensions must be considered regularly and carefully if students are to progress successfully through this instructional stage. At the end of this stage, students should be ready to transfer their facility with the strategy to materials that are more difficult and that approximate those found in the regular class setting.

The first dimension that must be taken under consideration to achieve successful implementation of the Controlled Practice and Feedback Stage relates to appropriate use of instructional materials. Initially, the stimulus materials used as students begin practicing the strategy should be devoid of many of the demands of the regular class setting (e.g., complex vocabulary and concepts, lengthy reading selections), so that students can focus their attention on learning the technique and can build confidence and fluency in performing the strategy steps. As students become fluent in applying the strategy to these easier materials, increasingly more complex materials for practicing the strategy should be provided. Thus, students learn to use the strategy when interacting with materials that gradually approximate the difficulty of those found in their regular educational settings.

For example, when practicing the Paraphrasing Strategy, students might first begin applying the strategy to reading materials that are well below their instructional levels but that address topics of high interest. Then, once students are able to perform the strategy when reading these easier materials, they are asked to apply the strategy to more challenging reading selections.

The second dimension that must be taken into consideration when implementing this stage relates to the context or conditions under which the strategy is practiced. During initial practice attempts, some students have benefited from working with the strategy in a *different* and *less complex* context. Many of the cognitive processes associated with performing a specific learning strategy can (and should) be practiced under conditions that do not require higher-order skills.

For instance, when learning the Paraphrasing Strategy, in which students (a) read a paragraph, (b) stop and ask themselves what the main idea and details are, and then (c) put the main idea and details into their own words, students might first learn to do the last two steps using the strategy in a reading-free context. The teacher might read the paragraph to the students and then ask them to perform the cognitive processes associated with identifying and paraphrasing main ideas and details. Later, they might practice performing the whole strategy in a reading context. Therefore, the practice session is not only controlled through the materials that are used but also through the conditions under which the student must perform to enhance strategy learning.

The third important dimension of this stage of strategy instruction relates to the amount of teacher/peer mediation that might be employed. The degree of assistance the teacher provides as students attempt to use the new procedure also should be carefully controlled. Initially, when students first practice using the strategy, the teacher provides ample cues and prompts to assure that students are performing the strategy steps appropriately and learning to use self-instruction. Then, as students become proficient at performing the strategy steps, teacher prompts are gradually faded until students can perform the strategy on controlled materials without assistance.

Like fading the use of prompts and cues, the teacher's role in providing feedback also shifts as students become proficient at using the new strategy. Initially, feedback is totally teacher-directed. That is, the student is explicitly informed about what he or she is doing effectively and how to perform more effectively. Later, the nature of the teacher's feedback shifts; the teacher simply cues the student or gives the student partial information with the expectation that the student will be able to participate in mediating his or her own learning. That is, rather than providing all of the corrective feedback and reinforcement to the student, the teacher cues the student to analyze his or her own performance and provide himself or herself with corrective feedback and reinforcement. Through cooperative group structures or other peer tutoring assignments (Johnson & Johnson, 1986; Kagan 1989; Slavin, 1989), students also can play a key role in mediating the learning process with each other. Later, the responsibility for learning and performance is deliberately and gradually passed from the teacher to the student.

The quality of feedback teachers provide is also a key factor in affecting the gains that students experience during controlled practice. Kline (1989) found "elaborated feedback" to be much more effective than feedback that merely provided students with "knowledge of results." Elaborated feedback entails categorizing the types of errors that students make and providing them with specific information that is both positive and corrective in nature. If necessary, it also can include the description and demonstration of a mini-strategy that may help the student avoid the same type of error in the future. The overriding purpose of elaborated feedback is to: (a) have students understand the types of problems they are encountering with tasks, (b) translate the information into a plan to solve the problem, and (c) implement the plan to alter and improve performance.

These three dimensions are taken into consideration as the three phases involved in the Controlled Practice and Feedback Stage are implemented. Because the Controlled Practice and Feedback Stage may last many days, the three phases described next detail how each practice session is conducted. Therefore, the three phases are repeated during each practice session. First, the teacher orients the students to the practice session. Second, the teacher carefully guides the entire group of students through practice trials to ensure that the strategy is being applied correctly and that students understand the practice activities. Third, the teacher prompts independent practice and monitors individual performance.

Phase 1: Orientation and Overview

As the Controlled Practice and Feedback Stage gradually moves from teacher-mediated to student-mediated instruction, students must be oriented to the purpose of the specific practice activity and must be informed of their progress thus far in this stage of instruction. In addition, before the practice session begins, the teacher should review the critical components of the strategy as needed and focus student attention on the most common types of errors being made. This orientation period also provides a good opportunity to discuss specific day-to-day instances in which application of the strategy might be beneficial. During this phase of instruction the teacher should:

1. Initially review the steps of the strategy before each practice session, and have students elaborate on what each step means. Gradually fade out the frequency of these reviews as students become proficient in describing the strategy steps.
2. Prompt students to review the results of previous practice attempts, and identify the areas in which improvement is needed.
3. Identify and discuss group progress and errors. If necessary, review or re-explain aspects or applications of the strategy that a student is consistently performing incorrectly.
4. Prompt students to describe how they could use or are using the strategy across different situations or settings.

Phase 2: Guided Practice

In the Guided Practice Phase the teacher is concerned with ensuring that students are correctly performing the strategy in the manner intended. Because the instructional materials, the context, and the level of teacher or peer mediation may be shifting throughout this stage, the teacher has to lead students through some of the practice activities before allowing them to work independently. During this phase of instruction, the teacher should:

1. Provide specific directions related to how the practice should be completed.
2. Model how the strategy is applied to the practice materials, using a demonstration that approximates the behaviors discussed in the Model Stage of instruction, described earlier. Model under the same conditions under which the students must perform the strategy. During the initial stages of practice, the model may be quite detailed and explicit. As the daily practice sessions progress, however, the teacher model can be shortened and the students can be enlisted in performing the model.
3. Prompt students to complete the practice activity as the teacher models application of the strategy on the practice materials.
4. Prompt students to gradually assume more responsibility for completing the practice activity on their own, without teacher guidance.
5. Provide clear and explicit instructions related to arranging peer-mediated practice sessions. Monitor practice activities and evaluate progress to determine the best groupings and conditions for arranging future peer-mediated practice sessions.

Phase 3: Independent Practice

In this phase of instruction, the teacher must allow the student to complete the practice activity independently, but the teacher should monitor performance and look for opportunities to provide individualized and direct instruction to students on specific aspects of the strategy. During this phase of the instructional process, the teacher should:

1. Inform students to work independently while applying the strategy.
2. Monitor performance by walking around the room to ensure that students are proceeding correctly.
3. When possible, provide additional information to students, individually, to prompt correct application of the strategy and completion of the task. If a student is having

difficulty performing the strategy, provide a model of the strategy, using the practice activity as a basis.

4. Occasionally, prompt a student to think aloud as he or she completes the practice activity. This will enable the teacher to evaluate how the student is thinking about and using the strategy under different conditions.

5. Differentiate on the Progress Chart those practice trials for which the teacher provided substantial assistance and practice trials that were completed without teacher assistance.

Stage 6: Advanced Practice and Feedback

The real test of students' mastery of a strategy is their ability to apply it to advanced assignments and materials that approximate those found in "criterion settings" (settings where they were unable to cope originally, such as the regular classroom or the workplace). This stage of instruction marks an important turning point in the overall learning process. Learning shifts from learning how to perform the strategy to learning how to apply the strategy to meet the various *real* demands typically found in the criterion environment.

During this stage of instruction, students learn to apply the strategy to these real-life tasks while still in a setting (e.g., a remedial class) that can offer support as needed. Thus, students learn how to proficiently use and adapt, if necessary, the strategy to a wide variety of materials and assignments and to discriminate when the strategy is appropriate for meeting specific types of problems. As in the Controlled Practice and Feedback Stage, the amount and type of teacher mediation in the learning process should be faded out gradually over time. A deliberate change from teacher-mediated to student-mediated feedback must occur. Thus, as a part of this stage, the teacher should:

1. Provide a wide variety of grade-appropriate stimulus materials related to the setting demand. For example, if the setting demand the new strategy is designed to target is reading comprehension, students should practice applying the new strategy to a wide variety of reading materials (e.g., health and history textbooks, newspapers and news magazines) appropriate for the grade in which the student is enrolled.

2. Structure assignments that require students to adapt the strategy to meet different characteristics of instructional materials. For example, if students are learning a textbook reading strategy designed to enable them to use textbook cues, some textbooks should require students to focus primarily on one form of cue (e.g., visual aids), and others might require students to focus on organizational cues (e.g., introductions, summaries, headings).

3. Structure assignments that allow students to practice with materials (or in situations) that are poorly designed. Using the textbook reading example, students should be asked to use the strategy with poorly designed textbooks (e.g., those in which visual aids and organizational cues are present but provide relatively useless information).

4. Fade the instructional prompts and cues so that students become responsible for taking initiative in using and evaluating the strategy in a variety of contexts. This

involves having students ask themselves questions about their responses, thus enabling them to analyze the appropriateness of the strategy application and their performance.

The instructional phases that guide daily implementation of this stage are the same as those described in the Controlled Practice and Feedback Stage. That is, in the *Orientation and Overview Phase* the teacher should focus on reviewing progress, discussing the strategy as it is applied to advanced materials, and identifying critical errors that have emerged from applying the strategy to more difficult materials and circumstances. In the *Guided Practice Phase* the teacher should focus on helping students see how the materials are becoming more difficult and how to discriminate cues signaling strategy use. Finally, during the *Independent Practice Phase* the teacher should monitor the independent and correct application of the strategy in the advanced materials.

Stage 7: Posttest and Make Commitments

This stage in the strategy acquisition process focuses on students' documenting mastery of the strategy and building a rationale designed to involve students in promoting self-generalization of the strategy across settings. Whereas earlier stages of the instructional process are critical to the learning process, this stage is critical to the application process. Unfortunately, many teachers who are successful at promoting acquisition of a strategy have difficulty promoting generalization. In fact, many teachers often completely disregard generalization or attempt to address generalization merely through supplemental worksheets to be completed at the end of other lessons. As a result, many strategy-training efforts have failed to result in significant levels of generalization outside of the training setting because of the lack of teacher attention to the transition from the acquisition process to the generalization process. If the full benefits of strategy instruction are to be realized, significant instructional attention must be given to this transition.

This stage of instruction has two phases: The first focuses on confirming that the strategy has been mastered and affirming success. The second phase of this stage focuses on forecasting the generalization process and making commitments related to both the student's and the teacher's role in the generalization process.

Phase 1: Confirm and Celebrate Mastery

This phase of instruction provides an opportunity for the teacher and student to confirm and document that the student has acquired the procedural and strategic processes involved in the strategy. In practice, the student probably has already demonstrated mastery of the strategy as part of the Advanced Practice and Feedback Stage of the instructional process. Many teachers have reported that they simply use as the confirming posttest score the last advanced practice attempt in which the student met the mastery requirements. Nevertheless, once the student has met the expectations, requirements, and goals related to performance on routine and daily practice efforts involved in the Advanced Practice and Feedback Stage of the instructional process, the student should have an opportunity to prepare for and confirm, to the best of his or her ability and with maximum motivation and effort, that he or she can perform the strategy and meet the demand. Therefore, the student is allowed to create a "trophy" of which he or she can be proud and that can be used as documentation on educational planning documents such as the IEP.

The activities implemented in this phase should serve to prompt the student and the teacher to celebrate the results of their efforts and commitments. If the student has set goals related to acquiring and applying the strategy and has worked hard to meet these goals, time should be devoted to affirming progress and reviewing what did and did not work along the way. Both the student and the teacher should reflect and discuss their efforts and be prompted to say, "I did great." To accomplish these goals associated with this phase, the teacher should:

1. Prompt each student to identify that he or she has met the mastery criteria associated with the Advanced Practice Stage.
2. Arrange for a final confirmation of mastery when a student informs the teacher that he or she has met the specified mastery criteria.
3. Inform the student that he or she will have an opportunity to perform the strategy to confirm mastery and to prepare by reviewing the strategy.
4. Provide the student with the appropriate task, and allow the student to complete the task under appropriate classroom conditions.
5. If the student does not meet the mastery criteria, provide encouragement and feedback and arrange for continued practice. If the student confirms mastery by meeting the mastery criteria, congratulate the student.
6. Arrange for a special opportunity to talk to the student about his or her achievement, and review with the student all the effort and learning that contributed to his or her success.
7. Work with the student to identify and implement various ways to recognize the accomplishment.

Phase 2: Forecast and Commit to Generalization
Within this instructional phase, the student and the teacher should make commitments related to ensuring that the student generalizes the strategy across settings, situations, and time. As part of this process, the teacher must adopt an instructional philosophy in which the success of strategy instruction is defined only by the degree to which the student uses the strategy to meet demands across regular classroom and other natural settings. In addition, this perspective must be transferred to students. Therefore, the teacher must:

1. Explain the general goals of the generalization process.
2. Identify specific consequences related to focusing versus not focusing attention on the generalization process.
3. Explain the four phases of the generalization process and what will be involved in each of the four phases.
4. Prompt the student to make a commitment to participate in and put forth maximum effort in the generalization process.
5. Explain the commitments of the support-class teacher and regular-class teachers in assisting students in the generalization process.

Stage 8: Generalization

Students who have mastered specific strategies in the support class setting often do not automatically use these strategies to facilitate learning across content settings (Ellis et al., 1987a, 1987b). For strategy instruction to be worthwhile, students must generalize the strategy to other settings. Successful generalization requires active, independent application and adaptation of the strategy across settings and tasks that vary in complexity and purpose. Students also must be able to recognize naturally occurring cues across settings that signal appropriate opportunities for applying the strategy. Therefore, the instructional processes for promoting generalization must focus on enabling the student to: (a) discriminate when to use the strategy to meet everyday learning and performance demands, (b) develop methods for remembering to use the strategy appropriately, (c) experiment with how the strategy can be used across circumstances encountered across settings, (d) receive and use feedback to develop goals and plans to improve performance, (e) adapt the strategy to meet additional problems and demands, and (f) incorporate the strategy and various adaptations of the strategy into the student's permanent system for approaching problems across settings and time. To facilitate application of these processes, the Generalization Stage of the instructional process has been divided into four phases: orientation, activation, adaptation, and maintenance.

Phase 1: Orientation

The purpose of the Orientation Phase of generalization is to make the student aware of the necessity of applying the strategy purposefully to meet relevant setting demands and to help the student get prepared for the generalization process. As part of this process, the teacher prompts the student to evaluate the pros and cons of using the new strategy and to begin to explore how the strategy might be used beyond the context in which it was taught (Ellis, et al., 1987a, 1987b). During this phase of generalization, the teacher should prompt students to:

1. Identify rationales for using the strategy across settings.
2. Explain why specific attention to strategy transfer and generalization is necessary.
3. Identify which settings are most likely to require use of the strategy.
4. Discuss how students might remind themselves to use the strategy in different settings.
5. Construct cue cards on 3″ x 5″ cards, and place the cards in textbooks, notebooks, and other materials used in settings in which the strategy might be applied.
6. Specify cues that exist in specific settings and across settings that will signal use of the strategy.
7. Review different types of materials that might be encountered across settings, and discuss how the strategy might or might not be applied.
8. Deliberately evaluate materials where the strategy should not be applied, and discuss reasons why the strategy is not appropriate.
9. Discuss which aspects of the strategy seem to be most helpful and least helpful, and then discuss how this information can be used to increase performance.

10. Generate ways to improve or adjust the strategy to make the strategy more responsive to setting demands.
11. Identify other procedures that might be combined with this strategy to make the student more effective in strategy use and improve overall performance.
12. Make cards on which the students write affirmations that connect use of the strategy with success in meeting a specific setting demand (e.g., "I am a successful writer when I monitor my errors") and which are to be reviewed on a daily basis.

Phase 2: Activation

The purpose of the Activation Phase of generalization is to prompt the student to purposefully use the strategy, to monitor a student's application of the strategy across a wide variety of materials, situations, and settings, and to prompt appropriate application of the strategy when generalization does not occur. To accomplish this, the responsibility for promoting generalization, heretofore generally left to the support-class teacher and the student, must be shared by other individuals, such as the regular classroom teacher, with whom the student comes in contact across a variety of settings. Therefore, the activities in this phase of the generalization process must focus on a variety of interactions that must take place among the support-class teacher, the student, and the regular classroom teachers. Initially, the support-class teacher should prompt students to:

1. Apply the strategy to a specific assignment related to another class and, afterward, demonstrate and describe how the strategy was used to complete the assignment.
2. Apply the strategy to a variety of assignments that must be done at home or in the regular classroom setting, and demonstrate and describe how the strategy was used to complete these assignments.
3. Set daily and weekly goals related to increasing the use of the strategy to a variety of settings and situations and to improving performance.
4. Develop a plan related to how to increase application of the strategy to meet these goals.
5. Review their affirmation cards daily.
6. Monitor implementation of the plan and effects of using the strategy across different settings and situations.
7. Enlist the help of the support-class teacher or the regular-class teacher to solve problems related to applying the strategy.
8. Request feedback from regular-class teachers related to improved performance in the areas specifically addressed by the strategy.
9. Develop a chart and record progress related to applying the strategy and its results on related measures of classroom performance.
10. Reinforce progress and success in the form of self-congratulatory statements and, if necessary, extrinsic rewards.

Though part of the responsibility for ensuring generalization of strategies rests with the support-class teacher, the regular classroom teacher, who teaches subjects such as social studies, language arts, or science, also must assume responsibility for facilitating the generalization process. The main instructional goals related to promoting strategy generalization in the regular classroom are to: (a) help the student see the relationship between the demands of the setting and appropriate strategies, and (b) guide the student to automatically and independently identify and apply strategies to successfully meet setting demands (Lenz & Bulgren, 1990). Therefore, the key to facilitating strategy generalization rests in teachers' ability to assure the student sufficient opportunities to apply the strategy and to experience success in meeting setting demands.

As a result, the content teacher should be in communication with the support-class teacher to inform him or her of the demands that the student is not meeting. Although the content teacher's involvement in the intervention process may vary at this point, he or she must be informed of the types of strategies that the student is to acquire and what skills are involved in performing each strategy. Afterward, the support-class teacher and the content teacher should communicate regularly to determine the student's progress in generalizing the pertinent strategy.

Thus, the support-class teacher should be communicating regularly with the content teacher(s), providing feedback to the student on his or her progress in the generalization process, and helping the student to set and plan for long-term application of the strategy across settings. Each regular classroom teacher, however, should be prompted to monitor if the strategies being used are meeting the specific learning demands presented in or characteristic of his or her content area.

A number of systems have been discussed and developed in an attempt to accomplish these goals (e.g., Ellis et al., 1987a, 1987b; Deshler, Schumaker, & Lenz, 1984; Schumaker, Deshler, & McKnight, 1989; Lenz, Schumaker, Deshler, & Beals, 1984). Lenz and Bulgren (1990) presented the following synthesis of procedures based on research related to promoting generalization of strategies across settings. In general, the regular classroom teacher should be prompted to:

1. From the support-class teacher, obtain a short description of the strategy that the student has been taught, the conditions or criteria for correct and successful application, and what the student has been taught with regard to applying the strategy in content lessons.
2. Determine if the student has been taught to identify specific cues to indicate when a strategy or part of a strategy is to be used.
3. Evaluate teaching materials, presentation routines, and classroom activities to ensure that sufficient cues are available for the student to be able to identify when to use a specific strategy.
4. Determine which situations and activities in the content classroom best lend themselves to direct monitoring of strategy generalization.
5. Initiate direct generalization monitoring by simply *checking* to see if the strategy is being used. If this cannot be determined by direct observation or review of permanent products, the regular-class teacher should ask the student if the strategy was used and have the student explain how he or she used the strategy.
6. Cue use of the strategy if the student has not started to use the strategy after several checks. As part of generalization instruction the support-class teacher provides, the

student should have a 3″ x 5″ cue card with a list of the strategy steps written on it. The regular classroom teacher can check to see if this cuing system has been implemented and, if it has not, prompt the student to design his or her own cue card. More direct ways of cuing strategy use might include: (a) discretely telling the student to use a specific strategy; (b) informing the whole class to routinely use a given strategy; (c) putting the name of the strategy on the chalkboard or bulletin board and pointing to it at appropriate times; and (d) prompting peers who use the strategy to cue students who are just beginning to learn and apply the strategy.

7. If the student does not begin to respond to cues after a short time, ask the student to list the steps of the strategy and ask how the first step would be accomplished. Then, possibly, watch the student as he or she performs the first step.

8. If the student seems unable to perform the steps of the strategy, determine if the student can see the relationship between the strategy and the specific demands of a class. Perhaps model how the strategy can be applied to meet the content learning demand, and require the student to imitate the model.

9. Once the student is applying the strategy, provide feedback to the student on the outcomes related to use of the strategy, what the student is doing right, what the student is doing wrong, and how to improve performance. Develop and routinely use a written or verbal system for providing specific feedback to students, facilitate and then collaboratively work with students to plan how specific problems or errors can be reduced.

Phase 3: Adaptation

The purpose of the Adaptation Phase of generalization is to prompt students to explore the strategy by identifying the various cognitive strategies in which they are engaging as the strategy is performed and to begin to change and integrate elements of the strategy to meet new and different setting demands. As part of this phase of generalization, the teacher should prompt students to:

1. Describe the strategy and all of its parts as the teacher writes the features of the strategy on the chalkboard.

2. Discuss what they are actually doing and thinking about while applying each step of the strategy.

3. Identify, with teacher guidance, the various cognitive strategies embedded in the strategy (e.g., self-questioning, clustering, categorizing, monitoring, checking, predicting, summarizing, paraphrasing).

4. Describe, with teacher assistance, what cognitive processes are involved in each of those strategies.

5. Discuss how and where these cognitive processes/strategies are required across different settings.

6. Identify, with teacher assistance, how the strategy can be modified to meet additional setting demands (e.g., "How can we modify the Paraphrasing Strategy to help us in note taking?" "How could we make paraphrasing work in the social skill of carrying on a conversation?").

7. Write down the strategy modifications and how they can be used.
8. Repeat the necessary orientation and activation activities that might be necessary to learn to apply the modifications.

Phase 4: Maintenance

The purpose of the Maintenance Phase of generalization is to ensure that the student continues to use the strategy across time and contexts. In this phase of generalization, the student and teacher jointly develop plans related to promoting long-term use of the strategy. During this phase of generalization, the teacher should prompt students to:

1. Discuss rationales related to long-term use of the strategy.
2. Identify habits and barriers that might prevent students from continuing to use the strategy.
3. Determine how the students might monitor long-term application of the strategy.
4. Discuss ways in which the teacher can help to monitor long-term application and successful use of the strategy.
5. Set goals related to monitoring long-term application of the strategy.
6. Determine how many times a week the teacher should check use of the strategy.
7. Determine how this check will be conducted and if other teachers or students will be involved (e.g., peer checks, classroom products or assignments).
8. Specify, with guidance from the teacher, the criteria for successful performance of the strategy at the various "check" points.
9. Plan, with guidance from the teacher, the procedures that will be used to improve students' performance if they are not applying the strategy effectively or efficiently.
10. Review their affirmation cards daily.
11. Determine the length of time during which weekly maintenance checks will be required before implementing biweekly maintenance checks.
12. Discuss and identify when the strategy can be considered a permanent part of students' approach to meeting setting demands and when maintenance checks will be no longer needed.
13. Develop a chart, and begin to record the results of efforts to maintain use of the strategy.
14. Identify self-reinforcers or self-rewards that can be used in conjunction with successful maintenance of the strategy.

CONCLUSION

A growing body of research illustrates that teaching students to use task-specific learning strategies can markedly affect their performance in academic and nonacademic situations. This research suggests that several elements are essential to effective strategy instruction (Swanson, 1989). Central among these elements is the way in which task-specific learning strategies are taught to students. Regardless of the instructional stages discussed herein, the teacher obviously is the key ingredient in helping students make the transformation from ineffective, at-risk performers to effective, efficient strategy users. Not only must teachers carefully and skillfully follow the stages of instruction, but they also must pinpoint various problems that students encounter along the way and modify instruction accordingly. In addition, success of the learning process seems to depend, in large measure, on how much excitement and commitment the teacher brings to the learning situation. In short, teachers' instructional skills, as well as their mind set and enthusiasm for how much students can improve their learning by acquiring learning strategies, greatly enhance the instructional process.

REFERENCES

Bennett, R. F. (1987). *Gaining control*. Salt Lake City: Franklin International Institute.

Covey, S. R. (1989). *Seven habits of highly effective people*. New York: Simon & Schuster.

Deshler, D. D., Alley, G. R., Warner, M. M., & Schumaker, J. B. (1981). Instructional practices for promoting skill acquisition and generalization in severely learning disabled adolescents. *Learning Disability Quarterly, 4,* 415–421.

Deshler, D. D., & Lenz, B. K. (1989). The strategies instructional approach. *International Journal of Disability, Development and Education, 36,* 203–224.

Deshler, D. D., & Schumaker, J. B. (1986). Learning strategies: An instructional alternative for low-achieving adolescents. *Exceptional Children, 52*(6), 583–590.

Deshler, D. D., & Schumaker, J. B. (1988). An instructional model for teaching students how to learn. In J. L. Graden, J. E. Zins, & M. J. Curtis (Eds.), *Alternative educational delivery systems; Enhancing instructional options for all students*. Washington, DC: National Association of School Psychologists.

Deshler, D. D., Schumaker, J. B., & Lenz, B. K. (1984). Academic and cognitive interventions for LD adolescents: Part I. *Journal of Learning Disabilities, 17*(2), 108–117.

Deshler, D. D., Schumaker, J. B., Lenz, B. K., & Ellis, E. S. (1984) Academic and cognitive interventions for LD adolescents: Part II *Journal of Learning Disabilities, 17*(3), 170–187.

Ellis, E. S. (1986). The role of motivation and pedagogy on the generalization of cognitive strategy training. *Journal of Learning Disabilities, 19*(2), 66–70.

Ellis, E. S. (in press). A learning strategy for meeting the writing demands of secondary mainstream classrooms. *Teaching Exceptional Children*.

Ellis, E. S., & Lenz, B. K. (1990). Instructional techniques for mediating content-area learning: Issues and research. *Focus on Exceptional Children, 22*(9), 1–16.

Ellis, E. S., Lenz, B. K., & Sabornie, E. J. (1987a). Generalization and adaptation of learning strategies to natural environments: Part 1. Critical agents. *Remedial & Special Education, 8*(1), 6–21.

Ellis, E. S., Lenz, B. K., & Sabornie, E. J. (1987b). Generalization and adaptation of learning strategies to natural environments: Part 2. Research into practice. *Remedial & Special Education, 8*(2), 6–24.

Harris, K. R., & Graham, S. (1985). Improve learning disabled students' composition skills: Self-control strategy training. *Learning Disability Quarterly, 8,* 27–36.

Johnson, D. W., & Johnson, R. T. (1986). Mainstreaming and cooperative learning strategies. *Exceptional Children, 52*(6), 553–561.

Kagan, S. (1989). The structural approach to cooperative learning. *Educational Leadership, 47*(4), 12–16.

Kline, F. M. (1989). *The development and validation of feedback routines for use in special education settings*. Unpublished doctoral dissertation, University of Kansas, Lawrence.

Kuhn, T. S. (1970). *The structure of scientific revolutions*. Chicago: University of Chicago Press.

Lenz, B. K., Alley, G. R., & Schumaker, J. B. (1987). Activating the inactive learner: Advance organizers in the secondary content classroom. *Learning Disability Quarterly, 10*(1), 53–67.

Lenz, B. K., & Bulgren, J. A. (1990). Promoting learning in the content areas. In P. A. Cegelka & W. H. Berdine (Eds.), *Effective instruction for students with learning problems*. Needham Heights, MA: Allyn & Bacon.

Lenz, B. K., Bulgren, J., & Hudson, P. (1988). Content enhancement: A model for promoting the acquisition of content by individuals with learning disabilities. In T. E. Scruggs & B. Y. L. Wong (Eds.), *Intervention research in learning disabilities*. New York: Springer & Verlag, 122–165.

Lenz, B. K., Schumaker, J. B., Deshler, D. D., & Beals, V. L. (1984). *Learning strategies curriculum; The word identification strategy.* Lawrence: University of Kansas.

Litch, B. C., & Kistner, J. A. (1986). Motivational problems of learning disabled children: Individual differences and their implications for treatment. In J. K. Torgesen & B. Y. K. Wong (Eds.), *Psychological and educational perspectives on learning disabilities.* New York: Academic Press.

McCombs, B. L. (1984). Processes and skills underlying continuing intrinsic motivation to learn: Toward a definition of motivational skills training interventions. *Educational Psychologist, 19*(4), 199–218.

Nagel, D. R., Schumaker, J. B., & Deshler, D. D. (1986). *The learning strategies curriculum: The FIRST-letter mnemonic strategy.* Lawrence, KS: Edge Enterprises.

Palincsar, A. M., & Brown, A. L. (1984). Reciprocal teaching of comprehension fostering and monitoring activities. *Cognition & Instruction, 1,* 117–175.

Pressley, M., Goodchild, F., Fleet, J., Zajchowski, R., & Evans, E. D. (1987). *What is good strategy use and why is it hard to teach? An optimistic appraisal of the challenges associated with strategy instruction.* Unpublished manuscript, Department of Psychology, University of Western Ontario, London, Ontario.

Pressley, J., Borkowski, J. G., & O'Sullivan, J. (1985) Children's metamemory and the teaching of memory strategies. In D. L. Forrest-Pressley, D. MacKinnon, & T. G. Waller (Eds.), *Metamemory, cognition, and human performance* (pp. 111–153). San Diego: Academic Press.

Pressley, M., Goodchild, F., Fleet, J., Zajchowski, R., & Evans, E. D. (1989). The challenges of classroom strategy instruction. *Elementary School Journal, 89,* 301–342.

Pressley, M., Johnson, C. J., & Symons, S. (1987). Elaborating to learn and learning to elaborate. *Journal of Learning Disabilities, 20,* 76–91.

Pressley, M., Snyder, B. L., & Cariglia-Bull, T. (1987). How can good strategy use be taught to children?: Evaluation of six alternative approaches. In S. Cormier & J. Hagman (Eds.), *Transfer of learning: Contemporary research and applications,* Orlando, FL: Academic Press.

Putnam, M. L. (1988). *An investigation of the curricular demands in secondary mainstream classrooms containing students with mild handicaps.* Unpublished doctoral dissertation, University of Kansas, Lawrence.

Roehler, L. R., & Duffy, G. G. (1984). Direct explanation of comprehension processes. In G. G. Duffy, L. R. Roehler, & J. Mason (Eds.), *Comprehension instruction: Perspectives and suggestions* (pp. 265–280). New York: Longman.

Schmidt, J. L., Deshler, D. D., Schumaker, J. B., & Alley, G. R. (1989). Effects of generalization instruction on the written language performance of adolescents with learning disabilities in the mainstream classroom. *Journal of Reading, Writing, & Learning Disabilities, 4*(4), 291–311.

Schumaker, J. B. (1989). The heart of strategy instruction. *Strategram, 1*(4), 1–5.

Schumaker, J. B., Deshler, D. D., Alley, G. R., & Denton, P. (1982). Multipass: A learning strategy for improving reading comprehension. *Learning Disability Quarterly, 5*(3), 295–304.

Schumaker, J. B., Deshler, D. D., & Denton, P. (1984). *The learning strategies curriculum: The paraphrasing strategy.* Lawrence: University of Kansas.

Schumaker, J. B., Deshler, D. D., & McKnight, P. (1989). *Teaching routines to enhance the mainstream performance of adolescents with learning disabilities* (Final report submitted to the U. S. Department of Education, Special Education Services). Washington, DC.

Schumaker, J. B., Nolan, S. M., & Deshler, D. D. (1985). *Learning strategies curriculum: The error monitoring strategy.* Lawrence: University of Kansas.

Schumaker, J. B., & Sheldon, J. (1985). *The Sentence Writing Strategy.* Lawrence, KS: The University of Kansas.

Seabaugh, G. O., & Schumaker, J. B. (1981). *The effects of self-regulation training on the academic productivity of LD and non-LD adolescents* (Research Report #37). Lawrence, KS: The University of Kansas Institute for Research in Learning Disabilities.

Slavin, R. E. (1983). *Cooperative Learning.* New York: Longman.

Slavin, R. E. (1989). Research on cooperative learning: Consensus and controversy. *Educational Leadership, 47*(4), 52–56.

Slavin, R. E. (in press). Regular education under the REI: How must it change. *Remedial & Special Education.*

Swanson, H. L. (1989). Strategy instruction: Overview of principles and procedures for effective use. *Learning Disability Quarterly, 12*(1), 3–16.

Van Reusen, A. K., Bos, C., Deshler, D. D., & Schumaker, J. B. (1987). *Motivation strategies curriculum: The education planning strategy.* Lawrence, KS: Edge Enterprises.

Van Reusen, T., Deshler, D. D., & Schumaker, J. B. (1989). Effects of a student participation strategy in facilitating involvement of adolescents with LD in the individual education program planning process. *Learning Disabilities, 1*(2), 23–34.

Warner, M. M., Schumaker, J. B., Alley, G. R., & Deshler, D. D. (1989). Role of executive control: An epidemiology study of school identified learning disabled and low achieving adolescents in a serial recall task. *Learning Disabilities Research, 4*(2), 107–118.

Wittrock, M. C. (1986). Students' thought processes. In M. C. Wittrock (Ed.), *Handbook of research on teaching* (3d ed.). New York: Macmillan.

Wong, B. Y. L. (1985). Issues in cognitive-behavior interventions in academic skill areas. *Journal of Abnormal Child Psychology, 2*, 123–131.

Wong, B., & Jones, W. (1982). Increasing metacomprehension in learning disabled and normally achieving students through self-questioning training. *Learning Disability Quarterly, 5*(2), 228–238.

Edwin Ellis is affiliated with the University of Alabama. Donald Deshler, Keith Lenz, and Jean Schumaker are with the University of Kansas Institute for Research in Learning Disabilities. Frances Clark is with Wichita State University.

○ 10 ○

So much superstition abounds regarding the pros and cons of mainstreaming students that some practical, school-based research on the topic is refreshing. This article looks at the relationship between classroom behaviors and final grades of students with mild disabilities who have been mainstreamed in grades 3–9. Although the study does have a number of major findings, the most interesting is that students with mild disabilities passed all their mainstreamed courses, and often with little assistance from special education.

Academic Behavior and Grades of Mainstreamed Students with Mild Disabilities

Lee Ann Truesdell and Theodore Abramson

Since the implementation of Public Law 94-142 (1975), students with disabilities have participated with other students in various school programs. At first, mainstreaming occurred in noninstructional settings, such as the playground, assemblies, and lunch periods where students were integrated for social and emotional growth. Gradually, students with mild disabilities joined regular classes for music, art, and physical education. As school communities adjusted to the presence of special education students, students with mild disabilities have been mainstreamed into regular academic classes. In some instances, these students spend most of their time in a regular class and attend a special class or resource room one or more periods a day. In other instances, these students remain in special classes most of the school day and go to a regular class for one or more periods a day. With the increase in academic mainstreaming, the research focus has shifted from the socialization experience (Goodman, Gottlieb, & Harrison, 1972; Gottlieb & Budoff, 1973; Madden & Slavin, 1983) to examining the academic functioning and success of mainstreamed students (Kaufman, Agard, & Semmel, 1985; Truesdell, 1985; Zigmond & Kerr, 1985). The purpose of this article is to continue in this vein and also report the relationship between classroom academic behavior and academic achievement of mainstreamed students with mild disabilities.

Bloom (1974) estimated that 20% of student variance in achievement is accounted for by active participation in the learning process. Participation in class discussion requires (a) knowledge and competence in a repertoire of social interaction skills (Erickson, 1982), (b) an understanding of when to talk to whom and what to talk about (Green & Harker, 1982), and (c) an ability to attend selectively to information sources to define tasks and discover how to accomplish them (Doyle, 1983).

Participation in and completion of tasks may be more difficult for students with mild disabilities who typically show deficits in discriminating significant cues and problem-solving ability. Such students often act impulsively, fail to consider alternative solutions (Schumaker, Pederson, Hazel, & Meyen, 1983), spend significantly less time in task-oriented behavior, attend less to teachers when they give instructions (Bryan, 1974; McKinney, Mason, Pederson, & Clifford, 1975), and require more attention from their teachers than do average students (McKinney, McClure, & Feagans, 1982; Thompson, White, & Morgan, 1982). Because students who are mainstreamed may have one or more of these characteristics, they could have difficulty functioning in regular academic classes.

In a 3-year ethnographic study of mainstreaming, regular teachers described the success of mainstreamed students in terms of their classroom academic behavior: attendance, homework, attention, participation, preparation for class, basic skills, and scores on tests (Truesdell, 1985). That is, regular teachers reported mainstreamed students' classroom behavior in the same way that they recounted the behavior of their regular students. Furthermore, they were less concerned with mainstreamed students' social ability and peer relationships (Hersh & Walker, 1983; Kerr & Zigmond, 1985; Truesdell, 1985). Kornblau found considerable agreement among teachers across grade levels for the school-appropriate behavior they identified for "teachable" students (cited in Macmillan, Keogh, & Jones, 1986). In interviews with 36 teachers, prekindergarten through high school, Truesdell (1985) found that teachers perceived successful students as those who followed directions, completed tasks, were prepared for class, and paid attention.

Whereas teachers may view mainstreamed students as behaving appropriately in their classrooms, they may not expect mainstreamed students with disabilities to perform academic tasks as well as students without disabilities. Studies of mainstreaming found that despite mainstreamed students' doing poorly on teacher-made tests in the regular classes and failing to do homework regularly (Truesdell, 1985), nearly three quarters of high school students with learning disabilities passed their mainstream classes, perhaps as a result of teachers' inflating the grades of these students (Zigmond, Levine, & Laurie, 1985). In North Carolina, classroom teachers used different standards for grading report cards of mainstreamed students with mild disabilities and those of students without disabilities; these teachers emphasized effort, attitude, and attendance for the mainstreamed students and class performance for the other students (Calhoun & Beattie, 1984; Carpenter & Grantham, 1985).

Studies that compared the behavior and achievement of mainstreamed and regular high school students found that attendance and organizational skills related most strongly to achievement (Brown, Kerr, Zigmond, & Harris, 1984). Elementary mainstreamed students with mild mental retardation were on task 72% of the time, compared with 83% for regular students. Both groups had about the same number of cognitive interactions with the regular teacher (Kaufman et al., 1985). Studies at the elementary level of the Adaptive Learning Environment Model found that students with mild disabilities functioned well in classrooms with structure and choice (Wang, 1979).

Some students with mild disabilities lack proficiency in attending to tasks and other academic behaviors which could make for a difficult academic experience for both the students and the regular teacher who ultimately assesses student progress. While regular teachers describe mainstreamed students' success in terms of their classroom academic behavior, they may assign report card grades on the basis of their effort and attitude. This study, therefore, examined the relationship between the academic behavior and final grades of students with mild disabilities and also compared their reading ability to that of their peers without disabilities. This study goes beyond and expands earlier work by comparing the basic skill ability and final grades of both groups of students.

METHODS

One elementary school and two junior high schools with substantial academic mainstreaming for students with mild disabilities were identified by the Superintendent for Special Education in Queens, New York. These schools served a culturally, linguistically, and ethnically diverse population. Participants were 14 elementary and 19 junior high students in self-contained special education classes for students with mild disabilities who were mainstreamed for at least one academic subject every day and for whom parent permission was obtained. Table 1 reports the sample in terms of grade level, sex, ethnic background, and disability.

Although evaluation data were not available to the researchers, students' disabilities were determined by the Committee for Special Education, according to New York State Regulations, Part 200, which state in part that (a) students with learning disabilities have an imperfect ability to use spoken or written language and exhibit a discrepancy of 50 percent or more between expected and actual achievement and (b) students with emotional disturbances have an unexplained inability to learn and to maintain interpersonal relationships, and they exhibit inappropriate behavior or feelings, a pervasive unhappiness, or fears associated with personal or school problems.

In the elementary school, all academic mainstreaming occurred in reading. The school used a modified Joplin plan that reorganized all students across classes and grades for reading instruction during the first hour of the school day. Each teacher was assigned one or two reading levels; and all students reading at a particular level, regardless of their actual grade placement, reported to the teacher responsible for instruction at that reading level. Selected special education students were mainstreamed into reading classes based on their reading ability, as determined by their special education teacher and the Committee on Special Education. Special education teachers cited general ability (64%) and

TABLE 1   Characteristics of Mainstreamed Students with Mild Disabilities, by School Level

Variable	Elementary (*n* = 14)	Junior High (*n* = 19)
Sex		
Male	10	8
Female	4	11
Ethnic Background		
Black	3	5
Hispanic	4	2
Other	1	1
White	6	11
Special education category		
Emotionally disturbed	12	4
Learning disabled	2	15
Mainstream class		
Reading/English[a]	14	5
Math		4
Social studies		5
Science		5

[a]The English classes into which students were mainstreamed in the junior high schools were primarily basic skills reading and writing classes.

reading ability (71%) most frequently as the criteria they used to select students for mainstream reading instruction.

In the junior high schools, students were mainstreamed in their areas of strength into individual subject classes, often in the low track classes for low-achieving students. Special education teachers indicated that they recommended students for mainstreaming in particular subject areas, based on the students' general ability (83%) and interest (94%). Teachers also indicated that student conduct was an important consideration (83%).

As a comparison group, five students were selected at random in each of the regular academic classes into which the sample of students with disabilities were mainstreamed. Standardized reading test scores, final grades, and attendance data were collected for both groups from school records.

The dependent variable in this study was the final grade earned in the mainstream class, with grades at or above 65 as passing. Ratings of student behaviors, including attendance, participation in class discussion, homework, accuracy of written work, paying attention in class, and scores on tests and quizzes, were the independent variables. Reading ability of the mainstreamed and regular elementary students was also compared.

The regular teachers of the mainstream classes completed a brief questionnaire in May 1986, indicating the academic behavior of the mainstreamed students in the sample. The questionnaire used a 5-point Likert-type scale, in which teachers rated the subjects from excellent (1) to poor (5). Special education teachers also completed questionnaires, in which they indicated, from a list, the criteria they used to select each subject for mainstreaming. They also indicated whether they tutored students in the subject of the mainstream class. The questionnaires were distributed by the coordinator for mainstreaming in each school.

At the end of the academic year, data from school records included attendance of the mainstreamed students (total number of days absent in the school year), final report card grades in the mainstream subject, and standardized reading test scores administered in April 1986 for mainstreamed students and their regular class peers at both school levels. Data also included the standardized reading test scores administered in April 1985 for the two student groups at the elementary school. Reading achievement in 1985 was indicated on student records by a grade equivalency score measured by the California Achievement Test. In 1986, the Degrees of Reading Power (DRP) test was used to measure reading achievement. Scores were reported in DRP units, indicating the readability of text at the student's instructional level. The New York State Board of Regents had changed to the DRP because it reflected a language-based theory of reading and provided a more relevant database for instructional planning. Tests were administered at the grade level to which mainstreamed and regular students were assigned.

The final grades of the mainstreamed students and the regular students were compared, using the Mann Whitney U Test. The relationship of final grades to teacher ratings of academic behavior of the mainstreamed students was calculated using the Spearman Rank Order Correlation Coefficient. Differences between the reading ability of the mainstreamed and regular elementary students were evaluated using the analysis of covariance (ANCOVA).

RESULTS

At the elementary school level, significant differences between the standardized reading test scores of mainstreamed and regular students were found. In the ANCOVA test for differences in the means of the residuals, where residuals are differences between the 1986 scores and a regression quantity based on the 1985 scores as covariate, the differences were not significant. The nonsignificant residual indicates that variations in 1986 reading scores are probably attributable to prior reading achievement as indicated by the 1985 reading scores (Table 2).

When the final grades of the students with disabilities were compared with those of the regular students in the elementary mainstream classes, regular students achieved significantly higher grades (U = 35, $p < .05$) than their MH peers. In the elementary schools, regular students (in percents) received the following report card grades: A, 25.4%; B, 32.7%; C, 36.4%; D, 4%, and F, 2%. Mainstreamed students received these grades: A, 14.3%; B, 14.3%; C, 57%; and D, 14.3%. No elementary school student with disabilities, however, failed the mainstream reading class.

In the junior high schools, no significant difference between the grades earned by the mainstreamed and regular students was found.

Although mainstreamed students earned lower grades in elementary school, only one student with disabilities across all three schools actually received a failing grade in the mainstream class. Furthermore, the mainstreamed students passed their regular classes

TABLE 2   *Means, Standard Deviations, and F-Ratios for Reading Scores of Elementary School Students With and Without Disabilities*

	Students				
	With Disabilities ($n = 13$)		Without Disabilities ($n = 10$)		
Reading Test	M	SD	M	SD	F-Ratio
CAT (1985)[a]	4.03	1.36	5.98	1.37	11.58**
DRP (1986)[b]	43.15	10.22	54.96	9.82	7.41*

[a]California Achievement Test grade equivalency scores.
[b]Degrees of Reading Power units indicating readability levels.
*$p < .05$.
**$p < .01$.

without any special or extra assistance from their special education teachers, who indicated that they seldom helped mainstreamed students with the content of the regular class.

When classroom behaviors were correlated with final grades, all relationships were found to be significant except school attendance at both levels, homework at the elementary level, and accuracy of written work at the junior high school level (see Table 3). The significant correlations ranged from .58 to .87 and .42 to .64 at the elementary and junior high school levels, respectively.

DISCUSSION

The strong positive relationships between classroom academic behavior and final grades are consistent with earlier work, in which regular teachers described the progress of their mainstreamed students in terms of academic behaviors (Truesdell, 1985). Teachers seemed to use student participation and activity in class as indicators of progress in learning the subject matter. The mainstreamed students in this earlier study exhibited appropriate academic behavior in the mainstream class. The lack of a significant relationship between final grades and homework at the elementary level and accuracy of written work at the junior high level may be more indicative of the relative importance placed on these academic behaviors at the different school levels than on the behavior of mainstreamed students. Absenteeism for the combined group varied widely among the mainstreamed population ($\overline{X} = 12.6$, $SD = 17$) but apparently was not related to final grades. The five students with disabilities who were absent more than 20 days achieved C or better in their mainstream subject, and the six students with disabilities who were absent 11–20 days also achieved grades of C or better.

The comparison of final grades of regular and mainstreamed students indicates that, in the junior high schools, the students with mild disabilities were as successful academically as the regular students with whom they were placed and earned grades similar to their regular class peers. Mainstreaming in the junior high school placed students in subject area classes of their *strengths* and *interests*.

TABLE 3   *Correlations of Academic Behavior Variables and Final Grades of Mainstreamed Students with Mild Disabilities*

Variable	Elementary Students (*n* = 14)			Junior High Students (*n* = 19)		
	Mean (SD)	Rho	*p*	Mean (SD)	Rho	*p*
Attendance	13.43 (20.37)	−.298	NS	12 (13.45)	−.0004	NS
Participation in discussion	2.86 (1.35)	.5769	.05	2.8 (1.39)	.4224	.05
Paying attention	2.58 (1.05)	.8610	.001	2.53 (1.19)	.5950	.01
Homework	2.8 (1.11)	.4727	NS	2.4 (1.38)	.6414	.01
Accuracy of written work	3.1 (0.8)	.6429	.02	2.5 (0.94)	.2145	NS
Tests and quizzes	3.5 (0.77)	.8716	.001	2.9 (0.94)	.6320	.01

In the elementary school, students with mild disabilities earned grades lower than their regular class peers. In all but two instances, their grades were lower than the average grades of the five regular peers selected at random for comparison. This finding is consistent with the standardized reading comparison. The mainstreamed students were found to be significantly lower in reading ability than the regular students in the mainstream reading classes; therefore, it is not surprising that their final grades would similarly differ.

What is difficult to explain is why students with mild disabilities were mainstreamed into reading classes in which their classmates were reading at a level significantly higher than they were. Placements of students with disabilities into mainstream settings were guided primarily by the special education teachers' estimates of the students' reading ability. Teachers' estimates may have been inaccurate because the special education teachers had little knowledge of the reading ability of regular students with whom the students with disabilities were to be mainstreamed. Furthermore, in arriving at the decision to mainstream, teachers may have used data from the students' individualized educational programs (IEPs). Reading achievement data on IEPs were frequently based on results of the Wide Range Achievement Test (WRAT) (Jastak & Jastak, 1978), which assesses reading skill in letter recognition, letter naming, and pronunciation of words in isolation. These skill domains do not correspond to the full scope of reading instruction, especially in the upper elementary grades, where comprehension is emphasized. Furthermore, there may be some technical problems with the WRAT; Salvia and Ysseldyke (1985) have reported that the norms are inadequate and its reported reliability is unsupported by data.

The nature of the mainstream placement of students with mild disabilities in regular academic classes seems to influence these students' academic success. Although final grades of the students in the junior high schools did not differ significantly, many students with disabilities were mainstreamed into the lower track classes where lower expectations for student performance are found than in regular track classes (McDermott & Aron, 1978). The elementary school students with mild disabilities were less successful academically relative to their regular peers primarily because they were placed in reading classes with regular students functioning at levels above their current ability. At both school levels, academic achievement of mainstreamed students with mild disabilities may be a function of the match of the ability or skills level of the two student groups.

This study relied on teacher reports of students' classroom behavior. Research is needed to determine whether observed classroom behaviors discriminate successful and unsuccessful students with mild disabilities in regular classes. In a study of high school mainstreamed students, Zigmond and Kerr (1985) found that organizational skills and attendance explained only 39% of the variance between successful and unsuccessful mainstreamed students. They proposed that basic skills and higher cognitive processes may also contribute to differences between successful and unsuccessful mainstreamed students.

Successful mainstreaming experiences may depend on a combination of students' abilities and placement into classes that are of interest to them and in which they start with an adequate skill or knowledge base. If teachers award final grades of mainstreamed students on a standard different from that of regular students, it will be impossible to determine success accurately using final grades as a criterion. A more comprehensive measure of student success and performance over time will be needed for a more accurate estimate of success.

REFERENCES

Bloom, B. S. (1974). Time and learning. *American Psychologist, 29,* 682–688.

Brown, G. M., Kerr, M. M., Zigmond, N., & Harris, A. (1984). What's important for student success in high school? Successful and unsuccessful students discuss school survival skills. *The High School Journal, 68*(1), 10–17.

Bryan, T. S. (1974). An observational analysis of classroom behaviors of children with learning disabilities. *Journal of Learning Disabilities, 7*(1), 35–43.

Calhoun, M. L., & Beattie, J. (1984). Assigning grades in the high school mainstream: Perceptions of teachers and students. *Diagnostique, 9,* 218–225.

Carpenter, D., & Grantham, L. B. (1985). A statewide investigation of grading practices and options concerning mainstreamed handicapped pupils. *Diagnostique, 11,* 31–39.

Doyle, W. (1983). Academic work. *Review of Educational Research, 53*(2), 159–199.

Erickson, F. (1982). Classroom discourse as improvisation: Relationships between academic task structure and social participation structure in lessons. In L. C. Wilkinson (Ed.), *Communication in the classroom* (pp. 153–182). New York: Academic Press.

Goodman, H., Gottlieb, J., & Harrison, R. H. (1972). Social acceptance of EMR children integrated into a nongraded elementary school. *American Journal of Mental Deficiency, 77,* 412–417.

Gottlieb, J., & Budoff, A. (1973). Social acceptability of retarded children in nongraded schools differing in architecture. *American Journal of Mental Deficiency, 78,* 15–19.

Green, J. L., & Harker, J. O. (1982). Gaining access to learning: Conversational, social, and cognitive demands of group participation. In L. C. Wilkinson (Ed.), *Communication in the classroom* (pp. 183–221). New York: Academic Press.

Hersh, R. H., & Walker, H. M. (1983). Great expectations: Making schools effective for all students. *Policy Studies Review, 2*(Special #1), 147–189.

Jastak, J. E., & Jastak, S. R. (1978). *Wide Range Achievement Test.* Wilmington, DE: Jastak Associates.

Kaufman, M., Agard, J. A., & Semmel, M. I. (1985). *Mainstreaming: Learners and their environment.* Cambridge, MA: Brookline Books.

Kerr, M. M., & Zigmond, N. (1985). *Too much, too little, too late: The role of behavioral assessment in treating adolescent school adjustment problems.* Paper presented at the annual meeting of the American Educational Research Association, Chicago.

Macmillan, D. L., Keogh, B. K., & Jones, R. L. (1986). Special educational research on mildly handicapped learners. In M. C. Wittrock (Ed.), *Handbook of research on teaching* (pp. 686–725). New York: Macmillan.

Madden, N. A., & Slavin, R. R. (1983). Effects of cooperative learning on the social acceptance of mainstreamed academically handicapped students. *Journal of Special Education, 17,* 171–182.

McDermott, R. P., & Aron, J. (1978). Pirandello in the classroom: On the possibility of equal educational opportunities in American culture. In M. C. Reynolds (Ed.), *Futures of education for exceptional students: Emerging structures* (pp. 44–64). Reston, VA: Council for Exceptional Children.

McKinney, J. D., Mason, J., Pederson, K., & Clifford, M. (1975). Relationship between classroom behavior and academic achievement. *Journal of Educational Psychology, 67*(2), 198–203.

McKinney, J. D., McClure, S., & Feagans, L. (1982). Classroom behavior of learning disabled children. *Learning Disability Quarterly, 5,* 45–52.

Salvia, J., & Ysseldyke, J. E. (1985). *Assessment in special and remedial education* (3rd ed.). Boston: Houghton and Mifflin.

Schumaker, J. B., Pederson, C. S., Hazel, J. S., & Meyen, E. L. (1983). Social skills curricula for mildly handicapped adolescents: A review. *Focus on Exceptional Children, 16*(4), 1–16.

Thompson, R. H., White, K. R., & Morgan, D. P. (1982). Teacher-student interaction pattern in classrooms with mainstreamed mildly-handicapped students. *American Educational Research Journal, 19*(2), 220–236.

Truesdell, L. A. (1985). *Making it in the mainstream: Student behavior and academic success.* Unpublished manuscript, Queens College, City University of New York, Queens.

Wang, M. C. (1979). The development of student self-management skills: Implications for effective use of instructional and learning time. *Educational Horizons, 57*(4), 169–174.

Zigmond, N., & Kerr, M. M. (1985). *Managing the mainstream: A contrast of the behaviors of learning disabled students who pass their assigned mainstream courses and those who fail.* Manuscript submitted for publication.

Zigmond, N., Levine, E., & Laurie, T. E. (1985). Managing the mainstream: An analysis of teacher attitudes and student performance in mainstream high school programs. *Journal of Learning Disabilities, 18*(9), 535–541.

Lee Ann Truesdell is an associate professor and the coordinator of the Special Education Program and Theodore Abramson is a professor in the Department of Elementary and Early Childhood Education at Queens College, City University of New York, Queens, New York.

Part II:
New Practices

A farmer once was offered more training in farming and responded, "I already know far more about farming than I'm practicing." A similar comment could be made about teaching students with mild disabilities, whether they are labeled behavior disordered, learning disabled, or mentally retarded.

This section of the book highlights new practices that can materially improve instruction. Several articles examine assessment practices that are closely related to instruction. One deals with curriculum, and the remainder with a great variety of instructional approaches that are considered to be among the most effective.

Wesson, Otis-Wilborn, Hasbrouck, and Tindal provide one of the most practical articles in this series. It addresses two questions: (a) What should I teach students in terms of oral and written language? (b) How will I know if the instruction has been effective? The authors guide the reader through effective instruction in oral and written language.

The article by Shinn and Hubbard lays out the use of curriculum-based measurement, which is a set of practices employing samples of instruction to determine the effectiveness of instruction. Because assessment is linked so closely to instruction in this approach, teachers have no doubt about what they have taught or how effective they have been. CBM probably has more potential for elevating the achievement of special education and regular education students than any other approaches we know of.

Polloway, Patton, Epstein, and Smith review the three main curricular approaches of the past and then set forth their own recommendations. They show how curriculum and programming must be adjusted to the delivery system. This seems realistic because, at times in the past, students have been the recipients of a certain curriculum regardless of their placement. Likewise, the curriculum must change as the student goes through school.

Westby describes how special education can apply the whole language approach—one of the hottest topics of today. This approach, incorporating reading, writing, and oral presentations, is widely used in regular education. It seems like a natural for special education. The author provides a road map for incorporating the elements of this approach into special education.

What a teacher does often dramatically affects student learning. Graham and Johnson examine teacher-directed activities before, during, and after teaching lessons in reading. They present convincing research that shows much greater student achievement if teachers select the appropriate level of materials. The many suggestions, all based on research data, offer ways in which teachers can promote better reading performance in their students.

Ensminger and Dangel present an intriguing experientially based approach based on the Foxfire pedagogy, which came out of the North Georgia Mountains for instructing youth there. Typical high school students were encouraged to take part in setting the outcomes of their education, to select how they would collect and disseminate information. These students ended up accomplishing many of the usual objectives of high schools, and they did it through conducting community interviews that they wrote and talked about. Ensminger and Dangel see this didactic approach as appropriate for students with mild disabilities and especially as a way for mainstreamed students to be involved in their education. The actual accomplishment of Foxfire looks much like successful cooperative learning, which has been popular in recent years.

Probably the most difficult area to cover in a book such as this one is the teaching of math. Mercer and Miller offer one of the better articles on this topic. It is beneficial not only to special educators but also to regular educators who have mainstreamed students.

Teachers, especially at the high school level, are charged with helping students to acquire a variety of associated concepts and facts in content areas such as geography, social studies, and history. Teachers encounter some of the greatest difficulties in improving the memory and presentation of information for students with mild disabilities. Ellis and Lenz give excellent advice on assisting students in these areas. They recommend a variety of remedies from something as simple as reducing the amount of content that must be covered or mastered to limiting the verbal content to only the essential material we want the students to learn, without extraneous material. They suggest controlling the readability of textbooks, as well as study guidelines, audio texts, learning strategies, and mnemonics, to enhance content and make it more learnable.

Rounding out the articles, Lloyd and Keller address effective mathematics instruction. Much of their discussion centers on what is known about the ways children learn math, followed by suggestions regarding effective presentation to students with mild disabilities. For the special education teacher, their presentation is based largely on the direct instruction model, especially the steps proposed by Rosenshine and Stevens (1986). The authors also offer a variety of techniques including modeling, reinforcement, and corrections. The authors conclude by looking at the research on the two basic groups of field studies: fairly specific aspects of math content or skill and the effectiveness of comprehensive mathematics programs.

The articles in this section explore new practices. They offer special educators and regular educators of mainstreamed students a variety of approaches and suggestions for their use, backed by a research base for understanding both the advantages and the limitations of these approaches.

Rosenshine, B., & Stevens, R. (1986). Teaching functions. In M. C. Wittrock (Ed.), *Handbook of research on teaching* (3rd ed., pp. 376–391). New York: Macmillan.

○ 11 ○

The authors discuss teachers' use of assessment techniques useful after the student has been placed in special education. These informal techniques determine what will be taught and how effective the teacher is in developing these skills. The authors offer a variety of assessment strategies that should be within the capability of all teachers and that should improve oral and written language instruction.

Linking Assessment, Curriculum, and Instruction of Oral and Written Language

Caren Wesson, Amy Otis-Wilborn, Jan Hasbrouck, and Gerald Tindal

Two major instructional questions addressed by the assessment process, according to Zigmond and Miller (1986), are *what to teach* and *how to teach*. In their reconceptualization of the assessment process for instructional planning purposes, they concluded that both questions could be answered best through the use of various informal assessment strategies. They suggested a two-stage process of (a) identifying the broad curricular domain and, (b) selecting specific instructional objectives. Formal testing and functional analysis of environmental demands have been useful in selecting domains in which IEP goals are necessary for the individual exceptional student.

Selection of goals occurs prior to placement in the special education program. Once the student is participating in the special education program, the second stage, informal assessment for identifying objectives, must begin. This process includes:

1. Planning for assessment; selecting or developing a cluster of skills or behaviors that represent the domain, deciding at what point to start the assessment, and selecting or developing a set of tasks or context that reflect the skills or behaviors.
2. Administering informal assessment.
3. Analyzing the students' responses and determining which behaviors require further probes.

4. Administering more specific probes.
5. Using survey and probe results to specify objectives.

We refer to this process as *pre-instructional assessment* (PIA).

Zigmond and Miller point to continuous monitoring of student performance as the means for determining how to teach. Documenting the failure of attribute-treatment interaction research, they contend that a priori testing cannot lead teachers to reliably know what teaching methods are best for the individual student. Instead, they suggest "direct and frequent evaluation of student achievement" (p. 507) and reframing of the question "how to teach" to"how can good instruction be responsive to individual differences?" (p. 507). We refer to the assessment conducted to answer this question as *on-going monitoring of progress in the domain* (OMPD).

LINKING ASSESSMENT AND CURRICULUM

The precedence for PIA and OMPD is found in *curriculum-based assessment* (CBA) and *curriculum-based measurement* (CBM). CBA has become a common term in the special education literature. Differing interpretations and implementations of these terms, however, have caused some misunderstandings. Tucker (1985) defines CBA as using the material to be learned as the basis for assessing the degree to which it has been learned. Complications arise from the various ways in which people define what is to be learned (the curriculum) and how to assess. Because there is no agreement, the combined use of these concepts has led to many vastly different interpretations of CBA (eg., Coulter, 1985; Deno, 1985; Howell & Morehead, 1987; Marston & Magnusson, 1985).

In contrast, CBM (Deno, 1985) refers to the repeated use of standard probes that are based on the curriculum. Teachers graph and use the data from these probes to make decisions about the effectiveness of their instruction. Most CBA strategies do not necessarily involve time series analysis for using the data. Thus, CBM becomes a subset of CBA. Because the terminology is confusing and CBA is open to interpretation, we will use new vocabulary, PIA and OMPD, to clarify the two assessment questions to be addressed here. The questions are:

1. How does a teacher decide for an individual student what should be taught within the domain of oral and written language?
2. How does the teacher know if the instruction in oral and written language is effective for individual students?

To address the first question, special education teachers typically survey through informal assessment skills within the domain of interest. This PIA process, recommended here, will be discussed later.

Most teachers do not directly ask the second question on a regular basis but, rather, assess annually using a standardized test to determine the amount of progress in a general domain. With the research in CBM, educators have become more attuned to the idea of questioning the effectiveness of their instructional approaches. Teachers understand the rationale for this type of assessment because they realize that no direct relationship exists between the mastery of subskills and progress in the whole domain. A student may be able to master the skills of asking questions beginning with the words *when, where, how, what*, and *why*, for example, but not be able to use question forms in functional communication contexts.

This relationship between specific skills and progress in the whole domain is illustrated best with an example from spelling. All teachers have seen the student who consistently masters the weekly spelling test at 90%, yet fails to improve spelling in spontaneous written expression. Adding up the parts does not necessarily equal the whole.

LANGUAGE, THE CURRICULUM, AND INSTRUCTION

To clarify the relationship between language curricula and language instruction requires defining the language curriculum and aspects of language performance that signal change and improvement in language competence. Oral and written language provide observable means for examining competence.

Difficulties with language use, expressively and receptively, cause many students with handicaps to fail in school. Language competence (understanding) and performance (use) are based on a student's proficiency in English language syntax, semantics, and pragmatics, and are the basis for development of most school-related knowledge and skills. In addition, students often are asked to demonstrate their mastery of the school curriculum through oral and written expression.

There is a close relationship between oral language and written language. Oral language is a reflection of general language comprehension, cognition, and concept development, and written language is built upon general language knowledge and oral language expression (Bereiter & Scardamalia, 1982). For this reason, examination of a student's proficiency in written and spoken language in authentic communication contexts can help a teacher understand not only a student's general language knowledge but also the student's ability to use language in meaningful ways. The assessment procedures presented here, therefore, focus on writing and speaking and suggest that assessment in these two areas be used in language. Direct parallels between assessing oral and written language will be made.

Language typically is described in reference to four parameters—*phonology, syntax, semantics*, and *pragmatics*. Phonology refers to articulation, the phonetic and phonologic components in speech. It is not discussed here because the speech and language pathologist typically assesses and works on speech articulation. Also, handwriting and the use of conventions such as punctuation, capitalization, and spelling are not addressed. These skills are related to written expression as articulation is to oral expression. Although one cannot deny the relationship of phonology and the mechanics of writing to language, a more extensive discussion would be required. Thus, this article focuses on syntax, semantics, and pragmatics.

The development and use of language are complex phenomena, making the process of language instruction complicated. Identification of discrete language behaviors or skills that guarantee an impact on overall language proficiency is difficult. Concern with meeting specific objectives can overshadow the need to look at the effects of language instruction on the broad domain of language. Meaningful assessment of language instruction requires a teacher to take a broad look at language (OMPD) in addition to a narrow one (PIA). The following general process is suggested for designing, implementing, and assessing language instruction.

1. Assess general language functioning.
2. Identify discrete language errors, omissions, or delays demonstrated by the child.
3. Discriminate language "errors" that are developmentally appropriate.
4. Develop instructional plans for working on the discrete language errors that have the greatest impact on communication.
5. Assess general language functioning. Answer the question: Is overall language communication improving? If not, are the discrete skills selected for focus appropriate? Are the choices of instructional contexts or strategies inappropriate or ineffective?
6. Revise/make adjustments in the choice of discrete skills targeted for instruction or revise the instructional plan.

Throughout the process described above, attention also should be given to the student's cultural and linguistic environment. Differences in language patterns, for example, may be attributable to the influence of different cultures, languages, or dialects. This includes the influence of linguistic characteristics of Black English dialect and structure and phonology of foreign languages (Golden-Fletcher, 1986).

DEFINING THE CURRICULUM FOR ORAL AND WRITTEN LANGUAGE

The student's individual needs and cultural and environmental backgrounds as well as expectations regarding language performance in the school setting are factors influencing curricular content and language instruction. Relevant language curricula in oral and written language should be used to guide the pre-instructional assessment process.

Language objectives can be drawn from two sources:

1. Specific aspects that describe the nature and structure of language and communication within the normal language development process.
2. Content inherent in the academic and social environments.

Aspects of Normal Language

In lieu of an "official" or formal curriculum, the model most often used in assessing language is the normal language development sequence. This language development sequence, which grows in content and complexity, also is an appropriate model for examining written language. Research on the language development of children with various handicapping conditions has demonstrated that these children often follow patterns of development similar to those of nonhandicapped children (Johnston & Schery, 1976; Morehead & Ingram, 1973). Therefore, the normal language model forms the basis for an appropriate language curriculum for children demonstrating language disorders.

Language within this model is described in reference to syntactic, semantic, and pragmatic development.

Snytax refers to the grammatical structure and complexity of language (simple, compound, complex sentences), which are developed from the basic parts of speech (noun, verb, adverb, pronoun, etc.) and their functions (subject, predicate, direct object, etc.). Also included in syntax are morphological aspects, the smallest meaningful units of language; they include word endings (e.g., indicating plurality, tense, comparatives, prefixes, suffixes, articles, prepositions, and other function words (connecting parts of a sentence).

Semantics refers to the meaning of language at the levels of the lexicon (word) and the sentence. At the lexical levels, semantics involves word meaning or vocabulary. Knowledge and use of vocabulary is quite complex because it is related to a student's overall concept development. Its critical role in language learning recently has been reemphasized (Rice, 1989). At the sentence level, meaning is expressed through relationships built in word combinations (Bloom & Lahey, 1978).

Finally, *pragmatics* refers to ways in which language is used. Systems for classifying linguistic functions have been developed to describe the purpose or intent of communication and indicate the effectiveness with which speakers use their knowledge about the communication situation, the participants, and language to achieve the intent.

Pragmatics in written language refers to the functional use of writing. To paraphrase Graves (1983), writing helps us to transcend ourselves in space and time. Writing helps to leave a lasting impression, a remembrance of our thoughts and feelings. Writing is intended to communicate not only to others but also to ourselves. For written language to be understood, it must comply with many of the same standards required of oral language. Context-specific written language must be used, and it must be approximately correct and complete with respect to semantics, syntax, and the intent or purpose of the communication.

Academic and Social Curricula

Oral Language Curricula

Language objectives also can be identified by examining the various "curricula" within the environment. Because most children enter school already having acquired complex oral language communication skills, there is no oral language curriculum per se. For the most part, children are working on developing complexity and proficiency in oral language and communication.

Standard adult English, another model of language, is useful in identifying language differences. A child's language resembles adult language and continues to develop in syntactic and semantic complexity throughout childhood. Also, observing the language/communication models of peers provides useful information regarding developmentally appropriate language patterns for a specific age group. Discrepancies between language patterns in adult and peer language and that of an individual student can facilitate the identification of relevant language objectives.

As discussed earlier, oral language curricula may be determined by the linguistic demands of the school, social, and home environments. Academic language includes skills such as asking and answering questions and discourse skills (identifying a topic, commenting on and maintaining the topic, selecting and organizing relevant information, oral reporting). In addition, specific vocabulary is linked with the academic curriculum. Social communication includes various interactions with peers and adults, requiring cooperative group skills, taking turns, and the use of social conventions such as greetings and salutations. The development and use of syntactic, semantic, and pragmatic communication devices facilitate academic learning and successful social interaction.

Written Language

Academic written language curricular requirements include many tasks ranging from minute responses to broad-based projects. Students learn to fill in the blank with one word or phrase responses in content and comprehension exercises. Students often are required to write sentences or paragraphs of explanation to show understanding of what they read or heard in class discussions. They also write to express their own novel thoughts and ideas. As they mature, student writers compose stories and themes. Some districts require students to pass a theme-writing test prior to graduation. Other academic written language tasks may include some study skills, such as planning for completion of a project, time management, notetaking, and outlining.

Writing is used also for social interactions. The student must be able to communicate in writing to teachers, family, and peers. Social written language curricula include writing notes, such an invitations, thank-you notes, and postcards. Consumer-related skills include writing letters of intent or complaint. Letter writing for a variety of purposes and audiences is an important skill.

PRE-INSTRUCTIONAL ASSESSMENT

The procedure for assessing language for the purpose of developing specific objectives is broken down into four steps:

1. Identification/definition of relevant curricula (the pool of potential objectives).
2. Assessment of language performance through language sampling.
3. Development of formal objectives to direct language development.
4. Prioritization and selection of objectives for instruction.

The purpose of the language assessment process is to collect enough evidence to identify errors in what Bloom and Lahey (1978) have defined as the *form* (syntax/morphology), *use* (pragmatics), and *content* (concepts and ideas, including semantics) of a student's language performance. The assessment process should be based on observation of language, which allows for the identification of (a) developmental achievements, (b) linguistic contexts in which the form, function, or content of language is problematic, and (c) patterns of language performance in response to the demands of academic and social environments.

A direct method for assessing language is through language sampling and analysis. For oral language samples, the manipulation of materials, settings, and language partners and the observation of a student engaged in natural communication situations provide more relevant information for identifying objectives and planning for language intervention. Although a number of formal instruments are available to guide this process, they are limited regarding the parameters of language upon which they focus. Informal but structured methods for collecting, transcribing, and analyzing language samples are more flexible and can be designed to fit the specific focus of assessment and the student's language skill level. In written language, samples that require students to communicate for a variety of purposes and to various audiences form the basis for identifying language development and errors and pinpointing the objectives of instruction.

Oral Language Samples for PIA

General sampling requires observing a communication situation to elicit a large number of utterances reflecting a variety of syntactic, semantic, and pragmatic aspects of language for analysis. The larger the sample, the more "representative" it is of the student's communication abilities.

When collecting a language sample, several variables should be considered. Although the sample should not be limited to sentence-level productions, the majority of the sample should be made up of word combinations, when possible. Next, the setting and materials should be motivating and should provide many opportunities for the student to respond freely. A free-play situation generally is recommended for young children. Toys that a student can manipulate, such as a play house with people, cars, and furniture, are excellent tools. A fuller language sample is achieved if the teacher follows the student's lead regarding the topics discussed. Also, teachers should monitor their own language used to prompt the student. Questions should be open-ended and require more than a yes/no or one-word response.

The sample must be recorded, through a video or audio tape recorder. The teacher can provide comments throughout the tape that will help to identify the context, activity, or any utterances that may be difficult to understand.

The next step is to transcribe the taped records. For each sample, the date, time of day, setting, participants, and materials should be documented. Then, student's utterances should be listed. Utterances illustrating an error or omission in content, form, or function, should include the standard English equivalent, which helps to identify specific syntactic, semantic, and pragmatic concerns. Other items that should be documented include contextual factors that indicate (a) verbal or nonverbal stimulus, (b) activity that preceded, accompanied and/or followed the utterance, (c) other important information regarding the context of communication that helps explain the intent of the student's utterances. In assessing the intent of the utterance, the teacher should take a child's perspective, not an adult's, by considering all of the contextual factors in relation to the student.

Written Language Samples for PIA

For sampling written language, teachers should collect several samples of the students' writing before identifying the objectives. The samples should have varying intents; thus, they might include creative writing samples, themes, and letters. Eliciting several samples increases the likelihood of a representative sample.

For each sample, teachers should conduct some prewriting activity to activate the student's knowledge and imagination with respect to the topic. For creative writing, teachers could collect two types—fantasy situations (e.g., "Once I was marooned on a tropical island. On the other side of the island there lived a . . .") and reality-based situations (e.g., "My favorite chore around the house is . . . because . . ."). Before writing, the teacher may lead a discussion on the topic, bring in artifacts to stimulate interest, take the students on a visualization journey, or tell or read a related story. Students should have ample time to complete their stories but should do all the writing in school (rather than homework).

Analysis of the Oral and Written Language Sample

Analysis of the oral sample identifies aspects of the student's language that are present and developmentally appropriate, present but incorrect (errors), omitted but demanded by the communication situation (omissions), and omitted because of insufficient opportunity during sampling. Identifying errors or omissions is only the first step. The teacher also must determine the nature of the language error or omission because this will influence the kinds of language goals and objectives developed and the instructional approach taken. Ultimately, teachers have to prioritize the language objectives, taking into consideration their impact on overall communicative competence.

Survey of Sample

The language sample should be surveyed for specific syntactic devices that are used correctly, incorrectly, or not produced. Table 1 gives examples of the more frequent and useful devices available. Objectives that can be developed on the basis of this analysis might include (a) developing syntactic structures and devices for achieving more complex sentences, and (b) developing the use of specific grammatical devices that the student has omitted or used incorrectly.

The language sample should be surveyed to check for the number and variety of semantic roles used correctly. These are defined in Table 2. The student's use of a variety of roles indicates the range of meaning expressed at the sentence level. Table 2 could serve as a checklist.

Conduct a semantic "field-analysis" (Miller, 1981). The purpose of a field analysis is to examine the appropriate meaning conveyed within a sentence (referential meaning) and between sentences within a linguistic context (relational meaning). As teachers survey the overall language sample, they should pose the following questions:

1. Does the vocabulary used match the student's intent?
2. Do sentences fit together meaningfully?
3. Are sentences connected by linquistic references to aspects of time and space?

The objectives that can be drawn from a semantic analysis might include increasing vocabulary knowledge and use, developing understanding and use of various semantic

TABLE 1 **Syntactic, Semantic, and Pragmatic Language Skills**

Syntax/Morphology	Semantics/Vocabulary
noun phrase/verb phrase	*Vocabulary*
regular plurals	functional words
subject pronouns	reading material vocabulary
object pronouns	content area vocabulary
prepositional phrases	idioms/figurative language
adjectives	multiple meanings of words
interrogative reversals	influence of context on meaning
negatives	
verb "be" auxiliary	**Pragmatics**
verb "be" copula	*One-way communication*
infinitives	(oral and written)
determiners	expresses wants
conjunction "and"	expresses opinions
possessives	expresses feelings
noun/verb agreement	expresses values
comparatives	follows directions
wh- questions	asks questions
past tense	narrates event
future aspects	states main idea
irregular plurals	sequences events
forms of "do"	subordinates details
auxiliaries	summarizes
derivational endings	describes
reflexive pronouns	compares and contrasts
qualifiers	gives instructions
conjunctions "and," "but," "or"	explains
conjunctions	*Two-way communication*
indirect and direct objects	(oral communication)
adverbs	considers the listener
infinitives with subject	formulates messages
participles	participates in discussions
gerunds	uses persuasion
passive voice	resolves differences
complex verb forms	identifies speaker's
relative adverb clauses	biases
relative pronoun clauses	assumptions
complex conjunctions	formulates conclusions

Source: Reprinted with the permission of Merrill, an imprint of Macmillan Publishing Company, from *Diagnosing Basic Skills: A Handbook for Deciding What to Teach* by K.W. Howell and J.S. Kaplan, 1980, Columbus, OH: Merrill. Copyright 1980 by Merrill Publishing Company.

roles, and using referential and relational devices to create continuity between (a) words within sentences, and (b) sentences within paragraphs or discourse.

In analyzing pragmatic aspects of the student's language, the teacher is determining the variety of purposes or functions for which a student can use language, as well as the efficiency with which the student communicates intents. Using the language sample that has been collected, the teacher can survey the sample to identify the presence or absence of pragmatic elements. The pragmatic elements in Table 1 provide a number of examples. Elements that were required based on the context but not demonstrated should be noted.

TABLE 2   *Semantic Skills: Definitions of 21 Semantic Roles*

Action: A perceivable movement or activity engaged in by an agent.

Entity: (One-term utterances only) Any labeling of the present person or object regardless of the occurrence or nature or action being performed on or by it.

Entity: (Multi-term utterances only) The use of an appropriate label for a person or object in the absence of any action on it (with the exception of showing, pointing, touching, or grasping); or someone or something that caused or was the stimulus to the internal state specified by a state verb or any object or person that was caused or was the stimulus to the internal state specified by a state verb or any object or person that was modified by a possessive form. (Entity was used to code a possession if it met either of the preceding criteria).

Locative: The place where an object or action was located or toward which it moved.

Negation: The impression of any of the following meanings with regard to someone or something, or an action or state: non-existence, rejection, cessation, denial, disappearance.

Agent: The performer (animate or inanimate) of an action. (Body parts and vehicles, when used in conjunction with action verbs, were coded Agent.)

Object: A person or thing (marked by the use of a noun or pronoun) that received the force of an action.

Demonstrative: The use of demonstrative pronouns or adjectives, *this, that, these, those,* and the words *there, right there, here, see,* when stated for the purpose of pointing out a particular referent.

Recurrence: A request for or comment on an additional instance or amount; the resumption of an event; or the reappearance of a person or object.

Attribute: An adjectival description of the size, shape, or quality of an object or person; also, noun adjuncts that modified nouns for a similar purpose (e.g., gingerbread man).

Possessor: A person or thing (marked by the use of a proper noun or pronoun) that an object was associated with or to which it belonged, at least temporarily.

Adverbial:

   Action/Attribute: A modifier or an action indicating time, manner, duration, distance, or frequency. (Direction or place of action was separately coded as Locative, Repetition, and Recurrence.)

   State/Attribute: A modifer indicating time, manner, quality, or intensity of a state.

Quantifier: A modifier that indicated amount or number of a person or object. (Pre-articles and indefinite pronouns such as *a piece of, lost of, any, every,* and *each* were included.)

State: A passive condition experienced by a person or object. (This category implies involuntary behavior on the part of the Experiencer, in contrast to voluntary action performed by an Agent.)

Experiencer: Someone or something that underwent a given experience of mental state. (Body parts, when used in conjunction with state verbs, were coded Experiencer.)

Recipient: One who received or was named as the recipient of an object (person or thing) from another.

Beneficiary: One who benefited from or was named as the beneficiary of a specified action.

Name: The labeling or request for naming of a person or thing using the utterance forms: my (his, your, etc.) name is _____, or what's _____ name?

Created Object: Something created by a specific activity—for example, a song by singing, a house by building, a picture by drawing.

Comitative: One who accompanied or participated with an agent in carrying out a specified activity.

Instrument: Something that an Agent used to carry out or complete a specified action.

Source: Reprinted with permission from "Semantic Roles and Residual Grammatical Categories in Mother and Child Speech" by K. Retherford, B. Schwartz, and R. Chapman, 1981, *Journal of Child Lanuage, 81*(3), 583–608. Copyright 1981 by Cambridge University Press.

The appropriateness and effectiveness of pragmatic functions that were demonstrated should be determined.

In addition, points in the language sample where communication was not successful should be identified. The teacher should try to establish the reason for the breakdown in communication. Was it because the student did not understand the linguistic demands? Did the student have difficulty organizing ideas or sequencing activities? Objectives in the area of pragmatics can be developed that work toward recognition of the need for and the use of a variety of functions of language and development of communication strategies to facilitate successful communication.

Determining Nature and Consistency of Errors

Answering a series of questions assists in determining the nature of omissions and errors. If the correct linguistic form, function, or content is omitted but demanded, does this reflect (a) a normal language development pattern? (b) an overall delay in language development? (c) a gap in language development? (d) influences of cultural or linguistic differences resulting from the student's home environment? Also, if the child produces the linguistic form incorrectly, does this reflect (a) a novel form (e.g., "He goed to school")? or (b) cultural or linguistic influences? In addition, for errors, particularly, what linguistic strategies does the student appear to be using? ("Goed" indicates that the student may be using the rule for constructing past tense with regular verb forms that are regular: adding *d* or *ed*.) Specific probes should be conducted to support hypotheses.

Also during analysis, the teacher should determine the consistency with which the student produces errors and omission. A search through all available language samples and completion of specific language probes can determine if the child demonstrates errors consistently or inconsistently with some contexts eliciting correct usage. Usually, language forms that are correctly produced in some contexts are easier to teach than those that are never produced correctly.

Finally, for all errors and omission, the teacher should determine if appropriate language behavior can be elicited, and at what level. Can the student produce a correct form with a model? Is a prompt required or is it spontaneously used in some contexts? With information regarding the nature of the error or omission, the consistency of its production, and its potential for elicitation, development of objectives and instructional strategies is more closely aligned with individual needs.

ADDITIONAL PIA TECHNIQUES

Anecdotal Recording

Anecdotal recording of oral and written language is useful in providing a richer, more meaningful context for language samples. General techniques often do not provide opportunities for the child to use particular syntactic forms or language functions. For this reason, monitoring communication throughout the day can provide this information. Particularly important is to document the stimulus context, the student's utterance or writing, and other contextual factors that help to establish the student's intent.

Specific Language Probes

Probing the oral production of specific language forms, content, and functions can be done after a preliminary analysis. At this level, the teacher creates meaningful and authentic communication situations that prompt—for example, the use of a specific syntactic structure that should be in the student's repertoire or a language function demanded in the academic or learning context. Specific language probes can be developed to target syntactic, semantic, and pragmatic domains of language performance. For example, in oral language, to probe for the use of past tense, questioning or picture cues might be used to elicit what happened immediately following a recently completed activity. In probing the use of requests, the teacher might set up a motivating activity in which the student must ask for materials in order to complete the task. The responses should be recorded.

Following analysis of the general written language sample, teachers should prompt students to edit and make corrections (e.g., "Try to fix your wording by adding more descriptive words"). The edited versions should be analyzed so the teacher can decide which skills should be taught at the acquisition level and which have to be shaped to become automatic and fluent. Further specific probes to elicit untapped skills may be conducted. For example, if the student uses a limited vocabulary, the teacher may devise a synonym activity in which the student writes all the words he or she can think of that relate to words such as "cold" or "pretty." The teacher then can evaluate semantic skills.

MONITORING PROGRESS IN ORAL AND WRITTEN LANGUAGE DOMAINS

Assessment activities at this level require demonstration of the integration of a variety of discrete language skills. Assessment tasks also may combine reading, writing, and oral language with relevant academic and social content, which, again, emphasize or capitalize on the interrelationships between modes of communication. Potential assessment strategies for OMPD in language are described next.

Collecting Brief Oral and Written Samples

The teacher might collect an oral or written language sample using a picture stimuli along with the directions, "Tell me a story about what you think is happening in the picture" or "Describe what you see in this picture." As examples, the picture may be of an Indian girl looking down at a herd of horses, a boy looking up at the shapes in the clouds, a girl throwing a penny into a fountain, a dog sleeping under a porch, or two boys carrying fishing poles. Again, care should be given to the child's experiential background as related to the pictures. Teachers should use pictures that depict familiar scenes or story starters to elicit oral and written language. The length of time required for collecting this sample may be as short as 1 minute. Teachers should collect writing samples following a standardized process. Initially, two or three samples should be collected over a period of a few days.

A structured method for collecting a brief written language sample follows. Although students actually write for only 3 minutes, 10 minutes of class time should be allowed for each sample collected—for giving directions, answering questions, writing, and passing in papers. A stopwatch or a watch with a second hand is required, and each student will need a blank sheet of lined paper and a pencil. They then complete their stories, within a reasonable amount of time. Directions to students are:

> I want you to write a story. I will read the beginning of a story to you first. Then I want you to write a story about what happens next. You will have 30 seconds to plan what you will write. Use that time to decide what will happen in your story. You will have 3 minutes to write. At the end of 3 minutes, I will say "time" and you will mark a star on your paper after the last word you wrote. (Demonstrate on board.) If you like, you will then be able to finish your story and give it a title. Start your story with your own words. You should not write the words that I read to you. You won't write a title for this story until you are finished. Are there any questions? . . . Listen carefully. For the next 30 seconds I want you to think about a story that starts like this: (Example) "I went up to the old, deserted house. The door was open, so I walked in. Suddenly . . ."

During the time the students are writing, no questions can be answered regarding spelling or story ideas. The story starter may be repeated if necessary. Students should be encouraged to write for the entire time.

A similar procedure may be used in sampling oral language, using the story starter and giving students time (30 seconds) to think. Then they have 1 to 3 minutes (being consistent across samples) to complete the story orally. The teacher tapes, writes, or types the student's responses.

Analysis of Brief Samples

Syntax

The purpose of the following analysis procedure is to provide measures of syntactic complexity and use of specific syntactic devices. Mean length of utterance (MLU) and measures of sentence complexity are offered as suggestions.

Mean Length of Utterance (MLU). As a child begins to combine propositions, the sentence length grows. This measure is an indicator of syntactical complexity for children who are producing up to five MLUs. The MLU can be used to identify if the student is producing sentence lengths appropriate for his or her age (see Miller, 1981, for specific instructions). Also, MLU is associated with the development and use of specific grammatical morphemes. Brown (1973) has identified three stages associated with levels of MLU during which specific morphemes appear. In written language, T-unit length—the shortest complete, nonfragmented, segment of a passage—is used to assess syntax (Isaacson, 1988). T-unit length in written language is comparable to MLU in oral language.

Sentence Complexity. The number of simple, compound, and complex sentences the student produced in the sample is counted, and percentage of the total sample that each sentence type represents is computed. As language develops, students begin to use syntactic devices to combine sentences. For example:

Simple sentence level—The boy went to school. The girl went to school.
Compound sentence level—The boy and the girl went to school.
Complex sentence level—The boy and the girl who were good friends went
    to school first and then to the playground.

Semantics

Analysis of semantic aspects of a child's language provides information regarding vocabulary knowledge and use. The following procedure may help to monitor semantic development.

Vocabulary Use. Because a word is used in spontaneous oral or written language, it is assumed that the student has a basic conceptual knowledge of the word's meaning in the context in which it is used. Vocabulary knowledge, however, involves more. The knowledge and manipulation of known vocabulary can be evaluated by randomly selecting a few of the content words in the student's oral or written language sample and asking the student to: (a) use the words in another sentence, (b) give antonyms or synonyms for the words, and (c) provide examples or definitions for the words. These tasks can require oral or written responses. A record of the percent of correct responses should be graphed.

Integrated Measures

Integrated measures reflect a student's ability to integrate aspects of syntax and semantics. These measures include number of words produced, number of correct word sequences, and mean length of word sequences.

Total Words Produced. The first integrated measure involves collecting a one-minute sample in oral language and a three-minute sample in written language based on a story starter. The scoring procedure is to count the total words used in the sample (Deno, Marston, & Mirkin, 1982). This measure of written or oral fluency is best used until the students are writing or talking fairly fluently, at which point a different measure would be more helpful as the objective switches from saying or writing more words to saying or writing in a more meaningful way.

Number of Correct Word Sequences. This measure is used to calculate the mean length of correct word sequences. A correct word sequence is defined as a sequence of two adjacent correctly spelled words that is acceptable within the context of the larger phrase/sentence to a native speaker of the English language. The term "acceptable" means that the scorer judges the word sequence as syntactically and semantically correct and appropriate (Videen, Deno, & Marston, 1982). A caret mark (^) placed above and between the two words is used to indicate each correct word sequence. An unbroken sequence of carets may continue as far as the end of the sentence. Sequences stop at the end of sentences, before an incorrect conjunction, or whenever two adjacent words are not both syntactically and semantically correct (Parker & Tindal, 1988). If a conjunction is used improperly to link three or more clauses, the scorer must judge which pair of clauses fit best together, if any. The incorrect conjunction will be an error, with correct sequences ending at the extraneous conjunction.

Mean Length of Correct Word Sequences. A widely accepted objective for written language is for students to use expanded sentences to increase syntactic maturity (Isaacson, 1988). To score this aspect of students' writing, or oral language, parentheses are placed around each unbroken string of adjacent carets marking correct word sequences. The number of carets marking *unbroken sequences* within each set of parentheses is counted, and those numbers are summed. The sum is divided by the total number of sets for the mean length of correct word sequences (Hasbrouck, 1988). An example is:

(∧   ∧   ∧)   (∧   ∧)   (∧   ∧ ∧   ∧)
I seen a great huge monster and it was green and it started to attack me

(∧)   (∧   ∧ ∧   ∧   ∧ ∧ ∧   ∧   ∧   ∧)
and then I seen something that I could pick up to get the monster away

(∧)   (∧ ∧ ∧   ∧ ∧   ∧)
so bent down and I got it but it seemed to . . .

Correct Word Sequences = 26
Mean Length of Correct Word Sequences = 26/7 = 3.7

Pragmatics

When pragmatics in written language is the emphasis, two possible suggestions for OMPD are given. Both of these suggestions are speculative, as there is no research in on-going monitoring of pragmatic development. These scales may be used after the student has had time to generate an entire story in oral or written form.

1. Isaacson (1988) offers four aspects of content that could be rated using a holistic or analytic scale: *idea generation, coherence, organization,* and *awareness of audience.* Though these elements are designed for analysis of written language, they may also be applicable to oral language. A 4-point scale for each of the four items provides a 16-point range in which to chart progress. Figure 1 depicts this scale.

2. Graham and Harris (1986), as discussed by Isaacson (1988), list eight story elements that could be used as items on a rating scale if a story starter is used to elicit the sample. The elements of the story are main character, locale, time, precipitating event, a goal formulated by the main character, a planned action to achieve the goal, an ending, and a final reaction, as presented in Figure 1. Graham and Harris use scores indicating each element's inclusion and quality of development. A 0-, 1-, or 2- point scale is suggested here.

USING THE OMPD DATA

All of the OMPD data in oral and written language can be charted on a graph, and these graphic presentations of students' performances can be used to make decisions about the

Scale 1

Directions: Use the 5-point rating scale below to evaluate written or oral language sample. Circle the number that is appropriate. Use the student's "baseline sample" in evaluating the current sample. Add the total points across all four aspects for a total score.

1 = much poorer (or less) than baseline sample
2 = slightly poorer (or less) than baseline sample
3 = about the same as the baseline sample
4 = slightly improved over (or more than) baseline sample
5 = much improved over (or more than) baseline sample

Aspects		Rating			
1. Idea generation; amount of content included.	1	2	3	4	5
2. Coherence; all parts relate to the theme.	1	2	3	4	5
3. Organization; text has a beginning, middle, and end.	1	2	3	4	5
4. Awareness of the audience; takes characteristics and knowledge of audience into consideration.	1	2	3	4	5

Source: From "Assessing the Writing Product: Qualitative and Quantitative Measures" by S. Isaacson, 1988, *Exceptional Children, 54*(6), 528–534.

Scale 2

Directions: For each of the components of a sample story, evaluate if each is *NOT PRESENT BUT REQUIRED* (0 points), *PRESENT BUT INEFFECTIVE OR INAPPROPRIATE FORM USED* (1 point), or *PRESENT, EFFECTIVE, AND IN APPROPRIATE FORM* (2 points).

Component	Points		
1. Main character	0	1	2
2. Description of locale	0	1	2
3. Information about time	0	1	2
4. A precipitating event (story starter)	0	1	2
5. Goal formulated by main character	0	1	2
6. A planned goal-oriented action	0	1	2
7. Ending result	0	1	2
8. Final reaction of main character to the outcome	0	1	2

Source: From "Improving Learning Disabled Students' Composition via Story Grammar Training: A Component Analysis of Self-Control Strategy Training" by S. Graham and K. Harris, April 1986. A paper presented at the annual meeting of the American Educational Research Association, San Francisco.

FIGURE 1   *Pragmatic Rating Scales for Four Written and Oral Aspects of Language Sample*

overall effectiveness of instruction. There are many choices of procedures to use for analyzing the data. The main step for using the data are:

1. Decide on the OMPD domain to be used for each individual student, and prepare probes for each level.
2. Set up a measurement station containing all measurement stimuli, graphs, pencils, stopwatches, and a system for organizing the graphs.
3. Label graphs completely for all students.
4. Take baseline data for all students.
5. Given baseline data recorded on the graph, choose the strategy for making expectations for each student.
   a. Alternate interventions as in an applied behavior analysis single-case study research design, to determine which intervention is the most effective for each student. The graph would show baseline, followed by at least 6 data points in treatment A, 6 or more data points in treatment B, A, B, C, etc. Systematically vary the intervention (treatment) to ascertain which is most effective for the individual student.
   b. Set a line of expected progress and make decisions about the effectiveness of instruction based on how closely the student's performance data match the aim-line (line of expected progress drawn on the graph). Some teachers do this on an annual basis when using a OMPD system. The key to using the data in this manner is setting a reasonable goal. Teachers have to be careful to not set goals too low. Some teachers use the performance of mainstream students to set the goals for the special needs students. The teacher may consider, for example, that Joe will be mainstreamed into a fourth-grade class for writing next year and may decide to find out what the average performance in writing is in the current year's fourth-grade class. The assumption is that if Joe can catch up to that level, he will be ready in fall to attend that written language mainstream class. Other teachers pick a rate of progress they would like to see the individual student attain and set the goal according to that rate. For example, the teacher may expect Sally's oral expression skills to improve by one additional word per story she tells per week. So, if Sally tells an average of 22 words in her stories in the fall, the goal would be set at (22 + 36 [number of weeks in the school year x one word per week improvement] = 58) 58. The intersection of the last week in school along the horizontal axis and the rate of 58 along the vertical axis is the place to mark the X, which represents the annual goal. Connecting the median score of a 3-5 day baseline period to the x representing the goal provides teachers with the aimline.
6. After the graphs are set up, delineate the instructional context, specifying objectives, instructional strategies, motivational techniques, materials, and arrangements for developing language and communication (independent, one-to-one with teacher, small group). Routine implementation of specific strategies allows teachers to use the data to guide the instructional process.

7. After deciding on a strategy for using the data (5a or 5b), collect data twice a week. Data points are charted routinely; many teachers have the students chart their own data. On a weekly basis the teachers pause and reflect on the graphed data, deciding either that the intervention in place is effective and should remain or that a change in instruction is necessary.

8. Add a new strategy or replace a strategy. Whatever the change, it should be substantial and have the potential for making a difference in the student's performance. Slight alterations will have little effect on the student's performance and should be avoided.

After the system is in place, the routine is to collect data, evaluate the effects of instruction using the data, change the instructional plan as necessary, and continue collecting data.

ISSUES TO CONSIDER

Because of the nature and complexity of language, any of the tasks that have been recommended must be considered in light of other contextual factors that may be related to performance. For example, when synonyms seem problematic (e.g., determining appropriate reading miscues), teachers also must consider the student's (a) experience and knowledge of word concepts, (b) cognitive understanding of synonyms, (c) retrieval of words, and (d) understanding of the context in which this skill is used (reading, writing, speaking). Further, in written language, the teacher must consider the complexity of the task demands, the student's organizational abilities, visual motor skills for producing legible written products, skills in retrieval of words and sentences, skills in transferring thoughts to paper, and spelling demands.

If these measures are to be useful in determining the effectiveness of instruction, there is the need to develop techniques that meet the criteria of validity, reliability, and sensitivity. Research in similar measures in other academic areas has been successful in identifying measures that meet these criteria (Deno, 1985). The issue of sensitivity to change is most critical, and is especially so in language as language growth may be slow and diverse. Therefore, it is often difficult to document improvement.

Because language is so pervasive and critical to success in academic and social life, ways in which to develop, refine, and improve proficiency in language requires attention. The complexity of language, however, makes it difficult to monitor. Hence, the need for measures that can direct instruction in ways more efficient than "current practice" is great. Current practice includes the use of trial and error in instruction, instruction in language that is splintered from the rest of the curriculum or decontextualized, and language instruction that is without focus.

Efficiency of assessment strategies is another issue that must be addressed. Teachers should spend most of their instructional time teaching rather than testing. Therefore, the system for assessment has to be efficient. Ideas about how to decrease measurement time include having the students themselves prepare materials (select probes), setting up a measurement station, having assistants administer the measures, and having the students do self-charting (Wesson, 1987).

The progress monitoring measurement is done twice a week with students whose progress rate is less than expected. More frequently collected data allow for more effective instructional planning. For students who are making progress in the domain at an acceptable or expected rate, the frequency of measurement may be once a week or biweekly.

In the future, computerized language assessments may be available whereby teachers can type into the keyboard as the student dictates the story or gives the directions. For written language, students will type in their own stories. The software will score, chart, and print the graph. Various scoring options will be available for both written and oral language.

CONCLUSION AND SUMMARY

Assessment procedures that help educators make decisions about what to teach and about the effectiveness of their choices of teaching strategies are crucial. Traditional formal tests do little in this regard; they serve primarily as evidence for the necessity of special services (Deno, 1985). Educators express the need for assessment data that can be meaningfully used in formulating and evaluating educational interventions. In special education, where the legal mandate is for individualized instruction, this need is even greater. Special educators must systematically plan for and evaluate the effectiveness of the strategies they use with each student.

The assessment methods presented in this chapter help to survey and target language and communication behavior. There are, however, a number of other ways that in combination provide information about students' language and communication and informal instruction. These methods bridge formal and informal language assessment and can become a part of a portfolio reflecting a student's growth and achievement (e.g., Herbert, 1992). The more complete and ongoing a teacher's "picture" of a student's development, the more sound his or her educational judgments and decisions will be.

Teachers make a multitude of decisions. Effective teachers continuously question what they have done and what they should do with respect to instruction. Within each academic area, two of the most important questions special education teachers make about individual students are: (a) what do I need to teach this student? and (b) is my plan for teaching this student effective? The first question leads to the development of goals and objectives and ultimately to the teacher's daily lesson plans. Basically, the teacher assesses the student within a domain, such as reading or math, to determine what the student already knows. At the same time, the teacher also determines what skills and content should be taught and practiced. But, deciding on what should be taught is only one side of the coin. Special education teachers also must evaluate the effects of their instruction on student performance.

REFERENCES

Bereiter, C., and Scardamalia, M. (1982). From conversation to composition: The role of instruction in a developmental process. In I.R. Glasser (Ed.)., *Advances in instructional psychology* (vol. 2, pp. 1–64). Hillsdale, NJ: Laurence Erlbaum.

Bloom, L., & Lahey, M. (1978). *Language development and language disorders.* New York, NY: John Wiley & Sons.

Brown, R. (1973). *A first language.* Cambridge, MA: Harvard University Press.

Coulter, A. (1985). Implementing curriculum-based assessment: Considerations for pupil appraisal professionals. *Exceptional Children, 52* (3), 277–281.

Deno, S. (1985). Curriculum-based measurement: The emerging alternative. *Exceptional Children, 52* (3), 219–231.

Deno, S., Marston, D., & Mirkin, P. (1982). Valid measurement procedures for continuous evaluation of written expression. *Exceptional Children, 48,* 368–371.

Golden-Fletcher, D. (1986). Language of bilingual-bicultural children. In V. Reed, *An introduction to children with language disorders.* New York, NY: Macmillan, pp. 181–200.

Graham, S., & Harris, K. (April, 1986). Improving learning disabled students' composition via story grammar training: A component analysis of self-control strategy training. A paper presented at the annual meeting of the American Educational Research Association, San Francisco.

Graves, D.H. (1983). *Writing: Teachers and children at work.* Exeter, NH: Heinemann.

Hasbrouck, J. (1988). *Objective and holistic scoring of writing: A manual for collecting and scoring writing samples using holistic and 8 objective scoring procedures* (Module No. 20). Eugene, OR: Resource Consultant Training Program, University of Oregon.

Herbert, E.A. (1992). Portfolios invite reflections from students and staff. *Educational Leadership, 49*(8), 58–61.

Howell, K.W., & Kaplan, J.S. (1980). *Diagnosing basic skills: A handbook for deciding what to teach.* Columbus, OH: Merrill.

Howell, K., & Morehead, M.K. (1987). *Curriculum-based evaluation for special and remedial education.* Columbus, OH: Merrill.

Isaacson, S. (1988). Assessing the writing product: Qualitative and quantitative measures. *Exceptional Children, 54*(6), 528–534.

Johnston, J., & Schery, T. (1976). The use of grammatical morphemes by children with communication disorders. In D. Morehead & A. Morehead (Eds.), *Normal and deficient child language.* Baltimore: University Park Press.

Marston, D., & Magnusson, D. (1985). Implementing curriculum-based measurement in special and regular education settings. *Exceptional Children, 52*(3), 266–276.

Miller, J. (1981). *Assessing language production in children: Experimental procedures.* Austin, TX: PRO-ED.

Morehead, D., & Ingram, D. (1973). The development of base syntax in normal and linguistically deviant children. *Journal of Speech & Hearing Research, 16,* 330–352.

Parker, R., & Tindal, G. (1988). *Direct, objective measures of writing skills for middle school students with learning disabilities.* Unpublished manuscript, University of Oregon, Eugene.

Retherford, K., Schwartz, B., & Chapman, R. (1981). Semantic roles and residual grammatical categories in mother and child speech. *Journal of Child Language, 81*(3) 583–608.

Rice, M. (1989). Synthesis/commentary on language teaching and learning strategies. In M. Rice and R. Schiefelbusch (Eds.), *The teachability of language,* Baltimore, MD: Brookes Publishing Co.

Templin, M.C. (1957). Certain language skills in children: Their development and interrelationships. *Child Welfare Monographs, No. 26. Minneapolis: University of Minnesota Press.*

Tucker, J. (1985). Curriculum-based assessment: An introduction. *Exceptional Children, 52*(3), 199–204.

Videen, J., Deno, S., & Marston, D. (1982). Correct word sequences: A valid indicator of proficiency in written expression (Research Report No. 84). University of Minnesota: Institute for Research on Learning Disabilities.

Wesson, C. (1987). Increasing efficiency. *Teaching Exceptional Children, 20,* 46–47.

Zigmond, N., & Miller, S. (1986). Assessment for instructional planning. *Exceptional Children, 52*(6), 501–509.

Caren Wesson and Amy Otis-Wilborn are associate professors in the Department of Exceptional Education at the University of Wisconsin, Milwaukee. Jan Hasbrouck is an instructor and Gerald Tindal is an associate professor in the Department of Special Education at the University of Oregon.

○ 12 ○

Curriculum-based measurement (CBM) is a set of procedures with the potential to greatly improve instruction and evaluation of instruction in general and special education. Shinn and Hubbard explain the differences in curriculum-based measurement and curriculum-based assessment, two concepts that often have been used interchangeably in the field of special education. They explain how these practices can improve the linkage of information that is collected in the assessment process and the instruction of children with special needs.

Curriculum-Based Measurement and Problem-Solving Assessment: Basic Procedures and Outcomes

Mark R. Shinn and Dawn D. Hubbard

More than 15 years after the passage of the Education for All Handicapped Children Act (EAHCA), assessment and testing practices with students who have mild handicaps remain essentially unchanged. Testing is characterized by a high reliance on commercially available, published norm-referenced tests (PNTs) of aptitude, achievement, and specific "abilities" (Reschly, Genshaft, & Binder, 1987). The lack of change is disturbing to many educators, as historically these practices have generated considerable controversy and little evidence of efficacy (Bersoff, 1973).

Most of the controversy has centered on appropriateness of PNTs to identify students as learning disabled (LD), educably mentally retarded (EMR) or low achieving (Gerber & Semmel, 1984; Heller, Holtzman, & Messick, 1982; Ysseldyke, Algozzine, Shinn, & McGue, 1982; Ysseldyke & Thurlow, 1984). Their accuracy and efficacy to diagnose students differentially among disability categories has been the subject of many research articles and much special education placement litigation (e.g., Reschly, Kicklighter, & McKee, 1988c). The focus on PNTs in identification has obscured a more important question, however. Can the data derived from current testing practices be used to: (a) *develop* more effective interventions, and (b) *evaluate the effectiveness* of any specific in-

tervention implemented (Deno, 1986; 1989)? Measurement experts summarizing litigation (e.g., Reschly, Kicklighter, & McKee, 1988a; 1988b; 1988c) concluded that the link to intervention planning and evaluation is what will form the basis for promoting assessment practices as useful.

A number of resources detail why information derived from PNTs is difficult to link to intervention planning and intervention evaluation (e.g., Marston, 1989; Shinn, Nolet, & Knutson, 1990). Stated briefly, to be useful for planning instructional interventions, a test must provide information about what skills, task preskills, or problem-solving algorithms a student does and does not demonstrate that are essential for success in the curriculum the student is expected to learn (Howell & Morehead, 1987). Key features of tests to be used for these purposes include high content validity, enough items to reliably detect error and success patterns, and response formats that rely on production-type responses (e.g., writing answers to math problems). To be useful for evaluating effectiveness of the intervention, a test must be capable of being used to write long-term (i.e., annual) goals and be used on a repeated and frequent basis so that effective interventions are maintained and ineffective interventions are modified.

Key features again include content validity, a sufficient number of items drawn from the curriculum, and production-type responses. Content validity ensures that decisions are made on the basis of what students are expected to learn. A sufficient number of items is necessary so that the test is "sensitive" to change. Production-type responses allow for a careful analysis of a student's pattern of successes and errors that facilitates modifications of the current intervention, if necessary (Howell & Morehead, 1987).

As detailed in Figure 1, PNTs, at best, can be used to describe the severity of an academic problem relative to the academic performance of what is typically a nationally normed sample. The utility of this use of PNTs is most defensible when the test has high content validity. Even with PNTs that have high content validity, however, information for intervention planning and evaluation is lacking or must be extrapolated or collected via devices and methods in addition to or *after* a special education certification/eligibility decision has been made.

CURRICULUM-BASED ASSESSMENT AS A VIABLE ALTERNATIVE

One of the most frequently proposed solutions to using PNTs is curriculum-based assessment (CBA). CBA has been promoted because of its purported linkage of assessment and intervention (Reschly et al., 1988c) and because of its emphasis on data for intervention planning (Tucker, 1985). Unfortunately, CBA is *not* one set of unified testing strategies or procedures. Instead, CBA approaches range from testing procedures that resemble teacher-made criterion-referenced tests (Criterion-referenced curriculum-based assessment, C-R CBA, Blankenship, 1985) to procedures designed to determine a student's frustrational, instructional, and independent academic levels (Curriculum-Based Assessment for Instructional Design, C-BAID, Gickling & Thompson, 1985), and to a set of short-duration fluency measures of reading, written expression, spelling, and mathematics computation (Curriculum-Based Measurement, CBM, Deno, 1985, 1986; Shinn, 1989a).

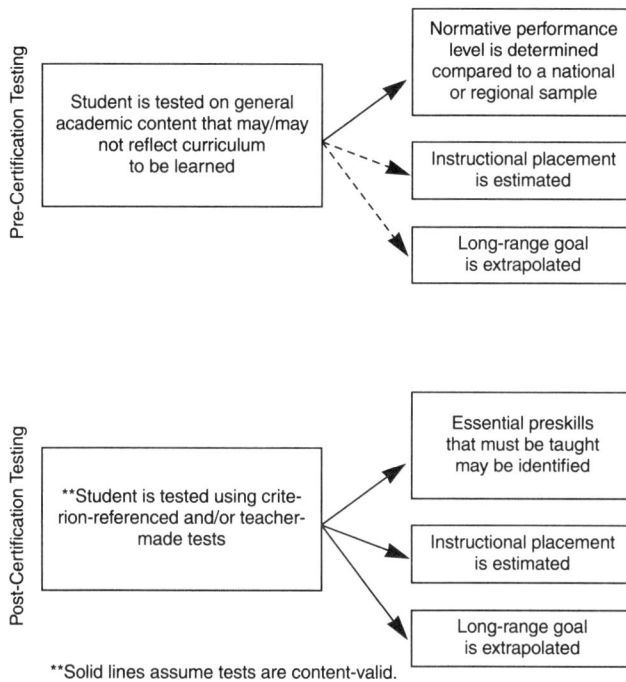

FIGURE 1   *Current Eligibility Determination and Intervention Planning Assessment Strategies and Potential Contributions to Problem-Solving Decision Making*

These CBA testing approaches are similar in that they rely on students' curriculum as the basis for constructing testing materials and decision making. The approaches differ on a number of critical dimensions, however, including philosophical assumptions underlying the assessment process, kinds of data collected, availability of technical adequacy data, and decision-making focus (for more detail, see Shinn, Rosenfield, & Knutson, 1989). Each CBA approach is designed to affect and improve academic interventions. Exactly how this is accomplished differs, though. Pragmatically, the approaches are not competitive; they can be used collaboratively and comprehensively to plan and evaluate academic interventions.

With the exception of CBM, CBA approaches emphasize the collection of student performance data for intervention planning that are not *directly* useful or validated for determining special education eligibility (Shinn, Rosenfield, & Knutson, 1989; Shinn & Good, in press). The procedures emphasize information useful for planning the instructional content (the "what to teach" component) of an intervention plan. The assessment strategies correspond to the kinds of information collected by special education teachers after the certification decision is made, as represented in Figure 1. Sequentially, the timing of CBA data collection need not occur after the eligibility determination, though.

At best, these CBA approaches contribute only indirectly to special education certification decisions. Therefore, the direct linkage between special education eligibility and intervention—one of the quality assessment indicators proposed by Reschly et al. (1988c)—is not evident. Furthermore, most CBA strategies have not been demonstrated to be useful for evaluating the effectiveness of interventions for specific students. As a result, they fail to meet Reschly et al.'s (1988c) second criterion for good assessment practice.

CURRICULUM-BASED MEASUREMENT

Curriculum-Based Measurement is the only CBA strategy to meet Reschly et al.'s criteria of linking information collected for eligibility determination to intervention planning and usefulness for evaluating intervention effectiveness. As developed by Deno (1985, 1986, 1989) and others (e.g., Fuchs, 1989, Fuchs, Hamlett, Fuchs, Stecker, & Ferguson, 1988; Germann & Tindal, 1985; Marston & Magnusson, 1985; Shinn, 1989a; Wesson, 1987), CBM is a set of short-duration (1–3 minutes) fluency tests in the basic skill areas of reading, spelling, mathematics computation, and written expression, used in a standardized manner to facilitate problem-solving assessment.

The basic CBM measures, testing durations, scoring metrics, and sample investigations of their technical adequacy (reliability and validity) are presented in Table 1. An extensive program of research has been conducted for more than 12 years supporting these measures as reliable and valid indicators of student progress in the basic skill areas. For example, in reading, the number of words read correctly has been validated as an accurate measure of a student's general reading skill, including reading comprehension. For more detail on technical adequacy, see the extensive review by Marston (1989).

In contrast to Figure 1, CBM links the assessment data collected for special education (or other special programs) eligibility to intervention by testing a referred student repeatedly in successive levels of the general education curriculum in which the student is having difficulty. This testing process is called Survey-Level Assessment (SLA). As with PNTs, data derived from CBM SLA may assist in determing a student's eligibility for special education services by providing an index of normative performance. Rather than testing referred students on tests assumed to be content-valid and making comparisons to a norm group that may or may not represent the referred students' learning experiences and opportunities within the specific curriculum, CBM tests students in the curriculum they are expected to learn. Performance is then compared directly to how other students perform in that curriculum. And while CBM provides equivalent, but more *direct* information for eligibility, the data also allow for initial decisions about intervention to be made, as presented in Figure 2.

By testing students in successive levels of the curriculum, the level in which a student performs *successfully* can be identified for instructional placement purposes. This strategy of directly testing students until they are successful is in stark contrast to PNTs, which usually confirm that the referred student is unsuccessful on the test tasks. SLA also facilitates discussion of the level of the curriculum in which the student would be expected to perform in 1 year. Once this curriculum level has been identified, the annual

TABLE 1 *A Description of the Basic Curriculum-Based Measures In Reading, Spelling, Mathematics Computation, and Written Expression*

Area	Testing Duration	Description and Types of Scores Derived	Sample Technical Adequacy Information
Reading	1 minute	Students read passages orally, and the number of words read correctly and errors are counted.	Deno, Mirkin, & Chiang (1982); Fuchs, Fuchs, & Maxwell (1988)
Spelling	2 minutes	Students write words that are dictated orally, and the number of words spelled correctly and correct letter sequences are counted.	Deno, Marston, Mirkin, Lowry, Sindelar, & Jenkins (1982); Marston, Lowry, Deno, & Mirkin (1981)
Mathematics Computation	2-5 minutes	Students write answers to computation problems, and number of correct digits are counted.	Fuchs & Fuchs (1987a); Marston, Fuchs, & Deno (1986)
Written Expression	3 minutes	After being given a story starter or topic sentence, students write a story. Number of words written, spelled correctly, and correct word sequences may be counted.	Deno, Marston, & Mirkin (1982)

goal of the individualized education program (IEP) can be written. Once goals have been established, the initial intervention plan can be evaluated on a continuous and frequent basis, allowing ineffective interventions to be identified and modified and effective treatments to be continued with confidence. Finally, the extensive amount of information about how the student performs (i.e., what the student does/does not do successfully) in the curriculum can be analyzed to form hypotheses about what essential curricular skills the student already has mastered and those that must be taught.

Basic Assumptions of CBM and Problem-Solving Assessment

The use of CBM is more than just employing a new set of "tests." Instead, it is a commitment to a new way of viewing school problems and their solutions through a Problem-Solving model (Deno, 1989; Shinn & Good, in press). The Problem-Solving model is predicated on seven assumptions.

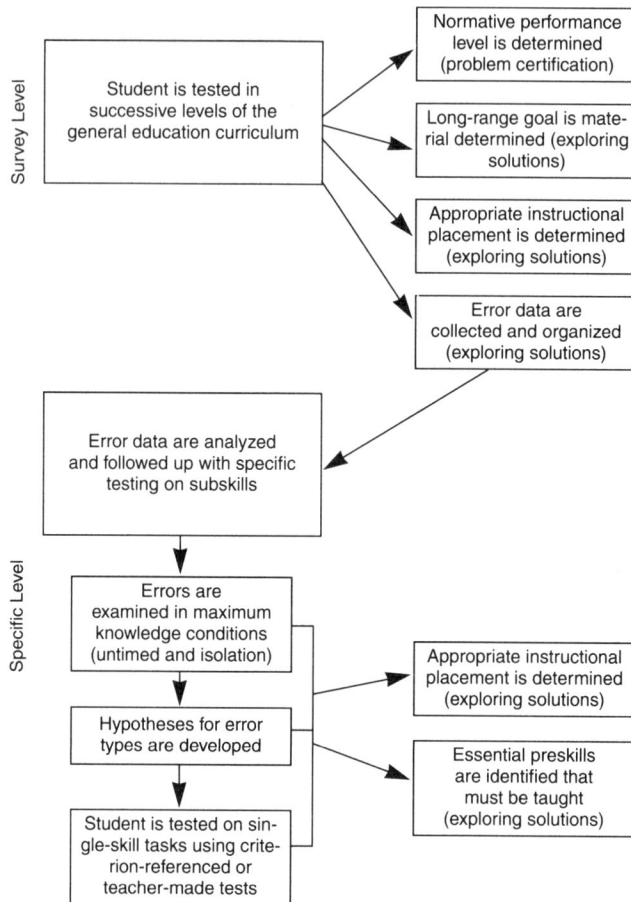

FIGURE 2   Linking Eligibility Determination and Intervention

First is an inherent assumption that special education, like other remedial programs, is a *problem-solving system* for general education. It is designed to remediate some of the problems that general education, as currently structured, is ill equipped to resolve. For example, general education in most schools is not designed to meet the needs of a population with diverse academic skills (Gerber & Semmel, 1984). Special education for students with mild handicaps attempts to remediate many of these problems.

Second, problems are *defined situationally*. A problem is defined as a significant discrepancy between what is expected in the environment and what occurs. Academic problems are defined by the lack of success for a specific student within a specific general education curriculum compared to students in that same environment who are performing successfully in the curriculum. Therefore, problems have to be defined by the discrepancy in the general education curriculum compared to peers rather than an internal discrepancy residing within the student. When situations change, what was a problem may no longer be one and vice versa.

Third, the Problem-Solving model takes a *value position* that some students need additional resources (e.g., special education) to profit from education. Although decisions about who needs additional resources can be data-based, changes in financial resources, service delivery models, or the knowledge base may result in a change in our conceptions as to who receives special education services.

Fourth, identifying problems is not enough; special education, in and of itself, is not an intervention. As a result, interventions have to be planned in detail.

Fifth, with our current assessment technology and scientific data base, unfortunately, we cannot predict with certainty an intervention that will be effective with any given student. Based on test results, we cannot identify a student as an auditory learner or a sequential learner and prescribe the intervention that is certain to work (for more information, see Deno, 1990).

Sixth, because of the uncertain effects of any intervention, the treatment outcomes for specific students must be evaluated frequently and in a timely manner. Effective interventions should be maintained. Ineffective interventions should be modified as soon as possible.

Seventh, problems are resolved when the discrepancy between what is expected and what occurs is no longer significant. For academic problems, typically, that means that a student performs in the general education curriculum at a level commensurate with peers in the same environment.

Steps and Issues

The Problem-Solving model is divided into five sequential steps, presented in Table 2. Each step is characterized by a different set of conceptual issues that dictate collection of different types of CBM data.

Specific CBM Problem-Solving Procedures

Problem Identification and Certification

A potential need for additional instructional resources to resolve an academic problem typically is stimulated by a general education teacher making a referral for assistance to a specialized remedial program such as Chapter 1 or special education. Referral to assistance programs such as Chapter 1 is relatively uncontroversial. Referral to special education has been and remains controversial, in large part because of the stigmatizing labels used and the testing procedures by which those labels are decided. Nevertheless, dramatic changes are needed in determining who receives special education services, and such services unfortunately must be accompanied by labels that place the problem solely within the student (e.g., learning disabilities).

As with any program with limited resources, educators must determine who needs specialized assistance so students may benefit from their education. It has been argued persuasively (e.g., Gerber & Semmel, 1984) and from a data-based perspective that

**TABLE 2   CBM Problem-Solving Model Decisions,
Measurement Activities, and Evaluation Activities**

Problem-Solving Decision	Measurement Activities	Evaluation Activities
1. Problem identification (Screening)	Observe and record student differences, if any, between actual and expected performance.	Decide that a performance discrepancy exists.
2. Problem certification (Eligibility determination)	Describe the differences between actual and expected performance in context of the likelihood of general education resources solving the problem.	Decide if discrepancies are important enough that special services may be required to resolve problems.
3. Exploring alternative solutions (IEP goal setting and intervention planning)	Determine probable performance improvements (goals) and costs associated with various interventions.	Select the program reform (i.e., intervention) to be tested.
4. Evaluating solutions and making modifications (progress monitoring)	Monitor implementation and student performance changes.	Determine whether intervention is effective or should be modified.
5. Problem solution (program termination)	Observe and record student differences, if any, between actual and expected performance.	Decide that exisiting discrepancies, if any, are not important and program may be terminated.

Source: From "Curriculum-Based Measurement and Alternative Special Education Services: A Fundamental and Direct Relationship" (p. 13) by S. L. Deno, 1989, *Curriculum-Based Measurement: Assessing Special Children*, edited by M. R. Shinn, New York: Guilford Press. Copyright ©1989 by The Guilford Press. Adapted by permission.

schools serve students with severe achievement needs in special education programs. For example, Shinn, Tindal, and Spira (1987) demonstrated that students referred by their general education teachers for learning disabilities services in reading typically perform below the 5th percentile, compared to local norms in the reading curriculum. Other studies have demonstrated that students actually placed in learning disabilities programs typically perform below the 3rd percentile, compared to local norms in the curriculum (Shinn, Tindal, Spira, & Marston, 1987).

The Problem-Solving model begins with a decision that a potential problem is *important enough* to investigate further. At the point that someone (often a general education teacher) has concerns over performance in the curriculum, CBM can be used to determine if the student's skills are sufficiently different from other students to warrant further investigation. As shown in Table 2, a problem is defined as a significant difference between expected performance in the general education curriculum and how the referred student performs. CBM is used to operationalize this conceptual model by having referred students take probes derived from the general education curriculum that typical students are expected to learn. The referred student's scores then are compared to local norms developed from same-grade peers using those same probes.

Consider the case of Desireé, a third-grade student referred because her classroom teacher had serious concerns about progress in reading and mathematics. Because no obvious reasons could explain the teacher's concerns (e.g., poor school attendance, vision or hearing difficulties), Desireé was tested using a series of probes derived from her general education reading (Ginn) and math (Heath) curricula. Typical third-grade students were expected to be reading Ginn Level 8, and school district norms had been developed on this level of the reading series (see Shinn, 1989b, for more detail on the local norming process). Desireé read three different passages each day for 3 days in a 5-day period. Her nine scores are presented in Table 3 and summarized by determining her median performance across the passages.

Desireé also completed three different forms of probes derived from the computational objectives for the Grade 3 Heath curriculum. Her scores on these probes also are presented in Table 3. To determine if a problem requiring further assessment existed, Desireé's scores were compared to third-grade peers in her school district. The median score of the third-grade local norms also is displayed in Table 3. In this example, if Desireé's scores consistently fell below half the level of typical grade-level peers, a problem worth warranting investigation would be identified.

To facilitate communication with general education teachers, parents, administrators, and the students themselves, the Problem Identification data are displayed graphically. Desireé's results are presented in Figure 3.

Desireé performed consistently below the cutting score only in the area of reading. Although her score in mathematics was below the median of her peers, it was not considered to be sufficiently different from other students to warrant additional investigation. Because all the math probes required Desireé to write answers to the computational problems, however, the specific responses could be analyzed to determine if she had areas of weakness that could be shared with her general education teacher for improved performance.

TABLE 3   Results of CBM Problem Identification for Desireé

Academic Area		Day 1	Day 2	Day 3	Median	Peer Median
Reading	Passage 1	22	16	11		
	Passage 2	14	15	11		
	Passage 3	18	12	14		
	Daily Median	18	15	11	15 WRC*	75 WRC*
Math Grade	3 Problems	19	20	14	19 CD**	26 CD**

*WRC= words read correctly
**CD= correct digits

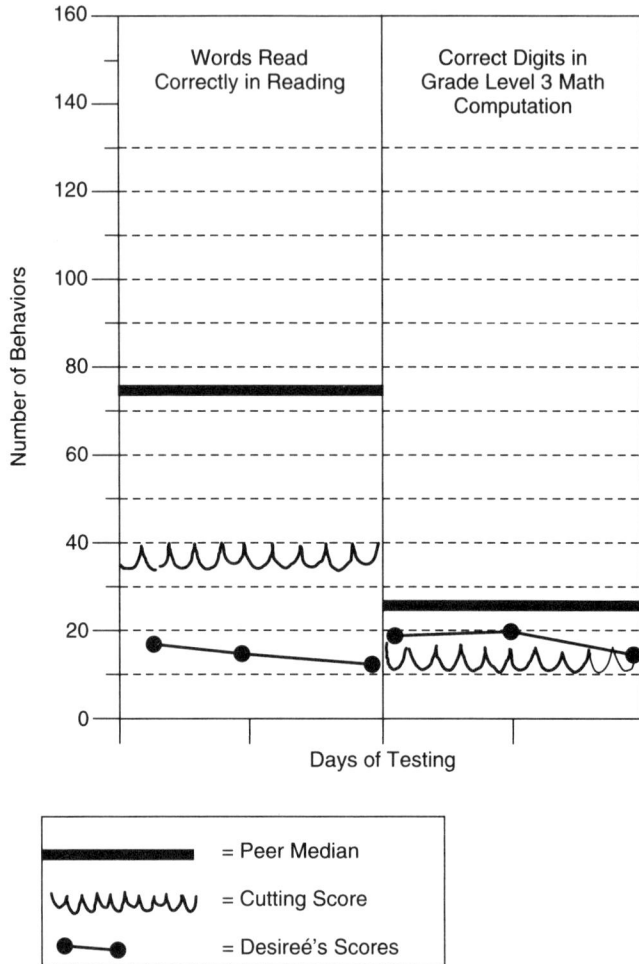

FIGURE 3   *Use of CBM Comparing Desireé to Same-Grade General Education Peers*

As a result of the Problem Identification decision-making process, a problem of potentially serious magnitude was observed only in reading. Consequently, Desireé was administered a Survey-Level Assessment from successive levels of her general education curriculum using CBM as part of the Problem Certification decision-making process. As shown in Table 2, Problem Certification is conceptualized as determining if the difference between expected performance and observed performance in the curriculum is serious enough that a multidisciplinary team considers it unlikely that the problem will be resolved in general education. Then the student may be considered eligible for special education, assuming that procedural state and federal requirements are met.

Consider a fifth-grade student who is placed appropriately in a fifth-grade reader. No additional resources should be required in general education for the student to acquire the expected reading skills, assuming instruction is adequate and the student is motivated. The need for additional resources is less clear for a fifth-grade student who is placed appropriately in a third-grade reader. The general education classroom should have resources (e.g., instructional alternatives, peer tutoring or cooperative learning programs, more individualized assistance) to accommodate that student in the general education classroom. In reality, however, the resources to accommodate the student may vary considerably from district to district and even from school to school. As currently structured, general education may not facilitate the student learning the reading curriculum, so additional resources outside of general education may be necessary.

Finally, consider the fifth-grade student who is placed appropriately in a beginning first-grade reader. It seems unlikely that in most settings, at least as currently structured, general education would have sufficient resources to facilitate the student mastering the reading curriculum. In this circumstance, the intensive and extensive resources provided by special education may be required.

The process of Problem Certification decision making using CBM relies on the SLA to identify the magnitude of the problem. In Desireé's case, she was given at least three randomly selected passages in each of a number of successively lower levels of the Ginn reading curriculum. Her scores in Ginn 8 were already available from the Problem Identification process, so the SLA began by testing her at the next lower level (Ginn 7). One of the major goals of the SLA is to determine a level of the curriculum in which Desireé is "successful."

This decision is operationalized in reading by identifying the highest level of the curriculum (i.e., instructional placement) where she could be placed and expected to profit from instruction. If the student were to be placed in third- through sixth-grade material, it would be desirable to be reading 70-100 words correctly per minute with no more than 4–6 errors (95% accuracy). If the student were to be placed in first- or second-grade material, it would be desirable to be reading 40–60 words correctly per minute with no more than 4–6 errors (90% accuracy).

On a single testing occasion, Desireé read passages beginning at Level 8 through Level 4. Her scores are shown in Table 4. For ease of interpretation, only the number of words she read correctly are included. According to the reading instructional placement guidelines, Desireé most likely should be placed in a Ginn 4 reader, material expected for typical first-grade students. One conclusion that can be reached is that Desireé performs about 2 years behind curricular expectations in reading.

The potential magnitude of the problem also is defined relative to local normative performance in the reading curriculum. Local norms were developed for the school district from the expected level of the Ginn series representative of each grade. For example, second-grade students were normed using Level 7 of the Ginn curriculum, the expected level representative of most second-grade students during the school year. The appropriate interpretive score is the percentile rank, also shown in Table 4. Desireé performed well below typical third- and second-grade students, but read above the median of typical first-grade students at this time of the school year.

**TABLE 4   Results of Survey-Level Assessment and
Problem Certification for Desireé**

Grade Material to be Learned	Level of Ginn Curriculum	Desireé's Median Performance	Grade-Level Peer Performance	Desireé's Percentile Rank
3	8	15	87	5
2	7	20	*	
	6	22	58	14
1	5	36	*	
	4	40	23	73

*Local norms, developed from only one level of curriculum per grade level. Therefore, no norms are available for these curriculum levels.

Decisions about Problem Certification using CBM usually are made on the basis of percentile rank criteria (Marston & Magnusson, 1988; Shinn, 1989b). In Desireé's school district, she could be considered eligible for special education if her scores were below the 16th percentile of students one grade-level below her current grade placement. In this instance, Desireé could be considered eligible because she performed at the 5th percentile of second graders, well below the 16th percentile. Desireé's results in reading compared to the range of reading scores from local norms are presented in Figure 4. The figure communicates clearly that she performs outside the range of typical third and second graders, but performs above typical first graders in the Ginn series.

Eligibility is but one part of the Problem Certification decision. The second part is *need*. A student may be eligible for special education, but not need the services. This decision is made only by examining Desireé's instructional needs in the context of resources available in general education that may be used to affect her learning positively. Only after it has been demonstrated to be unlikely that she could benefit from those resources should she be considered for special education. In this case, the multidisciplinary team decided it was unlikely that Desireé would benefit from reading instruction in general education regardless of what resources were brought to bear. Therefore, Desireé was provided special education with an IEP in reading.

Exploring and Evaluating Solutions
The data collected for Problem Identification and Certification decisions are linked directly to Exploring and Evaluating Solutions decisions. In Exploring Solutions, an initial intervention is planned with respect to the "what" to teach (e.g., content of instruction, type and level of curriculum to be used) and the "how" to teach (e.g., what teaching strategies will be used). CBM Problem Identification and Problem Certification data can assist in the intervention planning process by providing information regarding specific skills the student does or does not demonstrate (Howell & Morehead, 1987; see Figure 2). The major strength of CBM, however, is in evaluating outcomes. CBM was developed to provide teachers with a set of procedures so they may make frequent and routine decisions about whether and when to modify a student's instructional program (Deno, 1985).

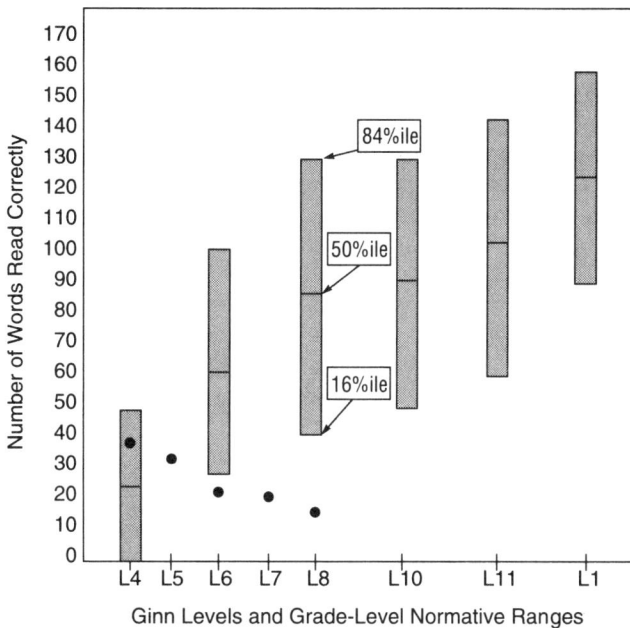

FIGURE 4 ***Comparing Desireé to Same- and Other-Grade General Education Peers in Reading***

In Exploring Solution decisions, the first task is to develop annual goals for the student. Fuchs and Shinn (1989) state that "specification of a goal precedes and defines the CBM monitoring of student progress and instructional effectiveness" (p. 130). A compelling reason to use CBM data to write goals comes from the Education for All Handicapped Children Act (1975). This act requires that an IEP identify each special education student's needs in terms of goals and objectives (Bateman & Herr, 1981) and identify "appropriate criteria and evaluation procedures" for determining progress toward these goals (Sect. 121a.316e). Yet, almost 16 years after implementation of the Act, current IEPs fail to demonstrate significant improvement in quality over initial implementation (Smith, 1990). Too often, IEP goals are written without current student performance data. IEP goals are frequently vague, lacking observable, measurable outcomes (e.g., "Will improve 1 year in reading"), or are overly specific and detail a series of short-term instructional objectives (e.g., "Will master C-V-C words with 80% accuracy"). As a result, *systematic* evaluation of an individual's special education intervention is precluded.

Writing IEP goals using CBM strategies employs a *long-term* approach to measurement (Fuchs & Deno, 1991). A decision is made about where and at what level of success in the general education curriculum the student would be expected to perform in 1 year if the student's program were considered successful. A basic format for IEP annual goals in reading, math, written expression, and spelling is illustrated in Table 5. The basic format includes the academic domain, conditions, student behavior, and criterion for success.

TABLE 5   *Basic Format for Annual IEP Goals in*
Reading, Math, Written Expression, and Spelling

Academic Area	Conditions	Behavior	Criterion
Reading	In *(number of weeks until annual review)*, when given a randomly selected passage from *(level and name of reading series)*,	student will read aloud	at *(number of words per minute correct/ # of errors)*.
Math	In *(number of weeks until annual review)*, when given randomly selected problems from *(level and name of math series)* for 2 minutes,	student will write	*(number of correct digits)*.
Written Expression	In *(number of weeks until annual review)*, when given a story starter or topic sentence and 3 minutes in which to write,	student will write	a total of *(number of words or letter sequences)*.
Spelling	In *(number of weeks until annual review)*, when dictated randomly selected words from *(level and name of spelling series)* for 2 minutes,	student will write	*(number of correct letter sequences)*.

Source: From "Writing CBM IEP Objectives" (p. 136) by L. S. Fuchs and M. R. Shinn, 1989, *Curriculum-Based Measurement: Assessing Special Children*, edited by M.R. Shinn. New York: Guilford Press. Copyright ©1989 by The Guilford Press. Reprinted by permission.

If we consider Desireé's SLA data, it was recommended that she be instructed in Level 4 of the Ginn basal series. After 1 year, if Desireé performs at the rate of progress expected of any student according to the publisher's scope-and-sequence chart, she would be expected to be placed in a Ginn Level 7 reader. The multidisciplinary team decided this expected rate of progress would be appropriate for Desireé. Thus, the long-term goal material identified for her annual IEP goal was Level 7. Next, the criterion for success must be identified. For Desireé, the multidisciplinary team used instructional placement standards (see Fuchs & Shinn, 1989, for more detail) and selected the upper end of the range for grades 1-2 material (60 WCM) as the criterion for success. After discussion of the SLA data, the Ginn scope-and-sequence expectations, and the specific expectations for Desireé, the following annual IEP goal was written:

> In 32 weeks, when given a randomly selected passage from Level 7 of the Ginn reading series, Desireé will read aloud at a rate of 60 words per minute correct with 4 or fewer errors.

One advantage of measuring Desireé's reading proficiency in long-term goal material is the emphasis on broad, rather than specific, curricular achievement (Fuchs & Fuchs, 1986a; Fuchs & Deno, 1991). In addition, measuring Desireé's performance in annual goal material, in contrast to short-term objectives, is more logistically feasible, assesses for retention and generalization, represents meaningful growth in the curriculum, and is supported by technical adequacy data (for more detail see Fuchs, in press; Fuchs & Deno, 1991).

Writing IEP goals using CBM data can be accomplished through a variety of strategies. The first set of strategies involves establishing the IEP annual goal(s) in the absence of local norms. These strategies include expert judgment, dynamic aim, and instructional placement standards.

The second strategy utilizes local norms to establish the criterion for success. All the strategies use the information collected from the SLA data, as this provides the legally required current performance data across levels of the curriculum.

Goal-writing strategies without local norms. The use of "expert judgment" is premised on the expectation that the student will "do more in more difficult material" in 1 year. The multidisciplinary team makes a "best guess" about the annual goal material, the level of the curriculum at which the student would be expected to be performing in 1 year. This level becomes the measurement material for evaluating student progress. A criterion for success also must be specified. As broad guidelines for using the expert judgment approach: (a) the annual goal material must be at least one curriculum level beyond the student's current instructional placement, and (b) the criterion for success must be higher than the student's current performance in the annual goal material (Fuchs & Fuchs, 1986a). In the case of Desireé, this strategy would require selecting, at the very minimum, Level 5 as the annual goal material and a criterion for success greater than 36 WPM. Goals written using this method usually are significantly more ambitious than these minimal standards. In the absence of more objective data (e.g., instructional placement criteria, local norms), this strategy is straightforward and encourages writing ambitious and realistic goals.

The *dynamic aim* approach is a variation of the expert judgment approach. This strategy originates with the original "best guess," but the criterion for success is adjusted based on the student's rate of progress. For example, suppose Desireé's IEP goal stated that in 1 year, given passages from Ginn Level 6, Desireé will read aloud at a rate of 50 WPM with 4 or fewer errors. The dynamic aim approach would require frequently evaluating Desireé's performance compared to the goal of 50 WPM and adjusting the criterion for success (i.e., 50 WPM) based on her projected rate of progress. If her rate of progress suggests that she will exceed 50 WPM, the goal would be raised. On the other hand, if her rate of progress suggests that she will not meet the goal, the 50 WPM goal would be retained and an instructional change would be made. Teachers who utilize a dynamic aim approach have been shown to raise goals more frequently, employ more ambitious goals, and obtain greater student achievement outcomes, as compared to teachers using an approach in which goals are not raised if rate of progress exceeds the goal (Fuchs, Fuchs, & Hamlett, 1989b).

A third strategy involves using *instructional placement standards* as guidelines for determining the level of the general education curriculum in which a student would be placed for instructional purposes, the annual goal level of the curriculum, and the criterion for success. To date, CBM instructional placement standards have been proposed only in the area of reading. This approach follows the same general guidelines that were set forth in the expert judgment strategy, but are more data-based. First, the level of the general education curriculum in which the student would be expected to be successful is identified. Although the special education student may not receive instruction in this curriculum, identifying instructional level serves as the index to current performance in the mainstream curriculum. Once that level has been established, the multidisciplinary team can discuss how much progress in the general education curriculum would be expected in 1 year, if the program were successful. The level of the general education curriculum where the student would be expected to perform corresponds to the annual goal material. The criterion for success equals the instructional placement standard for that level of the curriculum (for more detail, see Fuchs & Shinn, 1989).

As discussed in the section on Problem Identification and Problem Certification, for Desireé, the suggested instructional placement would be Ginn Level 4, because this was the highest level of first- or second-grade curriculum in which she read at least 40 WPM correctly. The instructional placement standards also are used as a guideline for determining criteria for success in the IEP goal material. If Level 7 were selected as the annual goal-level material, it would be recommended that Desireé read at least 40 WPM correctly as the criterion for success. In Desireé's case, the multidisciplinary team identified the upper end (60 WRC) of the instructional placement standards as the criterion for success.

Goal writing strategies using local norms. The availability of local norms assists with establishing more data-based criteria for success in the annual goal material. Expectations about student progress are tied to the performance of typical general education peers. Guidelines for this approach again require specification of the level of the general education curriculum in which the student would be expected to be performing in 1 year. The criterion for success in that material is the median score of typical general education students in that material. For example, if the multidisciplinary team decided that in 1 year Desireé would be expected to perform in the third-grade level of the curriculum (Level 8), the criterion for success would be 87, the normative score of students at that grade (see Table 5).

Evaluating Solutions

Procedures for Data Collection

Once data-based annual IEP goal(s) are written, a standard is provided for evaluating the initial intervention's effectiveness. Effectiveness is evaluated by routinely and frequently collecting and analyzing student data. Annual goals in the IEP are translated into a graph to provide a visual representation of the goal and actual student performance, as shown in Figure 5. The graph includes: (a) time frame (horizontal axis), (b) unit of measurement (vertical axis), (c) criterion for success, and (d) current performance data from the material specified in the annual goal (from SLA). The line drawn from the student's current performance data to the criterion for success represents the expected rate of progress, or *aimline*.

Frequency of measurement. Use of CBM is predicated on the notion that student outcomes are examined on an ongoing and frequent basis. Every time a student is tested, the results are graphed as shown in Figure 6. In Desireé's case, two times each week she was tested by reading a passage randomly sampled from the level of the curriculum specified in her annual IEP goal. In this instance it was Ginn Level 7. As shown in Figure 6, the initial instructional program implemented for 5 weeks was not effective. In fact, the inter-

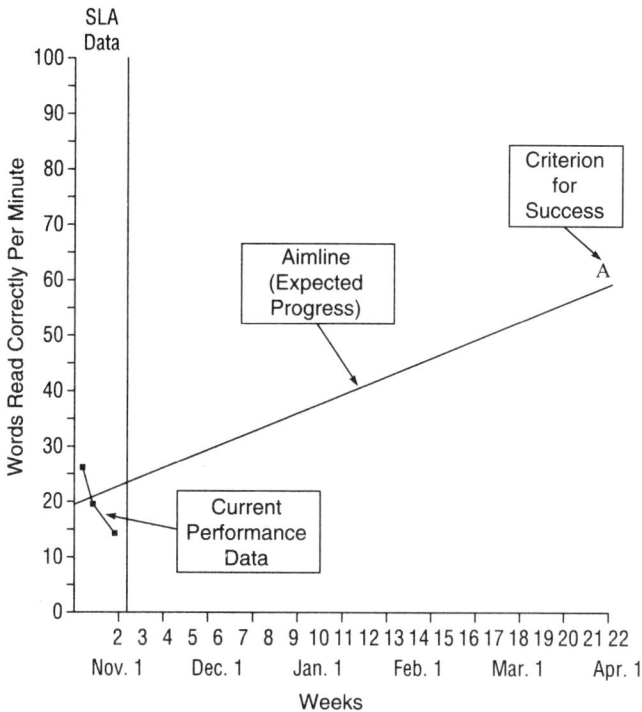

FIGURE 5 *Desireé's Annual IEP Goal Translated into a Graph for Monitoring Intervention Effectiveness*

vention was having a detrimental effect on her reading achievement. Her estimated rate of progress, shown by the *trendline,* was decreasing. The trendline is drawn through each of Desireé's scores to represent her estimated rate of progress. Because her actual rate of progress was much less than her expected rate of progress, a change in her instructional program was required.

The change in intervention was effective. Not only was Desireé now improving in her general reading skills, but her actual rate of progress was exceeding her expected rate. Collecting student performance data frequently allowed Desireé's teacher to change the instructional program when it was shown to be ineffective.

Determining how frequently CBM data should be collected involves appraising both technical and practical considerations. *Technical considerations* refer to evidence supporting the use of data to make reliable decisions regarding student progress. The major tool in making this decision is the trendline (Fuchs, 1989). Among the technical issues regarding use of a trendline are the number of data points required to estimate actual progress reliably and how to organize the data for interpretation. An ideal trendline would allow reliable decisions to be made with a few number of data points. This would enable teachers to avoid maintaining an ineffective instructional program for long peri-

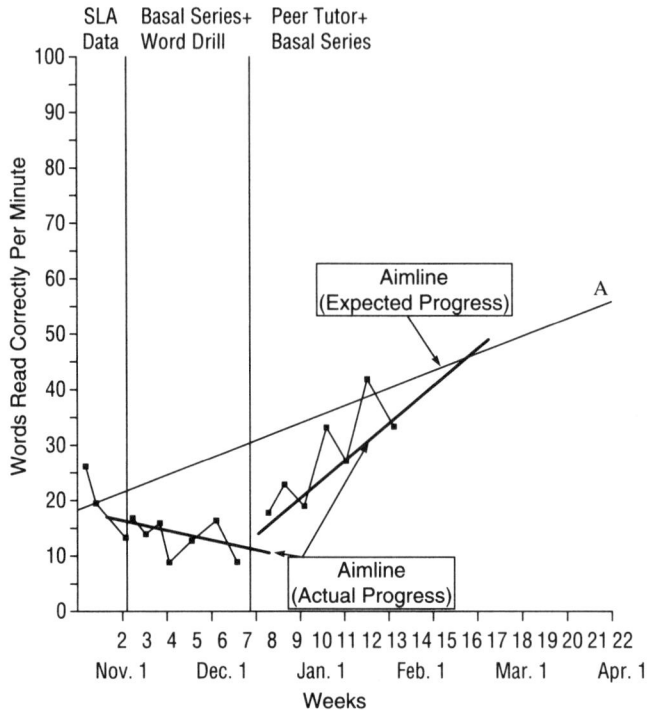

FIGURE 6   *Effectiveness of Desireé's Reading Intervention Relative to Rate of Progress Toward Annual Goal*

ods. A minimum of 10 data points (Good & Shinn, 1990) is necessary to estimate a reliable performance trend.

Practical considerations also are important. Although collecting data on student performance daily may be technically advantageous so that the minimum number of data points for trend estimation can accrue rapidly, this may not be feasible. Research has suggested that measuring student performance twice weekly may be sufficient to make appropriate decisions (Fuchs & Fuchs, 1986b). No additional student achievement benefits as a function of frequency of measurement were found for monitoring twice weekly or three times weekly or daily (Fuchs & Fuchs, 1986b). Therefore, it is recommended that special education practitioners collect student performance data twice weekly so the requisite 10 data points can be collected in a little over a month (5 weeks). This time frame allows adequate time for demonstrating instructional effects and the modification of ineffective programs.

Data collection strategies. Various methods have been utilized to collect CBM student performance data. Most frequently, teachers collect and score the data. The usefulness of having teachers meaningfully involved in collecting and evaluating student data has been documented in terms of greater positive effects on student achievement (Fuchs, Deno, &

Mirkin, 1984; Fuchs & Fuchs, 1986b). Some special education teachers, however, express reluctance, at least initially, to use CBM progress monitoring strategies because they perceive the amount of time involved to be excessive (Wesson, King, & Deno, 1984). The *perception* of progress monitoring being time consuming does not match the data, however. Fuchs (1987) found that teachers spent an average of only 2 minutes and 15 seconds collecting a 1-minute sample of reading, including preparation, administration, scoring, and graphing of student data. Other research corroborates these findings for teachers who monitor student progress using CBM (Marston & Magnusson, 1985; Wesson, Fuchs, Tindal, Mirkin, & Deno, 1986).

Although it is logistically feasible for teachers to collect, score, and analyze CBM data, other strategies may increase efficiency. One approach has emphasized computer-managed instruction (CMI; Fuchs, 1988), which uses computer software programs to collect, graph, and analyze student performance data (Fuchs, Hamlett, & Fuchs, 1990). CMI creates an information management system to assist teachers in evaluating students' progress towards the CBM annual IEP goal. In a study that compared utilizing the computer software program to teacher-managed CBM practices (Fuchs, Fuchs, Hamlett, & Hasselbring, 1987), teachers reported that computers were more efficient than scoring, graphing, and evaluating student data by hand. Although the teachers perceived increased efficiency by using the computer software program, the research results suggested that the use of computers actually decreased teachers' efficiency in charting student performance. Using the computer program, however, may minimize teacher time devoted to analyzing student performance (Fuchs, Fuchs, Hamlett & Hasselbring, 1987).

The use of student peers also has been investigated as an option to reduce teacher data collection time and allow teachers to devote more time to interpreting the obtained information. Moreover, it has been hypothesized that potential benefits to peer tutors from collecting student data may accrue in terms of their own achievement and self-concept gains. Research related to training general education students to monitor reading using CBM procedures suggests that they can be trained to be reliable data collectors. Trained student monitors have been shown to be as accurate as adults, with interrater agreement percentages between students and trained adults ranging from 96.6% to 97.7% (Bentz, Shinn, & Gleason, 1990) and 86.2% to 100% (Knutson, 1990). Concerns have been raised, however, about the amount of time needed to train and frequently monitor student data collectors to assure high levels of reliability over time (Knutson, 1990). Again, in making CBM procedures more time-efficient, the qualitative information that teachers gain through direct scoring of student protocols is forfeited and should be taken into account when considering alternatives.

Determining intervention effectiveness. Data are collected in an ongoing manner to provide information regarding a student's progress toward the annual IEP goal(s). Teachers ultimately must make *decisions* about whether a program is effective, based on the data. Program effectiveness decisions are made by summarizing actual student performance and choosing an evaluation framework, either goal- or experimental-based.

Summarizing actual student progress is accomplished in two ways: (a) using a split-middle trendline (SM) or (b) using an ordinary-least-squares trendline (OLS). The SM and OLS differ in the way they are calculated. The SM requires few calculations and is trained easily (White, 1974). The OLS requires a programmable calculator or a micro-computer. In a study comparing the accuracy of SM and OLS procedures, results indicated that the OLS method was superior to the SM method for reading CBM data (Good & Shinn, 1990). More specifically, the OLS estimates were superior in their ability to estimate with smaller numbers of data points (10) and for longer periods into the future (6 weeks). These data suggest that an OLS method for evaluating student performance and making instructional decisions is best.

Goal-based data evaluation is the most common evaluation approach (see Fuchs, Fuchs, & Hamlett, 1989b). In the goal-based evaluation framework, the annual IEP goal is translated into the aimline of expected rate of progress. This aimline is used as the reference for success and decisions are made according to the student's progress toward this line. This evaluation approach is illustrated in Figure 6. To determine whether Desireé is making progress toward her goal, decision rules are applied when a predetermined number of data points have been collected. The rules applied would be in accordance with the slope of the trendline (either exceeding or failing to meet projected aimline), as explained previously. A variation to using a trendline with this approach is the 3-day rule (see White & Haring, 1980). The 3-day rule states that if the student's data points fall below the aimline for 3 consecutive monitoring days, an instructional change is warranted. Conversely, if the data points fall above the line for 3 consecutive monitoring days, the goal should be raised.

An experimental-based approach to evaluating student performance (see Hamlett, Fuchs, Stecher, & Ferguson, Fuchs, 1988) also can be used to determine intervention effectiveness. This approach requires that an instructional change be made after collecting a predetermined number of data points (e.g., 10), regardless of student progress. Changes in student programs are made routinely to: (a) test the effectiveness of different instructional strategies, and (b) potentially effect a greater rate of progress than would be obtained even if an effective program were maintained (Fuchs, 1988). A student's slope of improvement for each intervention is compared to determine which intervention had the greatest effect on student progress. The teaching approach that had the greatest effect on student performance then is implemented. Research comparing the goal-based and experimental-based methods indicates that the goal-based approach has a greater impact on student achievement, and teachers using this approach implement the monitoring and data-management procedures more accurately (Fuchs, 1988).

Problem Solution
If interventions are effective, educators can expect that ultimately a problem will be resolved. In the Problem-Solving model, this decision is reached when the initial severe discrepancy between what was expected and what was occurring is no longer severe. In special education, this decision is akin to making a decision that a student no longer needs special education services and can benefit from education in the general education classroom. The limited research data on special education exit rates suggest that few students are returned to general education annually (Shinn, 1988; Rodden-Nord, Shinn, & Good,

1992). Whether this outcome is due to the limited effectiveness of special education intervention programs, poor assessment practices, or an interaction of the two has not been determined. Some school-based personnel (e.g., Allen, 1989) have argued that Problem Solution decisions are not made because relevant data are not collected to suggest that a special education student can perform successfully in the general education curriculum.

CBM can be used to assist in making Problem Solution decisions in two ways. *First*, student progress toward the annual IEP goal is examined formally. This process entails evaluation of the graphed data, typically in relationship to the expected rate of progress shown by the aimline. In Figure 6, failure of the intervention implemented initially to resolve Desireé's reading problem was identified as part of the Problem Solution decision in mid-December.

Second, CBM can be used to repeat quarterly the Problem Identification peer-referenced testing activities. Special education students are tested on one day in the typical level of the curriculum from their grade placement and compared to same-grade students. At the time the first peer-referenced testing took place, Desireé had not reduced the discrepancy from her third-grade students as she continued to score at the 5th percentile.

At the time of the annual review, special education students are given another SLA, in which they are tested in successive levels of the curriculum. These data allow decisions to be made regarding reduced discrepancies from same-grade and lower-grade students in the curriculum. The data also serve as current performance data for writing new annual IEP goals.

In Desireé's case, by the end of the school year, not only had she exceeded greatly her expected rate of progress on the IEP but she also had reduced significantly the discrepancy from her peers in the curriculum. At the beginning of the year, she had performed at the 5th percentile of same-grade peers. By the expiration of her IEP, she performed at the 38th percentile relative to same-grade peers. Because of her rapid rate of progress in special education, as evidenced by the IEP graph and her reduced discrepancy, Desireé was exited from special education.

RESEARCH OUTCOMES OF CBM AND PROBLEM-SOLVING MODEL IMPLEMENTATION

A number of studies have examined components of CBM implementation (e.g., the effects of specific goal-setting strategies on student achievement in reading) and on implementation of CBM in a Problem-Solving model for special education decision making. The current research results reported here are interpreted in a unit of analysis called *effect size* (ES). Effect size is determined by taking the difference in scores between group means (e.g., experimental and control groups) divided by the standard deviation of the control group (Kavale & Forness, 1987). ES will be used to discuss differences in CBM performance for descriptive and experimental studies. For descriptive studies, an ES represents the mean performance differences between groups of students.

For example, Shinn, Ysseldyke, Deno, and Tindal (1986) compared the CBM reading scores of fifth-grade students in learning disabilities programs and other low-achievers.

They found an ES of −1.3. This score is interpreted as meaning that the typical LD student performed 1.3 standard deviations below the typical low achiever on CBM reading probes. In terms of percentile ranks, an ES of this magnitude means that the typical LD student performed at approximately the 10th percentile rank of low-achieving students.

For the experimental studies, Fuchs and Fuchs (1986b) explain an effect size of approximately one-half standard deviation (.52) as meaning that "in terms of the standard normal curve and an achievement test scale with a population mean of 100 and standard deviation of 15, one might expect the [intervention X] to increase the typical achievement outcome score from 100 to approximately 107.5" (p. 436). Achievement gains of this magnitude suggest that a student who would be expected to perform at the 50th percentile without the treatment would be expected to perform at the 69th percentile with the treatment.

Problem Identification/Problem Certification Research Outcomes

Outcome investigations regarding the use of CBM to make Problem Identification and Problem Certification decisions have been undertaken in three broad areas: (a) the utility of using CBM measures to differentiate students with mild handicaps (e.g., learning disabilities) from low-achieving and typical general education students, (b) the effects on special education assessment and placement practices, and (c) effects on the practices of school psychologists.

Using CBM to Differentiate Groups of Students

Four studies have investigated the usefulness of CBM to differentiate students referred for or placed in special education from other groups such as low achievers (e.g., Chapter 1 students) and typical students. One study investigated the achievement characteristics of students referred for special education services in reading. Three studies examined whether CBM provides clear and reliable differentiation among students placed in special education, Chapter 1, and general-education-only students. If the measures are to be validated for Problem Identification and Certification decisions, differences should be observed among groups of students that educators classify differentially.

The achievement characteristics of students referred for special education because of reading problems were studied by Shinn, Tindal, and Spira (1987). They examined the performance of referred students grades 2–6 on grade-level CBM reading tasks compared to local norms of general education students in the same school district. ESs across grades ranged from −1.6 to −1.0. When translated into percentiles, these ESs ranged from the 5.5th to the 15.9th percentile. The typical referred student performed at about the 8th percentile of general education peers. The authors concluded that referred students are characterized by extremely low achievement in the general education curriculum compared to other students and that CBM reliably indexes these achievement differences.

CBM also reliably differentiates groups of students classified by more traditional procedures. As presented earlier, Shinn, Ysseldyke, Deno, and Tindal (1986) found significant differences between LD students and low achievers on CBM reading, spelling, and written expression problems. In reading, the typical fifth-grade LD student across five districts performed at the 9.7th percentile rank of low-achieving students. More than 90% of low achievers would be expected to earn CBM reading scores above the typical student placed in LD programs.

Shinn and Marston (1985) researched differences on CBM measures of reading, spelling, math computation, and written expression among students placed in programs for mild handicaps (MH), Chapter 1 students, and typical general education students in grades 4–6. ESs across grades showed that students in MH programs performed at extremely low levels compared to general education peers and Chapter 1 students. In reading, for example, ESs ranged from –2.3 to –2.4 relative to general education peers; the typical MH student performed at the 1st percentile of general education students. When MH students were compared to Chapter 1 students, ESs ranged from –.2 to –1.5, with the differences increasing by grade level; the typical MH student performed at the 17th percentile of Chapter 1 students. More than 83% of Chapter 1 students outperformed the MH students in reading. Chapter 1 students also were differentiated reliably from general education students. By grade, the ESs ranged from –.9 to –1.5, with the typical percentile rank corresponding to the 16th percentile compared to general education peers.

Finally, CBM was used to study potential CBM reading differences between all students in a school system, grades 1 to 6, who had been placed in programs for learning disabilities via traditional ability-achievement discrepancy procedures (Shinn, Tindal, Spira, & Marston, 1987) and Chapter 1 and typical general education students. When comparing LD students to general education peers, ESs ranged from –1.1 at grade 1 to –2.2; the typical LD student performed at the 3rd percentile of general education students. In comparison to Chapter 1 students, ESs ranged from –.2 at grade 1 to –1.5 with the differences increasing by grade level; again, the typical LD student performed at the 17th percentile of Chapter 1 students. As in the previous studies, Chapter 1 students were differentiated reliably from general education students. By grade, the ESs ranged from –.7 to –1.4 with the typical percentile rank corresponding to the 14th percentile compared to general education peers.

In each of these studies, the authors concluded that CBM could be used to differentiate groups into different types of educational services in much the same way as the school had classified students in the past, but more in line with the benefits of the Problem-Solving model approach.

Effects on Assessment and Placement Practices
Marston and Magnusson (1988) summarized the effects of using CBM within a Problem-Solving model on eligibility assessment and special education placement practices. The number of students referred for special education who actually were assessed for eligibility determination decreased by almost half when systematic Problem Identification decisions were made. In contrast to practices in which almost all referrals are tested for special education eligibility, Marston and Magnusson (1988) reported rates of 45 to 65% of referred students being tested. Actual eligibility rates also dropped to approximately 25 to 45% of all referrals—again a figure quite in contrast to national referral placement rates of 75 to 92% (Algozzine, Christenson, & Ysseldyke, 1982). Germann and Tindal

(1985) reported special education placement figures that closely paralleled their state and national levels.

Effects on School Psychology Practices
Changes in the assessment and service delivery practices of school psychologists after implementation of CBM within a problem-solving model have been noted by Canter (1991) and Marston and Magnusson (1988). Canter (1991) reported changes in school psychologists' assessment practices. Rather than routinely testing every referral to determine special education eligibility, in the Problem-Solving model school psychologists tested students only when there were specific assessment questions. Only half of the cases on the typical school psychologist's load involved testing, and only half of those involved assessment of learning aptitude (i.e., intelligence). In addition, Canter (1991) detailed qualitative changes in the types of data collected when testing was conducted.

With the decreased time in routine eligibility testing, Marston and Magnusson (1988) observed corresponding increases in school psychologists' consultation activities from 12 to 36% of their time within 3 years, and a similar increase from 1.5 to 10% for direct services (e.g., counseling). Canter (1991) reported that in subsequent years school psychologists' consultation time increased further to 52% of their time.

Exploring and Evaluating Solutions

The outcomes of using CBM to write data-based annual IEP goals and monitor intervention effectiveness have been examined in three broad areas: (a) student achievement outcomes, (b) changes in teaching practices, and (c) students' goal awareness. Most of the experimental work has been conducted by Lynn Fuchs and associates at Vanderbilt University and typically are interpreted as ES units.

Effects on Student Achievement

A number of studies have demonstrated effect sizes related to student achievement and CBM. These studies, summarized in Table 6, include the use of CBM procedures to monitor student achievement by having teachers collect CBM data: (a) without instruction on how to use the information (informal decision making), (b) with systematic rules for making intervention effectiveness decisions and instructional changes, and (c) by providing feedback about how the students' performed on specific required curricular skills (instructional enhancements).

These studies indicate, at a broad level, that the ESs associated with using CBM and data evaluation and decision rules produce significant and socially meaningful achievement gains. Most of the studies comparing the role of feedback systems (i.e., feedback regarding programmatic changes, qualitative feedback on student progress, and so on) indicate that teacher involvement in the evaluation process has a greater influence on student achievement than measurement that does not require teacher involvement.

Informal decision making regarding student progress. The process of collecting CBM student performance data without specific decision-making strategies for determining

TABLE 6   Summary of Effect Sizes Related to Student Achievement and Curriculum-Based Measurement

Study	Domain	Group or Experimental Conditions	Effect Size
Fuchs & Fuchs (1986b)	Meta-analysis of systematic formative evaluation	Effects on achievement using progress monitoring	Average = .70
		Effects on achievement using data evaluation and decision rules	Average = .91
		Effects on achievement using teacher judgment	Average = .42
		Effects on achievement using graphic display	Average = .70
		Effects on achievement using recorded data	Average = .26
Fuchs & Fuchs (1987b)	Meta-analysis of graphing student data	Effects on achievement using equal-interval paper	Average = .46
		Effects on achievement using ratio-scaled paper	Average = .53
Fuchs, Deno, & Mirkin (1984)	Reading	G1. CBM monitoring	Words read correctly = .92
		G2. Traditional monitoring	
Fuchs (1988)	Spelling	G1. Goal-based structure	*WSC = .67
		G2. Experimental structure	**CLS = 1.05
Fuchs, Fuchs, & Hamlett (1989d)	Reading	G1. Performance + quality feedback	Retell matched words = .67
		G2. Performance only	
Fuchs, Fuchs, & Hamlett (1989a)	Spelling	G1. Enhanced feedback CBM	1 vs. 3 = .45
		G2. Unenhanced feedback CBM	1 vs. 2 = .22
		G3. Control	2 vs. 3 = .23
Fuchs, Fuchs, & Hamlett (1989c)	Reading	G1. Measurement + evaluation	1 vs. 3 = .72
		G2. Measurement only	1 vs. 2 = .21
		G3. Control	2 vs. 3 = .36
Fuchs, Fuchs, & Hamlett (1989b)	Math	G1. Dynamic goal structure	1 vs. 3 = .52
		G2. Static goal structure	1 vs. 2 = .28
		G3. Control	2 vs. 3 = .25
Fuchs, Fuchs, Hamlett, & Stecker (1990)	Math	G1. Performance + skills analysis	1 vs. 3 = .67
		G2. Performance only	1 vs. 2 = .55
		G3. Control	2 vs. 3 = .26

*WSC = words spelled correctly
**CLS = correct letter sequences

when a program is ineffective and requires modification seems to have mild effects on student achievement. Overall, individuals whose progress is monitored using CBM over time can be expected to make modest gains (average ES = .36, increases from 50th to 63rd percentile) over those students whose progress is monitored using traditional methods (e.g., teacher judgment, student workbooks, and so on). In some circumstances, using CBM without specific strategies to make program improvements does not impact student achievement. For example, in a study by Fuchs, Fuchs, and Hamlett (1989c), an ES of .36 was found not to be reliably different from students whose progress was monitored using traditional methods. In a meta-analysis of systematic formative evaluation studies, ESs up to .70 (i.e., increases from 50th to 76th percentile) have been noted, but how many studies included a data collection-only group is unclear (Fuchs & Fuchs, 1986b).

Systematic decision-making strategies. Student achievement can be maximized by *using* CBM data and systematic decision rules to indicate *when* a change in an instructional program is required. Several studies have investigated systematic strategies designed to get teachers to make instructional changes in response to students' progress. The research has focused on feedback methods indicating to teachers that an instructional program is ineffective and a change is due, including: (a) the amount and type of feedback given regarding programmatic changes and student performance, and (b) the type of goal structure used.

Most frequently, computers have been used to indicate when an instructional change is required (e.g., Fuchs, Fuchs, & Hamlett, 1989d). The computer compares a student's actual rate of progress with the expected rate of progress toward the IEP annual goal. When actual progress is less than expected progress, the computer signals to teachers that a program change is required. Outcomes of using CBM and this computer feedback system are ESs in the magnitude of .72. This growth represents an increase from the 50th to the 77th percentile, compared to using traditional methods. Other research has explored using computer feedback after teachers make initial program effectiveness decisions. In the area of spelling, Fuchs, Fuchs, and Hamlett (1989a) provided feedback to teachers by the computer automatically or required teachers to make an initial decision about when and what to change. The computer then gave feedback regarding the correctness of the teacher's initial decision. Results indicated that spelling achievement was greater with students of teachers who were required to make initial decisions with subsequent computer feedback.

Varying computer feedback using different CBM goal structures also has been explored. Fuchs, Fuchs, and Hamlett (1989b) compared a dynamic goal structure approach to a static goal structure approach. The computerized feedback was the same for both groups, but the dynamic goal structure group received computerized feedback that required teachers to raise the goal when estimated student progress exceeded the aimline. The static goal structure did not require the teachers to increase goals in response to progress that exceeded the anticipated aimline. The results indicated that the dynamic goal approach had greater effects on student achievement than the static goal structure or the control group as measured by CBM math measures (Fuchs, Fuchs, & Hamlett, 1989b). The effect size magnitude associated with the dynamic goal CBM procedures was .52 (approximately one half standard deviation), or the difference from the 50th to the 69th percentile.

Instructional enhancements. Research on CBM and in Exploring and Evaluating Solutions, to this point, has examined the outcomes of collecting CBM data with informal and systematic decision-making strategies. The latter were designed to tell teachers explicitly that instructional changes are necessary because the current instructional program was not effective. The focus of decision making has been on the *when* to change rather than *what* to change. Use of CBM has been explored further in terms of providing specific information designed to tell teachers what parts of their instructional program to change. This type of information is referred to as a skills analysis, or an *instructional enhancement*. Most often, teachers have been provided with skills analysis information obtained from the student's performance on weekly probes. The skills analysis gives teachers specific information regarding skills required in the curriculum that have/have not been demonstrated. As shown in Table 6, research in this area corroborates earlier findings that teachers who use direct and frequent measurement affect student outcomes to a greater degree than teachers who use traditional means of monitoring progress.

In the areas of math and reading, teachers who use CBM *and* receive skills analysis information effected greater growth, compared to teachers who monitored and evaluated student progress and the control group (Fuchs, Fuchs, & Hamlett 1989d; Fuchs, Fuchs, & Hamlett, & Stecker, 1990). The skills analysis information for math included specific math problem types (e.g., addition basic facts, sums to 18) that were attempted at least 75% of the time on the probes with at least 85% accuracy. The ES magnitude associated with CBM skills analysis was .67 compared to the control group, and .55 compared to CBM teachers who did not receive the skills analysis. In reading, the skills analysis information consisted of a structured analysis of story components included in students' recalls. The ES magnitude associated with CBM skills analysis was .67 compared to CBM teachers who did not receive the skills analysis. In terms of the standard normal curve, this result would be associated with increases from the 50th to the 75th percentile.

Research in spelling indicates that CBM skills analysis can effect student achievment, but the skills analysis information does not have to include recommendations as to *what* to change (Fuchs, Fuchs, Hamlett, & Allinder, 1991a; 1991b). Fuchs, Fuchs, Hamlett, and Allinder (1991a) demonstrated support for earlier findings that CBM skills analysis effects greater student achievement. The skills analysis information provided teachers the lists of words administered to the student, the student's response, and the three most frequent types of errors the student had made. A variation of the skills analysis information in spelling was explored by providing the teacher a recommended teaching adjustment along with detailed instructions for how to implement it (Fuchs, Fuchs, Hamlett, & Allinder, 1991b). When compared to teachers employing traditional monitoring strategies, teachers who received skills analysis information versus teachers who received the revised skills analysis information both showed greater achievement gains, but did not significantly differ from each other. The comparability of the two CBM groups may suggest that in the area of spelling, specific recommendations for instructional planning may not be necessary or sufficient.

Effects on Students' Goal Awareness

Students' knowledge of their progress generally has been suggested as a means of making the student aware of teachers' expectations, offering motivation as a means of accomplishing their goal, and in some way serving as an exercise in self-monitoring. Erez (1977), for example, suggests that goals and knowledge of performance toward goals are necessary to improve student performance.

In a study examining the effects of CBM on teacher behavior and student achievement (Fuchs, Deno, & Mirkin, 1984), student awareness of learning also was examined. Awareness was measured by asking students if they knew their goals and if they could judge whether they would meet their goals. Results indicated that students who were monitored using CBM procedures in reading were more knowledgeable about their learning. Similarly, students using CBM in spelling described their goals more specifically than students who were monitored using traditional methods (Fuchs, Butterworth, & Fuchs, 1989). In addition, achievement gains were greater for students in the CBM groups than students being monitored using traditional methods. It was suggested that the differences in achievement gains were not attributable to differences in student perceptions of goal attainment but, rather, that they may be related to the student's knowledge of goals and perceptions of teacher feedback concerning progress (Fuchs, Butterworth, & Fuchs, 1989).

Effects on Teaching Practices

Although much attention has been directed at student achievement outcomes, teacher behavior also has been shown to be affected by CBM monitoring procedures. Changes have been demonstrated in terms of compliance with CBM procedures, responding to student data, and varying individual instructional planning and delivery.

The extent to which teachers implement CBM procedures has been determined most commonly using the Modified Accuracy of Implementation Rating Scale (MAIRS; Fuchs, 1986). This scale consists of 11 items assessing compliance with each component of the CBM procedure, ranging from placing students in goal-level material to changing instructional programs when told to do so. The degree to which teachers comply with the CBM procedures has been comparable across a variety of experimental conditions (Fuchs, Fuchs, Hamlett, & Allinder, 1991b; Fuchs, Fuchs, Hamlett, & Stecker, 1990; Fuchs, Fuchs, & Hamlett, 1989b; Fuchs, 1988). But differences in compliance have been found, relating to evaluation approach (e.g., goal- versus experimental-based) (Fuchs, Fuchs, & Hamlett, 1989a) and evaluation method (e.g., 3-day decision rule) (Fuchs, 1989).

Using CBM data to make progress monitoring and instructional effectiveness decisions has been shown to affect teachers' instructional planning and teaching. Teachers who received CBM data and qualitative feedback regarding student performance wrote more specific instructional plans (Fuchs, Fuchs, & Hamlett; 1989a; Fuchs, Fuchs, Hamlett & Stecker, 1990). In addition, teachers also increased their accuracy with identification of phonetic spelling errors (Fuchs, Allinder, Hamlett, & Fuchs, 1990).

The implications of this research are encouraging not only in terms of instructional planning, but also but with regard to changes in teaching. Teachers using CBM have been found to make more instructional changes in students' programs (e.g., Fuchs, Deno, & Mirkin, 1984; Fuchs, Fuchs, Hamlett, & Allinder, 1991b), which may be one of the variables associated with greater student achievement gains. The effect of progress monitoring on the structure of instruction also has been explored. Variables examined included instructional grouping, teacher-directed learning, active academic responding, and prompting (Deno, King, Skiba, Sevcik, & Wesson, 1983). Teachers who used CBM monitoring procedures demonstrated increased structure in instructional delivery (Fuchs, Deno, & Mirkin, 1984).

Teacher attitudes regarding student progress and instructional programs also have changed when utilizing CBM progress monitoring procedures. Teachers were more realistic about student progress (Fuchs, Deno, & Mirkin, 1984) and more open to trying new interventions when a student was not making adequate progress (Fuchs, Deno, & Mirkin, 1984; Marston & Magnusson, 1988).

Problem Solution Research Outcomes

Research on Problem Solution decisions for all assessment practices remains limited. Research on the use of CBM to make this decision is increasing and can be divided into two broad areas: (a) effects on percentages of students exited from special education, and (b) preliminary research on identifying potential candidates for reintegration into general education. Significant increases in special education exit rates have been observed when data relevant to performance in general education curriculum are used in decision making. Marston and Magnusson (1988) reported an increase in the percentage of students exited yearly from special education resource rooms to 20% from 4%.

Preliminary research on using CBM to identify potential candidates for reintegration shows promise. Shinn, Habedank, Rodden-Nord, and Knutson (in press) examined the percentage of special education students served in resource rooms with an IEP objective in reading who read grade-level curricular materials in the range of low reading group general education students from their grade placement. The outcomes estimated that approximately 40% of the special education students read as well as or better than at least one of the low reading group students. These data suggest that these special education students should be considered for return to general education for reading instruction. Rodden-Nord, Shinn, and Good (1992) researched the effects of these kinds of CBM data on general education teachers' attitudes about reintegrating special education students back into their classrooms for reading instruction. When provided with CBM data indicative of reading skills commensurate with low reading group students, general education teachers' attitudes about reintegration changed positively and significantly. Teachers reported that they were very willing to reintegrate the special education student.

CONCLUSION

CBM meets the criteria proposed by Reschly, Kicklighter, and McKee (1988c) for a useful assessment system, that the data collected for special education eligibility be linked to intervention planning *and* evaluation. CBM typically is used not as a series of tests added to an educator's testing "armament." Instead, it is to be used within a problem-solving model. Using CBM in this manner has a number of positive demonstrated outcomes for each of the five steps of the model proposed here. Most important, students' achievement is affected. When educators write data-based long-term goals and adjust their interventions as a result of students' rates of progress, significant and meaningful changes in student outcomes are observed. Given the legal requirement for evaluation of progress toward annual goals, the field of special education's documented lack of improvement in this area, and the strong potential for changes in student outcomes upon implementation, special education systems should place a high priority on training and implementing of CBM and problem-solving decision-making strategies.

Development of this paper was supported by grant no. 8029D80051–91 from the U.S. Department of Education, Special Education Programs, to provide leadership training in curriculum-based assessment. The views expressed within this paper are not necessarily those of the U.S. DOE.

REFERENCES

Algozzine, B., Christenson, S., & Ysseldyke, J. (1982). Probabilities associated with the referral to placement process. *Teacher Education & Special Education, 5,* 19–23.

Allen, D. (1989). Periodic and annual reviews and decisions to terminate special education services. In M. R. Shinn (Ed.), *Curriculum-based measurement: Assessing special children* (pp. 184–203). New York: Guilford.

Bateman, B., & Herr, C. (1981). Law and special education. In J. Kauffman & D. Hallahan (Eds.), *Handbook of special education* (pp. 330–360). Englewood Cliffs, NJ: Prentice Hall.

Bentz, J., Shinn, M., & Gleason, M. M. (1990). Training general education pupils to monitor reading using curriculum-based measurement procedures. *School Psychology Review, 19*(1), 23–32.

Bersoff, D. (1973). Silk purses into sow's ears. *American Psychologist, 10,* 892–899.

Blankenship, C. (1985). Using curriculum-based assessment data to make instructional decisions. *Exceptional Children, 52,* 233–238.

Canter, A. (1991). Effective psychological services for all students: A data-based model of service delivery. In G. Stoner, M. R. Shinn, & H. M. Walker (Eds.), *Interventions for achievement and behavior problems* (pp. 49–78). Silver Spring, MD: National Association of School Psychologists.

Deno, S. L. (1985). Curriculum-based measurement: The emerging alternative. *Exceptional Children, 52,* 219–232.

Deno, S. L. (1986). Formative evaluation of individual student programs: A new role for school psychologists. *School Psychology Review, 15,* 358–374.

Deno, S. L. (1989). Curriculum-based measurement and alternative special education services: A fundamental and direct relationship. In M. R. Shinn (Ed.), *Curriculum-based measurement: Assessing special children* (pp. 1–17). New York: Guilford.

Deno, S. L. (1990). Individual differences and individual difference: The essential difference of special education. *Journal of Special Education, 24*(2), 160–173.

Deno, S. L., King, R., Skiba, R., Sevcik, B., & Wesson, C. (1983). *The structure of instruction rating scale (SIRS): Development and technical characteristics* (Research Rep. No. 107). Minneapolis: University of Minnesota Institute for Research on Learning Disabilities.

Deno, S. L., Marston, D., & Mirkin, P. (1982). Valid measurement procedures for continuous evaluation of written expression. *Exceptional Children, 483,* 68–371.

Deno, S. L., Marston, D., Mirkin, P. K., Lowry, L., Sindelar, P., & Jenkins, J. (1982). *The use of standard tasks to measure achievement in reading, spelling, and written expression: A normative and developmental study.* Minneapolis: University of Minnesota Institute for Research on Learning Disabilities.

Deno, S. L., Mirkin, P., & Chiang, B. (1982). Identifying valid measures of reading. *Exceptional Children, 49,* 36–45.

Education for All Handicapped Children Act of 1975 (PL 94–142, 29 Nov. 1975) *United States Statutes at Large*, 79, pp. 27–52.

Erez, M. (1977). Feedback: A necessary condition for the goal setting-performance relationship. *Journal of Applied Psychology, 62*, 624–627.

Fuchs, L. S. (1986). *Effects of teacher training procedures on data-based instructional management implementation*. (Unpublished manuscript available from L. S. Fuchs, Box 328, Peabody College, Vanderbilt University, Nashville, TN 37203).

Fuchs, L. S. (1988). Effects of computer-managed instruction on teacher's implementation of systematic monitoring programs and student achievement. *Journal of Educational Research, 81*, 294–304.

Fuchs, L. S. (1989). Evaluating solutions: Monitoring progress and revising intervention plans. In M. R. Shinn (Ed.), *Curriculum-based measurement: Assessing special children* (pp. 155–183). New York: Guilford.

Fuchs, L. S. (in press). Enhancing instructional programming and student achievement with curriculum-based measurement. In J. Kramer (Ed.), *Curriculum-based assessment: Examining old problems, evaluating new solutions*. Hillsdale, NJ: Erlbaum.

Fuchs, L. S., Allinder, R. M., Hamlett, C. L., & Fuchs, D. (1990). An analysis of spelling curricula and teachers' skills in identifying error types. *Remedial & Special Education, 11*(1), 42–51.

Fuchs, L. S., Butterworth, J. R., & Fuchs, D. (1989). Effects of ongoing curriculum-based measurement on student awareness of goals and progress. *Education & Treatment of Children, 12*(1), 63–72.

Fuchs, L. S., & Deno, S. L. (1991). Paradigmatic distinctions between instructionally relevant measurement models. *Exceptional Children, 57*(6), 488–500.

Fuchs, L. S., Deno, S. L., & Mirkin, P. (1984). The effects of frequent curriculum-based measurement and evaluation on pedagogy, student achievement and student awareness of learning. *American Educational Research Journal, 21*, 449–460.

Fuchs, L. S., & Fuchs, D. (1986a). Curriculum-based assessment of progress towards long-and short-term goals. *Journal of Special Education, 20*, 69–82.

Fuchs, L. S., & Fuchs, D. (1986b). Effects of systematic formative evaluation on student achievement: A meta-analysis. *Exceptional Children, 53*, 199–208.

Fuchs, L. S., & Fuchs, D. (1987a). *Effects of curriculum-based measurement procedures in spelling and math*. (Unpublished manuscript available from L. S. Fuchs, Box 328, Peabody College, Vanderbilt University, Nashville, TN 37203).

Fuchs, L. S., & Fuchs, D. (1987b). The relation between methods of graphing student performance data and achievement: A meta-analysis. *Journal of Special Education Technology, 8*, 5–13.

Fuchs, L. S., Fuchs, D., & Hamlett, C. L. (1989a). Computers and curriculum-based measurement: Effects of teacher feedback systems. *School Psychology Review, 18*, 112–125.

Fuchs, L. S., Fuchs, D., & Hamlett, C. (1989b). Effects of alternative goal structures within curriculum-based measurement. *Exceptional Children, 55*, 429–438.

Fuchs, L. S., Fuchs, D., & Hamlett, C. L. (1989c). Effects of instrumental use of curriculum-based measurement to enhance instructional programs. *Remedial & Special Education, 10*(2), 43–52.

Fuchs, L. S., Fuchs, D., & Hamlett, C. L. (1989d). Monitoring reading growth using student recalls: Effects of two teacher feedback systems. *Journal of Educational Research, 83*(2), 103–110.

Fuchs, L. S., Fuchs, D., Hamlett, C. L., & Allinder, R. M. (1991a). The contribution of skills analysis to curriculum-based measurement in spelling. *Exceptional Children, 57*(5), 443–452.

Fuchs, L. S., Fuchs, D., Hamlett, C. L., & Allinder, R. M. (1991b). Effects of expert system advice within curriculum-based measurement on teacher planning and student achievement in spelling. *School Psychology Review, 20*(1), 49–66.

Fuchs, L. S., Fuchs, D., Hamlett, C. L., & Hasselbring, T. S. (1987). Using computers with curriculum-based progress monitoring: Effects on teacher efficiency and satisfaction. *Journal of Educational Technology, 8*, 14–27.

Fuchs, L. S., Fuchs, D., Hamlett, C. L., & Stecker, P. M. (1990). The role of skills analysis in curriculum-based measurement in math. *School Psychology Review, 19*(1), 6–22.

Fuchs, L. S., Fuchs, D., & Maxwell, L. (1988). The validity of informal reading comprehension measures. *Remedial & Special Education, 9*, 20–28.

Fuchs, L. S., Hamlett, C. L., & Fuchs, D. (1990). *Monitoring basic skills progress* [Computer program]. Austin, TX: PRO-ED.

Fuchs, L. S., Hamlett, C. L., Fuchs, D., Stecker, P. M., & Ferguson, C. (1988). Conducting curriculum-based measurement with computerized data collection: Effects on efficiency and teacher satisfaction. *Journal of Special Education Technology, 9*(2), 73–86.

Fuchs, L. S., & Shinn, M. R. (1989). Writing CBM IEP objectives. In M. R. Shinn (Ed.), *Curriculum-based measurement: Assessing special children* (pp. 132–154). New York: Guilford.

Gerber, M., & Semmel, M. (1984). Teachers as imperfect test: Reconceptualizing the referral process. *Educational Psychologist, 19,* 137–148.

Germann, G., & Tindal, G. (1985). An application of curriculum-based assessment: The use of direct and repeated measurement. *Exceptional Children, 52,* 244–265.

Gickling, E., & Thompson, V. (1985). A personal view of curriculum-based assessment. *Exceptional Children, 52,* 153–165.

Good, R. H., & Shinn, M. R. (1990). Forecasting accuracy of slope estimates for reading curriculum-based measurement: Empirical evidence. *Behavioral Assessment, 12,* 179–193.

Heller, K. A., Holtzman, W., & Messick, S. (1982). *Placing children in special education: A strategy for equity.* Washington, DC: National Academy Press.

Howell, K. W., & Morehead, M. K. (1987). *Curriculum-based evaluation for special and remedial education.* Columbus, OH: Merrill.

Kavale, K. A., & Forness, S. R. (1987). Substance over style: Assessing the efficacy of modality testing and teaching. *Exceptional Children, 54*(3), 228–239.

Knutson, N. (1990). *Teaching low-performing students to monitor the reading progress of their cross-age peers.* Unpublished doctoral dissertation, University of Oregon, Eugene.

Marston, D. (1989). Curriculum-based measurement: What is it and why do it? In M. R. Shinn (Ed.), *Curriculum-based measurement: Assessing special children* (pp. 18–78). New York: Guilford Press.

Marston, D., Fuchs, L. S., & Deno, S. L. (1986). A comparison of standardized achievement tests and direct measurement techniques in measuring student progress. *Diagnostique, 11,* 77–90.

Marston, D., Lowry, L., Deno, S. L., & Mirkin, P. K. (1981). *An analysis of learning trends in simple measures of reading, spelling, and written expression: A longitudinal study* (Research Rep. No. 49). Minneapolis: University of Minnesota Institute for Research on Learning Disabilities.

Marston, D., & Magnusson, D. (1985). Implementing curriculum-based measurement in special and regular education settings. *Exceptional Children, 52,* 266–276.

Marston, D., & Magnusson, D. (1988). Curriculum-based assessment: District-level implementation. In J. Graden, J. Zins, & M. Curtis (Eds.), *Alternative educational delivery systems: Enhancing instructional options for all students* (pp. 137–172). Washington, DC: National Association of School Psychologists.

Reschly, D. J., Genshaft, J., & Binder, M. S. (1987). *The 1986 NASP survey: Comparison of practitioners, NASP leadership, and university faculty on key issues.* Washington, DC: National Association of School Psychologists.

Reschly, D. J., Kicklighter, R., & McKee, P. (1988a). Recent placement litigation, Part I, Regular education grouping: Comparison of Marshall (1984, 1985) and Hobson (1967, 1969). *School Psychology Review, 17,* 9–21.

Reschly, D. J., Kicklighter, R., & McKee, P. (1988b). Recent placement litigation, Part II, Minority EMR overrepresentation: Comparison of Larry P. (1979, 1984, 1986) with Marshall (1984, 1985) and S-1 (1986). *School Psychology Review, 17,* 22–49.

Reschly, D. J., Kicklighter, R., & McKee, P. (1988c). Recent placement litigation, Part III, Analysis of differences in Larry P., Marshall, and S-1 and implications for future practices. *School Psychology Review, 17,* 39–50.

Rodden-Nord, K., Shinn, M. R., & Good, R. H. (1992). Effects of classroom performance data on general education teachers' attitudes towards reintegrating students with learning disabilities. *School Psychology Review, 21*(1), 138–154.

Shinn, M. R. (1988). Development of curriculum-based local norms for use in special education decision making. *School Psychology Review, 17,* 61–80.

Shinn, M. R. (Ed.). (1989a). *Curriculum-based measurement: Assessing special children.* New York: Guilford.

Shinn, M. R. (1989b). Identifying and defining academic problems: CBM screening and eligibility procedures. In M. R. Shinn (Ed.), *Curriculum-based measurement: Assessing special children* (pp. 90–129). New York: Guilford.

Shinn, M. R., & Good, R. H. (in press). CBA: An assessment of its current status and a prognosis for its future. In J. Kramer (Ed.), *Curriculum-based assessment: Examining old problems, evaluating new solutions.* Hillsdale, NJ: Erlbaum.

Shinn, M.R., Habedank, L., Rodden-Nord, K., & Knutson, N. (in press). Using curriculum-based measurement to identify potential candidates for reintegration into general education. *The Journal of Special Education.*

Shinn, M. R., & Marston, D. (1985). Differentiating mildly handicapped, low-achieving and regular education students: A curriculum-based approach. *Remedial & Special Education, 6,* 31–45.

Shinn, M. R., Nolet, V., & Knutson, N. (1990). Best practices in curriculum-based measurement. In A. Thomas & J. Grimes (Eds.), *Best practices in school psychology* (pp. 287–308). Washington DC: National Association of School Psychologists.

Shinn, M. R., Rosenfield, S., & Knutson, N. (1989). Curriculum-based assessment: A comparison and integration of models. *School Psychology Review*.

Shinn, M. R., Tindal, G., & Spira, D. (1987). Special education referrals as an index of teacher tolerance: Are teachers imperfect tests? *Exceptional Children, 54*, 32–40.

Shinn, M., Tindal, G., Spira, D., & Marston, D. (1987). Practice of learning disabilities as social policy. *Learning Disabilities Quarterly, 10*(1), 17–28.

Shinn, M. R., Ysseldyke, J., Deno, S. L., & Tindal, G. (1986). A comparison of differences between students labeled learning disabled and low achieving on measures of classroom performance. *Journal of Learning Disabilities, 19*, 545–552.

Smith, S. W. (1990). Individualized educational programs (IEPs) in special education: From intent to acquiescence. *Exceptional Children, 57*(1), 6–14.

Tindal, G., Fuchs, L. S., Christenson, S., Mirkin, P. K., & Deno, S. L. (1981). *The relationship between student achievement and teacher assessment of short- or long-term goals* (Research Rep. No. 61). Minneapolis: University of Minnesota, Institute for Research on Learning Disabilities. (ERIC Document Reproduction Service No. Ed 218 846).

Tucker, J. (1985). Curriculum-based assessment: An introduction. *Exceptional Children, 52*, 199–204.

Wesson, C. (1987). Increasing efficiency. *Teaching Exceptional Children, 20*, 46–47.

Wesson, C., Fuchs, L., Tindal, G., Mirkin, P., & Deno, S. L. (1986). Facilitating the efficiency of ongoing curriculum-based measurement. *Teacher Education & Special Education, 9*, 166–172.

Wesson, C. L., King, R. P., & Deno, S. L. (1984). Direct and repeated measurement of student performance: If it's good for us, why don't we do it? *Learning Disability Quarterly, 7*, 45–48.

White, O. R. (1974). *Evaluating educational process*. Unpublished manuscript, University of Washington, Child Developmental and Mental Retardation Center, Experimental Education Unit, Seattle.

White, O. R., & Haring, N. G. (1980). *Exceptional teaching* (2nd ed.). Columbus, OH: Merrill.

Ysseldyke, J. E., Algozzine, B., Shinn, M. R., & McGue, M. (1982). Similarities and differences between low achievers and students labeled learning disabled. *Journal of Special Education, 16*, 73–85.

Ysseldyke, J. E., & Thurlow, M. L. (1984). Assessment practices in special education: Adequacy and appropriateness. *Educational Psychologist, 9*, 123–136.

Mark Shinn is with the School Psychology Program, Division of Special Education and Rehabilitation at the University of Oregon, Eugene. Dawn Hubbard is a doctoral student in the School Psychology Program at the University of Oregon, Eugene.

○ 13 ○

These authors evaluate the approaches to curriculum that schools have tradi-tionally employed. They argue that the curriculum has to address the needs of students rather than the service delivery alternative in determining what a stu-dent is taught. For example, if a student needs to learn learning strategies, per-haps resource room services may be appropriate. This article is particularly important in that it stresses that curricular alternatives should be available and that the curricular option of choice should be determined after considering key decision-making variables.

Comprehensive Curriculum for Students with Mild Disabilities

*Edward A. Polloway, James R. Patton,
Michael H. Epstein, and Tom E.C. Smith*

The most critical programming consideration in classes for individuals with mild learning disabilities is, without question, what is to be taught—the curriculum. Regardless of the effectiveness and efficiency with which instruction may be provided, ultimately the over-all benefit of the school experience will be derived from the curriculum—that is, the planned learning experiences that have intended educational outcomes (Hoover, 1988). In considering the development of programs for students who are mildly handicapped, the importance of a *comprehensive* curriculum should be apparent inasmuch as the primary goal is to develop an outcomes-focus that is consistent with the diverse needs of these stu-dents. The focus of this article is on students with mild learning problems across all grade levels. Major curricular issues, however, become most significant at the secondary level. For our purposes, comprehensive curriculum is derived from a concept advocated by Pol-loway, Patton, Payne, and Payne (1989) and thus refers to a program that is:

—responsive to the needs of an individual student at the current time;
—consistent with the objective of balancing maximum interaction with nonhandi-capped peers against critical curricular needs;

—integrally related to service delivery option (i.e., resource programs, self-contained classes, and modified models);
—derived from a realistic appraisal of potential adult outcomes of individual students;
—focused on transitional needs across the life-span;
—sensitive to graduation goals and specific diploma track requirements.

The importance of this topic at the secondary level has been articulated by many teachers anecdotally, identified through studies of secondary special education settings (e.g., Halpern & Benz, 1987), and can be inferred from discouraging national statistics on graduation, drop-out, and employment rates (e.g., Department of Education, 1987; Edgar, 1987; Neel, Meadows, Levine, & Edgar, 1988). The recurring need is for innovative and relevant curricula that address the features listed above.

Three major topics are the focus of this article. Initially a description is presented of current and emerging curricular models for students with learning-related disabilities, accompanied by an evaluation of their effectiveness. Second, the decision-making process vìs-a-vìs curricular model selection is discussed. Third, the programmatic needs of identifiable subgroups of students with mild handicaps are reviewed and related to specific curricular models and combinations of models.

ALTERNATIVE ORIENTATIONS

Three general curricular orientations can be identified as a basis for programming with students who are mildly disabled (Polloway et al., 1989; Vergason, 1983). Although these orientations have been defined differently, they include: (a) *remediation* focusing on academic skills remediation and social adjustment, respectively; (b) *maintenance models,* including tutoring as well as programs emphasizing the acquisition and utilization of learning strategies; and (c) *adult outcomes,* inclusive of vocational training efforts and programs oriented to the transition from adolescence to adulthood. Figure 1 schematically presents the models in relation to traditional service delivery options. These three general orientations, discussed next, provide a basis for the subsequent discussion of the curricular needs of specific subgroups of students.

Remediation

Academic Remediation
A basic skills model primarily emphasizes the remediation of academic deficits, thus directly addressing apparent student needs. This approach provides the core for most elementary special education curricula. Reviews of student IEPs suggest that middle school programs are also primarily remedial/academic in focus (McBride & Forgnone, 1985). Basic skills programs have a long-term orientation because they presume that instruction in such skills ultimately will increase students' academic achievement levels and enable them, at least, to reach minimal functional literacy.

The major advantage of the remedial approach is that skill deficiencies are identified and intervention subsequently can be provided to increase performance in these prob-

Special Class	Resource Services	Regular Class

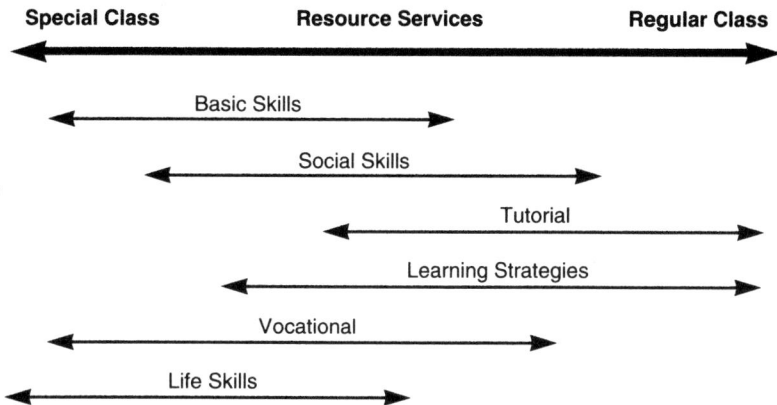

FIGURE 1   *Relationships of Curricular Orientations to Service Delivery Models*

lematic areas. Although not all basic skill programs have equal effectiveness, those that incorporate the tenets of effective instructional practice (Stevens & Rosenshine, 1981) have empirically demonstrated substantial gains in achievement. This issue is of greatest importance when consideration is given to programming for adolescents.

For example, the *Corrective Reading Program* (CRP; Engelmann, Becker, Hanner, & Johnson, 1980), based on the principles of direct instruction, was specifically designed for middle school and high school students who continue to experience difficulties in basic reading recognition and comprehension skills. A growing body of research on CRP (e.g., Campbell, 1983, cited by Becker, 1984; Gregory, Hackney, & Gregory, 1982; Polloway, Epstein, Polloway, Patton, & Ball, 1986; Thorne, 1978) offers evidence that it can be effective with older students identified as learning disabled or mildly retarded or those who are generically referred to as slow learners.

The research on Corrective Reading reinforces the premise that, when enrolled in intensive instructional programs, a large number of adolescents with disabilities may be able to benefit from academic remediation (Meyen & Lehr, 1980). It is instructive to consider what Meyen and Lehr (p. 23) identified as the characteristics of intensive instruction that would predict positive gains by students:

1. consistency and duration of time on task;
2. timing, frequency, and nature of feedback based on the student's immediate performance and cumulative progress;
3. regular and frequent communication by the teacher to the student of his or her expectancy that this student will master the task and demonstrate continuous progress;
4. pattern of pupil-teacher interaction in which the teacher responds to student initiatives and uses consequences appropriate to the responses of the student.

It can be concluded that remedial approaches may be successfully used with many students when attention is paid to certain principles of implementation. Additionally, benefits are enhanced when these approaches are balanced with attention to life skill needs. Even relatively small gains in certain skill areas such as reading may have a significant effect on a young adult's ability to function more competently in community settings.

Although the basic skills approach is in many ways attractive, several problems may emerge as a result of its use, especially when extended beyond the elementary school level. First, a remedial orientation often neglects students' specific strengths by focusing entirely on deficit areas. Second, it may fail to address issues of transfer of learning, whether defined as generalization to the regular class setting or to various post-school environments including postsecondary education and work settings. Additionally, sole reliance on a basic skills model without attention to other critical areas may be inappropriate for many students at the secondary level in that other skills (e.g., life skills, functional skills) are ignored or are only partially taught.

As a result of these concerns, more and more people have questioned the value of continued reliance on a basic skills model with adolescent learners (e.g., Alley & Deshler, 1979; Deshler, Schumaker, Lenz, & Ellis, 1984). Alternative programmatic options must be considered, especially for students who have been in an instructionally sound, intensive remedial program but who have failed to progress.

Social Skills and Adjustment

This remedial model is characterized by an emphasis on the development of social competence, typically recognized as critical to life adjustment (Epstein & Cullinan, 1987). The basis for classification as remedial is that it represents a deficit view of the traits of individual students. When this orientation has served as the core of curricular efforts, it most often has been within programs for students identified as emotionally disturbed or behaviorally disordered (Masters & Mori, 1986; Zigmond & Brownlee, 1980).

More generally, and of significant importance to special educators, the success or failure of students with mild disabilities in regular classes is related to social competence. For example, Gresham (1982, 1983, 1984), who reviewed over 40 studies on the integration of pupils with mild disabilities, reported that children with disabilities interact infrequently and, to a large extent, negatively with their nondisabled peers. He argued convincingly that many pupils have been placed in mainstream settings without the necessary social skills to succeed in these environments and to gain acceptance by their peers.

Three approaches have been associated with social adjustment: social skills acquisition, behavioral change, and affective education. Although each represents a somewhat distinctive focus, they are grouped together here, as all relate to the overall goal of social adjustment.

Social skills have been defined as "responses which, within a given situation, prove effective, or in other words, maximize the probability of producing, maintaining, or enhancing positive effects for the interactor" (Foster & Ritchey, 1979, p. 626.). Therefore, training efforts focused on *social skills acquisition* are concerned with the attainment of skills necessary for students to overcome situations in classrooms, on the job, and in other areas that prevent assimilation (Masters & Mori, 1986).

The *behavioral change* strategy focuses on identifying a target behavior and implementing a reinforcement system that will lead to permanent change in a behavior. Steps in the behavior change are: (1) selecting the target behavior, (2) collecting baseline date, (3) identifying reinforcers, (4) implementing a procedure for reinforcing appropriate behaviors; and, (5) evaluating the intervention.

Affective education differs in that it emphasizes self-control and the relationship between self and others in the environment (Shea & Bauer, 1987). A primary emphasis frequently is placed on emotional aspects of social adjustment.

Several considerations are important relative to the issue of effectiveness for the social adjustment orientation. First, any program should be accountable for observable and meaningful change in students. Unfortunately, some social adjustment programs, especially those focused on affective education, have generated little evidence of documented change in skills or behavior. Additionally, the effectiveness of most social skills curricula remains largely unknown (Epstein & Cullinan, 1987). A second concern has to do with generalizability of the programs. To justify their use, social adjustment programs must demonstrate that they can contribute to student success in subsequent environments. This may be defined in terms of transfer to regular classes or generalization to environments beyond the school setting.

For example, one program that stresses transfer is the School Survival Skills Curriculum, developed at the Learning Research and Development Center at the University of Pittsburgh (see Zigmond & Brownlee, 1980; Zigmond & Sansone, 1986). The curriculum includes attention to classroom behavior, study skills, and teacher-pleasing behaviors.

A beneficial approach to the issue of generalizability of program outcomes has come through the use of cognitive approaches to behavior change and social skills acquisition (see Meichenbaum, 1980,1983). Such programs, to the degree to which they can demonstrate meaningful and long-lasting behavior change, offer significant promise for social adjustment programming in the future.

Maintenance

Tutorial

The most common approach used with adolescents who have mild disabilities—in particular, in learning disabilities resource programs—has traditionally been tutoring. The objective of such a program is usually perceived as successful maintenance of students within the regular class curriculum. Thus the curriculum is focused on attending to their regular class needs.

A primary reason for the popularity of tutoring is motivational. Because students are concerned with success in the regular classroom, they often positively perceive it as a necessary form of support. In a related vein, they may prefer tutoring over other models (such as those with remedial foci) that are seen as more stigmatizing.

For similar reasons, regular class teachers, and parents, also tend to be supportive of a tutoring orientation. General education teachers may believe that tutoring enables them to meet the needs of students with special needs who require extra assistance. Parents typically like this model because it allows their children to remain in regular education settings and still receive special help. When tutoring achieves its major goal of maintaining a student in the regular classroom, it should have a positive effect on grades and thus, at the secondary level, assist in fulfilling graduation requirements.

Despite the potential advantages of tutoring, it has a short-term emphasis, offering little of lasting value to students. An additional concern is whether the material learned is relevant to the students' future needs. In terms of training, a serious concern is the possible undertraining of special education teachers who must provide instruction in subjects (e.g., chemistry) for which they are insufficiently prepared. Similarly, the issue of overtraining is a concern because, beyond knowledge in subject matter, tutoring requires little need for advanced training in sophisticated instructional techniques, and thus could be handled in many cases by paraprofessionals.

Tutoring's primary focus on short-term objectives underscores both its benefits and its most limiting disadvantage. Certainly all special education teachers must engage in some tutorial work to enhance their students' progress. For those students who require continual tutorial support, however, teachers should consider enlisting peers, paraprofessionals, and parent volunteers in the tutorial process.

Learning Strategies

The learning strategies concept emphasizes learning to learn and stresses the student's role as an active participant in the teaching/learning process (Weinstein & Mayer, 1986). It therefore derives from a cognitive focus with an orientation to the thought processes of students in the learning process. Additionally, it places primary emphasis on the importance of transfer or generalization to other learning situations (content, instructors, and settings).

A substantial amount of the work that has resulted in application of the learning strategies approach to programs for students with disabilities was derived from the research efforts of Deshler and his colleagues at the University of Kansas Institute for Research on Learning Disabilities. As presented by Alley and Deshler (1979), learning strategies are used most appropriately in resource programs in which the main goal is generalization of skills to the regular classroom—hence the reason why this approach has been classified in this article as a maintenance model. A necessary factor for this approach to be successful would be cooperation between special education and regular classroom teachers.

Alley and Deshler (1979) described adolescent students who appear to benefit most from a learning strategies approach (LSA) as possessing the following characteristics: reading achievement above the third-grade level; ability to deal with symbolic as well as concrete learning tasks; and demonstration of at least average intellectual ability, defined as scoring in the 85-115 IQ range. Although the target group was defined in this fashion, components of the model should be effective for groups beyond this population—for example, younger students, as well as students whose achievement and intellectual levels are not commensurate with the levels as defined. Nevertheless, empirical validation of this proposal has rarely occurred to date.

A number of individual strategies and related instructional methods have been developed by individuals concerned about the effectiveness of this model with students experiencing learning problems (see Deshler & Schumaker, 1986; Ellis & Sabornie, 1986; Ellis, Lenz, & Sabornie, 1987a, 1987b; Rooney, 1988). Deshler and Schumaker (1986) have suggested that a program of learning strategies instruction should provide training in approximately three or four strategies per year sequenced from within the three areas of acquisition, storage, and expression/demonstration of competence.

Given the work that has been done in developing the learning strategies approach, it now represents an appropriate programming option for older students. But certain considerations should be addressed when deciding whether to select this approach as a major component of the curriculum. First, if this type of model is used exclusively, it could result in limited attention to other curricular needs, especially in the area of functional skills. Second, many students with mild disabilities simply may not possess the entry-level skills necessary for successful acquisition and execution of strategic behaviors. Third, major consideration should be given to issues related to motivation in terms of "selling" to students the particular strategy being taught—especially given the difficulties that some students may have in becoming motivated to learn a strategy that provides primarily long-term rather than short-term benefits (Polloway et al., 1989).

Finally, the data base on the efficacy of this model (see Deshler & Schumaker, 1986) continues to need to be expanded, particularly as related to generalization. However, this is a universal concern about curriculum and could be voiced about many other curricula as well. An emphasis on explicit training in the use of learning strategies seems to be very appropriate for students with limited academic skills (Weinstein & Mayer, 1986).

Adult Outcomes

Vocational Training Emphasis

Although the two functional orientations—vocational training and life skills—are clearly interrelated, they have a number of distinctive key features that warrant their separate discussions here. Vocational training has a tradition of being associated with secondary programming for students with mild/moderate retardation (e.g., Kolstoe & Frey, 1965). Only recently have programs with vocational emphasis been considered more frequently for students identified as learning disabled or emotionally disturbed/behavior disordered as an alternative curricular focus at the secondary level.

The primary benefit of vocational training is its direct relationship to transitional efforts undertaken to prepare adolescents for postsecondary work environments. This feature may have motivational merit as well; for many students, enrollment in a vocational program may forestall the likelihood of dropping out of school. This concern is of particular importance given the fact that a substantial number of LD and BD students, in particular, are at risk for dropping out of school (Edgar, 1987).

Several related considerations are important to note at this point. Community-based learning opportunities are needed as an alternative to simulated vocational opportunities within a school setting. Community-based instruction implies programs that provide ideal environments for generalization and realistic job training opportunities. Similarly, a positive development in the vocational training domain has been the trend toward use of a supported employment model (e.g., Wehman, Renzaglia, & Bates, 1985). This approach places students on the job and provides them with direct assistance from employment specialists/job coaches that can be faded out gradually over time as students become increasingly independent.

Several possible disadvantages with a vocational training approach include students' getting locked into a vocational track early in their secondary school program with little chance of ever getting out; limited training options available in traditional vocational education programs; the training of skills that have no or limited community validity; the assumption that students with various labels should be channeled automatically into vocational programs; and the absence of instructional planning and instruction following vocational assessment.

Another disadvantage involves the exclusion of students who are in other curricular programs, especially diploma-track sequences. This is underscored by the reality that less than 4% of the enrollment in vocational education programs is composed of students with disabilities (Council of Chief State School Officers, 1986). Although these possible disadvantages can be overcome, they can present significant problems for the delivery of services to some students with mild disabilities.

Life Skills Orientation

A life skills orientation emphasizes a comprehensive life skills view of the postsecondary adjustment process. Although adult outcomes curricula may be focused less intensively on occupational training, they tend to be more responsive to varied concerns derived from the literature on adult adjustment (Cronin, 1988; Gerber & Cronin, 1982) and the demands of adulthood (Knowles, 1978). As such, the model can never be seen as distinctly separate from social adjustment and vocational concerns.

A life skills emphasis has a top-down orientation to curriculum development. This approach emphasizes skill development and knowledge acquisition that can be conceptualized as falling within two major domains (six topical areas), as represented in Figure 2, which must be considered in transitional planning (Patton & Browder, 1988). The *life* domains represent the principal ways in which people organize their lives; the *support* domains refer to areas that must be addressed before individuals can reasonably take on the other responsibilities and activities of adulthood.

An apt illustration of a life skills curriculum is the Adult Performance Level: Adaptation and Modification Project (APLAMP) (1975) (in LaQuey, 1981). This program contains 42 objectives, which form the basic elements for planning instruction and are associated with five general content areas: consumer economics, health, occupational knowledge, community resources, and government and law. The APLAMP serves as a core curriculum blending a focus on practical academics with direct applications to the specific demands of adulthood (Daniels & Wiederholt, 1986). The resulting matrix of basic skills X applications is similar in concept to other transitionally oriented curricula (see Cronin, Patton, & Polloway, 1992; Smith & Schloss, 1988).

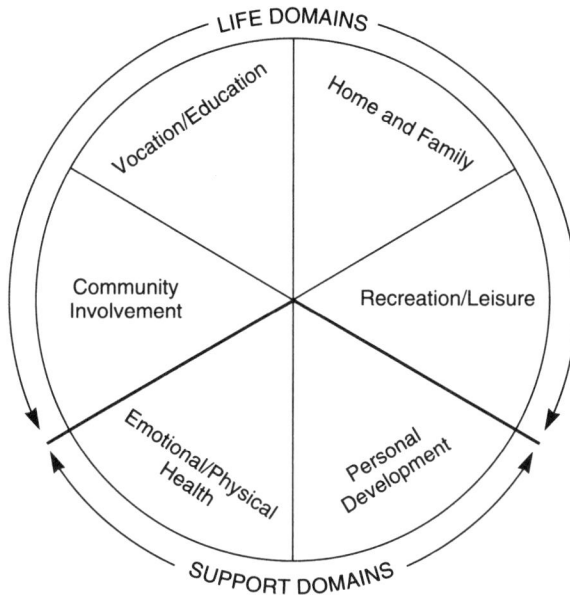

Source: From *Major Areas of Transition*, 1987, Honolulu: Hawaii Transition Project.

FIGURE 2   ***Adult Outcome Domains***

For students who have had learning difficulties in school over 10 years or more, a curriculum whose primary focus shifts away from longstanding academic deficits and toward current skill needs and future life demands has potentially significant value. Adolescents frequently perceive an approach that emphasizes adult outcomes as more attractive—and it may have positive motivational results; the noted trend toward students with mild disabilities dropping out of school is a most crucial motivational concern (Edgar, 1987; Lichtenstein, 1988).

A major caution that should be considered, however, is that *unsystematic* attention (i.e., inadequate scope and sequence) to adult outcomes may provide students with a curriculum of limited immediate or long-term benefit. Additionally, the definition of which community survival skills are most relevant has to be considered; attention to success within a given community therefore must be given serious consideration.

DESIGNING COMPREHENSIVE CURRICULA

The previous discussion highlighted alternative curricular models for consideration with students identified as mildly disabled. Without question, they seldom are present in isolation, and their relevance varies significantly when evaluated for an individual student in a given situation. Based on initial work by Dangel (1981, cited by Vergason, 1983) and modified by Polloway et al. (1989) and Vergason (1983), Table I outlines key variables

TABLE 1   Decision-Making Variables

1. Student Variables
   - cognitive-intellectual level
   - academic skills preparedness
   - academic achievement as determined by tests
   - academic achievement as determined by class grades
   - grade placement
   - motivation and responsibility
   - social interactions with peers and adults
   - behavioral self-control

2. Family Variables
   - short- and long-term parental expectations
   - degree of support provided (e.g., financial, emotional, academic)
   - parental values toward education
   - cultural influence (e.g., language, values)

3. General Education Variables
   - teacher and nondisabled student acceptance of diversity (classroom climate)
   - administrative support for integrated education
   - availability of curricular variance
   - accommodative capacity of the classroom
   - flexibility of daily class schedules and units earned toward graduation
   - options for vocational programs

4. Special Education Variables
   - size of caseload
   - availability of paraprofessionals or tutors
   - access to curricular materials
   - focus of teacher's training
   - consultative and materials support available
   - related services available to students

that should be considered in the process of making decisions with regard to general curricular orientations. These variables also influence choices related to combinations of the respective models for individual students or for groups of students with established similar needs.

Given the multiple variables to be considered, decision making clearly is not only an important, but also a complex, process. Matching a curricular model or models to traditional group labels represents an inappropriate practice reflecting the problematic nature of common labeling systems (Hallahan & Kauffman, 1977; Smith, Price, & Marsh, 1986). For example, the simple presumption that students with mild retardation cannot profit from remediation may prove to be just as invalid as the presumption that students with learning disabilities need primarily remedial programming regardless of age level.

Nevertheless, disregarding the area of exceptionality entirely may be fallacious because some cross-categorical differences have been empirically determined (e.g., Cullinan & Epstein, 1985; Edgar, 1987; Epstein & Cullinan, 1983, 1984; Epstein, Cullinan, & Gadow, 1986; Polloway & Smith, 1988). These differences are most relevant if modified by attention to *subgroups,* identified by instructional needs, across these respective areas of exceptionality. By focusing on identifiable subgroups, the emphasis can appropriately shift from categorical labels to relevant programming.

The discussion that follows provides an orientation to help the curricular needs of subgroups of students. In each instance, the discussion is intended to provide a basis for initial consideration of program design for groups of students, which then must be modified to accommodate the needs of individuals.

Elementary Students

Most students with mild and moderate disabilities in the elementary school have a need for primary curricular emphasis on basic skills instruction to maximize academic achievement. At the same time, virtually all students identified as mildly retarded, emotionally disturbed, or behavior disordered, and many students identified as learning disabled, coincidentally need attention to social skills acquisition (Cullinan & Epstein, 1985; Epstein, Bursuck, & Cullinan, 1985; Polloway, Epstein, & Cullinan, 1985; Zigmond & Brownlee, 1980). At the same time, however, these deficit-oriented models should be counter-balanced with emphasis on students' individual strengths and positive traits.

The nature of curricular needs for students at this level, as well as their needs for placement within the least restrictive environment, must be weighed against the benefits of cross-categorical programming. In most instances curricular needs may be sufficiently similar for students labeled LD, BD, and EMR so that overattention to labeling will be counter-productive to the student's development (Smith, Price, & Marsh, 1986). In addition, with appropriate modifications in programs within the regular classroom, and particularly with collaborative consultation (Idol & West, 1987; West & Idol, 1987), many of these needs can be met within regular class-based programs. Regardless of service delivery mode selected, two key programmatic elements need appropriate attention at this level: an introduction to career education with emphasis on career awareness and a focus on transitional variables as related to both placement in regular classes and movement to middle school settings (Epstein, Polloway, Patton, & Foley, 1989; Jaquish & Stella, 1986; Polloway, 1987).

Secondary Students

For our purposes here, secondary students are defined as including those who are enrolled in middle, junior high, and senior high schools. Curricular differentiation is most critical with this population. To provide a perspective on variant needs, the succeeding sections are organized into curricularly focused subgroups that suggest a system of program options. To some extent, these subgroups reflect the concept of alternative program foci, such as advocated by Minskoff (1971), in the formative years of the field of learning disabilities. As labeled here, the specific options are indexed against curricular needs for the subsequent environments into which the students are likely to proceed.

College-Preparatory Track

The population for whom curricular needs can be determined most clearly are students who have a reasonable opportunity of attending and being successful in postsecondary school settings. This population includes primarily students who currently are or previously were identified as learning disabled, as well as those labeled behavior disordered, who have acquired the academic prerequisites necessary for college admission and entry. Additionally, these are obviously students who, along with their parents, have the interest and commitment necessary for success at the postsecondary level. According to 1987 government statistics, 6.8% of college freshmen report having some disability—almost triple the number for 1978—and the percentage of self-identified college freshmen with learning disabilities is 1.2% (American Council on Education, 1987).

Development of an appropriate preparatory curriculum for these students should be in evidence during the middle school years and become a primary focus during high school. Curricular foci should include maximum participation in regular high school programs, not only for their generation of units toward a regular diploma but also for their attention to content necessary for college success. Second, attention should be given to the transitional needs of students moving into postsecondary settings. This should include attention to specific variables within the college setting that would require survival skills (e.g., time management and organizational skills) variant from those the individual students currently possess.

In terms of curricular focus, several general observations can be made. First, any needed remedial efforts should be broadly focused to include an emphasis on language development. In particular, intensive writing instruction should be encouraged because writing serves as the major basis for evaluation at the postsecondary level. A second key element of programming should be learning strategy training, especially with regard to organizational and study skills. Academic and career advising is a third necessary component of programming. Finally, college survival skills training, as alluded to earlier, would be a positive addition to the curriculum for these students (Patton & Polloway, 1986).

Community Preparation A

This option is for students with more significant learning problems and those with behavior problems whose difficulties within the regular school curriculum in middle and high school make them unlikely candidates for academic postsecondary programs, although they may participate in trade and technical training programs after high school. In addition, this focus may apply to students who can be characterized as "traditional EMRs" or as having "high mild mental disabilities" (Sargent, 1988). This cross-categorical group of students is placed together because of a common need for curriculum that will prepare them for success in environments other than that of higher education.

In many states virtually no students remain in EMR programs to whom this appellation would apply (e.g., California); in other states (such as Alabama and Iowa) because of higher prevalence rates and a higher IQ cutoff criterion, respectively, a large number

of students still classified as EMR are likely to be adaptive in terms of academic and social skills (see Patrick & Reschly, 1982, for a discussion of interstate variance).

Clearly, as individuals in this diverse group advance in age, intensive, relevant programming is increasingly needed. In many instances these needs will not be met easily in
regular class-based programs if they only offer a nonfunctional curriculum (Edgar,
1987). This concern is particularly apt given the reality that students with mild disabilities who are seen as being capable of being mainstreamed are at significant risk for dropping out of school (Lichtenstein, 1988). Teachers report that a primary concern is for access to functional data-based curricula in independent living and vocational areas
(Halpern & Benz, 1987). Particularly appropriate would be programs focusing on work
and transition to adulthood, and ecologically validated within the community.

Because social development is a key predictor of postschool adjustment (Epstein &
Cullinan, 1987), social skills instruction should be a core of the curriculum. Coincidentally, integration must take place at appropriate times in the instructional day so that these
skills can be generalized to interactions with students who are not disabled. The academic content of these programs should be designed and monitored for its potential contribution to mainstream success and adult outcomes.

Community Preparation B

This related option is designed for students with mild retardation in states and school divisions in which substantial declassification efforts have left behind individuals who are
"more patently disabled" (MacMillan & Borthwick, 1980, p. 155). With the declassification of students who might be considered adaptive and the concomitant inclusion of students traditionally placed in trainable classes, these programs are serving individuals
whose needs may be quite different from those found previously in EMR programs and
also quite different from students in other groups of students with mild disabilities
(MacMillan, 1988; Polloway, Epstein, Cullinan, Patton, & Luebke, 1986; Polloway &
Smith, 1988; Smith et al., 1986).

For this group, a transitionally focused curriculum is essential (Sargent, 1988; Smith
& Schloss, 1988). To promote transition, the curriculum must blend vocational training
and social skills instruction with an adult outcomes emphasis. Academic training without
direct, practical application, while justified for elementary and some middle school students, becomes an inappropriate focus for these students at the secondary level. An encouraging note is that few of these students apparently drop out of school (Edgar, 1987),
perhaps because they may be characterized as compliant vìs-a-vìs attendance and thus
are virtual "prisoners of the system" (Edgar, 1988).

Given the difficulty that some individuals may have with generalization, teachers must
avoid the "train and hope" philosophy (Stokes & Baer, 1977), in which few or no efforts
are made to facilitate transfer of learning. Key foci should include community-based instructional programming, occupational placement, and follow-up. For many students, job
coaching under the supported work model originally developed for individuals with more
severe disabilities could be incorporated. Sargent (1988) suggests that the goal for all of

these students should be part-time jobs prior to graduation. Given these considerations, educators can mold a curriculum to ensure its appropriate applicability for this population.

"Tough-to-Call" Track

The remaining subgroup of students with mild disabilities is one that continues to be difficult to categorize even within the admittedly loose designations listed earlier. This population would be considered inclusive particularly of learning disabled and emotionally disturbed/behavior disordered students at the middle school and early secondary school levels. Although most of these individuals subsequently will be likely to fall into a community preparation program, it cannot be discounted that some may be candidates for higher education. In many instances these are individuals with unconfirmed interests, marginal academic achievement, and absence of commitment to particular career directions. They are commonly at risk for dropping out of school and no doubt comprise a substantial portion of the 42% dropout rate that Edgar (1987) reported for LD/BD students. Given the fact that school dropout rates have been reported highest after ninth grade (Zigmond, 1988), this population clearly should be considered at risk.

Any decisions about curricular needs for these students are difficult, but several assumptions can be posited. Guidance in terms of future options must be a part of the efforts the school staff undertakes. A key element should be transition planning, which should be initiated around ninth grade and should emphasize the importance of a subsequent environments perspective.

In terms of curricular foci, several specific judgments seem justifiable. Continuing basic skills remediation should be based on demonstrated efficacy in terms of student improvement, qualified by the assurance that it is provided in the form of intensive instruction. But the virtually exclusive reliance on a remedial approach, documented in research in IEPs (McBride & Forgnone, 1985), should be modified to make the curriculum more comprehensive. Career education should be an important focus of curricular efforts, with particular attention to moving from the career awareness phase into exploration of alternative careers. Incorporation of a learning strategies approach should be entertained particularly to the extent that it may translate directly to success in the regular class curriculum. Because this population frequently is difficult to motivate, strategy instruction may have to be accompanied by motivational remediation with linkages between strategies learned and long-term benefits demonstrated.

Finally, as students move into the high school years, a shift in emphasis toward an adult outcomes model must be considered so that relevant life skills can become a major component of the curriculum. Given Edgar's (1987) report of an employment rate of only 30% for LD/BD dropouts, with 61% of the dropout population not engaged in employment or formal training, and Neel et al.'s (1988) similarly discouraging followup data on students with behavior disorders, it is imperative that preparation for life be initiated in middle school and become a priority in high school.

CONCLUSION

The commitment to comprehensive curriculum is an acknowledgment of the need for appropriate programs to meet both current and future needs. Decisions made about these programs should evaluate compatibility of curricular needs with programs that are categorical, non-categorical, or cross-categorical. Similarly, curriculum should be correlated with the specific service delivery model, with the initial decision made relative to curricular needs, followed by selection of the appropriate service delivery model. As Zigmond and Sansone (1986) noted, each student should be examined individually in terms of both the most appropriate educational setting and the most appropriate curricular model to be used.

REFERENCES

Adult Performance Level Project. (1975). *Adult functional competency.* Austin: University of Texas, Office of Continuing Education.

Alley. G.R., & Deshler, D.D. (1979). *Teaching the learning disabled adolescent: Strategies and methods.* Denver: Love Publishing.

American Council on Education. (1987). *American freshman: National norms for 1987.* Washington, DC: Author.

Becker, W (1984). Corrective reading program evaluated with secondary students in San Diego. *Association for Direct Instruction News, 3*(3), 1, 23.

Council of Chief State School Officers. (1986). *Disabled students beyond school. A review of the issues, a position paper and recommendations for action.* Washington, DC: Author.

Cronin, M.E. (1988). Adult performance outcomes/life skills. In G. Robinson, J.R. Patton, E.A. Polloway, & L. Sargent (Eds.), *Best practices in mental disabilities* (Vol. 2) (pp. 39–520). Des Moines: Iowa State Department of Education.

Cronin, M.E., Patton, J.R., & Polloway, E.A. (1992). Developing a life skills curriculum. Manuscript submitted for publication.

Cullinan, D., & Epstein, M.H. (1985). Teacher-related adjustment problems of mildly handicapped and non-handicapped students. *Remedial & Special Education, 6,* 5–11.

Daniels, I.L., & Wiederholt, J.L. (1986). Preparing problem learners for independent living. In D.D. Hammill & N.R. Bartel (Eds.), *Teaching students with learning and behavior problems* (4th ed., pp. 294–345). Austin: PRO-ED.

Deshler, D.D., & Schumaker, J.B. (1986). Learning strategies: An instructional alternative for low-achieving adolescents. *Exceptional Children, 52,* 583–589.

Deshler, D.D., Schumaker, J.B., Lenz, B.K., & Ellis, E.S. (1984). Academic and cognitive interventions for LD adolescents (Part 2). *.Journal of Learning Disabilities, 17,* 170–187.

Department of Education. (1987). *Ninth annual report to Congress on the implementation of the Education of the Handicapped Act.* Washington, DC: Author.

Edgar, E. (1987). Secondary programs in special education: Are many of them justifiable? *Exceptional Children, 53,* 555–561.

Edgar, E. (1988). *Pressing problems in practices with secondary level learning disabled students.* Paper presented at the 66th annual convention of the Council for Exceptional Children, Washington, DC.

Ellis, E.S., & Sabornie, E.J. (1986). *Teaching /earning strategies to learning disabled students in post-secondary settings.* Unpublished manuscript, University of South Carolina, Columbia, SC.

Ellis, E.S., Lenz, K., & Sabornie, E.J. (1987a). Generalization and adaptation of learning strategies to natural environments: Part 1. Critical agents. *Remedial & Special Education, 8*(1), 6–20.

Ellis, E.S., Lenz, K., & Sabornie, E.J. (1987b). Generalization and adaptation of learning strategies to natural environments: Part 2. Research into practice. *Remedial & Special Education, 8*(2), 6–23.

Engelmann, A., Becker, W.C., Hanner, S., & Johnson, G. (1980). *Corrective reading program.* Chicago: Science Research Associates.

Epstein, M.H., Bursuck, W., & Cullinan, D. (1985). Patterns of behavior problems among the learning disabled: 2. Boys aged 12–18, girls aged 6–11, girls aged 12–18. *Learning Disability Quarterly. 8,* 123–131.

Epstein, M.H., & Cullinan, D. (1983). Academic performance of behaviorally disordered and learning disabled pupils. *Journal of Special Education, 17,* 303–308.

Epstein, M.H., & Cullinan, D. (1984). Behavior problems of mildly handicapped and normal adolescents. *Journal of Clinical Child Psychology, 13,* 33–37.

Epstein, M.H., & Cullinan, D. (1987). Effective social skills curricula for behaviorally disordered students. *Pointer, 31*(2), 21–24.

Epstein, M.H., Cullinan, D., & Gadow, K.D. (1986). Teacher ratings of hyperactivity in learning disabled, emotionally disturbed, and mentally retarded children. *Journal of Special Education, 20,* 219–230.

Epstein, M.H., Polloway, E.A., Patton, J.R., & Foley, R. (1989). Mild retardation: Student characteristics and services. *Education & Training in Mental Retardation, 24,* 7–16.

Foster, S.L., & Ritchey, W.L. (1979). Issues in the assessment of social competence. *Journal of Applied Behavior Analysis, 12,* 625–638.

Gerber, P., & Cronin, M.E. (1982). Preparing the learning disabled adolescent for adulthood. *Topics in Learning & Learning Disabilities, 2*(3), 55–68.

Gregory, R.P., Hackney, D., & Gregory, N.M. (1982). Corrective reading programme: An evaluation. *British Journal of Educational Psychology, 52,* 33–50.

Gresham, F.M. (1982). Misguided mainstreaming: The case for social skills training with handicapped children. *Exceptional Children, 48,* 420–433.

Gresham, F.M. (1983). Social skills assessment as a component of mainstreaming placement decisions. *Exceptional Children. 49,* 331–336.

Gresham, F.M. (1984). Social skills and self-efficacy for exceptional children. *Exceptional Children, 51,* 253–261.

Hallahan, D.P, & Kauffman, J.M. (1977). Labels, categories, behaviors: ED, LD and EMR reconsidered. *Journal of Special Education, 11,* 129–149.

Halpern, A.W., & Benz, M.R. (1987). A statewide examination of special education for students with mild disabilities: Implications for the high school curriculum. *Exceptional Children, 54,* 122–129.

Hoover, J.J. (1988). *Curriculum adaptation for students with learning and behavior problems: Principles and practices,* Lindale, TX: Hamilton Publications.

Idol, L., & West, J.F. (1987). Consultation in special education (Part 2): Training and practice. *Journal of Learning Disabilities, 20,* 474–494.

Jaquish, C., & Stella, M.A. (1986). Helping special needs students move from elementary to secondary school. *Counterpoint, 7*(1),1.

Knowles, M. (1978). *The adult learner: A neglected species (2nd ed.).* Houston: Gulf Publishing.

Kolstoe, O.P., & Frey R.M. (1965). *A high school work-study program for mentally subnormal students.* Carbondale, IL: Southern Illinois University Press.

LaQuey, A. (1981). *Adult performance level adaptation and modification project.* Austin, TX: Educational Service Center, Region 13.

Lichtenstein, S. (1988). *Special education dropouts.* Washington, DC: ERIC Clearinghouse on Educational Management.

MacMillan, D.L. (1988). New EMRs. In G.R. Robinson, J.R. Patton, E.A. Polloway, & L. Sargent (Eds.), *Best practices in mental disabilities* (Vol. 2). Des Moines: Iowa State Department of Education.

MacMillan, D.L., & Borthwick, S. (1980). The new educable mentally retarded population: Can they be mainstreamed? *Mental Retardation, 18,* 155–158.

Masters, L.F., & Mori, A.A. (1986). *Teaching secondary students with mild learning and behavior problems.* Rockville, MD: Aspen.

McBride, J.W., & Forgnone, C. (1985). Emphasis of instruction provided LD, EH, and EMR students in categorical and cross-categorical programming. *Journal of Research & Development in Education, 18*(4), 50–54.

Meichenbaum, D. (1980). Cognitive behavior modification with exceptional children: A promise yet unfulfilled. *Exceptional Education Quarterly, 1*(1), 83–88.

Meichenbaum, D. (1983). Teaching thinking: A cognitive-behavioral approach. In *Interdisciplinary voices in learning disabilities and remedial education.* Austin, TX: PRO-ED.

Meyen, E.L., & Lehr, D.H. (1980). Evolving practices in assessment and intervention for mildly handicapped adolescents: The case for intensive instruction. *Exceptional Education Quarterly, 1*(2), 19–26.

Minskoff, J.G. (1971). Learning disabled children at the secondary level: Educational programming in perspective. In J. Arena (Ed.), *The child with learning disabilities: His right to learn.* Proceedings of the Eighth Annual International ACLD Conference, Chicago.

Neel, R.S., Meadows, N., Levine, P., & Edgar, E.B. (1988). What happens after special education: A statewide follow-up study of secondary students who have behavioral disorders. *Behavioral Disorders, 13,* 209–216.

Patrick, J.L., & Reschly, D.J. (1982). Relationship of state educational criteria and demographic variables to school-system prevalence of mental retardation. *American Journal of Mental Deficiency, 86,* 351360.

Patton, J.R., & Browder, P.M. (1988). Transitions into the future. In B.L. Ludlow, A.P. Turnbull, & R. Luckasson (Eds.), *Transitions to adult life for people with mental retardation: Principles and practices* (pp. 293–311). Baltimore: Paul H. Brookes.

Patton, J.R., & Polloway, E.A. (1987). Analyzing college courses: Academic planning for the LD college student. *Academic Therapy, 22,* 273–280.

Polloway, E.A. (1987). Early age transition: Transitional services for mildly retarded individuals. In R. Ianacone & R.A. Stodden (Eds.), *Transitional issues and directions for individuals who are mentally retarded* (pp. 11–24). Reston, VA: CEC-MR.

Polloway, E.A., Epstein, M.H., & Cullinan, D. (1985). Prevalence of behavior problems among educable mentally retarded students. *Education & Training of the Mentally Retarded, 20,* 3–13.

Polloway, E.A., Epstein, M.H., Cullinan, D., Patton, J.R., & Luebke, J. (1986). Demographic, social and behavioral characteristics of students with educable mental retardation. *Education & Training of the Mentally Retarded, 21,* 127–134.

Polloway, E.A., Epstein, M.H., Polloway, C.H., Patton, J.R., & Ball, D.W. (1986). Corrective reading program: An analysis of effectiveness with learning disabled and mentally retarded children. *Remedial & Special Education, 7*(4), 41–47.

Polloway, E.A., Patton, J.R., Payne, J.S., & Payne, R.A. (1989). *Strategies for teaching learners with special needs* (4th ed.). Columbus, OH: Merrill.

Polloway, E.A., & Smith, J.D. (1988). Current status of the mild mental retardation construct: Identification, placement and programs. In M.C. Wang, M.C. Reynolds, & H.J. Walberg (Eds.), *The handbook of special education: Research and practice* (Vol, 2, pp. 1–22). Oxford, England: Pergamon Press.

Rooney, K. (1988). *Independent strategies for efficient study.* Richmond, VA: J.R. Enterprises.

Sargent, L.E. (1988). Ideas for future programming in mental disabilities. In J.R. Patton, G.A. Robinson, & D. Browder (Eds.), *Setting our agenda. Proceedings of the Iowa Conference on futures in mental disabilities.* Des Moines: State of Iowa Department of Education.

Shea, T.M., & Bauer, A.M. (1987). *Teaching children and youth with behavior disorders* (2nd ed.). Englewood Cliffs, NJ: Prentice-Hall.

Smith, M.A., & Schloss, P.J. (1988). Teaching to transition. In P.J. Schloss, C.A. Hughes, & M.A. Smith (Eds.), *Community integration for persons with mental retardation* (pp. 1–16). Boston: College-Hill.

Smith, T.E.C., Price, B.J., & Marsh, G.E. (1986). *Mildly handicapped children and adults.* St. Paul: West Publishing.

Stevens, R., & Rosenshine, B. (1981). Advances in research on teaching. *Exceptional Education Quarterly, 2*(1), 1–9.

Stokes, F., & Baer, D.M. (1977). An implicit technology of generalization. *Journal of Applied Behavior Analysis, 10,* 349–367.

Thorne, M.T. (1978). "Payment for reading": The use of the "Corrective Reading Scheme" with junior maladjusted boys. *Remedial Education, 13*(2), 87–90.

Vergason, G.A. (1983). Curriculum content. In E.L. Meyen, G.A. Vergason, & R.J. Whelan (Eds.), *Promising practices for exceptional individuals: Curriculum implications* (pp. 127–142). Denver, Love Publishing.

Wehman, P., Renzaglia, A., & Bates, P. (1985). *Functional living skills for moderately and severely handicapped individuals.* Austin, TX: PRO-ED.

Weinstein, C., & Mayer, B. (1986). Learning strategies. In M.C. Wittrock (Ed.), *Handbook of research on teaching* (Vol. 3). New York: Macmillan.

West, J.F., & Idol, L. (1987). School consultation (Part 1): An interdisciplinary perspective on theory, models and research. *Journal of Learning Disabilities, 20,* 388–408.

Zigmond, N. (1988). *Pressing problems in practices with secondary level learning disabled students.* Paper presented at the 66th annual convention of the Council for Exceptional Children, Washington, DC.

Zigmond, N., & Brownlee, J. (1980). Social skills training for adolescents with learning disabilities. *Exceptional Education Quarterly, 1*(2), 770–84

Zigmond, N., & Sansone, J. (1986). Designing a program for the learning disabled adolescent. *Remedial & Special Education. 7*(5), 13–17.

Edward Polloway is a professor of education and human development and associate dean at Lynchburg College, Virginia. James Patton is an associate professor of special education at the University of Hawaii. Michael Epstein is a professor of special education at Northern Illinois University. Tom Smith is a professor of special education at the University of Arkansas, Little Rock.

◦ 14 ◦

One of the major literacy movements in regular education and special education is based on a philosophical and theoretical approach in which reading literature, discussing books, writing stories, and other activities are combined to promote learning. Westby describes how this whole language approach differs from traditional methods of instruction and, in particular, applies this technology to special education. This article is highly practical and should be of great value to special educators.

Whole Language and Learners with Mild Handicaps

Carol E. Westby

Schools are undergoing a number of paradigm shifts affecting school structure, student populations, and curriculum philosophies. The whole language approach to literacy is one of these—in this case, a shift from a basal skills approach to a literature-based language approach. A paradigm is a set of beliefs for viewing the world (Kuhn, 1970). Paradigms affect our decisions by influencing our perceptions and interpretations. A paradigm can be a magnifying lens that enables us to focus on relevant information.

The skills-based paradigm tells us that literacy is made up of a number of skills, such as decoding and identifying main ideas. The skills can be taught in isolation, and when they are all mastered, the student is literate. The whole language paradigm, in contrast, says that language should not be fragmented into skills. Language, including literacy, is learned by using language to accomplish goals in meaningful contexts (Froese, 1990).

Whole language is not a set of techniques but, rather, a philosophical and theoretical approach to education. A whole language approach to literacy involves more than reading children's literature, discussing books, writing stories, and corresponding with authors. These activities in and of themselves do not promote learning. Educators must translate the whole language philosophy and theory into a pedagogy or teaching strategies. They must consider both the content that is taught and the manner in which it is taught in terms of the specific social and cultural circumstances of students, their families, and their communities (Bloome, Harris, & Ludlum, 1991; Sawyer, 1991).

For maximum effectiveness, a whole language approach requires thorough understanding of language development—particularly for students with language learning difficulties. During the last half of the 20th century, we have witnessed paradigm shifts in our understanding of the components of language development and the nature of language learning disabilities. The language development paradigm has shifted from attention to vocabulary and articulation development in the 1950s, to sentence structure (syntax) in the 1960s, to meaning (semantics) in the 1970s, to language use (pragmatics) in the 1980s, and to discourse in the 1990s. The current paradigm shifts in educational and clinical settings are more encompassing than the previous ones in our approaches to language development. Our paradigms are changing in a number of ways:

1. *Changes in language testing:* From discrete point, decontextualized, standardized language testing to integrative, descriptive, naturalistic language assessment. Progress is no longer measured solely on the basis of test scores. Portfolios of children's work provide measures of language change. This shift in the testing paradigm is related to shifts in attitudes about what language learning is and is not. Language consists of more than the sum of its parts. Oral language involves more than the ability to comprehend and produce individual elements of phonology, syntax, and pragmatics; literate language involves more than the ability to decode. Mastering these parts does not assure students' ability to integrate them into meaningful communication.

   Standardized tests permit comparison of the performance of individual or groups of students on some set of selected tasks. They can predict which students may be at risk for academic difficulties. They do not, however, tell us *why* a student is at risk, and they do not tell us about a student's abilities in naturalistic contexts.

   To obtain information for appropriate programming in language and literacy areas, we are beginning to use authentic, ecologically valid assessments that present language or literacy tasks in ways in which language is used in the home or school (Garcia & Pearson, 1991). In authentic, ecological assessment, students talk to get needs met and to get things done, not to repeat what a teacher has said; they write to communicate a message, not to copy letters or words; they read for enjoyment and to gather information on an interesting topic, not to answer the questions in a workbook.

2. *Changes in persons served:* From student-centered to social systems intervention for the language-learning disabled student. The student is no longer the sole focus of assessment and treatment. Schools traditionally have located disorders or disabilities within the individual student and have not involved families in program planning. Increasing attention is being given to the role of students within their social systems—their schools, families, and communities. In some situations, the social system, not factors within the student, may be what creates the disorder (McDermott, 1974).

   The social systems paradigm requires an understanding of how students function with others in their environments. How do students' families, communities, and schools support or inhibit their performance? How do these systems vary among cultural and socioeconomic groups? How can these systems be used to facilitate a student's performance? Intervention may involve not only direct work with the identified student but also with others who relate to the student—teachers, parents, siblings. Families increasingly are being incorporated into school programs.

3. *Changes in our understanding of the relationship of oral and written language:* From separation of oral and written language to integration. The new paradigm views reading and writing as a natural part of normal language development for all children (Fillion & Brause, 1987). In the past, written language was viewed as developing after oral language. Oral language was thought to contribute to written language development, but written language was not viewed as contributing to oral language development. More recently, researchers have demonstrated an interdependence between oral and written language: Oral language nourishes students' literate abilities, and literate language influences oral language abilities (Kroll & Vann, 1981).

4. *Changes in service delivery:* From service provision along discipline lines to collaborative consultation. The roles and relationships between teachers and speech-language pathologists are changing for a number of reasons. We are aware that the school curriculum is a language curriculum; we have a better understanding of the relationship between oral language and literacy; and we place more emphasis on the regular education initiative and full inclusion of special education students in the regular classroom. As a result, speech-language pathologists are becoming collaborative consultants with teachers, and jointly planning and conducting lessons within the classroom environment.

5. *Changes in demographics:* From a focus on student similarity to an awareness of student diversity. The population of the 1990s is not the population of the 1960s. By the beginning of the 21st century, one third of the U.S. population will consist of minority groups, many from non-English speaking backgrounds. Culturally-linguistically different students often are unfamiliar with the interaction patterns required by traditional lessons. Teacher styles that work with one segment of the population may not work with another (Bloome, Harris, & Ludlum, 1991). Part of what children learn in school is how to "do school." They learn how to act like a student, think like a student, and talk like a student. To access literacy learning, students first must learn how to do school.

   When teaching culturally-linguistically different students, educators have to understand not only the content to be learned but also the ways in which the content could be taught. Delpit (1988) and de la Reyes (1991) have suggested that whole language approaches (as they are currently implemented) may not be particularly effective with Black and Hispanic students because the students are not used to or comfortable with the participant structures used in the whole language approach.

6. *Changes in teacher roles:* From teachers as transmitters of knowledge to teachers as facilitators of learning. Traditionally, teachers determined the content to be

taught, presented the content, and expected students to reproduce the material. In whole language approaches, learning is viewed as a process, not simply a product. The way in which students acquire and use the information is as important as, if not more important than, the information itself. What is taught to a given student depends on the teacher's perceptions of that student's present skills and the skills the student needs to understand the task.

Children acquire language through immersion in a language-rich environment. The teacher as facilitator assists students in this learning by providing models through personal communication and by listening and responding to students' communication attempts.

7. *Changes in the role of students:* From passive-learning students to active-learning students. Whole language programs view students as active learners who are given the opportunity to construct understanding of situations and events by selecting and organizing experiences. Rather than simply memorizing material, students plan and participate in field trips, hands-on art and science projects, and discussion of the activities and projects with their peers.

These seven paradigm shifts undergird the whole language movement. The whole language philosophy translates to an attempt to apply the transactional process observed in oral language learning to the process of literacy acquisition. To accomplish this, teachers must learn to be effective observers of individual students and sophisticated interpreters of their communication efforts. Educators also must understand the nature of language learning. They must recognize children's current skills and decide on ways to interact that will facilitate children's language development.

The tendency in whole language programs has been to assume that direct instruction is inappropriate and that simply providing interesting, motivating experiences will be sufficient. That approach probably will not be effective with learning disabled students. If it were sufficient, these students would not be exhibiting language learning delays or disorders. Students with mild handicaps can benefit greatly from whole language programs, but only if teachers are alert to the students' current language learning abilities and their language learning needs with respect to the curriculum.

Instruction in whole language classrooms for learners with mild handicaps (or any learner, for that matter) should be consistent with what Vygotsky (1978) described as the child's zone of proximal development. What should be taught, to whom, and when depend on teachers' and language specialists' perceptions of students' present language abilities and the abilities they need to accomplish certain tasks (Tharp & Gallimore, 1988). The teacher begins with activities that students cannot do alone but can do with assistance. The teacher models the process and scaffolds the task so the students can gradually take more and more of the responsibility of carrying out the task.

Compared to language during preschool years, language during the school years requires an increased variety of language functions, greater variety of discourse styles and organization, more abstract vocabulary, more complex syntax, and the ability to reflect on all these aspects of language.

ORAL LANGUAGE ABILITIES IN WHOLE LANGUAGE

In the 1990s, literacy involves more than being able to read printed words. Although the media proclaims the high illiteracy rate in the United States, more people than ever before are able to read print. The problem is not one of being able to read print but, rather, in being able to comprehend and think about what is read. The demand for increasing literacy skills is not a demand for more people to be able to read words; it is a demand for greater language skills in the service of thought. A whole language curriculum should seek to develop critical thinking skills, not simply the ability to read and write.

Whole language programs generally assume that students possess skill in oral language. This cannot be assumed for students with mild handicaps or disabilities in language learning. For these students, a whole language program must include development of oral language and thinking skills along with written language.

Language Genres

Whole language programs require that students communicate to their peers and the teacher. They must share ideas and interpretations about the activities they participate in and the books they listen to and read. To do so requires children to have an adequate command of the phonology, syntax, semantics, and pragmatics of oral language. They must be able to communicate a message that is intelligible, syntactically understandable, clear in meaning, and appropriate to the situation. These messages may be organized in different ways, called genres. Whole language programs must recognize that there is not just one way for children to communicate; there is not one type of conversation, one type of reading, or one type of writing. Each genre uses distinct vocabulary and syntactic structures (Black, 1985; Grabe, 1987; Graesser & Goodman, 1985; Kieras, 1985).

Narrative Genres
Narrative language is particularly important for success in the early school years. Most texts used in kindergarten through third grade are in a narrative format. There are a variety of narrative types (Heath, 1986a; 1986b). In addition to exposing students to fictional and biographical stories, teachers in whole language classrooms should provide opportunities for students to produce a variety of narrative genres such as:

1. *Recounts.* An adult requests that a child talk about something the adult and the child have shared. For example, the teacher says, "Tell Ms. Lopez (the librarian) about our visit to the zoo yesterday" or "Tell me what we discussed in history class." Adults can support children's recounting by asking "scaffolding" questions: "What did the gorilla do? What did you do when the bird landed on you? Who rode the camel?" The scaffolding questions adults ask guide students in the type of information they should include so they eventually can relate information without this assistance.

2. *Eventcasts.* Eventcasting is talking about what one is doing as one is doing it; it is talking aloud to oneself. Eventcasting has been related to segmentation abilities

and the development of self-regulatory speech. In eventcasting, children learn how to break behavior into its elements. Eventually, children learn how to segment sentences into words and words into phonemes. Older children and adults may eventcast to help them manage difficult tasks, for example: "What do I have to do today? Let's see. . . . I need to study for tomorrow's test, then work on my math assignment." Teachers can model eventcasting as they do the daily classroom activities: "I'm looking for my roll book. It's not under these papers. I'll look on the shelf. . . ." They can encourage children to eventcast (talk aloud) as they work on tasks: "I'm putting a puzzle together. I'm looking for a red piece." If children have difficulty talking aloud at first, teachers can eventcast for them: "You have a blue piece. You're fitting it into Miss Piggy's dress. It fits."

3. *Accounts.* Accounts are narratives about a personal experience a speaker offers to listeners who are unfamiliar with the experience. For example, a child may have gone camping with her parents on the weekend. On Monday she excitedly tells her teacher, who was not on the outing, about her experiences. Because the teacher did not participate in the experience, he cannot provide the type of scaffolding support he does for recounts. The child must organize the account with little or no assistance from listeners.

Teachers can provide opportunities for students to practice accounting. "Sharing time" is one frequently used activity. Accounting is often quite difficult for students with mild handicaps because they must talk about something that is not present, keep the topic in mind, sequence the information, and consider the listener's perspective. Teachers can design some ways to facilitate accounting. They can encourage parents to send notes or call them about special experiences the child has had so they will be able to encourage an account and have some knowledge about it. Teachers can select topics for accounting, such as *a time I got scared, inviting a friend home, my birthday party,* that everyone would likely have experienced. They can model talking about the topic. Students can be encouraged to join in with their experiences. In choosing a topic that everyone can talk about, modeling and asking scaffolding questions become easier and students can hear how others organize information about experiences similar to their own.

Schools rely heavily on stories, recounts, and eventcasts. Textbooks in the early grades usually are in story format. In most testing situations, students are expected to recount something that has been taught. In science, art, and activity-based language programs, children are expected to produce a running eventcast of their activities. Opportunities for accounts occur less frequently in the academic school environment than at home or on the playground. Because accounts commonly are used to initiate and precipitate social interactions, however, students should be able to give accounts.

Expository Genres

By mid-elementary school, students must master expository texts that require greater abstraction and generalization than narratives do. They must be able to discuss not only one experience of a vacation (a narrative) but also the characteristics of vacations in general (an exposition). They must be able to talk about not only their dog at home (a narrative) but also about dogs in general and dogs in relationship to other animals (exposition). They must master a variety of expository genres, such as the descriptive genre that describes types of dinosaurs, the comparison-contrast genre that compares plant-eating with meat-eating dinosaurs, the cause-effect genre that explains causes of the dinosaurs' extinction, the sequential-procedural genre that describes the steps in preparing dinosaur bones for exhibit, or the problem-solution genre that presents the problem of animals nearing extinction and what can be done to prevent their extinction.

A whole language program must expose students to a range of language genres. The focus of many whole language programs has been on high quality children's literature, primarily fictional literature. The ability to comprehend and produce fictional narrative texts does not assure the ability to comprehend the variety of expository genres. Teachers should make a point of exposing students to activities and texts that require a variety of expository genres. Teachers in whole language programs can prepare students for expository text by requiring the use of expository genres in familiar contexts as well as in printed texts. For example:

Sequential-procedural genre:	"Tell me how to make . . . (something familiar, e.g., lemonade, peanut butter and jelly sandwich)."
Cause-effect genre:	"What would happen at school if we didn't have rules for using the playground equipment?"
Problem-solution genre:	"Tell me all the things you did to find your dog when he ran away."

Language and Thought

The narrative and expository language genres of school require children to use language for increasingly abstract functions. The early language functions of young children are focused on meeting immediate needs. Children request objects they want or command people to do things for them (up, come, out, help), or they show objects they have. They talk about only what they see in the environment. Their language is tied to their perceptions. Eventually they talk about people and events they saw in the past or that they will see in the future, and later still they talk about ideas they cannot see at all.

Language Functions

The ability to use language for other than purposes of meeting needs is critical for the academic tasks schools require. In addition, children must use language to direct (including monitoring their own and others' behavior), to report, to predict, to project into thoughts and feelings of others, and to reason (Tough, 1979). Further, they must be able to use all of these functions in creating imaginary scenes in play and storytelling. Pretend play actually provides an ideal environment for using all of these language functions.

For example, a special education classroom teacher set up a McDonald's play area in her room. She programmed the classroom computer with the McDonald's menu, and she provided pretend food items and boxes, napkins, and paper cups donated by a local McDonald's restaurant. While participating in the play, she modeled the various language functions:

Requesting:	"I'd like a hamburger and a chocolate shake."
Directing:	"I'll get more bags." "Please enter Michelle's order on the computer."
Reporting:	"I put pickles, onion, lettuce, and tomato on your hamburger." "I burned myself with the grease from the french fries."
Predicting:	"There are lots of people here. I think we'll have to wait a long time."
Projecting into others' thoughts and feelings:	"She's in a hurry." "She's mad because you didn't give her the right change."
Reasoning:	"I don't have enough money, so I'll have to borrow some." "I can't find a place to sit because there are so many people."

The teacher observed that the children talked more and used language more for predicting, projecting, and reasoning when they were dealing with familiar themes in play than when they were talking about stories or other academic activities. As she encouraged more use of a variety of language functions in play, however, she was able to refer to these functions when discussing the behaviors, thoughts, and feelings of characters in stories.

Language-Thinking Hierarchy

Bloom (1956) recommended a hierarchy of language-thinking levels that should be part of a school curriculum. No ages were attached to these levels because, even in the elementary school, all levels may be required depending on the content of the course and the expectations of teachers. Each level requires the information and skills of the previous level. Students must be able to show they recognize and comprehend information, and they must be able to analyze, synthesize, and evaluate the information.

Table 1 explains each level and gives examples of questions asked in an elementary special education classroom. The questions in the science activity initially might seem quite difficult. The children, however, had had considerable firsthand experiences with geology. They lived in Albuquerque, New Mexico and had visited the mountains on the east side of the city and picked up pieces of granite rock containing fossils and rose quartz. They traveled around the mountains to visit an old coal mine. They went to the west mesa, walked down into an extinct volcano, and picked up pieces of basalt, obsidian, and pumice. Their teacher read the book, *The Magic School Bus Inside the Earth* (Cole, 1987). (This book describes a field trip in which children journey in a magical bus to see how rocks are formed inside the earth.) In the classroom they constructed papier mâché volcanos and used vinegar and soda to make them erupt. They collected rocks. They wrote about all their experiences.

TABLE 1   Sample Questions Using Bloom's Taxonomy

Level	Definition	Language Arts Examples	Science Examples
Knowledge	Memorizes and repeats information presented; answers simple questions.	What was the little girl's name in *Charlotte's Web*? Where did Templeton the rat live?	What kind of rock is made of mud and clay pressed together?
Comprehension	Demonstrates understanding by paraphrasing or stating in another form.	What was the story about? Tell me the story you just heard.	Explain how metamorphic rock is produced.
Application	Uses information, rules, methods, or principles in new but similar situations.	Charlotte and Wilbur are friends. How can friends help each other?	(after a discussion of the characteristics of granite) What could we use granite for?
Analysis	Identifies components, gives reasons, identifies problems.	How did Wilbur change over the course of the story?	How are limestone, shale, and sandstone alike?
Synthesis	Abstracts from previously learned knowledge to generate new solutions to problems.	What would have happened if Templeton hadn't found words for Charlotte to weave in her web?	How would the world be different if there were no volcanos?
Evaluation	Compares alternatives, states opinions, justifies responses.	Which character do you like best in the story, and why?	If you were commissioned to create a monument, what type of rock would you use, and why?

Oral Interactive Discourse

The activities involving these various genres and levels of thought require students to talk with one another and with teachers. Oral interactive discourse is not new to school-age children. The rules and the structure of these interactions, however, may change in school. In school, students are expected to participate in class discussions and work co-operatively in groups. Children must become more sensitive to their listeners, and they must know how to manage conversations. They must be able to get a turn in a conversation, initiate topics, maintain topics, give turns to others, respond to requests for conversational repair, and request repairs from others (Brinton & Fujiki, 1989; Donahue, Pearl, & Bryan, 1983; Fey & Leonard, 1983; Schneider, 1982). Deficits in oral interaction skills prevent students with language-learning disabilities from effectively participating in classroom discussions and group projects.

The accounting (sharing time) activity mentioned earlier provides many opportunities for conversational management. Students' comments should be related to the topic in some way. If there is no apparent relationship, the teacher might say, "We're talking about scary experiences. Are you talking about a scary experience?" The teacher may make explicit the rules for getting a turn in a conversation: "Wait until Brian has finished" or, "Look at the person talking so she'll know you're interested and may want a turn to talk." When she is unclear about what a student has said, the teacher may question with "What?" or requests for clarification: "Could you tell me more? Where did you say it happened?" When children are talking, the teacher may suggest clarifying questions that one child might ask another: "Jim, ask Andrew who else was at his birthday party."

LITERATE KNOWLEDGE FOR WHOLE LANGUAGE LEARNING

Students must bring their oral language skills to bear when reading and writing. Comprehension and production of texts requires that students use their pragmatic, semantic, syntactic, and phonological skills in more complex ways. Students also must have the language skills and knowledge to succeed with academic tasks. They must have a literate language style, schemas for content information, knowledge of text structures, metalinguistic skills, and metacognitive monitoring abilities (Lesgold & Perfetti, 1981; Marzano, Hagerty, Valencia, & DiStefano, 1987).

Schools use a more formal *literate language style* than the oral interactive language of the home or playground (Westby, 1984; 1985). Written language is not simply oral language written down. Written language uses more explicit vocabulary and complex syntax. Semantic information must be integrated into larger units or *content schemas*. Students must understand relationships among semantic elements. For example, not only must they understand what a spider is—its characteristics—but also what it does, where it lives, its relationship to other arachnids, its relationship to insects, the relationship of arachnids and insects to other animals, and so on. The information in these content schemas is presented in systematically organized patterns called *text structures* or *text grammars* (Anderson & Pearson, 1984; Meyer & Rice, 1984).

Reading and writing require *metalinguistic abilities*, or conscious awareness of language. Students must be able to separate words from the speech stream, segment words into sounds, and match phonemic sounds with grapheme symbols (Clay, 1975; Temple, Nathan, Burris, & Temple, 1988). Students must use *metacognitive monitoring abilities* to determine if they are comprehending oral and written information. They must use metacognitive strategies when they have failed to comprehend and when they are presented with complex learning tasks (Baker & Brown, 1984).

A strength in one knowledge area may compensate for a weakness in another area. For example, a student with weak metalinguistic skills may be able to use content knowledge to predict words; a student weak in content schemas may use metacognitive strategies to gain additional schema knowledge. All these aspects of literate language must be addressed in whole language programs for learning disabled, mildly handicapped students.

Literate Language Style

Reading and writing require a language style that differs from oral-interactive language in vocabulary, syntax, and organization. In an oral style, speakers may use nonspecific language (pronouns and words such as *that, this, here, there, stuff, things*) and short sentences. Ideas may be strung together in an associative style, with one idea leading to another but with little or no relationship among all the ideas. In the literate style, speakers and writers must use explicit vocabulary, complex syntax, and a topic-centered style that makes specific the interrelationships between elements of the text. When an adult and a child are looking at a picture in a book together, they understand if one says:

> He hit him. He ran away.

Without the context of the picture, however, these sentences make no sense. One does not know who did the hitting, who ran away, and why he ran. To understand what happened when no pictures are available, one may need to say or write:

> The boy who stole the bike hit the boy who was watching. Then the boy who saw the bike being stolen swiftly ran away because he was not strong enough to fight back.

In addition to the conjunctions *and, then,* and *because* used in oral conversation, literate language uses conjunctions such as *but, therefore, however, meanwhile, nevertheless, in addition*, adverbs (*swiftly, angrily, smoothly*), adverbial phrases (*when I finish my homework*), and relative clauses (The clever fox, *who tricked the coyote into holding up the mesa*, trotted off with the money).

Students with learning disabilities and mild handicaps frequently are exposed to less complex language. They may read "high interest, low vocabulary" books that use only familiar words and that simplify syntax by avoiding compound and complex sentences. Students acquire literate-style language only by exposure. Students with mild handicaps are capable of acquiring the literate language style when they have interesting, meaningful texts. Cumulative and predictive books provide a means of exposing them to complex vocabulary or syntax in ways they will remember and comprehend. For example, in the familiar story *Millions of Cats*, Gag (1928) repeatedly described the man's predicament in choosing a cat, using complex sentences with conjunctions and relative clauses:

> But then he saw a fuzzy grey kitten way over here which was every bit as pretty as the others so he took it too.

Content Schema

A content schema refers to organization of knowledge about a given topic or domain. Content schemas include semantic knowledge as well as cognitive knowledge of spatial, temporal, and causal relationships. One can have schemas for scenes (houses, jungles, schools), events (birthday parties, camping trips), and concepts/ideas (government, energy). A schema for a school might consist of classrooms, chalkboards, desks, chairs, books, teachers, principal, gym, restrooms. A schema for a birthday party could include

the person having the birthday, gifts, ice cream, cake, playing games, blowing out can-
dles, singing happy birthday. Event schemas also might include the scripts, or what people engaging in the event would say. A schema for energy could include sources of energy, location of energy sources, how energy is produced, pollution created by energy
generation, and so on.

Schema content can be developed by teaching in thematic units. Rather than reading
one book on a topic, or discussing a concept or theme in only one class, whole language
teachers present the theme in multiple ways throughout the day. For example, an elementary special education class did a unit on bears. The students listened to a variety of
stories about bears and read several versions of *The Three Bears*, including a classic by
Galdone (1973), a Hawaiian version, *Wili Wai Kula and the Three Mongooses* (Laird,
1983), and a wordless picture book, *Deep in the Forest* (Turkle, 1976), in which a bear
visits the peoples' house. They read stories about real bears, such as *Blueberries for Sal*
(McCloskey, 1948). They read stories about cartoon bears, such as *The Berenstain Bears
and the Messy Room* (Berenstain & Berenstain, 1983). They read stories about teddy
bears, such as *A Pocket for Corduroy* (Freeman, 1978) and *The Night After Christmas*
(Stevenson, 1981). And, of course, they read *Winnie the Pooh* (Milne, 1926).

The students compared and contrasted the bears in the stories. In math class they used
colored counting bears of different sizes. In science class they discussed where bears
lived and what bears needed to eat. That fall, because of a particularly dry summer, 21
bears came down from the mountains into Albuquerque looking for food. Students talked
about why the bears had to be captured and relocated. They planned a teddy bears' picnic. The children brought their own teddy bears from home, and they served foods bears
might like (e.g., blueberries, honey), although they rejected some foods bears might like
(such as bugs and raw fish). At the picnic they played Blind Bear's Bluff. Before being
blindfolded, the children looked carefully at all the bears. Then they felt a bear, used
words to describe the bear, and guessed who owned the bear.

Teachers also can assess and facilitate students' content knowledge by engaging them
in semantic webbing activities surrounding a topic or theme. Words or themes can be selected from the students' textbooks. The teacher writes the word or theme on the chalkboard and asks students to generate ideas related to the word or theme. As the students
give suggestions, the teacher requests information regarding the relationships among the
words and ideas they suggest. Children who are able to develop extensive webs for a
topic are more likely to be able to follow a topic of conversation or a theme in a text.

Text Grammars

The content of texts is organized or structured systematically. This structure is called a
text grammar. Students who are able to recognize text structures show better comprehension (Fitzgerald, 1989; Slater & Graves, 1989).

Components and Assessment of Structure

All narratives in Western cultures involve the same basic structure, which consists of:

Setting:	Describes the characters and the social, physical, or temporal context in which the story happens.
Initiating event:	A natural occurrence (e.g., earthquake, tornado), an activity of a character (e.g., stealing, threat), the perception of an event (hearing thunder), or changes in physiological state (hunger, pain), which triggers a response in characters.
Internal response:	The emotional state of the character in response to the initiating event.
Plan:	A character's strategy for obtaining a goal.
Attempt:	A series of actions the character intentionally carries out in an effort to achieve a goal.
Consequence:	The success or failure of the character in achieving a goal.
Resolution:	The character's feelings, thoughts, or actions in response to the consequences of attaining or not attaining a goal.
Ending:	A statement announcing the conclusion of the story, summarizing the story, or stating a moral or general principle.

By third to fourth grade, students are expected to be able to comprehend and produce a complete narrative episode that includes all these elements. If students do not recognize and understand these elements of stories, they will have difficulty in comprehending many of the books used in whole language literacy programs. Students' knowledge of the temporal and physical and psychological cause-effect relationships reflected in stories can easily be assessed by asking them to relate a story in wordless picture books. Many of the books by Mercer Mayer—for example, *One Frog Too Many* (1975), *A Boy, A Dog, and A Frog* (1967), *Frog Goes to Dinner* (1974), *A Boy, A Dog, A Frog, and A Friend* (1971)—are particularly useful for this purpose because they include all the elements of complete or complex episodes. The student is told, "Tell me the story that happened in this book. Make it the best story you can." If the student is hesitant to tell the story or has trouble organizing extended verbal responses, the examiner can ask questions that focus on the relationships:

Reporting:	"What was the boy doing here? What happened here? Tell me about this picture."
Projecting:	"What is the boy saying to the big frog? What is the frog thinking? How does the boy feel?"
Reasoning:	"Why is the frog thinking that? Why did the tree fall down?"
Predicting:	"What will happen next? What will the big frog do now?"

Teachers can evaluate the students' performance by considering the following questions:

1. Does the student simply label/describe pictures, or does she interpret the picture? That is, does the child use information in the pictures to generate schemas that go beyond the details of the pictures? For example, if a picture shows a boy carrying a pole, a bucket, and a net, does the student simply say, "The boy has a pole, and a bucket, and a net" or does she infer, "The boy is going fishing"?
2. Does the student indicate awareness of temporal relationships in stories? Does the child use temporal markers or conjunctions that indicate time relationships? (These include *just, already, always, before, after, while, then, when, now, as soon as.*)
3. Does the child recognize the characters' emotional feelings? What words does she use to describe the feelings?
4. Does the child explain relationships between characters' emotions and events in the story by using words such as *because, so, therefore*?
5. Does the child recognize the theme or reason for the characters' goal-directed behaviors? Does the child explicitly state the story theme?

The teacher can assess students' ability to integrate narrative relationships into an organized narrative structure by asking them to tell a story about a poster picture. Table 2 describes the developmental stages of storytelling and gives example stories for each level.

Students with learning disabilities and mild handicaps generally exhibit significant delays and disorders in narrative abilities. They may not understand the story content or relationships that underlie stories, and/or they may not be able to organize information into a cohesive and coherent story. To assure students' comprehension of narratives when reading stories, teachers have to be aware of a student's current narrative abilities. The teacher may want to select stories that will highlight specific aspects of story structure. For example, if a child produces a series of unrelated or temporally related actions, the teacher may want to introduce cause-effect relationships by presenting stories that make cause-effects explicit. For example, he may read *Round Robin* (Kent, 1982), the story of a robin who eats so much in the summer that when winter comes, it is too fat to fly south. Or he may read some of the *pour quoi* tales from other cultures that explain why things are as they are. For example, *Why the Sun and Moon Live in the Sky* (Dayrell, 1968) explains that sun and moon had to leave their house because when water came to visit, he overflowed the furniture, room, and house until the only place for them was in the sky.

Expository Text Grammars

Expository texts have more variety in structures than narrative texts do because the former are about a greater variety of ideas. Not only do different texts have different structures, but any text may also have several different structures. To comprehend expository texts, students must acquire a variety of text structures and be able to switch between these structures within a single text. Recognizing and comprehending key words that signal the various text structures and relationships among the text elements is an essential skill for reading and writing expository texts. Table 3 presents the major types of expository texts, their functions, and key words that signal the type of expository text. To com-

TABLE 2   Development of Stories

Content/Structure	Sample Story
Preschool Level	
Isolated description: Child labels or describes objects, characters, surroundings, or ongoing actions; no true sequence of actions.	There is a ghost and a pumpkin. The witch is a woman. She flies a broom. The witch is black. The witch chews Skol and makes cigarettes. The witch lives in California and Arizona. She does not come to Alamo.
Action sequence: Child lists actions that appear to be temporally sequenced; characters act independently of each other; story may have a central character or a central theme (actions that each character does).	Once there was some kids. And they were going to school. A giant bird flew over and landed. Then they got a piece of rope and put it in his mouth. The bird took off. And they had a good, good trip. They flew over the ocean, the mountain. Finally they came home.
Reaction sequence: One event or action automatically causes other events or actions, but no planning is involved.	There were two boys who went to China. And they made friends with a bird. And so they were flying around China. And they were going over a city where a statue was. But then a storm came. And the eagle's wings couldn't flap, so they crash landed in the trees.
Early Elementary School	
Goal-directed episode: The story character has some goal to achieve. There may be some reference to the character's feelings. The character engages in activities to achieve the goal, but the planning to achieve the goal is not explicit; the planning must be inferred.	A UFO came from outer space. Then the UFO came upon a big house. There were some scientists working in a building next to the big house. The UFO wanted to study earth people. One of the scientists was taken by the UFO and put in a big locker. Then the UFO went into a black hole and was never seen again.
Complete episode: The story describes the goals and intentions of the characters, and the characters' planning to achieve the goals is made clear.	For a whole month there had been a real big giant that had been throwing things in the houses and smashing houses and getting people and throwing them. But one day there was a man who wanted to solve this problem. So he got all the men. And they started up the mountain with torches to see what they can do about it. So they were about 10 feet from him. One of the men threw a torch at him and lit the giant on fire. And the giant fell down the mountain. And they never see him again.
Later Elementary	
Complex episode: At least one obstacle lies in the goal path (e.g., the first thing the characters try to reach a goal does not work and they must try something else).	Once upon a time there was a village in the mountains. And there was a gorilla that escaped from the zoo. And they went hunting for it. And it was on the top of a ledge. And they started chasing it with guns and swords. It run up the hill, and then it fell over the edge. And then the men tried to get it, but it jumped and it wrecked their house. And then they started chasing it up the mountain again. And he started to ski down 'cause he found a pair of skis at the top. And then the people got skis. So they chased him on skis. And they chase him right to the zoo. And he got back. He got caught in the zoo again.
Embedded episode: This is a story within a story. The first goal in the story is interrupted to accomplish a second goal. Then the first goal is accomplished.	A man named Mr. Dirt lived in the country all by himself and owns a farm. One calf got away and went to the woods and headed up the mountains. So Mr. Dirt went up the mountain after the calf. On the way a bear came after Mr. Dirt. He ran up a tree and the bear climbed up the tree after him. Mr. Dirt threw his ax at the bear and hit the bear in the head. Blood poured out of his head and the bear fell down and died. A few minutes later the calf ran over to Mr. Dirt.

TABLE 3   *Expository Text Grammars*

Text Pattern/Function	Key Words
Descriptive text: Tells what something is.	is called, can be defined as, is, can be interpreted as, is explained as, refers to, is a procedure for, is someone who, means
Collection/enumeration text: Lists things related to the topic.	an example is, for instance, another, next, finally, such as, to illustrate
Sequence/procedure text: Tells what happened or how to do something or make something.	first, next, then, second, third, following this step, finally, subsequently, from here . . . to, eventually, before, after
Comparison/contrast text: Shows how two things are the same or different.	different, same, alike, similar, although, however, on the other hand, contrasted with, compared to, rather than, but, yet, still, instead of
Cause/effect explanation text: Gives reasons why something happened.	because, reasons, then, therefore, for this reason, results, effects, consequently, so, in order to, thus, depends on, influences, is a function of, produces, leads to, affects, hence
Problem/solution text: States a problem and offers solutions to the problem.	a problem is, a solution is

prehend expository texts, students must comprehend these words, recognize that these words signal text organization, and then use knowledge of these structures to recognize the relationship among the concepts presented.

Metalinguistic Skills

The term *metalinguistics* refers to the ability to reflect on language or to use language to talk about language. Metalinguistic skills involve the ability to segment the sound stream into words and phonemes, to identify sound/symbol relationships, and to recognize that words and phrases can have multiple meanings.

Segmentation

Analyzing language into linguistic units is essential in learning to read. It is frequently assumed that children learn segmentation skills and sound/sound relationships simply by being exposed to print-rich environments. For many students this is true. Students with learning disabilities and mild handicaps, however, often have particular deficits in segmentation abilities and sound/symbols awareness (Kamhi, Catts, Mauer, Apel, & Gentry, 1988). Consequently, if they are to acquire these skills, they likely will require additional direct teaching.

Activities that involve rhyming and word substitutions in predictive texts can facilitate the ability to segment words from the speech stream. Children can be taught familiar rhymes and then assisted in varying them by substituting words, such as:

Humpty Dumpty sat on a *tack*.
Humpty Dumpty sat on a *chair*.
Humpty Dumpty sat on a *hill*.

Closely related to the ability of phonemic segmentation is the development of knowledge of sound-symbol association. Children from highly literate environments frequently acquire some awareness of sound-symbol relationships during the preschool years and will engage in spontaneous writing using invented spelling. Children match the way they produce the phonemes of the language with the way they say the letters of the alphabet. Many letters have a letter-sound match. For example, in B/*bi*/, F/*ɛf*/, S/*ɛs*/, L/*ɛl*/, the child produces the phoneme when saying the letter name. Hence, when asked to write "baby" or "soap," the child easily can produce "babe" or "sop" by relying on this letter-sound correspondence.

Many students with mild handicaps go through the same developmental sequence of writing as nonhandicapped students do if they are provided with meaningful writing activities (Westby & Costlow, 1991). Teachers can have students establish journals in which they write meaningful messages or notes to the teacher and to each other. As they master this interpersonal communicative writing, they can be encouraged to write personal stories, then fictional stories and expository texts. Initially, the focus is on communicating a message, and invented spelling is permitted and encouraged. As students deal with writing and reading for meaning, the necessary metalinguistic skills are introduced and discussed: What are words? How do you "sound out" words? What letters go with what sounds? How and why do you use punctuation?

Learners with mild handicaps, particularly some of those who have had a history of articulation problems, poor oral-tactile sensitivity, or poor auditory discrimination, may require direct teaching of sound-symbol relationships. These students should be introduced explicitly to the alphabetic principle that letters stand for sounds. They should be taught to name the letter, to give the sound of the letter, to note what they do with their lips and tongue when they say the letter or sound, and to give a word that begins with the sound. Highly structured phonetics programs, such as the Orton-Gillingham approach (Gillingham & Stillman, 1960), are appropriate and even essential for some students.

Multiple Word Meanings and Figurative Language

Developing multiple word meanings and figurative language is an aspect of both semantic development and metalinguistic development. Some multiple-meaning words refer to specific concrete objects or actions (e.g., lie on the river *bank*; put your money in the *bank*; *bank* the car on the sharp turn), as well as to figurative meanings (don't *bank* on it). Some multiple-meaning words refer to both physical and psychological attributes (a *sharp* knife and a *sharp* manager; a *crooked* nail and a *crooked* accountant).

Students with learning disabilities frequently understand only the physical meaning of words such as *sweet, sharp, crooked, soft, hard, warm, cold, bright,* or *deep,* yet comprehension of both the physical and psychological meanings is generally expected between 7 and 9 years of age, and by ages 9–10 students begin to be able to explain the relationship between the physical and psychological terms (Wiig, 1989). A similar pattern of development occurs with similes (*her eyes sparkle like diamonds*), metaphors (*sunshine of my life*), and idioms (*raining cats and dogs*).

Stories or books that play on multiple word meanings can be an amusing way to teach the concept. For example, in *Amelia Bedelia* (Parrish, 1963) Amelia makes many mistakes because she is unaware of multiple word meanings. When told to "draw the drapes," she makes a pencil sketch of the drapes; when told to "dress the chicken," she put pants and socks on it. In *The King Who Rained* (Gwynne, 1973), the child pictures her father with a small animal on his nose when he says he has a "mole" on his nose; she imagines that she will have to hold a locomotive when her sister tells her she can hold her "train" at the wedding.

Metacognitive Skills

Metacognition refers to the knowledge that learners have about their thinking and the strategies they use to monitor comprehension and production. Metacognitive thought requires a theory of mind and the development of metacognitive verbs (know, forget, remember, guess, doubt, infer, hypothesize, conclude, assume) are critical for children's learning and participation in school activities. According to Wellman (1985), the words *know, forget, remember*, and *guess* develop between ages 3 and 7 years. To carry out teachers' instructions, children must know if they understand what is expected, and they must ask questions or ask for assistance if they do not know. They must know if they have the necessary information or if they are guessing. And they must remember what they have been told to do and be aware if they have forgotten what they were told. Without this active awareness of knowing, remembering, forgetting, and guessing, children will not function independently.

Teachers can model these metacognitive words in daily activities:

"I think this is how Jennifer's aunt kneaded the bread."

"I forgot what Ms. Garcia did after she added the flour. Go ask her."

"I remember how good the bread smelled when it came out of the oven."

"I know how to make adobe bricks from clay, straw, and water."

"Good, you remembered to bring your permission slip for the trip."

If students have language deficits in the areas discussed so far, they are likely also to have metacognitive monitoring deficits, but students can have adequate skills in all other areas yet have trouble planning their behavior and oral and written productions, monitoring their comprehension, and generating and employing strategies for learning and remembering. In general, students with learning disabilities show little evidence of using effective strategies to meet task demands (Schumaker & Deshler, 1984; Torgensen, 1977a, 1977b). Some students do not have the oral language necessary for planning behavior; others have little awareness that mental acts exist; others may have the necessary language and awareness of mental acts but are not able to generate strategies to facilitate their performance; still others may be able to generate strategies but be uncertain of when to use them.

Throughout all activities, adults should model metacognitive strategies. They should talk aloud (eventcast) as they carry out activities. As they do so, they let students hear a variety of language functions and structures, and they also let children hear what task is to be accomplished, how the adult plans to approach the task, how the adult monitors performance, and what is done about success or lack of success (Meichenbaum, 1977). For example:

Problem definition:	"What do I have to do? Let's see. . . ."
Focusing attention and direction:	"Find step one. . . . Now find the piece shown in the picture. . . ."
Self-reinforcement:	"Good, I found that piece."
Self-evaluating coping skills and error-correcting options:	"This is the wrong piece. I need to look more carefully."

A similar strategy can be used during reading. The teacher asks the students to read along silently as the teacher reads the passage aloud and notes how they are thinking through the trouble spots. Davey (1983) suggested a number of points that can be made during this comprehension monitoring:

Making predictions:	"From the title, I think this will be about. . . ."
Describing the pictures you are forming in your head about the information:	"I have a picture of this scene in my head, and this is what it looks like. . . ."
Developing analogies (Show how to link prior knowledge with new information in the text):	"This reminds me of. . . ."
Identifying confusing points (Show how you monitor comprehension):	"This doesn't make sense."
Demonstrating fix-up strategies (Show how you make sense of the passage):	"I'd better reread this." "I'll read ahead and see if I can get some more information."

CONCLUSION

Determining school-age students' language learning needs for social and academic success in whole language programs requires assessment of their oral interactive language abilities, the language functions and genres they use effectively, the style, structure, and complexity of their language patterns, their content knowledge, metalinguistic skills, and metacognitive awareness and strategies. Teachers can help a student to benefit from whole language contexts by using oral and written language that is slightly above students' present language abilities. In conversational activities, teachers should model appropriate language functions, requests for clarification, conversational repairs, literate language style, and metacognitive monitoring. Students practice these aspects of language while working on group projects.

Throughout all school activities—art, science, social studies, language arts, math, gym—adults have to be alert to language functions and levels of language abstraction that students are using. They can assist students in using more diverse functions and higher levels of thought by making statements and asking questions. Literature and textbooks should be carefully selected to be within a range of the students' present comprehension abilities, yet challenging enough to facilitate language growth.

REFERENCES

Anderson, R. C., & Pearson, P. D. (1984). A schema-theoretic view of basic processes in reading. In P. D. Pearson (Ed.), *Handbook of reading research*. New York: Longman.

Baker, L., & Brown, A. L. (1984). Metacognitive skills and reading. In P. D. Pearson (Ed.), *Handbook of reading research*. New York: Longman.

Black, J. (1985). An exposition on understanding expository text. In B. Britton & J. Black (Eds.), *Understanding expository text*. Hillsdale, NJ: Erlbaum.

Bloom, B. (1956). *Taxonomy of educational objectives. Handbook 1: Cognitive domain*. New York: Longman.

Bloome, D., Harris, O., & Ludlum, D. (1991). Reading and writing as sociocultural activities: Politics and pedagogy in the classroom. *Topics in Language Disorders, 11*(3), 14–27.

Brinton, B., & Fujiki, M. (1989). *Conversational management with language-impaired children*. Rockville, MD: Aspen.

Clay, M. (1975). *What did I write?* Portsmouth, NH: Heinemann.

Davey, B. (1983). Think aloud: Modeling the cognitive process of reading comprehension. *Journal of Reading, 37*, 104–112.

de la Reyes, M. (1991). A process approach to literacy instruction for Spanish-speaking students: In search of a best fit. In E. H. Hiebert (Ed.), *Literacy for a diverse society*. New York: Teachers College Press.

Delpit, L. D. (1988). The silenced dialogue: Power and pedagogy in educating other people's children. *Harvard Educational Review, 58*, 280–298.

Dollaghan, C., & Miller (1986). Observational methods in the study of communicative competence. In R. L. Schiefelbusch (Ed.), *Language competence: Assessment and intervention*. San Diego: College Hill Press.

Donahue, M., Pearl, R., & Bryan, T. (1983). Communicative competence in learning disabled children. In H. Bialer & K. Gadow (Eds.), *Advances in learning and behavioral disabilities* (Vol. 2). Greenwich, CT: JAI Press.

Fey, M., & Leonard, L. (1983). Pragmatic skills of children with specific language impairment. In T. M. Gallagher & C. A. Prutting (Eds.), *Pragmatic assessment and intervention issues in language*. San Diego: College Hill Press.

Fillion, B., & Brause, R. S. (1987). Research into classroom practices: What have we learned and where are we going? In J. R. Squire (Ed.), *The dynamics of language learning*. Urbana, IL: ERIC Clearing House on Reading and Communication Skills.

Fitzgerald, J. (1989). Research on stories: Implications for teachers. In K. D. Muth (Ed.), *Children's comprehension of text*. Newark, DE: International Reading Association.

Froese, V. (1990). Introduction to whole-language teaching and learning. In V. Froese (Ed.), *Whole-language practice and theory*. Boston: Allyn & Bacon.

Garcia, G. E., & Pearson, P. D. (1991). The role of assessment in a diverse society. In E. H. Hiebert (Ed.), *Literacy for a diverse society: Perspectives, practices, and policies*. New York: Teachers College Press.

Gillingham, A., & Stillman, B. (1960). *Remedial training for children with specific disability in reading, writing, and penmanship*. Cambridge, MA: Educators Publishing Service.

Grabe, W. (1987). Contrastive rhetoric and text-type research. In U. Connor & R. Kaplan (Eds.), *Writing across cultures: Analysis of L2 text*. Reading, MA: Addison-Wesley.

Graesser, A. C., & Goodman, S. M. (1985). Implicit knowledge, question answering, and the representation of expository text. In B. K. Britton & J. B. Black (Eds.), *Understanding expository text*. Hillsdale, NJ: Erlbaum.

Heath, S. B. (1986a). Sociocultural contexts of language development. In *Beyond language*. Los Angeles: California State University, Evaluation Disseminations and Assessment Center.

Heath, S. B. (1986b). Taking a cross-cultural look at narratives. *Topics in language disorders, 7*(1), 84–94.

Kamhi, A., Catts, H., Mauer, D., Apel, K., & Gentry, B. (1988). Phonological and spatial processing abilities in language and reading impaired children. *Journal of Hearing & Speech Disorders, 53*, 316–327.

Kieras, D. E. (1985). Thematic process in the comprehension of expository prose. In B. K. Britton & J. B. Black (Eds.), *Understanding expository text*. Hillsdale, NJ: Erlbaum.

Kroll, B. M., & Vann, R. J. (1981). *Exploring speaking-writing relationships: Connections and contrasts*. Urbana, IL: National Council of Teachers of English.

Kuhn, T. S. (1970). *The structure of scientific revolutions*. Chicago: University of Chicago Press.

Lesgold, A. M., & Perfetti, C. A. (Eds.). (1981). *Interactive processes in reading*. Hillsdale, NJ: Erlbaum.

Marzano, R. J., Hagerty, P. J., Valencia, S. W., & DiStefano, P. P. (1987). *Reading diagnosis and instruction*. Englewood Cliffs, NJ: Prentice Hall.

McDermott, R. (1974). Achieving school failure: An anthropological approach to illiteracy and social stratification. In G. D. Spindler (Ed.), *Education & Culture Process*. New York: Holt, Rinehart & Winston.

Meichenbaum, D. (1977). *Cognitive-behavior modification: An integrative approach*. New York: Plenum.

Meyer, B., & Rice, G. E. (1984). The structure of text. In P. D. Pearson (Ed.), *Handbook of reading research*. New York: Longman.

Sawyer, D. (1991). Whole language in context: Insights into the current great debate. *Topics in Language Disorders, 11*(3), 1–13.

Schneider, P. (1982). Formal operations skills vs. explanation. *Psycholinguistic Newsletter* (Northwestern University), *8*, 16–23.

Schumaker, J. B., & Deshler, D. D. (1984). Setting demand variables: A major factor in program planning for the LD adolescent. *Topics in Language Disorders, 4*(2), 22–40.

Slater, W. H., & Graves, M. F. (1989). Research on expository text: Implications for teachers. In D. K. Muth (Ed.), *Children's comprehension of text*. Newark, DE: International Reading Association.

Temple, C., Nathan, R., Burris, N., & Temple, F. (1988). *The beginnings of writing*. Boston: Allyn & Bacon.

Tharp, R. G., & Gallimore, R. (1988). *Rousing minds to life*. Cambridge, MA: Cambridge University Press.

Torgesen, J. K. (1977a). Memorization processes in reading-disabled children. *Journal of Educational Psychology, 69*, 571–578.

Torgesen, J. K. (1977b). The role of nonspecific factors in the task performance of learning disabled children: A theoretical assessment. *Journal of Learning Disabilities, 10*, 27–34.

Tough, J. (1979). *The development of meaning*. New York: Wiley.

Vygotsky, L. S. (1978). *Mind in society: The development of higher psychological processes*. Cambridge, MA: Harvard University Press.

Wellman, H. M. (1985). The origins of metacognition. In D. L. Forrest-Pressley, G. E. MacKinnon, & T. G. Waller (Eds.), *Metacognition, cognition, and human performance*. New York: Academic Press.

Westby, C. E. (1984). Development of narrative language abilities. In G. P. Wallach & K. G. Butler (Eds.), *Language learning disabilities in school-age children*. Baltimore: Williams & Wilkins.

Westby, C. E. (1985). From learning to talk to talking to learn: Oral-literate language differences. In C. Simon (Ed.), *Communication skills and classroom success: Therapy methodologies for language-learning disabled students*. San Diego: College-Hill.

Wiig, E. (1989). *Steps to language competence*. New York: Psychological Corp.

CHILREN'S BOOKS

Berenstain, S., & Berenstain, J. *The Berenstain bears and the messy room*. New York: Random House.

Cole, J. (1987). *The magic school bus inside the earth*. New York: Scholastic Books.

Dayrell, E. (1968). *Why the sun and moon live in the sky*. Boston: Houghton Mifflin.

Freeman, D. (1978). *A pocket for Corduroy*. Cedar Grove, NJ: Puffin Books.

Gag, W. (1928). *Millions of cats*. New York: Coward, McCann & Geoghegan.

Galdone, P. (1970). The *three little pigs*. New York: Clarion Books.

Galdone, P. (1973). *The three bears*. New York: Scholastic.

Gwynne, F. (1973). *The king who rained*. New York: Young Readers Press.

Kent, J. (1982). *Round robin*. Englewood Cliffs, NJ: Prentice Hall.

Laird, D. (1983). *Wili wai kula and the three mongooses*. Honolulu: Barnaby.

Mayer, M. (1975). *One frog too many*. New York: Dial Press.

Mayer, M. (1967). *A boy, a dog, and a frog*. New York: Dial Press.

Mayer, M. (1974). *Frog goes to dinner*. New York: Dial Press.

Mayer, M. (1971). *A boy, a dog, a frog and a friend*. New York: Dial Press.

McCloskey, R. (1948). *Blueberries for Sal*. New York: Penguin.

Milne, A. A. (1926). *Winnie-the-Pooh*. New York: E. P. Dutton.

Parrish, A. (1963). *Amelia Bedelia*. New York: Scholastic Books.

Turkle, B. (1976). *Deep in the forest*. New York: E. P. Dutton.

Stevenson, J. (1981). *The night after Christmas*. New York: Greenwillow.

Carol Westby is a speech-language pathologist with the University Affiliated Program at the University of New Mexico, Albuquerque.

◦ 15 ◦

The authors of this article examine the activities of teachers before, during, and after instruction and the effects of teacher behavior and activities on individuals with learning disabilities. They present a model for teachers to use in assessing their effectiveness and in determining what works best in reading instruction. This article is a must for teachers of students with reading disorders.

Teaching Reading to Learning Disabled Students: A Review of Research-Supported Procedures

Steve Graham and LeAnn A. Johnson

According to a model presented by Graham (1985), several factors can jointly or independently affect students' pursuits during learning. The most important of these is the student's *entry behavior.* The knowledge, skills, motivation, and so forth that students bring to the task can have a powerful impact on learning. A student's *classroom peers* also can have a direct influence (either positive or negative) on pupil pursuits. In cooperative learning situations, for example, peers can affect a student's pursuits through encouragement or by offering assistance. The student's *teacher* represents a third and powerful factor that can directly affect a pupil's pursuits. Teachers can (a) direct and support the actions of students through the external provisions of the lesson; (b) attempt to change the student's entry behaviors into more preferred ones; and (c) develop arrangements that promote mutual assistance among students during learning. Although Graham's model only briefly mentioned the role of the family, the actions of a child's parents or guardians also can have a strong impact on student learning.

This article focuses primarily on the effects of teacher behaviors and activities. First, it examines research-based teacher-directed activities administered before, during, or after the lesson (or any combination of these). Next, it presents procedures that teachers can use to change students' entry behaviors (both reading skills and strategic behaviors). Finally, it discusses teachers' arrangement of peers and the impact of the student's family.

TEACHER ARRANGEMENT OF THE READING LESSON

Selecting Reading Material

One of the most important tasks in designing an effective lesson is to select or construct materials that are attractive, well organized, and at the appropriate level (Graham, 1985). In reading, teachers and researchers commonly classify materials as being at the student's *independent* (easy to read), or *instructional* (difficult enough to require teacher assistance), *or frustrational* (too difficult) level. Researchers have provided convincing evidence on the value of assigning materials that are at an appropriate level for LD students (Armstrong, 1983; Gickling & Armstrong, 1978). For example, when Gickling and Armstrong assigned instructional-level material to students functioning at the frustrational level on classroom reading assignments, the students' comprehension performance, on-task behavior, and task completion improved. Techniques that teachers can use to determine if materials are at a student's independent, instructional, or frustrational level have been presented by Graham (1983).

When selecting materials, teachers should be aware that the format or structure used to present information can affect a student's comprehension. Gold and Fleisher (1986) found that deductively organized text (main idea in the first sentence with details following) was easier for LD students to recall than inductively organized text (main idea presented later in the paragraph or left to be inferred). Because most reading materials contain both of these formats (as well as others), providing instruction on the organizing principles underlying common text structures may be advisable.

When selecting reading materials, another important factor involves illustrations. Although illustrations can make materials more attractive, and thus more interesting, some experts have argued that illustrations can have a detrimental effect on LD students' reading, particularly if students have poorly developed basic reading skills or if the pictures present ambiguous or inaccurate information (cf. Harber, 1983; Rose & Robinson, 1984; Rose, 1986). The most important questions regarding illustrations, however, may center on the quality of the picture. Mastropieri, Scruggs, and Levin (1987) reported that different types of illustrations are not equally beneficial; pictures containing information relevant to the desired outcome facilitated reading performance.

After reading materials have been selected, teachers also can consider how the materials should be displayed. For instance, reading materials can be presented directly on a computer monitor instead of the traditional format of the printed page. The use of computer-displayed text, over a short time period, does not appear to have a negative effect on LD students' comprehension processing, strategy use, or on-task behavior (Keene & Davey, 1987).

The display of text can be modified further by segmenting the material into smaller parts. O'Shea and Sindelar (1983) found that segmenting paragraphs into sequentially organized phrases improved the comprehension of poor readers. Although text segmentation is a time-consuming process, it may help to promote phrase reading and simplify the syntax of complex sentences, allowing the reader to concentrate on the relationship among phrases.

Teacher Activities Prior to Reading

Prior to having LD students read assigned passages, a teacher can use a number of activities or procedures to promote comprehension, fluency, accuracy, or a combination of these. Such activities may help students by directing or supporting what they do during the process of reading (Graham, 1985).

Setting Goals

Setting and selecting goals are central to the process of reading. Although teachers typically assume that the goal of reading is to construct meaning, students' goals actually may be to say the words right or answer the questions (Palinscar & Brown, 1988). Thus, identification of the purpose for reading by the student and the teacher is a commonly recommended instructional practice.

Research with LD students has concentrated on teacher-constructed goals; teachers set the purpose for reading and convey the goal through either a verbal or a written prompt. In a study by Pflaum, Pascarella, Auer, Augustyn, and Boswick (1982), a traditional purpose-setting aid ("This is a story about anteaters. You are going to read about how anteaters get food to eat, about their size, and about where they live," p. 111) was not effective in improving young LD students' recall. Similarly, O'Shea, Sindelar, and O'Shea (1987) found that instructing students to read quickly and correctly had no effect on LD students' fluency. They did find, however, that a cue to "remember as much as you can about the story" resulted in improved recall of story material.

In addition, Roberts and Smith (1980) found that giving LD students a specific purpose for reading (read more words correctly, reduce number of reading errors, or answer more comprehension questions), a strategy for meeting the assigned purpose, and reinforcement for accomplishing the goal resulted in improvement on a measure directly related to the assigned purpose. Finally, Wong, Wong, and Le Mare (1982) reported that LD students who were told explicitly why they were reading a passage (to take a test) performed significantly better on a comprehension test than did a control group of students who were not informed of the purpose of reading.

Another purpose-setting procedure used with LD students is the presentation of content-related questions prior to reading. Questions of this nature should help students focus attention on important text material. Bergerud, Lovitt, and Horton (1988) examined the effectiveness of assigning LD adolescents specific study guide questions to be answered while studying life science material. Although this particular technique was not effective, use of this general procedure should be investigated more fully. The effects of student-generated goals also should be examined.

Making Predictions

Asking students to make predictions about upcoming content requires them to draw and test inferences about the text to be read (Palinscar & Brown, 1984). Prior to reading a story, Sachs (1984b) asked students questions that required them to think about the goals and plans of the protagonist. These included: What is the main character in this story likely to want? How is the main character going to accomplish the goals? What do you think the main character should do? This procedure had a positive effect on LD students' comprehension of the story.

Activating Prior Knowledge

Helping poor readers activate relevant prior knowledge before reading should have a positive effect on reading performance (Holmes, 1983). Support for this proposition has been provided by McCormick and Hill (1984). They had poor readers write and "weave" together answers to teacher-prepared questions designed to help them relate their own background knowledge to the topic of the story and to make predictions about the story. Students were instructed further that during reading they should "combine knowledge they already have in their brains with predictions about what will occur in the story" (p. 222). The procedure was more effective than traditional reading instruction in improving comprehension. On the other hand, Pflaum et al. (1982) did not find that asking questions designed to activate prior knowledge, coupled with a cue to consider if anything new was learned, was effective in increasing the amount of information LD students recalled.

Using Advanced Organizers

Advanced organizers that provide an overview of the assigned passage prior to reading appear to offer an effective procedure for increasing comprehension. Idol-Maestas (1985) gave students the following prompts to be used with basal stories prior to reading: (1) What is the title? Does it give a clue as to what the story is about? (2) Look through each page of the story. Skim for clues. (3) Look for important words. Talk about what they mean. (4) Look for hard words. Practice saying them and talk about what they mean. (5) What is the setting of the story? When does it take place? Where did it take place? When directed to use these prompts, LD students' performance in answering factual, sequential, and inferential questions improved.

Darch and Gersten (1986) have developed an advanced organizer to be used with science and social studies curricula. Prior to reading, the teacher presents an outline consisting of the important facts and concepts included in the passage, as well as relationships among the various components. LD students receiving this outline scored higher on a comprehension measure than did those receiving traditionally oriented instruction.

Previewing

Teachers frequently ask LD students to read assigned materials outloud (Leinhardt, Zigmond, & Cooley, 1981). For poor readers, this can be frustrating, as they may not be very fluent or may make a lot of oral reading errors (cf. Graham, 1980). Previewing as a means for improving oral reading behavior involves exposing the student to a reading passage prior to required oral reading.

A series of studies by Rose reported the following findings: (1) allowing LD students to preview a passage silently prior to oral reading resulted in higher rates of word accuracy than a no-previewing condition (Rose, 1984; Rose & Sherry, 1984); (2) having LD students listen to a prerecorded tape of the material while following along silently prior to oral reading yielded higher rates of word accuracy than no previewing (Rose & Beattie, 1986); and (3) directing students to follow along silently while the teacher read the passage aloud prior to oral reading was more effective than no previewing or either listening or silent previewing (Rose, 1984; Rose & Beattie, 1986; Rose & Sherry, 1984).

Introducing Key Concepts and New Vocabulary

Another common prereading activity is to introduce and discuss key concepts and any new vocabulary presented in the reading material. Because students often encounter new words and ideas in assigned passages, the introduction of key concepts and words prior to reading is generally believed to facilitate comprehension.

In terms of prereading activities involving key ideas, Sachs (1983, 1984a) found that analyzing the main concept of a passage prior to reading had a positive effect on LD students' comprehension and oral reading speed and accuracy. The steps included: (1) the teacher writing out the central concept of the passage, (2) the teacher and students generating a list of examples and nonexamples of the concept, and (3) the student generating a definition of the concept based upon the examples and nonexamples.

Bos and her colleagues (Anders, Bos, & Filip, 1984; Bos, Anders, Filip, & Jaffee, 1985) have examined the effectiveness of *semantic feature analysis,* an activity that concentrates on both key ideas and vocabulary. With this procedure, the teacher first introduces a chart listing the major concepts presented in the passage across the top and the related vocabulary down the side. Each of the major concepts and vocabulary items then are briefly explained. Students rate each vocabulary item in relation to each concept as having a positive, a negative, or an unrelated relationship. Next, students read the passage to verify their rating and to clarify any questionable relationships. The procedure has had a positive impact on LD adolescents' recall of concepts and understanding of social studies text.

When only new vocabulary items are introduced, the results have not been as promising. Experiments conducted with LD students in the upper elementary grades have shown that learning the meaning of unfamiliar words in a story has not improved passage comprehension; these results were consistent across different methods of vocabulary instruction (Pany & Jenkins, 1978; Pany, Jenkins, & Schreck, 1982). Nevertheless, method of vocabulary instruction did have a differential effect on the learning of word meanings. The most effective procedure involved pairing an unknown word with either a definition or a synonym and a sentence containing the target item, followed by considerable practice in producing the correct definition or synonym. Simply telling students the meaning of the word after reading it in context had a positive, although weaker, effect on learning new vocabulary.

A Recap

In concluding this discussion, two comments seem to be in order. First, a broad combination of teacher-directed activities or procedures often has a powerful effect on pupil pursuits during learning (Graham, 1985). Thus, a sensible combination of several of the prereading activities presented could prove advantageous. Second, more attention has to be given to what students internalize as a result of teacher assistance immediately prior to reading a selected passage (or, for that matter, during or after reading).

Teacher Activities During and After Reading

Specific activities that teachers can institute during and after reading to affect LD students' performance on assigned materials are described next.

Reinforcing Specific Reading Behaviors

Although the use of contingent reinforcement is a popular and effective intervention (Harris, Prellor, & Graham, 1988), relatively few studies have examined its use in improving LD students' reading performance. A notable exception was a study by Jenkins, Barksdale, and Clinton (1978). They found that administering reinforcement to poor readers contingent upon either their comprehension or oral reading performances resulted in improvement in answering passage questions and oral reading accuracy, respectively.

In a study by Swanson (1981), LD students self-recorded their reading behavior and subsequently were reinforced contingent upon their performance. The combination of self-recording and reinforcement resulted in improvements in comprehension, silent reading rate, and oral reading accuracy when each was targeted for intervention. It is important to note that improvements in oral and silent reading behaviors had only marginal effects on comprehension. Similar results were reported by Jenkins et al. (1978).

Requiring Repeated Readings

A simple means for improving LD students' reading is to have them read the same passage more than once. O'Shea et al. (1987) found that having LD students read a passage *three* times resulted in better comprehension and more fluent reading as compared to a single reading.

Correcting Errors During Oral Reading

Considerable research has examined the effectiveness of various teacher-directed procedures for correcting LD students' errors during oral reading. Probably the most common method of teacher correction is to supply the correct response for the unknown word or error and then to have the student repeat the correct response. Although word supply has been found to be more effective in increasing correct oral reading than no correction procedures or a phonics correction procedure (cf. Jenkins & Larson, 1979; Rose, McEntire, & Dowdy, 1982), the effects generally have not been very powerful. As a result, researchers have examined how word supply might be augmented to make it more effective.

The most popular augmentation has been to combine word supply with drill; the correct response for each error is practiced following completion of the passage. In comparison to word supply, this procedure has proven to be effective in improving LD students' performance on word recognition in isolation and, to a lesser extent, in context (Jenkins & Larson, 1979; Jenkins, Larson, & Fleisher, 1983; O'Shea, Munson, & O'Shea, 1984; Rosenberg, 1986). The procedure, however, has only a small or marginal effect on comprehension (Fleisher & Jenkins, 1983; Jenkins et al., 1983). Other attempts to improve on word supply have included rereading the sentence after an error correction, reviewing all corrected errors at the end of the page, or telling the student the word meaning as part of the correction procedure. Each of these turned out to be only slightly better than word supply in improving LD students' word recognition performance (Jenkins & Larson, 1979).

Researchers also have tried to improve the word supply plus drill procedure. Fleisher and Jenkins (1983) found that supplementing word supply plus drill with comprehension questions at the end of each page did not result in an incremental improvement in LD students' reading. Rosenberg (1986) reported that modifying the drill procedure to phonics practice (sounding out) of the missed word did not result in improved oral reading behavior. In contrast, O'Shea et al. (1984) indicated that practicing the missed word within the context of the phrase in which it appeared was more successful in improving contextual reading than was flashcard practice.

Frequent teacher interruptions during oral reading may be counter-productive to the goal of self-reliant reading (Shake, 1986). They may interrupt the reader's line of thought and perpetuate an over-reliance on the teacher. We, therefore, recommend that teachers' corrections center primarily on miscues that disrupt meaning.

Inserting Questions into Text

Inserting questions into text provides a mechanism for directing students' attention to specific information and may promote retention of important information. In a study by Wong (1979), LD students were asked a single question just prior to reading each paragraph in a story. Students who were asked questions recalled more of the story than students who were not given questions.

In another study by Wong (1980), questions were inserted immediately after specific text material. Because the questions resulted in improved comprehension, they may have acted as prompts to remind LD students to apply constructive processing strategies.

Asking Post-Comprehension Questions

Asking students comprehension questions immediately following reading and encouraging them to "look back" in the text to locate the correct answers to missed questions constitute a common practice. Davey (1987), for example, asked poor readers to answer post-passage questions under two conditions: text-lookbacks allowed and not allowed. Poor readers were able to correctly answer more questions requiring a written response when lookbacks were permitted; lookbacks did not affect their performance on multiple-choice questions.

Promoting Text Summarization

Summarizing text consistently has been shown to result in improved recall of written content (Pressley, Johnson, Symons, McGoldrick, & Kurita, in press), even when students are directed to use very simple forms of summarization. For instance, Jenkins, Heliotis, Haynes, and Beck (1986) inserted a lined space after each paragraph of a story and directed LD students to write a brief sentence summarizing each paragraph after reading it. The restatement condition resulted in superior comprehension performance in comparison to two control conditions.

Focusing Students' Attention on Text Structure

Reading material such as conventional stories often share a general structure (Graham, Harris, & Sawyer, 1987). Idol (1987b; Idol & Croll, 1987) has investigated using text structure to improve LD students' comprehension. She had LD students complete a chart during or after reading, or both; the chart contained boxes for information on the setting, problem, goal, action, and outcome of the story. Use of the chart resulted in improved comprehension, and the students appeared to have internalized some components of the mapping procedure because most of them maintained acceptable levels of comprehension after the chart was discontinued.

Focusing Students' Attention on Important Information Using Charts or Graphics
Idol (1987a) also investigated the use of a mapping procedure with content area material. High school students who were poor readers were taught to complete a chart designed to accompany a history text; the chart contained boxes for information on important events, main ideas of the lesson, other viewpoints/opinions, reader's conclusion, and relevance to today. Use of the chart resulted in improved performance on the content material, and these gains generally were maintained once the chart no longer was used.

Bergerud et al. (1988) examined the use of graphics to improve LD students' retention of information in science text. The graphs contained a diagram (e.g., the heart) with blanks for important information (size, location, etc.). Students read the content passage, completed the graph, and discussed the answers with the teacher. In comparison to self-study or the use of a study guide, graphics resulted in greater content retention.

Circumventing Process Demands

At the secondary level, reading is primarily a tool for acquiring content area information. Although many LD students have the cognitive capability to understand the information presented in secondary text, their poor reading skills often make this task difficult (Deshler & Graham, 1980). An instructional alternative is to use teacher-directed activities designed to circumvent the processing demands inherent in reading. Alternatives include rewriting texts so that they are simpler, tape-recording textual material, or presenting text through the use of charts or other adaptations. The last two procedures have been investigated with LD students.

For chapter-length materials, verbatim text recordings used with or without the accompanying text do not appear to significantly affect LD adolescents' learning of chapter content (Schumaker, Deshler, & Denton, 1984; Torgesen, Dahlem, & Greenstein, 1987). Combining text recording with text study procedures, however, appears to be effective. Torgesen et al. (1987) found that coupling a verbatim recording and a highlighted text with a worksheet containing content questions resulted in improved performance. In addition, Schumaker et al. (1984) reported that verbatim text recording coupled with a highlighted text, worksheet activities, and the learning of a specific study strategy improved scores on chapter tests.

Finally, Darch and Carnine (1986) examined the effects of presenting information contained in content area text via visual spatial displays. The displays were designed so that relationships of content in the chapters could be presented visually with pictures and words. The display was first presented on an overhead projector, and the teacher described the ideas on the display and their interrelationships. Next students reviewed the material while working in small cooperative groups. In comparison to traditional instruction, the use of visual spatial displays resulted in greater learning of content.

IMPROVING STUDENTS' READING BEHAVIORS

Teacher activities just prior, during, or immediately after reading are designed to assist the student in reading and comprehending assigned materials. Such external provisions often produce immediate effects, but they are analogous to a "heart pacer" in that the teacher's manipulation does some or even most of the work for the student (cf. Graham, 1985). This is not meant to imply that the act of reading alone or in combination with such provisions does not result in new learning; reading and the effects of the external provisions of the lesson result in acquisition of new information and skills, as demonstrated by the studies reviewed in previous sections. Nevertheless, teachers of LD students often have to take a more direct course of action to change existing reading behaviors into more preferred ones. This involves altering students' entry behaviors so that their reading skills progressively improve and they become less reliant on teacher manipulations. Current research has concentrated primarily on improving LD students' basic reading skills and their strategic reading behaviors.

Reading Skills

Guthrie and Tyler (1978) recommend that instruction for poor readers should be directed at simultaneously improving as many deficient cognitive processes (as defined by underdeveloped skills) as necessary for reading to improve. As a group, LD students have difficulty with a wide variety of reading skills, including word recognition and decoding (cf. Manis, 1985), as well as comprehension (Hansen, 1978). We further agree with Guthrie and Tyler's recommendation that reading skills be taught directly and that sufficient instructional time be allocated for their mastery.

Word Recognition Instruction

Word recognition is a central and recurring part of reading. If students do not learn to recognize quickly and effortlessly the vast majority of words they will encounter in reading, comprehension processes are at risk (Perfetti, 1986). Probably the most common means by which LD teachers have tried to bolster students' word recognition skills is by improving their sight vocabulary. Research with LD students has primarily examined the effectiveness of procedures for teaching sight vocabulary presented in a list format. One of the more relevant findings is that instructional effectiveness can be increased through a judicious combination of teaching procedures.

For instance, Thorpe and Borden (1985), reported that the addition of either praise or letter tracing improved the effectiveness of a word study procedure that involved saying the word, sounding it out, and saying it again. Other researchers have indicated that learning of words can be facilitated through the use of games such as Bingo (Kirby, Holborn, & Bushby, 1981) or by pairing the target word with a picture (Jorm, 1977; Knowlton,

1980). The use of pictures may be advisable, however, only when used with high imagery words (cf. Jorm, 1977) or faded over trials (cf. Knowlton, 1980). Finally, Freeman and McLaughlin (1984) found that reading target words while listening to them on a tape recorder (presented at 80 words per minute) decreased LD students' word errors and increased correct rate of responding.

It is surprising that researchers have not placed more emphasis on having LD students apply sight word skills in context. Allington (1978) reported that the errors poor readers make in isolation are not predictive of errors they make in context, and vice versa. A study that did follow sight word training in isolation with contextual practice was conducted by Bryant, Fayne, and Gettinger (1982). They had LD students master small sets of words using flashcard training coupled with practice in discriminating the target words from similar nonsense words. The target words then were practiced in phrases, sentences, and stories. The procedures improved students' skills in recognizing words in isolation; unfortunately, performance in context was not examined.

Future research should examine what sight words should be taught to LD students. Frequency, meaningfulness, concreteness, and phonetic regularity represent some of the viable attributes in selecting words to be learned. Furthermore, more attention should be devoted to developing automaticity, particularly in applying new sight words in context.

Other procedures for improving word recognition skills include: (a) instruction in the use of the reading context as an aid in recognizing and determining the meaning of unknown words, and (b) repeated readings of passages as a means for reducing word recognition errors and promoting fluency. Dahl (1979) reported that poor readers who received training in the use of context or repeated reading practice read with greater word recognition and fluency than students who received flashcard instruction on sight words. Moreover, incremental effects were obtained by providing students with both types of training. Rashotte and Torgesen (1985) have sounded a note of caution regarding repeated reading practice, however. They found that repeated reading was no more effective than nonrepetitive reading if the passages used in repeated reading shared few words in common.

Decoding Instruction

An important goal for reading instruction is to help students develop a flexible and efficient decoding process. In addition to being able to recognize common words without effort, readers need a solid backup system for decoding words that are unknown (Perfetti, 1986). Although good readers often acquire decoding skills through exposure to printed words, poor readers are not as adept in discovering, without direct instruction, how our language works (Gaskins et al., 1988). Poor readers need to learn about alphabetic principles, specific orthographic patterns of the writing system, and specific mapping of print to speech; "this conclusion has been reached many times by thoughtful researchers in reading instruction" (Perfetti, 1986, p. 19).

One approach that researchers have used to improve LD students' decoding skills is to teach essential components of the decoding process. Bradley and Bryant (1985) found that training in phonological awareness resulted in improved reading achievement for young children with low categorization test scores. Instruction that involved arranging pictures of words according to their shared sound characteristics (beginning, middle, or ending sounds) plus forming words using plastic letters was particularly effective. Fayne and Bryant (1981) reported that direct instruction on a decoding strategy that emphasized clustering and blending the first two letters (CV) with the final letter (C) was more effective than several other alternative strategies, including letter-by-letter decoding. Henderson and Shores (1982) noted that training LD students to attend to suffixes while reading orally resulted in improved comprehension and reading fluency.

Other researchers have developed and field-tested instructional programs designed to teach a variety of decoding skills. Williams (1980) developed a program that provides instruction in syllabication, phoneme analyses and blending, letter-sound correspondences, and decoding various spelling patterns (CVC, CVCC, etc.). In addition, skills to be mastered initially were presented in context, and students were provided opportunities following instruction to apply target skills in context. LD students who participated in this program evidenced improvements in decoding skills and strategies.

A final decoding program that merits attention was developed at Benchmark School (Gaskins et al., 1988). It includes daily lessons that supplement the students' basal reading program. Decoding skills are taught using explicit modeling, and lessons are fast-paced and game-like. Students are informed why each targeted skill is important, how to do it, and when to use it. Preliminary results indicate that the program improves decoding performance.

Vocabulary Instruction

Students' vocabulary knowledge and their reading comprehension have a strong relationship (Pany & Jenkins, 1978). As a result, many educators have promoted the systematic and extensive development of students' vocabulary in the belief that such growth will have a reciprocal effect on reading comprehension (Pany et al., 1982). Surprisingly, few investigations on vocabulary instruction have been done with LD students. A notable exception is Mastropieri, Scruggs, and Levin's (1985) research. They have taught both general and specialized vocabulary to LD students using a mnemonic technique, the *keyword* method. To illustrate, a student is taught a keyword (doll) for a target word (dahlia—a flower) and then shown a picture depicting the keyword interacting with its corresponding meaning (doll sniffing a flower). The student is instructed to use the keyword and the picture to think of the meaning of the vocabulary item.

Although vocabulary instruction using the keyword method has proven to be effective for learning word meanings (cf. Condus, Marshall, & Miller, 1986; Mastropieri et al., 1985), questions regarding its acceptability remain. Developing keywords and interactive pictures is time-consuming, possibly precluding widespread use by teachers. These roadblocks can be bridged by having students develop the interactive pictures (Mastropieri, Scruggs, Levin, Gaffney, & McLoone, 1985) or through marketing commercial materials using this methodology.

To conclude this discussion of vocabulary instruction, reiterating some general recommendations of McKeown and Beck (1988) may be helpful. Effective teaching of vocabulary involves both definitional and contextual information, high frequency of encounters with each word, multiple exposures to target words in different contexts, and encouraging students to extend their use of new words outside the classroom. McKeown and Beck further recommend that a vocabulary program include the following two components: (1) introduction to a lot of words simply by establishing an association to a definition or synonym, and (2) rich instruction, as described previously, on a smaller set of words (e.g., words important to central ideas in a basal reader).

Comprehension Instruction
Another means for improving LD students' reading is to provide comprehension instruction. Only a few studies have provided comprehension training, but results from these investigations have been encouraging. White, Pascarella, and Pflaum (1981) improved LD students' reading comprehension by providing practice in arranging word cards into sentences. Students learned to construct sentences by first locating the sentence verb and then using a series of questions (who, what, when, where, why, and how) as cues for grouping other words around the verb. Students also noted if each unit was included, complete, and made sense. Williams (1986) tested an instructional program that trained identification of the general topic, the specific topic, and anomalous sentences in short paragraphs. Training resulted in improved performance on main idea comprehension. Finally, Darch and Kameenui (1987) found that direct instruction in using specific rules and strategies to detect instances of faulty arguments improved LD students' critical reading skills.

Strategic Reading Behaviors

Personal qualities such as attitudes and the strategies students use to learn can be altered so they exert a positive influence on performance (Graham, 1985). As Pressley et al. (in press) noted, reading performance can be improved by teaching students to independently use strategies involving summarization, mental imagery, self-questioning, question answering, and so forth. LD students appear to be prime candidates for strategy instruction, as their strategic reading behavior appears to be inefficient and inflexible (Wong, 1982).

Various self-questioning strategies have been found to be effective in improving LD students' reading comprehension:

- Stopping while reading to check to see if the material being read is understood (Graves, 1986)
- Generating several questions to ask an imaginary friend after reading the assigned text (Chan & Cole, 1986)
- Asking and answering "WH" questions (who, what, when, where, why) while reading; the student marks each answer so that the type of question asked is identified (Clark, Deshler, Schumaker, Alley, & Warner, 1984)

- Asking and answering questions related to the schematic structure of the text; e.g., "What does the main character want to do?" (Carnine & Kinder, 1985; Short & Ryan, 1984)
- Reading a question at the end of the passage, formulating a tentative answer, and confirming the answer based on text information (Holmes, 1985)
- Clarifying the purpose for reading, asking and answering questions about main ideas, and successively collating answers to new questions with answers to previous questions (Wong & Jones, 1982)

Other strategies that have been helpful in improving LD students' reading comprehension include *summarizing* (Jenkins, Heliotis, Stein, & Haynes, 1987; Rose, Cundick, & Higbee, 1983) and *visual imagery* (Rose et al., 1983; Clark et al., 1984). To illustrate, Jenkins et al. taught LD students to summarize by answering two questions: Who? and What's happening? Training resulted in an increase in the number of comprehension questions answered correctly. Similarly, Clark et al. (1984) found that training LD students to form and evaluate visual images for successive sentences resulted in improved performance in answering comprehension questions. Finally, Carnine and Kinder (1985) noted that summarizing and visual imagery can be used together; making and describing successive visual images of the reading material followed by summarizing the entire passage resulted in improved comprehension.

LD students' performance on both basal and content area materials has been improved by teaching them specific study strategies. Alexander (1985) found that teaching LD students a modified version of the SQ3R technique resulted in improved recall. Similar results with a particularly complex modification of the SQ3R procedures were noted by Schumaker, Deshler, Alley, Warner, and Denton (1982). Chan and Cole (1986) reported that comprehension performance was improved by using the traditional study strategy of underlining; students underlined interesting words after reading the passage. In a seminal investigation by Palinscar and Brown (1984), LD adolescents' performance in content area materials improved following training in four study activities: summarization, questioning, clarifying, and predicting.

A final strategy that we would like to highlight was developed by Pflaum and Pascarella (1980). They taught LD students rules for self-correcting their oral reading errors. When self-correcting, students learned to first focus on context cues and then graphic cues, and to ask if the correction helped the sentence make sense. Training in the strategy resulted in positive changes in reading behaviors, especially for students reading at second-grade level or higher.

Though the use of strategy training to improve LD students' reading has been promising, questions regarding generalization and maintenance remain. Researchers also should direct more attention to validation of instructional manipulations, confirmation of mediating responses, establishment of social validity, and efficacy of various treatment components. With regard to the latter, multicomponent instructional methods for teaching strategic behaviors have been described by Graham et al. (1987) and Palinscar and Brown (1984).

IMPACT OF PEERS ON PUPIL PURSUITS

LD students' immediate peers and other students often represent an untapped resource that can be used to affect pupil pursuits during reading. Peers can be trained to fulfill a variety of roles. These include administering prereading activities, providing assistance during and after reading, and teaching basic reading skills.

In terms of prereading activities, Salend and Nowak (1988) investigated the effects of having an LD student who was a more proficient reader orally preview a passage with an LD student who was a less proficient reader. While the previewer read a passage aloud, the other student listened and followed along using a photocopy of the passage. In comparison to silent previewing, peer-previewing resulted in a marked decrease in the number of oral reading errors committed by less proficient LD readers.

Peers also have been trained to provide assistance to LD students as they read. This generally has involved providing reinforcement for correct reading, feedback on the type of error that has occurred, correction of the error, practice reading the miscue successfully, or some combination of those (Jenkins, Mayhall, Peschka, & Jenkins, 1974; Sindelar, 1982; Trovato & Bucher, 1980; Willis, Morris, & Crowder, 1972). Usually, such procedures have had a positive impact on LD students' oral reading.

An interesting study was conducted by Fleisher and Jenkins (1978). Prior to reading, cross-age tutors had LD students practice isolated letter sounds followed by isolated practice of unknown words from the target reading material. Word practice consisted of the tutor directing the LD child to sound out the unknown word. When necessary, the tutor modeled the sounding-out procedure and had the tutee repeat the word. The prereading activities were followed by having the LD student orally read the target passage to the tutor. If the student made an error, the sounding-out and modeling procedure was used. The peer-directed activities resulted in an increase in the number of words read correctly in both isolation and context.

Research also has examined using tutors to teach specific reading skills. Most of this instruction has involved learning common reading words via flashcard instruction (Jenkins et al., 1974; Sindelar, 1982). Overall, the use of peers to teach sight vocabulary has yielded positive effects (Chiang, Thorpe, & Darch, 1980; Epstein, 1978; Jenkins et al., 1974).

A study of final interest was conducted by Sindelar (1982). Normal students taught LD students how to successfully predict upcoming words in both spoken and written context. Tutoring in word prediction was more successful in promoting comprehension than was having peers teach sight vocabulary. Also, tutors were as successful as teachers in administering training.

Prior to concluding this section, three caveats are in order. First, successful tutoring requires well trained tutors and close monitoring of the process. Second, we believe that tutors can learn to teach specific reading strategies to LD students. For example, in a study by Miller, Miller, and Rosen (1988), a modified form of reciprocal teaching was implemented in which "normal" students initially acted as the "teacher" to explain and model a variety of comprehension strategies. Third, cooperative learning arrangements represent a potentially powerful mechanism for having peers assist LD students during reading activities (see Slavin, Stevens, & Madden, 1988).

FAMILY IMPACT ON PUPIL PURSUITS

A student's family can have a powerful impact on a child's performance in school (Graue, Weinstein, & Walberg, 1983). Although extensive research examining the effect of the family on LD students' reading is lacking, some evidence suggests that parents can successfully deliver instruction and also can serve to reinforce their child's performance on school tasks. In terms of instruction, Gang and Poche (1982) taught parents of poor readers how to teach sounding and blending skills to their child when using a commercial reading program. Following 5 hours of group training, the parents were able to successfully apply the instructional procedures, and the instruction had a positive impact on reading performance.

With regard to delivering reinforcement, Trovato and Bucher (1980) asked parents to help select reinforcers and then administer reinforcement contingent on their child's performance during peer tutoring. Although both reading accuracy and comprehension were significantly increased by peer tutoring, home-based reinforcement doubled the observed increases.

In addition to administering reinforcement and teaching basic skills, a variety of parent-directed activities should have a positive impact on the LD child. These include reading together, modeling desirable reading behaviors, and monitoring (assisting when necessary) in the completion of homework.

CONCLUDING COMMENTS

The last 10 years have witnessed a substantial increase in instructional reading research conducted with LD students. Nonetheless, the current research base provides a somewhat narrow and tentative foundation for drawing instructional recommendations. We hope that the next decade will see an increase in research with LD students on promoting a positive attitude and the desire to read, developing effective and efficient systems for decoding, improving performance in content area materials, facilitating generalization and maintenance of learned skills and strategies, and examining what is internalized as a result of reading instruction

REFERENCES

Alexander, D.F. (1985). The effect of study skill training on learning disabled students' retelling of expository material. *Journal of Applied Behavior Analysis, 18,* 263–267.

Allington, R.L. (1978). Word identification abilities of severely disabled readers: A comparison in isolation and context. *Journal of Reading Behavior, 10,* 409–416.

Anders, P.L., Bos, C.S., & Filip, D. (1984). Effect of semantic feature analysis on the reading comprehension of learning-disabled students. In J. Niles (Ed.), *Changing perspectives on research in reading/language processing and instruction* (33rd yearbook of the National Reading Conference) (pp. 162–166). Rochester, NY: National Reading Conference.

Armstrong, S.W. (1983). The effects of material difficulty upon learning disabled children's oral reading and reading comprehension. *Learning Disability Quarterly, 6,* 339–348.

Bergerud, D., Lovitt, T.C., & Horton, S. (1988). The effectiveness of textbook adaptations in life sciences for high school students with learning disabilities. *Journal of Learning Disabilities, 21,* 70–76.

Bos, C.S., Anders, P.L., Filip, D., & Jaffee, L.E. (1985). Semantic feature analysis and long-term learning. In J. Niles (Ed.), *Issues in literacy: A research perspective* (34th yearbook of the National Reading Conference) (pp. 42–47). Rochester, NY: National Reading Conference.

Bradley, L., & Bryant, P. (1985). *Rhyme and reason in reading and spelling.* Ann Arbor: University of Michigan Press.

Bryant, N.D., Fayne, H.R., & Gettinger, M. (1982). Applying the mastery learning model to sight word instruction for disabled readers. *Journal of Experimental Education, 51,* 116–121.

Carnine, D., & Kinder, D. (1985). Teaching low-performing students to apply generative and schema strategies to narrative and expository material. *Remedial & Special Education, 6,* 20–30.

Chan, L.K.S., & Cole, P.G. (1986). The effects of comprehension monitoring training on the reading competence of learning disabled and regular class students. *Remedial & Special Education, 7,* 33–40.

Chiang, B., Thorpe, H.W., & Darch, C.B. (1980). Effects of cross-age tutoring on word-recognition performance of learning disabled students. *Learning Disability Quarterly, 3,* 11–19.

Clark, F.L., Deshler, D.D., Schumaker, J.B., Alley, G.R., & Warner, M.M. (1984). Visual imagery and self-questioning strategies to improve comprehension of written material. *Journal of Learning Disabilities, 17,* 145–149.

Condus, M.M., Marshall, K.J., & Miller, S.R. (1986). Effects of the keyword mnemonic strategy on vocabulary acquisition and maintenance by learning disabled children. *Journal of Learning Disabilities, 19,* 609–613.

Dahl, P.R. (1979). An experimental program for teaching high speed word recognition and comprehension skills. In J. Button, T. Lovitt, & T. Rowland (Eds.), *Communications research in learning disabilities and mental retardations* (pp. 33–65). Baltimore: University Park Press.

Darch, C., & Carnine, D. (1986). Teaching content area material to learning disabled students. *Exceptional Children, 53,* 240–246.

Darch, C., & Gersten, R. (1986). Direction-setting activities in reading comprehension: A comparison of two approaches. *Learning Disability Quarterly, 9,* 235–243.

Darch, C., & Kameenui, E.J. (1987). Teaching LD students critical reading skills: A systematic replication. *Learning Disability Quarterly, 10,* 82–91.

Davey, B. (1987). Postpassage questions: Task and reader effects on comprehension and metacomprehension processes. *Journal of Reading Behavior, 19,* 261–282.

Deshler, D.D., & Graham, S. (1980). Tape recording educational materials for secondary handicapped students. *Teaching Exceptional Children, 12,* 52–54

Epstein, L. (1978). The effects of intraclass peer tutoring on the vocabulary development of learning disabled children. *Journal of Learning Disabilities, 11,* 63–66.

Fayne, H.R., & Bryant, N.D. (1981). Relative effects of various word synthesis strategies on the phonics achievement of learning disabled youngsters. *Journal of Educational Psychology, 73,* 616–623.

Fleisher, L.S., & Jenkins, J.R. (1978). Effects of contextualized and decontextualized practice conditions on word recognition. *Learning Disability Quarterly, 1,* 39–47.

Fleisher, L.S., & Jenkins, J.R.(1983).The effect of word-and comprehension-emphasis instruction on reading performance. *Learning Disability Quarterly, 6,* 146–154.

Freeman, T.J., & McLaughlin, T.F. (1984). Effects of a taped-words treatment procedure on learning disabled students' sight-word oral reading. *Learning Disability Quarterly, 7,* 49–54.

Gang, D., & Poche, C.E. (1982). An effective program to train parents as reading tutors for their children. *Education & Treatment of Children, 5,* 211–232.

Gaskins, I., Downer, M., Anderson, R., Cunningham, P., Gaskins, R., Schommer, M., & Teachers of Benchmark School. (1988). A metacognitive approach to phonics: Using what you know to decode what you don't know. *Remedial & Special Education, 9,* 36–41.

Gickling, E.E., & Armstrong, D.L. (1978). Levels of instructional difficulty as related to on-task behavior, task completion, and comprehension. *Journal of Learning Disabilities, 11,* 32–39.

Gold, J., & Fleisher, L.S. (1986). Comprehension breakdown with inductively organized text: Differences between average and disabled readers. *Remedial & Special Education, 7,* 26–32.

Graham, S. (1980). Word recognition skills of learning disabled children and average students. *Reading Psychology, 2,* 23–33.

Graham, S. (1983). Selecting reading materials for learning disabled adolescents. *Pointer, 27,* 18–21.

Graham, S. (1985). Teaching basic academic skills to learning disabled students: A model of the teaching-learning process. *Journal of Learning Disabilities, 18,* 528–534.

Graham, S., Harris, K.R., & Sawyer, R. (1987). Composition instruction with learning disabled students: Self-instructional strategy training. *Focus on Exceptional Children, 20,* 1–11

Graue, E., Weinstein, T., & Walberg, H. (1983). School-based home instruction and learning: A quantitative synthesis. *Journal of Educational Research, 76,* 351–360.

Graves, A.W. (1986). Effects of direct instruction and metacomprehension training on finding main ideas. *Learning Disabilities Research, 1,* 90–100.

Guthrie, J.T., & Tyler, S.J. (1978). Cognition and instruction of poor readers. *Journal of Reading Behaviors, 10,* 57–78.

Hansen, C. (1978). Story retelling used with average and learning disabled readers as a measure of reading comprehension. *Learning Disability Quarterly, 1,* 62–69.

Harber, J.R. (1983).The effects of illustrations on the reading performance of learning disabled and normal children. *Learning Disability Quarterly, 6,* 55–60.

Harris, K., Prellor, D., & Graham, S. (1988, April). *Acceptability of cognitive-behavioral and behavioral interventions among classroom teachers* Paper presented at 1988 American Educational Research Association Annual Meeting, New Orleans.

Henderson, A.J., & Shores, R.E. (1982). How learning disabled students' failure to attend to suffixes affects their oral reading performance. *Journal of Learning Disabilities, 15,* 178–182.

Holmes, B.C (1983). The effect of prior knowledge on the question answering of good and poor readers. *Journal of Reading Behavior, 15,* 1–18.

Holmes, B.C. (1985). The effects of a strategy and sequenced materials on the inferential comprehension of disabled readers. *Journal of Learning Disabilities, 18,* 542–546.

Idol, L. (1987a). A critical thinking map to improve content area comprehension of poor readers. *Remedial & Special Education, 8,* 28–40.

Idol, L. (1987b). Group story mapping: A comprehension strategy for both skilled and unskilled readers. *Journal of Learning Disabilities, 20,* 1 96–205.

Idol, L., & Croll, V.J. (1987). Story-mapping training as a means of improving reading comprehension. *Learning Disability Quarterly, 10,* 214–229.

Idol-Maestas, L. (1985). Getting ready to read: Guided probing for poor comprehenders. *Learning Disability Quarterly, 8,* 243–254.

Jenkins, J.R., Barksdale, A., & Clinton, L. (1978). Improving reading comprehension and oral reading: Generalization across behaviors, settings and time. *Journal of Learning Disabilities, 11,* 5–15

Jenkins, J.R., Heliotis, J., Haynes, M., & Beck, K. (1986). Does passive learning account for disabled readers' comprehension deficits in ordinary reading situations? *Learning Disability Quarterly, 9,* 69–76.

Jenkins, J.R., Heliotis, J.D., Stein, M.L., & Haynes, M.C. (1987). Improving reading comprehension by using paragraph restatements. *Exceptional Children, 54,* 54–59.

Jenkins, J.R., & Larson, K. (1979). Evaluating error-correction procedures for oral reading. *Journal of Special Education, 13,* 145–156.

Jenkins, J.R., Larson, K., & Fleisher, L. (1983). Effects of error correction on word recognition and reading comprehension. *Learning Disability Quarterly, 6,* 139–145.

Jenkins, J.R., Mayhall, W.F., Peschka, C.M., & Jenkins, L. (1974). Comparing small group and tutorial instruction in resource rooms. *Exceptional Children, 40,* 245–251.

Jorm, A.F. (1977). Effect of word imagery on reading performance as a function of reader ability. *Journal of Educational Psychology, 69,* 46–54.

Keene, S., & Davey, B. (1987). Effects of computer-presented text on LD adolescents' reading behaviors. *Learning Disability Quarterly, 10,* 283–290.

Kirby, K.C., Holborn, S.W., & Bushby, H.T. (1981). Word game Bingo: A behavioral treatment package for improving textual responding to sight words. *Journal of Applied Behavior Analysis, 14,* 317–326.

Knowlton, H.E. (1980). Effects of picture fading on two learning disabled students' sight word acquisition. *Learning Disability Quarterly, 3,* 88–96.

Leinhardt, G., Zigmond, N., & Cooley, W.W. (1981). Reading instruction and its effects. *American Educational Research Journal, 18,* 343–361.

Manis, F.R. (1985). Acquisition of word identification skills in normal and disabled readers. *Journal of Educational Psychology, 77,* 78–90.

Mastropieri, M.A., Scruggs, T.E., & Levin, J.R. (1985). Maximizing what exceptional students can learn: A review of research on the keyword method and related mnemonic techniques. *Remedial & Special Education, 6,* 39–45.

Mastropieri, M.A., Scruggs, T.E., & Levin, J.R. (1987). Learning-disabled students' memory for expository prose: Mnemonic versus nonmnemonic pictures. *American Educational Research Journal, 24,* 505–519.

Mastropieri, M.A., Scruggs, T.E., Levin, J.R., Gaffney, J., & McLoone, B. (1985). Increasing the vocabulary of learning disabled students using mnemonic instruction. *Learning Disability Quarterly, 8,* 57–63.

McCormick, S., & Hill, D.S. (1984). An analysis of the effects of two procedures for increasing disabled readers' inferencing skills. *Journal of Educational Research, 77,* 219–226.

McKeown, M., & Beck, I. (1988). Learning vocabulary: Different ways for different goals. *Remedial & Special Education, 9,* 42–52.

Miller, C., Miller, L., & Rosen, L. (1988). Modified reciprocal teaching in a regular classroom. *Journal of Experimental Education, 56,* 183–186.

O'Shea, L.J., Munson, S.M., & O'Shea, D.J. (1984). Error correction in oral reading: Evaluating the effectiveness of three procedures. *Education & Treatment of Children, 7,* 203–214.

O'Shea, L.J., & Sindelar, P.T. (1983). The effects of segmenting written discourse on the reading comprehension of low- and high-performance readers. *Reading Research Quarterly, 18,* 458–465.

O'Shea, L.J., Sindelar, P.T., & O'Shea, D.J. (1987). The effects of repeated readings and attentional cues on the reading fluency and comprehension of learning disabled readers. *Learning Disabilities Research, 2,* 103–109.

Palinscar, A.S., & Brown, A.L. (1984). Reciprocal teaching of comprehension-fostering and comprehension-monitoring activities. *Cognition & Instruction, 1,* 117–175.

Palinscar, A.S., & Brown, A.L. (1988). Teaching and practicing thinking skills to promote comprehension in the context of group problem-solving. *Remedial & Special Education, 9,* 53–59.

Pany, D., & Jenkins, J.R. (1978). Learning word meanings: A comparison of instructional procedures. *Learning Disability Quarterly 1,* 21–32.

Pany, D., Jenkins, J.R., & Schreck, J. (1982). Vocabulary instruction: Effects on word knowledge and reading comprehension. *Learning Disability Quarterly, 5,* 202–215.

Perfetti, C.A. (1986). Continuities in reading acquisition, reading skill, and reading disability. *Remedial & Special Education, 7,* 11–21.

Pflaum, S.W., & Pascarella, E.T. (1980). Interactive effects of prior reading achievement and training in context on the reading of learning-disabled children. *Reading Research Quarterly, 16,* 138–158.

Pflaum, S.W., Pascarella, E.T., Auer, C., Augustyn, L., & Boswick, M. (1982). Differential effects of four comprehension-facilitating conditions on LD and normal elementary-school readers. *Learning Disability Quarterly, 5,* 106–116.

Pressley, M., Johnson, C., Symons, S., McGoldrick, J., & Kurita, J. (in press). Reading comprehension strategies that can be taught efficiently. *Elementary School Journal*

Rashotte, C.A., & Torgesen, J.K. (1985). Repeated reading and reading fluency in learning disabled children. *Reading Research Quarterly, 20,* 180–188.

Roberts, M., & Smith, D.D. (1980). The relationship among correct and error oral reading rates and comprehension. *Learning Disability Quarterly, 3,* 54–64.

Rose, M.C., Cundick, B.P., & Higbee, K.L. (1983). Verbal rehearsal and visual imagery: Mnemonic aids for learning-disabled children. *Journal of Learning Disabilities, 16,* 352–354.

Rose, T.L. (1984). The effects of two prepractice procedures on oral reading. *Journal of Learning Disabilities, 17,* 544–548.

Rose, T.L. (1986). Effects of illustrations on reading comprehension of learning disabled students. *Journal of Learning Disabilities, 19,* 542–544.

Rose, T.L., & Beattie, J.R. (1986). Relative effects of teacher-directed and taped previewing on oral reading. *Learning Disability Quarterly, 9,* 193–199.

Rose, T.L., McEntire, E., & Dowdy, C. (1982). Effects of two error-correction procedures on oral reading. *Learning Disability Quarterly, 5,* 101–105.

Rose, T.L., & Robinson, H.H. (1984). Effects of illustrations on learning disabled students' reading performance. *Learning Disability Quarterly, 7,* 165–171.

Rose, T.L., & Sherry, L. (1984). Relative effects of two previewing procedures on LD adolescents' oral reading performance. *Learning Disability Quarterly, 7,* 39–44.

Rosenberg, M.S. (1986). Error-correction during oral reading: A comparison of three techniques. *Learning Disability Quarterly, 9,* 182–192.

Sachs, A. (1983). The effects of three prereading activities on learning disabled students' reading comprehension. *Learning Disability Quarterly, 6,* 248–251.

Sachs, A. (1984a). Accessing scripts before reading the story. *Learning Disability Quarterly, 7,* 226–228.

Sachs, A. (1984b). The effects of previewing activities on oral reading miscues. *Remedial & Special Education, 5,* 45–49.

Salend, S., & Nowak, M. (1988). Effects of peer-previewing on LD students' oral reading skills. *Learning Disability Quarterly, 11,* 47–54.

Schumaker, J.B., Deshler, D.D., Alley, G.R., Warner, M.M., & Denton, P.H. (1982). Multipass: A learning strategy for improving reading comprehension. *Learning Disability Quarterly, 5,* 295–304.

Schumaker, I.B., Deshler, D.D., & Denton, P.H. (1984). An integrated system for providing content to learning disabled adolescents using an audio-taped format. In W. Cruickshank & J. Kliebhan (Eds.), *Early adolescence to early adulthood* (pp. 79–107.) Syracuse, NY: Syracuse University Press.

Shake, M.C. (1986). Teacher interruptions during oral reading instruction: Self-monitoring as an impetus for change in corrective feedback. *Remedial & Special Education, 7,* 18–24.

Short, E.J., & Ryan, E.B. (1984). Metacognitive differences between skilled and less skilled readers: Remediating deficits through story grammar and attribution training. *Journal of Educational Psychology, 76,* 225–234.

Sindelar, P.T. (1982). The effects of cross-aged tutoring on the comprehension skills of remedial reading students. *Journal of Special Education, 16,* 199–206.

Slavin, R., Stevens, R., & Madden, N. (1988). Accommodating student diversity in reading and writing instruction: A cooperative learning approach. *Remedial & Special Education, 9,* 60–66.

Swanson, L. (1981). Modification of comprehension deficits in learning disabled children. *Learning Disability Quarterly, 4,* 189–201.

Thorpe, H.W., & Borden, K.S. (1985). The effect of multisensory instruction upon the on-task behaviors and word reading accuracy of learning disabled children. *Journal of Learning Disabilities, 18,* 279–286.

Torgesen, J.K., Dahlem, W.E., & Greenstein, J. (1987). Using verbatim text recordings to enhance reading comprehension in learning disabled adolescents. *Learning Disabilities Focus, 3,* 30–38.

Trovato, J., & Bucher, B. (1980). Peer tutoring with or without home-based reinforcement, for reading remediation. *Journal of Applied Behavior Analysis, 13,* 129–141.

White, C.V., Pascarella, E.T., & Pflaum, S.W. (1981). Effects of training in sentence construction on the comprehension of learning disabled children. *Journal of Educational Psychology, 73,* 697–704.

Williams, J.P. (1980). Teaching decoding with an emphasis on phoneme analysis and phoneme blending. *Journal of Educational Psychology, 72,* 1–15.

Williams, J.P. (1986). Teaching children to identify the main idea of expository texts. *Exceptional Children, 53,* 163–168.

Willis, J.W., Morris, B., & Crowder, J. (1972). A remedial reading technique for disabled readers that employs students as behavioral engineers. *Psychology in the Schools, 9,* 67–70.

Wong, B.Y.L. (1979). Increasing retention of main ideas through questioning strategies. *Learning Disability Quarterly, 2,* 42–47.

Wong, B.Y.L. (1980). Activating the inactive learner: Use of questions/prompts to enhance comprehension and retention of implied information in learning disabled children. *Learning Disability Quarterly, 3,* 29–37.

Wong, B.Y.L. (1982). Strategic behaviors in selecting retrieval cues in gifted, normal achieving and learning-disabled children. *Journal of Learning Disabilities, 15,* 33–37.

Wong, B.Y.L., & Jones, W. (1982). Increasing metacomprehension in learning disabled and normally achieving students through self-questioning training. *Learning Disability Quarterly, 5,* 228–239.

Wong, B.Y.L., Wong, R., & Le Mare, L. (1982). The effects of knowledge of criterion task on comprehension and recall in normal achieving and learning disabled children. *Journal of Educational Research, 76,* 119–126.

Most of the studies included in this review were conducted with students in elementary or secondary schools who had been identified as LD by the researchers or the participating school system. A few studies were included that examined the effects of specific teaching procedures with disabled readers of average intelligence; these students had not been identified as LD. Not included in this review were studies examining the effects of available commercial programs (e.g., Distar), summer school instruction, or modality/learning style adaptations. Also not included were studies investigating the effects of indirect training (e.g., problem-solving training) on reading performance. The instructional procedures reviewed were presented within the framework of a model of the teaching-learning process proposed by Graham (1985). The central tenet of this model is that academic learning is a direct result of students' activities and pursuits.

Steve Graham is a professor and LeAnn Johnson is a doctoral candidate in the Department of Special Education at the University of Maryland, College Park.

○ 16 ○

An approach originated in the Georgia mountains to improve the learning of students who had not been motivated by the traditional curriculum, this concept, conceived by Eliot Wigginton, involved the students in an education that they more or less directed with teacher participation and guidance. The books that grew out of this approach were entitled "Foxfire." Ensminger and Dangel note the similarity to some of the pedagogy that has been used in special education, including cooperative learning, and describe how the Foxfire approach can be applied to special education.

The Foxfire Pedagogy: A Confluence of Best Practices for Special Education

E. Eugene Ensminger and Harry L. Dangel

Recent follow-up studies of students with learning disabilities as well as others with mild disabilities (behavior disorders and mild mental retardation) provide evidence that instructional programs designed for these populations have been less than effective. Several studies have reported high dropout rates for students with mild disabilities (Edgar, 1987; Hasazi, Gordon, & Roe, 1985; Hasazi, Gordon, Roe, Hull, Finck, & Salembier, 1985; Wolman, Bruininks, & Thurlow, 1989; Zigmond & Thornton, 1985). The dropout studies reviewed by Wolman et al. (1989) report dropout rates for students with mild handicaps as high as 50%, and in most cases the percentage is approximately twice the rate of nondisabled comparison groups.

Edgar's (1987) study of the post-school status of students in mildly handicapped programs in Washington state and his call for rethinking the educational programs for this population have provided a stimulus for curriculum reform. Whether they graduated or dropped out, most of the students previously enrolled in special education programs were receiving less than minimum wage. If the goal is a successful transition from secondary schools to post-secondary training or the world of work, the outlook, based on these results, is not promising with the present curriculum focus and instructional delivery designs. Edgar (1987) and Zigmond (1990) both have expressed the belief that the high dropout rates and the lack of post-school success for students classified as mildly disabled provide indirect evidence of the ineffectiveness of special education and call for rethinking the curriculum, especially for services offered at the secondary level. The need for curriculum and instructional reform in special education has focused largely on the secondary level (Affleck, Edgar, Levine, & Kostering, 1990; Halpern & Benz, 1987; Millward, 1987; Polloway, Patton, Epstein, & Smith, 1989; Wolman, Bruininks, & Thurlow, 1989; Zigmond, 1990). Recently, Polloway, Patton, Smith, & Roderique (1991) have recommended that curriculum and instructional reform occur, as well, at the elementary level for students with mild mental retardation.

The curriculum and instructional reform recommendations range from rethinking curriculum content to restructuring the way in which instruction is delivered (Polloway et al. 1989; Zigmond, 1990). Clough (1988) and Millward (1987), in Great Britain, advocate rethinking curriculum development for the "low attainer" and call for an integrated, experiential approach to instruction for the "special needs" student.

Although many factors contribute to the relatively poor school outcome for students with mild disabilities, this article addresses the student perspective of schooling, current instructional practices that thwart student motivation for learning, and emerging practices that potentially make learning more connected and purposeful for students with mild disabilities. The Foxfire approach to instruction described here incorporates the recommended practices of holistic thought, cooperative learning, and student self-determination in the instructional process.

PRESENT LEARNING ENVIRONMENTS

Schools and classrooms in the United States are reported to be unexciting for regular (Goodlad, 1984; Sizer, 1984) and special (Ensminger, 1991; Steinberg, 1991) education students. Goodlad, in *A Place Called School: Prospects for the Future*, and Sizer, in *Horace's Compromise: The Dilemma of the American High School*, provide a disconcerting view of America's schools. The general themes that emerge from these observational studies is that schools don't know what they are about, students are forced to be there, students and teachers don't have much control over what is to go on in the classroom (helplessness), the schools do not have a clear purpose agreed upon by various elements of society (home, community, church, business, technology), and lack an environment that enhances motivation for learning by relating instruction to "real-world" experiences.

In recent observations of special education classes, many of the themes are consistent with those identified by Goodlad and Sizer (Ensminger, 1991; Steinberg, 1991). In an attempt to understand the educational environment provided students with learning disabilities, Ensminger visited students and teachers in 10 high schools in five school districts in the Atlanta, Georgia, metropolitan area. Most of the students were attending resource classes for students identified as mildly disabled (behavior disorders, learning disabilities, and mild mental retardation). Typically, students were assigned individual work that corresponded with courses they were taking in the mainstream classes or they were completing a required Carnegie course within the confines of the resource room. The format for instruction was a textbook or worksheets, or both. Rarely were students conversing about the material with other students or the teacher. The environment, in most instances, could be described as a "study hall," with independent assignments and limited verbal exchanges.

Whenever students were invited to share their attitudes and beliefs about school and their perceived benefits of the special program, the vast majority of their responses indicated dissatisfaction. The most frequent comment students made was "school is boring." They were not excited about being in school or with the focus of instruction. They reported not seeing any connection between what was being taught and how it applied to their lives. They did not enjoy working alone on assignments and preferred having opportunities to discuss what they were studying with other students.

Similarly, Steinberg (1991) observed that students in classes for behavior disordered students were not *permitted* to talk with classmates, as school authorities believed this would lead to disruption. Ensminger concluded, "I had anticipated from the outset that neither students nor teachers were going to be terribly enthusiastic about what was going on, but I had no idea that the general climate in the secondary programs was as negative as I found it" (p. 46). Students with mild disabilities seem to have perceptions of schooling similar to those of the regular education population (Goodlad, 1984; Sizer, 1984).

In general, students served as mildly disabled are bored with school, they find little relevance of instruction to their everyday lives, and they desire more opportunity for cooperatively sharing with others in the learning experience. In our opinion, the present skill remediation and tutorial emphasis of instruction, frequently practiced in special education programs for students with mild disabilities, seems to promote amotivated students.

Current Instructional Practices

Special education, and particularly the field of learning disabilities, has been dominated by orientations that center on reducing the learning deficits of students to hypothetical constructs. These constructs are further used as explanations for the learning deficiencies. These reductionistic orientations place major emphasis on viewing the learner as the primary source of the dysfunctional learning, and the resulting instructional approach has been to bolster the learner's performance by concentrating on improving the deficit(s) identified (see Poplin, 1988b, for an excellent review of the issues surrounding reductionistic approaches to learning disabilities). The dominant instructional approach, then, has been to focus on students' disabilities rather than abilities. Our expectations of the learner have been determined by our documented limitations of the learner, and instruction tends to follow a "fix-it" orientation. The result is instruction that concentrates on specific skills or processes devoid of content and meaningful connection to relevant experiences and interests of students. The missing ingredient in instruction is the ". . . organic connection between education and personal experience" (Dewey, 1963, p. 25).

A Shift in Orientation

The educational approach to teaching students with learning disabilities (and other students with mild disabilities) is shifting to a more *holistic/constructivist* or *cognitive approach* that emphasizes the importance of connecting learning to student experience (Poplin, 1988a; Reid, 1988; Reid & Stone, 1991; Polloway, Patton, Smith, & Roderique, 1991). In addition is recognition of the need for empowering students by involving them in planning and executing instruction (Adelman & Taylor, 1986, 1990; Cohen, 1986; Deci & Chandler, 1986; Switzky & Schultz, 1988), and the importance of making learning a more cooperative experience (Hilke, 1990; Johnson & Johnson, 1983; Lloyd, Crowley, Kohler, & Strain, 1988; Sharan & Hertz-Lazarowitz, 1980).

The Holistic/Constructivist Approach

The holistic/constructivist orientation recognizes that learning is dependent on prior learning experiences. Of great importance to holistic or experiential learning is that skill and process instruction is integrated with information that matches the student's desires, interests, and experiences (Dewey, 1963; Poplin, 1988a). Instruction that incorporates holistic practices commonly uses thematic units or projects. The integrated experience unit or project approach to instruction is not new to the field of special education. In 1935, Ingram espoused the experience unit approach for working with slow learners. Her orientation was greatly influenced by Dewey's philosophy. Kirk and Johnson (1951) summarized Ingram's criteria for effective units of work as follows:

1) The units of work should evolve from real life situations of the children and grow out of the direct interest of the children.
2) The choice of unit should depend on the child's level of development in mental, social, and physical activities.
3) The unit should develop the individual as an individual and should further group activities in participation and co-operation.
4) The unit selected should be one that develops interest of basic habits and attitudes. These should include knowledges and skills necessary in social participation.
5) The unit selected should be one that develops interest in out-of-school activities. A unit that goes beyond the classroom participation into the home and community would be superior to a unit that exits only in the classroom.
6) The unit selected should include activities which utilize the tool subjects. Teaching reading, writing, and arithmetic should be correlated with the unit whenever possible.
7) The unit should be of such a nature that it provides children with a variety of experiences. (pp. 93–94)

Others have echoed the importance of the role of prior student experience in instructional planning. In his classic volume entitled *Teaching the Slow Learner,* Featherstone (1951) made the following observation about the nature of experience:

> The content of these experiences, that is, the subject matter, must possess characteristics which enable the pupil to tie it into past experience readily; otherwise he will be unable to "respond with meaning" to ideas he encounters in books, or to any life situation he encounters for the first time. (p. 42)

More recently, Meyen (1981) has advocated instructional units as the mechanism for organizing instruction for regular and special education students alike. He has noted that for students with deficient academic skills, the integrated experience unit is highly desirable.

> The primary learner characteristics that make [integrated experience] units highly desirable relate to the capabilities of embedding the teaching of skills, concepts, and information in experiences highly *meaningful* to the learner. (p. 6)

Whatever one prefers to call it—holistic, experiential, or cognitive instruction—the emphasis is on relating the learning of skill, knowledge, and attitudes to something meaningful in the student's life. The principles of instruction espoused by Ingram (1935), Featherstone (1951), and Meyen (1981) serve as an historical reminder of the importance of the experiential learning pedagogy for students with mild disabilities.

Human Motivation Theory

As Deci and Chandler (1986) have observed, motivation involves self-determination, competence, and relatedness. Students need to have some role in the decision-making process, to have some say about what they are studying and how they can best study it.

> Self-determination as a quality of behavior should be a goal of *all* education. . . . We would like the education of all children, including LD and other special population children, to be organized by the principles that promote self-determined functioning. Such functioning would capitalize on the intrinsically motivated behavior—behavior that is organized by interest and the desire to take on new challenges—and it would also facilitate the internalization and eventual integration of external regulations that are necessary for effective functioning in the social world. (p. 589)

Students with learning disabilities, after a history of school failure, frequently develop attitudes of "helplessness" (Smith, 1990). The typical strategy is to provide extrinsic rewards to maintain task orientation (completion), which quite likely enhances dependence on others to promote engagement in learning tasks (Deci & Chandler, 1986). The student usually is not given options for either the content to be studied or the opportunity to explore strategies for learning. With a limited opportunity to engage in the learning process at the decision-making level, it is not surprising that students develop a "don't care" attitude toward school and the learning process. Even when the decision is made about placement in special education programs, the student's opinion, feelings, and preferences are not usually explored. With the student being left out of the decision-making process, ownership and responsibility for learning is greatly reduced.

Cooperative Learning

The vast majority of students engage in an instructional activity without knowing its purpose, or how what they have been assigned connects with anything in their lives, and without an opportunity for self-assessment of what might be the best way to proceed with the task assigned. Self-determination is omitted from the instructional process. It does not offer students some choice of topics to study to which their learning objectives can be tied. In the absence of meaningful content that relates to student experience and interest, skill instruction is devoid of association with application. Objectives of the "basics" should be integrated with content that is useful to the student's present life experience and needs, and the student should engage in purposeful activities decided upon jointly by other classmates and the teacher. To further the process of involvement, the student needs to share the responsibility of accomplishing learning experiences with other classmates, thus advancing the opportunity to learn from each other. A byproduct of this cooperative learning is the socialization process it fosters.

Cooperative learning involves groups of students working together, in a common effort, to assist each other in completing a learning task or project. The various cooperative learning methods have a central purpose: to facilitate individual accomplishment by having the group members assume responsibility for each other's success (Slavin, 1990). Studies of the benefits of cooperative learning have demonstrated that students engaged with others in the learning process certainly develop more positive feelings about themselves, learn to interact in social situations, and in many instances show improved achievement (Hilke, 1990; Lloyd et al., 1988). In the study of students with and without handicaps, the cooperative learning approach was found superior to the competitive or individualistic approach (Johnson & Johnson, 1983).

Although we will not debate the mainstream versus resource delivery system here, we do point out that students learn from others who have previously mastered certain skills as well as how they approach solving particular learning tasks. To acquire new skills and knowledge, most students must have an "expert" to show them the ropes. Within any grouping of individuals with learning disabilities are students who have acquired skills and knowledge that other students have not. The cooperative approach also provides moral support to group members that enhances exploration and discovery, enhancing the motivation to maintain task orientation.

The Experiential Education Movement

The confluence of orientations of the holistic/constructivist theory, human motivation theory, and cooperative learning represents three of the key components in the experiential education movement. The student's prior experience and knowledge provide the base from which subsequent learning emanates. Learning is elaborated from past instances of knowing and gracefully spirals into new knowledge and the modification of previous understandings (Dewey, 1963; Poplin, 1988a). Having the opportunity to develop one's own approach to learning by making recommendations for topics or content that reflects the interests and desires of the individuals within a group promotes ownership and responsibility for performing and achieving, thus promoting self-determination (Deci & Chandler, 1986).

Learning processes are further elaborated by students working together for a common purpose, jointly sharing the process, the negotiation, and the final product of that learning relationship (Sharan & Lazarowitz, 1980). The ever-present fear of teachers is that permitting students to work together increases the risk of misbehavior. But, when students are permitted to have a role in setting the behavior standards, to determine the content to achieve the prescribed objectives, and to arrive at procedures for demonstrating mastery of learning, student misbehavior is greatly reduced (see Adelman & Taylor, 1990, for a review of the issues surrounding school misbehavior and the implications for intrinsic motivation in the intervention process).

THE FOXFIRE APPROACH

The components of holism, self-determination, and cooperative learning are fundamental tenets of the Foxfire approach to learning. Foxfire is an experiential approach designed to empower students and teachers in the learning process. Although it was initially developed for nonhandicapped Appalachian students, it incorporates the elements of best practices emerging in the education of students with mild disabilities.

The word Foxfire in the educational and lay communities is most commonly associated with a series of publications known as the Foxfire Books. This series (nine Foxfire books were published by Doubleday between 1972 and 1986) represents a compilation of student articles that either appeared in the *Foxfire* magazine or were prepared especially for publication in the various Foxfire books. The Foxfire books became best sellers as readers were fascinated by the customs, practices, and lore of the Appalachian Mountain people. The underlying pedagogy of instruction went essentially unnoticed.

In 1966, Eliot Wigginton became a high school teacher of English in a small private school in North Georgia. The students attending this school were a mix of those living in residence and, through an agreement with the Rabun County Board of Education, those living in the community. As a new teacher, Wigginton experienced students' apathy toward the traditional academic agenda and quickly recognized the need to involve them in determining the direction of the class and how the students and teacher were together going to achieve the objectives of the English class. Wigginton's account of the trials of getting students interested in learning, his growing understanding of the principles that guide student involvement in the learning process, and the administrative roadblocks to implementation of what is now referred to as the Foxfire approach to teaching, are documented in his award-winning book, *Sometimes a Shining Moment: The Foxfire Experience* (Wigginton, 1985).

Now, 25 years later, Wigginton (1989) continues to employ the pedagogy in his own classroom and, through the Foxfire Teacher Outreach Center, is expanding the application of the Foxfire pedagogy in classrooms across the United States (see the Appendix for locations of network centers). The Foxfire pedagogy has evolved into a set of core practices and procedures being used with all ages of students (including English as a second language classes at the college level) and with special education students (with moderate retardation, learning disabilities, and behavior disorders). (See Smith, 1989, for a description of classroom projects that teachers have developed as a result of the Foxfire courses offered through the Network Centers.)

Foxfire Core Practices

The core practices guide implementation of the Foxfire experiential approach to learning. These are not viewed as "scriptural" but, rather, as points to make learning meaningful, effective, and empowering for students (Wigginton & Smith, 1990). The ultimate goal is to have

> . . . students become more thoughtful participants in their own education, [and] our goal must be to help them become increasingly able and willing to guide their own learning, fearlessly, for the rest of their lives. Through constant evaluation of experience, and examination and application of the curriculum, they approach a state of independence, of responsible behavior, and even, in the best of all worlds, of something called wisdom. (p. 9)

Although these core practices are continuing to be reevaluated and revised, 11 practices currently highlight the intent of instruction guided by the Foxfire approach. The central element of the Foxfire pedagogy is that students are involved in decision making. Unlike traditional classrooms in which the teacher directs the work students are to do, in the Foxfire classroom students and teachers work together to determine the focus of instruction. In all instances the students and teacher determine the project or unit of study, plan the steps to achieve the project, connect the required learning objectives to the experience, design procedures for evaluating their work, and target the project for an interested audience.

Core practice 1: All the work teachers and students do together must flow from student desire, student concerns.
The interests, desires, and concerns of students ground the learning in experiences that are familiar and important to their lives. This practice is supported by the holistic view that "learners learn best from experiences about which they are passionately interested and are involved" (Poplin, 1988a, p. 405). Not only are student interests and the present context of their world brought to consciousness, but they also are encouraged to act upon these interests by democratically deciding upon, as a group, the work they will do together.

Core practice 2: The role of the teacher must be that of collaborator and team leader and guide rather than boss.
Giving the students the opportunity to have a voice in determining the area of focus and voting upon the choice of a project promotes ownership and, consequently, motivation for student action (Deci & Chandler, 1986). The teacher's role is to guide, to monitor the activities the students decide to engage in, to raise questions, to point out potential problems, to seek clarification, to become a partner in the learning process, and to assist students in meeting the required objectives of the curriculum.

Core practice 3: The academic integrity of the work must be absolutely clear.
A constant ingredient in the Foxfire approach is the academic agenda or curriculum objectives specified by the state, the school system and, in the case of special education students, the students' individualized education plans (IEPs). Students need to be informed of the curriculum objectives that must be achieved in their assigned program of study,

whether in the special program or in the mainstream class. In addition to being informed of the objectives to be achieved, they are invited to connect these objectives to whatever project they are doing. Rather than teaching objectives as isolated and fragmented skills, objectives are integrated with information and experiences relevant to students' lives.

In the Foxfire approach students are given the opportunity to review the learning objectives specified for the specific subject or course of study. These objectives are typically posted in the room on a large chart (done by the students or the teacher). After selecting a project for the group to initiate, the objectives are reviewed to determine the objectives that will be covered in the project. The students then identify how they will demonstrate that they have achieved the objective through the project.

Special education teachers include the IEP objectives as a part of this process. Students become partners in planning their achievement of these state, local, and IEP objectives. This fosters the connection of what must be learned to the students' present knowledge and experience. A criticism of special education instruction has been the isolated manner in which objectives have been taught (McGill-Franzen & Allington, 1991; Poplin, 1984). The Foxfire approach permits students to use their present background of knowledge to discuss these objectives in the physical and social context in which they exist for the students—as something more than abstract statements (Reid & Stone, 1991).

Core practice 4: The work is characterized by student action rather than passive receipt of processed information.

The population of students with learning disabilities has been characterized as passive learners (Torgesen, 1977), and students with mild mental retardation frequently fail to develop strategies for organizing and categorizing what is to be learned (Cegelka & Prehm, 1982). In the absence of action or choice, the traditional interventions of teachers' simply assigning worksheets, drill, and nonmeaningful repetition of isolated, basic skill instruction probably promotes this behavior of nonactive involvement (McGill-Franzen & Allington, 1991). The Foxfire approach is characterized by active participation in the learning process. Students engage in planning and developing a chosen project, analyze the project and determine tasks to be accomplished, and assist each other in executing the project.

Core practice 5: A constant feature of the process is its emphasis on peer teaching, small-group work, and teamwork.

During the entire process, students determine what is working and what is not working. They assist each other through peer teaching when a student needs help in acquiring an essential skill or task. Jones (1991), a teacher of an elementary interrelated resource program, had a class of first- through fifth-grade students choose to create a school store. The students surveyed the student body for items they typically needed, researched the best purchase prices for the items, negotiated with the school principal for permission to operate the store and for a location, set up the bookkeeping procedures, set the time schedule for operating the store, determined who would operate the store on different days, and so on. In the process of operating the store, student responsibility changed from time to time, allowing students to learn different aspects of the operation. On one occasion, an older, more able student forgot how to list the daily receipts into the ledger. A first-grade girl with an IQ of 65 quickly responded that she remembered how to do it and proceeded to guide the older student through the process. Jones quickly realized that the labels and the numbers we sometimes use to set expectations are meaningless.

Students using this experiential, active-participant approach to learning can demonstrate their strengths and gain great pride in being involved in a cooperative enterprise. The teacher is not viewed as the primary source of knowledge, and the teamwork provides an excellent opportunity for students to assist each other in acquiring or relearning skills and knowledge.

Core practice 6: Connections between the classroom work and surrounding communities and the real world outside the classroom are clear.
The activities in which students engage should always be connected to the real-world of the community in which the student resides. The context of home, school, and other components of the community provide the context from which learning can occur. As Poplin (1988a) has noted, "What students will learn next is what they already know and what interests them." The connection of real-world events, situations, and activities is what gives us the structure on which to attach new knowledge and to relate academic and social skills, because in the absence of such connections, knowledge and skills are meaningless. The connection of classroom work to real-world practice gives meaning to what otherwise might be viewed as irrelevant, nonuseful information.

Core practice 7: There must be an audience beyond the teacher for student work.
Foxfire teachers remain constantly vigilant to the need for students to identify an audience for their work. This may be other students, parents, community leaders—some significant others with whom to share. The chosen audience they seek to impress provides a focus for the project they have set out to complete. The importance of the audience goes beyond an opportunity for students to share what has been accomplished; it also provides an opportunity for students to have their work recognized as being significant and important.

An example of the role of an audience for a project is demonstrated by a primary class of students with learning disabilities, taught by Rice (personal communication, April 25, 1991). The students decided they wanted to plan a dinner party for their parents. For several weeks the students developed menus, visited a grocery store to determine costs of various ingredients, identified the roles played by different personnel in the grocery store, wrote reports of their visits, calculated the cost of the food and supplies they would need for their dinner party, and practiced preparing and serving the food. In addition they planned entertainment and a summary report of the process they went through in planning for the dinner party.

For this group of students, the parents provided a purpose for all the work they were doing together and an opportunity to share what they had learned in the process of planning and preparing the meal, and in providing entertainment that demonstrated the new academic skills and knowledge they had acquired. The students discovered from parental reaction that the work they did together was appreciated and that the effort they had put into this activity was worthwhile. This activity provided them with the opportunity to learn new words, to write, to compute, to practice social skills, and to connect their newly acquired knowledge and skills to the real-world of life. Students were no longer failures, but successful learners. They took on a challenge and came out winners.

Core practice 8: As the year progresses, new activities should spiral gracefully out of the old, incorporating lessons learned from past experience, building on skills and understandings that can now be amplified.
As new knowledge and skills are acquired, new questions evolve, and the newly acquired skills allow students to venture into other areas of interest. The conclusion of a project is to be viewed as the starting point for a new project or topic of study. It is a time to take stock of what has been accomplished, what students can do now that they couldn't do before they started the project, and how they can use what they have learned and the new skills acquired to do something new, different, and more difficult than what they have just completed. It is an opportunity to use the recent experience as a time to self-assess their current competencies and to build new connections from past learning to the achievement of additional objectives and newly developed interests.

Core practice 9: As teachers, we must acknowledge the worth of aesthetic experience, model that attitude in our interactions with students, and resist the momentum of policies and practices that deprive students of the chance to use their imaginations.
The learning climate must be conducive to promoting exploration and discovery. The teacher has to gain students' respect by promoting trust and exhibiting a positive regard for students as capable learners (Dewey, 1963; Poplin, 1988a). Teachers need to demonstrate their appreciation of student contributions, acknowledge newly discovered skills and knowledge students demonstrate, and, along with students, celebrate the work of each student. The caution implied by this core practice is that too frequently the recognition of student accomplishment is omitted in the daily routine and pressure of the moment to move on to other activities and experiences. In the rush to cover a specified set of objectives, teachers may fail to take the time to allow students to complete work that is aesthetically satisfying or to allow them to develop more creative and ingenious ways to complete activities.

Core practice 10: Reflection—some conscious, thoughtful time to stand apart from the work itself—is an essential activity that must take place at key points throughout the work.
Both during and at the conclusion of a project, students are encouraged to reflect on the experience. This is a time when students and teacher look back over what has been accomplished and ask themselves: What went well? What would they do differently? What changes should be made in the way we organize ourselves for accomplishing the necessary tasks? This reflection allows students to cooperatively assess the effectiveness of what they have been doing together and to determine what they have learned from their

interactions in this shared experience. What new skills and knowledge have they acquired? This is a constant process that keeps students reflecting on the purpose of schooling and the content of the subject matter studied. Based upon reflection of the worth of what has been accomplished and the knowledge gained in the project, students move on to new activities and projects.

Core practice 11: The work must include unstintingly honest, ongoing evaluation for skills and content, and changes in student attitude.
Evaluation of student progress in skills, knowledge, and attitudes must be regularly monitored and "unstintingly honest." As noted, students are made aware of the instructional objectives by identifying the objectives that the chosen project can meet. In addition, students are to identify how they will demonstrate that they have achieved the objectives. In some instances, teachers may develop checklists of specific skills to be acquired and regularly (weekly) record whether the student has demonstrated the skills specified. This student record of accomplishment is kept in a folder that the student retains, providing a ready reference for student self-assessment of progress. In addition, teachers may keep a journal describing student progress, special accomplishments, and general orientation to the work the students are doing.

The core practices represent a merger of many of the best practices proposed for students with learning problems. These practices promote self-determination by having students make decisions about what they would like to study together, in the planning and execution of the chosen project, and in the process of evaluation. The principles of cooperative learning, especially the method of group investigation proposed by Sharan and Hertz-Lazarowitz (1980), are an integral part of the Foxfire core practices. The core practices emphasize the importance of holistic/constructivist thought by focusing instruction on the learner's experiential background and constructing connections from those experiences to the prescribed objectives, thus bringing meaning and purpose to those objectives (Poplin, 1988a). The interactive nature of the process places a special emphasis upon shared learning and shared responsibility for academic growth and makes learning a social experience that students can enjoy.

The Foxfire Process

A set of instructional procedures has evolved to guide implementation of the Foxfire approach. This process incorporates the core practices into a sequential series of steps that guide the teacher and students in meeting state and local objectives established for a given area of study (Wigginton, in press). The process is quite different from the traditional approach in which the teacher generates the lesson plan, activities, resources, and procedures for evaluating the outcome of instruction. In the Foxfire process students and teacher together negotiate a topic of study, select a project to complete related to the topic, plan the steps to achieve the project, identify the instructional objectives that the project can meet, and document how they will demonstrate that they have achieved the objectives through activities in the project. Table 1 gives an overview of how a teacher

STEPS TO IMPLEMENTATION OF THE FOXFIRE APPROACH
(Wigginton, Foxfire course lecture, September 27, 1989).

Step 1   Students identify characteristics of the GOOD TEACHER.

Step 2   Students identify MEMORABLE EXPERIENCES and what characterize these experiences.

Step 3   Teacher reviews the ACADEMIC AGENDA. We need to deal with this and set the expectation that this is why we are doing what we are doing, and what we are to learn from the experience. These objectives are nonnegotiable.

PRETEST on content, skills, and attitudes.

Step 4   Teacher asks: *Where* do you see this? *Why* is it important? This makes the REAL-WORLD CONNECTION. The students are to bring the need to the level of consciousness.

Step 5   Students SELECT A PROJECT that will incorporate the Where? Why? (Step 4) and objectives from the Academic Agenda (Step 3).

Step 6   Students DEVELOP THE PLAN. Who is it for? What value will the project be and for whom is it being developed? What will the project do for others?

Step 7   Students refer back to the Academic Agenda to see which OBJECTIVES will be incorporated in project.

EVALUATION: How will you (the student) prove to me (the teacher) that you are achieving the objective? (e.g., by taking a chunk of this project and getting it published).

Step 8   Teacher provides opportunities for students to REFLECT and EXTEND. What's Next? So what? We need to review the skills, understandings we have. How are we doing in terms of the specified objectives (Academic Agenda)? How can we choose something else that uses the skills we have to do something different, more intriguing, more elegant?

Source: From Eliot Wigginton, Foxfire course lecture, September 27, 1989.

might cover objectives of learning spelling words using the Foxfire model, compared to traditional teacher-centered approaches

Although the procedures used in the Foxfire methodology seem to be very different from the traditional orientation of programs for students with a learning disability, the procedures actually incorporate effective instruction practices advocated by special educators. For example, the *Research To Practice: Lesson Structure* procedures distributed by the ERIC Clearinghouse on Handicapped and Gifted Children (1987) read like a Foxfire manual. Teachers of students with mild disabilities are advised to gain the learner's attention (Foxfire steps 1-8), review relevant past learning (Foxfire steps 1, 2, and 4), communicate the goals of the lesson (Foxfire steps 3 and 7), model a skill to be learned and prompt for correct responses (Foxfire steps 6 and 7), check for mastery (Foxfire steps

TABLE 1   Comparison of Traditional and Student-Directed Spelling Lesson

Traditional Approach	Foxfire Approach
The teacher says: "Our next spelling lesson is Lesson 12 on page 49. Open your books and turn to the first activity in Lesson 12."	The teacher says: "You have decided to write a letter to your parents to invite them to see your play. What do we need to be able to do to write a letter to them?" The students discuss the elements of a letter with the teacher, who lists the skills on chart paper. One of the skills the students note is "spelling the words right." The teacher asks: "How will we decide which words to learn?"
The teacher has each student use the trace, copy, cover, write, and check method to practice the 15 words in Lesson 12.	After writing a first draft of the letter, the students, with the teacher's help, identify high-frequency words that are misspelled. The class decides on a common spelling list of four high-frequency words that would benefit everyone. Each student adds four words unique to his/her list.
Each day the teacher assigns students another activity to use in memorizing the words (e.g., teacher uses the computer to produce crossword puzzles for students, assigns them to write the words in sentences, and gives them pre- and posttests).	The teacher asks: "What is the best way to learn these words?" Again, teacher and students discuss ways to help memorize words. They decide that copying spelling words isn't helpful but that two students working together could use their classroom computer and software to develop a crossword puzzle for the common words. Other students decide to play Hangman. The students vote to accept the teacher's suggestion of writing the words in sentences.
On Friday students take their spelling test and go on to the next lesson regardless of their performance.	The students write a letter of invitation to their parents during which they spell their words from memory. The teacher assigns a spelling grade based on the percentage of target words spelled correctly.

3 and 7), and close the lesson (Foxfire step 8). Foxfire differs from traditional approaches because it packages learning into a holistic, student-centered approach, rather than into a teacher-centered focus on isolated skill deficits.

Steps 1 and 2: Characteristics of the Good Teacher and Memorable Experiences
In the Foxfire approach the first two steps entail having the students identify the characteristics of the *good teacher* and the characteristics of *memorable experiences* based on their previous school experiences. These two steps provide the teacher and student with sets of markers to be used in evaluating what the students and teacher can do together to make the planned learning experiences another *memorable experience* in their lives.

The Good Teacher and Memorable Experience exercises are done as two separate activities in groups small enough to give each student ample opportunity for individual input.

Students are asked to list what they perceive as the characteristics of a "good teacher," and a student recorder (or teacher, if necessary) records their observations. If there are multiple groups, each recorder identifies the characteristics discussed by his or her group. These characteristics are printed on a chart for later reference by the whole class.

The students' Good Teacher list provides their teacher with a connection to the teacher qualities the students admire and appreciate. This list further serves as an excellent starting point to develop a checklist for the teacher to refer to evaluate his or her effectiveness.

Different groups of students show little variation in the teacher characteristics they identify (Wigginton, 1989). Students typically indicate they want a teacher who cares about them as individuals, can be trusted, has a sense of humor, is fair, makes learning fun, and is willing to help students when they need assistance.

Good teachers:
—never embarrass their students in class.
—know their subject well.
—are excited about their subject.
—love to teach.
—treat student work seriously.
—are fair. They give you a second chance.
—don't have favorite students or pets. (p. 10)

The characteristic of trust, in particular, seems to be critical in fostering self-determination among mildly disabled students (Adelman & Taylor, 1986; Deci & Chandler, 1986), for as Poplin (1988a) notes, "Few of us learn from those whom we distrust" (p. 409). When students trust the person who guides their learning, they are free to respond, make decisions, and act upon the learning experience with confidence.

The identification of memorable experiences is a component of the Foxfire approach that develops a linkage to those moments when the experience of learning was unforgettable. The focus of this activity is to extract the components of experience that made it memorable rather than to recall specific content or skills. A sophomore in a program for students with learning disabilities systematically reviewed his 10 years of schooling by naming each teacher without recalling any moments that were memorable. He then said, "Kindergarten was the most memorable, because we got to play, eat, and take a nap" (Ensminger, 1991).

This activity typically is carried out in small groups to maximize individual participation. After students have listed memorable experiences, they decide what it was about each experience that made it memorable, why it was special. Often students' experiences are memorable because they involved the opportunity to make something or see the real thing (e.g., "We made paper from wood pulp right in our classroom"), a chance to work cooperatively with classmates (e.g., "I remember how my friends and I drew a mural about dinosaurs in fourth grade), being able to share their work with others, an audience (e.g., "We sent our letters to the soldiers in Saudi Arabia, and they wrote back"), a chance to make decisions about how they did a project (e.g., "We planned the whole menu of what we were going to eat"), and an opportunity to accept responsibility (e.g., "We called police headquarters ourselves and asked if a detective would speak to our class").

The components that made for memorable learning experiences are listed on another chart as the students name them, and this list becomes another set of markers that are referred to as the learning experience progresses. The Memorable Experiences list serves as a reminder to students of components that have fostered learning in the past, and it promotes including these experiences in future learning. Through identifying students' memorable learning experiences, the teacher gains insight into the students' learning history. Identifying students' "shining moments" also gives teachers insight into how to individualize instruction and engage students in processes that match their individual learning style—taking advantage of possible student strengths such as learning from direct experiences or collaborating with others.

Step 3: The Academic Agenda

The third step in implementing the Foxfire approach is to review the objectives (the Academic Agenda) students are to achieve. This step sets the expectation for why the students are in this class and what is to be learned from the experiences they plan. The academic agenda may include the curriculum objectives mandated by state or local guidelines, the objectives for the special program to which the student is assigned, or the IEP objectives for each student. Whatever objectives have been specified, these become nonnegotiable requirements. But the students and teacher negotiate on *how* the objectives are to be achieved. Presentation of the academic agenda is a new experience for many students as they often are unaware that curriculum objectives exist or that IEP objectives have been developed for them. These objectives should be posted on another chart, and as students begin to develop their learning experiences, the objectives are reviewed to identify those that will be achieved by the experience.

To get an idea of students' level of performance on these objectives, each student's present level of functioning should be established using informal classroom-based procedures (e.g., pretests, work samples, and observations of performance in areas outlined by objectives). Information about the present level of performance may include an evaluation of student attitudes as well as content and skill mastery levels, as shown in Figure 1. These results are made available to the students, and they serve as a baseline for students to evaluate their progress through the learning experience.

	agree	1	2	3	4	5	disagree
I enjoy writing		1	2	3	4	5	
My writing is interesting to others		1	2	3	4	5	
I write more often now		1	2	3	4	5	
My writing has improved		1	2	3	4	5	

FIGURE 1   *Self-Assessment of Student Attitudes Toward Writing*

Step 4: Real-World Connections

To further assist students in making a real-world connection with the academic agenda, they are asked to identify instances from their experience in which they have seen the skill or content that is specified in the objective. The students should be guided to identify why this specific skill or knowledge is important. This is the phase of the implementation process that makes the objectives meaningful and purposeful and thus provides a connection between the academic agenda and the student's prior knowledge. As students identify where they have seen the objectives in real-life and why the objectives are important, these observations are recorded as a source of ideas to be used to generate projects that would address the objectives of the Academic Agenda. As in previous steps, the information the students provide should be placed on chart paper or overhead transparencies for later reference, as in Figure 2.

Step 5: Choosing a Project

After making the connections with previous memorable learning experiences and the learning objectives that must be achieved, the students identify the project on which they will work. Starting with the ideas generated when linking their objectives to the real-world examples of those objectives (Step 4), the students and the teacher brainstorm possible topics and projects of interest. As in previous steps, individual student contributions are valued and recorded as potential topics or projects to be explored. As in all aspects of the process, the teacher may contribute his or her ideas as well.

This part of the process usually takes some time because the class should explore all possibilities, and each student's contributions should be respectfully considered. Following the enumeration of possibilities, the students discuss the value of the proposed projects, who will be the recipients of the developed project and what it will do for them, and how it captures the elements from the memorable moments list. The students progressively narrow the possible list until one project or topic receives a majority vote.

For example, a teacher of a cross-categorical special education resource class in Georgia, in her first application of the Foxfire approach, told her fourth- and fifth-grade stu-

---

Objective: Use descriptive words and elaborative language

Where is this found?

Commercials use descriptive words, like a juicy hamburger

Talking about an exciting football game

Trying to convince your mother that a teacher was unfair

Telling about a movie or video that you liked—or the name of a movie

Making a story more interesting

Writing a good song

When you're trying to be interesting

Sometimes headlines in the newspaper

FIGURE 2   *Connecting Objectives to the Real World*

dents that they could study anything of interest to them if they would agree on one topic and then read and write about it. The students suggested the following topics:

How to get rich
Rockdale County history and people
How to write on the chalkboard
How to be a professional skateboarder
How to be a model
How to build a house (Jones, 1988, p. 29)

The students selected the topic "How to build a house."

Step 6: Planning the Project

Having selected a tentative topic for the project, students develop a plan for their project. They decide what has to be done, what steps are involved in doing the project, and who will do it. Just as important, they discuss the value of doing the project, identify what impact it will have, and consider what it might do for others. At this point, the final nature of the project remains undefined as students explore the components of what they need to do.

After Ms. Jones' class decided to do a project on "How to Build a House," they listed all the people associated with building a house (Jones, 1988). After generating a long list of people and careers associated with house building, one of her students noted that there were too many people to study and not enough time to do it (approximately 5 weeks remained in the school year). The class took another vote and decided to focus on how to design a house and develop blueprints. Ms. Jones told the students that if they wanted an architect to come to the class, they would have to make the arrangements. They identified a local architect and chose a student to call him. The students were unsure about what they should ask the architect, which led to a session on developing questions to ask the architect. Armed with the classmates' questions, the designated student made the call. The architect agreed to come but indicated that certain supplies would be needed and suggested that the students also contact a firm that could make the blueprints.

With that information, another student called a local supply company to get the cost of the materials the architect specified. A third student called a blueprint company to find out the cost to have the blueprints made. After the costs had been identified, the students wrote a proposal to the Foxfire Fund. In the letter the students specified the purpose of the project, the state, local, and IEP objectives to be achieved by the project, and a budget identifying the materials they needed to purchase (about $50). When the funds were received, another student was designated to serve as the bookkeeper and keep track of what was spent. Ultimately, the students learned about designing homes from the architect, and each student had the opportunity to see his or her design made into a blueprint.

As students plan the project, they identify skills and knowledge they might need and determine how to learn them, identify various resources available to them, create teams with responsibilities to complete specific tasks, plan activities, and set deadlines. Often a project requires getting special permission from the school administration. Students, with the teacher's guidance and support, develop and present their reasons why they should receive special permission for their project.

Step 7: Doing the Project

Along with planning the project (Step 6), the students and teacher refer back to the Academic Agenda (Step 3) and identify which objectives are incorporated into the project. The objectives identified by Ms. Jones' students to be achieved by their project were:

- Use descriptive words and elaborative language.
- Spell accurately using a dictionary and other spelling aids.
- Write a simple paragraph and identify the main idea and summarize the story.
- Write creatively.
- Participate in the writing process: prewriting, writing, editing, and publishing. (Jones, 1988, p. 29)

The students achieved many more objectives than those listed above, such as telephone skills, socially appropriate interaction, confidence in speaking to adults, new vocabulary, and practical math applications. Ms. Jones also noted that the students gained in self-esteem, effective peer teaching, and interaction.

In this example, students engaged in interesting activities and were in control of planning and coordinating the elements that went into their learning experience. The students never complained about the writing they were doing or objected to the assignments (the phone calls, the proposal for the project, and so on) (Jones, 1988).

Whenever students take ownership of what they are learning, they can frequently identify skills and content they need to learn (e.g., how to introduce themselves properly on the telephone and the types of questions to ask when making a "cold" phone call). The teacher becomes a valued collaborator in helping students develop the needed content and skills. The teacher may teach mini-lessons, direct students to other authorities, or suggest other resources available in the school and community. Textbooks are employed as resources that provide desired information rather than as the curriculum to be followed obediently.

Students and the teacher also decide how mastery of the objectives is to be demonstrated within the project. Here many opportunities are available to individualize for students with disabilities. Students might keep portfolios of their daily written work (e.g., team notes, letters to parents, calculations of expenses or measurements, drawings, and so forth). Much of the documentation of skills may be in the form of pictures, audiotapes of interviews, or videotaping, all done by the students. A checklist of skills the students develop with the teacher's help is often useful (e.g., Steps in the writing process include . . .), and peer review of work offers additional corrective feedback.

The final reports of their study of the design and development of blueprints written by Ms. Jones' students, along with their individual blueprints, were displayed in the front hall of the school near the office. This allowed other students and teachers to become an audience for their work and gave students an opportunity for others to appreciate what they had learned from this experience.

The students were engaged in a meaningful experience that permitted them to see a connection between what they were required to learn, but the experience was so rich that the students were not only achieving their objectives, but they were also going beyond them. Through the various assigned activities, the writing of letters, the negotiation with the architect and the blueprint company, and the final writing of the experience of designing and developing blueprints for a house, these students demonstrated that they had mastered their objectives. Because the students were able to specify the objectives achieved and how they knew they had achieved these objectives, the objectives became a meaningful and purposeful part of the experience.

Step 8: Reflecting and Extending
To provide multiple opportunities for students to reflect on what is being accomplished and what new skills are being acquired, students are asked throughout the project to think about their progress and if what they are doing reflects their memorable moments and achieves their academic agenda. Upon completing the project, Wigginton (personal communication, September 27, 1989) expresses the question that highlights the next step: "How can we choose something else that uses the skills we have (that will permit us) to do something different, more intriguing, more elegant?" That question leads to a recycling of the steps as students once again review their Academic Agenda and proceed to select a new topic and project that spirals gracefully out of their previous project.

A group of ten 7-year-old students with learning disabilities decided to master their objective on "matching rhyming words" by making holiday cards (Rice, 1991). As they reflected on their holiday card project and learning objective, the students decided to include listening to and copying lines from poems as part of their work on rhyming words. They soon were able to differentiate the styles of Shel Silverstein, Langston Hughes, and Robert Frost.

Even with their preparation, Rice reports that their initial efforts at writing were often disappointing: "Hope you're not sneezin' This holiday season." Although the verses did rhyme, the teacher repeatedly had to ask students to reflect on the purpose of writing a holiday card and the type of message they wished to send during the holidays. As a natural extension of their work, the students decided to sell their cards, and with the profits they purchased some of the necessities, such as mittens and school supplies, needed by children at a local shelter for the homeless.

IMPLICATIONS FOR TEACHER EDUCATION IN SPECIAL EDUCATION

Preparation for teachers of students with mild disabilities who wish to employ these procedures in a holistic, intrinsically motivating approach should include an orientation of:

  —changing the instructional focus from correcting deficits to that of enhancing learners' abilities.
  —viewing learners more holistically as individuals with knowledge, experience, interests, and desires.
  —moving away from the textbook and worksheet as the major media of instruction to the use of natural, real-world tasks.

—recognizing that curriculum objectives should be taught as they relate to the student experience rather than taught in isolation.

—promoting self-determination by collaborating with students in the decision-making process, thus relinquishing teacher control of instruction.

—viewing evaluation as something that goes on continuously in the learning act rather than as a measure obtained on a teacher-made or standardized test.

The deficit model of instruction that has guided the field of special education for the past three decades has promoted fragmented learning and dependence. Research rarely centers on what students with mild disabilities do well. The instructional approaches generally have been aimed at "fixing" the identified deficit. Eligibility reports and IEPs focus primarily on information about what students cannot do. Our direction of thought must be changed from looking for deficits to thoughts of what strengths and interests the student has and capitalizing on what the student *can do*.

Teachers must be guided to understand the importance of experience and to become familiar with students' past experiences as well as present interests in the world around them. Teachers must become acquainted with the students' culture and family life and fully assess each student's present home and community activities, what the student watches on television, what activities he or she engages in with family and friends, what he or she likes to eat, and so forth. Only through a full awareness of the student's knowledge, experience, interest, and desires can teachers form a clearer understanding of what life means to the individual learner.

And life, as Whitehead (cited in Sizer, 1984) has indicated, is the only subject matter of education. The use of life experiences is what gives meaning to all that is taught, for if instruction has no meaning, no application, it is useless because it has no foundation, no building base to which the information can be attached. Instruction dominated by textbooks and worksheets makes limited connections to students' lives and experiences. Because most of the students placed in special education have not succeeded previously in the textbook orientation of the regular classroom, they typically have developed a negative image of this media for learning. The opportunity to delve into a topic of current interest to students can provide the essential content from which curriculum objectives can be achieved. The textbook certainly may serve as a reference for students and teachers, but it should not dominate the plan of instruction.

The curriculum and IEP objectives should be integrated into the instructional experiences planned by the students and teacher. By viewing objectives as components of holistic experiences, the instructional task becomes one of guiding students to recognize the essential objectives as they engage in the planned experience. To spend inordinate amounts of time teaching objectives merely for the purpose of passing a test is patently unfair to students, yet this is a frequent practice in many secondary special education programs. Objectives that are taught in isolation from familiar content and have not been practiced in some real-life experience of the student is meaningless information—never mastered, soon to be forgotten.

Student motivation is a key ingredient in the learning process. Motivation should be inspired by interest and desire, not imposed or manipulated by extrinsic schemes. Students need to be provided the opportunity to assume responsibility and to take control of planning how they will achieve the academic agenda specified, whether it be from a state or local curriculum guide or their own IEP. Learning to allow students a role in the planning process will require teachers to be trained in collaborative, cooperative learning procedures. The case studies teachers report in various issues of *Hands-On: A Journal for Teachers* frequently mention the difficulty they have in letting go of control. The teacher models we have had and the pressure to maintain quiet, orderly classrooms have done much to promote teacher-dominated classrooms. Langston (1991), a teacher of students with behavior disorders, eloquently expressed her fear of chaos before implementing a Foxfire experience in her classroom. She soon discovered that her fears were ill founded when students are given the opportunity to establish rules of behavior and the responsibility for implementing them.

Teachers not only need training in the process of collaboration with students, but they also need peer and administrative support. The Foxfire Teacher Outreach Center, through the local networks, provides a support system that keeps teachers in contact with each other to share positive experiences and to learn from negative instances as well.

Evaluation of learning is an essential component of life. Teachers will need to become more flexible and creative in identifying ways students can demonstrate their accomplishments in learning. Each of us, as well as our students, must have some measure of growth and improvement in what we know and are able to do. Appraisal of new knowledge, skills, strategies, or attitudes cannot be obtained readily by paper-and-pencil tests. Procedures for documenting student performance must be more than some end-of-unit or standardized measure that focuses more on the product of performance. Students need to be involved in identifying ways they will be able to demonstrate that they have achieved specified curriculum objectives. This involvement should include the opportunity to design procedures for evaluation, record results, and report their progress through dialogue with the teacher and significant others. A portfolio with samples of student work, journal entries, and verbal self-descriptions of what they now know that they didn't know before can be used as a method of documentation. Students can be provided checklists with a place to note progress toward meeting specific objectives. Important to the holistic, experiential approach is to have students involved in evaluating what they do, to judge how well they are doing and to identify the targets for self-improvement.

In implementing the experiential approach, teachers should start out small by selecting a single subject or content area (e.g., reading, math, science, social studies) and following the procedures during that one period of the day. Perhaps the most intriguing aspects of observing teachers before and after they have been exposed to the Foxfire pedagogy is that they become energized as much as the students. In conversations with Foxfire-trained teachers (including special education teachers), they are constantly surprised at their students' capability to plan and carry out the development of projects, amazed at how few behavior problems occur, and are revitalized about teaching. Teachers, too, become bored with the standard textbook approach to instruction.

SUMMARY

An experiential, holistic approach to instruction that embraces students as partners in the learning process has much to offer. The Foxfire approach is one way of making learning more meaningful for students and teachers. The Foxfire approach incorporates many practices that meet the unique needs of students who have academic learning difficulties. The approach emphasizes the importance of connecting learning to student knowledge and experience. It incorporates opportunities for students to focus on content that is of interest to them and to plan for the development of a project that will be of value to themselves or others. It fosters social development through group interaction and models the democratic process of group decision making. Motivation is enhanced by the value of the student-selected content and the opportunity to make decisions about how the work will be accomplished (self-determination). In documenting the achievement of curriculum objectives, the student is constantly aware of progress as well as areas in need of improvement. The student takes ownership for what he or she learns and the process for learning.

The change in orientation from a textbook, isolated objective, instructional approach to one that emphasizes student-directed, holistic learning will require changes in teacher orientation. Support will have to be provided through training programs and peer networks if teachers are to gain the confidence to venture into an experiential approach, such as Foxfire.

REFERENCES

Adelman, H. S., & Taylor, L. (1986). *An introduction to learning disabilities.* Glenview, IL: Scott, Foresman & Co.

Adelman, H. S., & Taylor, L. (1990). Intrinsic motivation and school misbehavior: Some intervention implications. *Journal of Learning Disabilities, 23*, 541–550.

Affleck, J. Q., Edgar, E., Levine, P., & Kortering, L. (1990). Postschool status of students classified as mildly mentally retarded, learning disabled, or nonhandicapped: Does it get better with time? *Education & Training in Mental Retardation, 25,* 315–324.

Cegelka, P. T. & Prehm, H. J. (1982). *Mental retardation: From categories to people.* Columbus, OH: Charles E. Merrill.

Cohen, M. W. (1986). Intrinsic motivation in the special education classroom. *Journal of Learning Disabilities, 19*, 258–261.

Clough, P. (1988). Bridging "mainstream" and "special" education: A curriculum problem. *Journal of Curriculum Studies, 20*, 327– 338.

Deci, E. L., & Chandler, C. L. (1986). The importance of motivation for the future of the LD field. *Journal of Learning Disabilities, 19*, 587–594.

Dewey, J. (1963). *Experience and education.* New York: Collier.

Edgar, E. (1987). Secondary programs in special education: Are many of them justifiable? *Exceptional Children, 53*, 555–561.

Ensminger, G. (1991). Defragmenting fragmented learners. *Hands-On: A Journal for Teachers, 39*, 44–48.

ERIC Clearinghouse on Handicapped and Gifted Children. (1987). *Research to practice: Lesson structure* (ERIC Digest No. 448). Reston, VA: Council for Exceptional Children.

Featherstone, W. B. (1951). *Teaching the slow learner* (rev.) New York: Columbia University, Teachers College, Bureau of Publications.

Goodlad, J. I. (1984). *A place called school: Prospects for the future.* New York: McGraw-Hill Book Co.

Halpern, A. S., & Benz, M. R. (1987). A statewide examination of secondary special education for students with mild disabilities: Implications for the high school curriculum. *Exceptional Children, 54*(2), 122–129.

Hasazi, S. B., Gordon, L. R., & Roe, C. A. (1985). Factors associated with the employment status of handicapped youth exiting high school from 1979 to 1983. *Exceptional Children, 51*(6), 455–469.

Hasazi, S. B., Gordon, L. R., Roe, C. A., Hull, M., Finck, K., & Salembier, G. (1985). A statewide follow-up on the post high school employment and residential status of students labeled "mentally retarded." *Education & Training of the Mentally Retarded, 20,* 222–234.

Hilke, E. V. (1990). *Cooperative learning* (Fastback 299). Bloomington, IN: Phi Delta Kappa Educational Foundation.

Ingram, C. P. (1935). *Education of the slow-learning child.* New York: Ronald Press.

Jones, S. (1988, Summer). Fourth and fifth graders make blueprints from scratch. *Hands-On: A Journal for Teachers, 32,* 28–32.

Jones, S. (1991, Spring). You're over achieving, honey. . . *Hands- On: A Journal for Teachers, 39,* 49–54.

Johnson, R. T., & Johnson, D. W. (1983). Effects of cooperative, competitive, and individualistic learning experiences on social development. *Exceptional Children, 49,* 323–329.

Kirk, S. A., & Johnson, G. O. (1951). *Educating the retarded child.* Cambridge, MA: Houghton Mifflin/Riverside Press.

Langston, S. (1991, Spring). The fear of utter chaos . . . in a student-centered classroom. *Hands-On: A Journal for Teachers, 39,* 20–23.

Lloyd, J. W., Crowley, E. P., Kohler, F. W., & Strain, P. S. (1988). Redefining the applied research agenda: Cooperative learning, prereferral, teacher consultation, and peer-modulated interventions. *Journal of Learning Disabilities, 21,* 43–52.

McGill-Franzen, A., & Allington, R. L. (1991). The gridlock of low reading achievement: Perspectives on practice and policy. *Remedial & Special Education, 12*(3), 20–30.

Meyen, E. L. (1981). *Developing instructional units: For the regular and special education teacher* (3rd ed.) Dubuque, IA: Wm. C. Brown Co.

Millward, A. J. (1987). Old wine in discredited bottles? Curriculum development for the low attainer. *Oxford Review of Education, 13,* 297–306.

Polloway, E. A., Patton J. R., Epstein, M. H., & Smith, T. E. C. (1989). Comprehensive curriculum for students with mild handicaps. *Focus on Exceptional Children, 21*(8), 1–12.

Polloway, E. A., Patton, J. R., Smith, J. D., & Roderique, T. W. (1991). Issues in program design for elementary students with mild retardation: Emphasis on curriculum development. *Education & Training in Mental Retardation, 26,* 142–150.

Poplin, M. S. (1984). Summary rationalizations, apologies and farewell: What we don't know about the learning disabled. *Learning Disability Quarterly, 7,* 130–134.

Poplin, M. S. (1988a). Holistic/constructivist principles of the teaching/learning process: Implications for the field of learning disabilities. *Journal of Learning Disabilities, 21,* 401–416.

Poplin, M. S. (1988b). The reductionistic fallacy in learning disabilities: Replicating the past by reducing the present. *Journal of Learning Disabilities, 21,* 389–400.

Reid, D. K. (1988). *Teaching the learning disabled: A cognitive developmental approach.* Boston: Allyn & Bacon.

Reid, D. K., & Stone, C. A. (1991). Why is cognitive instruction effective? Underlying learning mechanisms. *Remedial & Special Education, 12,* 8–19.

Rice, E. (1991, Spring). When you're helping the poor, you're never finished. *Hands-On: A Journal for Teachers, 39,* 27–33.

Sharan, S., & Hertz-Lazarowitz, R. (1980). A group-investigative method of cooperative learning in the classroom. In S. Sharan, O. Hare, C. Webb, & R. Hertz-Lazarowitz (eds), *Cooperation in education.* Provo, UT: Brigham Young University Press.

Sizer, T.R. (1984). *Horace's compromise: The dilemma of the American high school.* Boston: Houghton Mifflin.

Slavin, R.E. (1990). *Cooperative learning: Theory, research, and practice.* Englewood Cliffs, NJ: Prentice Hall.

Smith, C. R. (1990). *Learning disabilities: The interaction of learner, task, and setting.* Boston: Allyn & Bacon.

Smith, H. (Ed.). (1989, Fall/Winter). What we have here . . . *Hands-On: A Journal for Teachers, 33,* 16–80.

Steinberg, Z. (1991). Pandora's children. *Beyond Behavior, 2*(3), 5–14.

Switzky, H. N., & Schultz, G. F. (1988). Intrinsic motivation and learning performance: Implications for individual educational programming for learners with mild handicaps. *Remedial & Special Education, 9*(4), 7–14.

Torgesen, J. K. (1977). The role of non-specific factors in the task performance of learning disabled children: A theoretical assessment. *Journal of Learning Disabilities, 10,* 27–34.

Wigginton, E. (1985). *Sometimes a shining moment: The Foxfire experience.* Garden City, NY: Anchor Books.

Wigginton, E. (1989). Foxfire grows up. *Harvard Educational Review, 59,* 24–49.

Wigginton, E. (in press). Prologue. In E. Wigginton, (Ed.). *Handbook series.* Portsmouth, NH: Heinemann, Boynton/Cook.

Wigginton, E. & Smith, H. (Eds.). (1990, Spring/Summer). The Foxfire approach: Perspectives and core practices. *Hands-On: A Journal for Teachers, 35/36,* 9–10.

Wolman, C., Bruininks, R., & Thurlow, M. L. (1989). Dropouts and dropout programs: Implications for special education. *Remedial & Special Education, 10*(5), 6–20.

Zigmond, N. (1990). Rethinking secondary school programs for students with learning disabilities. *Focus on Exceptional Children, 23*(1), 1–22.

Zigmond, N., & Thornton, H. (1985). Follow-up of postsecondary age learning disabled graduates and dropouts. *Learning Disabilities Research, 1,* 50–55.

APPENDIX A   Foxfire Teacher Network

Foxfire Teacher Outreach Center	Hilton Smith, Director of Network	P.O. Box B Rabun Gap, GA 30568 (404) 746–5318

Network Centers	Coordinator	Address/Telephone
Bitterroot Teachers' Network	Reva Luvaas-Hess	S-22385 Cave Bay Drive Worley, ID 83876 (208) 686–1444
Bristlecone	Donald Bear	Ctr. for Learning and Literacy College of Education University of Nevada–Reno Reno, NV 89557-0029 (702) 784–4951
Cascades	Donna Halverson	Chapman School 322 SW Cornwall Sheridan, OR (503) 843-3732
Crossties Teachers' Network	Connie Zimmerman	285 Lackland Court Dunwoody, GA 30350 (404) 804-8301
East Tennessee Teachers' Network	Sharon Teets	Division of Graduate Studies C.N. Box 1860 Carson-Newman College Jefferson City, TN 37760 (615) 471–3462
Eastern Kentucky Teachers' Network	Doris Miller	P.O. Box 452 Hindman, KY 41822 (606) 785–4858

APPENDIX A (continued)

Network Centers	Coordinator	Address/Telephone
Empire State Teachers' Network	Judy Kugelmass	3233 County Road 143 Interlaken, NY 14847 (607) 387–3464
Louisville Area Foxfire Network	Dotty Turnbull	9909 Glenda Court Louisville, KY 40223 (502) 339–9050
MountainFire West Virginia Foxfire Teacher Outreach Network	Ann Payne	Curriculum & Instruction 602 Allen Hall West Virginia University Morgantown, WV 26506 (304) 293–4769
MountainLaurel	Nancy Pfau	P.O. Box 8 Princeton Ave. Emory, VA 24327 (703) 628-1895
North Carolina Teachers' Network	Barbara Duncan	80 Lakeside Drive Franklin, NC 28734 (704) 369-7439
Partnership Teachers' Network	Marylyn Wentworth	R.D. 1, Box 1920 Kennebunkport, ME 04046 (207) 967–0862
PrairieFire Teachers' Network	Diana Nichol	290 Forest Avenue Glen Ellyn, IL 60137 (708) 858-5279
Sequoia	Tim Beard	ARC 310 Eighth St., Suite 220 Oakland, CA 94607 (510) 834–9455
SoundFire (Puget Sound Education Consortium Foxfire Teachers' Network)	Gayle McKnight Cheryl McGuire	PSEC, College of Education DQ-12 University of Washington Seattle, WA 98195 (206) 543-7267
Sunfire	Melody Starling	1581 Oneco Avenue Winter Park, FL 32789 (407) 628-4937

Gene Ensminger is a professor and the coordinator of the Undergraduate Program in the Department of Special Education at Georgia State University. Harry Dangel is an associate professor and the coordinator of the Learning Disabilities Program in the Department of Special Education, also at Georgia State University.

◦ 17 ◦

Students with learning disabilities and behavior disorders generally do not achieve well in school. Two studies reported here found that most twelfth-grade students with learning disabilities achieve at only the fifth-grade level. This article reports on instructional practices and components necessary for effective instruction of students with math learning problems. The article further describes the results of field tests on the strategic math series.

Teaching Students with Learning Problems in Math

Cecil D. Mercer and Susan P. Miller

Many students with learning problems have math deficiencies that result in practical and emotional problems. Daily living requires the application of math skills, for example, planning and monitoring time, computing percentages for on-sale purchases, making estimations, interpreting recipe measurements, measuring for carpet purchases, computing scores in games, handling banking transactions, and maintaining a checkbook. In school settings, math problems often result in school failures and lead to high levels of anxiety. Bartel (1990) stated that students with math deficiencies are as disabled as individuals with reading problems.

Research suggests that the math deficiencies of students with learning problems emerge in the early years and continue throughout secondary school. Cawley and Miller (1989) reported that the mathematical knowledge of students with learning disabilities tends to progress approximately 1 year for every 2 years of school attendance. Warner, Alley, Schumaker, Deshler, and Clark (1980) found that the math progress of students with learning disabilities reaches a plateau after seventh grade. The students in their study made only 1 year's total growth during Grades 7 through 12. Both studies report that the mean math scores of students with learning disabilities in the 12th grade is high-5th-grade.

In a survey of students with learning disabilities in Grade 6 and above, McLeod and Armstrong (1982) found that two of every three students are receiving special math instruction. From his survey of resource teachers, Carpenter (1985) found that both elementary and secondary learning disabilities teachers use one third of their instructional time to teach math. The importance of providing effective instruction for students with math difficulties is apparent; however, the challenge of improving instruction for these students intensifies when one examines the reforms being considered in math education. For example, the National Council of Supervisors of Mathematics (1988) and the National Council of Teachers of Mathematics (1989) are calling for reforms in math education that endorse higher standards of math achievement. Reforms that produce higher standards are certain to frustrate teachers and students who are struggling with current standards and the traditional curriculum.

Although many students with math deficiencies exhibit characteristics that predispose them to math disabilities (e.g., problems in memory, language, reading, reasoning, and metacognition), their learning difficulties are often compounded by ineffective instruction. Many authorities (Carnine, 1991; Cawley, Fitzmaurice-Hayes, & Shaw, 1988; Cawley, Miller, & School, 1987; Kelly, Gersten, & Carnine, 1990; Scheid, 1990) believe that poor or traditional instruction is a primary cause of the math problems of many students with learning problems. Numerous studies support the position that students with math disabilities can be taught to improve their mathematical performance (Kirby & Becker, 1988; Mastropieri, Scruggs, & Shiah, 1991; Peterson, Mercer, & O'Shea, 1988; Rivera & Smith, 1988; Scheid, 1990).

Given the poor math progress of students with learning problems and the call for a reform in math education to increase standards, a need clearly exists to design an effective math curriculum for these students. Without better math instruction, these youngsters will continue to face much frustration and failure. This article reports on the results of field-testing a math instructional design that incorporates research-supported procedures for teaching basic math facts to students with learning problems.

COMPONENTS OF EFFECTIVE MATH INSTRUCTION

The amount of research on teaching math has dramatically increased in the last decade, and it is now clear that both curriculum design and teacher behavior directly influence the mathematics achievement of students with learning problems (Good & Grouws, 1979; Kameenui & Simmons, 1990; Kelly et al., 1990; Mastropieri et al., 1991; Scheid, 1990). Although much remains to be learned about teaching math, it is important for educators to examine existing research and literature to determine *what* should be taught in a math curriculum and the best practices for *how* to teach it. Only through the systematic examination and application of what is known about math instruction can educators ensure that the achievement of students with learning problems is commensurate with their potential. The components of effective math instruction are presented next.

Select Appropriate Math Content

Math educators are recommending reforms in the content of the math curriculum. Although computation remains a vital component, experts agree that obtaining answers via written work is not sufficient. The ability to think critically and understand concepts, operations, and real-life applications are important goals of a math curriculum. In 1988, the

National Council of Supervisors of Mathematics released its official statement, *Twelve Components of Essential Mathematics*. The statement includes four components that directly relate to teaching facts to students with learning problems:

1. *Problem solving.* Learning to solve problems by applying previously acquired information to new and different situations is one of the primary reasons for studying math. Problem solving involves solving verbal (text) problems as well as nonverbal problems.
2. *Communicating mathematical ideas.* Students must learn the language and notation of math. They should present math ideas via manipulative objects, drawings, writing, and speaking.
3. *Applying mathematics to everyday situations.* Students should be encouraged to translate daily experiences into mathematical representations (i.e., graphs, tables, diagrams, or math expressions) and interpret the results.
4. *Focusing on appropriate computational skills.* Students must gain proficiency in using operations (i.e., addition, subtraction, multiplication, division) with whole numbers and decimals. Knowledge of basic facts is essential, and mental arithmetic is important.

Establish Goals and Expectancies

The teacher's effort to achieve an instructional match between student and task characteristics results in goal-setting. Thus, appropriate instructional goals are based on careful assessment of a student's learning needs. Basically, goals provide the basis for instruction. Student attention and achievement improve when teachers present clear goals and precise directions (Berliner, 1982). Moreover, goals communicate teacher expectancies, which, in turn, strongly influence student achievement. In their synthesis of research on good teaching, Porter and Brophy (1988) reported that good teachers are clear about their instructional goals and communicate both their expectancies and why the specific expectancies exist. In presenting goals, effective teachers explain what the student needs to do to achieve the goal and what he or she will learn in the process (Christenson, Ysseldyke, & Thurlow, 1989).

There is growing support for the premise that teachers tend to make goals too easy for students with learning problems (Anderson & Pellicer, 1990; Clifford, 1990; Fuchs, Fuchs, & Deno, 1985). Clifford (1990) reported that students need a challenge rather than easy success, and that tasks involving moderate risk-taking provide the best level of difficulty in setting goals. She recommended that instructional environments feature error tolerance and reward for error correction. A substantial research base (Locke & Latham, 1990; Locke, Shaw, Saari, & Latham, 1981) documents the premise that difficult but attainable goals lead to higher effort and achievement than do easier goals.

Provide Systematic and Explicit Instruction

Christenson et al. (1989) discussed four elements that relate to the quality of systematic instruction. First, a demonstration–prompt–practice sequence enhances student outcomes

(Carroll, 1985; Rosenshine & Stevens, 1986). This sequence occurs within an interaction format that involves the active participation and involvement of students and active teaching and monitoring by teachers. Second, explicit instruction is important for facilitating positive academic growth. Explicitness involves highly organized, step-by-step presentations that identify the target skill, cover why the skill is important, and discuss when the skill is useful and how to apply it. Third, effective instruction enables students to understand the directions and demands of the task. It is not sufficient for teachers to assume that students understand. It is important for teachers to conduct periodic checks (especially during independent practice) to ensure that students understand directions and task demands (Good, 1983). Fourth, the systematic use of learning principles is characteristic of effective instruction. Positive student outcomes occur when attention is maintained, positive reinforcement is used, spaced and varied practice occurs, and motivation is high.

Numerous investigators (Blankenship & Lilly, 1981; Deshler, Schumaker, & Lenz, 1984; Rosenshine & Stevens, 1986) support the use of systematic instructional procedures. Rosenshine and Stevens reported that an efficient teaching process involves three steps: demonstration, guided practice with prompts and feedback, and independent practice with feedback. These steps, coupled with an advance organizer, are inherent in the validated teaching sequence developed at the University of Kansas Institute for Research in Learning Disabilities. Moreover, these procedures (i.e., demonstration and practice) are consistent with the emphasis on teaching mastery of the skill at a generalization level. Some research suggests that demonstration, modeling, and feedback enhance the acquisition and generalization of academic skills (Deshler et al., 1984).

Numerous researchers have used these steps, and variations of them, to produce excellent mathematics achievement with students who have learning problems. For example, Blankenship (1978), Sugai and Smith (1986), and Rivera and Smith (1987) used a demonstration and permanent model technique to teach computation skills to students with learning disabilities. The technique involved a step-by-step teacher demonstration with the teacher leaving the completed problem with the student for use as a permanent model. The demonstration and permanent model technique proved to be very effective with students with learning disabilities. Also, Rosenshine (1983) reported that an 80% accuracy rate during the learning of new material is an important factor in improving the performance of low-achieving students.

Teach Students to Understand Math Concepts

During the acquisition of a computational or problem-solving skill, it is essential that the student be instructed in such a way that understanding is assured. Many authorities (Reisman, 1982; Suydam & Higgins, 1977; Underhill, Uprichard, & Heddens, 1980) believe that the use of the concrete–representational–abstract (CRA) sequence is an excellent way to teach students with learning problems to understand math concepts, operations, and applications. Several research studies (Hudson, Peterson, Mercer, & McLeod, 1988; Mercer & Miller, 1991; Peterson et al., 1988) reveal that the CRA sequence is an effective way to teach math to students with learning problems. Results indicate that large numbers of formal experiences at the concrete and representational levels are not necessary for students with learning problems to understand the basic facts. In this research, within six 30-minute lessons (three concrete and three representational), students at risk for school failure and students with learning and emotional problems demonstrated an understanding of the targeted math concept and generalized their learning to abstract-level (numbers only) problems. Moreover, the students retained the targeted skills during follow-up testing.

The learning of concepts and rules is also germane to facilitating a student's understanding of math. If a student memorizes that 8 + 6 is 14 but sees 6 + 8 as a new problem to memorize, he or she needs to understand a basic concept (in this case, the commutative property of addition) to learn addition effectively. Likewise, if a student understands the inverse relationship of addition and subtraction (i.e., a + b = c; c − b = a), the learning of subtraction is facilitated. Moreover, the concept of place value is difficult for many students and deserves much teacher attention. Finally, rules such as "Any number times zero is zero" help with learning multiplication facts. Concrete and representational experiences are excellent for demonstrating concepts and rules to students.

Monitor Progress

Monitoring progress involves the teacher frequently checking on the behavior and academic work of students and making instructional adaptations based on observations, to ensure that an appropriate instructional match is being maintained. Good and Brophy (1986) noted that active, frequent monitoring is the key to student learning. Active monitoring includes checking to see if students understand the task requirements and the procedures needed to complete the task correctly. To check understanding, the teacher asks the student to demonstrate how to complete the task. When the student performs the task, the teacher is able to pinpoint errors and help the student make corrections. Because these procedures enable the teacher to catch errors prior to extensive practice, high success rates are maintained (Christenson et al., 1989). Moreover, Rieth and Evertson (1988) reported that active teacher monitoring (i.e., moving rapidly around the classroom, checking work, and engaging in substantive interactions with students) increases the on-task academic responding of students with learning problems. In a review of programs for at-risk students, Slavin and Madden (1989) reported that the most effective programs involve frequent assessment of student progress and use of the results to modify programs according to individual needs. In a review of academic monitoring procedures, Fuchs (1986) reported that when students' academic programs were systematically monitored and developed formatively over time, the students achieved an average of .7 standard deviation units higher (equivalent to 26 percentage points) than those students whose programs were not monitored systematically. The research is replete with the positive effects of monitoring the math progress of students with learning problems and giving feedback (Fuchs, 1986; Lloyd & Keller, 1989; Miller & Milam, 1987; Robinson, DePascale, & Roberts, 1989).

Provide Feedback

A significant finding of the Beginning Teacher Evaluation Study (Fisher et al., 1980) is that academic feedback is positively associated with student learning. Rieth and Evertson

(1988) noted that all major reviews of effective teaching report that feedback is among the most essential teacher behaviors for promoting positive learning outcome. In a synthesis of research on good teaching, Porter and Brophy (1988) reported that good teachers monitor students' understanding via regular, appropriate feedback. Wang (1987) reported that feedback is important to promoting the following student outcomes: (a) mastery of content and skills for further learning, (b) ability to study and learn independently, (c) ability to plan and monitor learning activities, (d) motivation for continued learning, and (e) confidence in one's ability as a learner.

Gersten, Carnine, and Woodward (1987) reported that teachers who provide immediate corrective feedback on errors produce higher student achievement. Robinson et al. (1989) found that feedback helped students with learning disabilities complete more mathematics problems and improve accuracy from 73% to 94%. Moreover, Collins, Carnine, and Gersten (1987) noted that basic and elaborate feedback significantly improved student performance on reasoning skill tasks. In a comparison of basic and elaborative feedback, they found that elaborative feedback produced the greatest skill acquisition. Kline, Schumaker, and Deshler (1991) reported that elaborative feedback routines greatly improved the efficiency of academic instruction to students with learning disabilities. Although the literature is replete with studies that document the importance of feedback, studies analyzing the behavior of general and special education teachers report low frequencies of feedback to special education students (Rieth & Evertson, 1988).

Teach to Mastery

In this discussion, *mastery learning* refers to teaching a skill to a level of automaticity, which is usually obtained when an individual continuously responds to math problems without hesitating to think about computing the answer. (Most people operate at a level of automaticity when responding to questions such as "What is your address?" or "What is 6 + 2?") Rate of responding is regarded as an effective measure of automaticity (Hasselbring, Goin, & Bransford, 1987; Kirby & Becker, 1988; Lovitt, 1989). Reaching mastery on a skill provides numerous benefits, including improved retention and ability to compute and/or solve higher level problems. Other benefits include finishing timed tests, completing homework faster, receiving higher grades, and developing positive feelings about math.

Before mastery instruction or techniques are used, it is essential that the student possess the preskills and understand the concept related to the targeted skill. Once an understanding of a skill is achieved, mastery-level instruction becomes appropriate. Independent practice is the primary instructional format used to acquire mastery. Given that practice can become boring, the teacher must put forth an effort to make practice interesting or fun. Instructional games, peer teaching, computer-assisted instruction, self-correcting materials, and reinforcement are helpful in planning practice-to-mastery activities.

In establishing mastery rate levels for individuals, it is important to consider the learner's characteristics (e.g., age, academic skill, motor ability). For most students, a rate of 40 to 60 correct digits per minute with two or fewer errors is appropriate. Once a mastery level is achieved, the teacher and student are able to move to the next level skill with appropriate preskills and more confidence.

Teach Problem Solving

Since the National Council of Teachers of Mathematics (1980) made a statement noting that problem solving should be a top priority in math instruction, it has received more attention. Although problem solving has received a decade of attention from educators, its exact nature remains ambiguous (Engelmann, Carnine, & Steely, 1991). From an inspection of 10 books and problem-solving articles about students with learning problems, 37 different descriptors of problem solving were identified (Mercer, 1992). In addition, no definitions were offered, although some authors did infer that problem solving is analogous to doing word problems. The National Council of Teachers of Mathematics (1989) described problem solving as it relates to word problems and computation problems. It seems reasonable that a problem-solving activity is needed for any task that is difficult for the student. Thus, computation and word problems could both require problem-solving procedures. For skills in which automaticity has been achieved, problem solving is probably not a necessary procedure.

Most authorities (Cawley et al., 1987; Fleischner, Nuzum, & Marzola, 1987; Kameenui & Simmons, 1990) interpret problem solving within the context of word problems. From an analysis of the literature, it is apparent that problem solving includes some unifying components; for example, the student must (a) have a mathematical knowledge base, (b) apply acquired knowledge to new and unfamiliar situations, and (c) actively engage in thinking processes. These thinking processes involve recognizing a problem, planning a procedural strategy, examining the math relationships in the problem, determining the mathematical knowledge needed to solve the problem, representing the problem graphically, generating the equation, estimating the answer, sequencing the computation steps, computing the answer, checking the answer for reasonableness, self-monitoring the entire process, and exploring alternative ways to solve the problem.

Fortunately, in spite of the complexity of the concept, the problem-solving emphasis is generating research that provides insights into how to teach students with learning problems to solve word problems (Case & Harris, 1988; Montague & Bos, 1986; Nuzum, 1983). Paralleling the emphasis on problem solving has been a focus on strategy instruction. In this instruction, a strategy is taught that helps the student engage in the appropriate steps needed to recognize and successfully solve a word problem.

Teach Generalization

Generalization refers to the performance of the targeted behavior in different, nontraining conditions (i.e., across subjects, settings, people, behaviors, and/or time) that do not involve the same events that were present in the training conditions (Stokes & Baer, 1977). Students with learning problems typically have difficulty generalizing skills. A lack of instruction aimed at teaching these students to generalize math skills has contributed to their generalization problems. Ellis, Lenz, and Sabornie (1987a, 1987b) reported that generalization must be taught throughout the instructional process. Selected instructional practices to help students generalize math skills include:

1. Develop motivation to learn. It is believed that students who desire to learn a skill or strategy are most likely to generalize it. Motivation helps students feel responsible for their own learning and helps establish the independence needed to apply the new skill in settings without teacher support.
2. Throughout the instructional process, hold periodic discussions with students about the rationale for learning the math skill and in which situations (e.g., homework, recreational activities, shopping, etc.) it is useful.
3. Throughout the instructional process, provide students with a variety of examples and experiences. For example, vary the manipulative objects (such as cubes, checkers, and buttons) in concrete activities, and use a variety of pictures, drawings, and tallies in representational activities.
4. Teach skills to a mastery level so students can concentrate on using, rather than remembering, the skill.
5. Teach students to solve problems pertinent to their daily lives. This connects the skill to functional uses and promotes motivation and the need to generalize.

Promote a Positive Attitude Toward Math

Many students with learning problems have a history of mathematics failures. Consequently, they develop negative attitudes toward math learning and feel insecure about their capabilities to succeed in math. Attitudes, beliefs, and motivation play an important role in the learning of math. The National Council of Teachers of Mathematics (1989) and the National Council of Supervisors of Mathematics (1988) stressed the need to focus on the affective side of mathematics instruction. It is apparent that math instruction must be designed to ensure success and promote positive attitudes. Selected guidelines for promoting positive attitudes toward math learning include the following:

1. Involve students in setting challenging but attainable instructional goals. Goal-setting exerts a powerful influence on student involvement and effort (Locke & Latham, 1990).
2. Provide students with success via building on prior skills and using task analysis to simplify the instructional sequence of a math skill or concept.
3. Use progress charts to provide students with feedback on how well they are doing.
4. Discuss the relevance of a math skill to real-life problems. Use word problems that are part of a student's daily life.
5. Communicate positive expectancies of students' abilities to learn. Students need to sense that the teacher believes they will achieve in math.
6. Help students understand the idea that their own effort affects outcomes regarding achievement. Constantly point out that what they do influences both their success and their failure. This helps students realize that their behavior directly influences what happens to them and, consequently, that they are in control of their own learning.

7. Model an enthusiastic and positive attitude toward math and maintain a lively pace during math instruction.
8. Reinforce students for effort on math work.

BASIC MATH FACTS AND STUDENTS WITH LEARNING PROBLEMS

Math has a logical structure. Students construct simple relationships first and then progress to more complex tasks. As the student progresses in this ordering of math tasks, the learning of skills and content transfers from each step to the next. Reisman and Kauffman (1980) discussed the progression of math learning and its relationship to cognitive factors. The abilities to form and remember associations, understand basic relationships, and make simple generalizations appear to be basic cognitive factors that are needed before formal math instruction beings (Bartel, 1990). More complex cognitive factors are needed as the student progresses from lower level math skills to higher order ones. Moreover, the mastery of such lower level skills is essential to learning higher order ones; thus, the concept of *learning readiness* is important in math instruction. In their *Twelve Components of Essential Mathematics*, the National Council of Supervisors of Mathematics (1988) highlighted the need for students to be knowledgeable about basic facts and proficient in basic operations (addition, subtraction, multiplication, division). Many authorities (Kirby & Becker, 1988; Reisman, 1982; Underhill et al., 1980) claim that failure to understand basic concepts in beginning math instruction contributes heavily to later learning problems. Unfortunately, many students with learning problems fail to achieve an understanding of basic math facts or develop fluency in using facts.

Cox (1975) conducted a study of error patterns across skill and ability levels among students with and without disabilities. She found that the average percentages of systematic errors in multiplication and division were much higher for exceptional education students compared to nondisabled students. The majority of errors for all students occurred because of a failure to understand the concepts of multiplication and division. Moreover, Cox found that without intervention, many of these youngsters persisted in making the same systematic errors for a long period of time.

In a study of multiplication and division errors committed by students with learning disabilities, Miller and Milam (1987) found that the majority of the errors were due to a lack of prerequisite skills. Errors in multiplication were primarily due to a lack of knowledge of multiplication facts and inadequate addition skills. Errors in division included many subtraction and multiplication errors. The most frequent error in division was failure to include the remainder in the quotient. Miller and Milam concluded,

> Many of the errors discovered in this study indicated a lack of student readiness for the type of task required. Students were evidently not being allowed to learn and practice the skills necessary for higher order operations. The implications are obvious: students *must* be allowed to learn in a stepwise fashion or they will not learn at all. (p. 121)

Fleischner, Garnett, and Shepherd (1982) noted that the inability to acquire and maintain math facts at fluency levels sufficient for acquiring higher level math skills is common among students with learning problems. De Corte and Verschaffel (1981) and Russell and Ginsburg (1984) reported that unfamiliarity with basic number facts plays a major role in the math difficulties of students with math learning problems. Other researchers (Garnett & Fleischner, 1983; Thornton & Toohey, 1985) report that many students with learning disabilities lack proficiency in basic number facts. They note that these youngsters are unable to retrieve answers to math facts efficiently.

As noted previously, it is anticipated that reforms in math education will increase the overall complexity of the mathematics curriculum. It is essential that general and special educators work together to ensure that students with learning problems do not become victims of instructional reforms that are insensitive to their unique learning and emotional needs. Cawley and Miller (1989) reported that students with learning disabilities are capable of making progress in math throughout the school years, and comprehensive programming is needed to ensure their math progress. Given the problems that students with learning problems exhibit with lower level math skills (many students do not know the 390 basic math facts after 5 or more years of school) and the importance of these skills in overall math achievement, it is apparent that comprehensive programming to teach basic math facts is needed.

STRATEGIC MATH SERIES: PROGRAMMING FOR TEACHING BASIC MATH FACTS

Educators who have examined the mathematical deficits of students have suggested a number of initial teaching and remediation methods. Many of these methods feature the concrete–representational–abstract teaching sequence that has been found to facilitate math learning. Implicit in this method of instruction is an emphasis on teaching students to understand the concepts of mathematics prior to memorizing facts, algorithms, and operations. Although the CRA sequence is widely advocated for mathematical learning, it is rarely used in a systematic manner during math instruction. The Strategic Math Series (SMS) (Mercer & Miller, 1991) provides a systematic means of CRA instruction.

According to the CRA sequence, instruction begins at the *concrete level*, where the student uses three-dimensional objects to solve computation problems. For example, in solving the problem 5×2, the student is instructed to look at the first number, 5, and count that many groups, using circles or paper plates to represent the groups. Next, the student is instructed to look at the second number, 2, and place that many objects in each group (i.e., circle or plate). After being instructed to count or add the number of objects in all the circles, 10, the student says and writes the answer to the problem. After successfully solving several multiplication problems at the concrete level, the student proceeds to the *representational level*.

At the representational level, drawings are used to solve computation problems. For example, in solving the problem 7×3, the student is instructed to look at the first number, 7, and draw that many groups using circles. Next, the student is instructed to look at the second number, 3, and draw three tallies in each circle. The student then counts the tallies in the circles, 21, to arrive at the answer. Finally, the student says and writes the answer to the problem. After successfully solving several multiplication problems at this level, the student begins to work at the next level, the *abstract level*.

At the abstract level, the student looks at the computation problem and tries to solve it without using objects or drawings. The student reads the problem, remembers the answer or thinks of a way to compute the answer, and writes the answer. No objects or drawings are used in the computation unless the student is unable to answer a problem. Because success in math requires the ability to solve problems at the abstract level, it is essential that students achieve mastery at this level.

The Instructional Sequence

As presented in Table 1, the instructional sequence of SMS is divided into seven phases with 21 basic lessons. Student completion of all 21 lessons is important for two reasons. First, the lessons are sequenced and build upon each other in terms of complexity. Second, although most students acquire the respective computation skill (e.g., multiplication facts) when they reach the posttest, they need additional practice to maintain their knowledge and skills, to increase their fluency, and to ensure further development of their problem-solving skills.

Phase 1: Pretest
During this instructional phase a pretest is administered to the student to determine whether instruction is needed. Before the pretest, a rationale for assessing the respective basic facts is discussed with the student. If his or her score on the pretest falls below the mastery criterion (i.e., 80%), the student is informed that he or she needs to work on the targeted basic facts. The need for instruction is discussed, and a commitment to learn is obtained from the student via a signed contract.

Phase 2: Teach Concrete Application
The concrete phase of instruction includes Lessons 1 through 3. For each lesson, a sample script and learning sheets guide the teacher through the instructional sequence. During these lessons, students manipulate concrete objects to solve basic facts on their learning sheets. (A separate curriculum manual is used for each skill area—for example,

TABLE 1   *Instructional Phases of the Strategic Math Series*

Phase	Purpose	Lessons
1	Pretest	Pretest Lesson
2	Teach concrete application	Lessons 1–3
3	Teach representational application	Lessons 4–6
4	Introduce the DRAW strategy	Lesson 7
5	Teach abstract application	Lessons 8–10
6	Posttest	Posttest Lesson
7	Provide practice to fluency	Lessons 11–21

addition, subtraction, multiplication, or division.) Students also begin to solve word problems in which the numbers are vertically aligned, but blank spaces are provided after the numbers for students to write the name of the manipulative object (see Table 2). These concrete lessons act as a springboard for learning facts at the representational and abstract levels.

Phase 3: Teach Representational Application
The representational phase of instruction includes Lessons 4 through 6. Again, a sample script and learning sheets guide the teacher through each lesson. In this phase, students use drawings and tallies to solve basic facts on their learning sheets. Moreover, they continue to solve word problems in which the numbers are vertically aligned, but now they fill in the blanks after the numbers with the name of the drawing (see Table 2). Representational lessons help students understand the respective facts as they move toward the abstract level.

Phase 4: Introduce the "DRAW" Strategy
Many students with learning difficulties are passive when faced with a problem-solving situation (i.e., they tend to guess or quit working). However, these same students can become active, independent learners when they master a problem-solving strategy to facilitate computation. Thus, Lesson 7 introduces a math strategy called DRAW to help students solve facts at the abstract level. Each letter of DRAW cues students to perform certain procedures:

1. *D*iscover the sign.
2. *R*ead the problem.
3. *A*nswer, or DRAW a conceptual representation of the problem using lines and tallies, and check.
4. *W*rite the answer.

Phase 5: Teach Abstract Application
This phase of instruction is presented in Lessons 8 through 10. For each lesson, a script guides the teacher through the instructional sequence. Again, a learning sheet is provided to facilitate continued student practice of the targeted facts. During this time, students use the DRAW Strategy to solve abstract-level problems when they are unable to recall an answer. Students also begin to solve word problems in which the numbers are still vertically aligned but now include the names of common objects or phrases after the numbers instead of blank spaces (see Table 2).

Phase 6: Posttest
During this phase of instruction, a posttest is administered to each student to determine whether he or she has learned the basic facts and is ready to proceed to the phase of instruction designed to increase fluency (speed of computation) and further develop problem-solving skills. If the student's score on the posttest is below 90% he or she repeats one or more of Lessons 8 through 10. When the student achieves a score of 90% or

higher, the teacher informs the student that he or she is doing well and is ready for lessons in which students learn to increase their computation speed and solve more challenging word problems. The teacher also explains the need to solve facts at a rate that ensures success in various situations (e.g., classroom tests, classroom seatwork, homework, shopping, minimum competency tests, basal tests, and standardized tests).

Phase 7: Provide Practice to Fluency

The practice to fluency phase takes place in Lessons 11 through 21. Each lesson features a script to guide the teacher through the instructional sequence, plus a learning sheet to facilitate student practice of facts and word problems. Students work on three primary skills: (a) solving word problems, which become increasingly complicated as the lessons progress; (b) increasing the rate at which they can compute facts; and (c) discriminating previously learned facts from the newly acquired facts and accurately computing those problems.

To help students solve more complicated word problems, specific practice is provided in Lessons 11 through 21. Problems are presented in sentence form (as opposed to the numbers being vertically aligned with phrases written to the right of the numbers). As the lessons progress, students learn to filter out extraneous information and to create their own word problems (see Table 2).

To help students increase their rate of computation, a 1-minute timed probe, called *Addition, Subtraction, Multiplication,* or *Division Minute,* is given during selected lessons of this phase. A student is considered to be fluent or to have reached mastery on the *Minute* probes when he or she is able to write the answers to problems at the rate of 30 digits per minute with no more than two errors.

Finally, to help students discriminate between types of facts, during selected lessons of this phase all students receive a one-page *Facts Review,* containing two or more types of facts. Such practice not only checks the student's ability to discriminate facts when presented on the same page, but also provides important practice of previously learned facts.

The Instructional Procedures

To help teach basic facts, all lessons include a sequence of procedures that has proven to be effective with students who have learning difficulties. The primary instructional procedures are as follows: Give an Advance Organizer, Describe and Model, Conduct Guided Practice, Conduct Independent Practice, Conduct Problem-Solving Practice, Administer Minute Probe, Administer Facts Review, Conduct Pig Game Practice, and Provide Feedback.

Give an Advance Organizer

The first component in each lesson, the Advance Organizer, prepares the student for specific lesson activities. As presented in this curriculum, the Advance Organizer serves three purposes: (a) It connects the existing lesson to the previous lesson, (b) it identifies the target lesson skill, and (c) it provides a rationale for learning the skill.

TABLE 2   *Multiplication Problem-Solving Sequence in Strategic Math Series*

Lesson and Description	Example
Lessons 1–3 (two word problems) A computation problem is presented with the word *groups* written to the right of the first number and blanks beside the second number and the answer space.	6 groups of 3 _____ _____
The student writes the name of the manipulative objects used in the lesson in the blanks, solves the problem, and reads the statement, "Six groups of 3 checkers is 18 checkers."	6 groups of 3 checkers 18 checkers
Lessons 4–6 (two word problems) A computation problem is presented with the word *groups* written to the right of the first number and blanks beside the second number and the answer space.	6 groups of 3 _____ _____
The student writes the name of the drawings used in the respective lesson in the blanks, solves the problem, and reads the statement, "Six groups of 3 circles is 18 circles."	6 groups of 3 circles 18 circles
Lesson 7 (no word problems)	
Lesson 8 (two word problems) A computation problem is presented with the word *groups* written to the right of the first number and common words written to the right of the second number and the answer space.	6 groups × 3 apples apples
The student solves the problem and reads the statement, "six groups of 3 apples is 18 apples."	6 groups × 3 apples 18 apples
Lessons 9–10 (three word problems) A computation problem is presented with a noun or phrase (adjective–noun) written to the right of the first and second numbers and the answer space.	6 brown bags × 3 red apples red apples
The student solves the problem and reads the statement, "Six brown bags of 3 red apples is 18 red apples."	6 brown bags × 3 red apples 18 red apples
Lesson 11 (three word problems) A computation problem is presented with words on both sides of the numbers and the answer space. The numbers remain lined up in a vertical format.	Sue has 6 bags of __3 apples. She has ___ apples.

TABLE 2 (continued)

Lesson and Description	Example
Lesson 11 (continued) The student solves the problem and reads the statement.	Sue has 6 bags of _3_ apples. She has ___ apples
Lesson 12 (three word problems) A regular sentence word problem is presented in which the numbers are not aligned.	Sue has 6 bags. There are 3 apples in each bag. How many apples does Sue have?
The student solves the problem and writes the equation.	$6 \times 3 = 18$
Lesson 13 (three word problems) A sentence word problem including extraneous information is presented.	Sue has 6 bags. There are 3 apples in each bag. Bill has 2 pet turtles. How many apples does Sue have?
The student crosses out the extraneous information, solves the problem, and writes the equation.	Sue has 6 bags. There are 3 apples in each bag. *Bill has 2 pet turtles.* How many apples does Sue have?
Lesson 14 (three problems) The student is instructed to write or dictate his or her own multiplication word problems.	_____ _____ _____
The student writes or dictates a multiplication word problem, solves the problem, and writes the equation.	There are 3 puppies. Each puppy has 2 spots. How many spots are there altogether? $3 \times 2 = 6$

Lessons 15–21 (three problems)
Three types of word problems are presented, each including:
    1 problem without extraneous information
    1 problem with extraneous information
    1 problem to be created by the student
 	
The student writes or dictates the "creation" problem, solves the problem, and writes the equation.	

Describe and Model

The Describe and Model section follows the Advance Organizer section in Lessons 1 through 10 only. Because students usually understand the target facts by Lesson 10, demonstrations are no longer necessary after Lesson 10. As a result, this section is omitted in Lessons 11 through 21.

The Describe and Model component provides the teacher with an opportunity to describe and model the computation process, following two basic procedures. In Procedure 1, the teacher asks and answers questions aloud while demonstrating how to compute the answer for one or more problems on the learning sheet. In computing the problem, the teacher verbalizes his or her thoughts so students can better understand the thought processes involved. When the teacher arrives at an answer, he or she tells students the answer and instructs them to write it on their learning sheets. To enhance generalization across stimulus configurations, both horizontally and vertically configured problems are used as bases for the teacher's demonstrations.

In Procedure 2, the teacher continues to demonstrate how to solve one or more problems. While doing so, she or he asks questions and solicits student responses, using prompts and cues to facilitate correct responses. Thus, in Procedure 2, the teacher and the students work a problem together. When an answer is computed, the students say the answer and write it on their lettering sheets. Again, to enhance generalization across stimulus configurations, both horizontally and vertically configured problems are used.

Conduct Guided Practice

Guided Practice follows the Describe and Model procedures in Lessons 1 through 10 only. Students solve facts independently by Lesson 11; thus, Guided Practice is not included in Lessons 11 through 21. Guided Practice provides the teacher with the opportunity to instruct and support students as they move toward solving problems on their learning sheets independently. To enhance generalization across stimulus configurations, problems are written in both horizontal and vertical formats. During this time, the teacher follows two basic procedures designed to facilitate student independence in computing subtraction problems.

In Procedure 1, the teacher's role is to prompt and facilitate students' thought processes. Thus, the teacher no longer demonstrates the process unless further demonstration appears necessary. To facilitate correct responses, the teacher asks questions and solicits student responses, using prompts and cues. Through the use of this procedure, students are guided through each problem in a way that ensures success.

In Procedure 2, the teacher instructs students to solve the next few problems on the learning sheet, and offers assistance to individual learners only if needed. Thus, the teacher's role now is to step back, monitor student work, and provide assistance with thought processes only if needed.

Conduct Independent Practice

Independent Practice of facts is an integral component of the 21 basic lessons. It enables the teacher to determine if students can independently solve problems. The scripts for this component consist of simple directions, including a statement that reminds students to use previously learned skills and techniques to solve problems. During this time, the teacher does not provide any assistance.

Conduct Problem-Solving Practice

Like Independent Practice of computation facts, Problem-Solving Practice is an integral component of all lessons. To teach students the thought process involved in problem solving, the teacher uses a graduated sequence of word problems. For example, in Lesson 1, students begin solving problems involving three words, and by Lesson 21 they are writing their own word problems. Along the way, students learn to extract any information that is irrelevant to a problem. Thus, when they complete a facts program, they are able to solve word problems with and without extraneous information and to write their own word problems.

Administer Minute Probe

To help students increase their rate of computation, a 1-minute timed probe is given to them during Lessons 11, 13, 15, 16, 18, 20, and 21. (Depending on the needs of the students, the probe may be given during additional lessons in this phase.) The purpose of this probe is to provide the student with independent practice in quickly computing the respective facts. A student is considered to be fluent or to have reached mastery on a probe when he or she is able to write the answers to problems at the rate of 30 digits per minute with no more than two errors. For students with fine motor problems, this rate may be modified. Because each student is unique, some students will achieve mastery on the probe before completing all 21 lessons, while others will need to extend practice beyond the 21st lesson.

Once students have achieved mastery on their probe, instruction is altered in two ways. First, students who have reached mastery are allowed to skip the Independent Practice of computation facts in all following lessons, but *not* the Problem-Solving Practice. Second, after mastery is reached, the students' computation rates are checked using a probe at least every three lessons to ensure maintenance.

Administer Facts Review

To help students discriminate different facts from each other, a one-page Facts Review, containing both newly acquired and previously learned facts, is given to all students in Lessons 14, 17, and 19. (Again, depending on individual students' needs, the Facts Review may be given during additional lessons in this phase.) Such practice not only acts as an independent check of the student's ability to discriminate facts when presented on the same page, but also provides important practice of previously learned addition facts.

Conduct Pig Game Practice

Beginning in Lesson 11 and continuing through Lesson 21, additional practice of the respective facts is encouraged on the learning sheets under the heading, "Pig Game Practice." These problems are to be completed while playing one of several "Pig Games." These games feature the use of dice that include five numbers and one pig drawing on each die. The chance factor of the game (e.g., losing a turn, gaining an extra roll of the dice) is involved when the pig drawing appears. Although considered to be optional activities, Pig Games serve as an entertaining way to further practice the target facts.

Provide Feedback

Because proper feedback is critical to learning, a feedback component is found in all 21 lessons. This component allows the teacher to recognize and praise correct student responses, thereby preventing future errors. Feedback is facilitated through use of the Facts Progress Chart, whereby the teacher and the student plot the student's scores for the last 10 problems on a learning sheet, plus the total number of completed problems on the Minute probe and the Facts Review.

Research has shown that if teachers follow certain steps when giving corrective feedback, students will reach mastery in *half* the instructional time otherwise required when the steps are not used (Kline et al., 1991). Thus, the steps are important when giving feedback about a student's learning sheet, Minute probe, or Facts Review. To further facilitate student learning during instruction, the teacher should decrease her or his involvement in each phase of the feedback process and increase the students' involvement in assessing their progress through questioning techniques. The steps are as follows:

1. *Score the product for correct and incorrect responses; determine the total percentage of correct responses.* Ideally, scoring is completed as soon as the student has turned in the product. The teacher ensures that students understand the scoring system—how he or she marks errors, indicates the total number of correct and incorrect responses, and obtains the final percentage score.

2. *Individually meet with each student; help the students plot their scores on Progress Charts.* At the beginning of each meeting, the teacher makes at least one specific, positive statement about the student's work. For example, "John, you've really got a good handle on subtracting zero from any number." Next, the teacher helps the student plot his or her score on the Progress Chart. The teacher compares the student's score to the mastery goal line, noting any progress.

3. *Specify incorrect responses and corresponding error patterns, if they exist.* The teacher explains where errors have occurred and tries to avoid using the word *you*. For example, the teacher says, "These problems are incorrect." If an error pattern exists, the teacher might say something like, "John, I've noticed that these problems involving the number 9 are incorrect."

4. *Show the student how to perform the task.* For at least one problem missed, the teacher shows the student how to compute the problem correctly using the most recently instructed phase of the CRA sequence. For example, the teacher demonstrates how to compute the problem with concrete objects if she or he has been teaching the concrete lessons, with pictures or tallies if she or he has been teaching the representational lessons, or with the DRAW Strategy if she or he has been teaching the abstract lessons.

5. *Ask the student to practice the application.* The teacher asks the student to show how he or she will proceed in the future, using a different problem. "Okay, John,

now you try it using this problem. Think aloud so I can hear your thoughts as you do the problem." The teacher checks to see that the student correctly applies the current phase of the CRA sequence.

6. *Close the feedback session.* The teacher makes a positive statement about the student's performance in the feedback process and notes expectations for the future, for example, "John, you've done a super job and I know that the next time you see a 0, you'll do great."

Relationship of SMS and Components of Effective Math Instruction

An inspection of Table 3 reveals how the 10 components of effective math instruction were incorporated into the SMS instructional design. For each component, SMS includes from one to six instructional procedures or activities. Placement of effective teaching routines within a curriculum helps teachers translate research into classroom practices. In addition to facilitating best practices in math instruction, this procedure enabled teachers to provide feedback concerning how to improve the application of the components in their classrooms.

STRATEGIC MATH SERIES: FIELD TEST RESULTS

Concrete–Representational–Abstract Sequence

Although the CRA instructional sequence has been recommended in the math literature for decades, limited empirical data exist to support it. Thus, the initial stage of field-testing the Strategic Math Series involved testing the effectiveness of the CRA sequence.

A curriculum consisting of three concrete lessons, three representational lessons, and three abstract lessons was designed. Each lesson included a script that featured the following instructional sequence: Give an advance organizer, describe and model, conduct guided practice, conduct independent practice, and provide feedback. The lessons were used to teach place value (ones and tens) and basic facts (addition, subtraction, multiplication, and division) to students with learning problems. Each student was given a pretest, a posttest, and a retention test. The retention test was administered 5 to 10 school days after instruction was terminated. The results of the place value instruction are reported in several sources (Hudson et al., 1988; Peterson et al., 1988), and a summary of the place value data is presented in Table 4. The findings indicate that the mean gain on the place value scores was 68% and the mean retention score was 8% higher than the mean posttest score. The sample included 21 students with learning disabilities, 3 students with emotional handicaps, and 6 students identified as at risk for academic failure. Altogether, six teachers participated in field-testing place value. Given that students across all teachers and settings made substantial gains in $4\frac{1}{2}$ hours of instruction (nine lessons, 30 minutes each), it was concluded that the CRA sequence holds promise for teaching place value.

Next, the CRA sequence was tested for teaching basic facts (addition, subtraction, multiplication, and division). Again, nine scripted lessons were tested, and pretest, posttest,

TABLE 3   *Research Areas of Effective Math Instruction and Related SMS Curriculum Components*

Research Areas	Related Curriculum Components
Select appropriate math content	A graduated word problem sequence is used. Use of the mnemonic DRAW activates computation strategies. Computation problems are solved via objects, pictures, drawings, and numbers. Word problems are created. Basic facts are the target skill.
Establish goals and experience	Pretest ensures essential preskills. Pretest establishes need for target skill. Student signs a commitment to learn. Mastery or goal criteria are set. Progress on each goal is monitored.
Provide systematic and explicit instruction	Each lesson features the following steps: give an advance organizer, describe and model, conduct guided practice, conduct independent practice, and provide feedback.
Teach students to understand math concepts	The instructional sequence features the CRA sequence and the teaching of relationships and rules.
Monitor progress	Progress of each lesson is monitored on a chart. Percentage and rate scores are monitored against a mastery criterion.
Provide feedback	A teacher-directed, six-step elaborated feedback routine is used in each lesson.
Teach to mastery	After an understanding of the targeted concept is achieved, practice-to-mastery lessons are used to achieve a fluency criterion.
Teach problem solving	Problem-solving activities are used in each lesson. Students learn to solve problems with and without extraneous information and to create their own word problems.
Teach generalization	Students are provided multiple examples of the targeted math concept at the concrete, representational, and abstract levels. Problems are presented in vertical and horizontal formats. Students learn to a mastery criterion. Teachers and peers provide instruction. Rationales for the skill are discussed in each lesson.
Promote a positive attitude toward math	Success on each lesson is facilitated via explicit and carefully sequenced instruction. Goal-setting and goal attainment are included in each lesson. Elaborated feedback is provided in each lesson. Targeted math concepts are applied to students' daily lives. Practice-to-mastery activities feature high interest formats (e.g., Pig Games, peer teaching). Charts of progress provide visual displays of progress and encourage students to comprehend the relationship between their behavior and learning outcomes.

and retention measures were used. The results reported in Table 4 indicate a mean percentage increase of 70% from pretest to posttest. Also, the mean retention score reveals that the posttest achievement level was maintained. Altogether, eight teachers participated in the field testing. The student sample included 18 students identified as at risk for academic failure, 15 as learning disabled, 4 as emotionally disabled, and 3 as severely emotionally disturbed. Because the students made the substantial gains across all teachers and settings with $4\frac{1}{2}$ hours of instruction, it was concluded that the CRA sequence is effective for teaching the acquisition of basic facts. These results led to the inclusion of the CRA sequence in the Strategic Math Series curriculum for teaching basic facts.

Basic Facts Curriculum

The Strategic Math Series curriculum for basic facts has been field-tested primarily in special education settings. A total of 22 teachers from seven Florida school districts used SMS. Of the 109 elementary students who participated, 102 were identified as learning disabled, 5 as emotionally handicapped, and 2 as at risk for school failure. Field testing took place in small group (less than 7 students) and large group (7 to 18 students) instructional arrangements. Of the 22 teachers who participated, 21 (96%) indicated they would use the SMS curriculum again. Of the 75 students who were asked to complete follow-up questionnaires, 60% rated SMS as better than other math instruction and 31% rated it as equal to other math instruction. Thus, 91% rated the curriculum as equal to or better than other math instruction. Given the teacher and student satisfaction, it was concluded that SMS has positive consumer satisfaction.

Computation Acquisition and Generalization Data

Inspection of the results in Table 5 indicates that students were able to acquire the respective facts within Lessons 1 through 10 (i.e., 5 hours of instruction). For example, the total mean scores demonstrate that the average gain across skills was 59%. Moreover, the findings reveal that the students in the subtraction and multiplication groups were able to apply the DRAW Strategy to solve computation problems that they were not taught. For example, during the DRAW lesson, the students were taught to solve 3×4 by drawing lines to represent groups, and tallies to represent the number in each group:

TABLE 4 *Field-Test Results of CRA Sequence of Place Value and Basic Facts*

	Pretest	Posttest	Retention
Place value	20%	88%	96%
	$n = 30$	$n = 30$	$n = 30$
Basic facts	16%	86%	82%
	$n = 40$	$n = 40$	$n = 36$

TABLE 5   **Percentage Scores for Computation and Word Problem Data**

	Computation			Word Problem	
Fact	**Pretest**	**Posttest**	**Generalization**	**Pretest**	**Posttest**
Addition 0–9	40 $n = 4$	98 $n = 4$			
Subtraction 0–9	17 $n = 14$	95 $n = 14$	92 $n = 13$	28 $n = 9$	84 $n = 9$
Multiplication	43 $n = 52$	91 $n = 52$	96 $n = 52$	36 $n = 40$	92 $n = 40$
Division	9 $n = 19$	81 $n = 19$			
Total	32 $n = 89$	91 $n = 89$	95 $n = 65$	34 $n = 49$	91 $n = 49$

Note. The number of students in addition is low because fewer students in the field-test sites needed instruction in that skill. Data are not reported in selected areas due to absences, school-wide testing, field trips, and the ending of the school year.

$$3 \times 4 = \frac{\overline{/ / / /}}{\underline{\frac{/ / / /}{/ / / /}}} = 12$$

After the completion of all 21 lessons, students were asked to solve multiplication operations such as 12×3. Of the 65 students in multiplication and subtraction who were tested for the response generalization task, 62 performed the task successfully. Moreover, generalization testing was conducted by examiners whom the students did not know, in library, cafeteria, or classroom settings.

Word Problem Data

An examination of Table 5 indicates that students in subtraction and multiplication were able to learn word problems successfully. The pretest was conducted prior to Lesson 1, and the posttest was administered within 1 to 5 days after Lesson 21 was completed. The posttest included two problems with extraneous information and two problems without extraneous information, and it required the students to create two word problems and solve them. The posttest was conducted in library, cafeteria, or classroom settings by examiners whom the students did not know.

Computation Mastery Data

The initial rate data were collected after Lesson 8 (the first abstract lesson), and the posttest rate data were collected after Lesson 21. The follow-up data were gathered in library, cafeteria, or classroom settings 3 to 5 days after Lesson 21 by examiners whom the students did not know. Inspection of Table 6 indicates that the students were able to increase their rates for all skills. Across all skills the mean rate improvement was 132%

TABLE 6   *Rate-Per-Minute Scores for Mastery Data*

Fact	Pretest	Posttest	Follow-Up	Rate Correct Increase per Week	Percentage Increase per Week	Total Percentage Increase
Addition 0–9	10/.5 *n* = 8	18/.1 *n* = 8	18/0 *n* = 8	3.1	31	80
Subtraction 0–9	11/.9 *n* = 28	24/.4 *n* = 28	18/.6 *n* = 5	4.8	45	118
Multiplication	5/8 *n* = 46	14/2 *n* = 46	14/2 *n* = 37	3.5	69	180
Division	8/.6 *n* = 13	15/.4 *n* = 123		2.7	34	88
Totals	7.6/4 *n* = 95	17.6/1.2 *n* = 95	15/1.6 *n* = 45	3.8	51	132

Note. Number/number represents correct response/incorrect responses.

after Lessons 9 through 21. Given that 15% to 25% weekly improvement is considered an excellent criterion for improving rate of correct responses (White & Haring, 1980), these data are very positive. The mean weekly percentage increase was 51 across skills, with a range of 31% to 69%. In multiplication, the students significantly reduced their error rates and increased their digits-correct rates. In other skill areas, the beginning error rates were minimal. These data suggest that the students need additional practice to reach the target rate of 30 digits correct per minute with two or fewer errors.

Data Summary

Overall, the field test data indicate that students with learning problems were able to (a) acquire computational skills across facts, (b) solve word problems with and without extraneous information, (c) create word problems involving facts, (d) apply a mnemonic strategy to difficult problems, (e) increase rate of computation, and (f) generalize math skills across examiners, settings, and tasks.

These results were obtained with each student receiving approximately 11 hours of instruction within a group setting. This finding is significant in that many students with learning problems continue to have difficulty with these skills after years of traditional instruction. Moreover, consumer satisfaction data from teachers and students were positive. Finally, teachers in the field-test sites provided many recommendations for making SMS more "user friendly." Their changes have been incorporated into revised teacher manuals.

DISCUSSION

The SMS for basic facts represents an effort to incorporate research-based instructional factors into a curriculum for students with learning problems. The results of field testing indicate that SMS hold promise for teaching students with learning problems to acquire and understand basic facts and to apply them in problem-solving activities. Although these field test results are encouraging, several issues and questions need to be addressed.

1. The establishment of a rate criterion for mastery remains difficult. There is much variability in the findings on the fluency rate of specific math skills; however, the rate of 30 correct digits per minute with two or fewer errors is at the lower end of suggested fluency rates (Mercer & Mercer, 1989). In two studies (Gayler, 1988; Jones, 1990), the number of trials needed by nine first and second graders with learning problems to reach 30 digits correct per minute with two or fewer errors on subtraction facts 0 to 9 ranged from 632 to 1,168, with a mean of 840. More research is needed to guide the establishment of mastery rate criteria for specific math skills across individual learners of different ages and motor skills.

2. The most efficient applications of concrete, representational, and abstract level procedures continue to be examined. In teaching subtraction with regrouping. Evans and Carnine (1990) found that concrete representations and symbolic (abstract) activities were both effective, but symbolic instruction was more efficient. Moreover, they suggested that the symbolic–concrete sequence is more efficient than the concrete–symbolic sequence. The entire CRA sequence has been recommended in the literature for decades, but its effectiveness has not been systematically examined. As with the Evans and Carnine study, most researchers have compared components of the CRA sequence (concrete and abstract versus abstract; representational and abstract versus concrete and abstract, etc.) but have not systematically examined the three-component sequence. More research is needed to determine if the entire CRA sequence is more effective than any two-part combinations of the sequence, and if a different order of the three parts is more effective. Moreover, the CRA sequence and its various two-part and three-part combinations need to be examined in relation to math skills that vary in difficulty, maintenance of skills, generalization of skills, and problem solving. The field-test data for SMS suggest that the CRA sequence holds promise for teaching place value and basic facts to students with learning problems. Perhaps the progressive experiences coupled with the multiple examples across the various modalities enable students with learning difficulties to learn.

3. Although the individual components of SMS have research support, the relative effectiveness of the separate components on student outcomes is unknown. Script-guided explicit teaching, elaborated feedback, monitoring of progress, the DRAW strategy, the word-problem sequence, the Pig Games, the concrete lessons, the representational lessons, and the practice-to-mastery lessons are some components that warrant study. Investigations in these areas could lead to more efficiency.

4. SMS needs to be compared to other curricula to determine its relative effectiveness.

5. After students reach the practice-to-mastery lessons, alternative instructional delivery systems need to be explored to facilitate independent practice. From their research review, Mastropieri et al. (1991) reported that cooperative learning, computer-assisted instruction, peer tutoring, and interactive videodiscs have produced positive student outcomes in math.

6. When students reach mastery in fact computation, the inclusion of word problems that involve solving for different unknowns appears warranted. Also, word problems that require multisteps (e.g., addition and subtraction) are needed.

Many students with learning problems enter the upper grades without a functional knowledge of lower level math skills, such as place value and basic facts. Moreover, higher standards in math are likely to make the situation more threatening to these students. The research regarding how to teach math to these students is extensive. Educators are challenged with the task of putting best practices in the schools. One logical plan for promoting these practices is to develop and field test a curriculum that incorporates effective teaching routines. Sprick (1986) noted that less than 3% of commercial materials are field-tested before being published. For the benefit of all students and teachers, math materials that incorporate effective teaching practices need to be established in the nation's schools. If this happens, perhaps future efforts will not be directed toward reforming an ineffective math curriculum but toward refining quality instructional practices.

REFERENCES

Anderson, L. W., & Pellicer, L. O. (1990). Synthesis of research on compensatory and remedial education. *Educational Leadership, 48*(1), 10–16.

Bartel, N. R. (1990). Problems in mathematics achievement. In D. D. Hammill & N. R. Bartel, *Teaching students with learning and behavior problems* (5th ed., pp. 289–343). Austin, TX: PRO-ED.

Berliner, D. C. (1982, March). *The executive functions of teaching.* Paper presented at the annual meeting of the American Educational Research Association, New York.

Blankenship, C. S. (1978). Remediating systematic inversion errors in subtraction through the use of demonstration and feedback. *Learning Disability Quarterly, 1*, 12–22.

Blankenship, C., & Lilly, M. S. (1981). *Mainstreaming students with learning and behavioral problems: Techniques for the classroom teacher.* New York: Holt, Rinehart & Winston.

Carnine, D. (1991). Curricular interventions for teaching higher order thinking to all students: Introduction to the special series. *Journal of Learning Disabilities, 24*, 261–269.

Carpenter, R. L. (1985). Mathematics instruction in resource rooms: Instruction time and teacher competence. *Learning Disability Quarterly, 8*, 95–100.

Carroll, J. B. (1985). The model of school learning: Progress of an idea. In L. W. Anderson (Ed.), *Perspectives on school learning: Selected writings of John B. Carroll* (pp. 82–108). Hillsdale, NJ: Erlbaum.

Case, L. P., & Harris, K. R. (1988, April). *Self-instructional strategy training: Improving mathematical problem solving skills of learning disabled students.* Paper presented at the annual meeting of the American Educational Research Association, New Orleans.

Cawley, J., Fitzmaurice-Hayes, A., & Shaw, R. (1988). *Mathematics for the mildly handicapped—A guide to curriculum and instruction.* Boston: Allyn & Bacon.

Cawley, J. F., & Miller, J. H. (1989). Cross-sectional comparisons of the mathematical performance of children with learning disabilities: Are we on the right track toward comprehensive programming? *Journal of Learning Disabilities, 23*, 250–254, 259.

Cawley, J. F., Miller, J. H., & School, B. A. (1987). A brief inquiry of arithmetic word-problem solving among learning disabled secondary students. *Learning Disabilities Focus, 2*, 87–93.

Christenson, S. L., Ysseldyke, J. E., & Thurlow, M. L. (1989). Critical instructional factors for students with mild handicaps: An integrative review. *Remedial and Special Education, 10*(5), 21–31.

Clifford, M. M. (1990). Students need challenge, not easy success. *Educational Leadership, 48*(1), 22–26.

Collins, M., Carnine, D., & Gersten, R. (1987). Elaborated corrective feedback and the acquisition of reading skills: A study of computer-assisted instruction. *Exceptional Children, 54*, 254–262.

Cox, L. S. (1975). Diagnosing and remediating systematic errors in addition and subtraction computations. *The Arithmetic Teacher, 22*, 151–157.

De Corte, E., & Verschaffel, L. (1981). Children's solution processes in elementary arithmetic problems: Analysis and improvement. *Journal of Educational Psychology, 73*, 765–779.

Deshler, D. D., Schumaker, J. B., & Lenz, B. K. (1984). Academic and cognitive interventions for LD adolescents: Part I. *Journal of Learning Disabilities, 17*, 108–117.

Ellis, E. S., Lenz, B. K., & Sabornie, E. J. (1987a). Generalization and adaptation of learning strategies to natural environments. Part I: Critical agents. *Remedial and Special Education, 8*(1), 6–20.

Ellis, E. S., Lenz, B. K., & Sabornie, E. J. (1987b). Generalization and adaptation of learning strategies to natural environments. Part II: Research into practice. *Remedial and Special Education, 8*(2), 6–23.

Engelmann, S., Carnine, D., & Steely, D. G. (1991). Making connections in mathematics. *Journal of Learning Disabilities, 24*, 292–303.

Evans, D., & Carnine, D. (1990). Manipulatives—The effective way. *Direct Instruction News, 10*(1), 48–55.

Fisher, C. W., Berliner, D. C., Filby, N. N., Marliave, R., Cahen, L. S., & Dishaw, M. M. (1980). Teaching behaviors, academic learning time, and student achievement: An overview. In C. Denham & A. Lieberman (Eds.), *Time to learn.* Washington, DC: National Institute of Education.

Fleischner, J. E., Garnett, K., & Shepherd, M. J. (1982). Proficiency in arithmetic basic facts computation of learning disabled and nondisabled children. *Focus on Learning Problems in Mathematics, 4*(2), 47–56.

Fleischner, J. E., Nuzum, M. B., & Marzola, E. S. (1987). Devising an instructional program to teach arithmetic problem-solving skills to students with learning disabilities. *Journal of Learning Disabilities, 20*, 214–217.

Fuchs, L. S. (1986). Monitoring progress among mildly handicapped pupils: Review of current practices and research. *Remedial and Special Education, 7*(5), 5–12.

Fuchs, L. S., Fuchs, D., & Deno, S. L. (1985). The importance of goal ambitiousness and goal mastery to student achievement. *Exceptional Children, 52*, 63–71.

Garnett, K., & Fleischner, J. E. (1983). Automatization and basic fact performance of normal and learning disabled children. *Learning Disability Quarterly, 6*, 223–230.

Gayler, S. K. (1988). *The effect of the concrete to abstract mathematic instructional sequence with first graders.* Unpublished master's thesis, University of Florida, Gainesville.

Gersten, R., Carnine, D., & Woodward, J. (1987). Direct instruction research: The third decade. *Remedial and Special Education, 8*(6) 48–56.

Good, T. L. (1983). Classroom research: A decade of progress. *Educational Psychologist, 18*(3), 127–144.

Good, T. L., & Brophy, J. E. (1986). School effects. In M. C. Wittrock (Ed.), *Handbook for research on teaching* (3rd ed., pp. 570–602). New York: Macmillan.

Good, T. L., & Grouws, D. A. (1979). The Missouri Mathematics Effectiveness Project: An experimental study in fourth-grade classrooms. *Journal of Educational Psychology, 71*(3), 355–362.

Hasselbring, T. S., Goin, L. I., & Bransford, J. O. (1987). Developing automaticity. *Teaching Exceptional Children, 19*(3), 30–33.

Hudson, P. J., Peterson, S. K., Mercer, C. D., & McLeod, P. (1988). Place value instruction. *Teaching Exceptional Children, 20*(3), 72–73.

Jones, D. S. (1990). *Trials to mastery of basic subtraction.* Unpublished master's thesis, University of Florida, Gainesville.

Kameenui, E. J., & Simmons, D. C. (1990). *Designing instructional strategies: The prevention of academic learning problems.* Columbus, OH: Merrill.

Kelly, B., Gersten, R., & Carmine, D. (1990). Student error patterns as a function of curriculum design: Teaching fractions to remedial high school students and high school students with learning disabilities. *Journal of Learning Disabilities, 1*, 23–29.

Kirby, J. R., & Becker, L. D. (1988). Cognitive components of learning problems in arithmetic. *Remedial and Special Education, 9*(5), 7–15, 27.

Kline, F. M., Schumaker, J. B., & Deshler, D. D. (1991). Development and validation of feedback routines for instructing students with learning disabilities. *Learning Disability Quarterly, 14*, 191–207.

Lloyd, J. W., & Keller, C. E. (1989). Effective mathematics instruction: Development, instruction, and programs. *Focus on Exceptional Children, 21*(7), 1–10.

Locke, E. A., & Latham, G. P. (1990). *A theory of goal setting and task performance.* Englewood Cliffs, NJ: Prentice-Hall.

Locke, E. A., Shaw, K. N., Saari, L. M., & Latham, G. P. (1981). Goal setting and task performance: 1969–1980. *Psychological Bulletin, 90*, 125–152.

Lovitt, T. C. (1989). *Introduction to learning disabilities.* Boston: Allyn & Bacon.

Mastropieri, M. A., Scruggs, T. E., & Shiah, S. (1991). Mathematics instruction for learning disabled students: A review of research. *Learning Disabilities Research & Practice, 6*, 89–98.

McLeod, T., & Armstrong, S. (1982). Learning disabilities in mathematics—Skill deficits and remedial approaches. *Learning Disability Quarterly, 5,* 305–311.

Mercer, C. D. (1992). *Students with learning disabilities* (4th ed.). New York: Macmillan.

Mercer, C. D., & Mercer, A. R. (1989). *Teaching students with learning problems* (3rd ed.). Columbus, OH: Merrill.

Mercer, C. D., & Miller, S. P. (1991). *Strategic math series: Multiplication facts 0–81.* Lawrence, KS: Edge Enterprises.

Miller, J. H., & Milam, C. P. (1987). Multiplication and division errors committed by learning disabled students. *Learning Disabilities Research, 2*(2), 119–122.

Montague, M., & Bos, C. S. (1986). The effect of cognitive strategy training on verbal math problem solving performance of learning disabled adolescents. *Journal of Learning Disabilities, 19,* 26–33.

National Council of Supervisors of Mathematics. (1988). *Twelve components of essential mathematics.* Minneapolis, MN: Author.

National Council of Teachers of Mathematics. (1980). *An agenda for action: Recommendations for school mathematics of the 1980's.* Reston, VA: Author.

National Council of Teachers of Mathematics. (1989). *Curriculum and evaluation standards for school mathematics.* Reston, VA: Author.

Nuzum, M. (1983). *The effects of a curriculum based on the information processing paradigm on the arithmetic problem solving performance of four learning disabled students.* Unpublished doctoral dissertation, Teachers College, Columbia University, New York.

Peterson, S. K., Mercer, C. D., & O'Shea, L. (1988). Teaching learning disabled children place value using the concrete to abstract sequence. *Learning Disabilities Research, 4*(1), 52–56.

Porter, A. C., & Brophy, J. (1988). Synthesis of research on good teaching: Insights from the work of the Institute for Research on Teaching. *Educational Leadership, 45*(8), 74–85.

Reisman, F. K. (1982). *A guide to the diagnostic teaching of arithmetic* (3rd ed.). Columbus, OH: Merrill.

Reisman, F., & Kauffman, S. (1980). *Teaching mathematics to children with special needs.* Columbus, OH: Merrill.

Rieth, H., & Evertson, C. (1988). Variables related to the effective instruction of difficult-to-teach children. *Focus on Exceptional Children, 20*(5), 1–8.

Rivera, D. M., & Smith, D. D. (1987). Influence of modeling on acquisition and generalization of computational skills: A summary of research findings for three sites. *Learning Disability Quarterly, 10,* 69–80.

Rivera, D., & Smith, D. D. (1988). Using a demonstration strategy to teach midschool students with learning disabilities how to compute long division. *Journal of Learning Disabilities, 21,* 77–81.

Robinson, S. L., DePascale, C., & Roberts, F. C. (1989). Computer-delivered feedback in group-based instruction: Effects for learning disabled students in mathematics. *Learning Disabilities Focus, 5*(1), 28–35.

Rosenshine, B. (1983). Teaching functions in instructional programs. *The Elementary School Journal, 83,* 335–351.

Rosenshine, B., & Stevens, R. (1986). Teaching functions. In M. C. Wittrock (Ed.), *Handbook of research on teaching* (3rd ed., pp. 376–391). New York: Macmillan.

Russell, R., & Ginsburg, H. (1984). Cognitive analysis of children's mathematical difficulties. *Cognition and Instruction, 1,* 217–244.

Scheid, K. (1990). *Cognitive-based methods for teaching mathematics to students with learning problems.* Columbus, OH: LINC Resources.

Slavin, R. E., & Madden, N. A. (1989). What works for students at risk: A research synthesis. *Educational Leadership, 46*(5), 4–13.

Sprick, R. S. (1986). *Solutions to elementary discipline problems* (Cassette tapes). Eugene, OR: Teaching Strategies.

Stokes, T. F., & Baer, D. M. (1977). An implicit technology of generalization. *Journal of Applied Behavioral Analysis, 10*(2), 349–367.

Sugai, G., & Smith, P. (1986). The equal additions method of subtraction taught with a modeling technique. *Remedial and Special Education, 7*(1), 40–48.

Suydam, M. N., & Higgins, J. L. (1977). *Activity-based learning in elementary school mathematics: Recommendations from research.* Reston, VA: National Council of Teachers of Mathematics.

Thornton, C. A., & Toohey, M. A. (1985). Basic math facts: Guidelines for teaching and learning. *Learning Disabilities Focus, 1,* 44–57.

Underhill, R. G., Uprichard, A. E., & Heddens, J. W. (1980). *Diagnosing mathematical difficulties.* Columbus, OH: Merrill.

Wang, M. C. (1987). Toward achieving educational excellence for all students: Program design and instructional outcomes. *Remedial and Special Education, 8*(3), 25–34.

Warner, M., Alley, G., Schumaker, J., Deshler, D., & Clark, F. (1980). *An epidemiological study of learning disabled adolescents in secondary schools: Achievement and ability, socioeconomic status and school experiences* (Report No. 13). Lawrence: University of Kansas Institute for Research in Learning Disabilities.

White, O. R., & Haring, N. G. (1980). *Exceptional teaching: A multimedia training package* (2nd ed.). Columbus, OH: Merrill.

Cecil Mercer is a professor of special education at the University of Florida. Susan Miller is an assistant professor of special education at the University of Nevada, Las Vegas.

◦ 18 ◦

Learning strategy training may have limited impact on students who lack a basic working knowledge of the content subjects upon which the strategies are based. Content knowledge deficits may be due, in part, to the missed opportunities to learn social studies, science, and other content-area subjects while attending pull-out programs. This article reviews and questions a variety of approaches to content instruction that may compensate for student learning problems. One is content reduction—reducing the content load on students to only that which is perceived as essential. Another is the selection of more readable texts. The authors offer a variety of alternatives to facilitate student learning of content, including the integration and use of cognitive strategies with content instruction, graphic organizers, computers, and other technology.

Techniques for Mediating Content-Area Learning: Issues and Research

Edwin S. Ellis and B. Keith Lenz

Understanding and remembering associated concepts and facts presented in content-area classes (e.g., social studies, geography, health, history) and then applying and demonstrating mastery of these concepts and facts are the two core demands of secondary school settings. Many mildly handicapped and low achieving students often perform poorly in these areas because they (a) do not seem to employ effective strategies related to successful learning and performance (cf. Wong, 1985a, 1985b), (b) do not possess sufficient prerequisite subject-matter knowledge to learn readily by association (Wong, 1985b), and (c) must face instructional environments (e.g., teacher's instructional style, the manner in which a textbook is written) that often contribute to learning problems and do not facilitate mastery of the subject matter (Schumaker & Deshler, 1984). As a result, training students to employ various types of learning strategies that will promote more successful content-area learning has become an important instructional alternative for teachers of students with mild handicaps.

Teachers have quickly learned, however, that the power of both single and multiple strategies is often limited by a student's knowledge base. For example, a strategy to promote point-of-view writing is of limited value if, when attempting to state a position about the sources of racism in this country, students do not possess sufficient knowledge about racism. Also, a strategy for paraphrasing content in reading has limited value if the text contains extensive vocabulary and concepts that are unfamiliar to the student (e.g., metamorphosis in reptiles).

Clearly, an interdependence is present between the ability to employ effective learning strategies and the ability to retrieve important information from a knowledge base upon which the strategy is to be employed (Chi, 1981; Voss, 1982; Wong, 1985b). Unfortunately, because of the nature of many special education pull-out programs in elementary and secondary schools, many mildly handicapped students are denied opportunities to acquire content knowledge. Participation in resource room special education programs that focus on remediation of basic skills often has required students to miss content-area lessons (e.g., science, geography). As a result, opportunities to acquire important content-area knowledge frequently are reduced. (To paraphrase the prison guard in the movie *Cool Hand Luke*, "What we have here is a failure to accumulate.") Although strategy instruction holds great potential for many mildly handicapped and low-achieving students, simultaneous attention to direct instruction in content-area subjects continues to be a critical need.

Studies reviewed in this article were selected because each addressed topics directly related to teaching content-area information to low-achieving students or students with mild handicaps. Unless otherwise noted, the subjects identified as learning disabled were identified as having marked discrepancies (i.e., 15 or more standard score points) between intellectual ability and achievement. Each study employed either a true or a quasi-experimental design, and the efficacy of the techniques investigated was demonstrated by a minimum of .05 level of significance or, in the case of time-series designs in which statistical analysis was not appropriate, a replicated marked change in performance following stable baseline periods. The studies were selected for review here because they were representative of the empirical basis for the adaptive teaching procedure of concern; they are not intended to be inclusive of the entire body of research in this area.

MEDIATION OF CONTENT-AREA LEARNING

Mediation is the process involved in taking new (and sometimes difficult) information and translating it into a form that is meaningful and memorable. It also involves checking to assure that information is comprehended. Mediation occurs via the manner in which teachers and the tools they employ (e.g., textbooks, graphics, video documentaries, audio recordings) communicate subject-matter information and facilitate student interaction with the information in a manner that will promote student understanding and remembering. This mediation process may include the specific adaptations, modifications, or instructional techniques the teacher uses, or the tools the teacher selects, to facilitate learning and performance. The assumption is that the teacher's careful use of mediators will induce the student to process information more effectively and efficiently through the selection and use of targeted external stimuli.

Of course, not all procedures a teacher employs will be equally powerful in influencing learning. The power of a teacher mediator likely will depend on the extent to which it promotes internally generated mediation by the student. That is, the most effective teaching methods and materials are those that will promote the student's active learning through the emphasis and use of instructional cues, routines, or devices that will promote understanding, remembering, and organization. As a result, the more limited a student's ability to internally mediate learning through appropriate cognitive strategies, the greater the need will be for a teacher to promote successful learning and performance through the use of appropriate instructional cues, routines, and devices.

Although effective instruction has been the subject of considerable discussion with normal achievers (e.g., Brophy & Good, 1984; Joyce & Weil, 1980; Rosenshine, 1979), considerably less research has been generated examining the efficacy of these techniques as learning mediators for low-achieving students, and still less research has been conducted to examine the efficacy of these techniques for maximizing the acquisition of specific content-area knowledge. Even though the research on use of general techniques with this population remains vague, five clear instructional options related to promoting content-area learning have emerged from practice. These options provide an initial framework for discussing the relative merits and related research associated with these different approaches to content-area instruction. The five instructional alternatives are: (a) adjusting the curriculum so students do not have to learn as much, (b) selecting textbooks that are conducive to learning, (c) enhancing content through the use of study guides, graphics, and mnemonics, (d) using audio recordings of text material, and computer-assisted instruction, and (e) promoting the use of appropriate cognitive and metacognitive strategies during direct instruction of content-area subject matter.

Content Reduction

Reducing the quantity or changing the emphasis of a curriculum represents an approach to teaching content-area information to low-achieving students that schools commonly follow (Wiederholt & McEntire, 1980). Curriculum, as used here, is narrowly defined as the set of objectives that define what will be learned and the materials used to articulate the content. Reducing the breadth of the curriculum to enhance the acquisition of appropriate secondary content can be a valuable strategy for teachers. Reducing the curriculum may relieve frustration and provide success for some individuals who have been unsuccessful in secondary content learning.

Although this approach is a common practice in schools (Deshler, Lowrey, & Alley, 1979; Schumaker & Deshler, 1984; Schumaker, Deshler, & Ellis, 1986), a review of the research literature suggests that evaluation of this practice has been practically nonexistent. In the absence of research in this area, educators appear to rely on speculation and personal perspectives with regard to its efficacy.

It is also important to decide what types of curriculum modifications are ethically appropriate. For example, if the goal of a course is for students to attain 20 objectives, and a course adjustment is made that allows a learner to gain only one objective, the student will likely attain that objective. But, unfortunately, this strategy does not maximize the student's potential for learning. As a result, both learner and knowledge and "opportunity to learn" are lost. Therefore, if curriculum content is reduced, the amount or kind of information that can be acquired is limited even before learning can begin, regardless of the quality of teaching. The instructional question is whether this practice is implemented to appropriately meet the learning needs of students or whether it is implemented to meet the functional needs of teachers.

Regardless of the intent of this practice, some evidence suggests that reduced curriculum expectations may negatively affect the potential for future learning. For example, many adolescents with learning disabilities appear to be further handicapped by their limited background information in certain content areas. Lenz and Alley (1983) found that adolescents with learning disabilities had significantly less background knowledge of social studies content than their normally achieving peers, yet both groups were required to meet the same content classroom demands. This lack of background knowledge might be explained as the result of either an inability to learn the information or the absence of the "opportunity to learn" the information.

The cumulative effects of insufficient opportunity to learn could reduce the potential meaningfulness of information important for continued learning. As a result, the efficacy of reducing the quantity of material to be learned has not been researched adequately, and the practice of reducing the amount of content the low-achieving student must learn may actually limit opportunities to acquire knowledge.

Learnable Text

The problem of insufficient "opportunity to learn" can be illustrated by school district attempts to offer basic or modified curriculum courses. These courses often introduce controlled textbooks and materials as the primary means of curricular adjustment. Specifically, a school district or teacher selects an alternate text to the one used in the regular course. These textbooks and materials often feature a controlled reading level, shorter chapters, and an increased number of visual aids. Some research indicates, however, that these texts may not facilitate student learning.

For example, the methods used to control the readability levels of textbooks yield a number of problems. Popular readability formulas, which often guide the development of controlled texts, tend to emphasize word length, sentence length, word familiarity, and sentence complexity (Dupuis & Askov, 1982). Lovitt, Horton, and Bergerud (1987) noted that different readability formulas do not produce similar scores on the same text and a student's reading achievement scores on different standardized tests are typically inconsistent. Moreover, two texts can obtain the same readability scores but be markedly different in their comprehensibility because of the nature of their organization, use of visual aids, sentence structure, and so forth. In fact, if texts are modified based on the application of reading formulas, the elements that indicate important relationships may be eliminated in the process of achieving formula compatibility. The readability of a textbooks may involve considerably more than what readability formulas measure.

Anderson, Armbruster, and Kantor (1980) suggested that the readability of text should be based on structural coherence, unity, and audience appropriateness. These elements serve to cue the learner as to the various relationships between ideas in the text and those of the learner. The question of contextual relationship also emerges when larger topics or chapters are subdivided into shorter chapters. Whether these types of chapter configurations facilitate or inhibit content acquisition is unclear.

Another feature often included in controlled textbooks is the increased use of visuals (the increase may be in number or size, or both). This practice has been challenged by some researchers who have found that illustrations make text more difficult for some naive readers (Harber, 1983). Lenz, Alley, Beals, Schumaker, and Deshler (1981) found that visuals (pictures, graphs, charts, maps) used in controlled textbooks were harder for adolescents with learning disabilities to interpret for meaning than were visuals found in grade-level textbooks. Learning disabled adolescents were able to generate more statements relevant to the surrounding text from the visuals in grade-level texts than from those in controlled texts. An analysis of the visuals in the two types of texts indicated that the visuals in the controlled textbooks tended to be used for motivational or decorative purposes rather than to inform. The visuals also tended to supplant text rather than complement text, thus forcing students to make their own contextual generalizations. This finding is in contrast to research findings indicating that visuals are most helpful to readers when they are tied directly to the text in specific ways (Schallert, 1980).

Because textbooks play a major role in delivering content-area information to students, selection of texts should be based on the extent to which the book incorporates features that provide prompts and cues similar to those a teacher provides when mediating learning. Adjunct questions, objectives, advance organizers, summaries, pointer words, and textual highlighting are examples of textual mediators that have been found to be effective for poor comprehenders (Meyer, 1981). In an analysis of elementary- and intermediate-level textbooks, Armbruster and Anderson (1988) reported that most textbooks were deficient in structure (the manner in which ideas and relationships are organized in the text), coherence (the logical flow of ideas presented in text), and audience appropriateness (the match between the text and the reader's level of knowledge and skills).

Common problems with text structure tended to center on the texts' failure to employ organizational signals (e.g., introductory statements, pointer words such as "first," "second," "third," and textual cues such as boldface print words). In addition, the structure employed in the textbooks was often illogical. Rather than having a book with structures that mediated students' selection of critical information and facilitated its organization into a coherent concept, students' books often presented information that required the readers to "simply encode information as an unstructured list of ideas" (Armbruster & Anderson, 1988, p. 48).

With regard to coherence, Armbruster and Anderson (1988) reported that textbooks often presented information in a "list-like format which failed to convey the relationship inherent in the text" (p. 49). Transitions between topics were often sudden, and sequences presented in the text frequently were out of chronological order or occurrence in real time. Linguistic cohesive ties that help carry the meaning across phrases, clauses, and sentences tended to be a major shortcoming. To produce lower readability scores on textbooks, publishers seemed to shorten sentences by transforming compound and complex sentences into simple independent clauses by removing coordinating and subordinating conjunctions that served as cohesive ties. The result was that the material was more incomprehensible.

With regard to audience appropriateness, Armbruster and Anderson (1988) noted that many textbooks failed to account for the readers' limited amount of knowledge about the topic addressed by the text. Texts would "mention topics superficially" (p. 50) rather than provide sufficient explanation. Texts also tended to use words or phrases that failed to define important terms and used terms that were too vague to be of much use (e.g., "the *stuff* cells are made of . . .").

Armbruster and Anderson (1988) recommended carefully screening textbooks so that the textbooks most "considerate" to the reader are selected for use. They recommended texts that (a) were not characterized by the above limitations and (b) employed ample cues that would facilitate learning. The selection of "considerate" textbooks does not necessarily mean that students will capitalize upon these learning mediators, though. Schumaker, Deshler, Alley, Warner, and Denton (1982) found that students with learning disabilities did not necessarily use textbooks comprehension enhancing cues when reading. Students with learning disabilities tended to ignore cues such as titles, headings, and subheadings; boldfaced words; study questions; main idea statements; introductions; and summaries. But Schumaker et al. demonstrated that the effects of these types of textual variables could be maximized when adolescents with learning disabilities were taught how to identify and use them to facilitate textual learning. Therefore, curricular mediation appears to operate under the same conditions as teacher mediation in terms of learner awareness. Careful text selection may have to be accompanied by teaching students how to use cues effectively.

To summarize, selecting alternative textbooks thought to be controlled for reading difficulty is problematic because the quantity of material to be learned is reduced and the presentation of the content in controlled textbooks may actually inhibit, rather than enhance, the "learnability" of subject matter. A more desirable way to accommodate low achievers in content classes might be to make the subject matter more learnable by employing instructional procedures and materials that mediate learning experiences. Moreover, textbooks sometimes are inconsiderate to the learner because of limitations associated with structure, coherence, and audience appropriateness. Low-achieving students do not necessarily capitalize on learning cues when they are present but many of these students can be taught to look for and use these cues. Because up to 44% of the information for which students are responsible in learning is presented in textbooks (Zigmond, Levin, & Laurie, 1985) and because many textbooks appear to be inconsiderate (Armbruster & Anderson, 1988), teachers often have to provide additional instruction as an adjunct to the text to successfully mediate learning.

Enhancing Content

Study Guides

One of the ways teachers can cue the organization of information is by using structured study guides consisting of sets of statements or questions designed to accompany reading assignments or teacher's lectures. Three common types are (a) multi-level guides, (b) concept guides, and (c) pattern guides (Horton & Lovitt, 1987). Multi-level guides are designed to address literal, interpretive, and applied levels of comprehension, whereas concept guides are designed to make new information more memorable by facilitating conceptual links or associations between the new information and that previously learned. Pattern guides are designed to enable the learner to recognize patterns of information (e.g., enumeration, sequence, compare/contrast, cause/effect).

Study guides can be employed in many ways. Two common approaches are either to (a) give the student the study guide to use as he or she independently reads an assignment or to (b) use a teacher-directed approach in which the student first reads the passage and then is provided the study guide; the teacher directs a discussion of the questions from the study guide while working with an overhead projector. This discussion typically is followed by a short test on the content-area information. Thus, the student's use of the study guide is mediated by the teacher.

To determine the relative effectiveness of multi-level study guides under teacher-mediated conditions compared to self-study conditions, Horton & Lovitt (1987) developed multi-level study guides to accompany two chapters from textbooks for science and social studies middle school and high school classes. Further, the researchers developed tests containing 15 multiple-choice questions to accompany the chapters. Results of the study indicated that almost half the students in the self-study condition scored below minimal mastery levels (80%). But when these same students were exposed to the teacher-mediated study guide condition, at least 90% of them improved. More notable, with the teacher-mediated study guide condition 60% not only improved but also scored at or above the minimal mastery levels.

The researchers conducted a similar study to examine the relative effects of student-directed study guides in which the student is provided the study guide but the teacher does not mediate the learning process by conducting a discussion of the study guide questions. In this study, the students independently completed the study guides at their desks, participated in a 5-minute feedback session to check their accuracy, followed by a 5-minute study session, and then took a 15-item test. Results indicated that about half the students scored below the minimal mastery level following the self-study condition. In the student-directed study guide condition, 63% to 74% of these same students scored above the minimal mastery levels.

Unfortunately, the small number of students classified as learning disabled precluded a separate analysis of their performances, but the researchers reported that 13 of 16 of the students with learning disabilities improved with study guides, but only seven of these improved to levels at or above minimal mastery levels. Thus, the study guides helped considerably but were insufficient, in and of themselves, to facilitate mastery of the material. A possible explanation is that although the teacher may facilitate the learning process by providing organizational cues in the form of study guides and teacher-directed use of the guides, the learning process may continue to be impaired because of memory deficits or lack of cognitive learning strategies commonly attributed to students with learning disabilities.

In light of the considerable evidence suggesting that low achievers benefit from high levels of teacher-mediated instruction, they likely will benefit more from teacher-directed study guides than from student-directed approaches, but this remains an untested observation. Clearly, however, use of study guides is preferable to self-study conditions.

Use of Concept Maps and Graphic Organizers
Another important technique teachers can employ to mediate the learning experiences of their students with learning disabilities is to supplement textbook materials with graphics (e.g., charts, diagrams) that provide visual displays of the subject matter's organization or structure. The "organizational function of pictures" (Levin, 1981a) has been used in various ways, including "semantic maps" (Johnson & Pearson, 1978), "networks" (Dansereau & Holley, 1982), and what Scruggs et al (1985) referred to as "figural taxonomies," or graphics that display superordinate, coordinate, and subordinate relationships between concepts, facts, and details, or some combination thereof. Graphic representations can assist in making the material more learnable because students with learning disabilities often lack the basic reading skills to extract the information from texts (Torgesen & Licht, 1983) and the texts themselves are often "inconsiderate" because of poor structure and organization (Anderson & Armbruster, 1984).

Several studies have demonstrated that learners (with poor reading ability, low verbal ability, and underdeveloped vocabulary) performed better when graphics were used to supplement regular content area text chapters (Koran & Koran, 1980; Moyer, Sowder, Threadgill-Sowder, & Moyer, 1984). Recent studies have provided positive evidence that the use of graphics as supplements to textbook material can be more effective than individual study conditions when used with students with learning disabilities. Darch and Carnine (1986) demonstrated that upper-elementary students (grades 4, 5, and 6) with learning disabilities benefited from visual displays when they were mediated by the teacher. Here, the teacher used an overhead projector to present a display containing labeled cells. Students were taught using a teaching script describing the cells and their interrelationships. Later, the teacher mediated the information by guiding students through the information using a visual display in which the cells were not labeled. These students performed significantly better when compared to others in a self-study condition wherein the content was presented only by text and discussed by the teacher. The visual display group scored an average of 86% correct on probes, whereas the test group scored an average of only 56%. But the study also revealed that the students in the graphics condition did not readily self-mediate use of visual displays when presented with new text information; they remained dependent on the teacher to mediate use of the graphics.

In a related study, Bergerud, Lovitt, and Horton (1987) investigated the effectiveness of using graphics, as compared to study guides or self-study conditions, with high school students who were learning disabled. The students attended either a 9th-grade basic science class or one of three other study skills classes (grades 9-12) for students with learning disabilities. All of the classes were exposed to each of the three treatments. Passages were taken from a life sciences textbook, and 20-item multiple-choice tests were constructed for each passage. Graphics and study guides to be used in conjunction with the texts also were constructed.

Results of the study indicated that the graphics treatment was the most effective in helping students attain the highest scores (60.5% of the students had scores above the minimal mastery level of 80% on the tests when graphics were used to facilitate the organization of the material). In the study guide condition, 42.1% of the students attained minimal mastery level. When students were placed in the self-study condition, only 31.6% achieved mastery. Although the use of graphics proved to be the most effective in helping the greatest number of students, using either graphics or study guides was better than or equal to 98% of the students in the self-study condition.

Technological Alternatives to Textbooks

To supplement and even to supplant textbooks, many educators have resorted to various machines and media devices (e.g., tape recordings, films, television programs, microcomputers, laser disks for delivering content or modifying the content to be learned). Advances in technology over the past 10 years and the increased availability of technological products to schools have made these options popular, although not necessarily effective. The broad body of research on effective teaching methods for learning disabilities reviewed above indicates that many low-achieving students may not possess skills for internal mediation (i.e., metacognition) to be able to capitalize upon known learning strategies. Many students who are considered mildly handicapped in their ability to learn can effectively perform various learning strategies when cued to do so by others, but they often fail to employ the strategies when left to themselves. Some recent work has focused on using machines as supplements to the teacher's direct instruction, with promising results. The machines are used as mechanisms for providing students with cues to use various learning strategies.

Audio Recordings of Text

The audio recording method relies heavily on transferring knowledge to audio tapes and then playing the tapes for the student. Textbooks and lectures are audio recorded to circumvent a reading problem or to allow for repeated listenings that facilitate notetaking and comprehension of information. Although research on the effectiveness of audio recording textbook material with adolescents who have learning disabilities is sparse, the research in this area can be divided into three groups: (a) verbatim recordings, (b) variable-speed recordings, and (c) recordings combined with strategy instruction and active student responses.

Verbatim audio recording is a common method used to accommodate the reading problems of low-achieving students, but research has led to mixed results with regard to its effectiveness with adolescents who have learning disabilities. For example, Mosby (1979) reported that the use of verbatim tapes of social studies material resulted in increased year-end achievement test scores for students classified as "high-audio" students over those classified as "low-audio" students; however, significant improvement in students' social studies grades was not demonstrated across the group. Wisemen, Hartwell, and Hannafin (1980) also found that although listening facilitated content acquisition for some students, the listening condition actually caused poorer performance for some high- as well as low-functioning readers. Torgesen (1984) reported that verbatim tapes acquired through the American Printing House for the Blind produced significant gains in comprehension in an experimental group of adolescents with learning disabilities when compared to a control group of adolescents with learning disabilities. Unfortunately, the effects were not consistent for all experimental group subjects in the study. Torgesen suggested that verbatim tapes appeared to be most beneficial for adolescents with learning disabilities who demonstrated poor decoding skills in conjunction with relatively higher intellectual abilities.

Some researchers have investigated the effect of presenting content at *variable rates* (words per minute) to students with learning disabilities (D'Alonzo & Zucker, 1982; Sawyer & Kosoff, 1981). In these studies, tape recorders capable of presenting the content at expanded, normal, or compressed rates were used to present content to adolescents with learning disabilities. Findings from these studies suggest that presentation rate generally does not affect comprehension of content information. Factors similar to those associated with reading comprehension skills (e.g., students' prior knowledge of related content, vocabulary diversity) more likely account for learning variance. Because comprehension does not seem to be affected by rate of presentation, however, the use of time-compressed recordings (i.e., more content covered in a shorter time) may be more desirable because they are more efficient.

Rationales for using audio-tape formats are sometimes based on an "aptitude-treatment interaction" (Lloyd, 1984). A common application of this interaction is to design instruction around the perceived modality strengths of the student ("auditory" versus "visual" learners). Thus, students who are presumed to be auditory learners are provided with audio formats (Mosby, 1980). The effectiveness of this form of intervention has yet to be demonstrated. For example, Miller (1983) found that the performance of adolescents with learning disabilities on minimal competency tests did not differ significantly when the test was read to them versus when they had to read it without assistance. This compensatory (Deshler, Schumaker, Lenz & Ellis, 1984) approach is based on the assumption that students' modalities can be reliably and validly assessed, and that the treatment has both internal and external validity, but these assumptions have not been empirically supported (see Lloyd, 1984, for a review).

In addition, the model itself may be an over-simplification of the learning process and problems manifested in learning disabilities. Specific modality-based interventions often fail to incorporate well established principles of learning and motivation (e.g., opportunities for active involvement in the learning process). Verbatim audio-tape formats often suffer from these limitations as well as from a lack of time and training for teachers who would be responsible for producing the audio recordings (Schumaker, Denton, & Deshler, 1984). More important, verbatim recordings provide minimal cues for facilitating internal mediating processes. They do not facilitate or teach students to use various learning strategies that might be necessary to acquire and remember content-area information. If the student fails to employ basic cognitive and metacognitive strategies while listening to the recordings, minimal learning is likely to occur.

In response to these problems, Schumaker et al. (1984) developed a skill-assisted audio tape recording package that included procedures for audio taping content material and teaching adolescents with learning disabilities how to gain information from the audio-taped materials through the use of three specific strategies. The first strategy was designed to facilitate students' use of critical behaviors associated with previewing information to be learned from the tape and textbook. The second strategy was designed to facilitate application of various cognitive strategies (e.g., self-questioning, paraphrasing) for elaborating on information presented by the tape and textbook. The third strategy was designed to facilitate students' application of a rehearsal process for learning the material and the use of metacognitive strategies associated with monitoring whether what needed to be learned had been learned.

The audio-tape format varied so that cues to use the various cognitive strategies noted above were embedded on the recording. History textbook chapters were visually coded with a special marking system that appeared in the text margins. One code indicated a verbatim reading of a particular section; another code indicated that the section was paraphrased on the tape; a third code indicated that it was being skipped altogether; and so on. The students listened to the audio recording while following the visual codes noted in the textbook. Schumaker et al. (1984) reported that performance, as indicated by regularly administered classroom tests, was significantly better following training in the three strategies in conjunction with the specially recorded audio tapes as opposed to when they listened to verbatim tapes; moreover, they performed superior to a control group of students who listened to verbatim tapes. This gain was demonstrated over textual information that exceeded the reading ability of the students by as much as 7 years.

In summary, providing students with an alternative to traditional instructional delivery methods does not necessarily translate into the student's improved content learning. Results from research on audio taping content material indicate that some students can learn content from audio tapes, especially when the audio presentation contains cues to mediate learning processes in conjunction with student training regarding how to use these mediators.

Computerized Study Guides
Within content classrooms, computer-assisted instruction (CAI) can be used as an external mediator for teaching new knowledge and skills. Although much of the current software is inappropriate or only marginally helpful in acquiring new skills or knowledge (Carlson & Silverman, 1986) and few studies have investigated the role of microcomputers when used as a mediator of new skills or content (Ellis & Sabornie, 1986), the limited evidence suggests that the microcomputer may be effective when used to di-

rectly teach content and skills as a technological adjunct to textbooks in the form of computerized study guides.

Printed study guides containing questions and statements adjunct to textbook material (e.g., Anderson & Biddle, 1975; Herber, 1970; Riley, 1979; Reder, 1985) have been used with considerable success to assist students with learning disabilities in a variety of content-area information (Horton & Lovitt, 1987; Lovitt, Rudsit, Jenkins, Pious, & Benedetti, 1985). In a recent study Horton, Lovitt, and Givens (1989) demonstrated that CAI could be designed to incorporate the advantages of printed study guides and, in addition, present new material, provide opportunities for practice, and test students' knowledge of the information.

The CAI consisted of three segments: (a) an approximately 1,000-word passage taken verbatim from a history textbook; (b) a set of 15 short-answer questions based on main ideas from the reading passage; and (c) a multiple-choice test containing 15 questions. Students using the CAI were allowed 15 minutes to read the passage and then were required to silently answer the study questions twice during another 15-minute period, and finally were required to complete the test within a 10-minute period. When the CAI group was compared to a control group of students who were told to take notes and study the same passages, the CAI group performed significantly higher on the tests. Although the study demonstrated some promising results with regard to technological alternatives to textbooks, generalizability of the results is somewhat limited for the general low-achieving population because the subjects had an average silent reading rate of 140 words per minute. Another limitation of the study was that it did not compare the CAI study guide with a printed study guide, nor did the study compare groups of students using the CAI with groups that had mastered a specific notetaking strategy.

Promoting the Use of Appropriate Learning Strategies During Direct Instruction in Content-Area Information

A considerable amount of research has demonstrated the efficacy of using a systematic lesson structure as well as a set of key instructional behaviors that have come to be collectively called *direct instruction*. This form of instruction has demonstrated effectiveness with remedial learners (e.g., Becker, Engelmann, Carnine, & Maggs, 1982; Carnine & Silbert, 1979; Gersten, 1983). Direct instruction uses a variety of techniques to increase the number of student responses, including questioning students to elicit individual oral responses, *cuing* students to provide group unison responses, and cuing students to make individual or unison motor responses (e.g., "Everybody, look at your maps; put your pencil on the spot on your map that shows where the Boston Tea Party took place"). A key purpose of eliciting frequent responses from students is to maintain high levels of student attention on the subject matter.

With the direct instruction model brief acknowledgments of correct responses, tangible reinforcers (e.g., tokens or points that are redeemable), and positive and corrective feedback are employed frequently as *reinforcement*. The primary purpose is to reinforce student efforts at learning and to provide critical information with regard to correctness of the learning. These first two features (cuing for responding and reinforcement) can be conceptualized as the manner in which the teacher structures the climate to maximize learning of content-area information. The last feature, *repetition*, is characteristic of direct instruction because the model frequently requires learners to repeatedly recite information to be learned. Unfortunately, *less sophisticated* direct-instruction teachers encourage students to use repetition, or rote rehearsal, as the primary learning strategy (Scruggs et al., 1985). It is quite possible to elicit frequent responses from students while simultaneously cuing them to use more sophisticated learning strategies.

This brief analysis of the direct instruction model shows that the primary function of the content teacher is to structure the learning climate and to mediate students' use of learning strategies as content information is being taught. Our primary concern in this article is not with the manner in which teachers use techniques to manipulate the learning climate but, rather, to analyze what they can do to mediate students' use of optimal learning strategies for efficient learning and retention of the content-area information, and to identify what teachers can do to make information more learnable.

Three elaborative strategies that teachers can mediate are *paraphrasing, visual imagining,* and *questioning.* These strategies are elaborative in the sense that they require the student to elaborate on the content by transforming information to be learned into their own language structures, to construct images that depict the meaning of the material that is to be remembered (Pressley, 1977; Pressley, Johnson, & Symons, 1987), and to activate prior knowledge by posing questions about information to be learned. Ample evidence suggests that students can benefit from instruction in the use of these strategies (see Pressley, 1977, and Wong, 1985b, for reviews). The emphasis in this research has been on teaching students the strategies and then measuring how well students apply the strategies to master content-area information. Less research involving students with mild learning handicaps has investigated how these strategies can be incorporated into instructional routines (e.g., direct instruction models) in which (a) the emphasis is on mastering the content, not mastering the strategic skill, and (b) the more efficient strategies (e.g., paraphrasing) are substituted for less efficient ones (e.g., rote repetition).

Pressley, Johnson, and Symons (1987) noted that material often has to be restructured into a form that is "more learnable." This more learnable material is presented in such a way that (a) mnemonic elaboration is facilitated, (b) it is rich with structures, cues, and devices that facilitate learning, or both. Facilitating mnemonic elaboration of material involves processes that allow separate bits of information to be learned and remembered as units or as a whole. As discussed earlier, the use of specific structures, cues, and devices must direct the learners' attention to the critical information, should guide the student in how the information should be processed, and should be explicit or easily recognized by the learner. Combining the two approaches can be a particularly potent way to facilitate content learning. To illustrate pragmatic applications of these techniques, two forms of mnemonic elaboration are discussed below.

Mnemonics

Two mnemonic strategies that serve as elaborative techniques are the "key word" and the "peg word" methods. These are particularly useful for facilitating students' learning of vocabulary terms and lists commonly found in science, social studies, history, and health curricula (Atkinson & Raugh, 1975; Levin, 1981a, 1981b, 1983). The key word method involves teaching students to pair new vocabulary words with previously learned concrete words that phonetically sound like or look like the new word. Saying the new word cues the sound-alike familiar word, and then the association with the familiar word cues recall of critical features of the definition.

Peg words are used to recall an ordered list of words (e.g., the order of states that seceded from the union during the Civil War). Students are taught a group of rhyming words for the numbers 1–10 (e.g., one–bun, two–shoe, three–knee, etc). The ordered rhyming words are paired with the previously learned key words to recall a specific list of items in the correct order. Use of graphics in combination with teacher-mediated mnemonic instruction appears to be a promising way to increase mastery of science material by students with learning disabilities (Mastropieri, Scruggs, McLoone, & Levin, 1985; Scruggs et al, 1985). Combining graphics with key word and peg word mnemonic instruction allows the visual display to serve the organizational needs of learning, and the mnemonic features (use of key word and peg word mnemonics) of the graphic serve what Levin (1981a) termed the "transformational" function by facilitating the transformation of new, difficult information into a form that is easier to remember.

To facilitate learning of lists depicting four categories of information (mineral's name, color, function, and hardness rating), Scruggs first used key word mnemonics to facilitate knowledge of the first three categories of information for each mineral, and then used peg word mnemonics to facilitate knowledge of their order in terms of hardness ratings. Adding the dimension of graphic displays to further facilitate learning, the mnemonic information then was transferred into pictorial form. The mineral used in making cosmetics, calcite, with a hardness rating of "3," would be graphically illustrated by a picture of a cow putting gray cosmetics on her knee (to coincide with peg words for 3–"knee"). Mastropieri and her colleagues demonstrated that using mnemonic key words and peg words, in conjunction with graphic displays of the mnemonic features of the lists, proved superior to teacher-directed instruction and free study of a list of basic minerals, their color, hardness scale, and functional use.

In a related study Scruggs et al. (1985) compared the use of mnemonic-graphics as a means of facilitating the learning of science information using figural taxonomy cellular graphic displays paired with direct instruction and free study conditions. The 36 junior high students with learning disabilities were randomly assigned to one of the three conditions and then tested to determine the extent of mastery of the material. Scruggs et al. found that the graphic displays with accompanying teacher-directed instruction were not significantly more powerful than free study conditions—a finding different from those reported by Horton and Lovitt (1987). Students in the mnemonic graphic condition learned almost twice as much information as did students from either of the other two conditions.

Prompting Strategic Interaction with Content Subject-Matter

When teaching content-area information, teachers can promote strategic learning by prompting students to employ various cognitive processes while interacting with the subject-matter. These processes include paraphrasing, summarizing, identifying main ideas and important details, predicting, generating questions, imagining, and relating new information to personal experiences and interests. These strategies can be prompted during verbal presentations of material presented in class using the "instructional pause procedure" (Rowe, 1976, 1980, 1983).

To use the procedure, the teacher provides direct instruction on the content subject-matter for approximately 8 minutes and then initiates an activity that requires students to use various cognitive learning strategies (e.g., "Talk among the other members in your group and decide what was the main idea and two of the most important details of what I just taught" or, "Talk among the other members in your group and make a prediction about what will happen when I add sulfur to this mixture. Then we'll see if your prediction is correct" or, "Decide what would be a good way to remember. . . ."). The teacher then allows the students about 2 minutes to formulate their response and picks one group to express its response to the entire class. The other groups compare their response to the one expressed to class. By frequently utilizing the instructional pause technique to prompt strategic interaction with the material to be learned, students employ general elaboration strategies (e.g., paraphrasing) as they discuss the topic among themselves, as well as the specific strategy cued by the teacher (e.g., main idea generation, predicting), and they employ monitoring strategies when they compare their responses to those of other groups.

The empirical validity of the pause procedure in a classroom situation is promising, but only a few studies have investigated this option as applied to mildly handicapped or low-achieving students in secondary school settings (e.g., Hawkins, 1988; Hudson, 1987; Hughes, Hendrickson, & Hudson, 1986). Hawkins (1988) investigated the effects of using the instructional pause technique on the mastery of verb-identification skills by eight 7th- and 8th-grade students with severe behavior disorders. A multiple-baseline across student dyads designed was used. Results of the study showed moderate increases in verb-identification skills in seven of the students and a statistically significant response generalization as indicated by correct use of these verbs when writing. Hawkins noted that the procedure was particularly appropriate for students with short attention spans, low frustration tolerance, and limited impulse control.

Providing a Metacognitive Orientation to Learning Content Subject-matter

A technique that has received relatively little research attention involves having the teacher model metacognitive processes during content-area instruction and prompting students to use it when learning (Ellis & Sabornie, 1989). When teaching, metacognition can be modeled by making covert thoughts overt, or by thinking out loud to illustrate for students the thought processes associated with analyzing what is to be learned and what is the best way to go about learning it. To prompt students' use of metacognition, the teacher can provide students with a listing of information to be learned, and then work with students to prioritize the information, organize it, and decide the best way to learn it, decide which parts will be most difficult and easy to learn, and predict how much study time different parts of the material will require. Here, the content teacher acts both as an information source for the subject-matter and as a collaborator in the learning process.

The application of cognitive learning strategies also can be modeled by the teacher using a form of didactic, or reciprocal teaching, instruction (e.g., Palincsar & Brown, 1984). Here, the teacher provides a lecture about the content-area information while modeling the use of predicting, question generating, summarizing, and clarifying strategies. The teacher then prompts students to perform these strategies. Critical to this process is not just modeling and prompting students to use various strategies but also discussing with students why they are using them, when to use them, and how effective they seem to be working. The process is not limited to teaching students simply to use the strategies but also to reflect more on the demands of a given task, how to address these demands, and how to monitor the effectiveness of the chosen strategy for meeting these demands.

To date, little empirical research has been generated demonstrating the effectiveness of providing a metacognitive orientation to learning content in classroom situations. The procedures currently employed are commonly adapted from various instructional models that have a discovery learning (e.g., Ausubel, 1961), didactic (Palincsar & Brown, 1984) and repeated modeling of strategies (Rosenthal & Zimmerman, 1978) orientation. These procedures are often further enhanced by providing students with a direct explanation (Roehler & Duffy, 1984) about why, when and where to use metacognitive thought processes and various learning strategies.

Cuing Students to Use Previously Mastered Specific Strategies in Remedial Settings

Instruction in the use of task-specific learning strategies is becoming an increasingly more common form of intervention in secondary special education programs (Deshler & Lenz, in press). These task-specific strategies focus on how to perform specific routine tasks commonly found in content-area classes (e.g., reading textbooks, preparing for and taking tests, writing themes or essays, test taking). For example, because many content-area classes require students to answer essay questions or write reports, resource room students might learn the "DEFENDS" strategy (Ellis, Courtney, & Church, in press) for writing point-of-view paragraphs.

When students learn task-specific strategies in special education settings, the primary role of the mainstream content-area teacher is to cue students to use these strategies to complete tasks. This can be accomplished via verbal cues (e.g., "This is a good time to use the DEFENDS strategy") and by integrating cues to perform the strategies in the course media. For example, explicit overt cues to use the DEFENDS writing strategy can be incorporated into study guide and test questions (e.g., "Use the DEFENDS strategy to state why you think the South lost the Civil War"). Several studies have demonstrated that when students have been taught task-specific strategies in remedial settings, providing cues to employ them in the targeted setting can have a dramatic effect on their use of the strategy and performance in the mainstream classrooms (for a review, see Ellis, Lenz, & Sabornie, 1987a, 1987b).

IMPLEMENTATION ISSUES

For various adaptive teaching procedures to have a positive and sustained impact on the lives of students with mild handicaps, the intervention must have empirical validity, teachers implementing the intervention must be sufficiently trained in its critical features, and the climate in which the intervention is to occur must be conducive to implementation. Teachers' perceptions of (a) competence in using the technique, (b) its value relative to attaining instructional goals, and (c) ease in which the intervention is employed are critical variables that influence this climate and will logically have a significant impact on whether teachers actually employ the procedure in their content-area classrooms.

Ellis and Sabornie (1989) investigated these variables in relation to six adaptive teaching procedures oriented toward facilitating the use of cognitive learning strategies in content-area classrooms. The differences of 13 content-area teachers' perceptions of familiarity, value, use, assistance needed to routinely implement, and reasonableness of being expected to routinely implement six cognitive strategy-based adaptive teaching procedures for facilitating mastery of content-area information were investigated. The teachers were systematically trained in each adaptive teaching procedure and were asked to implement each procedure in their content-area classrooms. Following implementation, the subjects were queried using a forced-choice Likert instrument and a structured interview format.

The six adaptive teaching procedures investigated were the strategic enhancement of content-area information through (a) using organizational devices, (b) using mnemonic devices, (c) promoting strategic interaction with content subject-matter, (d) providing a metacognitive orientation to learning content subject-matter, (e) cuing students to use task-specific learning strategies mastered by students in remedial settings, and (f) integrating instruction in task-specific learning strategies with content-area instruction. Results of the social validity study indicated that teachers who had been systematically trained and were relatively confident in employing the adaptive teaching procedures in their classroom situations generally placed a high value on all six procedures and reported routine use of them. With regard to ease of implementation, the teachers reported that outside help would be beneficial but was not crucial to successfully implementing each of the six options, and that content-area teachers should be expected to routinely employ these procedures as part of their repertoire of instructional tools.

Qualitative data indicated that the teachers were significantly more confident with the concrete procedures (e.g., enhancing content-area information through organizational devices and mnemonic devices) than with those that placed greater demands on their ability to communicate information-processing skills to others (i.e., providing a metacognitive orientation to learning content subject-matter). The metacognitive instructional orientation, however, received significantly higher ratings of value over the mnemonic forms of instruction. Teachers perceived the use of first-letter, key-word, and peg-word mnemonic devices as having relatively short-term benefits that were not likely to produce a sustained impact on students' knowledge base. Although teachers placed high value on the use of mnemonic devices when the information to be learned was limited in quantity, this form of adaptive teaching was valued less when extensive amounts of content information were to be learned (i.e., several different vocabulary terms, several different groups of items to be mastered for a single test).

As previously noted, although teachers viewed positively the use of adaptive teaching procedures, some teachers also indicated that they perceived teacher-directed instruction as somewhat incompatible with modeling metacognition and cognitive strategies. They also indicated perceived pressure from school district officials to "finish the book" and were reluctant to take the extra time they believed was necessary to adequately address the thinking domain associated with learning content-area information.

Ellis and Sabornie (1989) reported that the qualitative data reflected two overriding concerns. First, teachers expressed considerable concern about the time required to prepare lessons incorporating these adaptive teaching procedures, particularly when they would require critically analyzing the curriculum to prepare organizational and mnemonic devices. Comments were particularly critical of textbook publishers. Teachers believed commercial publishers should have the responsibility to supply them with preconstructed concept maps, figural taxonomies, and mnemonic devices, as well as to write texts rich with cues to employ cognitive reading strategies. Teachers also were concerned about how to make instruction simultaneously appropriate for low-achieving and high-achieving students enrolled in the same class. Teachers indicated that they believed the adaptive teaching procedures would be beneficial to all students, but they also expressed a concern that many normal and higher achieving students would quickly become bored with the instruction and that their learning might be compromised as a result.

Clearly, some adaptive teaching techniques may be more powerful than others in facilitating the mastery of content-area information, but little research has been conducted examining the relative power of various techniques. From a teacher's perspective, some fundamental questions must be addressed by future research: Which of the various techniques are the most powerful while requiring the least amount of energy to use? Which can be implemented on an individual basis without preparing special materials prior to delivering the content? Which of these adaptive teaching techniques can be readily integrated into traditional approaches to teaching content, and which require radical change?

THE CONTENT ENHANCEMENT MODEL

To address some of these concerns, a model for promoting successful content learning through the careful selection, organization, and delivery of information is being developed currently by researchers at the University of Kansas Institute for Research in Learning Disabilities (Bulgren, Schumaker, & Deshler, 1988; Deshler & Schumaker, 1988; Lenz, Alley, & Schumaker, 1987; Lenz & Bulgren, in press; Lenz, Bulgren, & Hudson, in press; Lenz & Mellard, 1990; Schumaker, Deshler, & McKnight, in press). The model being developed by these researchers is called the Content Enhancement Model. Lenz, Bulgren, and Hudson (in press) define content enhancement as the process of teaching scientific or cultural knowledge to a heterogeneous group of students in which: (a) group and individual learning needs both are met; (b) integrity of the content is maintained; (c) critical features of the content are selected, organized, manipulated, and complemented in a manner that promotes effective and efficient information processing; and (d) the content is delivered in a partnership with students in a manner that facilitates and enriches learning for all students.

To accomplish this, several major assumptions have been made.

1. The content teacher has the responsibility to present information that will promote student understanding and remembering of content to low-achieving students.
2. The process of planning, teaching, and evaluating for learning should be based on careful consideration of the information-processing demands placed on the teacher as well as the student.
3. Enhancements, consisting of carefully planned instructional routines and devices, should be utilized to enhance the delivery of content information.
4. The teacher must inform students of the enhancements that are to be used to enhance the delivery of information, and as a result, student learning.
5. The teacher must cue students when specific enhancements are being used to promote learning.
6. The teacher must purposely implement the enhancement in a partnership with students.
7. The teacher should induce himself/herself and the students to reflect on the enhancement and to evaluate its roles in learning and whether it has been an effective teaching/learning experience.

Therefore, great responsibility is placed on the teacher to become the primary instructional organizer.

The model consists of three major components. The first includes specific teaching routines that might be used to enhance or guide the delivery of major chunks of a content lesson, (e.g., routines designed to orient the students to information that will be learned, routines designed to help students understand concepts, or routines to promote active learning of new material). The second component consists of instructional devices that might be embedded in a routine to further enhance the delivery of content (e.g., devices designed to help the student understand, remember, or organize information). The third component consists of procedures for planning instruction and organizing the content enhancement process daily and over time under both planned and spontaneous circumstances, (e.g., guidance in identifying important information, analyzing prior knowledge requirements of the students). This third component seeks to address how teachers might be able to incorporate adaptive techniques into their normal teaching plans and reduce the negative impact of additional preparation required by some adaptive techniques. (For review of this model, see Lenz, Bulgren, and Hudson, in press, and Schumaker, Deshler, and McKnight, in press).

Although the development of different approaches and models for delivering content to low-achieving students in a more successful manner may be available in the future, the success of current efforts to improve the instructional situation rests in the hands of classroom teachers and publishers. It seems clear that teacher-mediated techniques associated with using study guides, concept maps, graphics, and various mnemonic techniques (e.g., perusing the content to determine the organization of material, producing concept maps and mnemonic graphics, study guides, tests), will require curriculum development activities prior to instructional delivery. If textbook publishers would supplement their texts with materials providing these kinds of instructional aids, teachers would be more likely to employ them in their classes. Unfortunately, publishers rarely include these types of materials. Therefore, individual teachers must produce them or teams of teachers who teach the same course must produce them. But the structure and climate of many schools do not encourage this type of collaboration. If the task is left to individual teachers, however, the task may be overwhelming.

As an alternative, teams of individuals could divide the task into manageable components with each member assigned a specific section of a textbook to develop instructional materials for students to use in mediating the learning process. These members then would share and explain their work with other team members. The process can have many inhibitors as well. For example, many educators who teach content classes in which large numbers of low-achieving students and students with learning disabilities are enrolled often do so as only part of their instructional load. In addition, course material and content may change, and reaching agreement across teachers on general development goals for a specific discipline may be difficult.

SUMMARY AND CONCLUSION

In summary, it seems clear that educators must attend to content acquisition as well as to skill acquisition in developing appropriate educational programs for low-achieving students and students with mild handicaps. But, with the exception of some of the research efforts described in this article (and possibly others not referenced herein that are consistent with the purposes of these studies), current conceptualizations regarding how skill and content acquisition might be appropriately addressed in a balanced fashion have been unimpressive. Previous efforts have focused either on skill acquisition, with little or no attention to content-area generalization, or on content acquisition through tutoring or content reduction, with little or no concern for skill application or attainment. Neither of these alternatives seems appropriate or acceptable. Concurrently, concern for the decrease in scientific and cultural literacy levels of all students has reached national proportions. Attention to how content can be successfully promoted in the face of student diversity has become an educational issue broader than the concerns expressed by special educators.

In effect, the current attention on content-area instruction could set the stage for unprecedented change over the next 10 years in how instruction in the content areas is accomplished. This change could result in an increase or a decrease in teacher attention to learner-sensitive instruction. In essence, a decrease in an emphasis in learner-sensitive instruction would have devastating effects on the success of low-achieving students in content-area classes. But, prompting a change toward instruction that is more learner sensitive, as discussed in this article, cannot be accomplished through the initiative of special educators alone. Such a change can be realized only when content-area teachers support such a change, embrace the goals of strategic learning and performance, demand instructional environments that promote such an orientation, and, as a result, create their own initiative for improved content-area instruction. The task of concerned special and regular educators is to begin sowing the seeds for such a change.

REFERENCES

Anderson, R. C., & Biddle, W. B. (1975). On asking people questions about what they are reading. In G. Bower (Ed.), *The psychology of learning and motivation* (Vol. 9, pp. 90–132). New York: Academic Press.

Anderson, T. H., & Armbruster, B. B. (1984). Studying. In P. D. Pearson (Ed.), *Handbook of reading research.* New York: Longman.

Anderson, T. H., Armbruster, B. B., & Kantor, R. N. (1980). *How clearly written are children's textbooks? or, of bladderworks and alfa* (Reading Education Report No. 16). Urbana: University of Illinois Center for the Study of Reading.

Armbruster, B. B., & Anderson, T. H. (1988). On selecting "considerate" content area textbooks. *Remedial & Special Education, 9,* 4–52.

Atkinson, R. C., & Raugh, M. (1975). An application of the mnemonic keyword method to the acquisition of a Russian vocabulary. *Journal of Experimental Psychology: Human Learning & Memory, 104,* 126–133.

Ausubel, D. P. (1961). Learning by discovery: Rationale and mystique. *Bulletin of National Association of Secondary School Principals, 45,* 18–58.

Becker, W. C., Engelmann, S., Carnine, D. W., & Maggs, A. (1982). Direct instruction technology: Making learning happen. In P. Karoly & J. J. Steffen (Eds.) *Improving children's competence: Advances in child behavioral analysis and therapy (Vol. 1),* (pp. 151–204). Lexington, MA: Heath.

Bergerud, D., Lovitt, T., & Horton, S. (1987). *The effectiveness of textbook adaptations in life science for high school students with learning disabilities.* Unpublished manuscript, University of Washington, Seattle.

Brophy, J., & Good, T. (1984). Teacher behavior and student achievement. In M. Wittrock (Ed.), *Third handbook of research on teaching* (pp. 328–375). New York: Macmillian,

Bulgren, J. A., Schumaker, J.B., & Deshler, D. D. (1988). Effectiveness of a concept teaching routine in enhancing the performance of LD students in secondary-level mainstream classes. *Learning Disability Quarterly, 11,* 3–17.

Carlson, S. A., & Silverman, R. (1986). Microcomputers and computer-assisted instruction in special classrooms: Do we need the teacher? *Learning Disability Quarterly, 9*(2), 105–110.

Carnine, D., & Silbert, J. (1979). *Direct instruction reading.* Columbus, OH: Charles E. Merrill.

D'Alonzo, B. J., & Zucker, S. H. (1982). Comprehension scores of learning disabled high school students on aurally presented content. *Exceptional Children, 48,* 35–36.

Dansereau, D. F., & Holley, C. D. (1982). Development and evaluation of a text mapping strategy. In A. Flammer & W. Kintsch (Eds.), *Discourse processing,* (pp. 536–554). Amsterdam, Netherlands: North Holland.

Darch, C., & Carnine, D. (1986). *Content area instruction: The role of information organization, learner strategies, and task structure.* Paper presented at annual meeting of American Educational Research Association, Chicago.

Deshler, D. D., & Lenz, B. K. (in press). The strategies instructional approach. *International Journal of Disability, Development, and Education.*

Deshler, D. D., Lowrey, N., & Alley, G. R. (1979). Programming alternatives for learning disabled adolescents: A nationwide survey. *Academic Therapy, 14,* 415–421.

Deshler, D. D., & Schumaker, J. B. (1988). An instructional model for teaching students how to learn. In J. L. Graden, J. E. Zins, & M. J. Curtis (Eds.), *Alternative educational delivery systems: Enhancing instructional options for all students.* (pp. 391–411). Washington, DC: National Association of School Psychologists.

Deshler, D. D., Schumaker, J. B., Lenz, B. K., & Ellis, E. S. (1984). Academic and cognitive interventions for LD adolescents: Part 2. *Journal of Learning Disabilities, 17*(3), 170–187.

Dupuis, N. M., & Askov, E. N. (1982). *Content area reading.* Englewood Cliffs, NJ: Prentice-Hall.

Ellis, E. S., Courtney, J., & Church, A. (in press). A learning strategy for meeting the writing demands of secondary mainstream classrooms. *Teaching Exceptional Children.*

Ellis, E. S., Lenz, B. K., & Sabornie, E. J. (1987a). Generalization and adaptation of learning strategies to natural environments: Part 1—Critical agents. *Remedial & Special Education, 8*(1), 6–21.

Ellis, E. S., Lenz, B. K., & Sabornie, E. J. (1987b). Generalization and adaptation of learning strategies to natural environments: Part 2—Research into practice. *Remedial & Special Education, 8*(2), 6–24.

Ellis, E. S., & Sabornie, E. J. (1986). Effective instruction with microcomputers: Promises, practices, and preliminary findings. *Focus on Exceptional Children, 19,* 1–16.

Ellis, E. S., & Sabornie, E. J. (1989). *Strategy-based instruction in content-area classes: Social validity of six options.* Unpublished manuscript, Program for Exceptional Children, University of South Carolina, Columbia.

Gersten, R. (1983). *Direct instruction with special education students: A review of evaluation research.* Unpublished manuscript, University of Oregon, Eugene.

Harber, J. (1983). The effects of illustrations on the reading performance of learning disabled and normal children. *Learning Disability Quarterly, 6,* 55–60.

Hawkins, J. (1988). Antecedent pausing as a direct information tactic for adolescents with severe behavior disorders. *Behavior Disorders, 13*(4), 263–272.

Herber, H. L. (1970). *Teaching reading in content areas.* Englewood Cliffs, NJ: Prentice-Hall.

Horton, S. V., & Lovitt, T. C. (1987). *Information organization for secondary students: Study guides.* Unpublished manuscript, University of Washington, Seattle.

Horton, S. V., Lovitt, T., & Givens, A. (1989). Teaching social studies to learning disabled and remedial high school students in a mainstreamed setting: Effects of a computerized study guide. *Journal of Learning Disabilities, 22,* 102–107.

Hudson, P. J. (1987). *The pause procedure: A technique to help mildly handicapped students learn factual content.* Unpublished dissertation, University of Florida, Gainesville.

Hughes, C. A., Hendrickson, J. M., & Hudson, P. J. (1986). The pause procedure: Improving factual recall from lectures by low and high achieving middle school students. *International Journal of Instructional Media, 13,* 217–226.

Johnson, D. D., & Pearson, P. D. (1978). *Teaching reading vocabulary.* New York: Holt & Co.

Joyce, B., & Weil, M. (1980). *Models of teaching.* Englewood Cliffs, NJ: Prentice-Hall.

Koran, M. L., & Koran, J. (1980). Interaction of learner characteristics with pictorial adjuncts in learning from science text. *Journal of Research in Science Teaching, 1,* 477–483.

Lenz, B. K., & Alley, G. R. (1983). *The effects of advance organizers on the learning and retention of learning disabled adolescents within the context of a cooperative planning model.* Final research report submitted to the U.S. Department of Education, Office of Special Education, Washington, DC.

Lenz, B. K., Alley, G. R., Beals, V. C., Schumaker, J. B., & Deshler, D. D. (1981). *Teaching LD adolescents a strategy for interpreting visual aids.* Unpublished manuscript, University of Kansas, Lawrence.

Lenz, B. K., Alley, G. R., & Schumaker, J. B. (1987). Activating the inactive learner: Advance organizers in the secondary content classroom. *Learning Disability Quarterly, 10*(1), 53–67.

Lenz, B. K., & Bulgren, J. A. (in press). Promoting learning in the content areas. In P. A. Cegelka & W. H. Berdine (Eds.), *Effective instruction for students with learning problems.* Needham Heights, MA: Allyn & Bacon.

Lenz, B. K., Bulgren, J.A., & Hudson, P. (in press). *Content enhancement: A model for promoting the acquisition of content by individuals with learning disabilities.* Proceedings of the Division of Learning Disabilities 1988 Research Symposium, Purdue University, Lafayette, IN.

Lenz, B. K., & Ellis, E. S. (in press). *Designing effective interventions for learning disabled adolescents.* Boston: College Hill Press.

Lenz, B. K., & Mellard, D. P. (1990). Content area skill assessment. In R. A. Gable & J. M. Hendrickson (Eds.), *Error patterns in academics: Identification and remediation.* White Plains, NY: Longman.

Levin, J. R. (1981a). The mnemonic 80's: Keywords in the classroom. *Educational Psychologist, 16,* 65–82.

Levin, J. R. (1981b). On functions of pictures in prose. In F. J. Pirozzolo & M. C. Wittrock (Eds.), *Neuropsychological and cognitive processes in reading* (pp. 203–228). New York: Academic Press.

Levin, J. R. (1983). Pictorial strategies for school learning: Practical illustrations. In M. Pressley & J. R. Levin (Eds.), *Cognitive strategy research: Educational applications* (pp. 213–237). New York: Springer-Verlag.

Lloyd, J. W. (1984). How shall we individualize instruction—or should we? *Remedial & Special Education, 5,* 7–15.

Lovitt, T., Horton, S. V., & Bergerud, D. (1987). Matching students with textbooks: An alternative to readability formulas and standardized tests. *British Columbia Journal of Special Education, 11*(1), 49–55.

Lovitt, T., Rudsit, J., Jenkins, J., Pious, C., & Benedetti, D. (1985). Two methods for adapting science materials for regular and learning disabled seventh graders. *Learning Disability Quarterly, 8,* 275–285.

Mastropieri, M. A., Scruggs, T. E., McLoone, B., & Levin, J. R. (1985). Facilitating the acquisition of science classifications in learning disabled students. *Learning Disability Quarterly, 8,* 299–309.

Meyer, B. J. F. (1981). Basic research on prose comprehension: A critical review. In D. F. Fisher & C. W. Peters (Eds.), *Comprehension and the competent reader: Interspeciality perspective.* New York: Praeger.

Miller, K. (1983). *An analysis of minimal competency testing requirements as applied to learning disabled students.* Unpublished doctoral dissertation, University of Kansas, Lawrence.

Mosby, R. (1979). A bypass program of supportive instruction for secondary students with learning disabilities. *Journal of Learning Disabilities, 12,* 187–190.

Mosby, R. (1980). The application of the developmental-by-pass procedure to LD adolescents. *Journal of Learning Disabilities, 13,* 21–22.

Moyer, J. C., Sowder, L., Threadgill-Sowder, J., & Moyer, M. B. (1984). Story problem formats: Drawn versus telegraphic. *Journal for Research in Mathematics Education, 15,* 342–351.

Palincsar, A. M., & Brown, A. L. (1984). Reciprocal teaching of comprehensive fostering and monitoring activities. *Cognition & Instruction, 1,* 117–175.

Pressley, M. (1977). Imagery and children's learning: Putting the picture in developmental perspective. *Review of Educational Research, 47,* 586–622.

Pressley, M., Johnson, C. J., & Symons, S. (1987). Elaborating to learn and learning to elaborate. *Journal of Learning Disabilities, 20,* 76–91.

Reder, L. M. (1985). Techniques available to author, teacher, and reader to improve retention of main ideas of a chapter. In S. F. Chipman, J. W. Segal, & R. Graser (Eds.), *Thinking and learning skills: Vol. 2, Research and open questions* (pp. 37–63). Hillsdale, NJ: Erlbaum.

Riley, J. D. (1979). The effect of reading guides upon students' literal, interpretive, and applied level comprehension of word problems. In H. L. Herber & J. D. Riley (Eds.), *Research in reading in the content areas: Fourth year report* (pp. 79–97). Syracuse, NY: Syracuse University Reading and Language Arts Center.

Roehler, L. R., & Duffy, G. G. (1984). Direct explanation of comprehension processes. In G. G. Duffy, L. R. Roehler, & J. Mason (Eds.), *Comprehension instruction: Perspectives and suggestions* (pp. 265–280). New York: Longman.

Rosenshine, B. (1979). Content, time, and direct instruction. In P. L. Peterson & H. L. Walberg (Eds.), *Research on teaching: Concepts, findings, and implications* (pp. 28–56). Berkeley, CA: McCutchan.

Rosenthal, T. L., & Zimmerman, B. J. (1978). *Social learning and cognition.* New York: Academic Press.

Rowe, M. B. (1976). The pausing principle: Two invitations to inquiry. *Research on College Science Teaching, 5,* 258–259.

Rowe, M. B. (1980). Pausing principles and their effects on reasoning in science. *New Directions in Community Colleges, 31,* 27–34.

Rowe, M. B. (1983). Getting chemistry off the killer-course list. *Journal of Chemical Education, 60,* 954–956.

Sawyer, D. J., & Kosoff, T. O. (1981). Accommodating the learning needs of reading disabled adolescents: A language processing issue. *Learning Disability Quarterly, 4,* 61–68.

Schallert, D. L. (1980). The role of illustrations in reading comprehension. In R. J. Spiro, B. C. Bruce, & W. F. Brewer (Eds.), *Theoretical issues in reading comprehension: Perspectives from cognitive psychology, linguistics, artificial intelligence, and education* (pp. 503–524). Hillsdale, NJ: Lawrence Erlbaum Associates.

Schumaker, J. B., Denton, P., & Deshler, D. D. (1984). *The learning strategies curriculum: The paraphrasing strategy.* Lawrence: University of Kansas.

Schumaker, J. B., & Deshler, D. D. (1984). Setting demand variables: A major factor in program planning for LD adolescents. *Topics in Language Disorders Journal, 4,* 22–44.

Schumaker, J. B., Deshler, D. D., Alley, G. R., Warner, M M., & Denton, P. (1982). Multipass: A learning strategy for improving reading comprehension. *Learning Disability Quarterly, 5,* 409–414.

Schumaker, J.B., Deshler, D. D., & Ellis, E. S. (1986). Intervention issues related to the education of LD adolescents. In J. K. Torgesen & B. Y. K. Wong (Eds.), *Psychological and educational perspectives on learning disabilities* (pp. 239–365). Columbus, OH: Academic Press.

Schumaker, J. B., Deshler, D. D., & McKnight, P. C. (in press). *Teaching routines for content areas at the secondary level.* Washington, DC: National Association for School Psychologists.

Scruggs, T. E., Mastropieri, M. A., Levin, J. R., McLoone, B., Gaffney, J. S., & Prater, M. A. (1985). Increasing content-area learning: A comparison of mnemonic and visual-spatial direct instruction. *Learning Disabilities Research, 1,* 18–31.

Torgesen, J., & Licht, B. (1983). The learning disabled child as an inactive learner: Retrospect and prospects. In J. D. McKinney & L. Feagans (Eds.), *Topics in Learning Disabilities* (Vol. 1). Rockville, MD: Aspen.

Voss, J. F. (1982, March). *Knowledge and social science problem solving.* Paper presented at AERA meeting, New York City.

Wiederholt, J. L., & McEntire, B. (1980). Educational options for handicapped adolescents. *Exceptional Education Quarterly, 1,* 1–10.

Wisemen, D. E., Hartwell, L. K., & Hannafin, M. J. (1980). Exploring the reading and listening skills of secondary mildly handicapped students. *Learning Disability Quarterly, 3,* 56–61.

Wong, B. Y. L. (1985a) Metacognition and learning disabilities. In T. G. Waller, D. Forrest-Pressley, & E. MacKinnon (Eds.), *Metacognition, cognition and human performance* (pp. 137–180). New York: Academic Press.

Wong, B. Y. L. (1985b). Potential means of enhancing content skills acquisition in learning disabled adolescents. *Focus on Exceptional Children, 17*(5), 1–8.

Zigmond, N., Levin, E., & Laurie, T. (1985). Managing the mainstream: An analysis of teacher attitudes and student performance in mainstream high school programs. *Journal of Learning Disabilities, 18,* 535–541.

Edwin Ellis is affiliated with the University of Alabama, Tuscaloosa. Keith Lenz is affiliated with the Institute for Research in Learning Disabilities, University of Kansas, Lawrence.

○ 19 ○

This article reviews the instructional strategies found to be most effective for math instruction. It includes what is known about the learning of math and effective instructional technology. Teachers of students with mild disabilities will become more effective if they implement direct instruction as described in this article.

Effective Mathematics Instruction: Development, Instruction, and Programs

John Wills Lloyd and Clayton E. Keller

We see effective instruction as having three important characteristics:

1. It is based on empirical evidence about development and use of the knowledge and skills that comprise the area to be taught.
2. It is delivered using instructional procedures that have been shown to have positive effects on pupil outcome.
3. It uses programs that have been empirically validated.

At a minimum, providing content instruction requires some way of delivering that content. But, to the extent that we can incorporate knowledge about the ways people act and think when correctly and efficiently handling that content (point 1), we can make instruction more effective. Of course, other things being equal, we assume that people (teachers, parents, administrators, students, and others) would prefer to have students taught by teachers who use effective instructional techniques to deliver the content (point 2). Similarly, we assume that people would prefer to have students taught using the most effective instructional programs available (point 3); that is, we presume that people would favor instructional materials that have a demonstrated record of success.

Along these lines, our purpose in this article is to illuminate what is known about providing effective instruction in mathematics. We begin with some illustrations about the growing understanding of children's thinking in mathematics, follow that with a discussion of the application of effective teaching procedures, and conclude with an examination of research about effective procedures and programs.

COGNITIVE DEVELOPMENT IN MATHEMATICS

Much of the current research in mathematics education and cognitive psychology focuses on what pupils know and do when solving mathematical problems. In this section we illustrate this research by describing how students develop basic knowledge about numbers and strategies for manipulating them. Because one of the most thoroughly studied areas concerns the algorithms that preschool and primary-grade students use when solving simple addition problems, we highlight this area but also make references to more sophisticated types of performance. Researchers have considered (a) differences in the strategies learners use, and (b) knowledge about numbers and arithmetic procedures needed to use the strategies (Pellegrino & Goldman, 1987).

Strategies

To some extent, nonhandicapped learners apparently develop their own algorithms for solving problems involving numbers (Romberg & Carpenter, 1986), whether they are left to their own devices (e.g., Groen & Resnick, 1977) or are provided specific instruction in the use of certain algorithms (e.g., Houlihan & Ginsburg, 1981; Russell, 1977). Carpenter and Moser (1983) described three levels of development in addition strategies.

In the first level, called *counting all with models,* children use strategies in which physical objects (including fingers) represent the addends of the problem. Objects are set out for each addend, the sets of objects are combined either physically or conceptually, and then they are counted (starting at one).

At the second level, called *counting sequences without models,* learners do not depend on objects. In the first strategy at this level, called *Sum* (Groen & Parkman, 1972), the children use the counting-all-with-models strategy but do not use physical models of the addends. The second strategy at this level is called *counting on from first.* The pupil begins counting by naming the first addend and then counts on from the starting place the number of counts indicated by the second addend. For example, to solve the problem 3 + 5, the child would say "3," then count "4, 5, 6, 7, 8." The third strategy at this level is counting on from larger or *Min* (Groen & Parkman, 1972). Although this strategy is similar to the previous one, it is slightly more efficient. The child first determines which addend is larger ("3 plus 5 . . . 5 is larger"), names that addend ("5 . . ."), and counts on for the other, smaller addend ("6, 7, 8"). It is called Min because it requires the minimum number of counting steps.

Strategies at the third level use *number facts* that the learner knows (Carpenter & Moser, 1983). Children can recall some facts—doubles or ties (e.g., 4 + 4)—rapidly, even at a relatively early age (Groen & Parkman, 1972). In the strategies at this level, they use these known facts to solve other problems; for example, the child might think, "5 plus 6 . . . 5 and 5 is 10, and 6 is one more than 5, so my answer has to be one more . . . 11." Eventually, most children will solve simple problems just by using known facts. Use of this strategy becomes predominant around the third grade for children with normally developing arithmetic skills (Ashcraft, 1982).

Development of these strategies permits some generalizations to be made about the acquisition of mathematical skills (Carpenter & Moser, 1983). First, each succeeding strategy builds on strategies learned previously. Second, as learners progress through the levels of strategies, they become more flexible in using strategies to solve various kinds of addition problems. Last, the strategies increase in abstraction and efficiency; for example, in later strategies pupils simply let a numeral stand for a number of objects, whereas in an earlier strategy they put out a number of objects for each numeral.

Although learners gradually adopt more efficient strategies, they do not always use the most efficient strategies available to them (Carpenter & Moser, 1983). In fact, they use different strategies, often depending upon the particular addition problems they encounter (Houlihan & Ginsburg, 1981; Russell, 1977; Siegler & Robinson, 1982). In a longitudinal study of pupils in first through third grades, Carpenter and Moser (1984) found great variability in the use of strategies both within a testing session and from one session to another. For example, some children who were capable of efficient counting strategies such as Min would use less efficient strategies if manipulatives were available. But no clear patterns of strategy use emerged relative to type of word problem or size of the numbers involved.

Also, research suggests that students with difficulties in mathematics, such as some learning disabled students, may use the same strategies that competent math students use but may use them in ways that contribute to problems with the tasks. Geary, Widaman, Little, and Cormier (1987) found that students with disabilities in math (including learning disabled students in the sixth grade) seemed to use counting strategies instead of memory-retrieval strategies to solve basic addition facts, took longer to execute these counting strategies, and had difficulties monitoring the execution of the strategies. Svenson and Broquist (1975) suggested that poor achievers' slow reaction times for solving basic addition fact problems might be the result of difficulty in determining which addend was larger and where to start the counting process when using the Min strategy.

Conceptual Knowledge

Along with examining the procedures of addition strategies, researchers (e.g., Resnick, 1983; Fuson, 1982; Secada, Fuson, & Hall, 1983) also have studied learners' understanding of numbers and addition. When using Min (or any other mathematics strategy), learners manipulate the parts of arithmetic problems and numbers. According to Resnick, these strategies "provide evidence that children understand the structure of numbers and are able to partition and recombine with some flexibility" (pp. 121–122). Such understanding and ability are possible because children organize their knowledge about numbers into a representation or schema. The child, however, does not have to be able to describe his or her representation.

Schema can develop from everyday experiences such as counting things and noticing the relationships between parts and wholes. Numbers do not have to be involved in the origin of the representation. Simple forms of the representation that do involve actual numbers, however, could be related to simple procedures (e.g., counting up from a given number) for solving problems. Experiences with numbers then lead to further development of the representation and of new procedures.

In sum, two major points that have implications for instruction appear in the research about cognitive processes.

- As children become more proficient in addition, they develop strategies that are (a) based on previous strategies, (b) more efficient than earlier ones, and (c) likely to be similar to patterns of development in other individuals. Ideally, in choosing strategies to teach, one probably should choose strategies that are the most efficient. But can the most efficient strategies be taught without previous exposure to the preceding sequence of less efficient strategies?

  Often, we teach pupils something akin to the counting-all-with-models strategy and then go directly to teaching them to memorize each combination as a fact. Might this be the source of some of the problems that pupils experience in mathematics? Can atypical learners skip the intermediary steps as readily as their peers?
- Conceptual and procedural knowledge are linked and change together. Thus, although the stress is usually on teaching pupils how to perform arithmetic operations, instructional approaches maybe should teach concepts while attempting to change procedural strategies.

EFFECTIVE PRESENTATION

Many features of *how* teachers present material influence the learning of pupils being taught. These include providing adequate opportunities to learn, emphasizing academic learning, communicating expectations that the pupils can learn, actively leading instruction, and so forth (Brophy & Good, 1986). This model is generally referred to as the *direct instruction* approach (Rosenshine, 1976).[1] In addition, some more molecular aspects of teaching presentations (e.g., reinforcement) increase pupil performance. In this section we first discuss the overall model of effective teaching as it applies to mathematics instruction and then describe some of the more detailed techniques.

---

[1]Following the form of others (e.g., Becker & Carnine, 1981), we must discriminate between the version of *direct instruction* described by Rosenshine (e.g., 1976) and the model proposed by Engelmann, Becker, and Carnine (e.g., Becker, 1986; Engelmann & Carnine, 1982)—labeled the "Direct Instruction Model" during the late 1960s and early 1970s as a part of the Follow Through Project. Current, everyday use of the term "direct instruction" in educational circles probably is more similar to Rosenshine's than to Engelmann, Becker, and Carnine's. Our use here is tied to citations of the source.

Direct Instruction

Although educators may differ about the relative emphasis on parts of the model, they generally agree that teachers who are teaching orderly subjects such as mathematics are more likely to be effective if they:

- Begin a lesson with a short review of previous, prerequisite learning.
- Begin a lesson with a short statement of goals.
- Present new material in small steps, with student practice after each step.
- Give clear, detailed instructions and explanations.
- Provide a high level of active practice for all students.
- Ask a large number of questions, check for student understanding, and obtain responses from all students.
- Guide students during initial practice.
- Provide systematic feedback and corrections.
- Provide explicit instruction and practice for seatwork exercises and, when necessary, monitor students during seatwork. (Rosenshine & Stevens, 1986, p. 377)

Application of these broad guidelines to mathematics instruction is clearly illustrated in a part of the Missouri Mathematics Effectiveness Project (e.g., Good & Grouws, 1979; for an extensive set of recommendations, see Good, Grouws, & Ebmeier, 1983). In this project teachers implemented their mathematics instruction for 4 months according to the guidelines for teaching given in Table 1. The results showed that the percentile scores of students in the experimental classrooms increased over 30 points.

A particularly important aspect of the findings from this project was that the treatment program had especially beneficial effects on lower-performing students (Ebmeier & Good, 1979). Major reviews emphasize the importance of these teaching behaviors for low-performing students. Brophy and Good say that "low-achieving students need more control and structuring from their teachers: more active instruction and feedback" (1986, p. 365). Rosenshine and Stevens (1986) make similar observations. Additional support for the importance of this approach with atypical learners is available in the literature on specific parts of teachers' instructional behavior.

Specific Teaching Behaviors

Among the many other things that teachers should do, they must present a fact, concept, or procedure in some way. This usually is done by *modeling* the fact, concept, or procedure. Then, when pupils practice using the fact, concept, or procedure, the teacher must provide consequences that are related to their performance—particularly *reinforcement* and *corrections*. The effects of modeling and reinforcement have been studied extensively.

Modeling
Modeling or demonstrating is a time-honored teaching mechanism. Models occur in any of many different forms. The teacher may use modeling by:

**TABLE 1   Recommendations for Effective Instruction
From the Missouri Mathematics Effectiveness Project**

Daily Review (first 8 minutes except Mondays)
  (a) review the concepts and skills associated with the homework
  (b) collect and deal with homework assignments
  (c) ask several mental computation exercises

Development (about 20 minutes)
  (a) briefly focus on prerequisite skills and concepts
  (b) focus on meaning and promoting student understanding by using lively explanations,
       demonstrations, process explanations, illustrations, etc.
  (c) assess student comprehension
       (1) using process/product questions (active interaction)
       (2) using controlled practice
  (d) repeat and elaborate on the meaning portion as necessary

Seatwork (about 15 minutes)
  (a) provide uninterrupted successful practice
  (b) momentum—keep the ball rolling—get everyone involved, then sustain involvement
  (c) alerting—let students know their work will be checked at end of period
  (d) accountability—check the students' work

Homework Assignment
  (a) assign on a regular basis at the end of each math class except Fridays
  (b) should involve about 15 minutes of work to be done at home
  (c) should include one or two review problems

Special Reviews
  (a) weekly review/maintenance
       (1) conduct during the first 20 minutes each Monday
       (2) focus on skills and concepts covered during the previous week
  (b) monthly review/maintenance
       (1) conduct every fourth Monday
       (2) focus on skills and concepts covered since the last monthly review

Source: From "The Missouri Mathematics Effectiveness Project: An Experimental Study in Fourth-Grade Classrooms" by T.L. Good and D.A. Grouws, 1979, *Journal of Educational Psychology,* 71. Reprinted by permission.

- Stating a fact or rule (e.g., "Any number times zero equals zero").
- Performing a task (e.g., "Watch me. I'm going to do this long division problem. First, uhmm, I estimate how many times this [pointing to the divisor] will go into this [pointing to the dividend]. Let me see, 19 is almost 20 and 20 will go into 50 about 2 times. . .").
- Having students observe a shill (another student or teacher) answer a question (e.g., "Let's see if Jane knows this one—Jane, what's another way to say 10^3?") or perform a task (e.g., "Watch Jeff; he's going to show us how to multiply a binomial").

Simply modeling appropriate performance can have surprising effects on student behavior in mathematics. For instance, Smith and Lovitt (1975; see also Rivera & Smith,

1988) found that supplying learning-disabled boys with a demonstration and a permanent model (a problem and its solution written on the boys' worksheets) markedly improved the boys' performance. Not only did the boys' performance on the target problems improve, but it also improved on other problems for which they had not received models.

Reinforcement

As in most other learning, operant reinforcement plays an important role in acquisition of arithmetic skills and knowledge. In the early stages of learning, correct responses that are reinforced are more likely to recur. In later stages of learning, reinforcement also may be useful. For example, if students answer too slowly (not automatically) or inconsistently, reinforcement of higher rates of responding or more accurate responding can improve their performance (e.g., Hasazi & Hasazi, 1972; Smith, Lovitt, & Kidder, 1972).

Reinforcement is of lesser value when students do not know *how* to perform a task. Studies with handicapped learners have shown that the effectiveness of reinforcement contingencies depends upon students' being capable of performing the target response (Grimm, Bijou, & Parsons, 1973; Smith & Lovitt, 1976).

In addition to the forms of reinforcement with which we are all familiar (praise, token rewards, and so on), reinforcement can take subtle forms. For instance, Fink and Carnine (1975) found that having students maintain graphs of their progress reinforced their levels of performance in arithmetic. Furthermore, simply acknowledging that an answer is correct probably serves as reinforcement. Thus, teachers who nod, say "yes," or repeat students' correct answers are appropriately providing reinforcement.

Corrections

When students answer questions or perform algorithms incorrectly, they provide perhaps one of the most important opportunities to teach. Corrections are the teaching actions that teachers take under such circumstances. Corrections should neither be viewed as punishment nor delivered in a punishing fashion. When the incorrectly answered question is simple or factual (e.g., the teacher points to a numeral and says, "What number is this?"), the most appropriate correction is to model the correct answer for the student. When the mistaken response is made after the student has completed an algorithm or strategy, probably the most appropriate correction is to model the correct use of the algorithm.

Mistakes that students make on algorithmic problems are often systematic, revealing a mistaken strategy (Brown & Burton, 1978; Cox, 1975; Ginsburg, 1977; Lankford, 1972; Young & O'Shea, 1981). By analyzing these errors, teachers can ascertain on which specific part of a solution algorithm they should focus correction procedures.

Some additional procedures that have been studied in the area of mathematics may be useful when students make errors. For example, two studies have used interventions that cue pupils' access to appropriate procedural knowledge for computation problems. Lovitt and Curtiss (1968) required a student to read each problem aloud before writing the answer to it. This procedure produced beneficial effects on the student's arithmetic performance. Similarly, Parsons (1972) required pupils to both circle and name the operation symbols (a plus or a minus) of a problem prior to performing the arithmetic operation. This technique increased accuracy among students who had often performed the wrong operation.

In short, effective mathematics instruction must incorporate aspects of teaching behavior that have been shown to be related to achievement. We have solid information about the general form of these behaviors, such as was described in the Missouri Mathematics Effectiveness Project. And we know that the use of specific procedures such as reinforcement have very clear, immediate effects on performance. Effective programs should incorporate these.

PROGRAMS

Information about how pupils think has implications for the content and organization of effective instruction. This information and the information about effective teaching procedures, when combined with what is known from field studies of teaching mathematics, outlines effective teaching. Two major groups of field studies of mathematics are pointed out in this section. In one, researchers have focused on teaching some fairly specific aspect of mathematics content or skill. In the other, comprehensive mathematics programs have been studied.

Target Skills and Knowledge

Studies focusing on specific skills illustrate how interventions can address access to appropriate content knowledge or increase content knowledge. The content knowledge may be declarative (for example, knowing facts about numbers and their relations), or it may be procedural (knowing how to perform solution algorithms). These studies are summarized in Table 2.

One challenge that teachers face is teaching declarative content to students. Haupt, Van Kirk, and Terraciano (1975) described a simple method for increasing declarative knowledge and automatic recall of number facts. Gradually they obscured the answers to simple subtraction problems by covering each answer with cellophane. This condition was contrasted with a control condition in which the student received traditional drill-and-practice instruction in addition. Haupt et al. found that the fading procedure (combined with reinforcement) resulted in the child reaching criterion nearly twice as rapidly and making five times fewer errors than the control condition. Similarly strong results were observed at follow-up testing.

Sometimes, as the developmental literature on addition indicates, knowledge of basic facts is best taught as procedural knowledge at first and only later brought to the automatic level. Several studies have examined how to teach pupils procedural knowledge. In one model of how to teach procedural knowledge—academic strategy training—teachers model the steps of an algorithm that students use to solve a specific type of problem (Cullinan, Lloyd, & Epstein, 1981; Lloyd, 1980; Lloyd & de Bettencourt, 1982). According to this approach, a task analysis of the skills needed to solve a class of problems is completed. Then students are tested to ascertain which, if any, of the requisite skills

TABLE 2   Studies Focusing on Content Knowledge

Study	Math Content	Intervention and Cognitive Purpose
Albion & Salzberg (1982)	addition	general and task-specific self-instructional training (metacognition to guide procedural knowledge)
Cameron & Robinson (1980)	addition and subtraction	task-specific self-instructional training (metacognition to guide procedural knowledge)
Davis & Hajicek (1985)	decimal multiplication	teacher model, attention to task, self-reinforcement (train procedural knowledge, metacognitive strategies)
Haupt, Van Kirk, & Terraciano (1975, Exp. 1)	subtraction (basic facts)	cover answers with cellophane (increase declarative knowledge, automaticity)
Haupt, Van Kirk, & Terraciano (1975, Exp. 2)	multiplication (basic facts)	cover answers with tracing paper (increase declarative knowledge)
Johnston, Whitman, & Johnson (1981), Johnston & Whitman (1987), Whitman & Johnston (1983)	addition and subtraction	self-instructional training (metacognition to guide procedural knowledge)
Lloyd, Saltzman, & Kauffman (1981)	multiplication and division (basic facts)	teach solution algorithm (train procedural knowledge)
Lovitt & Curtiss (1968)	computation problems	read problems aloud before answering (cue access to procedural knowledge)
Montague & Bos (1986)	two-step word problems	paraphrase, visualize, detect information, locate question, hypothesize, estimate label, check (train procedural knowledge metacognitive strategies)
Parsons (1972)	addition and subtraction	circle and name operation sign (cue access to procedural knowledge)
Schunk (1981)	division	teacher model, corrective feedback (metacognition to guide procedural knowledge)
Schunk & Cox (1986)	subtraction	students verbalize aloud, attribution training (metacognition to guide procedural knowledge)
Thackwray, Meyers, Schleser, & Cohen (1985)	addition	general and task-specific self-instructional training (metacognition to guide procedural knowledge)

they have learned. Finally, they are taught the unknown skills and how to link them together to solve the problems. An example of the use of a strategy of this sort is shown in Table 3. Research has revealed that:

- Atypical students can learn algorithms for simple tasks such as number-numeral equivalences (Grimm et al., 1973) and more complex tasks such as long division (Rivera & Smith, 1988).
- Pre-teaching of the component skills of a strategy prior to learning how to use the skills in concert leads to greater generalization (Carnine, 1980).
- Failure to pre-teach component skills prior to teaching the students how to use the strategy inhibits generalization (Lloyd, Saltzman, & Kauffman, 1981).
- Students can learn closely related strategies for closely related tasks (e.g., multiplication and division) without confusing the strategies (Lloyd et al., 1981).
- During acquisition of strategies, teachers should prompt the use of each step in the algorithm, but as the pupils approach mastery of the algorithm, teachers should decrease the level of prompting until the students are functioning independently (Paine, Carnine, White, & Walters, 1982).

Various authors have used other variations on strategy training. For example, Montague and Bos (1986) studied adolescents working on two-step word problems. The strategy training program incorporated many components— "paraphrasing, visualization, detecting relevant information, locating the question, hypothesizing, estimating, labeling, and checking" (p. 26)—and was expected not only to improve pupils' performance but also to affect the way they thought about approaching problems.

In a study of the arithmetic performance of pupils with behavior disorders, Davis and Hajicek (1985) also called one of their treatment conditions "strategy training." In this program, the teacher demonstrated an algorithm for solving multiplication problems involving decimals. Then the teacher had the students imitate the strategy. In a later condition the teacher repeated modeling of the strategy and added to it a combination of steps to promote pupils' attention to task and self-reinforcement.

Schunk (1981) investigated the effects of demonstrating to low-achieving pupils an algorithm for solving division problems. Students observed a trainer solving division problems and verbalizing the steps in the strategy. Later they practiced the strategy and received corrective feedback that included modeling of the steps. In a related study, Schunk and Cox (1986) found that when learning disabled children were required to verbalize as they solved problems, they obtained higher scores on similar tasks.

Johnston and Whitman evaluated the effects of self-instructional programs with mentally retarded children (Johnston, Whitman, & Johnson, 1981; Whitman & Johnston, 1983) and with children who had low levels of prior knowledge about arithmetic operations (Johnston & Whitman, 1987). Self-instruction, which usually includes self-verbalization of a procedural algorithm for approaching certain kinds of problems, often includes components of self-monitoring and self-reward as well. The programs that Johnston and Whitman used included instruction in the use of strategies for solving specific types of arithmetic problems. In all three studies the results indicated that this inter-

TABLE 3   *Example of a Solution Algorithm for Finding Equivalent Fractions*

Step	Description	Action	
1: Read	Pupil reads problem to him- or herself.	"Let's see . . . um, 9/17ths is equal to how many 102nds?"	$\frac{9}{17} = \frac{?}{102}$
2: Plan	Pupil describes general process to him- or herself.	"Okay, I've got to multiply 9/17ths by some fraction that's the same as 1, and then I can get the number of 102nds that it equals."	$\frac{9}{17} = \frac{?}{102}$
3: Rewrite	Pupil rewrites problem, providing space for work. Note: This step can be completed while performing step 2.	"Here's my workspace . . . ."	$\frac{9}{17}\left(-\right) = \frac{?}{102}$
4: Identify known part	Pupil identifies part of equivalence for which numbers are known.	"Okay. I've got two out of three numbers here (pointing to denominators), so I can start on that part."	$\frac{9}{17}\left(-\right) = \frac{?}{102}$
5: Solve known part	Pupil uses prior knowledge to solve for missing multiplier.	"So, 17 times something equals 102 . . . um . . . I'll just figure that out . . . 17 is almost 20 and 20 goes into 100 five times, so I'll try that . . . nope, 17 leftover, so it's 6 times . . . great! It's even."	$\frac{9}{17}\left(-\right) = \frac{?}{102}$ $17\overline{)\begin{matrix}5\\102\\95\\\hline 17\end{matrix}}$
6: Substitute	Pupil uses information derived in Step 5 to complete fraction in equation.	"And that means this (writing) is 6 over 6 . . . which is the same as 1, so . . ."	$\frac{9}{17}\left(\frac{6}{6}\right) = \frac{?}{102}$
7: Derive missing numerator	Pupil solves for missing numerator using information from Step 6.	"Now, I can just multiply these 'cause I've got two out of three and . . . 6 times 9 is 54, sooo. . ."	$\frac{9}{17}\left(\frac{6}{6}\right) = \frac{?}{102}$
8: Read	Pupil reads completed problem.	"9/17th is equal to 54/102nds."	$\frac{9}{17}\left(\frac{6}{6}\right) = \frac{54}{102}$

vention had clear and substantial effects on the students' arithmetic performance. Others (e.g., Albion & Salzberg, 1982; Leon & Pepe, 1983; Cameron & Robinson, 1980; Thackwray, Meyers, Schleser, & Cohen, 1985) also have used self-instructional principles when teaching pupils algorithms for solving arithmetic problems.

An important feature of some of these studies (e.g., Johnston & Whitman, 1987) is that they have evaluated the teaching of algorithmic knowledge within the context of other instructional components as well. The results of these studies indicate that, although teaching students an algorithm or a strategy is terribly important in their mastery of a mathematical skill, incorporating other factors (e.g., general self-instruction, self-evaluation of answer accuracy) can be beneficial, too. In general, more complete instruction—instruction that teaches all of the steps that pupils will need to function independently—is more effective than less complete instruction (Lloyd, 1988).

Instructional Packages and Programs

Some instructional packages incorporate recommendations about helping pupils to develop strategies for solving mathematics problems. Examples of these are given in Table 4. In addition, teachers should examine basal mathematics programs such as those published by Holt *(Holt School Mathematics),* Scott, Foresman *(Mathematics Around Us),* Addison-Wesley *(Elementary School Mathematics),* and Laidlaw *(The Understanding Mathematics Program)* to determine the extent to which they teach strategic behaviors.

Our previous discussion should help to guide the evaluation of programs for use with atypical learners. We think that instructional programs that are to be used with atypical learners should have several features. They should:

- Include lesson descriptions that permit teachers to adopt and use principles of effective teaching (e.g., frequent student responding on tasks relevant to short- and long-term objectives that are directly related to outcome measures).
- Build mathematical skills in a manner that is consistent with what is known about children's mathematical thinking.
- Teach students explicit algorithms for solving problems, making sure that those algorithms are integrated with related algorithms and that students are taught to use them flexibly.

TABLE 4   *Selected Commercially Available Arithmetic Programs That Teach Strategies*

Program Name	Publisher	Grade Levels
Corrective Mathematics Program	Science Research Associates	3-12
Structural Arithmetic	Houghton-Mifflin	K-3
Project Math	Educational Progress	K-6
DISTAR Arithmetic	Science Research Associates	K-2
Mastering Fractions	Systems Impact	4-8
Mastering Ratios and Equations	Systems Impact	4-9

- Demonstrate their effectiveness by submitting to rigorous field testing and evaluation.

Teachers who select instructional packages would be well advised to examine the available research about packages such as *Project MATH* (see Cawley, Fitzmaurice, Shaw, Kahn, & Bates, 1978), *DISTAR Arithmetic* (see Becker & Carnine, 1981), and *Mastering Fractions* (see Hasselbring, Sherwood, & Bransford, 1986; Kelly, Carnine, Gersten, & Grossen, 1986).

REFERENCES

Albion, F.M., & Salzberg, C.L. (1982). The effect of self-instructions on the rate of correct addition problems with mentally retarded children. *Education & Treatment of Children, 5,* 121–131.

Ashcraft, M.H. (1982). The development of mental arithmetic: A chronometric approach. *Developmental Review, 2,* 213–236.

Becker, W.C. (1986). *Applied psychology for teachers: A behavioral cognitive approach.* Chicago: Science Research Associates.

Becker, W.C., & Carnine, D.W. (1981). Direct instruction: A behavior theory model for comprehensive educational intervention with the disadvantaged. In S.W. Bijou & R. Ruiz (Eds.), *Behavior modification: Contributions to education* (pp. 145–210). Hillsdale, NJ: Erlbaum.

Brophy, J., & Good, T.L. (1986). Teacher behavior and student achievement. In M.C. Wittrock (Ed.), *Handbook of research on teaching* (3rd ed., pp. 328–375). New York: Macmillan.

Brown, J.S., & Burton, R.B. (1978). Diagnostic models for procedural bugs in basic mathematical skills. *Cognitive Science, 2,* 155–192.

Cameron, M.I., & Robinson, V.M.J. (1980). Effects of cognitive training on academic and on-task behavior of hyperactive children. *Journal of Abnormal Child Psychology, 8,* 405–419.

Carnine, D.W. (1980). Preteaching versus concurrent teaching of the component skills of a multiplication problem-solving strategy. *Journal for Research in Mathematics Education, 11,* 375–379.

Carpenter, T.R., & Moser, J.M. (1983). The acquisition of addition and subtraction concepts. In R. Lesh & M. Landau (Eds.), *Acquisition of mathematics concepts and processes* (pp. 7–44). New York: Academic Press.

Carpenter, T.R., & Moser, J.M. (1984). The acquisition of addition and subtraction concepts in grades one through three. *Journal for Research in Mathematics Education, 15,* 179–202.

Cawley, J.F., Fitzmaurice, A.M., Shaw, R., Kahn, H., & Bates, H., Ill (1978). Mathematics and learning disabled youth: The upper grade levels. *Learning Disability Quarterly, 1*(4), 37–52.

Cox, L.S. (1975). Diagnosing and remediating systematic errors in addition and subtraction computations. *Arithmetic Teacher, 22,* 151–157.

Cullinan, D., Lloyd, J., & Epstein, M.H. (1981). Strategy training: A structured approach to arithmetic instruction. *Exceptional Education Quarterly, 2*(1), 41–49.

Davis, R.W., & Hajicek, J.O. (1985). Effects of self-instructional training on a mathematics task with severely behaviorally disordered students. *Behavioral Disorders, 10,* 275–282.

Ebmeier, H., & Good, T.L. (1979). The effects of instructing teachers about good teaching on the mathematics achievement of fourth-grade students. *American Educational Research Journal, 16,* 1–16.

Engelmann, S., & Carnine, D. (1982). *Theory of instruction: Principles and applications.* New York: Irvington.

Fink, W.T., & Carnine, D.W. (1975). Control of arithmetic errors using informational feedback and graphing. *Journal of Applied Behavior Analysis, 8,* 461. (Abstract)

Fuson, K.C. (1982). An analysis of the counting-on solution procedure in addition. In T.P. Carpenter, J.M. Moser, & T.A. Romberg (Eds.), *Addition and subtraction: A cognitive perspective* (pp. 67–81). Hillsdale, NJ: Erlbaum.

Geary, D.C., Widaman, K.F., Little, T.D., & Cormier, P. (1987). Cognitive addition: Comparison of learning disabled and academically normal elementary school children. *Cognitive Development, 2,* 249–269.

Ginsburg, H.P. (1977). *Children's arithmetic: The learning process.* New York: D. Van Nostrand.

Good, T.L., & Grouws, D.A. (1979). The Missouri Mathematics Effectiveness Project: An experimental study in fourth-grade classrooms. *Journal of Educational Psychology, 71,* 355–362.

Good, T.L., Grouws, D.A., & Ebmeier, M. (1983). *Active mathematics instruction.* New York: Longman.

Grimm, J.A., Bijou, S.W., & Parsons, J.A. (1973). A problem-solving model for teaching remedial arithmetic to handicapped young children. *Journal of Abnormal Child Psychology, 1,* 26–39.

Groen, G.J., & Parkman, J.M. (1972). A chronometric analysis of simple addition. *Psychological Review, 79,* 329–343.

Groen, G.J., & Resnick, L.B. (1977). Can preschool children invent algorithms? *Journal of Educational Psychology, 69,* 645–652.

Hasazi, J.E., & Hasazi, S.E. (1972). Effects of teacher attention on digit-reversal behavior in an elementary school child. *Journal of Applied Behavior Analysis, 5,* 157–162.

Hasselbring, T., Sherwood, R., & Bransford, J. (1986). *Evaluation of the mastering fractions level one instructional videodisc program.* Unpublished manuscript, Tennessee Valley Authority.

Haupt, E.J., Van Kirk, M.J., & Terraciano, T. (1975). An inexpensive fading procedure to decrease errors and increase retention of number facts. In E. Ramp & G. Semb (Eds.), *Behavior analysis: Areas of research and application.* Englewood Cliffs, NJ: Prentice-Hall.

Houlihan, D.M., & Ginsburg, H.P. (1981). The addition methods of first- and second-grade children. *Journal for Research in Mathematics Education, 12,* 95–106.

Johnston, M.B., & Whitman, T. (1987). Enhancing math computation through variations in training format and instructional content. *Cognitive Therapy & Research, 11,* 381–397.

Johnston, M.B., Whitman, T.L., & Johnson, M. (1981). Teaching addition and subtraction to mentally retarded children: A self-instructional program. *Applied Research in Mental Retardation, 1,* 141–160.

Kelly, B., Carnine, D., Gersten, R., & Grossen, B. (1986). The effectiveness of videodisc instruction in teaching fractions to learning-disabled and remedial high school students. *Journal of Special Education Technology, 8*(2), 5–17.

Lankford, F.G., Jr. (1972). *Some computational strategies of seventh-grade pupils* (Final Report of Project No. 2-C-013, U.S. Department of Health, Education, and Welfare Grant No. OEG-3-72-0035). Charlottesville, VA: University of Virginia Center for Advanced Studies.

Leon, J.A., & Pepe, H.J. (1983). Self-instructional training: Cognitive-behavior modification for remediating arithmetic deficits. *Exceptional Children, 50,* 54–60.

Lloyd, J. (1980). Academic instruction and cognitive-behavior modification: The need for attack strategy training. *Exceptional Education Quarterly, 1*(1), 53–63.

Lloyd, J.W. (1988). Direct academic interventions in learning disabilities. In M.C. Wang, H.J. Walberg, & M.C. Reynolds (Eds.), *Handbook of special education: Research and practice* (Vol. 2, pp. 345–366). Oxford, England: Pergamon.

Lloyd, J.W. & de Bettencourt, L.J. (1982). *Academic strategy training: A manual for teachers.* Charlottesville, VA: University of Virginia Learning Disabilities Research Institute.

Lloyd, J., Saltzman, N.J., & Kauffman, J.M. (1981). Predictable generalization in academic learning as a result of preskills and strategy training. *Learning Disability Quarterly, 4,* 203–216.

Lovitt, T.C., & Curtiss, K.A. (1968). Effects of manipulating an antecedent event on mathematics response rate. *Journal of Applied Behavior Analysis, 1,* 329–333.

Montague, M., & Bos, C.S. (1986). The effect of cognitive strategy training on verbal math problem solving performance of learning disabled adolescents. *Journal of Learning Disabilities, 19,* 26–33.

Paine, S.C., Carnine, D.W., White, W.A.T., & Walters, G. (1982). Effects of fading teacher presentation structure (covertization) on acquisition and maintenance of arithmetic skills. *Education & Treatment of Children, 5,* 93–107.

Parsons, J.A. (1972). The reciprocal modification of arithmetic behavior and program development. In G. Semb (Ed.), *Behavior analysis and education–1972* (pp. 185–199). Lawrence: University of Kansas, Department of Human Development.

Pellegrino, J.W., & Goldman, S.R. (1987). Information processing and elementary mathematics. *Journal of Learning Disabilities, 20,* 23–32, 57.

Resnick, L.B. (1983). A developmental theory of number understanding. In H.P. Ginsburg (Ed.), *The development of mathematical thinking* (pp. 109–151). New York: Academic Press.

Rivera, D., & Smith, D.D. (1988). Using a demonstration strategy to teach midschool students with learning disabilities how to compute long division. *Journal of Learning Disabilities, 21,* 77–81.

Romberg, T.A., & Carpenter, T.P. (1986). Research on teaching and learning mathematics: Two disciplines of scientific inquiry. In M.C. Wittrock (Ed.), *Handbook of research on teaching* (3rd ed., pp. 850873). New York: Macmillan.

Rosenshine, B. (1976). Classroom instruction. In N.L. Gage (Ed.), *The psychology of teaching methods* (77th yearbook of the National Society for the Study of Education). Chicago: University of Chicago Press.

Rosenshine, B., & Stevens, R. (1986). Teaching functions. In M.C. Wittrock (Ed.), *Handbook of research on teaching* (3rd ed., pp. 376–391). New York: Macmillan.

Russell, R.L. (1977). Addition strategies of third-grade children. *Journal of Children's Mathematical Behavior, 1*(4), 149–160.

Schunk, D.H. (1981). Modeling and attributional effects on children's achievement: A self-efficacy analysis. *Journal of Educational Psychology, 73*, 93–105.

Schunk, D.H., & Cox, P.D. (1986). Strategy training and attributional feedback with learning disabled students. *Journal of Educational Psychology, 78*, 201–209.

Secada, W.G., Fuson, K.C., & Hall, J.W. (1983). The transition from counting-all to counting-on in addition. *Journal for Research in Mathematics Education, 14*(1), 47–57.

Siegler, R.S., & Robinson, M. (1982). The development of numerical understandings. In H.W. Reese & C.P. Lipsitt (Eds.), *Advances in child development and behavior* (Vol. 16, pp. 241–312). New York: Academic Press.

Smith, D.D., & Lovitt, T.C. (1975). The use of modeling techniques to influence the acquisition of computational arithmetic skills in learning-disabled children. In E. Ramp & G. Semb (Eds.), *Behavior analysis: Areas of research and application* (pp. 283–308). Englewood Cliffs, NJ: Prentice-Hall.

Smith, D.D., & Lovitt, T.C. (1976). The differential effects of reinforcement contingencies on arithmetic performance. *Journal of Learning Disabilities, 9*, 21–29.

Smith, D.D., Lovitt, T.C., & Kidder, J.D. (1972). Using reinforcement contingencies and teaching aids to alter subtraction performance of children with learning disabilities. In G. Semb (Ed.), *Behavior analysis and education–1972* (pp. 342–360). Lawrence: University of Kansas, Department of Human Development.

Svenson, O., & Broquist, S. (1975). Strategies for solving simple addition problems. *Scandinavian Journal of Psychology, 16*, 143–151.

Thackwray, D., Meyers, A., Schleser, R., & Cohen, R. (1985). Achieving generalization with general versus specific self-instructions: Effects of academically deficient children. *Cognitive Therapy & Research, 9*, 291–308.

Whitman, T., & Johnston, M.B. (1983). Teaching addition and subtraction with regrouping to educable mentally retarded children: A group self-instructional training program. *Behavior Therapy, 14*, 127–143.

Young, R.M., & O'Shea, T. (1981). Errors in children's subtraction. *Cognitive Science, 5*, 153–177.

John Lloyd is affiliated with the Department of Curriculum, Instruction, and Special Education at the University of Virginia. Clayton Keller is affiliated with Education and Human Service Professions at the University of Minnesota at Duluth.

Author Index

A

Abelson, A. G., 54
Abramson, L., 34
Abramson, M., 54
Abramson, T., 2, 189
Adelman, H. S., 30, 318, 321, 329
Affleck, J. Q., 316
Agard, J. A., 56, 189
Agran, M., 122
Albion, F.M., 404
Alexander, D. F., 98, 307
Algozzine, B., 54, 116, 221, 243
Algozzine, R., 83, 118
Aliotti, N. C., 15
Allen, D., 241
Alley, G., 82, 83, 85, 87, 91, 98, 100, 118, 151, 152, 156, 163, 171, 258, 260, 306, 307, 341, 371, 373, 374
Allinder, R. M., 247-249
Allington, R. L., 36, 304, 323
Ambert, A. N., 22, 23
Anderegg, M. L., 1, 3, 4
Anders, P. L., 299
Anderson, L. W., 343
Anderson, R. C., 282, 380
Anderson, T. H., 373-374, 376
Apel, K., 288
Aristotle, 127
Armbruster, B. B., 373-374, 376
Armstrong, S., 341
Armstrong, S. W., 296
Aron, J., 196
Ashcraft, M. H., 395
Asher, J. J., 24
Askov, E. N., 372
Atkins, R. E., 14
Atkinson, R. C., 382
Auer, C., 297
Augustyn, L., 297
Ault, M. J., 4
Ausubel, D. P., 384
Avila, D. L., 36

B

Baca, L., 22, 24
Bachman, J. G., 85
Baer, D. M., 267, 347
Baker, E. T., 66
Baker, L., 282
Ball, D. W., 257
Bandura, A., 137
Banikowski, A., 43
Banks, J. A., 24

Barden, R., 137
Barik, H. C., 15
Barksdale, A., 300
Barrett, D., 100
Bar-Tal, D., 35
Bar-Tal, Y., 35
Bartel, N. R., 341, 349
Bateman, B., 233
Bates, H., III, 93, 405
Bates, P., 262
Bauer, A. M., 259
Bauwens, J., 50
Beals, V., 182, 373
Beattie, J., 190, 298-299
Beck, I., 90, 306
Beck, K., 301
Becker, L. D., 342, 346, 349
Becker, W., 5, 6
Becker, W. C., 257, 380, 405
Beery, R., 35
Begab, M. J., 118
Beimiller, A., 147
Benedetti, D., 380
Benedict, R., 30
Benjamin, L. B., 54
Bennett, R. F., 157, 159
Bentz, J., 239
Benz, M. R., 256, 267, 316
Bereiter, C., 128, 203
Berenstain, J., 284
Berenstain, S., 284
Bergerud, D., 297, 301, 372, 376-377
Berliner, D. C., 44, 343
Bernal, E. M., 22
Bersoff, D., 221
Bessette, K., 53, 56
Biddle, W. B., 380
Bijou, S. W., 399
Binder, M. S., 221
Birch, J., 56, 83, 118
Black, J., 277
Blampied, N. M., 7
Blankenship, C., 222, 344
Bloch, D., 116
Bloom, B., 280
Bloom, B. S., 4, 7-9, 190
Bloom, L., 205, 206
Bloome, D., 273, 275
Bonstrom, O., 104
Borden, K. S., 303
Boroski, J. G., 161
Borthwick, S., 267
Bos, C., 161
Bos, C. S., 299, 347, 402

Maggs, A., 380
Magnusson, D., 202, 224, 232, 239, 243, 244, 249
Maheady, L., 5
Mahoney, M., 140
Mahood, W., 85
Maldonado-Colón, E., 23
Manis, F. R., 303
Mare, R. D., 85
Margolis, H., 51
Mark, F., 54
Marsh, G. E., 264, 265
Marshall, K. J., 305
Marston, D., 8, 56, 202, 214, 222, 224, 228, 232, 239, 243, 244, 249
Martin, E., 53
Martin, J. E., 122
Martin, R. P., 29
Martin-Reynolds, J., 54
Maruzama, G., 7
Marzano, R. J., 282
Marzola, E. S., 347
Maslow, A. H., 31-33, 52
Mason, J., 190
Masters, J., 137
Masters, L. F., 258, 259
Mastropieri, M. A., 7, 9, 296, 305, 342, 364, 382
Mathey, J. P., 81
Mauer, D., 288
Mayer, B., 260, 261
Mayhall, W. F., 5, 308
McAllister, H. A., 16
McBride, J. W., 256, 268
McCloskey, R., 284
McClure, S., 190
McCombs, B. L., 160-161
McCormick, S., 298
McCoy, K. M., 52
McDermott, R., 196, 274
McDougall, W., 31
McEntire, B., 371
McEntire, E., 300
McGettigan, J., 51
McGill-Frazen, A., 323
McGoldrick, J., 301
McGue, M., 221
McIntosh, D. K., 53, 54
McKee, P., 221, 222, 249-250
McKenna, B. H., 57
McKenzie, R. G., 59
McKeown, M., 90, 306
McKinney, J. D., 67, 190
McKnight, P., 156, 182, 386, 387
McLaughlin, T. F., 43, 304
McLeod, P., 344
McLeod, T., 341
McLoone, B., 305, 382
McMillan, D. L., 24

McNeil, M., 104
Mead, M., 30
Meadows, N., 118, 256
Meers, G. D., 121
Mehring, T., 43, 129
Meichenbaum, D., 129, 147, 259, 291
Meister, G. S., 5
Mellard, D. P., 386
Mercer, A. R., 364
Mercer, C. D., 200, 341, 342, 344, 347, 350, 364
Mercer, J. R., 22, 23
Mertens, S., 52
Messick, S., 116, 221
Meyen, E. L., 4, 190, 257, 319
Meyer, B., 282
Meyer, B.J.F., 373
Meyer, M., 285
Meyers, A., 404
Meyers, C. E., 118
Milam, C. P., 345, 349
Miller, C., 308
Miller, J., 208
Miller, J. H., 342, 345, 349
Miller, K., 378
Miller, L., 54, 308
Miller, S., 201, 202
Miller, S. E., 100
Miller, S. P., 341, 344, 350
Miller, S. R., 305
Miller, T. L., 58
Millward, A. J., 316
Milne, A. A., 284
Minskoff, J. G., 265
Mirkin, P. K., 91, 214, 239, 245, 248, 249
Mithaug, D. E., 122
Montague, M., 347, 402
Moore, J., 54, 60
Moran, M. R., 103
Morehead, M. K., 24, 91, 202, 204, 222, 232
Morgan, D. P., 190
Mori, A. A., 258, 259
Morris, B., 308
Morrow, D., 83, 84
Mosby, R., 378
Moser, J. M., 394, 395
Moyer, J. C., 376
Moyer, M. B., 376
Moyer, R. H., 15
Munson, S. M., 300
Murray, H. A., 31
Murtaugh, M., 123
Myers, B., 15
Myklebust, H. R., 80
Myles, B. S., 2, 49, 51, 54, 56-60

N

Nagel, D. R., 152
Nagle, R. J., 29

Subject Index

A

Academic achievement
  of learning disabled students, 84-85
  of mainstreamed students, 54-55, 190-196
Academic behavior, of mainstreamed students, 190-196
Academic remediation, 256-258
Accounts, 278
Achievement, 45. *See also* Academic achievement
Administrator attitudes
  assessment of, 75
  modification of, 25
  toward exceptional children, 54
Adult outcomes
  life skills emphasis for, 262-263
  vocational training emphasis for, 261-262
Adult Performance Level: Adaptation and Modification Project (APLAMP), 262
Advanced organizers, 298-299
Affective education, 259
Anecdotal recording, 211
Anxiety, 35-36
Aptitude treatment interaction, 378
Assessment. *See also* Curriculum-based assessment (CBA); Curriculum-based measurement (CBM); Language assessment
  of exceptional children, 56
  for instructional planning purposes, 201
  linked with curriculum, 202-203
  as measure of program effectiveness, 55-57
  self-, 139-140
  steps in pre-instructional, 201-202
Assessment practices
  bias in, 23
  used for bilingual exceptional children, 22-23
Attitudes
  regarding mainstreaming, 54-55
  toward mathematics, 348-349
Attributions, 33-34
Audience, 324-325
Audio recordings, 377-379

B

Basic skills instruction, 86-93
Beginning Teacher Evaluation Study, 345-346
Behavior control activities, 93-96
Behavior disordered students
  community preparation curriculum for, 266-267
  learning environment for, 317
  motivation to learn in, 30
  as peer tutors, 5
  study of arithmetic performance in, 402
  vocational training for, 261
Behavioral change strategy, 259
Bilingual exceptional students
  development of relevant and appropriate programs for, 23-24
  identification and assessment of, 22-23
  teacher and administrator expectations and attitudes regarding, 25
Bilingual programs, 14, 24
Bilingualism
  effect on cognitive performance, 14-22
  research on, 18-19
  varying perspectives regarding, 13-14
Black English, 204
Bloom's task taxonomy, 7
Bridges Model, 117
Bureau of Education for the Handicapped (BEH), 80

C

Child Service Demonstration Centers (CSDC) experiments, 80-82
Class discussion, 190, 281-282
Class size, 57
Classrooms
  competitive vs. noncompetitive structures in, 42
  modifications for mainstreamed students, 57-60
  unidimensional and multidimensional, 42-43
Cognitive behavior modification, 7
Cognitive performance
  effects on bilingualism on, 14-22
  learning strategies and, 9
  mathematics instruction and, 396
Cognitive theory, 33-35
Collaborative consultation, 57-58
Collaborative teaching, 77
Collaborative teaching model
  evaluation and data collection in, 74-77
  implementation of, 72-74
  pilot program selection for, 68-69
  pre-implementation activities of, 69-72
  program design of, 67-68
College-preparatory track, 266
Community preparation curricula
  for learning disabled and behavior disordered students, 266-267
  for mildly retarded students, 267-268
Competitive classroom structures, 42
Comprehensive curriculum
  alternative orientations for, 256-263
  decision making for, 263-265
  for elementary students, 265
  overview of, 255-256
  for secondary students, 265-268
Computer-assisted instruction (CAI), 279-280
Computer use, for language assessment, 219
Concept guides, 375
Concept maps, 376
Concrete-representational-abstract (CRA) sequence

420

Language probes, 212
Language-thinking hierarchy, 280, 281
Learned helplessness, 34
Learning
 evaluation of, 336
 factors affecting, 295
 factors influencing motivation for, 35-39
 link between motivation and, 29-30
 motivation and process of, 37-38
 use of incentives for, 38-39
Learning disabled students
 achievement levels for, 84-85
 changes in special education for, 79-80
 characteristics of, 323
 Child Service Demonstration Center experiments with, 80-82
 community preparation curriculum for,
  266-267
 completion of required courses for graduation
  by, 98-100, 104-106
 comprehensive curriculum for, 255-256
 dropout rate for, 82-84, 315
 effective programs for, 85-86
 instructional approaches for, 86-93, 317, 318
 mathematics and, 341-342, 349-350
 motivation to learn in, 30
 post-high school planning for, 101-102
 survival skills for, 93-98
 teaching reading to, 296-309
 understanding of word meanings by, 289-290
 use of self-regulation procedures for, 128, 134
 vocational training for, 261
Learning readiness, 349
Learning strategies
 conclusions regarding, 184-185
 effectiveness of, 9
 for instruction in content-area information,
  380-384
 instructional model for teaching, 166-184
 instructional principles for, 161-165
 for mildly learning disabled students, 260-261
 overview of, 161-163
Learning structures, 42
Least restrictive environment (LRE), 117
Life styles orientation, 262-263
Literacy, 88-89
Locus of control, 34
Low-achieving students. *See also* Behavior disordered students; Learning disabled students;
 Mildly handicapped students
 mediation for, 270-371
 needs of, 397
 teacher expectations and, 37
 understanding of, 85

M

Mainstreaming
 advantages of, 53
 attitudes of teachers and administrations tied to
  success of, 54
 classroom modifications supportive of, 57-60
 early efforts in, 189

improvements in system of, 53
Maintenance
 learning strategies concept and, 260-261
 tutorial, 259-260
Males, employment of graduates of special education programs, 118
Mastering Fractions, 405
Mastery learning, 8, 9, 346-347
Mathematics
 activities for learning disabled students in,
  91-93
 cognitive development in, 394-396
 deficiencies in, 341-342
 learning disabled students and, 349-350
 studies of target skills and knowledge in,
  400-404
Mathematics instruction. *See also* Strategic Math
 Series
 effective presentation of, 396-400
 establishment of goals and expectations for,
  343
 mastery learning for, 346-347
 monitoring progress in, 345
 need for systematic and explicit, 343-344
 promotion of positive attitude toward mathematics during, 348-349
 provision of feedback during, 345-346
 selection of appropriate content for, 342-343
 studies of instructional packages and programs
  for, 404-405
 teaching generalization in, 347-348
 teaching problem solving during, 347
 and understanding of mathematics concepts,
  344-345
 use of strategic mathematics series for,
  350-365
Mean length of utterance (MLU), 213
Mediation, 270-371
Mentally retarded students
 academic behavior and achievement of mainstreamed, 191
 characteristics of, 323
 community preparation curriculum for,
  267-268
 employment of graduates of special education
  programs, 118
 motivation to learn in, 30
 study of self-instructional programs used by,
  402, 404
Mentor programs, 122-123
Metacognitive processes
 learning content subject-matter and, 383-384
 whole-language approach and, 282, 290-291
Metalinguistic skills
 explanation of, 282
 multiple word meanings and figurative language as, 289-290
 segmentation as, 288-289
Middle schools. *See* Junior high schools; Secondary schools
Mildly handicapped students
 academic behavior and grades of main-

appropriateness for handicapped students, 221-222

curriculum-based assessment as alternative to, 222-224

Q

Questioning, 381, 383

R

Reading, 309

Reading instruction

for learning disabled students, 89, 104

selection of materials for, 296

teacher activities during and after, 300-303

teacher activities prior to, 297-299

use of peers for, 308

Reading material, 296. *See also* Textbooks

Reading skills

comprehension instruction to improve, 306

decoding instruction to improve, 304-305

strategic instruction to improve, 306-307

vocabulary instruction to improve, 305-306

word recognition instruction to improve, 303-304

Recounts, 277

Reflection, 325-326

Regular education initiative (REI), 3, 107

Reinforcement, 399. *See also* Self-reinforcement

Remediation

description of, 256-258

social skills and adjustment and, 258-259

Repetition, 381

Report cards, 75

Resource rooms, 4

Restructuring movement, 106-107

S

Schemas

content, 282-284

development of, 396

School reform movement, 106-107

School Survival Skills Curriculum, 259

Schools. *See also* Elementary schools; Junior high schools; Secondary schools

development of emotional and motivational problems in, 29

missions for, 117

present learning environment in, 316-317

Secondary schools. *See also* Schools

achievement of mainstreamed students in, 190-191

components of successful programs for learning disabled students in, 85-102

comprehensive curriculum for, 265-268

curriculum issues for learning disabled students in, 255, 256

dropout rate from. *See* Dropout rate

programs for learning disabled students in, 79-80, 102-110

required courses for graduation and learning disabled students, 98-100, 104-106

service delivery models for learning disabled programs in, 102-110

Segmentation, 288-289

Self-assessment, 139-140

Self-concept

of handicapped vs. non-handicapped students, 56

and motivation to learn, 36

in young children, 34-35

Self-control curriculum, 7

Self-fulfilled prophecy, 36

Self-instructions

description of, 129-130

forms of, 130-133

levels of, 133

teaching students to use, 7, 133-136

used with mentally retarded students, 402, 404

Self-monitoring

proactive considerations for use of, 144

self-assessment as dimension of, 139-140

self-recording as dimension of, 140

teaching students to use, 140-144

Self-motivation techniques, 160-161

Self-questioning strategies, 306-307

Self-recording, 140

Self-regulation

goal setting for, 136-139

overview of, 127-128

rationale for, 128-129

Self-reinforcement. *See also* Reinforcement

explanation of, 144-145

practical considerations regarding, 146-147

teaching students to use, 145-146

Self-speech, 129, 130

Semantic development, 17

Semantic feature analysis, 299

Semantic knowledge

explanation of, 155-156, 158

for written language, 282

Semantics

analysis of, 214

examples of elements of, 209

explanation of, 203, 205

roles of, 210

Sentence complexity, 213-214

Sentence Writing Strategy, 162

Social integration, 56

Social skills, 258-259

Special education

current data base on outcomes in, 118-119

development of alternative systems to, 123-124

effectiveness of, 119-120

list of recommended programs in, 4-9

purpose of, 116-117

and teacher preparation in high school content areas, 109

Split-middle trendline (SM), 239-240

Strategic Math Series (SMS)

and components of effective mathematics instruction, 359, 360

explanation of, 350-351